T5-ARJ-247

Imagining Native America in Music

MICHAEL V. PISANI

Imagining Native America in Music

Yale University Press
New Haven
& London

Set in Sabon type by Keystone Typesetting, Inc.
Printed in the United States of America by Sheridan Books.

Library of Congress Cataloging-in-Publication Data

Pisani, Michael.
Imagining native America in music / Michael V. Pisani.
p. cm.
Includes bibliographical references (p.) and index.
ISBN-13: 978-0-300-10893-4 (hardcover : alk. paper)
ISBN-10: 0-300-10893-1 (hardcover : alk. paper)
1. Music—America—History and criticism. 2. Music—Social aspects—America.
3. Exoticism in music. I. Title.
ML3549.P57 2006
781.5′9—dc22

2005019915

A catalogue record for this book is available from the British Library.

The paper in this book meets the guidelines for permanence and durability of the Committee on Production Guidelines for Book Longevity of the Council on Library Resources.

10 9 8 7 6 5 4 3 2 1

To Ralph P. Locke
Teacher, Mentor, Friend

And to Christopher and Tim,
My Two Steadfast Braves

Contents

Acknowledgments

The idea for this book began in 1992 in a graduate seminar on musical exoticism with Ralph P. Locke at the Eastman School of Music. Little did I realize the scope of what I had set out to do, or that it would take me twelve years to arrive at a coherent means of describing so much material. I am deeply grateful that the person who sparked this interest so long ago is still an enthusiastic supporter of the project. Ralph, you are a constant source of inspiration and a wealth of ideas and insight. Thanks also to my wonderful editors at Yale University Press, especially Keith Condon and Mary Pasti, and to Duke Johns for careful copyediting. I am grateful to the Theodore Presser Foundation, the Elsa T. Johnson Fellowship in musicology at the Eastman School of Music, and the Dale Fund at Vassar College for their generosity in funding my research.

This journey of discovery would have been much impoverished without the knowledge and guidance of many other individuals, institutions, and organizations. I am grateful for the doors opened to me by the remarkable staffs at the Library of Congress, the American Folklife Center, the Smithsonian Institution, the British Library, the Sibley Music Library at the Eastman School of Music, the Boston Public Library, the Houghton Library of Harvard University, the Edwin A. Fleisher Collection at the Free Library of Philadelphia, the Edward E. Ayer Collection at Chicago's Newberry Library, the Northwestern University Library (especially for its WPA card index to music periodicals before 1930), the University of Arizona Library, the Bancroft Library at the University of California, Berkeley, the Southwest Museum of Los Angeles, and the UCLA Library, as well as at the historical societies of New York, Iowa, Nebraska, Missouri, Wisconsin, and Minnesota. Certain research librarians were particularly helpful, especially Wayne Shirley in the Music Division at the Library of Congress; Jeanette C. P. Eisenhart, assistant archivist of the Cadman Collection of the Pennsylvania State University Library; Annette Fern at the Harvard Theatre Collection; James A. Smith at the University of Kansas; Sergeant Mike Ressler, librarian of the United States Marine Band; Special Collections archivists Ted Honea and David Coppen at the Sibley Music Library; Michele Clark and Jim Shea of the Longfellow National Historic Site, Cambridge, Massachusetts; and Noelle Carter at the Warner Brothers Archive, University of Southern California.

Many individual scholars not associated with libraries freely gave of their time and ideas, especially Philip J. Deloria, Anne Dhu McLucas, Ellen Koskoff, Vera Brodsky Lawrence, Adrienne Fried Block, James Kimball, Edward Berlin, Paul Charosh, and Victor Fell Yellin. For helpful replies to my many inquiries, I wish to thank Thomas Stoner, James Parakilas, Margery Morgan Lowens, Victoria Levine, Rayna Green, Richard Crawford, Michael Broyles, Edward R. Reilly, Paul O'Dette, Tara Browner, Jonathan Bellman, A. Peter Brown, Nicholas Tawa, Philip Carli, William Scott Ball, Judy Tsou, Jarold Ramsey, Delmer D. Rogers, Wilma Reid Cipolla, John Doyle, S. Frederick Starr, Robert Fink, Frederick Roffman, Don Fisher, George Foreman, Simon During, Kim H. Kowalke, and Jurgen Thym. Special thanks are due to Vassar colleagues who offered assistance or instructive criticism along the way, especially Sarah Kozloff in film, Lucy Johnson and Thomas Porcello in anthropology, James Merrell in history, Margaret Stewart in geology/geography, Brian Mann and Kathryn Libin in music, Jannay Morrow in psychology, and Jeff Schneider in German. And to my students at Vassar, who are a constant source of inspiration, thanks for engaging me on so many ideas related to this book and for not letting me off easy in the classroom.

Where does one's work stand without the encouragement and support of friends? I couldn't ask for a better group of colleagues than those in the music department at Vassar, who fully understand how it is possible to be deeply committed to both teaching and scholarship. Heartfelt thanks to Karen Robertson (for being my Pocahontas), John Koegel (for years of sharing a love of history and music of the Americas), Peggy Monastra (for her gift of the *Shanewis* vocal score so many years ago), and also to Antonius Bittmann, Anthony Teso, Mark Stubis, Steve Laitz and Anne Marie Reynolds, John Sheridan and Walter Zimmerman, Edward Jurkowski and Colleen Bakker, Dorothy Griffiths, Tim Long, Thomas Elston, Orly Krasner, Peter Straus, and

Lee Stern, all of whom have made my life richer and my approach to scholarship more rooted in experience. Deepest gratitude always to my beloved parents, Mario and Dolores Pisani of Crown Point, Indiana, and to my dear "alternate parents," Walter and Irene Huebner of Waterloo, Ontario. Last, but most assuredly first, thank you to my two closest and dearest friends, Tim Hochstrasser of the London School of Economics and Christopher Huebner of Rochester, New York, both of whom instinctively understood the kind of dedication this book needed and who provided me with more strength and support than they will ever know.

Notes for the Reader

Terms

Since every reader will not necessarily have a background in music theory, I include here a brief explanation of the systems of musical reference used throughout this book. I frequently indicate scale degrees ($\hat{1}$–$\hat{2}$–$\hat{3}$–$\hat{4}$–$\hat{5}$–$\hat{6}$–$\hat{7}$–[$\hat{1}$]) in lieu of pitch names (for example, C–D–E–F–G–A–B–[C]). This approach allows for easier comparison in the relationships between works. Scale degrees are always rooted in the key or mode of the work under discussion. In other words, in the key of G minor, G is $\hat{1}$ and D is $\hat{5}$. If a scale degree goes below $\hat{1}$, as in the descending melody D–C–B♭–G–F, the root and the degrees below it are underlined: $\hat{5}$–$\hat{4}$–$\flat\hat{3}$–$\underline{\hat{1}}$–$\flat\underline{\hat{7}}$.

Theories associated with pentatonic or five-note scales are presented in detail in chapter 7, where the repertory of late nineteenth-century settings demands a more nuanced approach. The principal theoretical terms used throughout this book (and clarified at their first occurrences) are: simple and compound meter; iambic rhythm (or reverse-dotted rhythm); diatonic (or medieval) modes; pentatonic, tetratonic, chromatic, and whole-tone scales; Arabic maqam; standard chord names for triads such as tonic (I), dominant (V), subdominant (IV); quadrads such as dominant sevenths and diminished sevenths; and harmonic progressions and cadential expressions such as plagal cadences (IV–I). Diatonic modes are usually cited with their roots, as in E-Phrygian.

List of Works

Originally, this book was to include a list of "Indian"-based works as an appendix. It quickly became obvious that such a list would constitute a book in itself. The list has been made available online at the following address: http://IndianMusicList.vassar.edu.

Imagining Native America in Music

Introduction: A Language for Imagining Native America

In Samuel Goldwyn's film musical adaptation *Whoopee!* (1930), the principal character, a nervous white upper-middle-class hypochondriac played by comedian Eddie Cantor, becomes embroiled with an Indian tribe that, incidentally, manages near the end of the film to stage a musical extravaganza entitled "Song of the Setting Sun." This production number was designed and choreographed by Busby Berkeley and Florenz Ziegfeld. It featured not only Ziegfeld's ubiquitous long-legged dancing girls—as lovely Indian maidens—but also stalwart males in splendid Sioux regalia, a blazing sunset (an early experiment in Technicolor), thundering tom-toms, a chieftain with an operatic baritone voice, and, of course, a live (though invisible to us) Hollywood orchestra.

What was it about the music and the emotion of this obviously theatrical number that nevertheless made this scene linger in my mind long after Cantor's antics faded from memory? Perhaps it was the dignity with which the "Indian" characters carried themselves here, as opposed to the absurd manner in which they were portrayed in the rest of the film. Or perhaps it was because Walter Donaldson's richly orchestrated music evoked in me a dimly perceived sense of fascination with ancient America. Were these reactions different from the reactions of those who saw the film when it was first released? In 1930 a film set partly on an Indian reservation could draw upon the living memory of those in the audience who had themselves, perhaps as small children, made the long journey westward in the nineteenth century and who might have been able to recall the not-so-distant threat of uprisings and skirmishes. By the time I first saw *Whoopee!* I no longer expected to run into a tribe of war-mongering Indians. So the music did not reactivate any sensations of thrill or danger associated with the subject as much as it suggested sheer adventure or even an idealistic longing for a wild and unspoiled America.

The medium of television served as my informant about native America and the Old West during my impressionable youth, as I imagine it did for many people. Here Indians were often persistent antagonists, as in John Ford's *Stagecoach* (1939), where John Wayne miraculously defended a speeding coach against a sustained Apache attack. Had I turned the picture off but left the sound on, I would have realized even then that this compelling action was accompanied by evocative and allusive-rich music that held my attention in a viselike grip. Moreover, frontier Westerns such as *Broken Arrow* (1950) or *Man from Laramie* (1955) included music that often signaled Indian characters' identity long before they actually appeared on-screen. Through these films, and the music accompanying them, I was seduced by what I gradually came to realize was largely an imagined native America.

Music, which plays such an extraordinary role in organizing and shaping our societies and our social values, remains an unspoken and too often unacknowledged contributor not only to the social history of America, but to the creation of its folkways and myths as well. Cultural historians, while they may acknowledge the relevance of music to the subjects of their study, more often than not shy away from discussing music and its power to effect social and political change. Robert Berkhofer's *The White Man's Indian,* for example, is one of the key studies in the perception of America's indigenous peoples during the country's years of development and expansion. Berkhofer vividly demonstrates how literature and images contributed to this perception. Music, he inadvertently seems to imply, played little part in this construction. Yet it actually had a significant role in shaping the ideas of the American people (as James MacPherson duly acknowledges with regard to the Civil War). Music did not simply contribute to a generic depiction of "Indians" or "Indianness," but rather offered multiple views in which emphases shifted from century to century, from decade to decade, from work to work, and, in some cases, even within individual works.

I wanted to turn my attention to a study of these manifestations of American culture with my ears open, especially since it was music that had captured my imagination in the first place. At its most specific, then, this book is an investigation of music used to evoke North and South American Indians, but also, in a more general sense, aspects of national identity and specifically American national identity—often an all-embracing concept that in fact obscures many "identities." In addition to exploring a variety of musical sources, I also examine the nature of the attraction to this subject by composers and musicians who, in their efforts to evoke symbolically rich places such as the American West or the precolonial American past (or even a present location that is supposed to be somehow "genuine"), tend to rely upon distinctive musical combinations and effects.

In my search for the musical roots of "America's Indian," I returned to the earliest musical representations. These were composed in both Europe and its American colonies. They were inspired by Dryden and Rousseau's early modern construct of the noble savage, or by visiting Brazilians or Cherokees to the courts of Europe, or by Osages "performing" at French fairgrounds or on New York stages. This book thus begins by examining pale-faced imitations of Native American music and ritual as rendered in the royal courts, the opera house, the theater, the salon, and the exhibition hall (to cite some of the most prominent). In chapters 1 to 3 I focus principally on the years between 1650 and 1850, before a context for America's indigenous music and ritual had been established outside the communities in which they originated. Chapter 4 brings this investigation into the middle nineteenth century, into a period of rising interest in folklore and the creation of Indian-inspired Americana such as *The Song of Hiawatha* and its musical offshoots. Chapters 5 and 6 focus on the late nineteenth century, the decades of "scientific" study of North American Indian life sponsored by institutions or undertaken by individual anthropologists and ethnologists, and I examine the effects that these had on musical transcription and representation. The last three chapters focus on the twentieth century, when, with the physical conquest of Indian territories at an end and the American frontier a place of mythic construction, the exotic representation of Indians and Indian life became intensified and enriched with a sense of "authenticity," in part as a result of the anthropologists' work, but in part as one attempt to fill a spiritual void created by the nervous energy of modernism and the diminishing roles of religion and high culture. In the final two chapters I focus principally on song, musical theater and vaudeville, some opera, and film—largely the popular genres, as these seemed to me the dominant spheres of musical expression in which native America was and is invoked.[1]

In the course of my pursuit, I noted the changes that took place in musical description as various types of indigenous styles became available, first through live performance, then through written transcriptions, and finally through recordings and film. Some of this music might seem, at times, moving, like the many songs and arias written for Cora, the *belle Péruvienne* for whom Spanish soldiers nearly abandoned the conquest. Some of it, like the World War I song "Indianola" ("Me much like to kill, Scalp old Kaiser Bill"), may be offensive. This music's breadth and variety—more diverse than is generally acknowledged—is often astonishing. Music written to describe the wild "prehistoric" worlds of "primitive" America, for example, sounded in some cases more vigorous than traditional European-derived styles. Above all, this music's distinctively and self-consciously ethnic focus seems to define a space where, especially in the so-called melting pot of late nineteenth-century America, artists struggled to accommodate influences from differing and sometimes opposing cultures.

From our present, more informed, time, it might appear a simple matter merely to cite examples of Native American music—or to refer to specific recordings or other documentation—and then illustrate how "Indian music" fashioned for plays, operas, concert music, and narrative films bore little if any relation to indigenous sources. But that would be a pointless and repetitive task. My goal is more substantive: to analyze these products and to raise questions—sometimes unsettling ones—about what they might represent. I wish to examine closely what the "Indianness" of the music suggests, what cultural tools (in this case, what elements of music) are fused to achieve a coherent form of expression, and what this expression reveals, not only about the process of creativity, but about America's ongoing preoccupation with its own identity.

Music is too often ignored in cultural studies of this subject. This book bridges that gap and will appeal to those with an interest in American history and culture (who wish to know more about the roles that music played) as well as musicians (who wish to understand more about this music's deep roots in history and culture). The practical apparatus of publication meant that the book could not contain notated musical examples for every work I discuss. I therefore included these selectively. Some examples need not be quoted here, as facsimiles are easily available in Victoria Lindsay Levine's recent *Writing Indian Music: Historic Transcriptions, Notations, and Arrangements* or online at sites such as the Lester S. Levy Collection of American Sheet Music (Johns Hopkins University) or Music for the Nation (Library of Congress).

National Margins and Exotic Stereotypes

From 1986 to 1990 I lived in Winnipeg, Manitoba, where I witnessed the strange and painful marginalization of the Métis, a Canadian ethnic group descended partly from French fur traders but whose ancestors are also Cree, Ojibwe, and other indigenous tribes. I couldn't understand why these people, who had such a remarkable history and at least one memorial statue of a hero erected in town, were now the underdogs of society, essentially living in poverty and victims of a community rife with rowdiness and drunkenness. The years of hardship I saw on the faces of many of these people remained in the back of my mind as I turned to writing the kind of history of Indian representations that I as a musician could do best.

I sensed a disconnect between Indians such as the Métis and many other tribal groups across North America, who seemed positioned on the fringes of society, and the encoding process in the ballets, songs, and films that I examined, which often put Indians at the very center of the culture. I was intrigued by this process and became committed to understanding it. Part of the disconnect had already been engendered in the way seventeenth- and eighteenth-century Europeans classified "Indians" by their geographical, racial, and historical characteristics. Race served as an essentializing category not only in politics, journalism, and literature, as is well known, but also in music. Until the twentieth century, most racial categories remained stubbornly tied to notions of geographical origin (i.e., "Caucasian," "Ethiopian," "Asian," and so on). It is peculiar that today informal nineteenth-century racial categories such as "black" or "white" are still considered acceptable, while "red" or "yellow" seem particularly derogatory. (On the other hand, author Richard Rodríguez has recently opted for the designation "brown" for Latino peoples.) I have grappled with these issues in the course of planning this book and found it difficult to account for every inconsistency of nomenclature. While, for example, the label "Indian" has since Columbus's time traditionally signified a particular group of people (first the misconstrued "Indians" and then all native peoples of the Americas) as perceived by another group (Europeans), "Indian" has been reclaimed today as a term of unity among many First Peoples. Partly in response to these inconsistencies, I shifted my original focus from "Imagining Indians" (which is fairly common in the literature), to "Imagining native America" (which is not). This takes the emphasis away from the people as subjects and places it more generally on the worlds, or supposed worlds, that they inhabit. (Why, for example, are suns always setting in representations of native America?)

From the Revolutionary period to the early twentieth century, native America gradually shrank in size. Its confinement and oppression were exacerbated by a growing nation that flourished due to pioneer determination. But the swiftness of American expansion also relied heavily on connotative ideologies of Manifest Destiny, which effectively projected an imagined nation onto the geographical space. (I will return to this topic in a discussion of the American frontier in chapter 3.) National identities naturally lead to stereotypical perceptions (German orderliness, Scottish frugality, and so forth). A nation, defined on the one hand by Benedict Anderson as "an imagined political community," is not so much a thing, a space with physical margins, as a concept, no less real but constructed and maintained through discourse. (Consider, for example, the semantic complexity of "the Oneida Nation"—an entity that has social, cultural, and legal parameters but is not constrained by geographical borders.) How that nation is defined, and what it includes and excludes, forms the discourse of nationalism. Music, like social and even political discourse, establishes, reinforces, and redefines the cultural margins of even "imagined communities," serving to establish boundaries between various peoples and nations.[2]

America's cultural margins can be seen reflected in the history of its music. In the eighteenth century, much American music was inherited directly from British culture, in sacred hymnody as well as in patriotic and theatrical genres. Though the United States parted ways politically with Britain, the two cultures hardly became distinct immediately. Even American folk music in the first seventy-five years of the country's history was indebted to the words and tunes of the British ballads and dances. Most American music before the 1830s tended to reflect, as did Federalist architecture of the time, an elegant but utilitarian art whose style, like the relatively undifferentiated design of churches, schools, homes, and state buildings, strove toward classical form and unity of expression. With new immigrants and their musical traditions, however, American music began to reveal a struggle with its margins. The modal tunes of Irish folk songs or the graceful chromaticism of Italian bel canto were easily absorbed into American music of all genres, and their popularity lent an extraordinary impetus to sheet music publishing and distribution. But aspects of African American music were filtered and reshaped into minstrel songs, reflecting the first major discomfort with the margins of national musical culture. With the European revolutions of 1848, America gained vast numbers of German immigrants, whose ideas concerning culture exerted a powerful force on the American musical scene. Along with other central and eastern Europeans, Germans brought with them deeply rooted notions of nationalism and exoticism and effected the transplanting of these cultural ideas to America. Embedded in German philosophies of music were also persuasive Hegelian formulations of idealism and the romanticism of German poets and writers. It was largely at this stage, as Lawrence Levine has pointed out, that the hierarchical splintering of American musical culture into categories of "art" and "popular" began to occur. In the decades following the Civil War, diversity of immigration and a greater influx of influences led to the collapse of any serious efforts to incorporate these within the margins of a single musical culture, whether classical or popular. What would be considered musically "American," from the 1870s to the 1940s, formed the subject of countless fascinating debates, from those surrounding Dvořák and nationalist sentiment in the 1890s, to those in the 1920s about the role of jazz in the arts, to the politicized issues arising from classical composers' use of American folk music in the 1930s and 1940s. All of these controversies dealt with "boundary" issues—what could and what could not be absorbed into the "nation-space" of American musical consciousness.[3]

While America grappled with issues of cultural identity, American Indians themselves were continually relegated to the margins. In the nineteenth century, Indian characters were common in popular fiction, though they were usually bloodthirsty warriors or traitorous scouts. Other Indians were common foils in popular culture: occasionally a noble chieftain or a dark, mysterious maiden, both high-minded individuals and usually of few words. Generally, Indians were portrayed either in subservient positions, such as a faithful friend and companion (television's Tonto was a later instance), or as low-life types: the murderous thief, the idler and drunkard, or the embittered "half-breed." When Indian characters turned up in plays, burlesques, and operettas, as they often did, they were always played by white actors and, as a rule, spoke pidgin English and were simple-minded and easily outwitted. An "Indian" by the name of "Lo" appeared in Edward Everett Rice's 1874 musical extravaganza *Evangeline; or, The Belle of Acadie.* In this play, which has been described as "the most popular American stage work of the decade," "Lo" was billed as "the *lo*west and *lo*nest Indian of them all, such a dealer in human hair as it is hoped you *may ne'er* meet on any stage but this." "Lo" was a creation of Bret Harte (Francis Brett Hart), one of the mythmaking storytellers of the Gold Rush years, who in turn had derived it from a distorted reading of Alexander Pope ("Lo, the Poor Indian"). Throughout the nineteenth century (and into the twentieth), "Lo" remained a derogatory term that was meant to keep Indians in their place, at the very bottom of the social stratum.[4]

The irony, of course, is that while Indian stereotypes persisted, the idea of "the Indian" continued to serve as an almost iconic national image. In the 1850s, for example, the United States government issued several new coins with such images: Liberty in an Indian headdress on the one- and three-dollar gold pieces (1854) and the Indian-head penny. During these years, however, Indians had no civil rights compared with even the most indigent immigrant. An 1872 Thomas Nast political cartoon for *Harper's Weekly* shows a blanket-draped chieftain turned away at a voting poll inundated by a conglomerate of ethnicities.[5] For most of United States history—and to some degree still today—the indigenous peoples of America were situated, culturally if not also physically, outside the boundaries of American nationhood. (Complicating the matter, of course—but also confirming Anderson's thesis—is the fact that some Indians choose to remain outside the American nation while living on American soil.)

Perhaps the cornerstone work on racial and ethnic representation, problematic though it may be, is Edward Said's *Orientalism* (1978). Said noted that traits by which others are represented are not found in the fidelity of the representation to some original, but occur as stylistic evocations, figures of speech, narrative devices, and so on. He could have included music here, too—and did in his later *Culture and Imperialism* (1993)—for clearly music played a critical role, for example, in "orientalizing" the Middle East for Europeans in the eighteenth and nineteenth centuries, thereby making parts of it open to colonization. With the rise in the nineteenth century of political nationalism and music's crucial role in defining the perceived existence of national character, the musical portrayal of exotic others extended from Russia to Spain and to the New World, and a fascinating body of literature has grown around this subject.[6]

Said sees orientalizing as a persistent and unchanging value, whereas I see the ethnic representation of American Indians as a complex and changing process. Unlike Said, I found identification and representation in the case of American Indians—like nationalism and exoticism—to be mutually constitutive, a point to which I will be returning throughout this book. To begin with, the languages of nationalism and exoticism are often conspicuously related. Why does it seem obvious, for instance, that John Philip Sousa's *Liberty Bell* march (1893) sounds more authentically "American" than the same composer's "Red Man" (from his *Dwellers in the Western World* suite, 1910)? Clearly they come from the same imagination. The musical languages of each, though they are often understood as separate dialects, are closely related, and the latter dialect would not be possible without the former. In the second edition of the *New Grove Dictionary of Music and Musicians,* Richard Taruskin's essay on nationalism is nearly eight times as long as Ralph P. Locke's on exoticism. This disparity may have been editorial, as the discourse of nationalism has abundant precedents, whereas exoticism is a relatively newer field. Moreover, one could argue that there have been several important "nationalist schools" of musical composition and no comparable "exoticist schools."[7] Yet some nationalist composers (if there *are* such exclusive people) are often exoticists, because the musical language of nationalism also serves the dual roles of representation and identification. For example, Glinka is generally acknowledged by Russian nationalists as having composed the first piece of truly distinctive Russian classical music—*Kamarinskaya*—and also as having written an early work of internationally recognized "Spanish" classical music—*Jota aragonesa*. Similarly, Aaron Copland, whose *Appalachian Spring* is among the most important classical pieces that defined a style of Depression-era "Americana," preceded this phase of his development with *El salón México*, a work based on Mexican folk tunes and which enjoyed great success, even in Mexico City. Are the ideological issues of musical borrowing and cultural appropriation fundamentally different in the contrasting works of these composers?[8]

Carl Dahlhaus would have said no. "It is misleading to claim," wrote the musicologist in 1980, "that a gaping chasm separates the musical expression of [one's] own 'national spirit' from a picturesque rendering of a foreign milieu." Though writing from a distinctively European perspective, Dahlhaus identifies the cultural ambiguities of nation-space. Musical nationalism is generally rooted in folk music, which consists of elements, melodies, and structures that are local and regional in origin but also, as Dahlhaus points out, incorporates other features that migrated throughout the whole of Europe. A folk music tradition, therefore, can rarely be said to represent one nation and one nation only. As Béla Bartók so elegantly put it: "neither new borderlines nor old, changed back and forth on the map, could ever raise any barricade to the wind that went on carrying the pollen and the seeds effortlessly over those expanses of land . . . wafting the songs, too, for centuries." The issue is no less complicated in the relationship between European folk and American Indian musics, since these traditions have affected one another since the point of contact. This perhaps explains why exoticism, even more than nationalism, has remained elusive as a tool of analysis. It is still all too easy to fall into the trap of relying upon generalizations. The tendency toward fuzzy carelessness in discussing sources of musical exoticism, as Miriam Whaples argued in 1958, is still prevalent.[9]

If exoticism creates imaginary worlds of dangerous or alluring others, then artistic nationalism is no less imaginary in that it reflects back to a people the constructs of its nation-space. Musical nationalism in "classical music" is often discussed as a largely nineteenth-century European phenomenon, as Dahlhaus does above. But if we allow ourselves to remove conceptual boundaries between American classical and popular music—boundaries that were to a large extent forcefully constructed in the nineteenth century—as well as boundaries established in the early twentieth century between folk and popular music, we see that nationalism and exoticism are persistent ideologies in the arts as well as politics. Issues of exoticism are just as relevant today—when American hip-hop artists sample recordings of non-Western musicians, as David Hesmondhalgh has noted—as they were in the eighteenth century, when German composer Georg Philipp Telemann incorporated Polish melodies in his polonaises.

Like nationalism, exoticism also traverses boundaries of classical, popular, and folk, a point to which I will also be returning repeatedly.[10]

Music historians have not given the portrayal of American Indians much attention, probably because there appears to have been no music comparable to the exotic works of, say, Mozart, Verdi, Saint-Saëns, or Rimsky-Korsakov. Nevertheless, the large amount of surviving songs and instrumental music about native America—including some intriguing "war dances"—has rarely been acknowledged, let alone examined. This repertoire falls loosely into the category of popular culture, though the application of this modern concept to an earlier period unfairly undermines the genuine interplay between musics of all social classes. In the early nineteenth century, musical style cut across the disciplines of parlor song, concert music, opera, and theatrical and dance music. We can read Jon Finson's insights into American parlor songs and Wilbur Maust's taxonomy of Anthony Philip Heinrich's programmatic instrumental music as points of departure for a much wider purview of musical depiction of Indian subjects, thereby discovering some important relationships between genres. Music also brings a performative dimension to our understanding of humans interpreting the actions and characteristics of other humans.

For urban Americans in the nineteenth century, the only American Indian music likely to be heard was that of native touring groups that performed in exhibitions, circuses, or medicine shows or as variety features between the acts of plays. Before this time, few Americans appear to have concerned themselves with the roles that music played in the lives of American Indians. This began to change in the late nineteenth century with ethnographic writing, a development that raised as many questions as it answered. What are we to conclude about the impulses of white ethnographers such as Alice Fletcher among the Omahas, George Boas among the Kwakiutls, or Walter McClintock among the Blackfeet? Are their writings—like those of explorer Frank Cushing, who traveled to the Southwest in the 1880s to participate in Zuni societies—manifestations of exoticism? What were they seeking by "going primitive" (as Marianna Torgovnik might put it)? Analogously, how would we classify certain early twentieth-century musical compositions that seek the primitive in the national, among them Bartók's *Allegro barbaro* (Hungarian), Stravinsky's *The Wedding* (Russian), or Arthur Farwell's *Navajo War Dance* (American), works that do not so much condescend to portray their subjects as picturesque Others as to find points of identification with them? Is this much different from, say, the impulse that drove writers and painters such as Herman Melville, Robert Louis Stevenson, and Paul Gauguin to the South Pacific? While I would argue that primitivist compositions such as these do draw on the established rhetoric and syntax of musical exoticism, they also succeed in conveying a kind of raw, unmediated experience while challenging listeners to bypass stereotypical formulations and to listen in new ways. I am therefore interested in showing not only how imagined Indians are completely cut off from real Indians, but also how music tries to come to terms with the complex (and varying) relationships between the two.

A Semiotics of Musical Representation

In order to understand how music—a medium of communication largely based upon abstract sounds—could be used to label, stereotype others, and even shape attitudes, we need to explore music's metaphorical relationship to representation.[11] In the first two chapters we will explore the important rhetorical features that were engaged in portraying native America. What is distinctly exotic about musical settings from Vivaldi's *Montezuma* (1733) to Félicien David's "Lullaby of an Indian Mother" (1844) was that these composers had no more understanding of their subject matter than did their audiences. The musical language used to evoke New World Indians from 1700 to the early nineteenth century consisted largely of an increasingly expanded collection of available musico-rhetorical devices, few derived from actual Indian sources and most taken from the works of other Western musicians.

From about 1790 to 1840 the rhetorical language of much European music, especially music used to depict self and others, began to expand. I would like to argue for a paradigm shift during these years—particularly for music of a descriptive nature—from an emphasis on rhetoric to an emphasis on grammar, with its attendant syntactic and semantic properties. This shift involved a gradual turning away from the generalized language of musical rhetoric common in the eighteenth century to the increased use of what might best be described as linked syntactical devices, analogous to tropes in figures of speech. Musical rhetoric relies upon allusion (e.g., a slow march in a minor mode metaphorically implies "funereal"), whereas musical syntax relies upon turns of phrase, graphic depiction, specific narrative devices, and so on. Syntactical systems in the early nineteenth century were connected with the older system of rhetoric in that they were also rooted in the effective communication of ideas, but they were new in the sense that these ideas embodied more specific (and specifically realistic), rather than merely poetic, content. The effect of thunder in Beethoven's and Rossini's musical storms serves as an obvious example of attempts at realism rather than metaphorical rhetoric (compared with, for example, Vivaldi's "storm" in *The Four Seasons*). Before the nineteenth century, syntactical devices—such as the so-called "Scottish snap" (in "The Death Song of the Cherokee Indians") or "hopping minor thirds" (in Reinagle's "Indian March")—were rarely used connotatively. When, where, and why this shift occurred is difficult to pinpoint. It certainly originated in continental Europe, though it was soon applied to American subjects (in addition to, for example, Scottish ones).[12]

I used the term *metaphor* above in lieu of the more comprehensive *semiotic,* a form of interdisciplinary analysis that evokes diverse, and sometimes confusing, possibilities. Yet metaphors are in fact semiotic representations, as are all other forms of nonidiomatic speech that similarly can be recognized as modes of communication. While this book is not strictly a semiotic study, I have found that methods and terms developed in this field are particularly useful for exploring the connotative richness of this music. For example, recent research by musical semioticians reveals a hierarchy of grammatical components at work: basic semantic units (specific musical devices) combine to form meaningful collections (musical tropes). Some examples of these are the tropes of heroism in Beethoven or the macabre in Liszt (both of which are the result of multiple devices). A musical trope is therefore more syntactically complex than a rhetorical topic. It functions as a category of signifiers and usually consists of several basic semantic units occurring simultaneously rather than individually. Chapters 1 and 2 explore important early modern topics of Indianism, while chapters 3 and 4 explore musical tropes that developed after about 1790. The nineteenth-century tropes of Indianism are roughly equivalent to *intonations,* a term coined by Boris Asafiev. He used intonation theory to discuss the absorption of folk music into Russian national styles, as well as composers' imitation of natural characteristics and use of programmatic narratives. (We'll explore this useful concept in chapter 6.)

Tara Browner offers a compelling semiotic model in her study of American Indian music and twentieth-century classical composers. Drawing on concepts from pioneer semiotician Charles Peirce, Browner grouped musical works based on Native American subjects into three categories: symbolic (merely native-inspired), indexical (attempting to approximate native sounds), and iconic (using materials from native music). Like Browner, I think these three categories work effectively for a larger discussion of musical borrowing among different cultural groups. They refer to general types of musical works, as symbols, indexes, and icons identify the relationships between sign and "object" in Peirce's triadic theory. A painting of a war dance, for example, is an iconic sign that resembles the actual dance. A "war dance" composed for Western musical instruments is an indexical sign, as it relies upon known conventions that evoke in the listener either an actual war dance or an iconic image of one. I also unravel the meaning of this music by taking into account all parts of the musical sign: its dynamic features (conventions), its referents, and its reception. The music examined in chapters 1 and 2—court ballets and operas and English-American theatrical songs—would correspond largely to the category of symbolic; in other words, the meaning is conveyed solely through established conventions of the genres. Chapters 3 and 4 turn to the development of indexical works, identifying the principal features of musical syntax that were involved in this indexography. Where possible, I also take into account the connotative quality of indexical works, keeping in mind the recurring use of basic semantic units that are combined in specific ways to form tropes relevant to native America (the "Resistance Indian," for example). Because these tropes are often linked with questions in the broader sphere of ideas, we can learn more about this music by examining it within the context of cultural history, a dimension usually ignored by musical semioticians. Chapter 3 is in part driven by two questions: what semiotic components constituted the tropes of the frontier in early nineteenth-century America, and how were these different from other non-Indian "frontiers"? Such a formulation can be meaningfully applied to music produced during this period. For example, why would someone want to use music "to approximate native sounds"? Questions of meaning are essential in any discussion of music as a language of communicative signs. What are the conventions through which musical signs point? What do they point to? How were they read (to the extent that we can know)? Our focus here, to paraphrase Edward Said, is on *how* native America is portrayed (and by what means) in order to understand better *why*, not on whether it is accurately portrayed or to what degree native source material is appropriately used.[13]

Most of the music explored in this book, like the production number in *Whoopee!* was composed or adapted for specific media or performed under particular circumstances. Without taking these into account, this music would seem, as it often does interpreted out of context, little more than incompetent imitation or, at best, a patently absurd or parodistic reduction of what originated as meaningful expression. Obvious parodies in musicals, such as the Indians in *Annie Get Your Gun* or *Peter Pan,* are relatively straightforward to analyze, given their predecessors in nineteenth-century burlesques. Much more problematic are the various "Indian marches," the nostalgia-laden nineteenth-century parlor songs, the "Indian laments" and instrumental war dances, the character pieces "based on Indian themes," the "Indian intermezzos" and ragtime songs, and even the operas with tragic Indian figures. I approach each of these by asking the same two questions: (1) what do the construction of this music and the circumstances of its composition and performance communicate to us about how native America was observed and interpreted? and (2) does this music present a coherent message, and, if so, what do these conventions reveal about the society that fostered (and in some sense still continues to foster) such attitudes? This book, with its chronological pursuit of these questions, uncovers a wide variety of cultural moves made through the language of music. It explores both real and imaginary Indians and asserts the important role that music plays in constructing relationships between the two.

PART I

New World Americans

1

Noble Savagery in European Court Entertainments, 1550–1760

When Columbus first encountered the welcoming Tainos of the West Indies in the 1490s, he called them *Indios,* thinking he had met the Indian peoples of the Far East. "Indian" became and remained a term by which people in the Western Hemisphere identified the native peoples of the Americas. It has also remained, to some extent, the term by which many of American Indian descent have chosen to identify themselves. "Native American," a liberal derivation that originated in the 1970s and that would seem to be a modern political correction of the original "Indian" misnomer, is in fact a reversion to the colonial frame of reference. Between 1507, when the word "America" first appeared on a globe of the world in Saint-Dié, France, and the colonists' declaration of independence in 1776, "Americans" from the European perspective meant specifically the native peoples of the continents. The tension that arose between Spanish, Portuguese, Dutch, French, and British colonial interests—and the "savages" who resisted these invasions—stimulated much of Europe's endless fascination with the New World.

When the final lavish entrée of the ballet *Flore* unfolded before Louis XIV at the Grand Salon of the Tuileries in 1669, it was intended to reflect the major racial groups of the world. Each section represented one of the "four corners" of the earth: the Europeans, the Africans, the "Asiatics," and the Americans. The music, still surviving in manuscript, was by court composer Jean-Baptiste

Lully. From this and from other balletic entrées for "Americans"—"Zelmatide, le Prince du Pérou" in *Ballet d'Alcidiane* (Lully, 1658), Louis's equestrian carrousel of 1662, *Le temple de la paix* (also Lully, 1686), and the *ballet des nations* that concluded *Isse* (Destouches, 1697)—it is evident that French court composers knew nothing of any actual Native American music (or at least did not attempt to imitate the style).[1] This does not mean, however, that indigenous cultures of America were entirely unfamiliar to the French royal court, for the design of the costumes and the peculiarities of movement in each of the entrées were crafted by Louis's dancing masters, based on their study of the peoples of each region. Yet in 1669, while histories of the Americas were rich in detail about the customs and behavior of "the Americans"—or *les sauvages américains,* as the French sometimes called them—little was commonly known about the music.[2] It is essential to understand how noble savagery developed in the musical language of France from Louis XIV's time to the years before the Revolution as a foundation for later representations of native America. France's role was significant, but not singular. England, as the principal agent in the colonization of North America in the seventeenth century (alongside Spain), followed a similar path and established much of the culture in North America until the 1840s. It was largely at that point that French and other continental influences broke through the hold that English music had on the cultural imagination of the new republic. These issues, then, particularly the literal struggle between France and England for North America (or its cultural equivalent), reveal tensions in the way culture was first imposed upon, and then took root in, the North American continent.

European Observers in America

Putting aside the content of Lully's ballets for Louis XIV for a moment, we might ask what educated Europeans in the 1660s would have known about music and the practice of music among the indigenous peoples of North America. The simple answer is probably very little, as far as most Europeans were concerned. But if we phrase the question another way—what would an educated person living in Europe in the 1660s have been able to learn about the music of *les sauvages américains* ?—then the answer leads us to the roots of musical exoticism.

According to Ramón Pane, a Catalonian cleric writing in 1496, the Tainos of Hispaniola sang religious chants in a call-and-response pattern (*arieto*), and these island Indians danced to the accompaniment of a two-keyed slit drum called the *mayohayau.* Placed directly on the ground, Pane informs us, the drum could be heard as far away as "a league and a half." From the Caribbean to the far westerly reaches of New Spain, some form of the hollowed-out log drum was used to accompany singing or dancing, as the early European explorers observed. Shortly after the Spanish conquest of Mexico, the texts of over one hundred Nahuatl songs were written down, most of them to be sung to the accompaniment of the *teponaztli*—again a notched log drum. In Aztec culture the drum was normally slit to have two keys—like the *mayohayau*—but some drums resembled the xylophone and had a range of up to five. While many Spaniards recorded their observations of Aztec music making, there were some, such as Juan de Zumárraga, first archbishop of Mexico, who authorized the destruction of ancient books and pictographic documents. Such plundering left later Spanish chroniclers with a limited basis for an understanding of Aztec culture, including music and worship.[3]

The Spanish explorers also noted a wide variety of other instruments as they made their way across the North American continent. In the 1530s Cabeza de Vaca (writing from an area that is now western Texas) remarked on the importance of gourd rattles, not just for keeping rhythm but also for the virtue that many Indians of the region believed resided in them. In the Sacramento Mountains of what is now California, Andrés de Carrança thought it important to mention copper jingle bells, again noting the spiritual value that they held for the local tribes. Flutes of all sizes were described by many of the Spaniards. Antonio de Mendoza wrote of the importance of flute playing among the Zunis. The highest pitched flutes—what today resemble piccolos or fifes—Mendoza called flageolets, and in 1540 Francisco Vásquez de Coronado reported a warm and sonorous welcome by the Pecos with flageolets and *atambores* ("drums"). In sixteenth- and seventeenth-century European civilization, drums as well as pipes had largely military associations, and as such they were considered the responsibility of the royal stable (*écurie*), not the church or court. But in the Americas, drumming was a means of providing continuity for a large portion of musical life—worship and inauguration ceremonies, celebrations, and seasonal holidays among them.

On this same expedition, Pedro de Castañeda noted a remarkable incident among women who sang while grinding corn. "One crushes the maize, the next grinds it, and the third grinds it finer," Coronado's chronicler wrote. "While they are grinding, a man sits at the door playing a flageolet, and the women move their stones, keeping time with the music, and all three sing together. They grind a large amount at one time." Songs, even those unaccompanied by rhythm instruments such as drums or rattles, were not just for work or worship, but were employed in times of conflict. Hernando de Soto's team, settling uncomfortably among the Natchez in roughly what is now Arkansas, noted that the tribe used songs to taunt the Spaniards, hoping to drive them away. The Natchez, the central group of mound builders whose villages bordered the Mississippi River, were one of the richest cultures in North America and still relatively intact as a civilization at the time of the Spanish expeditions. Partly dispersed from the ancient city of Cahokia (and perhaps related culturally to their Toltec neighbors to the south), they were also sun worshipers. According to chronicler Garcilaso de la Vega, when they greeted the rising sun, they did so with a great clamor and clatter of voices, trumpets, drums, fifes, shells, and other loud instruments. At the same time, they could be fierce when singing to no other accompaniment than the sound of the waves of their canoes and of their oars hitting the water. De la Vega describes how only a portion of De Soto's men escaped, the Natchez angrily pursuing them down the Mississippi toward the Gulf of Mexico while singing canoe-rowing songs to maintain their remarkable speed.[4]

These are some of the important examples of Indian music making that the Spanish described in their travel diaries during the first fifty years of European exploration in the Americas. There are similar English accounts from different regions. Shortly after the British landed on the East Coast and established the colony of Virginia, William Strachey wrote about dancing and singing (1609), noting that the Algonquian word for "dance" and "song" was the same: *cantecante.* He mentioned rattles of various sizes, also small gourds or pumpkin shells (with different pitches or ranges) and pipes or "recorders" made from cane. The latter were gentle and were played "without great strayning of the breath." He also described their singing and dancing in some detail, adding that rattles sounded in different pitches and mingled with their voices, "sometymes 20 or 30 togither." He called their love songs tuneful and their "angry songs" full of taunting strophes, meant to drive away the *Tassantasses,* as they called the invading English. Though Strachey's descriptions are vivid, the musical sounds from the civilization of Pocahontas and Powhatan are perhaps forever mute.[5]

Neither the Spanish nor the English explorers had the skill (and perhaps not even the desire) to notate any of the American music they heard. The French were the first to do so, beginning with the Calvinist pastor Jean de Léry (the "patriarch of transcribers," according to Roger Savage). Accompanying Admiral Villegaignon on his expedition to Brazil in 1557, Léry heard singing Tupinambá near modern-day Rio de Janeiro. Although he admitted that he could not fully capture the "ravishing" sound of some 500 voices, Léry did notate the text and music of the song's simple refrain and went on to transcribe several other songs as well. He published five of these in 1585. Seven years later, Théodore DeBry's published account of travel in Brazil included a more elaborate report on the music of the nomadic Tupinambá. DeBry was an engraver by trade, but his travel writings are protoethnomusicological in that he not only transcribed melodies but also based his analysis on recognizable patterns, among these the fixed range of a fifth and the internal repetition of short melodic phrases. From the French perspective, the Brazilian "Tupí" were an extraordinarily graceful and musical people, and it was they who received the first invitation to dance before the French court in 1613. The French in general were much more interested in the musical culture of "the Americans" than either the Portuguese or the Spanish. On an expedition to Acadia (modern-day Nova Scotia), Marc Lescarbot observed and notated some Micmac songs, ones he allegedly obtained from Membertou, a medicine man. Gabriel Sagard, traveling in 1632 in the Georgian Bay area, wrote about the Wyandot Hurons. He did not think much of Huron singing and generally found it disagreeable. On one occasion, however, he overheard the singing of a group of *sauvages* preparing for a feast. They sat around a stewing pot, singing sweetly rather than forcefully. First one led off, then all sang together, eventually singing the same music in alternation. Sagard found himself "carried away with admiration" by the singing. He also took many notes on Huron dancing, observing a variety of round dances. He was especially pleased to watch the dancing of young Huron women, whom he likened to nymphs, and rhapsodized over their lightness of foot.[6]

Sagard, a Recollet lay brother, was a missionary of extraordinary perception and courage. Many of his observations have been corroborated and hold up today. Not all observers focused on sweet singing and delicate female dancing, however. An anonymous Jesuit writing from Quebec (published in 1659) noted the distinctiveness of the Amerindian body, and he drew on concepts like vigorous and violent to describe the physical motions of the dancers. The author noted how the Hurons repeatedly struck the ground with their feet "as if determined to make it tremble." In 1655 Jesuit missionary Claude Dablon wrote similarly of dancing among the Iroquois. One of the songs sustained a "rhythmic tattoo sounded by tribesmen beating their feet, hands, and pipes against the mats."[7]

In 1636 the Franciscan and music theorist Marin Mersenne quoted a "Chanson Canadoise" in his *Harmonie universelle,* saying that it had been sent to King Louis XIII by one of his "captains" in New France. Mersenne also noted that reports from Canada indicated that the *sauvages américains* were beginning to sing songs they had learned not only from other Indians but also from the French traders settled among them. Similarly, the Jesuit missionaries Dablon and Chaumonot among the Iroquois noted in 1655 that the Indians were creating songs in their own language that were clearly European in style. The Iroquois tribesmen greeted them at Onondaga with "six airs, or chants, which savored nothing of the savage." To seventeenth-century European ears, each air expressed "the divers passions they wished to portray." Less than a hundred years after the French first began to send missionaries to North and South America, a process of acculturation was already under way. Not only European observation but also European participation in this process would problematize the very nature of mapping indigenous Indian cultures. When Dablon notated an Illinois melody in Winnebago County in 1670, he admitted that he could no longer be sure to what extent the tune was truly native to the Americans in question.[8]

An Exchange of Cultures?

Even if musicians in seventeenth-century Europe had not known any of the writings that contained descriptions of American Indian music (and these expensive books were not widely available), they certainly would not have missed the numerous reports of New World visitors to the royal courts of Europe. In 1500, only a few years after the Portuguese began their exploration of South America, Pêro Vaz de Caminha sent several Tupinambá to the king at Lisbon. The distinctive features most often written about the Brazilians were the feathers that adorned their headpieces and cinctures, their bows and arrows, their strong bodies, and of course the amount of exposed bare flesh. The strength and beauty of the Amerindian male body quickly became a source of fascination and drew hundreds of onlookers wherever these New World visitors appeared. In 1527 Hernán Cortés similarly sent a group of Aztec males to Charles V. The king was amazed at the physical strength they displayed in their synchronized dancing. Encouraged by this success, Cortés the following year brought more Aztecs to Europe, where their reputation as skilled jugglers had preceded them. They never failed to dazzle their courtly audiences, and Christoph Weiditz's 1528 sketch of a young Aztec male spinning a log in the air with his feet depicts one of the first American performers in Europe. But Cortés brought these people to Europe for other reasons: the Aztecs served to convince skeptical Europeans of his discoveries; their subjugation demonstrated his authority over the Mexican people; and with their presence he hoped to allay the church's fears that he was a ruthless murderer.[9]

For most Europeans at this time, Indians were *sauvages* (or *Wilden* in German), not necessarily in the pejorative sense but as childlike and unaffected creatures from an untamed, often idyllic, wilderness. The possibility of actual Indian delegations—groups of Indians led by representative chieftains who visited Europe to further diplomatic relations—did not exist until the eighteenth century. The extraordinary fascination with the "savages" could also be attributed to the fact that since Europe first encountered the New World, ideas about a separate genesis for the native peoples of America took hold, first among alchemists in the sixteenth century, then in theological writings, and finally among incipient anthropologists. Indigenous Americans inadvertently activated the belief in polygenism, a concept that was central, as George Stocking points out, to pre-Darwinian anthropology. The polygenetic account held the races to be irreducible to one origin; hence the peoples of the New World shared nothing in common with those of the Old. Asians and Africans had long been mapped on the old Greco-Roman and biblical taxonomy, argues Jonathan Smith. But the *sauvages* were not descended from Adam and hence were not tainted by original sin. Although the term appeared much later, the belief in polygenesis appears to have been quite common by the seventeenth century and heightened the sense of alterity (or otherness) that Europeans felt when in their proximity.[10]

For much of the sixteenth and seventeenth centuries, the French seemed in amazement of this alterity and were particularly fascinated by the Tupinambá. At Rouen in 1550, an entire "Brazilian village" was re-created, exposition-style, as part of the entry festival for Henry II and his wife, Catherine de Médicis. A "jungle" was created on the banks of the Seine in which parrots, monkeys, coatis, and other South American animals frolicked. Two villages of thatched cabins included fifty "authentic Brazilians" who, with 250 painted and costumed Frenchmen, engaged in pantomimes of idyllic life in Brazil—practicing archery, swinging in hammocks—but who also staged mock battles, ostensibly between the Tupinambá and their enemies, the Tobajaro. The Brazilian fad encouraged other French explorers to deliver more South Americans. In 1560 several Peruvians participated in court ceremonials. By the early seventeenth century, Native American dancing constituted a distinct style to the French, and in the *Ballet de la reine,* offered before Henry IV and his queen on 31 January 1609, the first entry featured "Les américains." Wearing Brazilian plumage, the dancers of the court imitated the movements of the so-called *enfants sans soucy.* (One of these dances was published in Praetorius's *Terpsichore.*)[11]

Four years later, one of Richelieu's commanders, François de Rasilly, returned from Brazil with six Tupinambá from the coastal region of Maranhão. Thirteen-year-old Louis XIII persuaded them to "perform their native dances" before the court. The poet François de Malherbe, who recounted this incident in his *Oeuvres,* made no mention of instruments or any specific details of Tupinambá music. He did note, however, that "they danced a kind of branle without holding hands and without moving from one place." Among the many dances of the French *ballet de cour,* the branle (of which there are at least four types—all of them round dances in which couples held hands and formed a line or circle) was considered a peasant or folk dance, not one that originated among the aristocracy. (Lully used very few branles in his court ballets and none before 1665. The French branle was common in the early seventeenth century, however, and Michael Praetorius included several in his 1612 *Terpsichore*, including a "Ballet des Amazones.") Branles were generally notated in a compound meter, usually consisted of alternating 1 + 2 and 2 + 1 rhythms, and illustrations reveal that a *timbale* was sometimes used to mark the pulse. Malherbe's observation curiously tries to account for the nature of Tupinambá dancing by comparing it with this round dance. But his comparison was probably based more on the movements themselves than on any actual musical similarities. Nevertheless, Malherbe was sufficiently interested in Tupinambá singing to ask the well-known French lutenist Ennemond Gaultier to compose a piece based on their music. Gaultier's response was not specifically a branle, but rather the related sarabande, a rough-hewn Spanish folk dance also in a compound meter (and little known outside Spain in 1613). Gaultier's sarabande has not survived (or at least is not recognized as such among his intabulated sarabandes). But Malherbe was quite explicit in confirming that the lutenist had indeed based his work on a tune obtained *sur la danse des Toupinamboux*. Gaultier probably used the Brazilian tune as a ground bass, as Miriam Whaples surmised, improvising a series of *double* variations over it. This was common practice among lutenists at the time, and Gaultier would certainly have been on the lookout for new and unusual basses.[12]

Seven years later, in the *Ballet de l'amour de ce temps représenté par les enfants sans-soucy* at the royal court, an apparently naked Tupinambá (or a French dancer painted as one) "titillated the women spectators" by coming forward and addressing the audience: "Beauties, my name is Topinambou, I've come from a foreign, far countree." Naked Brazilians, it seems, were now a standard feature of the French court, and it was well known that in the warm Brazilian paradise, the Tupinambá lived unencumbered by much clothing. Yet Tupi immodesty was often exaggerated. Another account of this same ballet notes instead "his almost entire lack of costuming." "Nakedness" with respect to the *sauvages américains* seems to have been largely a construct used for its rhetorical power as a marker of childlike innocence in the Indian character. Since the Brazilians had never been driven from Eden, it could be argued, they had never learned physical modesty. Moreover, sophisticated Europeans allowed themselves the pleasure of contemplating the bare flesh and taut exposed limbs of innocent *sauvages* to a degree that would have been generally unacceptable had the dancers been identifiably European.

A few years later, another "Tupinambá" appeared before the court. This

Figure 1. Daniel Rabel, *Le Roy Atabalipa* as depicted in the *Ballet de la douairière de Billebahaut* (1626). Pen, wash, and gouache. Louvre, Dessins, Inv. 32 633. Cliché Musée National, Paris.

time it was in the *Grand Bal de la douairière de Billebahaut* ("the Dowager of Bilbao"), a *ballet des nations* danced before Louis XIII at the Louvre on 11 February 1626. The *Bal,* which took the form of a *réception burlesque,* consisted of not four but five parts representing the principal continental regions of the world—America, Asia, the Arctic, Africa, and Europe—each preceded by a leader. Could this "leader of the American people" have been the same Tupinambá dancer? Now he had a name beyond that of his tribal affiliation: "Atabalipa." The Peruvian king, as depicted in a drawing by Daniel Rabel (fig. 1), rides in a divan hoisted by two bare-breasted slaves. He wears both a crown and a traditional headdress of burnt-edged feathers. This same hydrocephalic dwarf, who would seem to have been in France since the late sixteenth century, is mentioned in Banchieri's *La Nobiltà dell'asino Attabalippa dal Perú* (1599). By 1626 Atabalipa had become a stage name for the Peruvian king. According to Lionel de la Laurencie, this figure was "destined to achieve a long career in French literature" by popping up in several places over the next several decades. At times he billed himself—or was billed—as "Atabalipa, King of Cusco." At other times he was "Atahuallpa, King of the Incas." The original Atahuallpa, of course, never left Peru, having overthrown his own brother to obtain the Inca throne. He was emperor at the time of the Spanish conquest in 1532 and was executed under Pizarro. This apparent namesake of the Peruvian emperor, as Laurencie noted, was probably the first in a long line of European actors pretending to be Americans.

Rabel's drawing shows "Atabalipa" moving his legs to the accompaniment of his own music, which he plays on a hurdy-gurdy.[13] The linkage between a powerful South American king and an instrument associated with peasantry is an intriguing one. The hurdy-gurdy was known in Europe as early as the tenth century. In the Middle Ages its associations were mostly with the nobility, as it was fashionable for minstrels to use the drone instrument to accompany their singing at princely courts. But by the fourteenth century, perhaps because of the development of more sophisticated instruments, its reputation fell, and discarded hurdy-gurdies were adopted by the poor and indigent. Many paintings from the Renaissance, for example, show blind beggars cranking away. Was this European dancer, with his grotesque Peruvian mask, poking fun at American simplicity? It would seem so, and the French nobility might certainly have understood it this way. In a later seventeenth-century engraving by Martin Engelbrecht, the artist shows three country musicians and includes this verse:

> Limited as is their intelligence,
> So are their instruments.
> Shawms, hurdy-gurdies, and bagpipes,
> Playing naught but the tune.
> The effect is so charming
> One wants to hold his ears.

A 1672 example of a *branle de Bresse* shows the melody played by a single-reed chalumeau and the drone bourdon sustaining open fifths, hurdy-gurdy style. In the eighteenth century, composers drew on the simple drone basses of the hurdy-gurdy and musette as a rhetorical device for the pastoral. (Later "Indian music," as we will see, also maintained this connection.) In the eighteenth century, however, the nobility sometimes revived the hurdy-gurdy for its *primitif* Arcadian associations. But this was a later affectation. In 1626 the French court would have been principally aware of its annoying and persistent droning. In fact, the musical emphasis of *Le Grand Bal* was on parody. For the Asian entrée (which was set in the Middle East), the libretto specified cacophony: the oboes were to play *mal d'accord* with the violins. The effect of the music throughout the first episodes was no doubt to prepare the way for the superiority of the final European entrée with its elegant dancing and fine *chanteurs.*[14]

It is typical of French attitudes toward dance that drones could be incorporated into the rustic dances performed at court. By the early seventeenth century, French court dances constituted a compendium of styles brought together from across Europe and the world. Dances such as the canarie, a dotted 6/8 pattern thought to be from the Canary Islands, were not necessarily danced only in contexts reflecting their cultural origin. Nor were court dances in the early seventeenth century necessarily differentiated by movements, as Marie-Françoise Christout has argued. Meter, time, and tempo defined dance style, even though dance types were sometimes transported with their cultural attributes. One of the dances singled out most frequently in the early seventeenth century for its degree of exoticism was the moresca (or morisque). As its title implies, its origin was Moorish (and it represented a conflict between two fighters). In moderate tempo, it featured a driving four-beat rhythmic pattern (𝅗𝅥 ♩♩), a distinctive long–short-short accompaniment. The moresca was found all over Europe, including England, where, as Curt Sachs has shown, it developed into the Morris dance. The moresca was probably first mapped onto native America in 1641, in a *Ballet de M. le Cardinal de Richelieu.* While France continued its colonization of the New World, French dancers of the royal court dressed as American Indians for entrée no. 26 ("les Américains") and danced to the throbbing rhythm of a moresca, although the subject of the G-major tune was of course no longer Moorish.[15]

While the French court marveled at *sauvagerie,* visiting native Americans were elsewhere increasingly displayed more as curiosities, expected to exhibit the characteristics of savagery sensationalized by reports from the New World. In 1644 two former members of the Dutch West Indies Company and one Hermanus Meyer formed a partnership to display a "wild Indian named Jacques," an Iroquois from the Dutch colonies. That same year, Governor Johan Maurits of Brazil, who prided himself on his good relations with the Indians, returned to the Hague bringing six Tapuia with him. Maurits asked his Brazilians to offer a war dance at a reception in the Mauritshuis. According to John Hemming, a scholar of Brazil's indigenous population, the sight of stark naked, painted Indians "caused much amusement and giggling among all sorts of people." Hemming doesn't mention the Tapuia music, which must have contributed to the heightened response. By this time the practice of publicly exhibiting American Indians was already over a century old. But the Dutch reception appears to have been the first recorded occasion on which an American Indian war dance was performed on European soil.[16]

The manner in which the seventeenth-century French wrote of the American

Indians already demonstrates a binary opposition between the pure and child-like versus the vicious and heathen. The latter originated in tales of cannibalism from the West Indies ("Caniba"). Woodcuts depicting human portions hung in preparation for a feast had already appeared in Augsburg, Germany, shortly after Columbus's return. At the same time, the woodcuts exaggerated the precious stones on the headdresses of the Indians, establishing a connection between danger and desire, wealth and conquest. In 1580 the essayist Montaigne questioned the pejorative connotations of the term *sauvage* in his essay on cannibals, finding the term inappropriate for the Americans. But many of his compatriots, as Harry Liebersohn noted in *Aristocratic Encounters,* "continued their un-self-conscious, usually contemptuous use of it." In the sixteenth and seventeenth centuries, the concept of "savage" seemed to be based on a few clearly identifiable markers of appearance and behavior. The first of these was nudity (but not through lack of vanity, as "savages" were observed to decorate their bodies with tattoos or jewels and other objects of acquisition). Though nearly all Indians of North and South America wore clothing of various kinds, the majority of Indians brought to Europe in the first two centuries of contact were from warm southerly regions. Warfare served as another distinct marker of savagery, especially given the Americans' growing reputation for ambushes and other stealth tactics. More important, however, savages were pagans. In 1537 Pope Paul III had issued a proclamation that all Indians were "true men," and this initiated the sustained effort over the next three hundred years to bring Christianity to the natives, thereby aiming to eradicate one aspect of their "savagery."[17]

In 1583 the Franciscan Bernardino de Sahagún published Aztec Christian psalms at Mexico City. These were, according to Robert M. Stevenson, sacred lyrics that may have been sung in Nahuatl to native tunes (tunes that were not notated and therefore are lost to us today). This clever use of native music in the process of evangelization, however, offered a means of presenting the unfamiliar through familiar media. Franciscans, Jesuits, and others also brought European instruments with them to Mexico. Beginning around 1620, Franciscan missionaries even in the farthest northern regions of New Spain could boast organs, bassoons, *cornetti,* and a collection of music books for singing and instruction. Conversion of the American Indians also involved the teaching of Latin and Gregorian chant. Many missionaries even offered lessons in part-singing. According to seventeenth-century records, instrumental music and a rich polyphonic tradition throughout New Spain resulted in what is often referred to as the "Mexican Baroque." Moreover, polyphonic singing of sacred music became for the Franciscans and Jesuits across North and South America an important aid in the conversion of the Indians.[18]

In keeping with this practice, Sagard in 1636 harmonized three of Lescarbot's earlier notated Micmac songs. Along with a harmonized version of one of Léry's transcriptions, he published these in *Histoire du Canada,* a revision of his earlier *Grand voyage.* Although Sagard called these four songs representative of "Huron Music," the first three were Iroquois (Micmac) in origin and the latter Brazilian. Sagard had enough interest in the nature of the tunes to make some observations about their similarities and differences, even as he diluted these by setting the tunes in a standard four-part harmonization, thereby submitting them to the theoretical discipline of sacred French missionary music. Despite his comments on the music, however, Sagard failed to note a crucial difference between the three Micmac songs and the Brazilian one (as Whaples points out). Léry's Tupinambá refrain appears to be diatonically (or modally) oriented and therefore distinctly European-sounding, whereas the Micmac songs with their "gapped" scales are decidedly pentatonic (a natural five-note ordering system used in folk musics around the world). As composers would continue to do for generations, Sagard set the pentatonic melodies to diatonically derived accompaniments, thereby "westernizing" them in the process. Mersenne published Sagard's four-part harmonizations, along with the previously mentioned "Chanson Canadoise." When over a century later Jean-Jacques Rousseau compiled his *Dictionnaire de Musique* (Paris, 1768) he quoted the Tupinambá song from Father Mersenne. Rousseau also noted its similarity to European music and added that some may doubt its authenticity. By the middle of the eighteenth century, "authenticity" had become an important consideration in the study of all ethnically centered music. But in the seventeenth century, questions of authenticity—at least as far as music of the Americas was concerned—were just beginning to be raised.[19]

"Indians," Lully, and the Court of Louis XIV

This brief overview of the sixteenth- and seventeenth-century observance and exchange of cultures between Europe and the native peoples of the New World suggests the limited and sometimes conflicting information that circulated among educated Europeans of Lully's generation. Hardly more than a symbolic understanding of what constituted Indian music could have been available to Lully and his librettist Francesco Buti when they fashioned *Les Indiens,* entrée no. 8 in *L'Amour malade,* an evening of ballet for Louis XIV and his queen given in the Grande Salle of the Louvre on 17 January 1657. Even for the eighteen-year-old king, culture and politics were classically united in *ballets de cour,* and the king himself had danced as Apollo in a 1653 allegorical ballet to celebrate the victory of the royalist forces in the Frondes.[20] *L'Amour malade,* interspersed with Italian narrations and delivered by "Reason," consisted of forty-seven separate dances, grouped into nine themed entrées. The Peruvian sequence featured six Indian men and six Indian women. The women, though *"basannez"* (sunburned), carried parasols. These are the first New World inhabitants represented on a European stage with music by a major composer. (Surprisingly, Atabalipa shows up again in this ballet, dancing as "the King of Peru and of the Indians.")

This entry contains only two musical numbers, an air and a ritournelle. The air, marked *très gai,* is a lively dance in what would later be called French overture style. The stately opening passage with its dotted rhythms is followed by a contrasting section (marked *gracieusement*) in three. The texture is that of Lully's standard five-part writing. The air opens plainly enough with a cheerful phrase and is followed by three simple *doubles* that are each repeated. Lully uses music here (and in the ritournelle that follows) to emphasize symbolically the "Indians" in the ballet. There are no indexical references to "drums" for marking the beat and no use of rattles or chanting to provide local color. Nothing signifies Peruvian, American, or, in this case, "Indian" in either the melody, the ornamentation, the bass line, the harmonies, or the texture (five principal features of Western musical style), nor does Lully's music suggest difference in the way that the dancers' dress and movements in the *ballet des nations* suggested difference. Yet one feature should be noted here (and for future reference): Lully had some preoccupation with choice of key and mode. Although the single flat in the key signature suggests otherwise, this air is firmly in G minor (with an occasional pull to B♭ major). G minor, with its modally inflected lowered seventh, is a key that Lully generally reserved for dark moods, for tragedy (as in his motet "De Profundis"), and for the mysteries of imaginary worlds. For Benserade's ballet *Alcidiane,* given at the royal court the following year, Lully wrote airs for "Prince Zelmatide" and the "Peruvians" in G minor and B♭ major. Much of Lully's music for that ballet—peopled as it is by Turks, Moors, Peruvians, supernatural figures, and monsters—is, as Whaples points out, dominated by the key of G minor. With the possible exceptions of the similarities between Peruvian round dancing, the peasant branle, and similar uses for the "dark" key of G minor, Lully uses no indexical language—indeed, he would not have had access to any—to mark the American Indians as musically different from the other groups of dancers.

Symbolic representation remained standard for most ballets at the court of Louis XIV, with Americans included in entrées largely to demonstrate the breadth of the king's empire. A *ballet des nations* in 1662, for example, was designed to celebrate one of Louis's equestrian carrousels. It opened with a

Roman procession (headed by Louis himself) and included a panorama of many distant nations, among them Persians, Turks, (East) Indians, and Americans. *Flore* of 1669 is unique in that its panorama is not of nations but of continents, whereby America receives equal status with Europe. When all four groups (Europeans, Africans, Asiatics, and Americans) are eventually united on the stage, they dance together to the music of a canarie. Dictionaries of dance, such as that of Charles Compan (Paris, 1787) normally describe the dancers of a canarie to be costumed as savages and simulating a mock combat, approaching and recoiling from one another. The canarie that closed *Flore,* however, almost certainly underscored the sense of denouement through harmony of gesture, rather than suggesting conflict. Lully used canaries in other exotic contexts and used other dances in "Indian" contexts. In 1685 his dramatic ballet *Le temple de la paix* contained a rondeau (F major, 6/4) for the entry of the "Sauvages de l'Amérique" and concluded with a chaconne, another dance of American origin. *Le temple* was first produced at Fontainebleau, repeated at Versailles and Paris, and performed again in 1686. In his preface Lully wrote that "the Peace which Your Majesty has given so generously to his conquered enemies is the subject of this ballet." Verses referred to the expedition of Ferdinand de la Salle, who only four years before had explored the Mississippi River Valley and claimed the region, which he called Louisiana, for Louis XIV.[21]

Opera and Representations of the New World after Lully

If there were a single word or idea that could appropriately describe the nature of ballet at the French court during the seventeenth century, it would be *ménagerie.* The far-flung sumptuousness of the *ballets de court* reflected not only an interest in diversity but more importantly a sense of marvel and wonder, to paraphrase Stephen Greenblatt. This sustained period in the European experience emerged out of contact with the New World and then became pervasive in representation. The French royal court did not initially seem interested in narrative accounts of international conquest. No musical dramatizations of the encounter between Europeans and the New World, for example, exist in France before Rameau's *Les Indes galantes* (1735). The allegorical subjects of French court ballet (and subsequently those of English, Italian, and other courts) instead reflected amazement at the New World. Recognition of this sense of marvel and wonder is critical to understanding the question of meaning in historical context. Conquest does not seem to have been a major thrust of French involvement, and perhaps for this reason, relationships between many Indian tribes and the French remained strong well into the nineteenth century. Discovery of gold and other resources, on the other hand, clearly drove most colonial interests. In major European centers, representations of the Discovery were played out on the operatic stage. Like Lully's ballets, these works are largely symbolic of the empire—and even of local politics—and are rarely if ever musically expressive of "Americans" themselves.[22]

In Italy, Pietro Ottobone's dramma per musica *Il Colombo ovvero l'India scoperta* with music by Bernardo Pasquini recast the Italian explorer as a modern-day Odysseus. Performed in Rome's Teatro di Tordinona in 1690, the opera relied on spectacular stage machinery to depict the mythological perils of the ocean voyage. Once Columbus arrives in his mythical land, the opera unfolds in a series of ludicrous love intrigues between fictional characters of opposing sides. At the time that he created his dramma per musica, Ottobone served as cardinal nephew to Pope Alexander VIII, which put him in rank next to the pope himself. Jürgen Maehder suggests that this dramatization of discovery, political intrigue, and seduction served as an allegory both to demonstrate the influence and power of the Ottobone family as well as to reflect the political aspirations of the cardinal himself. The operatic conflict is naturally resolved, however, and conquest is thereby achieved in the end through a joyful marriage that unites the two sides. Columbus dazzles the Americans with gifts that display the wealth and scope of the Spanish empire, a dramatic convention that necessitates the inclusion of a panoramic *ballet des nations*.[23]

Columbus might seem the most obvious choice for a "discovery opera," especially in a centennial decade like the 1690s. But in the late seventeenth and early eighteenth centuries, the most dynamic New World librettos centered on the confrontation between Cortés and Moctezuma, adversarial figures often allocated equal stature. John Dryden, who in 1670 coined the epithet "noble savage" in *The Conquest of Granada,* had already explored this vital Mexican confrontation in two of his previous verse plays. The subject was pursued in masques by Purcell, in a play by Voltaire, and in operas by Vivaldi and Karl Heinrich Graun, court composer to Frederick the Great. While Cortés and Moctezuma's equal status did not preclude remarkable exotic touches in costuming, there are relatively few features in Purcell's and Graun's operatic music (Vivaldi's score is lost) that suggest "difference" between the Spaniards and the Mexicans. In fact, these works were allegorical and not necessarily about the struggle for Mexico, as scholars have shown, although they set the stage for Rameau's magnificent *Les Indes galantes,* which can arguably be shown to reflect colonial anxieties in the Americas and elsewhere. Though the music of these "discovery operas" is largely symbolic in portraying the New World, they do share some features that contributed to the stylistic rhetoric of Indianism that would develop in the eighteenth century.

In 1664 John Dryden and Robert Howard's *The Indian Queen,* a heroic verse tragedy with occasional songs, enjoyed enough success in London that they followed it with *The Indian Emperor* in 1665. Pelham Humfrey, a singer and composer for the Chapel Royal who is believed to have studied with Lully, wrote music for both plays. Only a single song from *The Indian Emperor* survives in a 1675 publication. Humfrey's continuo aria ("Ah, Fading Joy") was sung by an unnamed Aztec woman to entertain the Spanish conquistadors. The aria does not feature any unusual vocal or instrumental devices (although it's impossible to know what a singer might have added at the time). The song *is* in G minor, however, and, like Lully, Humfrey may have turned to this key as a rhetorical marker of dark and imaginary worlds. In 1691 Henry Purcell, who had likewise studied with Humfrey, composed music for a new production of *The Indian Emperor,* of which also only one number remains, that for a non-Indian spirit.[24]

Purcell's complete score for an adaptation of Dryden's *The Indian Queen* for a production at His Majesty's Theatre survives intact, however.[25] The music is some of Purcell's finest, though it is written, as is customary in the English masque, for secondary and allegorical characters rather than for the principal actors. Dryden's play focuses on the Mexican Queen Zempoalla and her Peruvian enemies to the south. According to Curtis Price, Purcell transformed this fantastical account into a powerful tragedy by focusing most of the attention on Zempoalla, the usurping queen. Though she never sings, "she is surrounded by music that conveys her unspoken turmoil and guilt."[26] Like Humfrey, Purcell offers no special characterization for the South Americans. The music for neither the Indian boy and girl opening the first masque nor the High Priest and Aztec chorus closing Purcell's last completed masque (nor for any of the allegorical characters in between) bears any of the seventeenth century's few identifying "Americanisms": marked rhythmic accompaniments, unusual instrumentation, darkly hued modes, or distinctive ornamentation. Indeed, no composer had yet thought of using them together for this purpose.[27]

There is one scene, however, in which the most delicate exotic touch is incontestable. At the opening of act 3, Zempoalla celebrates her soldiers' defeat of the Incas. According to Howard's instructions, she appears "seated upon her slaves in triumph, and the Indians, as to celebrate the victory, advance in a warlike dance." At first glance, there is little that appears "warlike" about Purcell's music. It is in B♭ major, in a brisk cut time, and scored for violins, bass, and continuo. B♭ major, of course, uses the same key signature as G minor, and in fact Purcell's two-part dance occasionally slips into G minor in its B section. But this touch, even if it could be proven to be related to Lully's use of the same mode, is so deft as to be seem largely coincidental. (It should be noted, however, that the dance continues uninterrupted into the Conjurer's Song—one of Purcell's most famous tunes—"You twice ten hundred deities," and that this recitative-aria is in G minor.[28]) Perhaps more distinctive than key or mode, however, is the dance's accompanying rhythm. It is reminiscent of a sixteenth-century moresca, with its strong emphasis on one, its lack of a marked second pulse, and the sharp quarter upbeat. (Morescas often had two quarter-note upbeats instead of one.[29]) Though there is no percussion specified in Purcell's dance, the incessant repetition of the rhythm (𝅗𝅥. ♩) assumes an inevitable and driving quality. As in a presentational moresca, this dance would have called for the performers to exhibit a display of weaponry—perhaps a brandishing of swords and knives—and even perhaps an illustration of mock combat. Were it not for the brisk tempo, this dance could be compared with some of the contemporary mock combats "fought to the slow beat of a special drum," which Dablon noted during his visit to the Americas.[30]

The circumstances surrounding the creation of a libretto by Girolamo Giusti for Antonio Vivaldi on the American conquest (and slated for performance at the Teatro di Sant'Angelo, Venice) are less clear. Giusti's *argomento* reveals that his synopsis of the work is derived from the historian Antonio De Solís and that for dramatic purposes he would restrict the focus to Montezuma and his court's reception of Cortés. "I have imagined the friendship, though feigned, which grew up between the two nations, the reasons for the breaking of the truce, and I show in the present drama the calamities of the last day," Giusti added. In other words, Giusti's scenario adopts a harsher and more realistic stance toward the brutal confrontation between two communities, one indigenously American, the other a powerful invader. Giusti's libretto ends with the destruction of Tenochtitlán. Though we will have to wait for an edition of the recently found manuscript of 1733, we can reasonably conclude that Vivaldi's music, as for the Turkish and Egyptian subjects in his *La verità in cimento* and *Il Giustino,* probably did not intentionally characterize Mexico. Vivaldi, as had Purcell before him, generally subjugated notions of alterity to the normative idioms of Baroque musical style. By the time that Giusti and Vivaldi created their depiction of the Aztec world, Mexico City had become a European-style capital with its own cathedral and even its own theater. These Italians were writing about an "ancient" city that was nearly as far removed from them in spirit as were those of classical Greece from Herodotus. As Venetians in the 1720s and 1730s were losing interest in mythological operas and preferred historical subjects instead, the Aztec ruler would have been interesting to Venetian audiences for his pivotal role in the downfall of the last ancient civilization.[31]

Compared with *Montezuma*'s dark political undertones, Voltaire's roughly contemporaneous play *Alzire, ou les Américains* (1736) depicted the New World as a terrestrial paradise. According to Maehder, "no references to human sacrifice disturb the vision of a well-organized country living in harmony with its rulers." Voltaire, inspired partly by Dryden's *The Indian Emperor,* was concerned with portraying three distinct groups in postconquest Mexico and South America: Catholic Spaniards, Christianized Aztecs, and pagan Aztecs.[32] Voltaire assumed the inevitability of the conquest but questioned the validity of religious intolerance, not in the essence of Christianity but as practiced by the Spaniards. True Christians are loving and forgiving, Voltaire lectured, not violent, deceitful, and murderous. The "problem" of this play was the question it raised: is the religious conviction of the church (Spanish Catholic) superior to innate virtue (Mexican Aztec, i.e., noble savage)?[33]

For three years (1750–52), Voltaire shared an intense friendship with Frederick the Great, which led Frederick to create his own dramatic elaboration on the Moctezuma-Cortés conflict, this time as a full-fledged opera with Karl Heinrich Graun providing the music. The opera that opened the Berlin Winter Carnival of 1755 pitted Montezuma and his (fictional) general Pilpatoé against Cortés and his own menacing and ruthless accomplice Navrès, thereby increasing the military conflict. The work has a decidedly anti-Christian message: Montezuma and his queen refuse to give up their "pagan idols," while Cortés and his aides are portrayed as religious bigots who intend to make Christians of the Mexicans at any price. Frederick's scenario was unambiguous about the moral dilemma, however: because Queen Eupaforice did not forsake her false gods and marry Cortés, the Aztecs were slaughtered. *Montezuma* has often been noted by scholars as the finest of Graun's thirty-some Italian operas written for Frederick's court. Especially moving are Montezuma's prison scene at the opening of act 3 and Eupaforice's final dramatic suicide monologue. According to Ernest Helm, Frederick identified with the nobility of Aztec culture and interpreted the coalition of powers surrounding Prussia allegorically as the barbarous Spaniards.[34]

Like Purcell sixty years before him, Graun did not use music to differentiate between the Aztecs and Spaniards. That was left to the costumes. In Graun's aesthetic, as for his fellow North German opera composers, the gestures of music emanated directly from the characters' emotional and psychological states (signified by the so-called *Affekten*).[35] The surface details of his music vary in degrees of virtuosity and principally to convey the right affect, not to suggest gender, ethnic, national, racial, or even class difference. (Of course Metastasian conventions fully in place by the 1750s would have forbidden members of different classes to interact on the stage.) The music that Graun

Figure 2. Anonymous dance excerpt ("Tambourin") from Karl Heinrich Graun's *Montezuma*. From *Denkmaler Deutscher Tonkunst* 15 (1904), 226.

composed for an aria of Eupaforice, for example, bears no audible differences in style from that of an aria written for the Spanish captain Navrès, who, like Cortés, loathes the Aztec "heathens." Among the principal defining stylistic features of music—melody, ornamentation, bass lines, harmonic setting, texture, and choice of key and mode—none of Graun's operatic music in *Montezuma* defines binary *musical* opposition between the Spanish or Aztec characters.

A big surprise occurs, then, when we discover ethnic markers in the *balli* danced by the Mexicans (omitted from the only recording of the work). There were three divertissements—one for each act—added and presumably composed by the unnamed dancing master. In the allegro dance at the conclusion of act 1, as Whaples pointed out in 1958, there is evidence of an attempt to create an "authentic primitivism" in the use of a drone bass and the "monotonous melody and rhythm of the refrain."[36] I would add that the two tambourins (one in act 2 and another in act 3) exhibit additional markers of early primitivist musical rhetoric. These devices include not only the use of G minor, but also other characteristics that became increasingly prominent in later works. Figure 2 shows that many phrases have short, reiterated passages that seem halting and intentionally rough-hewn, certainly compared with the other dances. Given that the tambourins were to be performed quickly, the leaping octaves in the bass, both upward and downward, stand out as angular, athletic markers of wild, rather than stylized, courtly dancers.

Rameau and Baroque Musical Rhetoric

In Baroque discovery operas, then, it was almost exclusively in the dance numbers where any unusual stylistic markers could be found. This would seem to make sense, given that court dances already had distinguishing physical characteristics as early as the sixteenth century. In 1719 Jean-Baptiste Dubos defined the term *danse de caractère* as referring to a dance whose "melody and rhythm *imitate a specific style* and which is, therefore, assumed to be *appropriate for certain peoples*."[37] (The emphases are mine.) This statement implies that different national or regional styles in music—styles that could be imitated—did exist in 1719, whether or not Baroque composers chose to use them or not. Dubos also suggests that "character" in dance music could serve to mark the national (or idiomatic) character of a people.

In a letter Jean-Philippe Rameau wrote to a friend in October 1727, he described a new keyboard work, "Les sauvages," as "characterizing the song and dance of the savages who appeared at the Théâtre-Italien a year or so ago."[38] The appearance of two dancers from Louisiana actually took place in September 1725 and was described by an eyewitness in the *Mercure de France*. The dancers were then about twenty-five years old. One appeared to be a tribal chief with a great feather-plumed crown, while the other dressed as a simple warrior. Their dance consisted of three parts: First came a dance of peace, when one presented a calumet (peace pipe) to the other. Next came a war dance, "depicting a gathering of savages bent on waging war with an enemy tribe." Third came a pantomime in which the warrior, armed with a bow and quiver of arrows, went in search of his enemy while the other sat on the ground beating a drum, one compared to a small kettledrum (*timbale*) the size of a hat. On discovering the enemy, the warrior returned to the chief and acted out the combat in which he defeated his foe. After this, the two danced a victory dance together.[39]

Claude Jean Allouez noted in *Relations de Nouvelle France, 1666–67* that one might easily mistake the calumet dance for pantomime-ballet. One contemporary account of the calumet ceremony as performed in America, *Le premier voyage qu'a fait le Père Marquette* (copied by the Jesuit Joseph-François Lafitau in 1724), divided it into "scenes." Lafitau judged that the combat scene was "done so well—with slow and measured steps, and to the rhythmic sound of the voices and drums—that it might pass for a very fine *entrée de ballet* in France." This was only one year before the Louisianans reenacted the ceremony in Paris. In all accounts, the combination of events in a calumet dance served as a drama or play in which the spectators were also participants.[40]

Rameau's "Les sauvages" is a rondo; the thematic design is A-B-A-C-A in G minor, with only the B section in the relative major. In addition to the key and mode, which are older Baroque markers of the exotic, the use of octave leaps in the bass line stands out as a new eighteenth-century device. (This feature, as we will see, is more meaningful within the larger context of American Indian portrayal than within a stylistic analysis of Rameau's exoticism.) Roger Savage points out a few other indexical features that could possibly have been influenced by the Americans: one- and two-measure units introduced by strong half notes; phrases featuring descending scales in eighth notes; and support given to the vocal monody by the imitation of "insistent drumbeats." Several phrases also tend to describe a series of irregular descending arcs, each with its center rather lower than the one before. Rameau was not so much as transcribing Indian music, Savage argues, as "translating it into a sophisticated European idiom." (The strong half notes on the downbeats of every other bar—followed by two quarters—again draw attention to the similarity perceived between the moresca and Native American dancing.)[41]

In 1735 Rameau and librettist Louis Fuzelier decided that their new work for the Académie Royale, *Les Indes galantes,* should have an entrée set in the Americas. They began their opéra-ballet with a scenario entitled "Les Incas du Pérou," forty-two years before Jean-François Marmontel would publish his highly influential and semihistorical *Les Incas.* Fuzelier's characters (Huascar the priest, Phani the princess, and Don Carlos, Phani's Spanish lover) were fictional. Fuzelier designed the plot around a festival of the sun—an important New World ceremony for peoples as far north as the Natchez—and this strategy offered spectacular opportunities for theatrical effects. Huascar's aria and chorus, "Brillant soleil," worships the sun with great majesty and sweeping grandeur; it is one of the opera's musical highpoints. At the end of the entrée, the jealous and vengeful priest is killed by the very volcanic eruption that he himself had invoked.[42] A Turkish entrée was also part of the original production; a Persian one was added a little later. The following year, for the Paris Opéra, Fuzelier and Rameau added a final entrée, "Les sauvages," this time set in the Louisiana territories. The scene is "a grove in the forests of America." The conflict between the Spaniards and the French provided the background for the story, and an ironic twist occurs when Zima, the "Amazon" chieftain's daughter, rejects both her Spanish and French suitors and takes the hand of a young Indian brave, Adario. As a female "noble savage," Zima prefers the simplicity of Indian life to the temptations offered her by the Europeans. *Les Indes galantes* ends happily as the would-be conquerors join the Indians in the great ceremony of the peace pipe. Though Fuzelier's libretto initially met with much criticism (over style, not content), the opera was an astounding success and remained in the Opéra's repertoire until the 1770s. The locales were

Example 1. Two sections from Jean-Philippe Rameau, "Les sauvages," from *Nouvelles suites de pièces de clavecin* (1728).

exotic, *Indes* referring not just to the Indies, West or East, but to all faraway places. Yet instead of appealing to the mind (*esprit*), as Charles Dill argues was typical of most opéra-ballets, the characters of *Les Indes* appealed to the heart.[43] Rameau's music, even in the trumpet-timpani flourishes that were more evocative of Louis's court than of the Louisiana colony, served to elevate the Americans, making them worthy of serious drama.

As with his predecessors, Rameau used little overt exoticization of the American characters in the airs or recitatives. The most recognizable features of otherness occur in the ballet sequences that close the work. The dance representing the peace pipe ceremony, as Whaples has noted, is so different from anything else in the opera that it is impossible not to read "exotic intent" in the "luxuriant combination of chromaticism, sinuous melody, and long-unresolved dissonance."[44]

In his *New Discovery of a Vast Country in America* (1683; English trans., 1698), Louis Hennepin gave a detailed account of the pipe ceremony as practiced by the Illinois.[45] He wrote that they used it to entertain any nation that came to visit them, and hence it served as the equivalent of a diplomat's ball. The "scenes" are broken down roughly as follows, with Hennepin's wording in quotes. Modern equivalents for the dances appear in brackets.

Greeting of the chief, the guests, and the icon (stone, bird, serpent, etc.) that is the *Manitoa,* or spirit.

The "Preludium": Accompanied by singing, the dancers blow smoke over the *Manitoa* and pass the calumet from person to person, each of whom dances with it.

"Scene 1": Leader begins the dance, offering the pipe to the sun, then dances with it, finally offering it to the spectators to smoke, one after the other. [Pipe Dance]

"Scene 2": "the fight" ("with vocal and instrumental musick"); drum beats out the rhythm while the leader acts out a fight with one of the warriors [Dance of Discovery]; he then gives a "speech" [Striking the Post], recounting the battles he has fought and the prisoners he has taken; he receives a gift from the chief of the ball [Give-Away]; he then passes the calumet to another who enacts the same sequence; this continues until the calumet returns to the leader.

Conclusion: Leader presents the pipe to the visiting nation and invites them to a feast.

Fuzelier and Rameau's design for the calumet ceremony closely follows this structure, with a few important divergences. The libretto specifies that the scene begins with Zima, Adario, French maidens dressed as Amazons, French and Indian soldiers (*sauvages*), Indian women (*sauvagesses*), and shepherds of the colony. Rameau begins with an instrumental *prélude* in D minor that continues into Adario's aria to the Indians. "Banish all grievous alarm!" he sings. "Our conquerors restore our peace. Share their pleasures, fear their arms no more! Upon our shores let love alone forever cause his fires to glow and launch his darts!" The Indians sing Adario's words to the same music. There are no further specifications in the libretto, but this section corresponds to the sung "Preludium" and the passing of the calumet. The actual "Danse du Grand Calumet de la Paix" (now indicated as a rondeau in the score) begins with an orchestral version of the harpsichord "Les sauvages," again in G minor. The entire rondeau is played once through in an instrumental version. Then the A section is played twice (but only with *doux* strings and continuo) to accompany Zima and Adario's duo. They ask that "unrequited love never trouble our hearts here" in these "peaceful forests . . . created . . . to harbor innocence and peace." The "chorus of savages," singing the same words, repeats the entire rondeau, again with fuller orchestration.[46]

At the conclusion of the sung ceremony, there immediately follows a minuet for the warriors and the Amazons (corresponding to the Dance of Discovery). The minuet is in ternary form, beginning in D major, followed by a second minuet in D minor as a kind of trio, and completed by a reprise of the first minuet. The timpani, silent in the ceremony until now, play a great flourish during the minuet. Rameau's use of timpani here corresponds with both Hennepin's description of the drums in the Dance of Discovery and the use of "the small kettledrum" noted by the *Mercure de France* for the Paris dancer's battle pantomime.

Then, with a very fast *prélude* (*assez vif*), Rameau launches an *aria da capo* for Zima. This is the most important divergence in the calumet scenario. Instead of the warriors recounting their victories in battle or receiving gifts from the leader, the heroine of the entrée—the chieftain's daughter and therefore of noble stock in the eyes of the European audience—sings gloriously about the triumph of nature's laws in the lives of the Indians: "All that wounds tenderness is unknown to our ardors. May nature, who made our hearts, take care to guide them for evermore." Zima's expression of integrity comes straight out of the writings of Hennepin, who had lived among the Louisiana tribes in 1681–82 and observed that while the Europeans may have called them barbarous, they had "more humanity than many nations of Europe."[47]

The ceremony concludes with a rousing and energetic chaconne in D major in which all dance, in lieu of a final smoke and feast. (The *chacona* was an erotic New World dance accompanied by guitars, castanets, and tambourine. It appears to have originated in Mexico, though in its modification for court ballet and opera it lost much of its bawdy component.) In one passage Rameau evokes the sound of the musette, a droning effect in a *danse de caractère* (and evocative of the hurdy-gurdy). Usually intended for shepherds, it serves here as an allegory for the pastoral. As Dubos might have put it, Rameau imitates a certain style that is assumed to be appropriate for the characters onstage. This peaceful moment in the midst of the otherwise brilliant chaconne, the first in a long line of musico-rhetorical topics—here the "pastoral Indian"—serves allegorically as the authors' reminder of the natural simplicity and inherent good in the lives of shepherds and American savages alike.[48]

While *Les Indes galantes* continued to run at the Paris Opéra, Rousseau published his *Second Discourse on the Origin and Inequality among Men* in 1755 (in which he formulated his now-famous doctrine of primitivism). It would seem, however, that despite Diderot's later contributions, noble savagery was about to reach its apex in European political thought. Parodies of *Les Indes* appeared in the vaudeville theatres, and in 1767 Voltaire tossed off *L'ingénue,* a satirical romance about the quintessential noble savage. The following year Marmontel and composer André Grétry adapted Voltaire's satire into an opera, *Le Huron.* The hero, a Canadian savage, is brought to France. His simple, frank, and naturally good qualities amuse the French, who also observe their violent contrast with the conventional mores and religious convictions of their "civilized" society. Ironically, however, the "Huron" turns out to be a French nobleman taken into captivity at birth, so the joke is on his compatriots. Unlike Baroque opera seria or opéra-ballet, the form of *Le Huron,* with its interspersed dialogue and seriocomic touches, resembles the French vaudeville or the English ballad operas of the 1720s and 1730s. The libretto occasionally alludes to the Huron's primitive life in the wilds of North America, but Grétry did not attempt to suggest to his audience at the *Comédie-Italienne* any difference, in musical terms, between the "savage" and the "civilized."

Yet by the early eighteenth century, several defining features had already been used to musically identify "Americans" in European ballet and opera, although composers did not necessarily apply these stylistic markers with consistency. The features were those of the peasant branle, first noted in 1613, with, in the same year, the addition of a ground bass and sarabande rhythm. In 1626 "Atabalipa" was shown playing the hurdy-gurdy, and—though there are no written sources from that period to demonstrate it—the use of the drone bass for "Americans" along with other pastoral figures became increasingly prominent. Lully's use of G minor as a dusky "Indian" mode was replicated by Humfrey, Purcell, and Rameau, among others. The musette, associated with shepherds, was sometimes applied to dwellers of the American forests. The *ballet des nations* seemed to favor particular rhythmic accompaniments for American dances—the canarie, the sarabande, the moresca, and the chanson—some of which were carried over into theatrical *danses de caractère.*

These devices were largely symbolic, with composers borrowing them mostly from each other. As an eyewitness to a war dance, Rameau was among the first to attempt an indexical representation of American Indians. None of the indigenous instruments cited in American sources, however, were replicated in European music from 1500 to 1800. No xylophone-like instruments were modeled after the *mayohayau* or *teponaztli,* nor percussion after the Tupinambá *maracas,* nor tambourine-rattles after the Québec *montagnard* (as described by Léry and Paul Le Jeune in the 1630s). Nor were flutes, pipes, or flageolets used specifically in conjunction with American subjects. *Timbales* (timpani) were rarely used, although Rameau added them in his "Les sauvages" entrée for the American warriors, where the *timbales* were meant to accompany the trumpets as they did in typical French military style.

The first known attempt to use any indigenous American instruments in a European musical composition was that of Gaspare Spontini in his operatic treatment of the conquest, *Fernand Cortez* (1809). Representations of the Discovery, while they occurred with relative infrequency on operatic stages after 1776, were still a subject of occasional interest by composers such as Spontini and even Verdi in the nineteenth century (*Alzira*), as well as by Roger Sessions and Philip Glass in more recent times.[49] Popular English-language theater of the late eighteenth century, however, suddenly appeared flooded with versions of the Discovery, inspired by Marmontel's 1777 retelling of Pizarro's conquest of Peru. Music served a crucial role in intensifying these legends.

2

Death, Defiance, and Diplomacy: Resistance in British-American Theater and Song, 1710–1808

Several prominent court entertainments in the seventeenth and early eighteenth centuries—as we saw in the last chapter—depicted and imagined the Americas through music. These ballets and operas shared at least three things in common: First of all, by positioning "Americans" (i.e., personified American Indians) in aristocratic roles, Europeans during this time attempted to elevate their status within a hierarchy of civilization. Second, the symbolic representation of American Indians in European courts and royal theater served as political allegory. It would be oversimplifying the situation, however, to say that all such representations served predominantly to justify colonial enterprises. For many of these, the implications for court politics were far more crucial. Finally, we reviewed a number of important works and identified in them musical materials by which European musicians designated Indians as Americans. These materials provide the basis for a developing musical rhetoric (many would call it a stereotypical musical rhetoric) that served as the basis for representation.

Music and the British Colonial Imagination

In the Anglo-American theater of the eighteenth century, this representation assumed different stylistic qualities. The ruthlessness of conquest and the heroism of the Native Americans who resisted began to surface as dominant themes. The American subjects for the ballets and operas in the seventeenth century were based principally on Spanish and French encounters with Indians in South and Central America. For Great Britain in the eighteenth century, the focus shifted northward to reflect England's growing preoccupation with the Cherokees, the Iroquois, and other disaffected North American tribes. Fear and mistrust between the Indian peoples of America and the English began as early as 1590, when John White, the governor of Virginia, returned to Roanoke to discover a "lost colony" of vanished settlers. "This could be no other," White wrote, "but the deed of the savages our enemies." In general, the English seemed to take little interest at that time in the Indian villages that were slowly desiccated or evacuated owing to settlers' encroachments; instead, rumors proliferated of cannibalism and human sacrifice. Though the English colonists tried to distance themselves from cruelties practiced (wittingly or unwittingly) by their Spanish and Portuguese predecessors, they found that conflict with the indigenous tribes over land, culture, and religion was inevitable. As the English built new villages, they cut off trade routes long held dear by the tribes. When the Indians fought to defend their land rights, using ancient customs of warfare, the British demonized them for the perpetration of "inhuman" acts. The New England Indians scalped their enemies; the British hung, quartered, and burned theirs. The Indians worshiped spirit gods; the Puritans practiced a severe form of radical Calvinism and deferred only to biblical authority. To complicate matters, some New England Indians had converted to Christianity, and colonists' inability on occasion to tell the difference between a "good" and a "bad" Indian resulted in disastrous consequences. When in 1676 the Wampanoag chief Metacom (or "King Philip") launched his all-out attack on the residents of towns across Rhode Island, Connecticut, and Massachusetts—a war in which hundreds of Narragansetts, Wampanoags, and English settlers were killed and dozens of towns and villages destroyed—Dryden's formulation of the "noble savage" in *The Indian Queen* of only six years before would have seemed to the colonists little more than a taunting irony, a blatant case in which England's court poets betrayed little understanding of human behavior or the nature of life in colonial America.[1]

While audiences in Restoration England enjoyed "Indians" frolicking in court masques, William Hubbard in his *Narrative of the Troubles with the Indians in New England* (1677) portrayed them as "children of the devil" and the "dross of mankind." And roughly ten years later, while *les sauvages de l'Amérique* danced a rondeau in Lully's *Temple de la paix* at Fontainebleau, Iroquois fighters murdered twenty-four French settlers at Lachine near Montréal. In turn the French captured six Iroquois and burned them at the stake to give the Indians "a taste of the torture they themselves devised." If Europeans could continue to foster ideas of noble savagery in their exotic entertainments, the English and French colonists living in North America experienced a more direct experience with savagery and their own liminal role in its proliferation.[2]

A profound attitudinal sea change occurred, however, in just three quarters of a century. In 1704, for example, Narragansetts and Mohawks, with the assistance of the French, massacred the English colony at Deerfield, Connecticut. The English reaction was of course outrage, interpreting this attack as another in the series of perpetrations that would ultimately result in the French and Indian Wars. But when James Adair published his *History of the American Indians* in 1775, its instant notoriety demonstrated that the British were beginning to recognize the cultural role that indigenous North Americans played in the identity of the colonies. To begin with, Adair identified with the heroism in Indian narratives, and he related such powerful experiences as witnessing an Indian "death song," a song of defiance in the face of torture and possible death. Only a few years later, a "death song" became one of the most popular pieces of British (and American) music in the late eighteenth century, Anne Home Hunter's "Death Song of the Cherokee Indians" (ca. 1780). It's essential to understand that this song, which will be examined in detail later in this chapter, was not a Native American work. Any relationship between this composition and an actual Indian death song is relatively superficial (and also impossible to substantiate). What *is* most significant about it, of course, is Hunter's text, its social implications, the expressive quality of the tune and its accompaniment, and the song's reception. While this is generally referred to as an air (a sung work), it embodies the stylistic characteristics of a march. Presumably because of this, it was used after 1780 for many occasions—both in Britain and America—where feelings or demonstrations of patriotism ran high. For this reason, Hunter's air is central to this chapter, not only for the cultural implications surrounding its popularity, but also for its role in inspiring many other resistance works.

The words to Hunter's "Death Song" reflect a particular concept of noble savagery that developed in England in the eighteenth century, one that purported to align itself more with Indian views than with those of the colonists. To sing such songs also allowed the British and colonists an opportunity to assume the role and "voice" of an Indian, even if, at the same time, it reflected their ambivalence about an emerging American identity. While the music for French court ballets manifested Europe's marvel and wonder of contact with the New World, the music of songs and plays in late eighteenth-century Britain had much more to do with transatlantic colonialism—no longer reflecting wonder, but rather utility, diplomacy, display, and ultimately displacement. The increasingly complex relationships between Britain, the young United

States, and the indigenous peoples of North America can be sensed behind these songs, which in both text and musical rhetoric express the celebration and the anxieties of the colonial enterprise. While these ideas first took root in the songs and musical plays produced by English actors and musicians, these English products were imported into America, thereby reflecting the source of this ambivalence back onto itself.

North American Indians in Eighteenth-Century British Song

Despite the territorial conflicts between American Indians and colonial settlers, the English grew increasingly fascinated with Indians throughout the eighteenth century. In 1710 a delegation of four representatives of the Iroquois League—under the auspices of four colonial naval officers—visited the court of Queen Anne. "Americans" had been displayed in European courts since the early 1500s, as we have seen, but this was the first time that a group of Americans arrived in Europe to discuss foreign policy. The court described the delegation as the "Emperor of the Mohocks" and three "Indian Kings." Such titles, though probably exaggerated, provided them with a stature normally allotted only to foreign dignitaries. The four Iroquois created a sensation in London, and their activities were reported in the newspapers. They were billeted at the spacious home of the upholsterer Michael Arne (father of composer Thomas Arne) and were royally entertained by lord commissioners, dukes, and duchesses.

The purpose of the Iroquois visit to London was twofold: On the one hand, they came to request additional missionaries among their confederation, according to contemporary sources. At the same time, they wanted to assure the queen of their allegiance to the English against the French, who, descending from Canada, were pushing aggressively into their lands. While the aristocracy treated the visitors with courtesy, the delegation met with a varied reception in public circles. The *Tatler* reported that the chiefs had been persuaded to make the visit because of increased pressure from the Jesuits to turn the Iroquois against the English and support the French. In Richard Steele's infamous *Spectator* essay, the editor made the Iroquois sound more like noble savages and used them to attack what he saw as the corruption of European society. The visitors were commonly referred to as "Mohocks"—a term that in England came to be applied to "a class of aristocratic ruffians who infested the streets of London at night." According to Jonathan Swift, this usage first began around 1711, not unrelated perhaps to the visit of the "Mohock Kings." Although the Iroquois delegation had their images engraved by John Simon (after Jan Verelst's portrait), they apparently inspired no musical responses.

They are known to have made music for their hosts on the ship, however. According to the admiral, each sachem took turns singing a song and dancing, "while the rest sat down and hummed and hollow'd [hollered] at distinct periods of his dance, with a tone very odd and loud, but yet in time." One of the Mohegan singers also made an English visit later in 1740, where he was again royally received, this time by George II. Another of the four was grandfather to Joseph Brant, a Canajoharie Mohawk, who would travel to London to meet George III in 1775.[3]

Like the Iroquois, the Cherokees developed strong diplomatic ties with England, their first delegations visiting George II between 1730 and 1733 under the sponsorship of Alexander Cuming, an Englishman who had lived among the Cherokees, married a Cherokee woman, and learned the language. Like those of the Iroquois, the Cherokee visits had crucial political overtones. As South Carolina steadily grew in economic strength and became increasingly oppressive toward the Indian nations of the Southeast (map 1), the Cherokees pursued trading options in England with an eye to future independence. (The Creeks from what is now Alabama, following the lead of the Cherokees, also sent a delegation to London in 1734.)

By the early 1730s, British representations of the "Americans" seemed to crop up with increasing frequency in popular venues such as taverns, public houses, and theaters. The first Indian character to appear on the British stage was actually an adaptation from a French *commedia dell'arte.* Louis-François Delisle de la Drevetière's philosophical farce *Arlequin sauvage* (Théâtre Italien, 1721) initiated a tradition of including American Indians on the French stage. The satire was adapted for the British theater in October 1734—perhaps in part stimulated by the Creek delegation that year—and it was produced at the Little Theatre in the Haymarket and starred Francisque Moylin, a French-born acrobat and actor. As one later synopsis put it, the savage Harlequin is brought to England "from some barbarous country" by a European merchant. Since he is of course completely unfamiliar with European customs, he "commits a thousand extravagencies [*sic*] which are highly entertaining." *Arlequin sauvage* ran intermittently until June 1735. Many harlequinades after that featured at least one incidental Indian character or two. Following a harlequinade at Goodman Fields Theatre in 1744, there was even a "dance of Indians" to conclude an entertainment viewed by some seven hundred people.[4]

Somewhere in the middle of the eighteenth century, an important distinction emerged in Europe: a kind of Janus-faced representation. American chieftains continued to be received royally as a gesture of their acknowledged nobility (also reflected in some of the music written about them). In the 1750s the British went to war with France over American territories, and the French

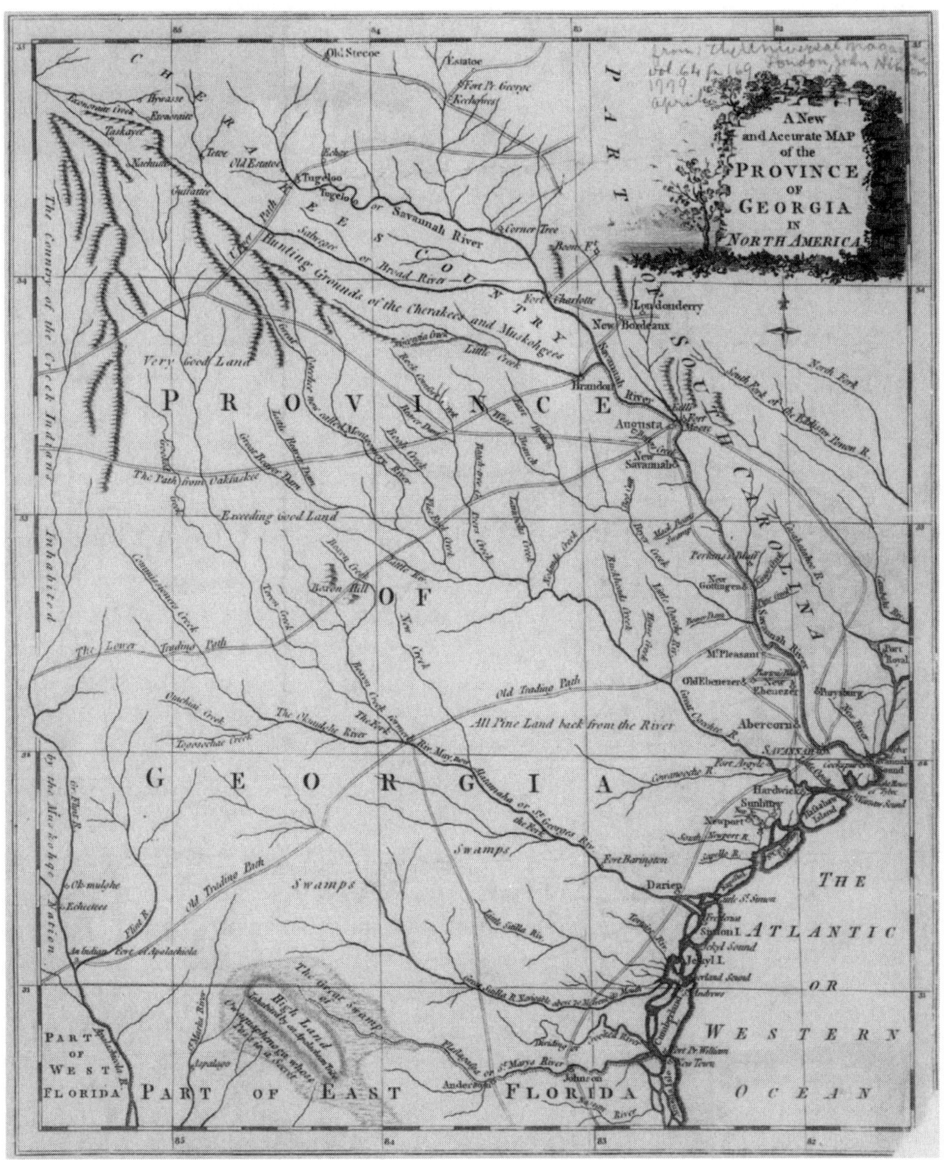

Map 1. The "Cherakees Country" between the "Province of Georgia" to the south, South Carolina to the east, and the "Country of the Creek Indians" to the west. Historical map originally published in *Universal Magazine* 64, no. 169 (London, 1779). Courtesy of Hargrett Rare Book and Manuscript Library, University of Georgia Libraries.

allied themselves with many American tribes. Hence French portrayals of Native Americans during this time tend to be more sympathetic than British ones. Earlier in the century, Voltaire (in *Alzire*) had portrayed Peru as a kind of idealized empire; his "Americans" were a harmonious people with philosopher kings as rulers. In 1755 Rousseau elaborated on such a sublime and virtuous existence in his *Second Discourse*. Even the "savages" of the world, Rousseau noted, took pride in personal possessions as did their European counterparts. But they had not yet degenerated into the inequalities of wealth, inequalities he believed arose from advances in technology that set Europeans apart from one another. In 1767 Voltaire sought to undercut Rousseau's fatalism with humor. The protagonist of his *L'Ingénu* (and also of *Le Huron*, Marmontel and Grétry's subsequent opera) is brought from Québec to an aristocratic European environment and proves to be more "noble" than the nobles. As Harry Liebersohn expressed it, he "disrupts polite expectations in eighteenth-century France with his direct expressions of feeling, his insistence on justice, and his indifference to titles."[5]

Despite these noble sentiments, however, fears of Indians as wild and hatchet-waving were still exploited. In the public eye, the native inhabitants of America were less interesting as ambassadors than as savages in captivity, arousing curiosity and condescension for their manner of dress or behavior. Capitalizing on this fascination, New York entrepreneur Hyam Myers transported three Mohawks to England in March 1765. They arrived not for presentation to the king, but as "warriors" for exhibition in the London taverns. After a few months of raking in some profit, however, Myers received official orders to take the Indians home. One of the Mohawks, Sychnecta, was even sold off by his interpreter in Amsterdam like a piece of property. (Myers searched for Sychnecta but apparently never did find him.)[6]

Perhaps the most famous appearance of American Indians in England in the eighteenth century, however, was the visit of the three "Cherokee chiefs" to King George III in 1762. This controversial and highly symbolic meeting followed shortly after the British suppression of the Cherokee rebellion (which had lasted from 1758 to 1761). Two of the three visitors, Cunne Shote and Chief Ostenaco, sat for portraits by Francis Parsons and Joshua Reynolds. It was also the first visit of Americans in which specific music was noted as a part of their experience. As the ship arrived in Southampton port, Ostenaco ("painted in a frightful manner," according to Lieutenant Henry Timberlake) sang a prayer of thanks in a loud voice. Timberlake, who called the song a "dirge," noted that Ostenaco's singing and appearance "attracted boats full of curious spectators from ships in the harbor."

Since the bloody rebellion in America had created a minor scandal in the

British press, it was no surprise that the visit of the three chiefs received sensational treatment in stage and song. They were invited to plays at the Haymarket in September (their intention to attend even was announced on the playbills). In honor of their visit, James Dance, manager of the Drury Lane Theatre, produced *The Witches, or Harlequin Cherokee* (23 November 1762). In this comic work Harlequin (played by Edward Rooker) is now a European merchant. He goes to America to capture Indians and brings them back to England to display them. The gist of the humor surrounds the astonishment of the Indians at such things as an orchestra, a mill, and a festive ball. Robert Sayer engraved a scene from the play, with Harlequin dressed as an Indian chief against a backdrop of Saint Paul's Cathedral. The "Cherokees" were rendered by actors Grimaldi, Vincent, Lochery, and other prominent comedians, who concluded the pantomime with the Cherokees' safe return, landing, and reception in America. (The surviving "comic tunes" for *The Witches* by Walter Claggert unfortunately contain no specific reference to the Indians, either musically or by title.) Meanwhile, Ostenaco and the other Cherokee visitors were also invited to rival theaters, where their acceptance of such was again billed in advance.[7]

Not everyone was impressed with the national reception of the Cherokees, however. A broadside appeared by the "versifier and scribbler" Henry Howard, poking fun at all the attention the visitors were receiving, particularly from British women. In one of the stanzas, Howard obviously got his geography confused:

> The Ladies, dear Creatures, so squeamish and dainty
> Surround the great Canada Warriors in plenty;
> Wives, Widows and Matrons, and pert little Misses,
> Are pressing and squeezing for Cherokee Kisses.
> Each grave looking Prude, and each Smart Looking Belle, Sir
> Declaring no Englishman e'er kissed so well, Sir.[8]

Howard's "A New Humorous Song" (in the Lester S. Levy Collection, Johns Hopkins University) was to be sung to the tune of *Caesar and Pompey were Both of Them Horned.* Instead of reflecting on the dignity of the visitors, the verses allude to scalping and savagery, linking the two with sexual mores. In a moment of crude humor, it even inquired of the women if Cherokees kiss or "f - - k" any better than British men. Howard is a somewhat shady figure in eighteenth-century English theatrical history. Although he only made one professional appearance, he was a notorious personage around the London theaters, a fact that earned him an entry in the *Biographical Dictionary of Actors, Actresses, Musicians, Dancers, Managers, and Other Stage Personnel in*

London, 1660–1800. He was said to posses "some humour in the club room [though apparently] none on stage." Howard's broadside sold for sixpence and could be purchased from the author "opposite the Union Coffee House in the Strand, near Temple-Bar" and from "all the print and pamphlet sellers." It shamelessly included a full-length sketch of the three Indian visitors in the headpiece. As art historian Stephanie Pratt has noted, this was the most widespread image to result from the Cherokee visit of 1762, and it represented the delegations as "emissaries from an exotic land who were by that same token primal creatures only barely restrained by European civilization from outrageous behaviour." The irreverent Howard probably sang his reactionary editorial in many of the public taverns he is reported to have frequented, and it no doubt provoked much laughter.[9]

In 1764 Henry Timberlake tried to capitalize on the notoriety of the 1762 visit by escorting yet another party of Cherokees to England. Cheulah of Settico headed the three-man delegation. Again, the sachems were billed as "kings" or "chiefs." Timberlake hadn't received official British sanction for the delegation, and so the chiefs received no royal audience and comparatively little attention in the press. According to Stanley Hoig, the Cherokees' reputation suddenly escalated when they presented some gold apparently brought from America. They were presented to the Lords of Trade and Plantations in February 1765 and received invitations around town. It was probably this visit for which the engraver-dramatist Samuel Boyce (d. 1775) wrote his "New Song on the Arrival of the Cherokee King and His Chiefs." While Boyce's song does include notions of religious conversion, it also humanizes the Cherokee in ways that the harlequinade and bawdy songs such as Howard's did not:[10]

> From Regions wild and drear we come, Britania's [*sic*] Isle to see;
> Oh that our Nations left at Home, knew half so much as we:
> Chorus: No more they'd cut and scalp and slay
> But all for GEORGE AND ENGLAND pray.

The Puritans in the seventeenth century had struggled to convert—as Jill Lepore put it—preying Indians to "praying Indians," and Boyce seems to be drawing on the same analogy here, ascribing to the Cherokees the desire to lay down their scalping tools. The anonymous tune—perhaps by the author's more celebrated son, William—is a bisectional melody accompanied by a figured bass in the broadside. It does not imitate Indian chanting but rather is a lusty tune in D major that might rouse English loyalists in the wake of colonial rebellion to nationalist fervor. The song goes on to describe how "rapine and the wreaking knife" are not to be found in Britain and that "no horrid face of war glooms here." In Boyce's poem, the Cherokees freely give their wampum belts (used as colonial currency) and would rather live as Britons instead. In a final twist, the British switch places with the Indians: if the Indians would only give up their warfare and way of life, so the last verse espouses, then for certain will "GEORGE and CHARLOTTE reign at ease, and all be loyal CHEROKEES."

What was truly new about Boyce's song — besides its stirring melody — was that it was the first to turn away from the humorous portrayal of the Cherokees as either cruel or simpleminded, and he found a quality of heroism in the Indian resistance. Boyce (or whoever wrote the music) conveyed this by evoking the tempo, rhythms, and spirit of a march. In the early eighteenth century, marches were still in the French style (usually in three) and served a largely military function. The march was brought into court ceremonials, played for the entrances of royal guests, and finally expanded to include the accompaniment of processions of all kinds, though it usually embodied political or moral overtones suggestive of military victory and heroism. The English march gradually assumed a popular flavor, but not for nationalist purposes until after the French Revolution and the popularity of "La Marseillaise." In the late eighteenth century, marches served to open ballet performances, ceremonies, and stage presentations, and were illustrative of authority and of the cavalier and manly virtues of the battlefield. As a rhetorical marker of the military (and hence of nation), the march as a style topic also permeated late eighteenth-century music generally, as Leonard Ratner has demonstrated.[11] While I certainly would not assert that the march in itself is suggestive of American Indians, I think it is necessary to recognize that in an American Indian context, the march, and especially the patriotic English-style march, developed specific associations and rhetorical meanings that continued to accrue from the 1760s until at least the 1830s. For example, in Sheridan's afterpiece *Robinson Crusoe,* performed at Drury Lane in 1781, Crusoe observes the "savages landing" to the accompaniment of a march in C major. While he is apprehensive about the new visitors to his island, the music, by Thomas Linley, depicts the arriving Indians nobly in a pert and proper march (including thirty-second-note upbeats, dotted rhythms, and the standard rhythmic cadential figure: (♩♪.𝅘𝅥𝅯♩). For British — and later, American — music after 1760, we can therefore add "in march style" to our ongoing list of rhetorical devices to portray Indians, while acknowledging that in an isolated context — as is true for any of the rhetorical devices discussed in this book — the referent is not automatically Indians.

Few eighteenth-century songs on American Indian resistance subjects had the extended impact of "The Death Song of the Cherokee Indians." It was first published anonymously, ca. 1780, but the text is by the Scottish-born poet Anne Home Hunter, who later included it in her published collection of poems in 1802. In a note on the masthead of the published song, the author informs us that "the simple melody was brought to England ten years ago by a Gentleman named Turner who had (owing to some singular events in his life) spent nine years amongst the natives of America." The note goes on to say that the melody "was peculiar to that tribe or nation called the Cherokees." ("Ten years ago" would have been about 1770; nine years before that would have been 1761. By then, a few Europeans were known to have made their homes among the Cherokees, the most famous perhaps being Christian Priber in 1736. Turner in 1761, however, would have found himself right in the midst of the rebellion, during which he may have been taken captive.[12]) Hunter's preface continues with "the words here annexed have been thought something characteristic of the spirit and sentiments of those brave savages. We look upon the fierce and stubborn courage of the dying Indian with a mixture of respect, pity, and horror; and it is to those sentiments in the breast of the hearer that the Death Song must owe its effect."

Mrs. Hunter's poem was not the first European source to eulogize the courage of a dying Indian warrior. The North American practice of singing a song of defiance in the face of torture had also been noted earlier, particularly in Joseph-François Lafitau's 1724 study of customs among the Iroquois. The Jesuit missionary wrote that "captives are free to say whatever they may wish. They sing of their high deeds of arms and those of their tribe. They spit forth a thousand imprecations against their tyrants. They try to intimidate them by threats. They call their friends to their help to avenge them." Lafitau even noticed children playing games in which they tested their courage against one another "while singing their death song." (He doesn't comment on the strangeness of this or on what constituted a "death song" to a child.) He related the death song to the ancient tradition of the Hebrews in captivity, citing Psalm 186 as an example of a death song.[13] James Adair, who had a similar point of comparison, also observed the death-song tradition in his *History of the American Indians* (1775). In fictional sources, Jean-François Marmontel created a moving death song in *The Incas of Peru* (1777) for an elderly Peruvian chief who is overtaken and burned at the stake by roving Spaniards. Hunter's "Death Song," however, was certainly the first to reach such a wide audience through its dissemination in a musical setting. Aside from the title and the identification of one chieftain — Alknomook — the words are generalized enough to be applicable to many situations:

The Death Song of the Cherokee Indians

The sun sets in night, and the stars shun the day;
But glory remains when their lights fade away!
Begin, ye tormentors! Your threats are in vain,
For the son of Alknomook shall never complain.

Remember the arrows he shot from his bow;
Remember your chiefs by the hatchet laid low;
Why so slow? Do you wait till I shrink from the pain?
No, the son of Alknomook will never complain.

Remember the wood where in ambush we lay,
And the scalps which we bore from your nation away.
Now the flame rises fast, you exult in my pain;
But the son of Alknomook can never complain.

I go to the land where my father is gone;
His ghost shall rejoice in the fame of his son;
Death comes like a friend, he relieves me from pain;
And thy son, Oh Alknomook! Has scorn'd to complain.

The identity of the Alknomook referred to in this text has never been discovered—or even questioned, to my knowledge—and, like Atabalipa in the seventeenth-century courts, he appears in several guises, as we will see. Here his son sings in defiance of being captured and burned at the stake by another Indian tribe. The images he paints are rooted in memories of warfare and peace as they may have been understood in tribal terms—the scalps "we bore from your nation away" refer to military victories of one tribe over the other, the "hatchet laid low" perhaps recall truces declared by tribal chieftains. The warrior here not only welcomes death as a form of release from his torturers but also demonstrates an extraordinary amount of courage and defiance in refusing to grant his enemies the pleasure of witnessing his moral capitulation, even in the face of extreme pain. His death song is the ultimate triumph of resistance.

Hunter's use of the plural for Indians in the title probably led to the misconception that all imperiled Cherokee warriors might sing the same song. According to surviving accounts among northeastern tribes (which are all by Europeans and elusive about their sources), an American Indian might compose his own death song in anticipation of possible capture. While he would practice the song on his own (reinforcing his courage), it was probably not something he'd share with his family or even closest allies. (Lafitau's account of a chieftain leading his warriors into battle by singing his death song demonstrates the vagueness of this term's use in colonial sources.[14]) For this reason, it seems odd that Hunter's gentleman from America would have had access to this song, unless he had witnessed such a torture and death.

In the 1802 edition of her poems, Hunter further explained that the origin of the song occurred when she heard the gentleman Turner "sing a wild air, which he assured me it was customary for those people to chaunt with a barbarous jargon, implying contempt for their enemies in the moments of torture and death."[15] Hunter's account of the circumstances surrounding the "Death Song" in both these instances has been quoted on numerous occasions to substantiate her authorship. Her comments merit closer scrutiny, however, since the underlying philosophy is a persuasive one that would dominate Anglo-American thought for nearly a century. To begin with, Hunter's comments imply that an artist possesses the creative means to impart "something of the characteristic spirit and sentiment" of a Cherokee under torture from one of his enemies. Aside from "Mr. Turner's" eyewitness account, Hunter could have made certain assumptions about the death-song tradition by reading other sources, particularly in Adair's very recent summary. (In 1791 John Long included the text "of a typical death song" in his *Voyages and Travels,* but Hunter's "Death Song" was already well known in both Britain and America by then.) Secondly, Hunter calls the original Cherokee tune "wild"—or perhaps passes on the description given to her. Yet the prosody of her text adheres closely to a metrically and rhythmically disciplined melody. "Wild" is a term akin to "savage," one she also uses. It suggests that the Cherokee style of performance lacked the control and refinement of European singing. ("Wild" and "savage" seemed to be used interchangeably in eighteenth- and nineteenth-century sources. As previously noted, the German for "savages" is *Wilden.*) It is unknown if Hunter had had the opportunity to see and hear any of the Indians upon their visits to England. She certainly had not made the perilous journey to America. The fascination at this time with a kind of music that was customary for "those people to chaunt" leads me to ask at least two questions: (1) why was Hunter interested in turning a wild American Indian song into a genteel English one that engendered "a mixture of respect, pity, and horror"? and (2) why was the song so popular? Hunter's intentions for this song can never really be known, of course. But we can explore its impact and influence.

The process of collecting and adapting North American Indian music to European tastes was not new. We have seen how Gabriel Sagard set some Huron songs to four-part accompaniment in 1636. On the other hand, the idea of "authenticity" in ethnically centered music was a relatively recent notion in 1780. French and German scholars had already begun publishing transcriptions of American Indian music with extensive commentaries. For his remarks on Iroquois music and the melodies he transcribed, François Picquet drew on eleven years experience, 1749–60, in which he assisted in the management of an Iroquois colony. Within a few years Friedrich Marpurg had reprinted these remarks in his 1762 study of music with a German translation of Picquet's essay. In 1768 Jean-Jacques Rousseau quoted Mersenne's 1736 "Chanson Canadoise" in his *Dictionnaire de Musique,* adding that, because of

The Death Song of the Cherokee Indians.

Figure 3. "The Death Song of the Cherokee Indians," voice and continuo (London: Longman and Broderip, [1784]). A. K. Bell Library, Perth, Scotland.

its similarity to European music, some might doubt its authenticity.[16] For most people in the 1780s, however, "The Death Song of the Cherokee Indians" probably held considerable allure, suggestive as it was not only of the New World but also of the revolutionary spirit of the age. I also believe that it exudes just enough of a hint of otherness that eighteenth-century British audiences would have been inclined to accept it as an adaptation of authentic North American Indian song.

We can only come to an understanding of this song's popularity by situating it within the production of British and American culture. Hunter was wise to specify that she had "annexed" words to a received melody and probably thus avoided the ridicule that was heaped upon older collections of folk literature. In the process of compiling his two volumes of *Scotish Songs* (*sic*, 1794), Joseph Ritson, among those who began to adopt more rigorous methods in song collecting, decided to include the "Death Song" only after first consulting with the author about matters of provenance. According to Ritson, Hunter composed not only the text but also the bass line. And so he ultimately included the song—but only its melody and text, as he did for the others in his collection.[17]

The version shown in figure 3 is from an undated publication by Longman and Broderip. The "Death Song" is appended to *Nine Canzonetts for Two Voices; and Six Airs with an Accompanyment for the Piano-Forte by A Lady.* The A. K. Bell Library of Perth, Scotland, dates it 1784, but others believe 1782 to be more accurate. It is not difficult to see why this song became so popular. The rhythms are snappy. The melody has logic, drive, and purpose. The antecedent and consequent phrases of the first period are beautifully balanced, the consequent essentially being a slightly ornamented version of the antecedent, lowered sequentially by a whole step. The second period follows the same rhythmic pattern as the first, but its antecedent phrase is thematically related to the consequent phrase of the first period and begins in a similar downward sequential pattern. The tune itself isn't overly repetitive, but it contains just enough of a motivic and rhythmic hook to be catchy. The melody also has a decided Scottish flavor, including the descending third on the word "threats," which is also rhythmically marked by an iambic rhythm, the so-called Scottish snap.

A feature that stands out in Hunter's version is the elegant bass line. It is so beautifully tailored—with its climax in mm. 5–6 and its dramatic plunge downward from the seventh of the dominant (A♭) to the final tonic—that it's almost a singable melody in itself. The skills of counterpoint and melodic construction evident in Hunter's version reveal the classical priorities of an eighteenth-century musical mind. Though the details of Mrs. Hunter's education are scant, it is known that from an early age she studied the harpsichord in addition to writing music.

Since many dominant features of this air seem clearly derived from English or Scottish folk song, as well as British military music, we might be inclined to overlook some of its peculiarities. Given its remarkable popularity and staying power in both British and American culture, however, it is essential to consider what in the song may have been heard as musically distinctive. Two features of this song—features that have never been pointed out in the literature—are indeed common to many American Indian styles, certainly the North American styles with which "Mr. Turner" might have been familiar. First of all, the continuation of the first antecedent phrase (C–B♭–A♭–F–F–F), with its gapped pentatonic inflection and repeated final notes, is a standard cadential figure in Iroquois and some other North American Indian styles as well. (The third of Chabanon's four *Chansons des Sauvages d'Amérique septentrionale,* published in Paris in 1785, contains this identical figure.[18]) Secondly, the first six of the eight measures begin high and follow a downward pattern, traversing a full octave. In many Indian cultures from the Plains eastward, chanting often begins high and gradually descends an octave or more. These two features, though they no longer stand out as distinctively Native American, certainly must have done so when this song first became popular in the late eighteenth century.

The version used in the example above is from the earliest known printing. By 1785 the song had already been published in the United States, both in the southern *Charleston Evening Gazette* and the northern *Massachusetts Spy.* Several American versions titled the song "The Indian Chief," beginning with a Rhode Island manuscript source as early as 1783, and it appeared under this title in 1787 in the *Boston Gazette* and in 1789 in the *Philadelphia Songster*, among other publications.[19] Musicologist John Koegel has found fifty-seven separate printed and manuscript sources of the "Death Song of the Cherokee Indians" in England and the United States dated between 1780 and 1855 (and suggests that there are likely more to be found).[20]

In the United States, the death song as a tradition remained a fascinating subject among poets and writers until the mid-nineteenth century. Washington Irving's "Traits of Indian Character" (*Sketch-Book* of 1819) and John Treat Irving's *Indian Sketches* of 1835 are only two of many early nineteenth-century sources to highlight its significance in literature. Koegel observes that "The Indian Chief" was mentioned in children's novels of Maria Edgeworth (1769–1849) as "The Son of Alkomook Shall Never Complain." Edgeworth used the song for instructive purposes, demonstrating that children sang it believing it was a real death song of an Indian chief.[21] According to Henry Broadus Jones, who wrote a study of the death song tradition in 1911, it was sung by schoolchildren even as late as the turn of the twentieth century. Elements of resistance in the death song no doubt underpinned many moral lessons in nineteenth-century teaching.

None of the surviving versions after Mrs. Hunter's, however, contain her elegant bass line. Not only are most less artful, but some are downright crude. It is probably the case that many American editions were prepared either from Ritson's 1794 edition in *Scotish Songs*, vol. 2, which did not contain a bass, or from Gilfert's New York version of around 1800, attributed to James Hewitt (the version probably best known in recent years as it was reproduced in Marrocco and Gleason's 1964 anthology *Music in America*).[22] This doesn't explain the amateur bass line and voice leading in the early Rhode Island source, however. "The Indian Chief" is one of seventy-four songs and dance tunes for keyboard copied in 1783 by Sally and Eliza Marchant. It is unknown whether this copy was made in England or the United States and whether it was copied from an existing publication or by ear. Were the source indigenously American, that would suggest that there is a yet-undiscovered predecessor for both the Marchants' and Hunter's versions. The source of the tune that Mrs. Hunter set has never in fact been identified. Could it be possible that "Mr. Turner" brought back a song sung not by a Cherokee but by other Europeans in America, a political song of resistance constructed to allude to Indian heroism? I'll return to this hypothesis later, in the context of the Tammany Society. Regardless of its origins, "The Death Song of the Cherokee Indians" played a substantial role in theatrical productions in the decades following its appearance in print. As a stylistic topic, it also influenced other music for Indian characters in these plays.

Tales of Conquest in British and Early American Theater

Beginning in 1781 with *Robinson Crusoe*—and fueled by the popularity of George Colman and Samuel Arnold's *Inkle and Yarico* in 1787—dozens of plays based on Native American subjects followed over the next fifty years and attained popularity in the United States as well as in Britain. Most of these were loosely based on historical events, and some reenacted conflicts that led to the development of the United States as a nation. They also began to establish many of the character types of American Indians that persisted for over a hundred and fifty years. In the seventeenth century, there were principally two literary possibilities: the noble Indian chieftain or princess (such as Pocahontas) and the aboriginal savage (as in Shakespeare's Caliban). In the early eighteenth century, captivity narratives and island romances opened up the possibilities to include at least two new character types. One of these was the faithful friend, such as Defoe's Friday (*Robinson Crusoe,* 1719) or Pohetohee and Cawwawkee in John Gay's *Polly* (1729). The other was the beautiful, steadfast, and wronged Indian bride, already partially evident in Smith's construction of Pocahontas but made more palpable in the fictional Yarico, a character that captured eighteenth-century English imaginations.[23]

Inkle and Yarico was derived from a story published by Steele in a 1711 issue of *The Spectator,* retold from Richard Ligon's 1657 *True Exact History of the Island of Barbados.* Because of the work's controversial and apparently irreconcilable position in the late eighteenth century—it was an indictment of slavery and slaveholders—Roger Fiske has called it one of England's first problem plays. It also bears some similarity to the Pocahontas legend, with a concluding twist. Yarico, an Indian woman, saves the life of Thomas Inkle, a young English merchant on the run from some hostile Indian warriors. She falls in love with him, but once he's nursed back to health his greed takes over and he tries to sell her on the slave market. For the stage adaptation, Colman added some other characters but also intensified the young white merchant's ultimate humiliation. Inkle is a character blinded by racism and hubris, and he gets his comeuppance in the end. The comic opera version opened at the Little Theatre in the Haymarket on 4 August 1787. Composer Samuel Arnold made no attempt to situate the work musically in America. In one air ("Our Grotto Was the Sweetest Place"), Yarico sings a gentle melody as she recounts first meeting her lover and feeling the first pangs of fear as she attempted to conceal him from her people. The most distinctive piece in Arnold's score, however, is "Wampum Swampum," a comical courtship number for Wowski (Yarico's black servant) and Trudge (Inkle's cockney servant). Although the duet uses what I will call "hopping fourths" as well as other marking devices, such as telltale leaping octaves in the voice parts and a few drone basses, the inclusion of these characters is an influence from the harlequinade. The gestural music seems to burlesque their naïveté and foolishness: the black and the cockney servants are both subjects of the same class humor. Still, *Inkle and Yarico* was probably the first major play to feature a romantic relationship between a white man and an Indian woman. (Colman eliminated the baby they were supposed to have had.) The play was extraordinarily popular. Within a few years it had performances all over the British colonies—even in Calcutta, India. Odell's *Annals of the New York Stage* shows that it ran at various theaters in New York from 1789 until as late as 1844. The American productions could be quite elaborate. In 1797 at Ricketts' Circus in New York, Yarico was *The American Heroine* and was billed as a "heroic pantomime . . . [with] grand military evolutions, single combats, new decorations, etc." Several "Indian Chiefs" were added to the cast, and the play concluded with a "Grand Indian Dance." I could find no record of the music for this dance nor what President John Adams, who attended one of the performances, thought of it.[24]

Meanwhile, Hunter's "Death Song of the Cherokee Indians" stimulated other death songs not based on Hunter's original, among them Charles Dibdin's "Indian Death Song" as sung in *The Wags, or The Lamp of Pleasure* (one of Dibdin's popular "table entertainments" given at the Lyceum in 1790).[25] Hunter's song itself made an appearance in Royall Tyler's play *The Contrast* (John Street Theatre, New York, 1787), where it was sung in a drawing room setting by Maria, a young woman disconsolate over her forthcoming marriage to a man she does not love. Maria's remarks after singing the "Death Song" offer some insight into its reception in America:

> There is something in this song which ever calls forth my affections. The manly virtue of courage, that fortitude which steels the heart against the keenest misfortunes, which interweaves the laurel of glory amidst the instruments of torture and death, displays something so noble, so exalted, that in despite of the prejudices of education I cannot but admire it, even in a savage.

As in later popular theater and eventually film, songs were inserted into the narrative not solely because of their dramatic relevance but also for their topical appeal, and audiences then as now took pleasure in the recognition. Of course onstage pronouncements such as "even in a savage" remind us of the extraordinary condescension prevalent on the part of white Americans toward Indians at this time. Yet Tyler's inclusion of this song in his play—a song which could hardly have been more than six or seven years old—and his description of this character's relationship to it suggests to us that many people in 1787 found its evocation of nobility and honor in the face of misfortune compelling.

Hunter's "Death Song" turned up again in John Scawen and Samuel Arnold's short-lived comic opera *New Spain, or Love in Mexico* (Little Theatre in the Haymarket, 1790). The story involves one Leonora who, disguised as a soldier, follows her departed lover Don Garcias to Mexico. There—while still in disguise—she is promoted to the rank of lieutenant governor and becomes embroiled in an Indian uprising. The Mexican Indians are given familiar names: Zempoalla (from Dryden's *The Indian Queen*) and Alknomoak, the captured chieftain (presumably no longer Cherokee). Alknomoak sang his by-now well-known song of resistance—which Arnold calls a march—while bound in chains. The subtitle "march" is of course highly ironic in this context, but it makes explicit the inherent military quality of the piece (the "manly virtue . . . which steels the heart" identified by Tyler) as well as the patriotic context in which it would become increasingly used.

Beginning with *New Spain,* the decade of the 1790s saw several prominent plays about the New World. The complex genre of British popular theater, with its increasing emphasis on spectacle and a prominent role for music, began to develop throughout the decade. None of these works, even those with extensive music, could be called "operas" by modern standards. By the early nineteenth century, works of these types had split into many subgenres, although *burletta* was the British legal term for any stage play from the 1790s to 1843 that incorporated songs, dances, and incidental music. The year 1792 marked the three-hundredth anniversary of Columbus's voyage. At least two English authors, Thomas Morton and Anne Julia Hatton, each contributed a popular burletta to the British and American stage to honor Columbus; Stephen Storace fashioned an "opera" on a Cherokee subject; and Richard Brinsley Sheridan and Michael Kelly turned again to the subject of the Incas in Peru for their musical play. Each of these, along with specific features in their musical numbers, reminds us of both the celebration of the new nation and the anxieties inherent in the representation of native America.

The first of the Columbian plays was Thomas Morton's *Columbus, or The Discovery of America,* produced at Covent Garden in December 1792 and then in Philadelphia and New York in 1797.[26] The published version of Morton's play (London, 1792) notes that the "pathetic tale of Cora and Alonzo" is taken from Marmontel's *Incas.* Morton drew much of his substance from August Kotzebue's play *Sonnenjungfrau* (*The Virgin of the Sun,* 1791) that was in turn drawn on incidents from Marmontel. Though I have not found any extant music for Kotzebue's original production of *Sonnenjungfrau* (apparently by Zumsteeg), there is one piece—a death song, no less—surviving by Franz Xaver Gerl for its sequel, *Die Spanier in Peru.*[27]

Jean-François Marmontel's novel *Les Incas, ou la destruction de l'empire du Pérou* (1777) had an enormous impact when it first appeared. It was not just a two-volume account of a historical event, but one interwoven with intriguing fictional characters and dramatic situations. Like Frederick the Great and Graun's slightly earlier *Montezuma* of 1755, Marmontel used the allegory of a two-hundred-year-old American encounter to speak out in defense of freedom of religion. Marmontel's *Incas* served in part as his reaction to censorship of a chapter on religious tolerance in his earlier *Belisarius*. As one source notes, Marmontel retorted "by tracing the cruelties in Spanish America to the religious fanaticism of the invaders."[28] The book was important not only in France, but in England and other European countries as well. Most important, Marmontel's historical novel dramatized Pizarro's ruthless conquest of Peru from the perspective of the Incas. It also introduced an affecting love interest, that of Cora and Alonzo. This romance must have created a sensation, because it was replicated in many stage plays and songs well into the 1840s. Cora's parents relinquish her as a young girl to be brought up as a high priestess. (Marmontel hints at an older tradition of sacrificing virgin victims, though this was no longer practiced in the sixteenth century.) When the Spaniards land on Inca shores several years later, one of them, Alonzo, proves to be sympathetic to the Incas' cause. He falls in love with the priestess Cora during ceremonies at the Temple of the Sun (at Koricancha), and she in turn becomes enamored of him. He abducts her but leads her safely back after they consummate their love. In the eyes of Inca law she is defiled and must pay the price, although "Ataliba," the Peruvian monarch, says the law does not apply to a Spaniard and thus Alonzo is free to go. With Cora's father begging for mercy, Alonzo pleads her case, and in a remarkable twist of events, the monarch and his tribunes pardon Cora and release her from her sacred bonds. These incidents amount to just a few pages in Marmontel's elaborate history. But for many they were the most compelling—and human—part of the story.

No subsequent version, however, adhered exactly to Marmontel's original. Kotzebue intensified the romantic conflict by introducing a new character and rival to Alonzo, the noble Peruvian Rolla. Rolla was such a successful creation with audiences that the Austrian dramatist followed this play in 1795 with *The Spaniards in Peru, or Rolla's Death*. Cora, Alonzo, and Rolla were among the most popular roles for two generations of actors. There were at least seven international versions of *The Virgin of the Sun* and at least eleven adaptations of *The Spaniards in Peru*. In Morton's version, the conquistador was replaced by Columbus—in celebration of 1792—despite the anachronism. In Kotzebue's version and Morton's adaptation, Alonzo marries Cora and, instead of abducting her, saves her from the temple during an earthquake. (Morton's adaptation also owes a debt for this sensational episode to Fuzelier and

Rameau's *Les Indes galantes,* 1735, in which a Spaniard saves his Peruvian lover from an erupting volcano.)

The original British music was probably by Karl Baumgartner, Covent Garden's music director. Alexander Reinagle provided music for the 1797 Philadelphia production, James Hewitt for New York the same year, and Peter Van Hagen for Boston in 1800. The Philadelphia production, which opened on 30 October, was by all accounts quite a spectacle. According to a review from a local newspaper, *Columbus* included a procession of Indians, the landing of the explorer, a representation of a storm and an earthquake, a grand eruption from a volcano, a sacrifice, and a grand pageant.[29] Reinagle's "Indian March," no. 16 "of the much admeired american play caled Columbus," was arranged for keyboard and printed in Philadelphia by C. Hupfeld. According to the specifications for music in the published version of the play, Reinagle's no. 16 was probably used in act 1, scene 4. The scene begins at the seacoast. Three ships are seen at anchor. To the accompaniment of "Martial Music" (presumably no. 15), Columbus, Alonzo, Roldan, Valverdo, the English tar (sailor) Harry Herbert (Morton's comic addition), and the rest of the Spanish adventurers emerge from the boats. In a short scene, they stake their claim. Before long, "Indian Music" is heard, starting offstage (no. 16). The Indian music continues for the arrival of Orozimbo, Cora, and the Indian warriors. (Although the location of Columbus's landing is not specified, the details are similar to Marmontel's Peruvian setting.)

Not surprisingly, the "Indian Music" is a march. Reinagle's short piece consists of three phrases (ABC), of which B and C are to be repeated, presumably until all the party is onstage. The march begins with a slight ambience of mystery, the minor mode and unison doublings portending some uncertainty. The next phrase begins *piano* and is more overtly threatening. The last phrase, however, bursts forth in a bright, heroic tone. Reinagle's music is a curious blend of standard eighteenth-century rhetorical topics and syntactical devices that presage the tropes of nineteenth-century exoticism. The "hopping" pattern of minor thirds in the opening phrase functions indexically unlike any other "Indian" music we have heard so far. The rocking-style form of the minor chords in the accompaniment of phrase B, however, was commonly used in the late eighteenth century to represent the clanging of a Turkish Janissary band.[30] The repetitive five-note melody of phrase B suggests a primitive tune (especially with the open fifths in the bass), and from the clangorous style of accompaniment it is easy to imagine cymbals, triangle, and bass drum keeping the beat (a feature common to many "Turkish" numbers in 1780s Vienna). The *alla turca* style, however, quickly resolves to the major key (phrase C) and to the patriotic sounds more typical of the English march and

16.

INDIAN MARCH.

of the much admeired american play: caled

COLUMBUS.

Arranged for the Piano Forte printed and fold Philadelphia by C: Hupfeld .

Figure 4. Alexander Reinagle, "Indian March" from *Columbus* (1797; Philadelphia: C. Hupfeld, [1799]). Library of Congress, Music Division.

other genres popular in the early American republic. Divorced from its theatrical context, I would argue, this work probably does not convey any distinctive associations with American Indians. But this "Indian March" was clearly written to be heard in a dramatic context, and it is necessary to reconstruct the visual presentation in order to understand how the march's specific musical features were perceived at the time.

Reinagle was music director from 1792 to 1809 for the Chestnut Street Theatre in Philadelphia — the theater President Washington attended regularly. Like Linley at London's Drury Lane, Reinagle composed and adapted much music for his theater. This English-born composer arrived in Philadelphia with his musical tastes largely formed. (He studied in Scotland under Raynor Taylor, became a member of C. P. E. Bach's circle in Hamburg, and came to the United States in 1786.) Since this "Indian March" is the only published item from the score of *Columbus* for which copies survive in several libraries, it was no doubt well known. It may even have been used, given its distinctive title, on other dramatic occasions when "Indian" music was required.[31]

In 1794, seven years after Tyler's *Contrast*, Hunter's "Death Song" again made an appearance on the same stage in a different play, and with revised words. The authors of *Tammany, or the Indian Chief* (1794) were also both British-born and -educated. Anne Julia Hatton came to America in 1794, and her play was produced at the John Street Theatre under the auspices of the New York Tammany Society. James Hewitt, musical director of the theater, wrote the overture and "accompanyments." Neither the text of Hatton's play nor Hewitt's music has been found. But the Tammany Society of New York, which sponsored the production, published a booklet that included the song texts, and these were sold at the door for one shilling.[32] Eyewitness accounts inform us that the title character was a noble chief (of no identifiable tribe, though situated in Pennsylvania) whose lover, Manana, is threatened with abduction by Ferdinand, a ruffian member of Christopher Columbus's band of explorers, who have just landed. When Tammany rescues Manana, Ferdinand vengefully sets fire to their wigwam and destroys them. Tammany and Manana sing their death song, after which the Indians lament the loss of their noble leader and his lady. The catastrophe of this play is not exactly Hatton's original construction. It owes a great deal to the history of Tammany Societies in eighteenth-century America. The mascot for this white organization was Tamanend, the seventeenth-century Delaware chief who granted William Penn access to the rivers and woods of what is now Pennsylvania but was ultimately burned at the stake by colonists.

According to Philip Deloria, Tammany followers from New York to South Carolina reenacted Tamanend's mythic end in ritual ceremonies. In his study of the Tammany Society's evolution, Deloria revealed the desire of colonial Americans (in the middle colonies) to act out both the bacchanalian excesses of European carnival and (in the northern colonies) Old World misrule traditions. It was this latter form of political protest, for example, that drove republican patriots in 1774 to dress as Mohawks, board British vessels -in Boston Harbor, and shout the war whoop while dumping British tea overboard. "Whether aimed at British officials or colonial landlords," Deloria writes, "misrule traditions, often performed in Indian dress, remained a vital mode of American political protest for more than a century."[33] Traditions of European carnival took root in such activities as those of the Schuylkill Fishing Company of Pennsylvania, which proclaimed May 1 as "King Tammany's Day" and which gathered for celebrations that featured songs, tobacco, a huge dinner, and prolific toasting with bowls of potent alcoholic punch. Deloria quotes the *New York Journal and Patriotic Register* of 1792, which recounts one such celebration in Charleston:

> At about 4 o'clock they sat down to a plain and plentiful dinner, and after imbibing a suitable quantity of Indian drink proceeded to the solemnity of burning the Old Chief, who being placed in the Wigwam and having sung the death song, fire was set thereto and the whole immediately consumed. A dance, after the Indian manner, concluded the ceremonies of the day.

Deloria argues effectively that Tamanend's death was a metaphor for the destruction of the old order—Indian rulers in the land—and a new era in which successor white Americans would take control. But he does not comment on the peculiar strangeness of this 1792 notice. Who was the "Old Chief"? Presumably there was an effigy placed in the tent. But if so, who sang the death song? An official of the society? Which death song did he sing? And what sort of dance constitutes "after the Indian manner?"[34]

Tammany societies existed in America since the early eighteenth century, and these rituals were enacted long before the appearance of Hunter's "Death Song." Yet it is curious that, at the John Street Theatre, Tammany and Manana sang Anne Hatton's words to a melody "adapted," as the published text tells us, "from the old Indian song." Though the text begins the same ("The sun sets in night"), the song diverges in one important and critical respect: the antagonists are not other Indians, but white European colonists. ("You white men, deceivers your smiles are in vain, / The son of Alkmoonac shall ne'er wear your chain.") This raises the interesting supposition that perhaps the melody of this "old Indian song" may have been a Tammany tune that "Mr. Turner" picked up and brought back to England in the 1770s. Sources for the Tammany Society provide texts for some Tammany songs but unfortunately no music. (During the Revolutionary War, the Tammany Society became overtly political, hence its role in later Philadelphia and New York politics.)

The character of Tammany received much applause for his independent and noble spirit, as theater historian Eugene Jones has noted, and the spoken prologue and epilogue "were brim full of the present popular notions of liberty and of course [they] went down with great éclat." Jones describes an audience of "industrious members of society" along with "poorer classes of mechanics and clerks."[35] According to Odell's *Annals* (vol. 2, 346), *Tammany* was turned into a symbol of republicanism, "and as such was patronised by the hot-heads of New York, to the utter rout of the aristocrats." The play ran on selected nights in March and April 1794. After performances in Philadelphia that same year, in New York in 1795, and in Boston in 1796—all probably at the behest of Tammany Societies—the fervor for its republican message faded.

According to the *Tammany* playbill, the show—like the ceremonies on which it was based—also featured an "Indian Dance" by Messrs. Durang and Miller. John Durang was an acrobat who, like Francisque Moylin, made his reputation in harlequinades. We will encounter more American actors posing as Indian dancers in the next chapter; simply put, however, the dramatic rise in the level of Indian performers onstage after about 1795 makes it difficult to tell from accounts which are the Indians and which are the actors. Again, the liminal nature of Indians in American culture played an important role, particularly in their increased exoticization in the early nineteenth century.[36]

In Britain, Cherokees still dominated the public imagination, and James Cobb produced an "opera" entitled *The Cherokee* at Drury Lane in 1794 with music "principally composed" by Stephen Storace. Surprisingly, no Cherokee death song appears in this play, although, as in *Columbus,* there are "Indian marches." Like the rescue operas then in vogue in France, *The Cherokee* marks a decided shift toward gothic melodrama, with its gloomy settings, symbolic thunderstorms, secret plots, and a hero arriving in time to save the heroine. As Cobb's published text reveals, two Cherokee leaders become antagonists over their passion for Zelipha, who is in secret an Englishwoman living with a young son. A British expedition is sent to suppress this exploding rivalry, but Malooko, one of the two chieftains, discovers Zelipha's son and kidnaps him. (This situation inspired Storace to compose a magnificent vengeance chorus led by Ontayo, the other rival, to bring down the first-act curtain.) An "Indian messenger" allied with the British rescues the boy, which only further infuriates Malooko. Eventually it is discovered that the colonel of the expedition is actually Zelipha's estranged husband. The colonel tries diplomacy, but he ultimately kills both Malooko and Ontayo. Even the young boy manages to shoot a Cherokee in order to save his mother and father in the final skirmish.

The singer-composer Michael Kelly played the colonel. There were eighteen

Figure 5. Stephen Storace, Two Marches from *The Cherokee* (London: J. Dale, 1795).

performances the first season but only one in the next. James Gray of the *Morning Chronicle* liked the way the Indians were characterized and said he would have been happier "had the wild manners of these Indians oftener possessed the scene."[37] The play was produced in the United States at the Boston Haymarket Theatre in June 1799, and actor John Kemble revived it in 1802 as an afterpiece at Drury Lane, where it was renamed *Algonah* and contained some additional music by Kelly.

In one confrontational scene in act 2, the Indians and the British meet in a forest grove to decide whether conflict can be averted. In accordance with the spectacle nature of the gothic melodrama, each of the groups enters separately to their own music. To the accompaniment of a "Cherokee March," the two chieftains and their retinue enter with Patomac, "an old ally," and several Indians bearing the hatchets of war. The British officers, soldiers, and artillerymen enter to a "British March." Neither march seems particularly characteristic of its group. But it is curious, given the violent nature of the Indians in the play, that the "Cherokee March" exhibits perfect symmetry and balance, poise and elegance, compared with the "British March," which features a rattling Alberti bass line and clunky five-measure phrases. Storace seems to be taking advantage of the order of presentation — the British second — by emphasizing "difference" between the two in this way. There is clearly an innate nobility of expression in the Cherokee march that the British one lacks.

At the conclusion of act 1, Ontayo alludes to a tempest to stir his men to battle:

> Oh pow'r unknown who in the Storm
> Shrowdest on high thy aweful form
> For vengeance, for vengeance, for vengeance we implore
> Give us revenge, we ask no more.

The chorus itself (sung by the full Drury Lane forces, SATB) begins in E♭ minor. But Storace, in a harmonic twist that foreshadows Beethoven's heroic style, dramatically modulates to C major for the victorious battle cry: "And grant that like thy thunders sound / Our war whoop may the foe confound." In his *Reminiscences,* Kelly called this chorus one of the grandest ever composed and the effect of it "sublime." Like his theatrical predecessors, Storace used music to represent native America symbolically, rather than using any indexical gestures to situate his characters *musically* in North America.

PIZARRO

Certainly one of the most elaborate representations of native America in this period—and the longest lasting of the New World plays to emerge on the cusp of the new century—was *Pizarro,* Sheridan's version of Kotzebue, which opened at Drury Lane in 1799. The music for the production was quite a tour-de-force. Michael Kelly prepared the musical pastiche for the onstage action (which included marches by Gluck and Drury Lane's music director Thomas Shaw, as well as choruses taken from works by Sacchini and Cherubini), and he composed a few glees, choruses, and marches himself. Jan Ladislav Dussek, a Czech pianist and composer living in London in the 1790s, composed the overture and "characteristic pieces as played during the entr'actes," each of these dramatically foreshadowing events in the following acts ("Preparatory to Battle," "Expressing Despair and . . . Leading to the Dungeon," and so on).[38]

Pizarro again brought the characters Alonzo, Rolla, and Cora to the stage. It was extraordinarily successful, even more than *Columbus,* and the play remained in British and American repertories for fifty years or more. In Kotzebue's and Sheridan's versions, Cora and Alonzo are married and have a child. Though he does not sing a death song, Rolla heroically sacrifices his life to Pizarro's soldiers in the climactic scene in order to allow Alonzo and his infant to escape. The title character, as realized by William Barrymore, emerged as one of the first—and for many decades the most compelling—villains of early melodrama.[39] Music figured most highly during the scene of the Temple of the Sun—which was virtually a short opera in itself—and near the end for Rolla's funeral sequence. The setting for the temple (fig. 6) combined ancient New

Figure 6. James Winston, *The Temple of the Sun Scene in Pizarro.* Drawing in ink and watercolor, unsigned (n.p., 1799). Harvard Theatre Collection, Houghton Library. Used by permission.

World symbols, Baroque spectacle, and even contemporary Greek revival in a scene of great pageantry.

Compared to Reinagle's and Storace's theater music, Kelly's contributions to *Pizarro,* such as the "Grand March in the Temple of the Sun," the "Distant Military March and Chorus of Peruvians," and the "Dead March" for Rolla's funeral are relatively simplistic, offering little more than embellishments of a tonic-dominant harmony with repetitive generic British military flourishes. "Pomp and bombast without much distinctiveness" might be a good way to describe them. Despite Dussek's rousing curtain-raisers, King George III thought *Pizarro* "a poor composition." But the public that crowded the theaters paid no attention to His Majesty's opinion. Roused by stirring battle music and moved by heroic marches and mournful processionals, audiences on both sides of the Atlantic cheered the noble efforts of Rolla and Cora and hissed the savage cruelty of Pizarro. As Michael Kelly noted, *Pizarro* "for years afterwards proved a mine of wealth to the Drury Lane treasury and, indeed, to all the theatres in the United Kingdom." As late as 1882 *Pizarro* was still listed in Samuel French's catalog of plays with music for hire, clearly demonstrating its enormous longevity.[40]

What did the influential *Pizarro* have to say about British views of native America? Though it contained no death song, it nonetheless embodied the display and diplomacy evident in the earlier British songs. To begin with, Sheridan's play, like the earlier *Inkle and Yarico,* was anti-imperialist. One journal accused Kotzebue of trying "to render the upper classes of society objects of indignation or contempt and to confine all virtue, and every noble quality, to the lower classes of the community."[41] In addition, Sheridan's play was actually set in a "gothic" rather than an Indian Peru, as theater historian George Rowell noted. Paul Ranger has also observed that "solitary places [were] made terrifying by thunderstorms in which the lonely figure of Cora could hide; the Valley of the Torrent with its fragile bridge spanning the ravine brought a familiar image to the stage; and the dungeon, although translated to South America, had lost none of its massive strength."[42]

Furthermore, many of the characters were also of gothic stock, particularly the greedy tyrant and the helpless heroine. As a key Indian figure, Rolla represented the archetypal hero of resistance. And yet, according to Ranger, he also represented all stands made against advancing foes, a critical topic as England began to mobilize its forces to repel Napoleon's awaited attacks. In this sense, *Pizarro,* at least in Great Britain, resonated with domestic issues. For example, Fintan O'Toole has effectively demonstrated that Sheridan's defiant speeches for Rolla were taken from contributions to the Warren Hastings trial, and he argues that the besieged Peruvians served as an allegory for the Irish, a subject dear to Sheridan's heart. It would seem that the conquest (and defense) of America conveniently provided a theatrical soapbox upon which to address political situations at home, much as it had for the royal "discovery operas" of the seventeenth and early eighteenth centuries, while avoiding the sharp pen of the royal censor.

We could compare the first, politically oriented production of *Pizarro* with a very different one from some fifty years later. At the Princess's Theatre in 1856, Charles Kean attempted to bring to Sheridan's play all the lavish visual splendor of Prescott's recent history, *The Conquest of Peru* (1847). In the 1850s Kean's focus was not on allegory but on *authenticity:* how to recreate a Peru at the time of contact that was consistent with historians' and scholars' accounts. Although he permitted Kelly's original glee "Fly Away Time" to be sung in the production, the rest of the music was completely rewritten by John Hatton and based on "Indian airs . . . founded on melodies published in Rivero and Tschudi's work on *Peruvian Antiquities* as handed down to us by Spaniards after the conquest."[43] It is beyond the scope of this chapter to examine the many productions of *Pizarro* in detail. But clearly Europe's interest in these ancient civilizations continued to increase, particularly as the newly independent nations of the Americas began to assume economic and political power in the modern world.

Productions of *Pizarro* in the young United States served yet another purpose. The play's continued success marks the beginning of a new phase of "Indianism": mythmaking, particularly that of establishing a "prehistory" on which to build a modern history. The play was adapted by William Dunlap and first produced at the Park Theatre, New York, in 1800. James Hewitt, who had already had some experience at imagining native America in 1797 with his song "The Wampum Belt," prepared the music, adding at least one march, if not other numbers, of his own. During this phase the resistance Indian, used as a rhetorical marker for heroism throughout the eighteenth century, became an increasingly dangerous topic. According to Eugene Jones, nineteenth-century playwrights avoided recently controversial personalities by choosing a subject from the distant past. *Pizarro,* set as it was in an earlier place and time, held the stage well into the age of border wars, even inspiring later plays such as *Metamora* (about King Philip) that drew upon the earlier tradition of resistance dramas.[44] At a certain point, as we will see in the next chapter, what were once considered proud Indian dramas cheered by audiences changed in just a few decades to works laughed or booed off the stage.

THE INDIAN PRINCESS

In the light of the extraordinary popularity of these melodramas, Barker and Bray's *The Indian Princess, ou La Belle Sauvage,* important as the first complete musical score to a theater work to be published in America, seems merely a footnote in theatrical history. James Nelson Barker and composer John Bray again turned to the distant past to retell the Pocahontas story with songs and pantomime. The play opened in April 1808 at the Chestnut Street Theatre in Philadelphia and received a few performances the same year in New York and in Baltimore. It ran in Charleston a year later and was also produced in London at Drury Lane. *The Indian Princess,* however, could probably be included within the tradition of literary historical dramas more read than seen or heard since their premieres, along with *Ponteach* of Robert Rogers (1766) or the later *Yemassee* of William Gilmore Simms (1835). Susan Scheckel has written extensively about the play, emphasizing the role that the title character plays in portraying the successful conquest of Virginia although, surprisingly, she never even hints that specific music—not to mention a host of wonderful songs—was associated with the play. According to Scheckel, because the Indian princess rebels against her father and heroically rescues Smith, "Pocahontas's goodness is signaled by her intuitive recognition of the superiority of the conquerors and their values."[45] The emphasis by 1808 had clearly begun to shift away from the idea of Indian resistance—and it is here too (in Pocahontas's rescue of John Smith) that we see an important trope of musical Indianism beginning to emerge.

Bray, a singer-actor as well as a composer, was born in England in 1782 and came with his singer wife to Philadelphia in 1805 to work for the Chestnut Theatre. Bray's music brings both a tone of noble savage heroism to the melodrama as well as the requisite sense of "hurry" in the action scenes. Though the music to *The Indian Princess* may be overlooked in literary sources, its survival in print offers some examples of dances that might have been common in the decades bordering 1800 (John Durang's, for example).

The climax of the drama—Pocahontas's famous rescue—occurs at the opening of act 2. Bray's music runs throughout this scene, in typical melodramatic fashion—words alternating with short musical statements for mime. "Behold the white being," King Powhatan proclaims. To pizzicato strings in F major, Captain Smith is brought before the council. Miami, a prince, and Grimosco, a priest, argue for the white man's death. As the king deliberates, music once again ensues. Powhatan decides that Smith must go to the block, and with Pocahontas's outcry "Shall that brave man die!" the orchestra plays a melancholy tune in C minor (*Andante affettuoso*). As she pleads with her father for his release, the orchestra switches to a more lyrical 3/4 but remains in C minor, the melody—perhaps played by a mournful oboe—plaintive and supplicating. "Is thy child dear to thee, my father?" Pocahontas asks. Bowing down to Powhatan, she firmly asserts that "thy child will die with the white man." After a few moments, the king yields, offering his daughter a string of white wampum. While the orchestra bursts out in a *vivace* G minor passage in 2/4, Pocahontas rushes ecstatically toward Smith with the beads, shouting "Captive! Thou art free!" (See musical example in chapter 3, table 3.) In this moment of "Indian joy," Bray decided to avoid a bright key or major mode (more consistent with the eighteenth-century resistance Indian) and instead cobbled together the components of a trope that would become increasingly common in the nineteenth century: the war dance. The pulsing minor chords in the orchestra and the sharp rhythmic gestures in the melody are indexical of Native American singing and drumming. They suggest mixed sadness and joy and simultaneously reflect Miami and Grimosco's displeasure. (The gods are offended, this music seems to imply, and the Virginians will have to pay a price for their king's weakness.)[46]

For generations of eighteenth-century Europeans, American Indians defined the essence of "American," and tales of conquest and heroic resistance proved to be some of the most compelling works to hold the popular stage. The style of the march served as an important and often eloquent marker of Indian nobility, courage, and heroism when used in this context. It is ironic that in early nineteenth-century America the "Indian march" came to mean something quite different. In an instrumental version of Hunter's "Death Song" from the 1840s entitled "The Indian Chief," the tune was given a plodding and repetitive bass line. In this setting—one found in several editions throughout the nineteenth century—the air is robbed of its gentility and elegance, and its simplistic alternating tonic-dominant bass pattern is an accompaniment more suitable for regimentation than exciting the "sensations" that Hunter wrote about.

As we will see, the distinctions that began in the eighteenth century between the noble resistance Indian and the untamed provocative savage continued to be projected in the United States but were now intensified through the lens of American desire for more land and resources. The intensification also occurred musically, due to an increasing variety of stylistic influences flowing into the United States as well as a growing body of knowledge and familiarity with Native American music and performance ritual.

PART II

Exotic Peoples, Exotic Sounds

3

Imagining the Frontier, 1795–1860

One morning in 1803, John Rodgers Jewitt, armourer for the *Boston,* a ship anchored in Nootka Sound off the coast of Vancouver Island, suddenly found himself alerted to a scuffle on deck. The ship had been overtaken by several Nuu-chah-nulth, a formerly amicable tribe that was suddenly annoyed by the intruders. Chief Maquinna ordered the American sailors killed but spared Jewitt because of his ability to clean and repair guns. Jewitt and another surviving companion were enslaved for almost three years, during which time he learned the Nootkan language and took careful note of the customs, rituals, and music of the Indians. Eventually Jewitt was able to escape to freedom when another American vessel came into the sound. Upon his return, he published his memoirs (1815), and this most recent in a long line of captivity narratives created quite a stir. "There is scarce any relation of savage manners," a review in *Analectic Magazine* read, "which can lay higher claim to authenticity."[1]

James Nelson Barker, author of *The Indian Princess,* thought the account a thrilling story for dramatic adaptation, and *The Armourer's Escape, or Three Years at Nootka Sound* opened at Philadelphia's Chestnut Street Theatre in 1817, the very year the Seminoles began their bloody retaliation against settlers in Florida. Barker's *coup de théâtre* was having Jewitt, who was already something of a literary celebrity, appear as himself in the play. "Pains have been taken," the playbill announced, "to represent faithfully the costume, manners, ceremonies and superstitions of these extraordinary people." A ballet-pantomime capped the first scene of act 2. This "Ludicrous Ceremonies of the Bear" contained a war dance by "Nootkians," Jewitt singing the "Nootkian War Song" (the words of which he had already translated in his book), and continued with a scene in which Jewitt was forced to choose a wife—Princess Yuqua being the lucky lady. The ballet concluded with a dramatic finale in several parts: a dance of young Nootkan girls; the entrance of an enemy tribe masked with heads of animals to carry the girls off; their rescue by young chieftains; and a general dance.

The music for this astonishing sequence of events was compiled and arranged by John C. Lefolle, violinist and music director of the theater.[2] Neither text nor music seems to have survived, however, and our knowledge of the performances is based only on the playbill and newspaper accounts. Perhaps Lefolle did not write any original music but instead drew on existing works available to him in Philadelphia. The play itself did not last more than a few performances. But it is tempting to consider what must have nevertheless been quite a sensational event in the theater. Despite the missing music, it is clear that *The Armourer's Escape* was a far cry from *Inkle and Yarico* or *Pizarro* in its exotic portrayal of American Indians. The Nootkas weren't "noble savages" but rather a very real tribe living at some point on the distant frontier. What made the Nootka ceremonies exotic was not just that they were representations of imagined communities but that they were billed to audiences as authentic recreations. Exoticism, like myth, enfolds its subject enigmatically within layers of imprecise meaning that hint suggestively at the kernels of truth at its core; hence its allure. In order to understand music's persuasive power, we need to peel back some of those layers in early nineteenth-century musical works about native America.

If eighteenth-century songs and plays reflected the celebration of colonization, musical works of the early nineteenth century reflected conquest and its ambiguities. It has therefore been necessary to structure this chapter around three overlapping time periods, each with its own distinct emphases. The first segment, covering ca. 1795 to 1818, deals with emerging issues concerning American political and cultural identity (i.e., a consideration of Native American culture within the context of the new nation's search for an identity). The second, roughly encompassing 1818 to 1832, focuses on the expanding frontier and its relationship to the idea of nationhood (i.e., geography rather than people). The third, extending from about 1832 to the 1850s, involves the emerging formulation of a distinctly American cultural identity, perceived and even imitated by those outside the United States (in which native America achieved less of a subsidiary role as an increasingly antithetical cultural element). The degree to which many North American tribes were caught up in these phases, either as real or as imaginary Indians, shifted dramatically.

The Exotic American Frontier

Two key developments led to an increased exotic representation of Indians in the early nineteenth century. The first of these was the United States' westward expansion beyond the Ohio Valley, particularly Jefferson's purchase and annexation of the vast Louisiana territory in 1803, as well as the territories of Missouri and Oregon over the next four decades. This gradual mapping of the continent resulted in thrilling tales from the frontier. The second major development, beginning in 1823, involved the evacuation of Indians from their homelands, particularly the forced removal of five southeastern Indian nations that took place in the 1830s under Andrew Jackson's administration. These were especially difficult years in Indian-white relations, given the large number of Indian deaths due to a smallpox epidemic—despite the availability of inoculation—and the ruthless uprooting and exile of so many Indian peoples.[3] Tribal cohesiveness in the eastern half of the continent began to deteriorate rapidly as Indians were driven west of the Mississippi River. Though the interactions between white explorers, Indians, settlers, and the United States government during this time were far more complex than is possible to summarize here, the systematic endeavors of exploration and removal served as the principal background for how Indians were perceived, interpreted, and represented. When depicted in a sympathetic light, as Indians sometimes were in plays or parlor songs, the male or female "savage" usually appeared as a character of naive temperament, who—like Zima in *Les Indes galantes* or Cora in *Pizarro*—still roamed in an unpolluted romantic landscape, a "child of nature" whose uncivilized way of life could be sentimentalized. Swept aside by colonization and a westward drive, American Indians also led the way for further European exploration. They were both navigators of this exploration (hence "friend of the white man") and its obstructors (hence "enemy of the white man"). The two polar views of noble Indians (those that accepted or even facilitated American expansion) and heathen Indians (those that forcefully resisted it) served as compelling musical as well as literary tropes.

We might well ask why American Indians were increasingly demonized for their resistance to conquest when for over two centuries they had often been praised and emulated for it. This question could be addressed differently from

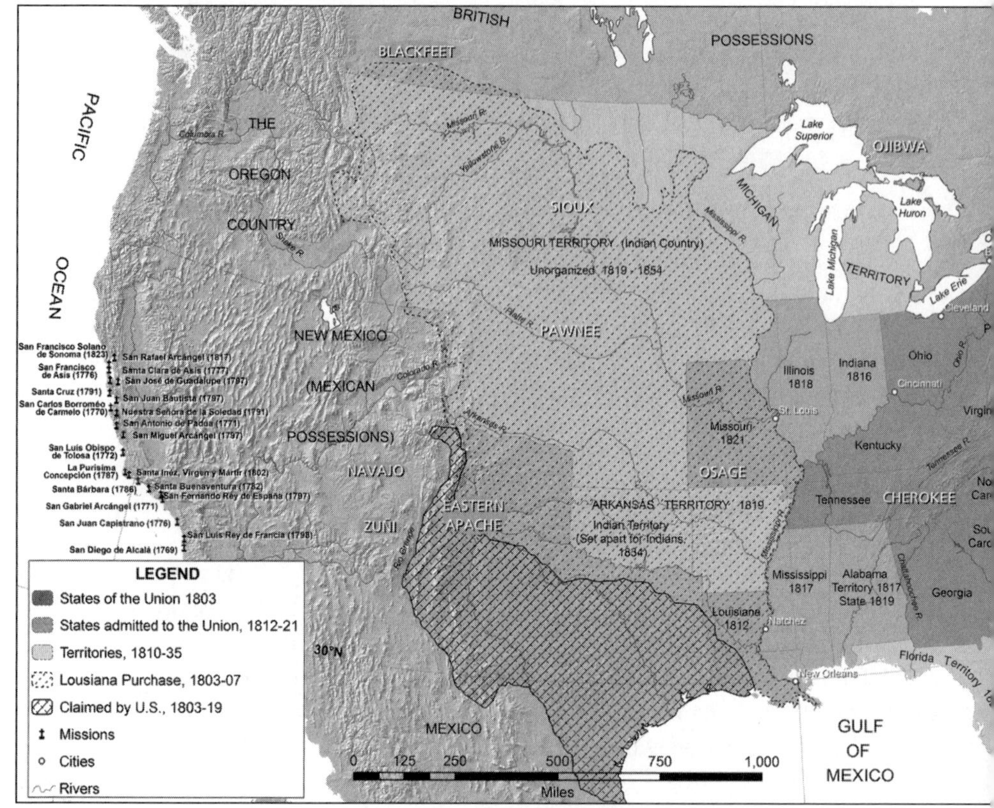

Map 2. Louisiana Purchase and western territories from 1803 to the 1830s, with select Indian homelands shown in capitalized white letters. Modified from William R. Shepherd, *Shepherd's Historical Atlas,* 9th ed. rev. (Totowa, N.J.: Barnes and Noble Books, 1964), 203; *The American Heritage Pictorial Atlas of United States History* (New York: American Heritage Publishing, 1966), 128–29; and select maps from the *Illustrated Atlas of Native American History* (Edison, N.J.: Chartwell Books, 1999). Cartography by Meg Stewart.

economic, social, and cultural perspectives. The frontier Indians as depicted in *The Armourer's Escape* were no doubt terrifying to the urban East Coast audiences of 1817. Since the Nootkas lived at the opposite end of the continent in what was then little-explored Oregon Country (map 2), the physical distance from the spectators as well as the barbaric onstage representation magnified the degree of exoticism and perceived danger. Philadelphia residents, whose economy and cultural values were still largely tied to those of Europe, might have been more inclined to accept romanticized notions of the frontier.

Yet the very concept of "frontier," a potent force in the history of American ideas that would be much debated at century's end by Theodore Roosevelt, Frederick Jackson Turner, and Owen Wister, changed its meaning based upon the location of the observer. For residents of Ohio or Kentucky, for example, the frontier around 1800 proved an ontological challenge to one's resourcefulness. In a place where contact between settlers and Indian tribes still formed a part of the social and economic welfare, the frontier had pragmatic associations more connected with issues of survival than with romance. Residents of Boston, Philadelphia, New York, or Charleston, on the other hand—not to mention London, Paris, or Berlin—lived the American frontier vicariously, through a somewhat filtered medium. This "frontier"—the borders of the "nation-space"—became important as an *idea* while its physical location continued to shift.

The sheer size of the realm played a significant role in defining the frontier, especially given the natural beauties and sublime perils this unexplored territory was believed to contain. It was not yet possible at this time to wrap one's mind around the geographical idea of America; hence various metaphorical levels served as intermediate stages in the process. Saint-John de Crèvecoeur provided such a metaphor of the frontier and its borders in his *Letters from an American Farmer* (1782), one of the most influential books for several generations of American readers. He envisioned a "realm of domesticated nature," a utopian environment cultivated by American farmers, that would be unlike eastern cities, where merchants exploited the limits of commercialism (with all its attendant vices), or the wilderness, the region of the Indian (where hunting and warfare were the principal means of existence. Between this ideal space and the wilderness were the "borderers," dangerous outlaws who fought with Indians and, perhaps inadvertently, kept them at bay from the frontier farms. This metaphor of the frontier was no doubt compelling precisely because it was *not* a community based on existing European models. In this world, nature shaped the individual, not the other way around. Along the same lines, John Filson's influential *Kentucke* (1785) mythologized the adventurous Daniel Boone as a folk hero and, inspired by Colonel Boone's own accounts of a "second paradise," painted the territory as a wild and exotic landscape complete with unusual rock formations, brilliant flowers, buffalo herds, and rich forests teaming with animal life.

Others preferred even more fantastical writings about the frontier. In this regard, nothing surpassed Viscomte François-René de Chateaubriand's *Atala, or The Love and Constancy of Two Savages in the Desert,* published in 1801. Loosely based on impressions during the author's travels across the Ohio Valley in 1791, *Atala* revealed an exotic countryside tingling with blue herons, green flamingos, and bears drunk from eating grapes. Chateaubriand mingled the flora and fauna of widely disparate regions, but he succeeded in presenting a coherent, almost psychedelic image of nature. His evocation of the frontier —written in the first-person singular—was so vibrant that it made readers desire to see the wilderness themselves. Chactas, the romance's narrator, is rescued from being tortured and burned at the stake by Atala, a young Christianized Indian woman. As they make their escape up the Tennessee River, Chactas recalls seeing

> the Indian village of Stico with its pyramidal tombs and ruined huts on the left; on our right we passed the vale of Keow, bounded by a view of the cottage of Jore, situated on the declivity of a mountain of the same name. Gliding down the river, we now passed among towering rocks, the summits of which were brightened by the rays of the setting sun. These profound solitudes were undisturbed by the presence of man. We only saw an Indian hunter, who, resting on his bow and standing motionless on the point of a rock, resembled a statue erected on the mountain to the genius of these wilds.

("Old Stecoe" was still on late eighteenth-century maps. See the uppermost point on map 1, chapter 2.)

In *Atala, René* (1802), and even the later *Natchez* and *Travels in America* (both 1826), Chateaubriand, as Harry Liebersohn put it, "provided subsequent travelers with a style, a vocabulary, a cast of characters, and a set of landscapes" for imagining the frontier and the Indians for which it was home.[4] *Atala* and *René,* first published in France, strongly influenced the way Europeans imagined America, much as had Marmontel's writings in the previous century. Of course, productions of *Pizarro* continued on European and American stages. As with Marmontel, Chateaubriand's emphasis was not on a contemporary America, one that Tocqueville, Dickens, and others would soon pursue. His Indian subjects instead evoked an "ancient America," a locus of European romantic ideals that allowed escape from the political and economic uncertainties of an emerging industrial society by affirming the existence of an Arcadia preserved among the relics of a ruined past.

These romantic ideals stimulated the creation of many operas and musical plays for European theaters. *Atala* was set by Thomas Thollé (Théâtre Jeunes Artistes, Paris, 1802) and Giovanni Pacini (Teatro Nuovo, Padua, 1818). Subjects from *Pizarro* were elaborated in Johann Baptist Lasser's *Cora und Alonzo* (Munich Hoftheater, 1801), [Johannes] Simon Mayr's *Alonso e Cora* (La Scala, Milan, 1803), Guilbert de Pixérécourt's "mélodrame historique" *Pizarre, ou La conquête du Pérou* with music by Henri Darondeau (Théâtre de la Porte St.-Martin, Paris, 1802), and Henry Bishop's *Virgin of the Sun* (Covent Garden, London, 1812). And both Columbus and Cortés were celebrated by Ignaz von Seyfried (Theater an der Wien, Vienna, 1804) and Karl Wöber (Royal Theatre Berlin, 1809), in Gaspare Spontini's *Fernand Cortez* (Paris Opéra, 1809) and J. R. Planché's "historical drama" *Cortez, or The Conquest of Mexico* with music by Bishop (Covent Garden, London, 1812), by Pixérécourt and Darondeau (Théâtre de la Gaité, Paris, 1815), and in at least three settings of Felice Romani's libretto *Il Colombo alla scoperta delle Indie:* Francesco Morlacchi (Genoa, 1828), Vincenzo Fioravanti (Naples, 1829), and Luigi Ricci (Parma, 1829).

Songs, both art and popular, were also written in Europe on American Indian subjects. Perhaps due to the more intimate level of communication between a solo performer with keyboard or small orchestra and an audience, the subjects were not necessarily those of "ancient America" but sometimes evoked glorified resistance Indians or romanticized natives in the American forest. Among these were two songs by Johann Zumsteeg—"Grablied" (after Kotzebue, 1789) and especially "Nadowessische Totenklage" ("Sioux Death Song," after Schiller, 1801)—as well as John Moorehead's "My Name Be Umba," the "favorite Indian ballad" in George Colman's *La Perouse* (London, 1802), Thomas Thorley's "Poor Eliza, or The Indian Captive," (1802), William Horsley's "When Shall We Three Meet Again?" (1815, with poetry "by an American Indian"), Franz Schubert's "Cora an die Sonne" (1815), Henry Bishop's widely popular round "Yes, 'tis the Indian Drum" from *Cortez* (1823), J. C. Gladstanes's glee *The Indian: They Made Her a Grave* (1830), and George Rodwell's "Love a Captive" from Richard Brinsley Peake's "melodramatic entertainment" *The Wigwam, or The Men of the Wilderness* (also 1830). A surprising number of rondos or variations for piano and other instruments also appeared in London: not only Felix Yaniewicz's strikingly original *Indian War Hoop* (1815), but also Stephen Rimbault's elaborate variations on the "Cherokee Indian Death Song" (1816) and several fantasias on Bishop's "Indian Drum" and the "Indian Rondo" from *Paul et Virginie,* including one by Johann Nepomuk Hummel (1825).[5]

Most surprising on this list, perhaps, are the lieder by Zumsteeg and Schubert. Schubert composed his simple, rather delicate strophic song in E♭ major in a *Volkston* style, its only audible trace of primitivism. I have found no Schubert scholars who have mentioned the Peruvian connection, so there is perhaps nothing in the poet's sources to suggest that Gabriele von Baumberg was influenced by the Cora of Kotzebue's play. Any educated Viennese living through the last two decades of the eighteenth century, however, would have known about Cora, the Virgin of the Sun, and the Spaniard whom she loved, and further explication would have been unnecessary. Schubert, who in his last year showed an interest in the novels of James Fenimore Cooper, no doubt also knew Marmontel's Cora via Kotzebue—if not from the original—although his diatonic musical setting does not seem to evoke Peru either symbolically or metaphorically.[6]

Henry Bishop's extraordinarily successful 1823 round, on the other hand, exhibits marked features of otherness.[7] It also demonstrates the paradigm shift from musical rhetoric to a more indexical lexicon of "Indianism" that took place in the early nineteenth century. The text by James Robinson Planché is based on simple alliteration: "Yes! 'tis the Indian Drum; The woods and rocks around / Echo the war-like sound, they come, they come, they come!"

Bishop combined three syntactical features to evoke a "war-like sound": the dotted rhythms and regimental character of an English military march; a simple yet ominous effect of a reiterated note broken by a quick alternation of a fourth or fifth; and the pulsating, drumbeat-simulating chords in the accompaniment. These are of course all derived from the larger rhetorical categories summarized in the last chapters. But this is perhaps their first use in combination. Moreover, for the key and mode of this "Indian" round, Bishop chose G minor, an older symbolic shading for the exotic that originated—as we've discussed—in the seventeenth century.

Bishop, remembered most as the composer of the Italianate "Home, Sweet Home," was foremost a theater musician, and in this capacity he wrote music for dozens of plays and operas at Covent Garden. Much of his music therefore is descriptive, and much of it, compared with, say, Handel's of a century earlier, was written for a society that, in the first two decades of the nineteenth century, came face to face with the cultural diversity of its expanding empire. Some of Bishop's theatrical works, among them *A Voyage to India* (1807), *The Aethiop* (1812), *Haroun al Raschid* (1813), *Arabian Tale* (1816), *The Slave* (1816), *The Law of Java* (1822), *Nigel, or The Crown Jewels* (1823), *The Fall of Algiers* (1825), and *Aladdin* (1826), clearly reflect English colonial preoccupations. The imaginative Bishop also used this wide range of exotic topics to expand the musical rhetoric in English opera.

Musical rhetoric in nineteenth-century European music, like stylistic diversity, is often linked with the development of emerging nationalist schools. Exoticism, however, would seem to have preceded the rise of nationalism in some cases. Mozart's style, for example, reflects the classical features of Enlightenment thought—balance, symmetry, elegantly shaped phrases, and a cogent "argument" in its thematic and harmonic design. No ideological "Austrian nationalism" pervades his style. Around 1800 this style could be found as an international language of music from Lisbon to St. Petersburg, with varying levels of competence and eloquence, of course. Yet when Mozart wrote descriptive or characteristic music on Turkish subjects, he pointedly reached

Figure 7. Henry Bishop, "Yes! 'tis the Indian Drum" (1823). The Lester S. Levy Collection of Sheet Music, Special Collections, The Sheridan Libraries of the Johns Hopkins University.

outside or rather beyond the norms of his musical style. This departure involved more than just the use or suggestion of the typical *alla turca batterie:* bass drum, cymbals, and triangle. As Mary Hunter has pointed out, instrumentation (or timbre) is only one of two categories in the Janissary topos of Mozart and his contemporaries. The second category includes melodic, rhythmic, harmonic, and phraseological devices that are analogous to figures of speech. Among those Hunter isolates are oscillating or "hopping" thirds, turn figures, frequent or repeated neighbor-note patterns—all of these found in Mozart's well-known *Rondo alla turca* from his Piano Sonata in A Major, K. 331—static harmonic patterns, unison writing, "jangling" ornaments, and a heavily accented first beat in a duple rhythmic pattern. The imitative devices in the *alla turca* trope also participate in a much larger orientalizing mindset, Hunter argues, and serve as "a set of principles of translation."[8]

In the generation or two after Mozart, especially with the ebbing of the Ottoman presence in Europe, the *alla turca* topos eventually yielded to other "translations" of musical traditions. Some of the details of the *alla turca* style were adapted to that of Hungarian "gypsy" music, as Jonathan Bellman has shown, establishing for many central and eastern European composers a set of musico-stylistic features linked with that group. After the Napoleonic Wars, Russians such as Glinka traveled to western Europe. He composed his *Recollections of Castile* for audiences back home, translating not only surface features of the Spanish music he heard but also conveying the visceral quality of experiencing this music in a faraway place. *Recollections* attempts to portray what David Brown called "a wide variety of impressions in kaleidoscopic succession."[9] France, on the other hand, increased its involvement across the Mediterranean. French composers from Félicien David to Saint-Saëns searched for more flexible musical language to translate their own encounters with North Africa, some of which allegorized the comparative "ancientness" of Middle Eastern cultures or illustrated the nomadic life of the bedouin, the solemnity of a dervish ritual, or the seductive dance of an *almah*.

As a nation still largely without a distinctive cultural profile, the United States in the first decades of the nineteenth century was similarly engaged in exploratory, expeditionary, and colonial enterprises. The regions to be traversed, mapped, and, if necessary, conquered were no less mysterious to Anglo-Americans than were the Orient and the Far East to the French and the English. In fact, except for what could be gleaned from crude Spanish and French maps, the area north of New Spain was shrouded in even greater mystery. Literary works like *Atala* were thus successful not solely for their vivid imagery and exquisite language but also simply because the author himself had been to the western territories. Only five years after Bishop and Planché introduced their "Indian round," illustrations of American Indian drums (referred to as "tom-toms") appeared in the British periodical *Harmonicon* (vol. 4, no. 37; Jan. 1828), while "Yes, 'tis the Indian Drum" continued in popularity, with editions available as late as 1894. Again, the most truly exotic works of the early nineteenth century were those supposedly rooted in geographical, cultural, or ethnographic data. It would be arrogant for us to assume that Americans of this time were more gullible than those of today. But they were undoubtedly avid consumers of information—often contradictory information, it is true—about the western frontier.

Performing Indians; Performing "Indian"

Accounts from the West filled American newspapers. Detailed information about geography, animal life, and the Indian tribes that inhabited the regions of the frontier was increasingly made available through such writings as Bradbury's *Travels,* Lewis and Clark's *History,* James's account of Long's expedition, Prince Maximilian of Wied's journals, and a growing numbers of literary sources.[10] Eastern Americans were curious about the western tribes that, it was believed, still adhered to unbroken and uninfluenced traditions dating back to ancient times. More important, easterners increasingly had opportunities to see for themselves representative inhabitants from these territories. In 1802, for example, a group of Shawnee and Delaware chieftains visited Philadelphia to meet with members of Congress. An enterprising theater manager, Thomas Wignell, convinced the Indians that Philadelphians wanted to see and hear their native dances, and for several August evenings, sounds of native America filled the Chestnut Street Theatre.

The appearances of delegations from western tribes, though sometimes controversial, almost always caused a frisson of excitement, as they had for Europeans in the eighteenth century. They also sparked considerable controversy. Suspicion of Indian rituals—even dancing—was deep-seated in Anglo-America's Calvinist ethics. In 1778 John Carver had written that the hideous yells, cries, and war whoops used by the Plains Indians during their war dances made it "impossible to consider them in any other light than as an assembly of demons." Between 1795 and 1818, these two contradictory values began to emerge with considerable clarity. Those who thought themselves worldly and sophisticated welcomed the experience of seeing Indians recreate traditional songs and dances. Indians were also seen as highly sexually charged, as the eighteenth-century English assumed of their Cherokee visitors, and the amount of bare skin exposed in these ceremonies also appealed to voyeurs. Many religious leaders, of course, were horrified at both the perceived affront to modesty as well as, in their view, the blatant display of paganism.

In 1804, for example, the dancing of some Osages and Pawnees in Baltimore sparked a range of reactions. (See map 2 for these tribal homelands.) The group was among the few to receive an invitation to visit Washington, an old strategy less concerned with stimulating cooperative dialogue, according to historian John Joseph Mathews, than with impressing the chieftains with the power of the white Americans.[11] The mayor of Baltimore prevailed upon the Osages to gratify his citizens' curiosity "by representation of their grand national War Dance." The local clergy were outraged, and the ensuing debate was recorded in the pages of *The American* and *Plain Truth*. Several clerics referred to the performance as "indecent" and lectured that public displays of war dances should not be tolerated, let alone enjoyed. All attention, these voices sternly pronounced, should be directed toward suppressing any form of paganism and toward converting these "Indians from the West" to Christianity. Not all agreed, however. John Hargrove, a cloth weaver, defended the Indians' right to dance:

> This singular and bloodless scene was exhibited at Mr. Leaman's Rural Gardens in the presence of near 2000 spectators of both sexes, among whom most of the principal characters in the city were recognized, and it can be truly added that the utmost order and decorum prevailed during the whole scene, in which the rude affections of savage nature were displayed to the life, and were worthy the attention of the *Historian*, the *Philosopher*, and the *Divine* [italics in the original].[12]

In a footnote Hargrove added that "the War Dance is one of the most solemn religious rites of the nation, and I understand it was with reluctance that they consented to gratify the wish of our citizens by performing it." Reluctant or not, this same Osage troupe could be seen in New York two weeks later offering war dances at the Vauxhall Summer Gardens.[13]

Indian performers in these decades could attract large crowds, a point not lost on wily entrepreneurs. Few Indian social practices were as closely associated with the notion of the frontier as were tribal dances intended to incite a hunger for war. Like the pipe ceremony explored in chapter 1, war dances were part of an ancient legacy of induction and survival. An 1830s white traveler who observed war dances among the Sauk and Fox described how these ritual events were group-oriented, yet individualized:

> The war dance, in which the warriors only engage . . . is a ceremony, not a recreation, and is conducted with the seriousness belonging to an important public duty. . . . The dancers pass around in a circle with the bodies uncouthly bent forward . . . uttering low, dismal, syllabic sounds, which they repeat with but little perceptible variation throughout the exhibition. The songs are, in fact, short, disjointed sentences, which allude to some victory, or appeal to the passion of revenge, the object of which is to keep alive the recollection of injury, and incite hatred of the tribe against their enemies. From the monotony of most of these dances there are, of course, exceptions. Sometimes the excitement of a recent event gives unwonted life and spirit to the ceremony, and occasionally an individual, throwing talent and originality into the representation, dramatizes a scene with wonderful force and truth.[14]

"War dances," a socially acceptable form of boasting, demonstrated a warrior's prowess while "scalp dances" usually celebrated the warriors' successful return. "In these dances," Oliver LaFarge explained, "each warrior dramatized in stylized form what he would do or had done, bending low to track the enemy, leaping to the attack, going through motions of combat." The music for these dances always involved drumming and singing. Before a war, the rhythm was usually slow and the melodies hypnotic. For a scalp dance, LaFarge noted, "the footwork was light and fast, [and danced] in time to fast, cheerful songs almost always pretty and often beautiful, and to the rapid beat of a high-toned drum."[15]

The large crowds that Indian dancers drew suggested that urban Americans were interested in seeing the Osages for themselves, not simply in reading about them in novels, newspapers, or travel journals. Performing troupes like the Osage dancers' began to increase in frequency and demand. On 22 March 1808, just one month before the premiere of Barker's *The Indian Princess,* five "Indian chiefs" traveling through New York apparently also consented to offer war dances. An advertisement announced that they were to "sing the war whoop" at Dyle's, a hotel next to the Park Theatre. According to Odell's *Annals of the New York Stage,* "the Indians whooped and danced for over three weeks." Although details are scant, such groups must surely have been paid in cash or hard goods in order to appear under these circumstances. This practice continued what had already begun in England in the eighteenth century: visiting Indian delegates for whom dancing and performing ceremonies served as an extension of courtesy and diplomacy.

Some theatrical managers even incorporated Indian dancing into a stage production, making it difficult to ascertain whether the dancers were Indians or white actors. In 1805 "Indian warriors" in New York performed a war dance in a grand historical pantomime commemorating Captain Cook's voyages. Within such a framework, war dances fulfilled the obligatory balletic component of pantomime or burletta, as they had done since the late eighteenth century. (The "Dance of the Savages" in *Robinson Crusoe* is one example noted in the previous chapter.) In the first decade of the nineteenth century, pantomimes were fast becoming popular theater, and managers were always on the lookout for new and sensational subjects. Harlequinades were now old hat, and blackface minstrelsy, partly a reconfiguring of the harlequinade, would not devolve into its recognizable popular form until some twenty years later. The depiction of frontier Indians as in *The Armourer's Escape* therefore served as a form of escapist entertainment, and the fashion of non-Indians "getting up" in native costume to pass for Indians may have begun in America as early as 1797. As part of *The American Heroine* at Rickett's Circus, for example, several "Indian Chiefs" were added to the cast, and the play concluded with a "Grand Indian Dance." It may be impossible to know whether any of these "chiefs" were consenting Indians or actors paid to "play Indian." Yet some events from earlier that year may shed some light on this phenomenon. In the summer of 1797 Ricketts traveled northward to Canada with his circus and his star actor-mime John Durang. Durang notes that they occasionally met Canadian Indians on their travels. While acting in a benefit in Montréal, he decided to stage an "Indian characteristic dance." He was able to borrow some native clothing for the cast directly from the Northwest Trading Company. His own outfit, Durang noted, was "purchased from an Indian" in exchange for some rum. It included "chichicoes"—dried beans strung together and tied below his knees—to produce a rattling similar to castanets. In his posthumously published memoir, Durang wrote:

> I performed the Pipe Dance. The manner is gracefull and pleasing in the nature of savage harmony. Next, the Eagle Tail Dance. I concluded with the War Dance, descriptive of their exploits, throwing myself in different postures with firm steps with hatchet and knife, representing the manner they kill and scalp and take prisoners with the yells and war hoops.[16]

Durang reported that he learned these dances from some Chipway [Ojibwe] and Naudowessie [Sioux] chiefs. Apparently the officer from the company who lent the clothing told Durang that he was very good but that his dancing was far more elaborate than any Indian dancing he had seen. That fall, the dancers of the "Grand Indian Dance" in New York may well have been actors from Ricketts's troupe trained by Durang.

Nevertheless, some American Indians were apparently persuaded to don their most elaborate regalia, paint their faces, and appear onstage in many eastern cities. In 1812, for example, a delegation of Osages, Sioux, Iowas, and other Indians were visiting Washington when the new manager of the Chestnut Street Theatre, William Warren, offered the party $100 to journey to Philadelphia to perform. The group was large, apparently "thirty-six warriors," including chieftains billed as Black Storm, Hard Oak, and others. A Russian visitor then in Philadelphia attended the performance. When the curtain rose that night, Pavel Petrovich Svinin recalled seeing upon the stage "groups of these savages with their wives and children":

> The performance opened with a sacred dance called the ring dance, with which the Indians usually celebrate New Year's Day, [and] which occurs in the month of August, when all the fruits have ripened.
>
> Nothing can be more dreadful and more revolting, nothing so well expresses the bestial savagery of these sylvan children of Nature, as their war dance. . . . With this they celebrate their return from a campaign. To this

festival are brought the booty and the prisoners, who are put to death in a horrible manner, being burned at the stake, etc., the mode depending on the degree of hatred inspired by the enemy.

When the curtain rose again, we saw on the stage only Indian women with children. Soon from behind the back drop there came a long drawn-out and piercing roar, repeated three times: Hown, hown, hown! . . . Three Indians with hands tied behind their backs impersonated prisoners. A fire was built on the stage, at which they were to be burned. On this occasion the dancing represented solely a crowd of barbarians leaping, or rather tossing like possessed ones, in savage joy, and roaring and bellowing to the sound of drums, rattles and pipes. Among these frantic cannibals, the prisoners, wrapped in flames, sing war songs in which they usually extol their own feats, accuse their tormentors of cowardice and treachery, and end their lives with fortitude amid tortures. The least weakness on the part of the sufferer is reckoned a disgrace to his entire tribe and calls down upon him the abjurations of the very women and children.

It is hard to imagine that any of the tribal delegates would have participated in such a blatant form of staged exoticism. Nevertheless, audiences that night likely witnessed the appearance of *some* Indians who had likely been convinced to participate in this interlude before a predominantly white audience. Given the small children involved, the Russian visitor must have surely seen native families in a kind of *tableau vivant,* a protoanthropological display with live specimens.[17]

There could also have been some white dancer-actors onstage who acted out the pantomimes. Still, the stage performers were understood by the audience to be "savages," primitive people living in the distant forests and plains. Svinin's comments indicate that some Europeans still thought of American Indians as cannibals, even though the pantomime offered no suggestion that the enemy would be eaten. Svinin also confused a war dance—a rallying ritual before a battle—with a victory or scalp dance—a celebration of the spoils of war. Nevertheless, an account such as this one and the numerous indications of Native Americans as performers in the theatrical playbills of these decades suggest that these were for the most part actual American Indians and not white actors. This has never been proven otherwise, although it is reasonable to suppose, along with theater historian Rosemarie Bank, that in many cases the Indians could have in fact been white actors in redface and makeshift Indian garb.[18]

The appearance of American Indians in public gardens, theaters, museums, and even hotels during this time provided a form of exotic entertainment. It answered a need for sensation, for pantomime with music in some cases.

Moreover, Native American singing and drumming offered audiences a kind of raw unbridled power that they could not find elsewhere in Anglo-America's somewhat straitlaced culture. Many traditional Indian singing styles involved piercingly high falsettos, phrases that unlike European music usually began extremely high, like an eagle in flight, and swooped downward, sometimes for almost two octaves. They also included sliding pitches and pulsating tones sung on vocables (nonlexical syllables) and were accompanied by a persistent drumbeat, sometimes even in a different meter from the singing. In addition, the melodies were rooted in different tuning systems from modern European music and oriented most often toward pentatonic rather than modal or diatonic scales. As in all exotic entertainment, the representations of American Indians onstage were framed in ways that made them seem more real or more "authentic" than the surrounding material. (This kind of exaggerated representation can still be seen in some twentieth-century Broadway musicals, for example in the "Small House of Uncle Thomas" ballet in *The King and I* and the "Indian Dance and Ceremonial Chant" in *Annie Get Your Gun.*)

Even more remarkable than the Osage pantomime at the Chestnut Theatre was an onstage placard bearing the words to the "Death Song of the Cherokee Indians" in large print. According to John Koegel, Anne Hunter's well-known words were probably invoked to help the audience identify with the action of the Indians on the stage by associating the dramatic events with a familiar song.[19] Such an addition seems incongruous to us today, but it suggests that these audiences heard this tune as authentically Indian. Moreover, the "Death Song"—already by 1812 something of a Revolutionary era classic—celebrated the Indians' "heroic" past. And turning backward with a sense of nostalgia was part of the romanticism in Euro-American culture that began to intensify after 1812.

Frontiers between Real and Imaginary

It seems peculiar that Philadelphia audiences could see Osages, Sioux, and Iowas singing and dancing, and yet five years later in the same theater witness white American dancers sensationalizing the Nootkan "Ceremonies of the Bear." But as the nation's demographics began to reflect a growing immigrant population, fewer and fewer Americans could be said to have any first-hand knowledge of Indian cultures, and they therefore became increasingly reliant upon stereotypes. Stereotypes were of course nothing new. Many of the ideas that surrounded the principal character types of American Indians that had developed in eighteenth-century popular theater, however, had usually been positive if constraining ones: faithful, honest, ennobled, innocent of western vices, and so forth. Such views, though generalized here, had often facilitated diplomacy between the English and French colonial powers and many Indian tribes.

In the next generation's fight for expansion west of the Mississippi River, other, more pernicious stereotypes emerged as part of the American discourse of conquest and savagism. One of these, "the Indian hunter," seemed benign on the surface (and also in its pastoral musical rhetoric) but embodied the hidden ideologies of Manifest Destiny. While "the son of Alknomook" went to the land where his "father had gone," he resisted death to a stirring march of great dignity. Though Chateaubriand's hunter resembled a statue, he still held his ground as he rested on his bow. But the Indian hunter of British poet Eliza Cook (and the poem's many musical settings) imagined a homeless wanderer, reliant upon natural resources over which he no longer had any freedom, and in which he must instead find refuge from the white man's pursuit. The hunter trope, as we'll see later in its musical manifestations, reflected a subset of a larger trope in American culture, that of the "vanishing Indian."

Gottfried Duden, a German immigrant who settled on the Missouri frontier between 1824 and 1827, doubted that many in his homeland would believe him when he wrote that no Indian had been sighted in his area for some ten years. Apparently, they were in fact disappearing. Settlers could occasionally see Indians who came into St. Louis to exchange wares or collect annuities for relinquished areas. But they were not seen on the roads to and from town. "Fifteen English miles from here to the south side of the Missouri," Duden wrote, "a Shawnee town of about fifty houses existed. Some time ago they abandoned their settlement and moved about a hundred miles farther west."[20] For many settlers of formerly Indian territories, then, it would seem that the idea of "vanishing Indians" was more than just a literary trope. As early as 1784 Crèvecoeur had noted that "they have all disappeared, either in the wars which the Europeans waged against them, or else they have mouldered away, gathered in some of their ancient towns in contempt and oblivion. Nothing remains of them all." Already in the anonymous ballad "Yarrimore," published in Philadelphia in 1794, the noble Indian sings farewell to his European friends in nostalgic couplets:

> My poor heart flutters like the sea
> Now heaving on the sandy shore;
> It seems to tell me you shall see,
> Never again your Yarrimore.

By 1819 Washington Irving believed that "scarce any traces remain of [Indians] in the thickly-settled States of New England, excepting here and there the Indian name of a village or a stream." Sooner or later, Irving ominously warned, the same fate would come to the other tribes that skirt the frontiers. "They will vanish like a vapor from the face of the earth," he wrote. "Their very history will be lost in forgetfulness. . . . If, perchance, some dubious memorial of them should survive, it may be in the romantic dreams of the poet, to people in imagination his glades and groves, like the fauns and satyrs and sylvan deities of antiquity."[21] In Irving's opinion, the only "Indian" that would eventually be left in America would be the Indian of the white man's imagination.

In Richard Emmons's 1836 play *Tecumseh* (Walnut Street Theatre, Philadelphia), the Shawnee warrior's last line before expiring (presumably to stirring applause) was "I die—the last of all my race." (For the final tableau over which descended the Stars and Stripes, the band struck up a victorious "Hail Columbia.") For Ralph Waldo Emerson, Indians were only a "picturesque antiquity."[22] One heard of Massachusetts, Shawmut, and Samoset, Emerson noted, but where were the men? By 1846 John Hutchinson and his touring New England family of musical performers had little reason to doubt the words of *The Indian's Lament* when they sang: "I stand alone as the last of my race, / Upon this earth I feel I no more have a place."

The widespread belief that Indians were vanishing grew increasingly difficult to dispel, and it placed the surviving Indians and their ways of life in a perilous state. The prevailing notion, instrumental in the creation of museums and exhibitions such as George Catlin's Indian Gallery, was that Indians were to be seen, their histories chronicled, and their cultures categorized before they would soon disappear from the earth, wiped out by advancing civilization. Catlin's idea for a Museum of Mankind in 1840 was "to contain and perpetuate the looks, manners, and history of all the declining and vanishing races of man."[23] Catlin, though a protoethnologist, furnished an exoticism par excellence. He vividly captured the spirit of several North and South American tribes in his paintings and, like Jewitt and Barker a generation before him, he displayed his wares to urban audiences hungry to experience the sensationalism of the frontier.

The one to respond to Irving most literally, of course—and also the most influential and widely read purveyor of romantic frontier ideology in the early part of the nineteenth century—was James Fenimore Cooper, beginning with his novel *The Pioneers* in 1823 and continuing with four others, including *The Last of the Mohicans* in 1826. In these tales of the eastern regions of New York State, Cooper drew from John Heckenwelder's history as the backdrop to his eighteenth-century frontier narrative. Neither the white man Natty Bumpo ("Hawkeye") nor the Mohegan Chingachgook were idealized romantic heroes in the sense formulated by the early romantic essayist Thomas Carlyle (and that perhaps reached its apex in World War II Hollywood cinema, as illustrated in the 1942 film portrayal of General Custer). In *The Last of the Mohicans,* a novel set during the French and Indian Wars of the 1750s, Cooper divided the Northeastern Indians into two camps: the "good Indians" (Algonquin-Delaware, peace-loving peoples from which Chingachgook and his son Uncas derive) and the "bad Indians" (Iroquois-Huron, the restless warmongers). *Mohicans* tells a story rooted historically in the past, but for many readers at the time, it inverted the hierarchies of the colonial world once that world was left behind and the novel's Europeans entered the realm of the wilderness.

Part of the romantic impetus that gradually began to take hold in America (as it had already in Europe) involved a turning backward and a reassessment of the past as a partly historical, partly mythical source upon which a future culture could be built. In the first few decades of the nineteenth century, mythologies of America's first frontier (such as Cooper's) sprang up during the exploration of the second frontier, in part justifying and reinforcing the enterprise. Cooper's novels were extraordinarily popular throughout much of the nineteenth century. They helped to spur generations of Americans (and many abroad) to believe that a "frontier" was central to American character and identity, a belief that coincided with emerging romanticism in all the arts. Consider, for example, Thomas Cole's 1828 painting, *Scene from "Last of the Mohicans."* Cole painted the Indians as tiny figures on a cliff, and his canvas is dominated by picturesque nature and the sublimity of the rough landscape. Along with those of Asher Durand, Washington Allston, Thomas Doughty, and other artists of the Hudson River School, Cole's Indian subjects, though minuscule by comparison with the nature around them, were intrinsically connected with the idea of American land. "Romantic Indianism" as an impulse in American arts can be seen in two distinct phases. The first, with its emphasis on identification, spanned from about 1818 to 1832. During this period Euro-Americans still perceived Indians to be a part of American culture. The second began about 1832 and was associated with issues of removal.

The first phase of romantic Indianism yielded some of the most important literary, theatrical, and artistic events of early nineteenth-century America. In 1818, while five Wyandots appeared as guests in Philadelphia and New York theaters, Mordecai Noah's adventure-drama *She Would Be a Soldier* (Park Theatre, New York, 1819) featured as its central character an Indian chieftain modeled after the great Shawnee leader Tecumseh, who was defeated and killed by General Harrison's army in 1813. The play featured a young Edwin Forrest in his first of several Indian roles. In 1820 poets James Eastburn and Robert Sands published *Yamoyden: A Tale of the Wars of King Philip,* an epic poem. The same year, several Pawnees on official business in Washington—"painted horribly," one observer noted—attracted a crowd of several thousand people when they danced, whooped, and performed war dances before the president's house. In 1821 Henry Rowe Schoolcraft (another protoethnologist) published his *Narrative Journal of Travels . . . through the Great Chain of American Lakes*. But this ethnographic report was immediately followed by Cooper's *Pioneers* (1823) and *Mohicans* (1826), both novels appearing in several languages in Europe as well. Meanwhile, performances such as *The Indian Heroine* at the Vauxhall Gardens in New York featured a "grand ballet," while Bishop's "Yes, 'tis the Indian Drum" from *Cortez* (1823) became as popular in America as it had been in England.

Not all actors playing theatrical Indians, it should be noted, were white. In June 1823 the African Grove Theatre, a black American company located on Mercer Street in New York, gave several performances of Henry Brown's *Drama of King Shotaway*. The play, noted as the first in American history to be produced by a black writer, was set in the West Indies. The noted black Shakespearean actor and singer James Hewlett played the role of the Prince. Like *The Armourer's Escape* and *The Indian Heroine, King Shotaway* included a ballet. Odell's *Annals* describes the sections of the ballet as a "Grand combat between the Prince and the Chieftain," an "Indian War Dance" (danced by Hewlett himself), and a pantomime of the "Grand Battle of Susquehannah." (The battle didn't seem to have anything to do with the subject of the play, the insurrection of the Caravs on the island of St. Vincent. But the insertion was topical; Cooper's *Pioneers,* based on the Susquehanna battle, had just come out earlier that year.)[24]

This strange mix of half realism/half exoticism continued for several years, with Indians taking center stage in American culture. In 1824 several Indian groups traveled across the East, including six "Sons of the Forest" who performed war dances and pantomimes at Castle Gardens in New York and elsewhere. In 1825 William H. Keating offered an account of Stephen H. Long's experiences among the Sioux, published as *Narrative of an Expedition*. That same year George Washington Custis's play *The Indian Prophecy* opened in Philadelphia and many other cities; an old chieftain in this work ultimately conforms to Jefferson's idea of a "good Indian" ("Good man has changed Menawa," he concludes). Cooper's 1827 novel *The Wept of Wish-ton-Wish* was based on a true story of an abduction of a young white girl by an Indian tribe, though she grew up among them and suffered their fate. In 1828 President Monroe hosted a large delegation of trans-Mississippi Indians, and in response to the government's hospitality, the visitors presented a three-hour public ceremony that included a mock council, a war dance, and an exhibition of scalping and tomahawking. Meanwhile, several representatives from the Iroquois Confederacy, threatened by white encroachment, visited New York continually from 1826 to about 1832, performing the peace pipe and other ceremonies in many theaters. In 1828 Red Jacket, using an interpreter, spoke in New York's Masonic Temple and elsewhere, and the following year William Apess, a Christianized Pequot, published his autobiographical *Son of the Forest.* The phenomenally successful *Metamora* began its fifteen-year run in 1829, and this dramatization of the first frontier served as the stylistic model for other "Indian plays" in the 1830s, including a *Pocahontas* by Custis that was heralded as "a National Drama" and performed to great acclaim in Washington and other cities. In 1831 a dramatic version of Cooper's *Wept of Wish-ton-Wish* opened in New Orleans and then New York, starring the much-adored actress Céline Celeste as Naramattah, the abducted young Puritan woman. These incredibly rich years of American romanticism (from about 1818 to 1832) essentially involved an engagement and identification with Native American subjects.[25]

From 1832 to 1855, however, literature, art, and music romanticized native peoples through distancing, a more pernicious enterprise fueled by tropes of the vanishing Indian ("vanishing" in reality either through hiding, death, or cultural assimilation). When the United States had established its government some fifty years earlier, settled nations such as the Iroquois, the Shawnee, and the Five Nations in the Southeast (Cherokee, Creek, Choctaw, Chickasaw, and Seminole) were still in control of their own lands. By 1832, however, tribal authority had been seriously eroded, and within a decade it would be eliminated in these areas altogether. Most important, Indians were no longer perceived as "Americans," as they had been for nearly three centuries. Indian peoples were not only physically displaced; they were displaced in the ideas and ambitions of the white Americans. For this reason, even the exceptional nature of Indians singing and dancing in theaters across the country did little to convey the sense that native peoples were alive and well.

As noted earlier, there remains the question—often unanswerable from surviving sources alone—as to when performing Indians in the early part of the nineteenth century were actually Indians. One night in February 1836, during the second act of Custis's *Pocahontas* in Washington, "Ten Cherokee Chiefs" appeared representing the delegation onstage. Their purpose was to show their gratitude for the "national drama" by dancing a war dance and demonstrating a ceremony of scalping. Even a review in the *Washington Globe* indicated that the audience was delighted by the appearance of "John Ross and his 'merrie men.' " Meanwhile, the actual John Ross, political leader of the Cherokees, wrote to the *Globe* insisting that neither he nor any

Cherokee to his knowledge had appeared on the stage. He added: "we have been occupied with matters of graver import than to become the allies of white men forming the dramatic personae. We have too high a regard for ourselves — too deep an interest in the welfare of our people — to be merry-making under our misfortunes." The stunt turned out to be an apparent deception of white actors impersonating Indians.[26]

Other events during these years continued the distancing effect. In April 1832 the Black Hawk–led resistance erupted in war. By August, his people along the Mississippi had been massacred, and the chief himself was taken prisoner and paraded through the streets like a captive animal. But Black Hawk, enraged with the injustices done to his people, lectured publicly to audiences in New York and in 1834 published his diary in Boston, a city with a growing concern for civil rights causes, including those of American Indians. Among these idealists was a young Henry Wadsworth Longfellow, who in October 1837 wrote to his father:

> There is a grand display of Indians in Boston. Black-Hawk . . . and some dozen other bold fellows, all grease and red paint: war-clubs, bears-teeth, and buffalo scalps in profusion: hair cut close, like a brush, and powdered with vermillion: one cheek red, one black: forehead striped with bright yellow, with a sprinkling of flour between the eyes. This will fit almost any of them. They are to have a pow-wow on the Common tomorrow.[27]

This image remained with Longfellow, so much so that eighteen years later, when he penned his narrative poem *The Song of Hiawatha* (1855), he conveyed the intensity of this experience in his characterization of the irascible Pau-Puk-Keewis, shaping him partly in the image of the Sauk fighter.

These years coincided with emerging musical Romanticism in America and, as in art, frontier ideologies fueled some of the earliest musical examples, such as the Italianate parlor songs of Henry Russell or the more elaborate tone paintings by Anthony Philip Heinrich. Heinrich turned to Indian heroes of the past, Pocahontas, for example, but also to more recent heroes who resisted Manifest Destiny and remained true to their ancestral heritage, among them Pontiac, Yamoyden, and Chief Logan. While Heinrich would seem to have revived the resistance Indian, neither of these composers' works, as we will see, manifested any points of identification with their subjects.

What makes the decades of the 1830s and 1840s the significant period of Indian exoticism is that these were the most crucial years of debate (until those of recent times) about land rights for Indians and whether surviving Indians were entitled to territories granted to them by ancestral heritage. These decades produced the most sustained representations of Indians in nearly all the popular arts, particularly in the burgeoning new industry of sheet-music publishing, where line drawings of imaginary Indians on the covers were particularly evident. It would seem that icons of Indianism, to paraphrase Eugene Jones, increased in the commercial entertainment industry in an inverse ratio to the degree in which actual Indians were being removed from the centers of those industries. Just as nationalism works to define the margins of culture, exoticism often serves to represent culture(s) perceived as beyond that margin.

In one of the first "Indian parlor songs" in this period—"The American Indian Girl" (1835) by J. M. Smith and the English-born composer Charles E. Horn—a young woman finds herself torn between physically vanishing and assimilating. Her only escape from this predicament is to long nostalgically for the past. This is the narrow window through which these creative artists allow us to see their subject. An epigraph for the published version of this song states that the girl, "residing in one of the early settlements," was asked if, in the course of her education, she did not think her present situation and prospects happier "than when wandering in ignorance among the weeds." It would seem that anyone in this situation would have to offer some sort of qualified response to such a begged question. And yet the young girl replied "in the following strain of feeling and pathos":

> O give me back my forest shade,
> Where once I roam'd so blithe and gay,
> Where with my dusky mates I stray'd,
> In childhood's blest and happy day.[28]

Such a song, while gently beckoning its listeners with a sweet Italianate lyricism, ominously portends the outcome for this young woman. In the second stanza, we learn that she is unmoved by the teachings of western civilization and, as Jon Finson put it, "suffers like a wild animal in captivity."[29] The year of this song's appearance, 1835, is decisive. If assimilation is not successful, so says the unspoken narrative, then removal is the only option.

Salvaging Indian Culture

The decades in which many Indians were driven physically to the margins of American culture did lead, as many would see it, to one important outcome: the development of ethnography, that is, scientific methodologies for studying cultures that are not one's own. The valorization of folk cultures had of course begun much earlier in Europe, fueled partly by the idea of noble savagery. "The remnants of the old folk way of thinking are rolling with a hastening final rush into the abyss of the past," warned Johann Gottfried

Herder in the late eighteenth century.[30] Herder himself penned one of the most influential formulations of folklore in *Voices of the People in Songs* (1789). Fashioned for a literate audience, folk legend traditionally was to have originated in illiterate sources. Though printed and duplicated by machines and read by the educated bourgeoisie, folk legends told stories of peasants whose world was rural, whose work was done by hand, and whose stories were passed on and embellished by word of mouth and by the singing voice. The impetus that led to the systematic collecting of Indian folk song in America did not begin until the 1870s, nearly a century after Herder's directive. But the emerging of an ethnographic sensibility that would lead ultimately to what some scholars have called "salvage ethnography"—capturing the essence of a culture before it disappears—could be found in the 1830s and 1840s in the writings of Schoolcraft and Catlin.

The French and Spanish had always had an interest in recording New World cultures, including music, and this continued into the nineteenth century. While living at the San Juan Bautista mission in California (see map 2), the Franciscan friar Felipe Arroyo de la Cuesta transcribed some two hundred songs in the Mutsun and Yokut languages. Among these were "hiding songs" and "gambling songs," the latter sung as consolation after losing a bid. But Felipe worked alone and without the benefit of an established methodology, and his songs were notated only in manuscript. Henry Rowe Schoolcraft, on the other hand, was among the first to transcribe, publish, and thereby popularize the stories, customs, and songs of the greater eastern Algonquin tribes. Marrying into a family of Chippewa descent at Fort Brady (Sault Ste. Marie), he studied the Ojibwa language, began to record Indian legends and folklore, and founded the Algic ("Algonquin") Society to publish and disseminate this information. Although he did not demonstrate much interest in notating the music surrounding the folklore, as would later ethnographers, Schoolcraft's transcription of a "War Song of the Chippewas" is among the first music transcriptions to appear in a scholarly study of American Indian cultures.[31]

Although George Catlin showed little interest in the musical culture of the Indians he otherwise painstakingly documented, it was a stage performance of Indians dancing and singing that convinced him to devote his life to this pursuit. Catlin was a portrait artist at the Pennsylvania Academy of the Fine Arts in 1824 when he saw and heard six young "Sons of the Forest"—the oldest was twenty-five—then touring eastern cities. He was bowled over emotionally by the experience. He decided that the American Indians were "themes worthy of the lifetime of one man, and nothing short of the loss of my life shall prevent me visiting their country and of becoming their historian." Between 1832 and 1836 Catlin traveled into the heart of Indian country (later organized as the

Figure 8. George Catlin, "War Dance of the Apachees [*sic*]" (1855). Oil on card mounted on paperboard. Paul Mellon Collection, National Gallery of Art. Washington, D.C. Used by permission.

Missouri Territory; see map 2) with his notebook, easel, and paints, capturing Indian life wherever he could find it. His paintings were the first means by which many Americans in the eastern states saw representations of the Pawnees, the tall Blackfeet and Crows, the Sioux, and the wild Comanches. As he later wrote, "They saw wide prairies teeming with buffalo, the turbulent Missouri River, and the giant grizzly bear. They saw villages of hundreds of graceful teepees and peered into the dim interiors of comfortable earth lodges, and witnessed the four-day torture ceremony of the Mandans."[32] Unlike their cousins on eastern reservations, the Indians beyond the Mississippi—so Catlin's portraits asserted—still lived proudly and freely amid the beauties of unspoiled nature. Paintings made on later trips, such as *War Dance of the Apachees* (ca. 1854), almost suggest a return to the "awe and wonder" of the centuries of first contact.

Because of his ability to represent their likenesses on canvas, the Plains Indians bestowed Catlin with the title of "Great Medicine Man of the Pale Faces." His *Letters and Notes on the Manners, Customs, and Conditions of the North American Indians* (1841) sold many copies and earned him a reputation as one of the most important scholars of American Indian life. This two-volume narrative appeared on the coattails of his Indian Gallery, an exhibit that opened in September 1837 at Clinton Hall in New York. It included several hundred portraits of western Indians, as well as paintings of villages, dances, buffalo hunts, and religious ceremonies. The paintings were sumptuous in their breadth of scope and brought to easterners the vividness of the frontier and of ancient America. Catlin accompanied his artworks with lectures, his recollections serving as ethnographic proof of contact with these cultures. He also took his gallery to Washington, Philadelphia, Boston, and then—at the end of 1839 —London, where it created a sensation at Egyptian Hall in Piccadilly Circus. On one occasion Catlin, his nephew, and his traveling companion Charles Murray dressed up as Indians to attend a "Caledonian Ball." They used a small drum, a rattle, and their voices to enact a Sioux war chant. The hosts were pleasantly surprised by the three impersonators—the house rang with applause and the "Indians" were showered with bouquets of flowers—and Catlin, a salesman as well as an ethnographer, decided to hire twenty men and women to don Indian regalia and create *tableaux vivants* as a permanent part of his exhibit. One reviewer was surprised that Catlin's nephew had learned to imitate the war whoop so effectively. The *Morning Post* observed that "his warlike appearance and dignified movements seem to impress the assemblage more strikingly with a feeling of the character of the North American Indian than all the other evidences which crowded the walls." Like John Durang, the young man appeared able to "out-Indian" the real Indians.[33]

Building on this success in London, Catlin took the exhibit to other major British cities. Surprisingly, small groups of Ojibwa and then Iowas, apparently stranded in the country, linked up with Catlin's group. He realized the potential for increasing the notoriety of his show with the genuine article, and for five months some of these Indians traveled with the gallery, eventually earning enough money to return home. One of Catlin's specialties was to open the exhibit to large audiences of children. The children were always frightened by the men in Indian paint, he recorded in his journal, but they went home after the lecture imitating the war whoop. In 1843 Catlin took the gallery to Paris, where he entertained such visitors as Delacroix and George Sand.[34]

Catlin's *tableaux vivants* were important in bringing a modern ethnographic sensibility to the depiction of a war ceremony followed by that of the peace pipe. Table 1 lists the order of performances in two evenings of Catlin's Indian Gallery.

Catlin's programs demonstrated his familiarity with Plains Indian cere-

Table 1. George Catlin's Tableaux vivants

First evening, War Scenes

1. Group of Warriors and Braves, in Full Dress
2. Warriors Enlisting (by smoking from the pipe)
3. War Dance (the "swearing in" ceremony)
4. Foot War-party on the March ("Indian file" going to war)
5. War-Party encamped at Night
6. War-Party in Council
7. Skulking (advancing cautiously upon the enemy to take them by surprise)
8. Battle and Scalping (mode of taking the scalp)
9. Scalp Dance (celebration of a victory—women hold up the scalps on sticks, the men dance around them "in the most frightful manner")
10. Treaty of Peace (chiefs and warriors of the two hostile tribes smoke the calumet)
11. Pipe-of-Peace Dance ("this picturesque scene will be represented by the warriors all joining in the dance, uniting their voices with the beat of the Indian drum, and sounding the frightful war-whoop")

Second evening, Domestic Scenes

1. The Blackfoot Doctor, or Mystery-man
2. Mr. Catlin at the Easel in the Mandan Village painting the portrait of Mah-to-toh-pa, a celebrated Mandan chief
3. An Indian Wedding
4. Pocahontas rescuing Captain John Smith, an English Officer
5. Wrestling
6. Ball Play ("the most beautiful and exciting of all Indian games")
7. Game of Tchung-kee
8. The Night Dance of the Seminoles

Source: Catlin's Notes, vol. 1, p. 98.

monies and also his desire to infuse his entertainments with considerable dramatic interest. He provided some vivid details about audience reactions during the first evening:

> The drum was beating, the rattles shaking, war clubs and tomahawks and spears were brandishing over their heads and all their voices were shouting (in time with the beat of the drum and the stamp of their feet. . . . With the exception of some two or three women (whose nerves were not quite firm enough for these excitements, and who screamed quite as loud as the Indians did as they were making a rush for the door) the audience stood amazed and delighted with the wildness and newness of the scene that was passing before them.

Despite the audience's interest in the wildness, Catlin remarked that it was the pipe dance (the dance of peace), rather than the war and scalp dances, that was the favorite of the Ojibwe who toured with him.[35]

Ignoring the Indian in "Indian Music"

Catlin's ethnographic responsibility toward representing Indian peoples in art provides the background for later musical portraits of Indians by European and Euro-American composers, particularly in one-movement miniatures or character pieces and parlor songs. But the distancing effect in musical compositions about Indians in the 1830s and 1840s involved more than just the limitations of western musical languages. There was nothing especially "Indian" about the Indian marches of the late eighteenth century, and yet these had been composed to glorify the spirit of resistance of America's indigenous peoples. How and why did distancing occur in these relatively new musical genres? Large concert works whose subject was the frontier—works equivalent to Cooper's novels or Catlin's themed exhibitions—were extremely rare before Edward MacDowell's celebrated "Indian" Suite of 1896. Those of Anthony Philip Heinrich prove notable if eccentric exceptions.

Heinrich was a Bohemian composer who came to America in 1805. This "maniac musician," as his contemporary John Hill Hewitt called him, was known during his lifetime as a violinist and pianist who also composed lengthy, turgid, and utterly incomprehensible music.[36] In 1817, the year of *The Armorour's Escape,* Heinrich found himself drawn to Kentucky—perhaps not having found eastern cities sufficiently receptive to his creativity—and he fearlessly set out by foot from New York for the frontier he knew largely from reading Filson and Chateaubriand. There he made a lifelong friend in the naturalist John J. Audubon. In a log cabin in the "isolated wilds of nature," decades before Thoreau's *Walden,* Heinrich composed *The Dawning of Music in Kentucky; or, the Pleasures of Harmony in the Solitudes of Nature,* an oddly assorted collection of programmatic works for different combinations of instruments. Though it is difficult to measure his success in these attempts, Heinrich tried to capture in his music the spirit and sounds of the great wilderness: the breaking of the frozen river Niagara, for example, or a "Migration of Wild Passenger Pigeons."

Heinrich was fascinated with American Indians and wrote no fewer than nine large symphonic works and several piano pieces on Indian subjects.[37] There is no evidence that shows to what degree he had contact with Indians in Kentucky or elsewhere. He may have traded with them or, like other European immigrants, perhaps saw them in eastern theaters. Heinrich's lengthy compositions often had mysterious or elaborate titles, such as *The Mastodon* (1845, unpublished), an orchestral symphony of three "musical portraitures": (1) "Black Thunder, the Patriarch of the Fox Tribe," (2) "The Elkhorn Pyramid or the Indian's Offering to the Spirit of the Prairies," and (3) "Shenandoah, an Oneida Chief." In some ways his works were written in the spirit of Catlin's Indian Gallery and may also have been inspired by Charles Bird King's illustrations accompanying McKenney and Hall's *History of the Indian Tribes of North America* (1836–44). Despite the earnest titles, however, Heinrich's musical canvases spun wildly imaginative fiction out of the barest scraps of historical accounts. (Too bare, it would seem, to stimulate much interest in his time.)

Heinrich's compositions, as Wilbur Maust has pointed out, demonstrate his preoccupation with three areas of Indian life: (1) historical events based on early meetings of Indians and whites (e.g., the heroic actions of Pocahontas or the signing of treaties between William Penn and the Indians); (2) portraits of Indian leaders (Pushmataha, Shenandoah, or Logan, all chiefs glorified or depicted as noble savages); and (3) Indian customs and religions (usually quite loosely based on fact). The last area is reflected in works such as "The Elkhorn Pyramid," "A Bacchanale among the North American Indians," and the large symphony *Manitou Mysteries.* Deliberately or not, Heinrich was vague about his sources. He describes his *Pushmataha* as composed "under peculiar circumstances which have given it great wildness," but he never says what the circumstances were, or what, like Catlin, he meant by "wildness." The actual Pushmataha (Choctaw) met with Lafayette in Washington and made his famous speech there in 1824. Heinrich's "fantasia instrumental," as he called it, was composed while on a visit to London in 1831. There is nothing in the expression of this work, however, that is redolent of the earlier historic event. It is curiously light-spirited, a rather syrupy waltz that vacillates between C major and E♭ major. Unfortunately, it is not possible to determine what Heinrich's contemporaries might have thought of this musical portrait: *Pushmataha,* like most of his instrumental works, never got any further than the paper he wrote it on. In 1846, however, at Boston's Tremont Temple, conductor Henry Schmidt led a benefit concert for Heinrich that opened with *Tecumseh, or The Battle of the Thames.* This large symphonic work, written ten years after Emmons's play of the same name (and perhaps even devised in part for a production of it), began with an "Overture Héroique." It was followed by an "Indian War Council" and concluded with a finale depicting a "War Dance, the advance of the Americans, the skirmish and battle, and Tecumseh's fall."[38]

According to William Treat Upton, Heinrich's biographer, reviews of the concert were generally favorable. A young John Sullivan Dwight, however, writing for *The Harbinger* (the official journal of the Transcendentalists), found what he called a lack of genuine feeling in the music. His observations are worth quoting in full since they touch on many of the issues we have been dealing with here, especially the impression that America could make on an immigrant composer in these years:

> Mr. Heinrich belongs to the romantic class who attach a story to everything they do. Mere outward scenes and histories seem to have occupied the mind of the composer too much and to have disturbed the pure spontaneous inspiration of his melodies. We are sorry to see such circumstances dragged into music as the "Indian War Council," the "Advance of the Americans," the "Skirmish" and "Fall of Tecumseh.". . . It is true that everything about America and American history was ideal to the warm-hearted and liberty-loving enthusiast when he came here. It was to him a new world; and in his log cabin in the forest solitudes of Kentucky, there must have been as much to inspire and people a musician's fancy, as in the most fabulous region of the world. . . . The vanishing hosts of the Red Man ministered to his passion for the picturesque and marvelous. This was so far well and can be conceived to have cooperated finely with his musical labors, had he only composed from the sentiment with which they filled him, instead of trying to compose tone-narratives and tableaux of them.[39]

Dwight, perceptive as usual, underscored an important criticism of program music in general, that mere musical picture painting does not lead (in fact, Dwight might argue, *cannot* lead) to a satisfying expressive level. Heinrich's reaction to this criticism is captured in a letter to a friend, where he partly blames a poor performance: "I cannot see why I should not introduce into a work which I choose to call "Tecumseh" . . . the clacking of cymbals, triangles, etc. in proper places for the feats of a savage." The anachronism of the Janissary sound he evokes, by 1846 long an *alla turca* cliché, apparently did not seem in any way illogical to him.[40]

Despite his wild imagination and his naive assessment of the political situation, it was Heinrich's inability to find a musical language on an emotional and intellectual level with his subject matter that lends his works their extraordinary air of eccentricity. *The Moan of the Forest, or The Cherokee's Lament* was an explicit response to President Jackson's removal policy. Heinrich published it privately in New York in 1849, though it was probably written earlier. The programmatic descriptions above each significant tempo and mood change (presumably to be narrated by the voice mentioned on the title page) make it quite clear that each subsection was to be linked narratively with the story he wished to tell (table 2).[41]

Heinrich's boldness lies in his combination of stylistic idioms. He embroi-

Table 2. Movements in Anthony Philip Heinrich's The Moan of the Forest, or The Cherokee's Lament *(1849)*

I. *Adagio* (introduction)
"Command of the United States Government for the removal of the Indians from the country of their birth, which their fathers had possessed from the earliest ages."

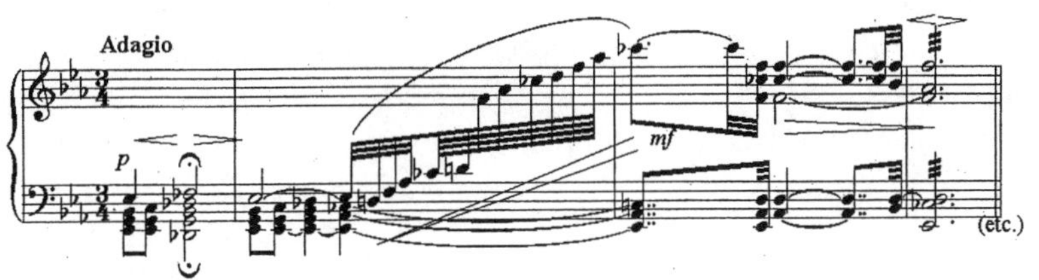

II. *Andante* (in the cantabile style)
"Anguish at being forced to resign their native land."

III. *Più adagio*
"Prayer for future repose and peace."

IV. (*alla fantasia*)
"Aspiration for the oblivion of all discontents."

V. *Allegro fugato*
"Exultation in the hope that no future aggressions will interrupt their renewal of the wild sports of their ancestors."

VI. *Andantino* with an *Allegro assai* coda
"Vows of permanent good will hereafter, between the red race and the white."

Source: From *Mý m Slovanský m Bratrů m v Europè!* ("To my Sclavonian [*sic*] Brethren in Europe"). New York: Published by the author, 1849. Library of Congress, Music Division.

ders a florid bel canto in cantabile passages with an occasional patch of complex pianistic figuration (at times displaying a Beethovenian fury). The style of each subset reveals different facets of Heinrich's imagination. First, the theatrical opening gesture with its "tragic chord" (*Adagio*) suggests the intensely melodramatic treatment of the piano as storyteller. Second, a melodically symmetrical lyric phrase (*Andante,* in major mode) depicts Cherokee "anguish." The *Allegro fugato* in subsection 6 demonstrates the concentrated intensity sustained by the virtuoso handling of the piano. The treatment of the keyboard medium is certainly dramatic, though the work's unrelenting E♭ major would seem to undercut the programmatic intent of lamentation. Nevertheless, Heinrich's social concern and appeal to public sympathy represent unusual ideals for musical composition. Unfortunately, we can surmise from the limited reception for *The Moan of the Forest*—I have been unable to find any reviews—that this already nostalgic nineteenth-century composition, clearly predicated on one European American's unique interpretation of a recent political crisis, probably did little to elicit much help for the Cherokee peoples, who at the time were struggling to survive in Indian Country.

At least one other visiting composer was fascinated initially by American Indians. Unlike Heinrich, the English-born songwriter Henry Russell was seen as a mirror of the age. He was not only a prolific songwriter, having written about eight hundred vocal works, but he was a dynamic entertainer and gave scintillating concerts by singing illustratively from the piano. His songs could be long, through-composed, and intensely dramatic—"Ship on Fire," for instance—or they could be strophic and sentimental, as in "Woodman! Spare That Tree!" Sometime in the mid 1830s, inspired by reading Cooper, Russell asked George Catlin if he could accompany him on one of his trips to the Far West in the hopes of hearing "some original Indian melody." The two began their journey by carriage from Troy to Buffalo, then continued by boat across Lake Erie to Cleveland, then by wagon to Cincinnati. They formed a small party with some servants and then set out on foot, sleeping on the ground "under the stars." After six days a group of Missouri Indians came upon them and, after exchanging a few words with Catlin, welcomed the small party to their camp. For Russell, of course, this whole journey was the adventure of a lifetime. Yet he tells it with surprisingly little expression or sense of revelation. Catlin asked if some of the braves would sing for their musical guest. With a cue from the chief, "the surrounding braves started to their feet," Russell recalled, "and burst out with what I suppose they called song." Russell found the high falsetto yelling "truly fearful." In the end, he was thoroughly disenchanted and regretted having made the trip. In the braves' singing he heard only "hideous noises." When he confided his disappointment to Catlin, the artist replied, "I could have told you that none of the tribes have any idea of music." Despite Russell's discomfort after that morning, the team remained for several weeks while Catlin made sketches of the chiefs. Russell wrote about this trip some fifty years later. Looking back, he remembered the Indians that he encountered as still "hardy children of the forest, possessing some ideas on the subject of honour and of gratitude," not reservation Indians, as he would see them later, living a deteriorating life destroyed by too much "fire-water."[42]

Four of Russell's five songs on Indian subjects were written in the sentimental style and drew on the conventions of Italian opera as Charles Hamm has defined them: diatonic but expressive melodic lines, expressive use of appoggiaturas and octave leaps, and arpeggiated accompaniments.[43] By way of England and then America, Russell, who always sang his own songs, anglicized the Italian-opera style, forging it into a language of American parlor song that influenced a generation of younger composers. Shortly after his return from Missouri, he came across a book of poems by Eliza Cook, the nineteen-year-old British poet. Though Cook had never been in America nor had ever had any contact with its native peoples, she styled "The Indian Hunter" from an Indian point of view:

> Oh why does the white man follow my path
> Like the hound on the tiger's track?
> Does the flush on my dark cheek waken his wrath?
> Does he covet the bow on my back?

Russell composed a melody for this poem in fluent Italianate bel canto style. The 6/8 meter and the dotted rhythms of the accompaniment, as Jon Finson has pointed out, reveal the work's kinship to the romanza, a genre of operatic aria reserved for characters telling fanciful, often nostalgic tales. In the last quatrain of each verse, Russell sets the syllables "yha, yha, yha" to a rollicking Swiss-style *ranz des vaches,* as if the Indian hunter is calling from one mountaintop to another. It offers no hint that Russell's Indians are anything other than imaginary. Other composers of parlor Indian songs adopted Russell's mimicking of Indian vocables, including William Dempster in his 1848 "Song of the Indian Woman" (composed to John Greenleaf Whittier's *The Bride of Pennacook*).

Russell's "The Soldier and His Bride" (1841) is a retelling of the Jane McCrae captivity and murder of 1777, still a grisly tale of frontier folklore. Russell preceded his performance of this song with a description of the historical sources, which he included as a lengthy epigraph on the first page of the printed music. The words, by George Morris, begin:

The tomahawk is raised to crush
'Tis buried in her brow!
She sleeps, she sleeps,
Beneath that pine tree now!

Russell set these lines to a slowly rolling, arpeggiated accompaniment in 6/8. Given the ominous text, the unremitting E♭ major mode deeply sentimentalizes this trope of the Indian hunter, rather than seeking to identify with the pain of exile:

The frown of the Great Spirit fell
Upon the redmen like a spell!
No more those waters slake their thirst,
Shadeless to them that tree!
O'er land and lake they roam accurst,
And in the clouds they see
Thy spirit! thy spirit unavenged, McRea!

Morris's lyrics in effect punish all Indians for the McCrae perpetration. The final lines of the song also seem to suggest that the removals and the Indian campaigns are retribution for this sixty-year-old tragedy. Russell, like Heinrich, did not find much to identify with in his subjects. When in the 1850s he encouraged his British compatriots to immigrate to America with the seductive song "A Life in the West," Indians were so eliminated from his memory that they received no mention whatsoever.

Neither Heinrich nor Russell turned to musical figures of speech beyond those of their own styles, as had Mozart and David for their Turkish and Arabian subjects. They neither drew on older rhetorical practices in their methods nor attempted an indexical interpretation of indigenous American experience. Nevertheless, Russell's songs inspired many of the touring family singers of the 1840s to include at least one song on behalf of the Indian crisis. These politically minded groups traveled the country performing in theaters, meeting houses, churches, on steamboat excursions, and even in prisons, and they carried temperance, antislavery, and other messages about social and political justice. In this context, the "Indian hunter" trope shifted toward the "wronged Indian." Of the many singing ensembles, no fewer than eight—the Baker Family, the Orphean Family, the Gibson Troupe, the Harmoneon Singers, the Bohannans, the Amphions Excelsiors, the Washington Euterpeans, and, the most famous, the Hutchinson Family—included in their programs "Indian laments" or laments in all but name. (One group, the Neiss Family, even appeared together with six Iroquois at Peale's Theatre in 1845.) Most of these songs imagined a lone Indian wandering in the forests (a variation on the

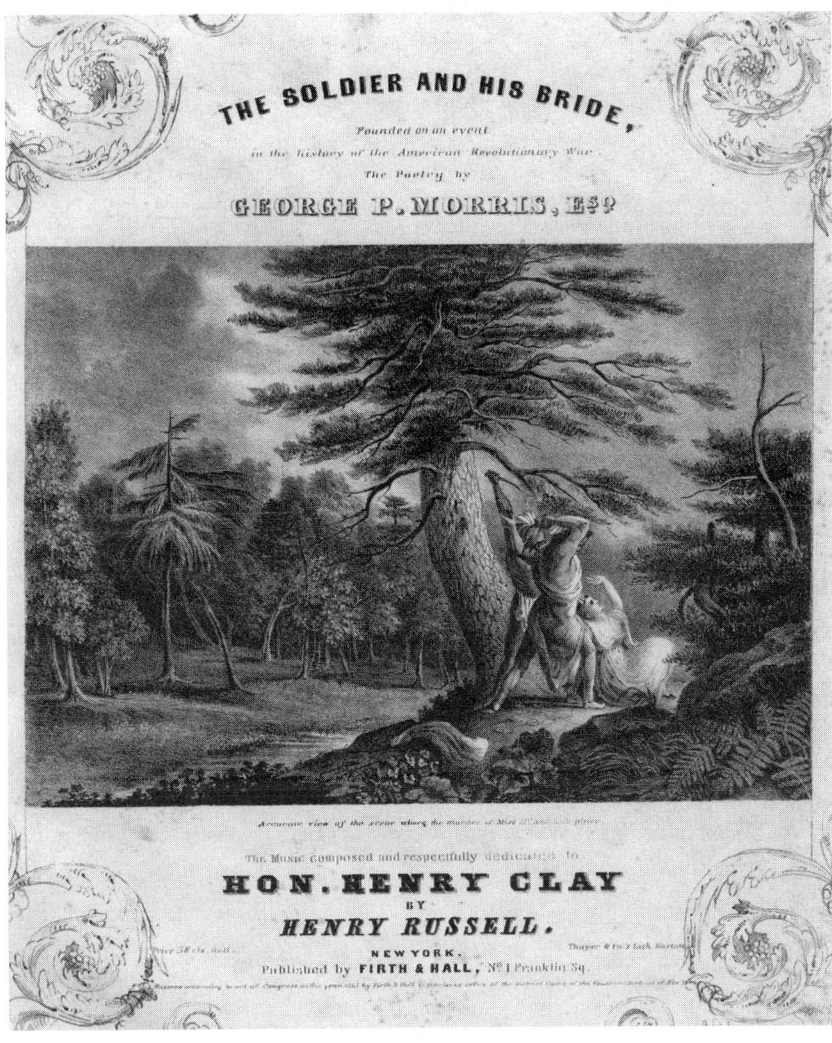

Figure 9. "The Soldier and His Bride" (1841). Cover. The Lester S. Levy Collection of Sheet Music, Special Collections, The Sheridan Libraries of the Johns Hopkins University.

hunter trope) or longing to be once again in a lost homeland. In "The Red Man's Chant," the Gibsons sang "Let me go to my home in the far distant West. Let me go, let me go, let me go." Several of the songs were songs about death. Led by Sophia Baker, the Baker Family sang "The Burial of an Indian Girl" in 1845. The Harmoneon Singers added Marshall Pike's "The Indian Warrior's Grave" in 1850 and mourned the ignominious death of a hero, as was fashionable at the time, in quartet harmony. In "The Red Man's Requiem" (1855), the Excelsiors sighed "they are gone, they are gone."[44]

By then the Hutchinson Family had already performed Russell's "The Indian Hunter." Sometime in the mid–1840s John Hutchinson composed "The Indian's Lament" for the group. Modeled after Russell, the beautiful Italianate melody floats in 6/8 time over a rolling F-major broken arpeggio accompaniment. "I once had a sister, the pride of the vale," went the lyrics, "and a brother whose features were ruddy and hale, / who often would join me in innocent play, / but the steel of the white man has driv'n them away." Sweetly sung as a solo to the accompaniment of a flute and guitar, this lament must have touched liberal-minded audiences wherever the Hutchinsons performed it, if it did not make them feel downright duplicitous in banishing American Indians from their homes. Many took the song and its sentiment to heart, singing it in their drawing rooms. Indeed, Pennsylvania Representative Samuel A. Purviance recalled how General Sam Houston's daughter, who possessed a voice of "exquisite tender sympathy," the kind that "distils the secret tear and bids it flow," often sang Russell's "Indian's Lament" to her own accompaniment.[45] The sentiment of these songs, though written about eastern Indians, could also have been applied by extension to those tribes who would soon be endangered in the West. Among the Hutchinson's audiences in their home state of New Hampshire may have been a young Alice Fletcher, who later devoted her life to the cause of native peoples.

Most writers of parlor songs throughout the nineteenth century clearly sympathized with American Indians. "Lyricists endowed them with the virtues of beauty, courage, steadfastness, and fidelity," comments Finson, "and many authors disapproved the injustice done them by the rapacity of European civilization."[46] It is significant, however, that most of these songs were written and performed well after the period of eastern removals. Of the fifty-nine parlor "Indian songs" and instrumentals published between 1835 and 1860 in Boston, New York, Philadelphia, Baltimore, Cincinnati, Louisville, and St. Louis that I was able to examine (see appendix 1), only two songs and two instrumentals were composed specifically in the minor mode. The rest were all consistently in major modes throughout. Flat keys in general were far more numerous, although G major was also common: thirteen are in G major, twelve in F major, and twelve in E♭ major.

The two minor-mode songs were both published in New York about the same time: Herrman Saroni's "The Pequot Brave" (1844) and Henry Philipps's "The Huron Prayer" (1845). The tone of these two songs is surprisingly defiant, and the minor mode (and frequent use of diminished chords in Saroni) would seem to underscore the bitter irony of this defiance. "For every drop of thy father's blood," an Indian mother cautions her son in "The Pequot Brave," "let a white heart bleed in the silent wood." I have been unable to trace the origins or performance history of these two songs. Their covers are plain and do not bear the lithographic images of noble savages common to sentimental songs of this period. The musical style of these two seems closer to the "war dance," an important but distinctly separate trope.

Unlike "The Huron Prayer" or "The Pequot Brave," most of the sentimental Indian parlor songs clearly reflected the sensibilities of an age of genteel expression. Yet it still seems odd that songs about a young girl separated from her people or a solitary Indian hunter going to his grave should be so relentlessly set in major modes, cradled in warm, contented keys, and sung to romanza-like arpeggiated accompaniments. By the time these songs were written and performed, thousands of America's indigenous people had been moved literally outside the borders, their culture no longer a part of the nation-space, to use Homi Bhabha's metaphoric phrase. Only this cultural climate could bring about the popularity of such a venomous play as Robert Montgomery Bird and Luisa Medina's *Nick of the Woods* (1838), which ran successfully throughout the 1840s. It depicted Indians as lying, cheating, and as otherwise loathsome savages. *Nick* appeared on American stages just at the point when many families in Georgia and Tennessee were rounded up in stockades to be prepared for removal, demonstrating in retrospect how and when stereotypes of warmongering and scalping Indians could also be devastating to the culture as a whole. What seemed appropriately "national" before 1800—for example, the portrayal of resistance Indians in heroic marches—now seemed entirely inappropriate. On the contrary, some music publishers began to produce parodies: Indian topics incorporating the quickstep, the new vigorous military march in 6/8 meter. In the 1840s sheet-music publishers turned out dozens of marches that seemed to mock the Indian situation, among them the "Osceola Quickstep" and "Black Hawk Quick Step," and Allen Dodworth even converted one of Russell's sentimental songs into an "Indian Hunter Quickstep."

At 120 beats per minute, quicksteps were normally used for military purposes and occasionally for dancing. It is difficult to assess under what circumstances an "Osceola Quickstep" would have been played. The Seminole chief was captured in the mid–1830s; he had put up a formidable resistance, and when he was finally arrested he was incarcerated, treated harshly, and died in prison in 1838. It seems incongruous that there should be a quickstep named after him in the early 1840s. The Black Hawk tribute is perhaps more understandable, given that he was known to have appeared in military parades, probably for the symbolic nature of both his heroism and defiance as well as the authority it lent the army in displaying a captured rebel. (I have found no record of specific occasions on which the "Black Hawk Quick Step" was played.) Many more wars would be fought on the American frontier in the name of Indian campaigns. If military quicksteps—"Garry Owen," for example—were played to inspire men to go into battle, quicksteps titled after captured (or dead) Indians may have allowed the soldiers to identify with the ideals of the Indian heroes, even if the heroes themselves had to be suppressed. (The cover of Louis Wallis's "Sioux March" from St. Louis, 1856, bears a lithograph by E. Robyn of mounted U.S. troops attacking a Sioux camp.) One cannot hear these brisk, inspirational marches, anchored as they are by their titles, without hearing in them an attempt to bury the trope of the noble savage.[47]

Writing War Dances

Like the Baroque composers of previous centuries, Russell's music was affective and rarely reached beyond the cohesiveness of his musical language to suggest ethnic or racial differences. Looking forward sixty years or so, however, John Crook's songs and dances for Neverland's Indians in J. M. Barrie's *Peter Pan* (London, 1904) exhibit extraordinarily specific features of Indian otherness. A few of these, as we've discussed, were already incipient in Bishop's "Yes, 'tis the Indian Drum" round. The comparison suggests that the indexical features available to Crook (and countless other twentieth-century composers) accrued over the course of the nineteenth century. These first emerged in the musical trope of the war dance. Unlike antebellum parlor songs about Indians, most of which were written in the United States, the most prominent instrumental "war dances" were largely European. These were semiotically richer than the parlor songs of the same period, and instead of relying on the syntax of pastoral or lament they drew on older tropes associated with pagan rites, moral deviancy, sorcery, cannibalism, even devil worship. This is the first time, however, that such tropes can be heard unmistakably in music. This manifestation parallels the rise of European musical exoticism (particularly orientalism) as well as the romantic interest in the supernatural, heard in such popular works as Paganini's *Le streghe,* Berlioz's "Dream of a Witches' Sabbath" in the *Symphonie fantastique,* Liszt's *Mephisto Waltz,* Gounod's "Walpurgis Night" from *Faust,* and Saint-Saëns's *Danse macabre.* Many such "Indian war dances" were published without such specific contexts, but in some cases these can be reconstructed.

The *Indian War Hoop* by the Polish violinist and composer Felix Yaniewicz stands out immediately as an unusual "characteristic piece," even though the rondo and variations that follow the theme are typical of amateur salon works of the time (including even parallel *minore* and *majore* variations in sixteenth notes). The variations are not indexically Indian in any way nor are they graphic, picturesque, or narratively structured. But the theme itself (see table 3) *does* have iconically North American Indian characteristics: it is pentatonic and it covers a full octave, starting high and moving downward.[48] At the same time it borrows from an established rhetoric in its use of a drone bass—the pedal G (an old hurdy-gurdy–related device). The *War Hoop* stands as a remarkable example, perhaps the first, in which a composed work of music bears such an unmistakably indexical relationship to North American Indian music. How Yaniewicz may have come up with this theme is unclear, for comparable Indian transcriptions did not appear in any published source up to that time. Perhaps he heard Native American performers in England. Aside from the fact that Yaniewicz, a composer and teacher who ran a musical instrument warehouse in Liverpool, may have written it for a piano student (it is dedicated to "Miss Aspinal"), I have not been able to determine the genesis of this piece, nor to locate a source for its unusual tune.

We can presume with some certainty, on the other hand, that composer Auguste Panseron probably saw and heard the six Osages who were visiting Paris as guests of David Delauney, French inspector of the Arkansas-Missouri Territories. The Osages, who resided in France from 1827 to 1830, had an audience with King Charles X, were invited to some of the fashionable salons, and attended the opera and the theater at Rouen.[49] As they were Christian Indians, they also visited the bishop of Montauban. When interest started to wane, according to John Joseph Mathews, historian of the Osages, Delauney arranged a *fête extraordinaire* and advertised that the Indians would perform the "savage dances of the Missouri," after which their chief would then be taken up in a hot-air balloon. Mathews writes:

> Every maker of things in Paris embraced the opportunity. Vendors on the street were selling Indian dolls dressed in native costume, and shops were selling work bags with pictures of the six Osages embroidered or otherwise decorating them, as well as bronze groups of them which the students used as paperweights. Even the bakers seized the opportunity and sold Indian figures made of spiced bread.[50]

Mathews doesn't mention music. But in 1830 Panseron, who had composed a number of works for the Opéra-Comique and was now teaching at the Conservatoire, was undoubtedly inspired by the "savage dances" of the Osages. Perhaps he went to the *fête* with the intent, as had many other musicians before him, to transcribe some of the Indian music. The published music's headpiece clearly depicts six Indians dancing in an open field. One is holding what looks like a tambourine (perhaps a "chichiguoan," a small drum with skins over each side and pebbles inside for shaking).[51] The text, in Osage, praises the valor of Chief Kaniké. The instrumental introduction begins with chords moving down in parallel motion, something a professor of music would never sanction without pointed intent. In the voice part Panseron included abrupt leaps of fifths and octaves, hardly attractive vocal writing. The large intervals simulate vocal breaks in the Osages' singing. Unlike Henry Russell's parlor songs, Panseron's "national song of the Osage" works against the lyricism of European bel canto by emphasizing the registral breaks in the voice.

In the early eighteenth century, leaping intervals, except perhaps for the octave, would not have been affective of a particular emotion. Beginning in the later eighteenth century, however, fifths and octaves began to accrue meaning with more consistency, especially in certain descriptive contexts. We can identify these for their gestural quality in a semiotically rich musical language, one that also includes linguistic derivatives such as mottos (simulating ululation), distinctive accompanimental textures such as rolling arpeggios or throbbing beats (simulating tom-toms), and onomatopoeic figures. The semantic units we have encountered so far contributed to established nineteenth-century tropes or categories of signifiers. First was the nature-loving pastoral (the Indian hunter), with its roots in Baroque rhetorical devices: drone-supported naive melodies and moresca accompaniments. Second was the virtuous and wronged Indian, with Italianate melodies, delicate chromatic inflections, and major-key romanza accompaniments. Third was the warmonger—the "war-like sound" of Indians preparing to attack—with its emphasis on open intervals (fourths and fifths) in the melody, minor-mode accompaniments, and pulsing "drumbeat" chords, against the general rhetorical device of the military march with dotted rhythms (as in Bishop's "Yes, 'tis the Indian Drum"). Fourth was the pagan savage, similar to the warmonger but with even more angular melodies and motivic devices, intense chromaticism, and increased use of diminished seventh chords, fast tempos, and driving rhythmic accompaniments.[52]

The important published war dances (table 3) illustrate the development of the pagan savage trope in the nineteenth century. Many of the syntactic devices used for war dances were reconstituted from piece to piece and most clearly appear in other non–war-dance repertories. But when used in specific combinations—and again it must be stressed, with the specific connotation suggested by title, subject matter, and function—they take on meanings stereotypically associated with American Indians. These are titles that have shown up as cataloged in music collections of major libraries. There were, no doubt, many more throughout the later nineteenth century, especially for circuses, carnivals, music halls, vaudevilles, and Wild West shows.

CHANT NATIONAL DES OSAGES.

Dédié au Grand KANIKÉ

Musique de Mr. AUGUSTE PANSERON.

Propriété

Professeur à l'Ecole Royale.

Prix 2f.

A Paris, chez AULAGNIER Professeur et Editeur de Musique. Rue de la Paix N°. 9.

Figure 10. Auguste Panseron, "Chant national des Osages." Item no. 262. Lithographie de Leborne. Non daté. Bibliothèque Nationale. Mus Vm7 86451. Used by permission.

Table 3. A Century of Selected Music Written for "War Dances" or in War-Dance Style, ca. 1780–1880

1781	Thomas Linley, *Robinson Crusoe.* Drury Lane pantomime. No. 10: "Dance of the Savages." [D major, 4/4] 
1790	War Dance by the young D'Egivilles at the conclusion of *L'amour au rendevous; or the Conflict of Love,* Drury Lane Theatre, London.
1797	John Durang's "Indian War Dance" in *The Ghost.* Montréal.
1808	Barker and Bray, *The Indian Princess.* New York. "[War] Dance and March" at conclusion of act 2. [E♭ minor, 2/2] 
1809	Gaspare Spontini, "Ballet of the Mexicans" from *Fernand Cortez, ou La conquête du Mexique.* Théâtre de l'Académie Impériale de Musique, Paris.
1815	Felix Yaniewicz, *Indian War Hoop,* rondo for the pianoforte. London. [G major, 2/4] 
1817	Mr. Lefolle, "War Dance" in the play *The Armourer's Escape, or Three Years at Nootka Sound.* Philadelphia.
1823	Anonymous, "Indian War Dance" in the *Drama of King Shotaway.* Danced by J. Hewlett. New York.
1823	Henry Bishop, "Yes! 'tis the Indian Drum" from *Cortez, or The Conquest of Mexico.* London, Covent Garden. [B♭ major/G minor, 4/4]
1835	Auguste Panseron, *Chant national des Osages.* Paris. [G major, 2/4]
1837	Adolphe Adam, *Les mohicans* (ballet). Paris.
1844	Félicien David, "Danse de sauvages (*Air de ballet*)," from *Christophe Colomb, ou La découverte du nouveau monde.* Paris. [A minor, 4/4] 

845 "The Real and Original Native Kickaraboo or Indian War Dance, by the sole proprietor of the Caravan, and a Beautiful Indian Princess" in the production of Buckstone's *The Green Bushes*. New York.

846 Anthony Philip Heinrich, "Indian War Dance" in *Indian War Council*. Boston.

852 John Hill Hewitt, *The Indian Polka*. Baltimore. [A minor, 2/4]

858 Ernest Gagnon, *Stadaconé: Danse sauvage pour piano*. Canada. [A minor, 2/4]

859 Robert A. Stoepel, "Pau-Puk-Keewis's Dance" from *Hiawatha,* "Indian Symphony." Boston. [D minor, 4/4]

860 Hans Christian Lumbye, "Indian War Dance" from *Fjernt fra Danmark*. Copenhagen. [D minor, 2/4]

863 William Vincent Wallace, "Indian March and Chorus" from *The Desert Flower*. New York.

872 George Frederick Bristow, "Indian War Dance" from Symphony No. 2 ("The Pioneer"). Brooklyn. [A minor, 2/4]

873 Horace Poussard, *Danse des Sauvages Polka* for piano. Paris. [C major, 2/4]

875 Frédéric Clay, "Dance of the Red Indians" from *Princess Toto* (W. S. Gilbert). London. [D minor, 4/4]

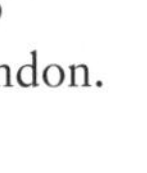

877 Gustav Satter. No. 10, "War Dance of the Indians" from *Douze souvenirs pour piano*. Leipzig.

The performers in Catlin's Gallery in Paris may have inspired the Indian dances of Félicien David's highly popular "ode-symphony" *Christophe Colomb, ou la découverte du Nouveau Monde,* performed in 1847. David was a noted French orientalist. He had traveled to Egypt with a small group of Saint-Simonians in the 1830s and there transcribed Egyptian melodies, incorporating some of them in his magnificently panoramic *Le désert* (1844). *Christophe Colomb* was a popular work with audiences, if not with the critics, and enjoyed performances well into the 1860s.[53] In four large parts, it portrayed the journey from Spain to the New World, including a dramatic scene with a thwarted mutiny of sailors. Upon arrival in Hispaniola, Columbus is greeted by Indians who welcome him with dancing. (He also comes across a "Lone Indian Mother 'neath the Tree," whose song—a "melancholy little masterpiece," according to Dorothy Hagan—prompted the audience at the premiere to demand an encore.) For Columbus's first encounter with the New World inhabitants, David's *danse des sauvages* instantly characterizes them with distinctive music, a very different tactic from the Baroque "discovery operas." Few observers today, however, would detect much that is "savage" in the harmony and rhythm of David's dance, which at first glance seem rather conventional, or in the melody, which climbs in simple diatonic three-pitch cells (marked with arrows in table 3). But one conspicuous semantic device (marked by brackets) stands out prominently: the isorhythmic accompaniment (♩♪♪). A second, not shown in table 3, is a pattern of three descending sixteenth notes ($\hat{5}$–$\hat{4}$–$\hat{3}$ or $\hat{3}$–$\hat{2}$–$\hat{1}$), the first always accented (♬ 𝄾). The rhythmic accompaniment is a feature, as we have noted, of the sixteenth-century moresca (and, by extension, of the later Morris dance). The descending three-note melodic figure, while common in late eighteenth-century instrumental music without connotation, was later used in the context of the Middle East, notably in bedouin dances, by David himself in *Le désert* and later by Grieg in *Peer Gynt.* The syntactical role of this musical gesture is highlighted through repetition.

The musical language of the European "war dance"—a virtual toolbox of signifiers to connote savagery and paganism—emerged with startling clarity in American sources by the 1850s. These were heady years of wagon trains and railroad building across the West but also of endless skirmishes between whites and Indians over land transgressions. John Hill Hewitt, whose father James had written a number of "Indian" works himself, composed his "Indian Polka" in 1852 for one of his students at the Young Ladies Collegiate Institute of Baltimore. There are no forlorn Indian figures gracing the cover of the publication, as found on most of the sentimental parlor songs of the time. They would have been incongruent with this warlike trope. Hewitt's music draws on an accumulating syntax: hopping fifths in the introduction and leaping octaves in the principal melody; the quick sixteenth-note gesture, which alternates between hands, then becomes more insistent until finally bursting into the principal melody (see table 3), of which it is now an expressive part. Hewitt also adds grace notes, another semantic marker. Grace notes, of course, were standard inflections in some polkas. But this feature was also a common flourish in the *alla turca* style and had been used with pointed reference by both Mozart and Beethoven in their Turkish marches. (Verdi also used grace notes as a marker of the Orient to ornament the most "exotic" oboe/piccolo melody in his *Aida* ballet music.) Clearly, then, the combined use of leaping fifths and octaves, the quick three-note descending figure, and the added grace notes contributes to the trope of "Indians engaging in the pagan ritual of dancing for war." Hewitt's opening left-hand rhythm, tricky to play on the piano because of the fast repetitions, could be interpreted as a kind of drumming effect similar to Bishop's. The minor mode, which increases as an essential component of "war dances" after this time, also imparts an aura of mystery (and perhaps even a tinge of danger) to Hewitt's portrait.[54]

By the late 1850s, the wild American West was becoming as much a European preoccupation as an American one. Stereopticon images, or magic lantern slides, in mid-nineteenth-century Europe often featured pictographic tours of the western United States. One firm to produce such images from photographs and paintings was the Continent Stereoscopic Company, whose "Ancient War Dance of the Apaches" (1877)—unlike Catlin's noble rendering—depicted Indians in macabre pagan rites with a rising full moon. The animal skin of one dancer even suggests a demonic "horns and tail" (fig. 11).

Even in a festive European locale like Copenhagen's Tivoli Gardens, it could be fashionable to emulate such a ritual. In Hans Lumbye's "Indian War Dance" of 1860, the basic components of a kind of pagan Indian trope were fully in place. The piano reduction reproduced here does not convey the frightful orchestration of this wild cymbal-crashing dance in its evocation of the primitive. Lumbye, "the Strauss of the North," was one of Denmark's most prominent nineteenth-century composers and orchestra leaders. He wrote descriptive music for parades, dances, celebrations, and other civic events. His "Indian War Dance" was originally part of a vaudeville/ballet about the New World—*Fjernt fra Danmark* ("Far from Denmark")—to which Lumbye contributed music. This "Polka Marsch" features octave leaps downward in the melody (accentuated by grace notes at the beginning), and again three quick descending notes. Lumbye's music abounds in imagery, some of it prompted by the work's associative title. The sharply falling octaves suggest wild leaping dancers; the quick descending notes (as Lumbye uses them here) almost seem to convey a kind of musical shiver. Several measures later he added a dramatic

Figure 11. "An Ancient War Dance of the Apaches." Continent Stereoscopic Company (1877). Reprinted in Enoch Conklin, *Picturesque Arizona: Being the Result of Travels and Observations . . .* (New York: Mining Record Printing, 1878), 276. University of Arizona Library.

effect of two pauses following ominous diminished seventh chords (themselves melodramatic markers of suspense or reversal). The pauses were essential. They gave the dancers at the Tivoli a chance to shout the war whoop (as they do in one modern recorded reconstruction). Not evident in the piano score but heard on the recent recording is the tambourine, an instrument comparable to the "chichiguoans" heard in connection with the Osages in Europe. While we can't expect that Bristow or Poussard or other later composers of war dances would have known all the works I've discussed here, by the 1870s the syntax of musical paganism had developed into a recognizable (and memorable) musical language, one that would long serve to portray warmongering Indians.[55]

Looking back over these musical tropes of Indians and the American frontier, we might ask why such clear distinctions emerged. Are these not vast, almost ridiculous, oversimplifications in the way Euro-American musicians perceived Indians? To some extent, Indian peoples were more individuated in Cooper's novels, Catlin's paintings, and in the later novels of the German author Karl May. The rather crude musical categorizations between 1820 and 1860 (and beyond) suggest that, in the popular sense at any rate, music fell far behind the other arts in subtlety of expression when it came to musical portraiture. At the same time, the artistic retreat from allegory and toward realism tended to favor more sensationalized depictions, and "war dances" were certainly some of the most sensational forms of popular music at the time. Next to American Indian performers, war dances allowed non-Indians to participate in imaginary thrills of the frontier with the kind of sensuality and immediacy that is unique to music. From the 1850s on, Bishop's "war-like sound" began to reverberate in American society as the country battled against the Indian peoples of the West. It is perhaps not surprising that it is precisely during this period when such a clear expression of an idea, albeit it a negative one, embedded itself deeply in American culture.

4

"In the Glory of the Sunset": Singing and Playing Hiawatha

Arriving at the climax of the distancing phase of American Indians in antebellum American culture, Henry Wadsworth Longfellow's *The Song of Hiawatha* (1855) in effect answered Irving's call most succinctly, for its protagonist was one of the most resilient imaginary Indians of all time. *Hiawatha*, appearing as it did in times of growing political animosity between the North and South, would seem to have been dead in the water, a throwback to an earlier stage of noble savagery and romantic literature. And yet few works of American poetry had its endurance. Within a decade it was translated into dozens of languages and was published all over the world. The poem resonated particularly deeply in New England, where for much of the nineteenth century Longfellow was virtually the poet laureate. Dramatic readings of *Hiawatha* proliferated in private clubs and drawing rooms. By the late 1850s, according to one critic, readings had reached the level of a "public nuisance." Actress Julia Barrow's appearance to narrate the poem on the stage of the Boston Theatre in 1856 costumed as Minnehaha was only one of many such events. Readers committed long sections of the poem to memory as late as the first decades of the twentieth century. Even in the 1950s, an *I Love Lucy* episode parodied a dour thespian woman's intoning of "By the shores of Gitche Gumee . . ." In the 1850s, however, *Hiawatha* was not just highbrow culture. It easily meshed with America's middle-class popular culture: the models were high-minded, but the verse was direct and satisfyingly unambiguous. Though Longfellow was later criticized for his sentimentality, the clever Harvard don knew how to address the aesthetic and emotional needs of his large readership.

Today many consider *The Song of Hiawatha* a dusty Victorian relic or, as wrote one editor of an edition of Longfellow's poems, "a liberal complacent-sympathetic construction of Indian culture as noble, exotic, and doomed." The 1820s, '30s, and '40s—Longfellow's early adulthood—were some of the most difficult years in Indian-white relations, as we have noted. By the time Longfellow's poem appeared, Indian cohesiveness in the East had been destroyed and many eastern tribes had been driven west of the Mississippi River. In New York State, Indian advocates such as Lewis Henry Morgan worked to save the scattered tribes of the Iroquois Confederacy. But white New Englanders no longer had much direct association with Indian peoples, at least nonassimilated Indian peoples. In a newly emerging social order—one structured around commercialism and industry—the renewed manifestation of a noble savage for modern readers reminded Americans of the simple, natural life that many cherished.[1]

Longfellow's models were partly the chivalric romances of the early nineteenth century, not only those of folklorists such as the Grimm brothers but also French, German, and Scandinavian medieval and folk epics. In the American South, struggles for social justice and eventual war held the cultures of this region within a tight grasp. But the prosperous northern cities such as Boston were free to continue entertaining heady ideas of frontier life and westward expansion. In the 1850s and 1860s *Hiawatha* answered the call for a specifically American type of growing folk literature, and its bucolic setting was part of the appeal. The poem's "numerous descriptions of the sylvan landscape," in the words of an early reviewer, helped open readers' minds to the (real or imagined) wonders of the vast western territories, even if these were based on Longfellow's woolly knowledge of anything further than the Ohio valley.[2] Yet at the same time that Longfellow's poem mythologized America's lost innocence, it exoticized the natural unspoiled beauties of the West, making it more accessible to political domination and economic penetration. In this sense, *Hiawatha* was not only a fairy tale with strong moral overtones but also an American form of orientalism, much like *Lalla Rookh* or *Omar Khayyam.*

Longfellow drew largely from Schoolcraft's Algonquin legends. But he purged the tales of incongruities and indecencies, probably because he feared they would have offended the sensibilities of his readers. He engaged other sources—Heckenwelder's *Account of the History, Manners, and Customs of the Indian Nations* (1819) and the autobiographical *Narrative of the Captivity and*

Adventures of John Tanner (1830)—only to find himself having to "disentangle the legends" in order to adhere to the bildungsroman nature of his own epic. He chose a nonrhyming but singsong poetic form of eight-syllable trochaic verse. Critics immediately found this rigid and stultifying pattern identical to that of the *Kalevala,* the Finnish epic poem that Longfellow had encountered in 1842. (He knew it in German rather than Finnish; it was not translated into English until 1868.) Curiously, with the monotony of the meter—"Gítche Mánitó, the míghty, / Thé creátor óf the nátions"—Longfellow may have tried to capture some of the persistent rhythmic chanting of ritual, this ever-throbbing "drumbeat" functioning to remind readers of the native roots of the subject matter.[3]

In a biography of Longfellow published in the year of his death (1882), William Sloane Kennedy observed that *The Song of Hiawatha,* along with the author's other poetic works, had "furnished topics to the sculptor, the *littérateur,* the ethnologist, and the philologist." Kennedy didn't mention music, which he perhaps considered more ephemeral than some of the other art forms. A good deal of the author's poetry, including sections of *Hiawatha,* had in fact by this time already been set to music, although many of the more famous musical versions of *Hiawatha* were yet to come. *Hiawatha* is central to this book, as its many musical adaptations contributed substantially to the subject's longevity and to the ways in which native America was imagined.[4]

Michael Hovland's *Musical Settings of American Poetry* demonstrates that, next to Thomas Moore and Alfred Tennyson, Longfellow enjoyed the distinction of being the English-language author most often set to music. Why was this so? The "bard of Boston" was a gentleman poet who blazed his own imaginary trails; he forged no alliance with the Transcendentalists, New England's important literary school. But his flair for grandeur, his fondness for atmosphere, and his love of nature supplied composers with rich options for descriptive or evocative music. *The Song of Hiawatha* in particular was an eminently musical poem: music, song, and dance were integral to the Ojibwe history it proposed to relate. Longfellow's folklike adventures and the distinctively American-sounding character names and locales even attracted a few prominent European composers in the 1890s. Although Dvořák's "New World" symphony was heavily influenced by *Hiawatha* (as Michael Beckerman has demonstrated), the most famous, or infamous, work based on Longfellow's poem was certainly Samuel Coleridge-Taylor's cantata trilogy *Scenes from "The Song of Hiawatha"* (1898–1900).

Longfellow himself adored music. It is surprising that he would take so well to a musical setting of his *Hiawatha* by a relative unknown, but that was the case when Robert Stoepel, a German-born musician, approached him in 1858.

Longfellow followed the progress of Stoepel's *Hiawatha: A Romantic Symphony* and attended the first performance on 8 January 1859. This was only a few years after the poem's publication and still at the height of the Hiawatha craze sweeping American drawing rooms. This "dramatic symphony" was performed with great fanfare in Boston, New York, and even London. It was widely reviewed (the first work in this study to have achieved this level of critical attention), and many reviewers were surprised by the work's originality. Moreover, it engaged them in a fascinating debate about musical depictions of native America and expressions of cultural identity. For this reason, Stoepel's work and its reception merits some serious consideration here.

The Context for Hiawatha *in the 1850s*

Some of the attention Stoepel's symphony generated cannot entirely be separated from the polemics surrounding the reception of the poem itself. Longfellow—poet, translator, and (later in life) chair of modern languages at Harvard—completed his controversial narrative roughly a decade after William Prescott's *History of the Conquest of Peru,* the appearance of Catlin's Indian Gallery in Paris, and the sympathetic portrayals of American Indians by such well-known personalities as Henry Russell and the Hutchinson Family. Its empathetic tone may have served to assuage some of the guilt many felt over the removals and the subsequent hardships imposed upon American Indians in the 1840s and '50s. As one of a three-part trilogy of epic poems about early America—the other two were *Evangeline* and *The Courtship of Miles Standish*—its twenty-two lengthy cantos filled 316 pages of the first edition (150 pages in the Modern Library edition). Longfellow's saga depicts the union of the Chippewa (Ojibwe) and Dacotah (Dakota) nations under the leadership of Hiawatha, a legendary hero endowed with miraculous gifts. (The fictitious character is not to be confused with the historical Hiawatha, a relatively minor chieftain of the Iroquois Confederacy.) The poem concludes portending the eventual adoption of Christianity after the coming of the white man and with Hiawatha's return to his immortal origins.[5]

In seeking poetic models to describe North America's pre-European past, Longfellow turned to ancient North European sagas. He constructed his literate fable and aimed it toward the growing market for middle-class popular literature. With such "fakelore"—a term coined by Richard M. Dorson to describe fiction composed in the style of folklore—Longfellow resuscitated the noble savage in mid-nineteenth-century America and created one of its most durable embodiments. "Fakelore" also implies that such fiction deliberately obscures its latent ideological motives. For those of American Indian descent,

Hiawatha portrays a negative white image of Indian passivity. For many non-Indian Americans, Longfellow's allegory, and its presentation of humans interacting with archetypal nature gods, conveyed a story of an unspoiled Eden in which dwelled a primitive race, itself unspoiled by the sins of civilization. With its singsong narrative, Longfellow's poem seduced its readers into supporting an image of the past that may have been useful to America's territorial expansion but that also led to disastrous results for the Indian population.[6]

One of the first musicians to consider a concert version of the poem was Emile Karst, an Alsatian-born violinist living in the Midwest. His plan to link the Hiawatha subject to an 1858 St. Louis cultural event involved a selection of unrelated incidents drawn from the epic. Between his own musical settings of excerpts for voice and piano, Karst interpolated orchestral interludes on western American subjects written by his colleague, Jacques Ernest Miquel. Judging from the titles of these movements—the music itself is lost—Miquel composed what were perhaps among the earliest orchestral descriptions of a buffalo hunt and a steamboat traveling down the Mississippi. This strange compilation was performed several times by the Philharmonic Society of St. Louis in early September 1858 during the week of the Missouri Agricultural Fair, but it did not survive beyond this event. Except for a brief mention in Ernst Krohn's *A Century of Missouri Music*, the Karst-Miquel work has otherwise gone unnoticed in accounts of the musical life of nineteenth-century St. Louis. Moreover, the surviving libretto reveals little about the character of the music or the circumstances of the performances.[7]

In contrast with Karst's and Stoepel's grander settings, there were in Longfellow's lifetime numerous published songs—including some by the gospel-hymn writer Charles Crozat Converse—a five-part instrumental symphony by Ellsworth Phelps (1878, individual movements conducted in New York by Theodore Thomas), and a men's choral work that Frederick Russell Burton wrote for the Harvard Glee Club (ca. 1882). And of course there were parodies in New York theaters—Charles M. Walcot's *Hiawatha, or, Ardent Spirits and Laughing Water* (1856) and Edward Everett Rice's musical extravaganza *Hiawatha* (1880). Rice's burlesque—despite a stage wigwam and, behind it, an oil-painted diorama of a waterfall—had little to do with Longfellow and was more of a satire on tales of foraging westward (as in Augustin Daly's roughly contemporaneous play *Horizon*, 1871) or on "life among the savages" (as depicted in graphic dime novels such as Edward Ellis's *The Lost Trail: A Legend of the Far West*, 1864). The sections of Longfellow's epic most appealing to composers were those that dealt principally with Hiawatha's wooing of Minnehaha, their wedding feast, and Minnehaha's death from the winter famine. Many settings sought ways to translate into music Longfellow's nature imagery and also underscored the idea of Indian conversion at the poem's conclusion (a semihistorical account loosely based on Father Jacques Marquette's mission among the Ojibwas in the 1600s).[8]

Hiawatha proved to be a fertile source for music and spawned more than seventy-five settings. While scant information exists on most of these before the 1890s, the accounts of Stoepel's symphony, as well as a complete published piano-vocal score with details of instrumentation, affords us an opportunity to experience in some depth a significant contemporary musical reading of this once-classic yet problematic work of American fiction.[9]

An "Indian" Work in the Concert Hall

On 22 February 1859 Charles Bailey Seymour, critic for the *New York Times,* described Stoepel's *Hiawatha: A Romantic Symphony,* which he had heard the evening before. The performance had taken place at New York's Academy of Music at (Washington) Irving Place (near Union Square):

> When the instruments speak they mean something, even as the voices do. The composer's muse is graceful. . . . The melodies in this symphony are frequently strikingly beautiful, and we have no hesitation in saying that many of them will become eminently popular. The choruses are written with masterly skill, and without any of the irksome dullness and affectation which usually belong to the *cantata* style. "Hiawatha" is sufficient in every respect to place Mr. Stoepel among the best informed and most gifted composers of the day.[10]

Needless to say, Stoepel's melodies did not become "eminently popular." Yet his rendering of text and imagery as implied in this and many other reviews suggests a deft musical and theatrical hand.

Born in Berlin in 1821, Stoepel had moved in the 1830s to Paris, where he studied composition at the conservatory. His earliest known works—various waltzes and polkas published in London in the 1840s—established him as a significant composer of light music. While playing in the orchestra at Dumas's Théâtre Historique, he met the young Irish playwright Dion Boucicault and went first to London and then to America to serve as music director for his productions, conducting incidental music for genteel melodrama. His most important position was at Wallack's Theatre in New York, "the foremost English-language playhouse" in the world, according to Odell. In 1857 he married the American actress Matilda Heron, remembered as one of the major tragediennes on the pre–Civil War stage. Heron knew how to use her gut-wrenching, tears-in-the-throat projection to great emotional advantage in an age when audiences responded with gusto to such outpourings.[11]

Stoepel and Heron, like many Americans of recent European stock, were enamored of *The Song of Hiawatha.* Matilda found in the poem's exotic language the perfect vehicle for her throaty alto. Robert, too, was attracted to the poem's songlike text. The duality of the work's ostensibly American theme and its exoticism fired his imagination and afforded him an opportunity to present something musically substantial within a popular vein. Stoepel's career in the theater shows him to have been no pure idealist, but rather a shrewd and practical musician. It was clear to him that a composer would need to have major financial resources to undertake the writing and performance of a concert work, even one on a fashionable topic.[12]

New York in the 1850s was rich with musical and theatrical activity. Much of the music and drama was European in origin, though authors and managers sometimes experimented with American subjects. The music scene reflected New Yorkers' passionate love of opera. Imported Italian, French, and German opera towered in importance over the isolated efforts of those such as George Frederick Bristow, whose successful *Rip Van Winkle* (1855) must surely have seemed as exceptional then as it does now. Theater consisted largely of British imports, though a few director-managers sought out works with an American flavor. Boucicault's *The Octoroon* (1859), for example, dealt with black-white relations on a Louisiana plantation and boldly addressed injustices perpetrated in slavery-dependent America upon those with African blood. Boucicault was also fascinated with American Indians and recognized the emotional power that Indian characters could generate in works dealing with contemporary social history. He created a pivotal Indian character in *The Octoroon* (and acted the role himself). Wahnotee, as he is called, had been left behind by his tribe, presumably during their expulsion westward. Accused throughout the play of murdering a young black boy, he is vindicated, only to resort to murderous revenge upon the villain. The complexity of relationships between the property owners, the slaves, and the lone Indian figure shows Boucicault attempting to grapple with difficult social problems at a time when literary works of escapism and fantasy like *The Song of Hiawatha* were at their most popular.[13]

Yet for musicians such as Stoepel, Longfellow's *Hiawatha* was more than a work of fiction; it was a cultural event, its protagonist a culture-hero with supernatural connections. (He can be compared in some ways to Superman.) At a time when America was seeking musical artworks of its own to stand alongside those of Europe—and these expectations abounded in the musical journalism of the 1850s and '60s—this new immigrant leapt in to fill the void. Like Europeans coming to America to pan for gold, Stoepel probably also hoped to make a major international splash with his symphony on an "American" topic. What better subject on which to base it: the fictional work of an author "more interested in establishing its cousinship with the heroic poetry of the Old World," as Daniel Aaron noted, a tale with New World pretensions that adheres punctiliously to the themes and conventions of European epic literature? *Hiawatha* provided a model along the lines of the ancient Arthurian-Carolingian epics that a still-young nation lacked. Like the earlier writings of the ersatz Scottish folk hero Ossian, *Hiawatha* seemed already quite old by the time it was conceived.

Stoepel's unpublished letters reveal that his initial idea was to produce *Hiawatha* in Europe.[14] But he quickly realized Boston's centrality to this subject; the success of Longfellow's poem was nowhere greater than in New England. Boston's reputation as a "musical Athens" also made that city the perfect location for his idealistic venture. A musical setting, however, entailed preparing a selective libretto from Longfellow's enormous text. To secure rights for these changes, Robert and Matilda visited Boston in January 1858 and met the poet whom many New Englanders admired as an icon of American culture. One might have expected Longfellow — who, after all, in his passion for music shared intimate friendships with Liszt, Ole Bull, and other distinguished musicians — to have received these plans from a relative unknown with skepticism. But Robert and Matilda apparently wooed him with their natural charm and their affection for his work.

The first of several performances of the choral symphony took place on 8 January 1859 at the Boston Theatre, one of the most remarkable auditoriums of the day. Seating approximately three thousand, it was only a few years old in 1859 and ranked for decades as the city's premiere "place of amusement" featuring opera, melodrama, minstrel shows, and other forms of entertainment. With an extended stage that thrust well into the auditorium, the theater provided an ideal venue for actors and performers to come down center stage quite close to the audience.[15]

In addition to the chorus of the Handel and Haydn Society, Stoepel conducted an orchestra of about fifty musicians and three vocal soloists. The latter were mezzo-soprano Mrs. I. I. Harwood (who alternated between the two female roles of Nokomis and Minnehaha), tenor Harrison Millard (Hiawatha), and baritone J. Q. Wetherbee (who sang both the Great Spirit and the Arrow-Maker). Matilda Heron narrated, and some witnesses who felt that the readings made the evening much too long would have preferred hearing the symphony without them. The orchestra, however, was in top form, and the critics — including the irascible John Sullivan Dwight — uniformly praised Stoepel's work as a conductor. The *Hiawatha* symphony was generally considered a signal success and Stoepel a composer to be watched. Even the highbrow

Dwight, who had a decade earlier criticized Heinrich's *Tecumseh,* commented on the symphony's effectiveness as a sort of "occasional" work:

> As a form of art quite novel and peculiar, to-wit, the illustration of a poem, based on wild Indian life, by means of instruments and voices, with the aid of recitation, we found it deeply interesting to the end. There was a wild, romantic charm about it, entirely, as it seemed to us, in keeping with the poem.[16]

Comparing Stoepel's symphony with David's *Le désert,* a work performed in New York five years before, he added:

> "Hiawatha" seemed to us to have more meat in it; more musical material; more thought; more wealth of color; more variety. The instrumental portions were what pleased us most. Indeed Mr. Stoepel shows himself a master of orchestral combinations; he is at home there, to say the least.[17]

Rare indeed was such praise from Dwight's pen for a new work, especially one not by an established European master.

Longfellow himself was apparently delighted with Stoepel's music. He addressed the audience at the first performance and, in the words of one witness, expressed himself "highly pleased with the music to which Mr. Stoepel had married his immortal verse". According to Longfellow's published journals, the author noted that "[the *Hiawatha*] music is beautiful and striking; particularly the wilder parts, the War Song and the Dance of Pau-puk-keewis."[18]

Encouraged by this success, Stoepel brought *Hiawatha* to New York's fashionable Academy of Music the following month. There he marshaled orchestral forces from the Academy and his various theater orchestras and arranged for the combined participation of the Mendelssohn Choral Union and the Liederkranz Society. Attendance for the two performances, though neither one came close to filling the enormous 4,600–seat Academy, still surpassed that in Boston. Most of the critical attention again seemed to focus on the orchestral movements, and several reviewers expressed astonishment at the original and imaginative orchestration. Henry C. Watson, writing in the *Spirit of the Times,* noted that nearly everyone attending Stoepel's *Hiawatha* recognized "the marked individuality, the keen appreciation of national characteristics which [stood] out in bold relief, and the charm of the elaborate and exquisite instrumentation."[19]

Stoepel's *Hiawatha* was thus a unique venture at this point in America's cultural history. It attracted a broad audience that included fans of Matilda, fans of *Hiawatha* (and there were many), and concertgoers—hovering somewhere between skepticism and genuine curiosity—who expected to hear a substantial musical work that would offer some relief from the Italo-German sameness of much American concert music.

Stoepel and Heron eventually took *Hiawatha* to England, where, under the sponsorship of the impresarios Louisa Pyne and William Harrison, it was produced in London at Covent Garden on 11 February 1861. The orchestra and chorus of the Royal English Opera were led by the Adelphi Theatre's music director Alfred Mellon, whose own "Indian" music for the character of Miami in Buckstone's play *The Green Bushes* could still be heard only a few blocks away. Four singers for *Hiawatha* are mentioned only by surname in the reviews (Palmieri, St. Albyn, H. Corri, and Wharton). All in all, the British press found the work to be a startling musical achievement. Stoepel revived the symphony in New York two years later (November 1863) with a much grander orchestra, a fuller and more "efficient" chorus, and with a different cast of singers. About this same time, William H. Hall published a piano-vocal score with the title slightly revised to the more emphatic *Hiawatha: Indian Symphony.* The score was dedicated to L[ouis] M[oreau] Gottschalk, who may have been influential in securing the publisher's interest.[20]

In organizing his dramatic symphony—which combines narration, solo arias, descriptive choruses, and programmatic orchestral interludes—Stoepel maintained the chronological integrity of the original poem. Each of the fourteen movements corresponds to an episode, among them the Great Spirit Manito's prophecy, Nokomis's descent to earth, Hiawatha's birth and childhood, tribulations experienced during his coming of age, his wooing of Minnehaha and their marriage, the harsh winter famine, and Minnehaha's fatal illness. In addition, Stoepel chose cantos in which Hiawatha and his wife transform the quality of life for their people: for example, Hiawatha's constructing the first canoe and Minnehaha's midnight dance to ward off ravens from eating the newly grown corn. In this sense, Stoepel's portrayal of Hiawatha is more rounded dramatically than those of later composers, who generally focused on one or two episodes. More important, however, Stoepel ended the narrative without the critical denouement of Hiawatha's departure. The symphony closes with the coming of spring—the poem truncated at canto 21 just before the storyteller Iagoo reports having seen "the people with white faces."

In some of the passages, the bleak "Winter" sequence, for example, the writer for the *Boston Courier* noted the vividness of the music, claiming that one could hear "the wailing of the winds, the fierce blasts, the cries of despair." Reviewers for both the *Courier* and *Dwight's Journal* described the winter movement, with its dramatic evocations of the ghosts of Famine and Fever, as "sublime." Rather than portray this primeval American wilderness as something vastly different from European experience, Stoepel drew upon the emotional breadth of his European musical background to express movingly a world of hunger and fear, cold and hopelessness, oppression and devastation.[21]

Exotic Sounds in the Native Land

As Lully had done in the seventeenth-century *ballet de cour,* Stoepel employed dance and song forms, though by the nineteenth century these embodied more overtly nationalist traits: a barcarolle for no. 4, Hiawatha's "Canoe-Building Song," and a bolero accompaniment for no. 9, the instrumental "Magic Corn-Field Dance." In general, Stoepel's music does not essentialize the specific folkloric accent in Longfellow's Indian romance with "American-specific" styles—as Yaniewicz and David did in their war dances—but instead used those familiar to international audiences. The two movements singled out by Longfellow, however, unmistakably engage an exotic discourse that not only incorporates the "pagan trope" (discussed in the last chapter) but does so in a startlingly original manner. These movements, "The Fight with Mudjekeewis" (no. 5) and "Pau-Puk-Keewis' Beggar Dance" (no. 7), also present an odd paradox within the work. While the vocal and choral portions of the symphony generally rely upon a European stylistic eclecticism (not unlike Longfellow's poem), these two instrumental movements evoke, if not a distinctly "American" sound, at least the projection of a non-European one. It was not only Stoepel's use of pastoral and war-dance tropes but also his broader exotic palette that encouraged the comparison with David's orientalist *Le désert.*[22]

Critics noted this otherness, and their responses ranged from pleasant surprise to mortification. Dwight, for one, had little interest in the songs and dances of American Indians: "In spite of their picturesque life, and their romantic legends, there is a certain monotony, a certain faded, superannuated sort of feeling, that comes over us in reading of them. This savage, dying-out life lacks just that germinal vitality out of which poetry, and certainly all music springs." The critic for *Leslie's Illustrated* couldn't understand why any composer would find Indian subjects useful since, in his words, the only sounds of the "musical genius of our native savage" were limited to "monotones" and "tomtoms." Any attempt to incorporate such sounds would "perpetuate a horror too painful for modern ears." But while the writer did not advocate the use of Indian music, he suggested that the creative musician could derive inspiration from the "social character of the [Indian] people" and convey in musical form certain suggestive ideals, those "consonant with the received popular and poetical belief" (i.e., the world of Indian peoples as made known through Cooper, Irving, and Schoolcraft). The *Boston Courier* admitted a certain boldness in the setting of Longfellow's "poetically idealized" text in these two movements but added that "the little Indian music that we know of furnishes a very slight foundation for the composer to work upon, [it being] vague, rude, destitute of form or expression, and significant only of savage wildness."[23]

Semantic representations of the savage seem especially strong in Stoepel's instrumental movements. "The Fight with Mudjekeewis," for example, begins darkly and mysteriously with a fifth sonority in the basses, cellos, and horns. True to earlier semantic usage, this droning pedal ostinato occurs in the winds and strings (rather than in the tom-tom-like timpani, the latter a feature more common in twentieth-century stylizations). The timpani, meanwhile, plays a distinctive two-note figure, perhaps emulating water or barrel drums, or perhaps suggesting the actions of the characters, shifting from side to side. Stoepel continues this accompaniment for some time, allowing it to establish the stern mood and psychological sizing up of each man as the two prepare to fight. Sustained open fifths as a basic semantic unit—even, one might argue, a primordial foundational unit in music—have long-standing pre–noble-savage associations in other repertoires, of course. But Stoepel's syntactical use of a throbbing drone effect in combination with the minor mode demonstrates his familiarity with the relatively new syntax of the war dance (and, in fact, may have been a significant contribution to it): "Then began the deadly conflict, / Hand to hand among the mountains" (IV:189–90).

Almost inarticulately at first, a descending three-note figure for clarinet and violins in C minor begins over the throbbing drone. This obstinate figure starts higher each time, becoming more frenetic so that through the first thirty-five measures it encompasses the descending notes A♭–G–E♭–D–C–B♮–A♭–G–F–E♭–D–C. Oddly, this scale is closer to a maqam, a Middle Eastern mode, than it is to any American Indian modes, though as played against the bass and the timpani's distinctive pounding it evokes the pagan savage rather than an oriental trope.

The movement gains more momentum as the cosmic struggle grows more ferocious ("Till the earth shook with the tumult and confusion of the battle"). The tension finally breaks on a powerful melodic descent—likely played by trombones and lower strings—ending on an A♭-major chord (an exotic ♭VI color chord) before being resolved into an agitated coda in C minor. The final measures seem astonishingly fresh and both harmonically and rhythmically imaginative, as Stoepel several times repeats a minor-key plagal cadence (iv–i) in combination with the rhythmic vitality of a hemiola (a sudden shift in stress from two to three).

This evocation of native America inspired some of the most rhythmic and harmonically adventurous music written at that time for the American concert hall. Yet none of the critics referred explicitly to the poetic source itself: the test of wills between Hiawatha and his immortal father, the West Wind. Dwight

Example 2. Robert Stoepel, "Fight with Mudjekeewis" from *Hiawatha: Indian Symphony* (New York: William Hall and Son, 1863), 32.

found this a "very impressive" instrumental work. It began, he wrote, "with strange Indian-like balancings and approaches, as of first one party and then the other, indicated by short, rude, ponderous phrases, which are worked up with effective imitations, till the conflict becomes grand and exciting, and the piece ends with smart, crisp, fiery chords, reiterated with all the force of the instruments, in a manner that might remind one a little of one of Beethoven's fiery overtures."[24] The *Boston Courier* wrote that a listener might easily imagine himself "within the wild influence of a horde of untamed savages." But a reviewer for the *New York Times* perhaps best described the music's vividness: "The necessity of giving a purely Indian character to this piece, has led Mr.

Example 3. Stoepel, "Dance of Pau-Puk-Keewis" from *Hiawatha,* 42–43.

Stoepel into a vein of the most acceptable originality. There is war paint on the first bar [and] stolid determination and dogged obstinacy in the suggestion of every phrase and figure. Monotonous repetition being a feature of Indian music, Mr. Stoepel has preserved it, but as a circumstance around which rare effects may be hung. . . . It is certainly a triumph of musical painting."[25] Significantly, the two pointedly "Indian" sections in an otherwise European-sounding work received the most attention.

Pau-Puk-Keewis's "Beggar Dance" (no. 7) begins in a tone similar to that of the fight sequence. Pau-Puk-Keewis is the trickster in Longfellow's poem. His fancy dance at Hiawatha's wedding feast provokes considerable exhilaration, especially among many of the female guests. As an evocation of native America, however, the "Beggar Dance" differs from "The Fight with Mudjekeewis." The opening—a relentless drumbeat imitation in the bass with a minor-mode harmonic accompaniment—also includes several indexical features that could only have been acquired by hearing some American Indian music making: (1) the "snapping" iambic rhythm (here strongly emphasized with a thirty-second note), (2) the melodic range of one full descending octave, which, after two or three phrases, ascends to another third (and sometimes a fifth) above the original range, (3) the tendency of the melody to cascade downward through pentatonic rather than diatonic modes, and (4) several repetitions of the final note (the "tail"), often embellished by a few descending vocal-like ornaments. Stoepel's music closely follows the poem's imagery:

First he danced a solemn measure,
Very slow in step and gesture . . .
Treading softly like a panther (XI:97–101)

Remarkable here is the snappy ascending fourth (A–D) and the falling, mournful minor third (F–D) at the cadences, both suggesting some authentic pentatonic source. Furthermore, the ensuing pattern — two bars of solo melody and drumbeat accompaniment, two bars of a harmonized response — suggests an awareness of some native performing styles. It is impossible to know for sure whether Stoepel observed any of the dozens of traveling performing Indian troupes. Perhaps during his Paris years he may have gone to Catlin's Indian Gallery, where he might have seen and heard Ojibwas and Iowas dancing and singing. On the one hand, Stoepel's vivid depictions of nature (a blizzard, for example) demonstrate the romantic influence of Chateaubriand and Cooper, much more strongly than any of Heinrich's attempts. On the other, Stoepel's pentatonically inspired indexical music for an American Indian dancer is the first to convey a sense of musical "ancientness," linking Indian people with a long ancestral connection to the land. In this sense, Pau-Puk-Keewis's dance falls between earlier symbolic depictions of noble savages and iconic attempts in the 1890s to harmonize American Indian song.[26]

The darkly mysterious, mystic, even erotic mood of the opening is transformed dramatically into extremely high-spirited, less overtly exotic music.

Then more swiftly and still swifter
Whirling, spinning round in circles. (XI:102–3)

Once again, the melody of the *allegro* is pentatonic, though this time in a major key and quite folksy in character. A reviewer in Dwight's *Journal* detected that this part of the dance was "not unlike a Scotch *gigue* in character" but that Stoepel's setting was much more wildly Caribbean in nature, "reminding one of the *tambour* dance of Curaçao . . . [or] 'Dansa Habanero,' [where] the [music's internal] motion [is a] greater feature than the air or harmony."[27] As the music turns surprisingly to Kentucky fiddling style, the dance becomes more energetic and syncopated:

Leaping o'er the guests assembled,
Eddying round and round the wigwam,
Till the leaves went whirling with him,
Till the dust and wind together
Swept in eddies round about him. (XI:105–9)

It takes on a tone that, in the jubilation of Hiawatha's wedding festivities, begins to evoke an energetic New World spirit. The *Spirit of the Times* reviewer isolated this movement as a particular favorite with the audience and observed the demand for an encore.[28] Dwight, however, noted skeptically that "the jig-like movement [the 'hoe-down'?] . . . sounded a little too familiar; the Indians must have known rum and white men before they danced to such tunes." An anonymous writer came to the music's defense, although it's unclear whether the "we" here refers to New Englanders or immigrant Americans:

> You say . . . that "the Indians must have known rum and white men before they danced to such tunes." Here the misconception is palpable. We have nothing to do with tunes to which the Indians danced. The composer's idea was very far from that of reproducing the particular music which accompanied the wild dances of the Indians. . . . The composer's intention was poetic and ideal; the one you attribute to him is vulgar and prosy in comparison.[29]

The effect that Stoepel's music had on its audience, as well as on the current reception of Longfellow's poem, stemmed from its originality of musical expression, especially "American" musical expression, as Richard Storrs Willis noted decisively in the *New York Musical World:* "We think that, aside from the attractiveness of the music of 'Hiawatha,' there is that in the theme—its newness, its purely American character—which will give it something more than an ephemeral popularity."[30] From our present perspective, it seems odd that at this point in United States history—on the eve of civil war—a "purely American character" should have been identified in a *Hiawatha* setting. But it was precisely Stoepel's eclectic use of musical styles, evoking both ancient and modern, that seemed to generate so much enthusiasm. Here was an ethnic universe rooted in an allegorical Indian romance.

Other writings at the time went so far as to suggest that the musical *Hiawatha* was even more "American" than the poem itself. An anonymous London correspondent for *Dwight's Journal* who attended the Covent Garden performance in 1861 wrote at length about an unexpected relationship between Stoepel's score and his own personal experiences in the American Middle West:

> There is . . . a freshness and originality about it, very delightful. I have been for months at Lake Superior, have read all I could find in Schoolcraft and other writers of the Ojibway tales and traditions, and have perhaps greatly admired Longfellow's poem. . . . Stoepel seems not only to have caught the spirit of the poems but of the everlasting forest and cool bright waters of the lake. His music gave me an inexpressible longing to be there again. It touched my feelings, entered into my heart, gave me true musical enjoyment. . . . I have for a long time heard no work of this species, which gratified me so much.[31]

Judging from these and other accounts, Stoepel's *Hiawatha* symphony attained, however fleetingly, that rare success in setting an already popular American poem to music. William Henry Fry—a prominent composer and avid proponent of American music—proclaimed that Stoepel's work could easily take the place of "obsolete" Baroque oratorios in American concert halls.[32] Unlike works for the theater, which, as we have seen with Boucicault's *Octoroon,* were beginning to address some of the complex problems of race relations in America, the symphony's pseudomythological basis perhaps allowed it to succeed in Boston and New York concert halls on an allegorical level, when a work that depicted Indians in a historical context would probably have been dismissed.

Surprisingly, none of the commentaries mention Stoepel's lilting conclusion, which avoids Longfellow's denouement. By ending his musical narrative with a hymn to nature (complete with evocations of birdsong as "all the woodlands ring with music"), Stoepel minimized the extraordinary Indian passiveness embodied in the poem's conclusion. Longfellow himself did not appear to mind the omission. But then why would he? Stoepel's version remained true to the image of a primeval North America, described by one Longfellow critic as essentially a "transatlantic Arcadia, in which the quiet enjoyment of Theocritus's shepherds was combined with the valour of Homer's heroes."[33] The arrival of the "Black-Robe Chief" in canto 22 especially evokes historical events and would have again served as an uncomfortable reminder of the government's assimilationist policies and of the sense of conflict that American audiences must have felt in their sympathy toward the Indians' plight. The emphasis on "showers of rain" and "growing grasses" instead of on Hiawatha's departure afforded the opportunity to put aside this discomforting view of recent history and revel in a much simpler and more reassuring conclusion. Self-fulfilling futures, it seems, are often built upon a constructed and idealized past.

Although considerable notoriety and even cachet surrounded these performances of *Hiawatha,* they did not establish Stoepel as a major composer of concert music. This may explain why, when later composers and critics wrote about Indian subjects as a basis for musical composition, not a single one recalled Stoepel's earlier *Hiawatha* experiment. The work may also be another casualty of America's cultural amnesia about its antebellum past. Stoepel's symphony nevertheless remains a crucial work for understanding the way native America was imagined at the midpoint of the nineteenth century, as well as a fascinating instance of interaction between music and the literary culture of the age.

Dvořák and Hiawatha *in the Later Nineteenth Century*

Although Stoepel's "Indian Symphony" faded into the sunset, *Hiawatha* itself showed no signs of vanishing. The poem continued to sell at unprecedented levels in America and almost as well abroad. Within a few years editions were available in several languages, including Russian. One dedicated scholar even translated it into Latin as *Carmen Hiawathae* in 1862. In Bohemia, Longfellow's poem appeared in Czech translation in 1870, only a decade before Dvořák took an interest in it as a musical subject. During Edward MacDowell's sixteen-year residence in Germany, he wrote of plans to compose a symphonic poem to be called *Hiawatha and Minnehaha,* but evidence of a finished work has never been found.[34]

An idealistic thirty-two-year old Bostonian composer, Arthur Foote, participated in the continuing craze by fashioning a cantata for baritone solo, chorus, and orchestra, *The Farewell of Hiawatha* (1886). Boston had become an important center for choral music, especially sacred choral music. Unlike Stoepel's *Hiawatha* symphony, which depicted human relationships set against the forces of nature, *The Farewell of Hiawatha* portrays only the final episode, in which Hiawatha ascends to immortality just when his people would seem to need him most. Foote imparted to his opulent score a spiritual quality through the use of the diatonic church modes (specifically Aeolian and Phrygian), a rare instance of modality in American concert music before the 1890s.

The cantata was first performed by the Apollo Club, a Bostonian men's choral society, under its director, Benjamin Lang. Lang was New England's self-appointed Wagner emissary. With Foote he had attended the first Bayreuth *Ring* cycle in 1876. In *The Farewell of Hiawatha,* Foote enchanted his audience with Wagnerian moods and colors to suggest the bittersweet departure of a folk hero. Hiawatha thereby reveals his kinship with Wagner's Lohengrin or Tennyson's King Arthur—both of whom, like the fictional Ojibwa leader, depart for immortality in a skiff. The triumphant finale implies a moral: those who make way for the advance of civilization will be rewarded in the hereafter.

The lesser-known Louis Coerne, like Foote a student of John Knowles Paine, also turned to *Hiawatha,* although he completed his four-part symphonic suite in Munich while studying with Joseph Rheinberger in the early 1890s. Upon his return to the United States, Coerne led the Boston Symphony in the first and only known American performance of this work at Harvard's Sanders Theatre on 5 April 1894. Shortly afterward, Miles and Thompson of Boston published a four-hand version. Between the performance and the publication, the work is likely to have come to the attention of many Boston musicians, although it is not known whether important critics such as Philip Hale knew of it. Perhaps more than one attentive Bostonian might have remarked on the uncanny similarity between Coerne's programmatic *Sheherazade*-like Hiawatha suite and the controversial Hiawatha "program" of Dvořák's Symphony No. 9 in E

Minor ("From the New World"), a work that the Boston Symphony had performed for the first time some four months before.[35]

In many ways Coerne's music was an ideal match for Longfellow's aesthetic, since his Lisztian harmonic language and use of leitmotifs echoed Longfellow's own passion for the so-called New German school of composition. In addition to descriptive titles, the score contains running citations from the poem that resemble cues for spoken narration. The work thus either was designed to be performed as a concert melodrama or was programmatic in the most literal sense: each new phrase, each change of mood is supported by a specific quote from the poem. Like Foote's cantata, this *Hiawatha* also ends with the passage of the departure of the hero: "In the glory of the sunset, / In the purple mists of evening" (XXII:241–42).

More than any other musical setting of *Hiawatha,* Coerne's resembles the brilliantly colored oil painting on this subject, Albert Bierstadt's *Departure of Hiawatha* (1868). Bierstadt bathed the Ojibwa and Dacotah peoples in the intense glow of a setting sun. They wave farewell to their leader who, his mission now fulfilled, sails into immortality on his westward course. In Bierstadt's painting the sublimity of nature overwhelms the subject matter. Coerne similarly crowns his setting in a blaze of symphonic splendor: against swirling figures in the winds and strings, an organ intones a solemn hymn signaling the triumph of European civilization over the sunset world of America's pagan past.

Frederick Delius's *Hiawatha* was for him an early and unrefined experiment. The music, composed in 1887–88, no longer exists in its original state. The score, left only in incomplete manuscript, must be appreciated largely through contemporary accounts and a few printed examples included in the published literature on Delius. The British-born Delius composed the tone poem during a sojourn in Florida. According to Sir Thomas Beecham, *Hiawatha,* "a budding and not wholly unsuccessful attempt to capture the atmosphere of wild woodland life" was a longish piece "with two main sections of a serious and flowing character divided by a sprightly dance movement" (possibly intended either for Pau-Puk-Keewis's dance or Minnehaha's cornfield dance). The work ended with Hiawatha's departure. Beecham believed that its principal weakness was the orchestration. *Hiawatha* was never published nor apparently ever performed, and Delius pilfered large sections of it for later pieces. The fact that parts of this work could later be adapted by the composer Andrew J. Boyle as the soundtrack for a Norwegian nature documentary ("From the High Solitudes," 1984) may attest to a lack of specifically New World color in the original.[36]

Antonín Dvořák was clearly the most internationally famous composer to

Figure 12. Albert Bierstadt, *Departure of Hiawatha* (ca. 1868). Oil on paper. Courtesy of the National Park Service, Longfellow National Historic Site, Cambridge, Massachusetts.

turn his attention to *Hiawatha.* He came to America from Bohemia in 1892 and spent nearly three years of his life in the United States. At least two movements of his Ninth Symphony were inspired in part by Longfellow's poem. After the symphony's premiere in New York, the composer became increasingly evasive regarding this connection. Nevertheless, he was clear at the time about two points at least: the mood of Longfellow's "Indian romance" affected him deeply while he was at work on this symphony, and the sketches for a planned but abandoned *Hiawatha* cantata (or possibly even an opera) were apparently incorporated into its second and third movements. Notes by Arthur Mees for the first performance and critic Henry Krehbiel's lengthy essay in the *New York Tribune* made brief but unmistakable mention of the connection to Longfellow's poem. In general, though, both publications broadly emphasized a rich palette of possible influences. For many years the *Hiawatha* connection remained largely unexplored among scholars and the general public alike. In the past three decades, though, Dvořák scholars have returned to reveal the hidden Hiawatha within the pages of the "New World" Symphony.[37]

Shortly after Dvořák's arrival in New York as director of the National Conservatory of Music, founder and patron Jeannette Thurber suggested to him—according to the composer's secretary Josef Kovařík—that *Hiawatha* would make an excellent subject for an opera. Though a libretto had not been chosen (and never would be), Dvořák "became totally absorbed" in working on the music. The point here is not to argue for specific programmatic influences. The evidence that "Hiawatha's Wooing" (canto 10) and "Hiawatha's Wedding-Feast" (canto 11) inspired certain aspects of the second and third movements of this symphony seems incontrovertible. Scholars still disagree, though, about the *extent* of the influence. Michael Beckerman's Hiawatha program for the Scherzo is the most convincing. For the Largo, even Beckerman's well-argued suggestions—as well as James Hepokoski's different scenario—remain largely speculative (though Beckerman makes an excellent case for these).[38] The slow movement's beautiful and melancholy D♭-major theme is problematic for its almost immediate adaptation into a black spiritual. In the early 1890s there was still some general confusion among Euro-Americans as to differences between Native American and African American music. Some of this confusion had to do with similarities in the use of what were thought of as "primitive" scales and rhythms, though today we are more struck by obvious differences in the way the two cultures used these musical building blocks.[39] Even Samuel Coleridge-Taylor, a British composer of African descent, incorporated the tune of an authentic black spiritual, "Nobody Knows the Trouble I've Seen," into his *Overture to the Song of Hiawatha* (1899).

It is essential not to mistake Dvořák's preoccupation with *Hiawatha*—or that of any other composer writing before the mid–1890s—as reflecting an interest in American Indian musics. For Dvořák, as for the other composers cited here, Longfellow's classic served principally as a source of poetic folklore. For composers in search of uniquely American subject matter, the metaphoric language of "ancient America" could be found at the library or the corner bookstore. After 1900, of course, reference to Indian peoples in music was no longer marketable without a heavy dose of indexing and quotation. But that was a later phase, and it would be incorrect to apply this sensibility to works of the early 1890s.

Dvořák's Scherzo brings together three episodes from the wedding: Pau-Puk-Keewis's swirling dance, Chibiabos's love song, and Iagoo's tale of Osseo. The first two can be documented from notes in Dvořák's copy of the poem and his fifth American sketchbook, as Beckerman has demonstrated. Considering Dvořák's work here in the light of other *Hiawatha* settings allows us a perspective missing in studies of the "New World" Symphony alone. For example, the

Example 4. Antonín Dvořák, Symphony No. 9 ("From the New World"), mvt. 3, mm. 1–9.

opening of the Scherzo paints a very different picture of Pau-Puk-Keewis than Stoepel's. Instead of a "merry mischief-maker," beloved of all the women in his soft white shirt of doeskin with ermine fringe, Dvořák sees him as the "the Storm-Fool . . . skilled . . . in sports and pastimes." In the ferocity of the opening, Dvořák captures in part the "idle Yenadizze" (dandy) who entertains with his dance, but he also prepares us for Pau-Puk-Keewis's jealous fury when this character later (in canto 16) bursts into Hiawatha's empty lodge and kills his livestock. The fierceness of this opening therefore serves to characterize Pau-Puk-Keewis more completely. Dvořák, as any first-rate dramatist might do, paints a full musical portrait of this handsome but potentially dangerous character at his first appearance in this "operatic" symphony.

Other musical suggestions in the Scherzo have their origins in particular verses of the poem (XI:107–9), all noted by Beckerman. In the first four measures, Dvořák captures "the sound of drums and voices"; in measures 13 and following, "the sound of flutes and singing." In measure 21, the ambling violin countermelody suggests the whirling leaves and eddies of "dust and wind" as Pau-Puk-Keewis dances.[40]

A significant harmonic feature with repercussions for later evocations of Indian worlds, however, occurs in mm. 5–12. Between measures 5 and 8, four notes, each emphasized by a *sforzando* and an identical rhythmic pattern, stack up to form the chord that results in measure 8 (identified in ex. 4). The chord can be read as two interlocking perfect fifths, E–B and G–D′, but clearly the E of the lower fifth is treated as its functional root. Through incessant reiteration over twelve measures, the D (a $\hat{7}$ in the natural minor or Aeolian mode) becomes audibly embedded in the tonic E-minor chord. (The D merely seems to "color" the chord, and, unlike other dissonances in Dvořák's music, neither demands nor receives resolution.) Metaphorically, this pulsating "tonic-minor minor-seventh" chord (i^7) may seem not much more than a throbbing drumbeat accompaniment to the tune above it. But as we will see, its use as a tool of modal ambiguity extended beyond Dvořák to other composers of the 1890s (and beyond) to depict an exotic nostalgia, principally for ancient cultures such as those of Celtic lore (for example in the music of MacDowell) and, more importantly, in both popular and art music about native America in the early twentieth century.

In 1890s Boston, *Hiawatha* remained a persistent if controversial subject for musical treatment. Rubin Goldmark, a Dvořák pupil, completed his "Hiawatha" Overture in 1896; the Boston Symphony gave the first performance four years later. Samuel Coleridge-Taylor began his cantata trilogy on *Hiawatha* in 1898. In March 1900 Benjamin Lang led the Cecilia Society of Boston in the first American performance of *Hiawatha's Wedding Feast,* the first of the three cantatas. The following December, the Cecilia Society of Boston performed part three of the trilogy, *Hiawatha's Departure.* Coleridge-Taylor's sumptuous work struck a sonorous note in Boston, and within a year it was performed in Washington, Chicago, and other cities. Even as late as 1900, Longfellow's romance continued to fascinate both composers and audiences alike.

The "Hiawatha Man"

Coleridge-Taylor's cantatas, surely among the grandest manifestations of Indian exoticism, continued to be performed regularly until the Second World War. Coleridge-Taylor (1875–1912) was born in London, the son of an African physician from Sierra Leone. After graduating in 1890 from the Royal Academy of Music in violin, he began his own string orchestra while studying composition with Charles Stanford. In 1898, at the age of twenty-three, he became a violin instructor at the Royal Academy and in that year achieved immediate national attention with *Hiawatha's Wedding Feast.* The other cantatas followed, each a year after the other; thereafter they were understood as a trilogy whose parts could also be performed separately.[41] Coleridge-Taylor's lifelong preoccupation with Longfellow's poem has caused a recent biographer to designate him "the Hiawatha man." He was apparently drawn to this particular work through the assonance of the Native American words and names (e.g., Mishe-Mokwa, Nagow Wudjoo), many of which, as he noted, gave him considerable pleasure. (The vocal scores each contain a glossary and guide to "pronunciation of the Indian words.") His first *Hiawatha* composition was not vocal, however, but a set of *Hiawathan Sketches* for violin and piano (1896). And the work that preoccupied him for the last year of his short life was a *Hiawatha* ballet, in which the brief choruses were not from Longfellow but from his own original texts.

Coleridge-Taylor was also fascinated by the Indian subject matter. He was well aware of the controversy surrounding national themes that ensued during Dvořák's visit to the United States. As one of Dvořák's great supporters in England, Coleridge-Taylor continually programmed his works on concerts. It is uncertain, however, whether he had access to either of two studies of North American Indian music circulating during the 1890s: Theodore Baker's dissertation on Iroquois/Seneca music (1882) and Alice Fletcher's study of Omaha music (1893). Although MacDowell's "Indian" Suite (1896) was not performed by a professional orchestra in London until 1901, Coleridge-Taylor probably studied the published score, as certain passages in his *Hiawatha* cantatas reveal a familiarity with that work. As for other *Hiawatha* settings in England, the Covent Garden performance of Stoepel's cantata had occurred long before Coleridge-Taylor was born, and, though a vocal score existed in the British Library, the work was largely forgotten by the 1890s. It is unknown whether Coleridge-Taylor knew about Delius's *Hiawatha* (1888), especially since it was never published nor presumably even performed. Coleridge-Taylor did know Frederick Cowen's setting of "Onaway, Awake!" (1892), but this was apparently not until he had already written his now-famous tenor aria on that text.[42]

Coleridge-Taylor's cantatas therefore represent a crucial link in the way native America was imagined in Europe, and, in that sense, their roots go back to Purcell, Rameau, Spontini, and others. They never quite drew the fanatical response in America that they garnered in England. It may be difficult for a modern audience to fully appreciate the novelty of these works for British listeners in the last years of Victorian England. Oratorio and cantata dominated musical culture in nineteenth-century Britain, and some of these genres' finest proponents, including Arthur Sullivan, Charles Hubert Parry, and Edward Elgar, fashioned their works within what seems—for its time—a peculiarly monochromatic style, stylistically modeled on Mendelssohn and Gounod.[43] This is not to say that late nineteenth-century British choral composers did not occasionally dare to brush with the exotic. Sullivan and Frederic Clay each drew upon pseudo–Middle Eastern elements for, respectively, *On Shore and Sea* (1871) and *Lalla Rookh* (1877). For the most part, though, English choral music during these years was conspicuous for its uniformity of style and its extreme soft-pedaling of exoticism. Indeed, exotic color is muted even in Coleridge-Taylor's other "exotic" works: *Zara's Earrings* (1895), *Kubla Khan* and *African Dances* (both 1906), *The Bamboula* (1910), and *A Tale of Old Japan* (1911). *Hiawatha's Wedding Feast,* to be sure, contained some of the melodic shapes that he may have borrowed from Indian songs in Baker's or Fletcher's published collections: pentatonic melodies, long phrases cascading downward, and descending octave leaps. But these indexical Indian references could just as easily have been gotten from other Western composers. With only one major exception, as we'll see, they are woven subtly into the fabric of the music.

Coleridge-Taylor was virtually catapulted to fame following the success of the first performance of *Hiawatha's Wedding Feast* at the Royal College of Music on 11 November 1898 under Charles Stanford. Commissions for new works began to flow in, but the composer intended to continue with his *Hiawatha* project. The first performance of *The Death of Minnehaha* at the North Staffordshire Musical Festival in 1899 was a decided success, and the general assessment was that the new cantata was even more compelling than the first one. A commission from the Royal Choral Society initiated work on the third cantata, and the completed trilogy was performed by that group at the Royal Albert Hall in London, 22 March 1900, the composer conducting.

About this time, Coleridge-Taylor began establishing connections in America. A society of African American musicians formed in Washington, D.C., in 1901, and the composer was invited to conduct as well as to lend his name to the group. It would take Coleridge-Taylor three years before he could travel to the United States. The secretary of the organization wrote on 1 June 1903: "The [society] was born of love of your work, was christened in your honour, and for two years has studied your masterpiece inspired by the hope that you would sooner or later come to America and personally conduct its presentation. Should you visit us, we can assure you of a thoroughly competent chorus of no less than two hundred voices, all in love with *Hiawatha* and its creator."[44]

The first official performance of the complete cantata trilogy in America was in Easton, Pennsylvania, on 5 May 1903 by the Orpheus Oratorio Society under Charles Knauss. But the first actual performance (with two pianos) was by an all African American chorus for a largely African American audience of some 1,500 in April 1901 at the Metropolitan African Methodist Church in Washington, D.C., under John T. Layton.[45] Though Coleridge-Taylor sent his regrets (as well as his reservations concerning a two-piano rendition), he himself came to Washington in 1904 to conduct a complete *Hiawatha* with the U.S. Marine Band expanded to an orchestra in Constitution Hall. This performance—given that he must have been one of the first black symphonic conductors on an American podium—caused a sensation in the press. W. C. Berwick Sayers recalled that the "Coleridge-Taylor Festival"

> occupied two evenings at Washington and a third at Baltimore. The Washington concerts were held in the Convention Hall [*sic*], a building with a capacity for concert purposes of nearly 3000. . . . The first concert, on Nov. 16, was devoted to *Hiawatha*. His principals, as his chorus, were all coloured, the soprano being Madame Estella Clough, of Worcester, Massachusetts, a well-known operatic singer, the tenor Mr. J. Arthur Freeman, of St. Louis, perhaps the foremost of living Negro tenors, and the baritone Mr. Harry T. Burleigh. . . . The crowded audience was in the proportion of two-thirds coloured and one-third white, in itself an evidence that the intense interest in Coleridge-Taylor was by no means confined to his own race. . . . President Roosevelt had hoped to be present, but public engagement—the Presidential election had taken place only a few days before—detained him in New York.[46]

The African American educator Booker T. Washington, who attended this performance, later wrote of its "haunting melodic phrases, bold harmonic scheme, and vivid orchestration." In 1907 Coleridge-Taylor again returned to Washington for the festival's performance of *Hiawatha* on 22 November. This was apparently the thirteenth performance to date in that city. Other noted performances in America were by the Chicago Apollo Club under Harrison Wild—*Hiawatha's Wedding Feast* in April 1901 (with reportedly 400 singers in the Club, 300 boy singers from the local schools, and an orchestra of 102 musicians)—and in 1908 by the enterprising Litchfield County Choral Union Festival in Norfolk, Connecticut.[47]

Imagining Native America

Each of the Coleridge-Taylor cantatas draws on parallel sections in Longfellow's narrative: cantos 11 and 12 for the wedding feast, canto 20 for Minnehaha's death, and cantos 21 and 22 for Hiawatha's departure. *Hiawatha's Wedding Feast* opens with an accented open-fifth drone in a dancelike moresca/Morris dance rhythm (bracketed in ex. 5), a device that immediately evokes the pastoral topic. The sopranos and altos (not shown in the example) introduce the cantata's principal thematic germ ("You shall hear how Pau-Puk-Keewis, / How the handsome Yenadizze, / Danced at Hiawatha's Wedding"). The leaping fifths and octaves in this setting—also, as we have seen, an earlier indexical device—carry over into the voices from the earthbound

Example 5. Samuel Coleridge-Taylor, *Hiawatha's Wedding Feast* (London: Novello, 1899): opening.

accompaniment with a suggestion of elemental power. The strings rhythmically invigorate the choral statement with offbeat pizzicatos.

Coleridge-Taylor must have known the practice of many North American Indian singers of beginning melodies high and cascading downward, often through pentatonic scales. In a slightly later section (vocal score, p. 27) he uses a descending figure in the men's voices and then, twelve measures later, uses this same descending phrase in counterpoint to the surging lyrical soprano line ("'Til the leaves went whirling with him"). Coleridge-Taylor must also have known of the tail that rounds out the phrases of some Indian song, for that in effect is what he has given the men's voices in "Swept in eddies, round about him" (B–A–F♯–F♯, B–A–F♯–F♯). Coleridge-Taylor exaggerated the cascading effect, dramatically repeating it.

The Death of Minnehaha is naturally sterner in tone than the previous cantata and uses a different set of themes. In this scene from canto 20 ("The famine"), Minnehaha lies dying from cold and starvation. Hiawatha tries to comfort her, but in the manifestations of nature most dear to them—the earth, the air, the sky—they see only reflections of their own hunger. Even the stars glare down at them like the eyes of hungry wolves. The slow tempo of the opening (*Larghetto lamentoso*) and the belabored downbeat of each 3/4 measure emphasize sadness and hardship. Here the sopranos begin high and strong. But at the glaring of the stars the melody cascades down through a pentatonic scale.[48] Even the bass line descends downward with a sense of hopelessness and resignation. The principal theme of the cantata imbues this moment with a sense of sorrow and a heaviness of spirit (especially in the unusual harmonic modulation of C minor to an F-minor sixth and back again). The tragic tone of this movement seems to extend well beyond the two characters. Like the great landscape panoramas of romantic painters, the natural splendors of the American West sometimes formed the background for human suffering. Against backgrounds of often stunning beauty, Bierstadt, Edgar Paxson, Henry Cross, and John Innes depicted the hardships endured by displaced Indians and the devastation of the tribes since the vanishing of the buffalo herds. One can certainly hear the intense sadness of Coleridge-Taylor's *Death of Minnehaha* as a personal reflection of grief. But it can also be interpreted as a metaphor (depending upon the context of performance) for the late nineteenth-century oppression that many Indian people endured in America.

In one crucial passage, Coleridge-Taylor went beyond his generally conservative harmonic language to create one of the most powerful and memorable moments in the entire work. He also created a musical impression of native America that, to my knowledge, had never before existed and that, through imitation by others, has resonated down to the present time. Desperate with hunger and with the fear of losing Minnehaha, Hiawatha rushes into the forest to offer prayers to Manitou for help, prayers that will ultimately prove futile. Shortly before example 6, the mood and texture continue much the same as at the opening. During a short orchestral interlude, however, this changes. The melody is increasingly accented and grows less languid, the bass line becomes more active, and an accelerando leads to an *Allegro* in 4/4. Two startling events can be identified here at the double bar: first, the short accented two-note melodic interjections (B♭–G); and second, the resolution of these into open fifths (D–A). The fifths achieve a sense of thrilling climax, powerfully reinforced in the woodwinds and brass. Because of the sharp, biting rhythm of the melody and the sense of eruption growing out of the dramatic one-measure orchestral crescendos on open fifths, this commanding and even violent moment in the cantata evokes parallel nonmusical images: the representation of a fierce and vengeful primitive power (Manitou?) and the terrible forces of nature. (Unlike the pastoral drone fifths in the bass, these open fifths reinforced *fortissimo* throughout the entire orchestra suggest nature at its overwhelmingly most sublime. The two most famous romantic precedents for this effect are the furious open fifths at the beginning of Beethoven's Ninth Symphony and in Wagner's *Flying Dutchman* Overture, the latter signifying the unconquerable power of the wind and sea, as the reappearance of this material later in the opera makes clear.) Coleridge-Taylor doesn't miss the opportunity

Example 6. Coleridge-Taylor, *Death of Minnehaha* (London: Novello, 1900), 72–73.

to drive the force of this primitive experience home. The chorus enters ("forth into the empty forest"), echoing not only the open fifths but also a pentatonic minor (actually only four notes), the only such combination in the entire work. Here again is a musical "ancientness" (seen earlier in Stoepel) that, as we will see, will come to play a major role in Indian settings in the early twentieth century.[49]

Unlike in earlier *Hiawatha* settings, Coleridge-Taylor treats the chorus as a character. For example, the sopranos and altos assume the role of Nokomis in the dialogue at Minnehaha's bedside. Here, Nokomis's calming replies occur strophically, with the same music as Minnehaha's hallucinations about hearing the rushing of the falls. The only differences are that the choral responses are lower by a third, marked to be sung *tranquillo,* and harmonized in a contrasting major mode.[50] Coleridge-Taylor, as did Stoepel, has Nokomis repeat herself for emphasis at the end of each of her phrases. The somewhat presentational quality here, however—unlike the parallel place in Stoepel's work—formalizes these two characters into ritualistic figures. Like a Greek chorus, the unison responses of all womankind ("'No, my child,' said old Nokomis") hint at the tragic outcome of Minnehaha's delirium. The two characters seem less like actors in a drama and more like Jungian archetypal figures.

Coleridge-Taylor's setting throughout the three cantatas often lulls the listener into passivity with soothing, sometimes monotonous harmonies. He seems reluctant to provide too direct, too offensive an interpretation. Consequently, much of the cantata trilogy unfolds as if told in the sweet voice of a kind but impartial narrator. The composer rarely seems to "read" Longfellow's text. He is too closely Longfellow's counterpart; his music subdues as Longfellow's meter fatigues. Perhaps Coleridge-Taylor respected the poet too much.

For the conclusion of the trilogy, on the other hand, Coleridge-Taylor imparts a touch of remorse and sadness to Hiawatha's farewell. The baritone's Wagnerian majesty ("I am going, O my people") appears in dramatic counterpoint to the tenderness of certain orchestral passages in the minor mode. The composer also emphasizes the two lines "Listen to their words of wisdom; / Listen to the truth they tell you" by using the same chromatic musical phrase for both. He approach to this text is less melodic than Foote's in his *Farewell.* Instead, Coleridge-Taylor builds dynamically to the musical and dramatic climax of the cantata (at "From the land of light and morning!") with a triumphant return of the opening motive from *Hiawatha's Wedding Feast.*

Coleridge-Taylor's delicate brushstrokes did not achieve a long-lived success in the United States. But the trilogy was practically venerated in England. It was considered "the most popular English oratorio" between 1898 and

1912, and Coleridge-Taylor's publisher, Novello & Co., profited considerably from performance royalties and sales of the music. It was after 1924, however, that the cantata trilogy began to benefit from the new twentieth-century "Indian craze" then being fueled by the popular music and film industry. After several attempts by organizations in England to stage *Hiawatha* in operatic form, a British producer, Thomas Fairbairn, devised an extravaganza around the cantatas. For these events, beginning on 19 May 1924, he draped the whole vast arena of Royal Albert Hall, as well as the stage platform, in scenic decoration. Masking the organ, he suspended a backdrop of snow-clad mountains, pine forests, and wigwams. He costumed some five hundred choristers—"braves and squaws"—in full Indian regalia and war paint and directed them to make a dramatic first entrance with whoops and hollers, and to participate physically throughout the evening by arm waving and other gestures. He also engaged skilled lighting technicians who, among other things, created the illusion of falling snow at the opening of the second part. In addition, actors were hired to pantomime the various characters, since the original score called for only three vocal soloists. A corps de ballet of a hundred dancers directed by choreographer Kydia Kyasht also participated. Eugene Goossens presided on the podium, and the composer's son, Hiawatha Coleridge-Taylor, conducted an interpolated ballet for the *Wedding Feast* to music drawn from Coleridge-Taylor's *Three Dream Dances*. The performances were such a success with the public that they became an annual event. The spectacle reportedly continued even through World War II, after which it was discontinued. Conductor Malcolm Sargent later took over from Goossens, and at least one Native American, Oskenonton (Mohawk), sang the role of Hiawatha from 1925 to the 1940s.[51]

Coleridge-Taylor's *Hiawatha* produced a range of different responses, from that of the Duchess of Sutherland, who reportedly was deeply moved by the 1899 Hanley Festival performance, to the enthusiasm of the Washington, D.C., African American chorus, to the London audiences' fascination with the hyperexoticized Royal Albert Hall extravaganzas. By pointing to some of the work's musical features, we have identified a few elements of musical exoticism. But the music's strongest appeal did not lie in specifically syntactical or iconic devices. What made these cantatas so touching, as the composer's daughter later recalled, was the sense of conviction in Coleridge-Taylor's simple melodies.[52] Another rhetorical device of eighteenth-century primitivism, we might recall, was the element of simplicity and nobility in the portrayal of American Indians.

The work's popularity poses a challenge, however, especially in its Victorian-era treatment of a North American subject—a topic not so estranged from

British interests when we consider that the Ojibwa peoples are, and were then, as much a part of Canada as they are of the United States. The influx of foreign elements into Great Britain's society and culture during the nineteenth century was certainly one result of its colonial involvement in world affairs. The presence of such elements raises interesting questions about the nationalism-exoticism dialectic: Were the foreign elements in Coleridge-Taylor's work, for example, *heard* as markers of the other? Or did Coleridge-Taylor's rather homogenous musical style when applied to North American "Indian culture" seem more like the outward extension of British national styles toward foreign or even colonial subjects? These two possibilities for hearing *Scenes from "The Song of Hiawatha"* need not be mutually exclusive, despite England's strongly insular and uniform classical musical culture in the late nineteenth century. Coleridge-Taylor, as a visible and—as he himself reported with regret—often denigrated minority, had at some time in his life to face the consequences of reactionary insularity. In his embrace of Longfellow's poem, he may have been aiming to widen his country's sense of cultural identity. Perhaps his magnum opus, exotic trappings notwithstanding, was intended to be understood as a beachhead in the battle for mutual tolerance between peoples of diverse cultural and racial origins, all the more potent for being performed in the near-sacred national venue of Royal Albert Hall.

In the complexities surrounding Coleridge-Taylor's work we can see new options opening up. Exoticism here is no longer *only* about the making of meaning within a context of colonialism and conquest. There's a fascinating and contradictory movement here, from the symbolic modes of representation characteristic of contact to the iconic modes that we will explore in the next several chapters. With the rise of ethnographic disciplines in the nineteenth century, knowledge was being produced and with it the possibility of creating more "authentic representations" of native America. *Hiawatha* points us toward this development. At the same time, however, it presages that these hybrid representations will exist at a relatively greater distance from actual Indian people.

PART III

Nostalgia for a Native Land

5

Ethnographic Encounters

Longfellow's *The Song of Hiawatha* may have remained a popular representation of American Indians for many decades, but it reflected none of the realities of late nineteenth-century American life, especially those of a shifting economy based on the need for more land and natural resources. The settling of the vast and fertile Mississippi valley, for example, was vividly described by the *New York Tribune* editor Horace Greeley in 1869: "And to its luxuriant and still unpeopled expanse all nations, all races, are yet eagerly flocking . . . from every quarter, every civilized land, the hungry, the portionless, the daring . . . [come] to hew out for their offspring the homes of plenty and comfort denied to their own rugged youth. Each year . . . sees the cultivated portion of the Great Valley expand; sees the dominion of the brute and the savage contracted and driven back."[1] The immigrants and other Americans whose sturdy characters shaped the nineteenth-century frontier and who also created the towns that sprang up as if miraculously across the western half of the continent were little interested in romantic drawing-room notions of Indians.

Many of the attitudes formed in popular culture about Indians were created indirectly in the nineteenth century by government agencies, which often perpetuated hostilities between white settlers and local tribes. From the late 1840s, when gold was discovered in California and the transcontinental railroad was begun, until 1890, many American cavalry and infantry units fought decisively in the "Indian wars," violent encounters with tribes across the West who refused to comply with United States government restrictions (and also with many who did). The conflict was exacerbated by the increasing strength and fierce resistance of the Sioux Nation and its speedy communication via horse-backed messengers. Eventually, however, the telegraph proved faster and more efficient for the U.S. cavalry and more deadly for the Sioux. Partly in reaction to the 1862 Sioux uprising in Minnesota (then a four-year-old state), in which hundreds of Scandinavian and German settlers were slain—not to mention the violence that erupted (on the Indian side) after the Sand Creek massacre and the hostile reaction (on the American side) to Custer's defeat on the Little Big Horn in 1876—Congress effectively outlawed any attempts toward making treaties with the western Indian tribes as sovereign nations. The American Indian resistance, which had a long history, was finally broken at Wounded Knee in 1890. The massacre, as well as the mapping of the West by that year, effectively brought an end to what had been understood for over a hundred years as the American frontier.[2]

Defining the "Dominion of the Brute and the Savage"

By the middle of the century, efforts to dispel the noble savage idea of American Indians led in two principal and very different directions. The first of these involved government- and private-sponsored investigations into cultural practices of regional Indian life. These investigations seemed determined to offset fanciful notions of Indian cultures with scientific methodologies. Most important for music was the formation of progressive organizations modeled on European principles of classical archaeology. Those in the lead were the American Ethnological Society (Flushing, New York, 1842), the Smithsonian Institution (Washington, D.C., 1846), the American Association for the Advancement of Science (1848), Harvard's Peabody Museum (Cambridge, Massachusetts, 1867), the American Anthropological Society (Beloit, Wisconsin, 1879), and the Archaeological Institute of America (1879). These organizations galvanized the new disciplines of ethnography and anthropology around ideals of preserving the diverse cultures of the Indians, cultures that, as many believed, were in danger of being seriously eroded by the forced migration of dozens of tribes to Indian territory in present-day Kansas and Oklahoma. An extraordinary burst of energy—perhaps originating in what Renato Rosaldo has called "imperialist nostalgia"—surrounded the movement to collect and preserve Indian culture, including the category of music. Roy Harvey Pearce put it more bluntly: "The Indian, becoming the province of learned groups especially organized to study him, soon was a scholarly field in himself, just like a dead language."[3]

Crucial in these endeavors were new methods of research developed in response to the social Darwinism that was then beginning to influence scientific scholarship. In his *Synthetic Philosophy* (first volume, 1862), Herbert Spencer applied Darwin's theories of biological evolution to human behaviors, and in *Ancient Society* (1877), Lewis Henry Morgan detailed kinship structures in social evolution from primitive to modern civil societies. These writings proved to be foundational to the emerging disciplines of anthropology and sociology.[4] Ironically, the confinement of Indian tribes to reservations offered a relatively safe environment for the study of these cultures. Under the aegis of scientific accreditation, ethnologists went in search of, as critical anthropologists might describe it today, distilled concepts of pure authenticities that could first be cataloged and then disseminated. Significantly, ethnographers found the music of American Indians inseparable from their culture and developed methods for notating and recording it (thus becoming the first explorers to treat it in anything like a systematic way). Moreover, the ideologies that motivated the ethnologists also motivated composers to adopt similar procedures of transcription and adaptation and to form an alliance with ethnographers in the pursuit of indigenous musical resources.

The second reinventing of native America was subject to fluctuating tastes of consumerism. Entrepreneurs realized the marketing potential of Indian subjects in popular middle-class entertainment—pulp fiction about the West, for example, or outdoor western action dramas. "Wild West shows," conceived and billed more as exhibitions of national pride than as Barnum's or Hickok's brand of circus entertainment, depicted scenes and events characteristic of the American Far West frontier. Relying upon the patriotic sentiments of his audience and incorporating theatrical techniques of drama and suspense, "Buffalo Bill" Cody hit upon a simple but successful dramatic formula that eventually ossified into a sweeping mythology about the West: Indians were antagonists and the whites were victims and heroes. His scheme left no room for compromise when it came to placing the Indians at the lower social and cultural end of the evolutionary scale and elevating the Euro-American to the status of ultimate moral leadership, regardless of the amount of violence necessary to maintain such a status. For the general public, the Wild West shows undoubtedly reinforced negative opinion and attitudes toward Indians. They were nevertheless extraordinarily popular. These outdoor extravaganzas established the view of the expansion of America as a "shoot-'em-up" standoff between the Savage and the Civilized. Cody's spectacles also featured the sharpshooter Annie Oakley (later characterized as an adopted Indian in Irving Berlin's musical *Annie Get Your Gun*). Though Cody featured an enactment of Indian dances and ceremonies, he relied principally upon his wind band to play quicksteps or standard theatrical melodramatic music for the battle and rescue scenes. (Programs from the late nineteenth-century shows survive. But Indian "characteristics" do not appear until the early twentieth century, once Tin Pan Alley and other publishers began turning out new "Indian" pieces.) Cody's shows largely manifested the world of the dime novels. Sometimes these included an occasional noble red man or a beautiful Indian maiden, but they almost always featured a savage nemesis to the Anglo-Saxon protagonist. The basic ingredients of the dime Western remained fundamentally the same, persisting well into the twentieth century and showing up in quite different media as well. Cecil B. DeMille, one of early cinema's top producers, directed more than thirty silent Westerns between 1913 and 1918 that replicated many of the formulas.[5]

The basic influences that led to iconographic as well as increased indexical representation of Indian music in American culture therefore came from two directions: anthropology and popular middlebrow culture. As an important area of overlap between these, the music used to portray native America contributed to both "scientific" understanding as well as increased stereotypical views of Indian peoples.

The Indianists: Mapping Culture

The speed with which the United States expanded after the Civil War was less driven by Manifest Destiny than by the newly emerging political philosophy of progressivism. North American Indian beliefs are most often rooted in an understanding of the cyclical nature of human destiny. The emerging Euro-American worldview, on the other hand, implied the recognition of progressions: from ape to human, from chisel and stone tablet to typewriter, from superstition and mythology to scientific explanation, and from instinctive behavior to cultivation and refinement. According to Theodore Roosevelt (*The Winning of the West,* fourteen volumes, 1885–94), the energy that up until 1890 united Americans in the fight for the frontier would now have to be focused on other "frontiers," one of which was building the United States into a leading world power. According to Richard Slotkin, Roosevelt's accounts "use the history of the West to illustrate first the succession of savages by civilized races and then the succession of different classes or subdivisions of the white or Anglo-Saxon race that represent progressively higher stages of development" and leading to a heroic, elite class.[6]

On the other hand, historian Frederick Jackson Turner had his own "frontier thesis," one he delivered formally in 1893 in a paper at the World's Columbian Exposition in Chicago.[7] The twenty-five-year-old Turner rejected the hunter mentality and racism implicit in Roosevelt's view of the American character. Instead, he believed Americans would find a new frontier in the "realm of the spirit," principally through institutions of social reform. In both expressions, however, the mythic space of the frontier (or "the West") began to outweigh its importance as a real place and became identified with the fictions created about it. For urban readers, dime Westerns continued to offer an escape from the growing reality of urban congestion and discontent with industrialization. National expression in America took its cues from a set of dichotomies that crystallized around Roosevelt's and Turner's nationalist ideologies: science vs. superstition, progress vs. economic stagnation, civilization vs. wilderness, virility vs. sentimentality, industrial vs. agrarian, and imperialist vs. provincial.

These dichotomies were embedded in the philosophies of the Smithsonian as well as its offshoot the Bureau of American Ethnology, founded under John Wesley Powell in 1879. These organizations, along with the independently formed American Ethnological Society, were interested in bringing science to bear on the mapping of the West. They sponsored fieldwork among the various tribal cultures of America. At first, their anthropological and sociological publications were directed toward a highly specialized readership of scholarly monographs and journals. Gradually, however, some of this knowledge filtered into more general writing about Indian life in middlebrow publications such as *Scribner's, Harper's, Popular Science Monthly, Century Illustrated,* and the *Atlantic Monthly.* In splendidly detailed articles, these magazines treated Indian topics with the same curiosity and allure as they did, for example, Egyptian archaeology, early navigation of the Samoan Isles, or dancers in New Orleans's Place Congo. Informed citizens could not avoid encountering the growing body of knowledge about specific tribal cultures, much of it cast in the guise of folklore.

When the American Folklore Society was established in Cambridge, Massachusetts, in January 1888 under the supervision of the German-born Franz Boas and others, one of its primary objectives was to assist in the collection of "the fast-vanishing remains of folklore in America." The lore of the Indian tribes was one of four distinctively North American cultures earmarked for collection. In the first issue of the society's principal mouthpiece, the *Journal of American Folklore,* the traditions of the Indian tribes were cited as the richest and most abundant area for documentation.[8] This desire to preserve North American folklore no doubt stemmed in part from similar attempts on the part of Europeans to collect native folk music. As more and more Indians were pressured to assimilate into the dominant culture—largely through government-run centers such as the Carlisle Indian Industrial School in Pennsylvania or the Hampton Institute in Virginia—it became apparent that traditional Indian religions and rituals would eventually be forgotten.

Boas warned that the collection of folklore was not merely a source of amusement but an important and essential part of history. Moreover, "the habits and ideas of primitive races include much that seems to us cruel and immoral, much that it might be thought well to leave unrecorded. But this would be a superficial view. What is needed is not an anthology of customs and beliefs, but a complete representation of the savage mind in its rudeness as well as its intelligence, its licentiousness as well as its fidelity."[9] It was clear from the first issue of the *Journal* that music as part of this "savage mind" was to enjoy equal footing with customs and stories. Unlike the earlier work of Schoolcraft and others, who (like Herder in Europe) set about collecting the verbal texts of folklore, the goals of the society included collecting also the pitches and rhythms of the songs. It was therefore partly the task of the ethnologists who had musical training to dispel the notion that Indian music was little more than noise and war whoops, as Catlin might have expressed it, and to attempt to get inside the mind and experience of the Indians for whom music clearly constituted an important social fabric of their lives.

Many researchers, often working independently, undertook fieldwork among various Indian tribes in order to compile factual information about Indian life and culture. Theodore Baker's *Über die Musik der nordamerikanischen Wilden* ("On the Music of the North American Savages") still serves as the most compelling example. In the late 1870s and early '80s, Baker, born in New York, studied historical musicology in Leipzig. His analysis of Iroquois/Seneca music for his 1881 dissertation was the first systematic study of any Indian music repertoire. Published in German in 1882, this short but detailed book, though not without its controversies, was the first to draw attention in Europe and the United States to the variety and complexity of indigenous North American musics. Although it is often cited as the first major effort to notate Indian music, musical notation of Indian themes existed long before Baker, as we have discussed in the accounts of early Spanish and French sources. In his analysis of Baker's volume, Robert M. Stevenson has revealed the strange assortment that Baker brought together to present as authentic Indian melodies, including such wayward influences as English folk songs and old American hymn tunes.[10]

Baker's interest in Native American music was something of an exception at the time. His methodical approach, however, served as a yardstick for ethnographers who sought to include music in their research. In the 1880s, published studies of Indian music begin to circulate more widely, beginning with Baker in 1882 and continuing with transcriptions by noted Indianists such as Alice Fletcher, Franz Boas, and Benjamin Ives Gilman (and eventually Frances Densmore). Some recent critical theorists, among them Shari Huhndorf and Susan Scheckel, have asserted with some justification that the sympathetic Indianists, trained ethnographers and anthropologists who, in the nineteenth and early twentieth centuries, recorded the languages and beliefs of indigenous American peoples (which included music), inadvertently helped to map out the cultural territory for conquest. While this is partly true (perhaps more so in the engine of private sponsorship), the search for cultural understanding as evidenced in the writings of the Indianists exhibits greater moral conscience than, say, in any of the subsequent treaties over land rights.

Indianist, as the word appears in ethnology, refers broadly to those nineteenth-century activists who favored policies that supported native peoples. It can also be applied to anyone speaking on behalf of Indian culture as well, as novelist Helen Hunt Jackson did in *A Century of Dishonor,* her 1881 indictment of American Indian policy. Fletcher, Boas, Gilman, and Densmore, on the other hand, might be more accurately described as ethnomusicologists, although that term did not come into use until the 1950s and would be anachronistic here. "Indianist" is certainly one acceptable nonmusical designation, but the gap between Indianists and ethnomusicologists requires some clarification. The American branch of musicology in the nineteenth century spawned several related fields. One of these involved the collection of music as a vital component of folklore. In 1885 Guido Adler could refer to three separate disciplines that had branched out from a musicological center: traditional "historical musicology"; "comparative musicology," practiced by collectors interested in the basic data relating to music of other cultures; and "systematic musicology," indicating those fields that combined music with other disciplines such as psychology, philosophy, and education.[11] In the 1930s in the United States, comparative musicologists interested in folklore and non-Western cultures began to apply anthropological paradigms to the analysis of their fieldwork. By the 1950s this hybrid discipline led to more contextual evaluations of music performance and ritual. Despite differences in labeling and methodologies between these disciplines, it is clear that the study of the social context of music—which today's advocates of postmodernism hail as a recent discovery —has been a distinctive feature of American comparative musicology and folklore since the nineteenth century.

Several important ethnologists and comparative musicologists worked on behalf of government organizations—Franz Boas among the Kwakiutls of the Pacific Northwest, Benjamin Ives Gilman among the Hopis and Zunis of the Southwest, and Alice Fletcher among the Omahas and Nez Perces of Idaho. Hence the criticism they have faced in recent times. Some of the other major nineteenth-century ethnologists interested in Indian music were James Mooney, Jesse W. Fewkes, Walter James Hoffman, Washington Matthews, Frank G. Speck, J. D. Sapir, Natalie Curtis, and one Indian, Francis LaFlesche (Omaha-Ponca)—all in America—as well as Alexander Cringan in Canada and Carl Stumpf and John Cornelius Griggs in Germany. These Indianists devoted their efforts to documenting Indian culture while living among various tribes as "participant observers." Individual bulletins published by the Smithsonian's Bureau of American Ethnology and devoted to Indian studies during these years number nearly two hundred. Those scholars who took an interest specifically in music, however, were considerably smaller, though many sustained large reputations within the field.[12]

Some of the first major articles to record and translate Indian music in a spiritual context largely unknown to white America were Washington Matthews's "The Mountain Chant: A Navajo Ceremony" (1887), James Mooney's "The Sacred Formulas of the Cherokees" (1891), and Mooney's *Ghost Dance Religion* (1893), the latter an important study of this visionary movement written virtually at the moment of its emergence. The single most influential publication, however, was the benchmark *Study of Omaha Indian Music* (1893) by Alice Fletcher and Francis LaFlesche. This book was particularly significant for musical composition because it included transcriptions by the music historian and prototheorist John Comfort Fillmore, who proposed ways in which monophonic Indian chants could be harmonized and, as he saw it, made more palatable to "cultured tastes."[13]

In addition to government agencies, private sponsorship contributed enormously to the collection of musical information about American Indians. In the 1880s the Bostonian Mary Hemenway financed an eight-year expedition into the Southwest to document Pueblo cultures. J. Pierpont Morgan sponsored Edward S. Curtis's twenty-volume *The North American Indian,* a remarkable photographic display of native America. Later, the retail giant Rodman Wanamaker sponsored three "educational expeditions" (1908, 1909, and 1913) to pave the way for citizenship of the Plains Indians. Some "Indian hobbyists," as William K. Powers described the impulse, spent huge amounts of money on the pursuit of their passions. Edward E. Ayer, a Chicago businessman and an avid collector of Americana, began in the early 1870s to collect books (among other artifacts) dealing with American Indians. He could have had little premonition of the scope of his endeavor. By the 1920s over 11,000 volumes had been assembled, and they now make up the impressive Ayer Collection at the Newberry Library in Chicago, one of the most comprehensive collections of books and writings about the North American Indians.[14]

By the turn of the twentieth century, most Euro-American citizens had come to see the Indian peoples as a fast dwindling element of North American life, especially since most unassimilated Indians had long been relegated to the reservations. Over the previous forty years, various exploratory missions had been undertaken in the West to investigate little-known Indian territories recently acquired by the United States government. The aforementioned Hemenway Archaeological Expedition under the explorer Frank Hamilton Cushing was one such expedition. Cushing, often hailed at the time (incorrectly) as the "first white man to penetrate the Zuni nation" (see map 2, chapter 3), brought a host of ethnographers and photographers with him. One of his later musical confidantes, the evidently eccentric California musical entrepreneur Carlos Troyer, was himself an amateur ethnographer who had a reputation for his controversial renderings and explanations of Zuni music. Though the extent of Troyer's participation is unclear, he reportedly collaborated with Cushing in notating about forty Zuni melodies following the expedition, two of which he published in San Francisco in 1893. (His later so-called adaptations of some of these songs, however, are wildly imaginative.)[15]

After 1890 Thomas Edison's cylinder machines ("Ediphones") or Columbia's equivalent product ("graphophones") proved a great boon to more systematic approaches. Recordings could be made on location even by archaeologists with no musical training—such as Cushing did among the Zuni—and the cylinders sent home either to be deposited in an archive or transcribed by musicians. In 1890 Edward Curtis employed the services of classically trained composer Henry F. Gilbert to transcribe Indian music he had recorded with Edison's cylinders. One of these transcriptions—"Medicine-Song of the Morning Star" (Nez Perce)—can be seen in Victoria Levine's *Writing Indian Music*, along with many examples of the work of ethnologists discussed here. Though their attempts seem scientific enough, the musicians' efforts to transcribe what they heard were hampered by the limitations of Western musical notation—a system whose development since the seventeenth century was closely tied to instrumental discipline. There was little precedent for writing down the variable pitches and flexible rhythms of, for example, the Luiseños (Southern California) or Laguna Pueblo (New Mexico). This didn't phase Alice Fletcher, however. In an 1898 issue of the *Journal of American Folklore,* she argued that she could demonstrate convincingly that the Indian melodies she had recently recorded with a graphophone were identical with those she had transcribed on paper fourteen years earlier. The evidence suggested that Indian melodies did in fact constitute the basis of a continuous tradition, one that could be systematically documented. (These cylinder recordings, now at the Library of Congress, are, at the time of writing, available online.)[16]

By 1950 an extraordinary amount of recording, transcription, and analysis had been made of native singing. The ethnographic tradition in the twentieth century was led by Densmore of the Smithsonian, and was followed by ethnologists and musicians such as Helen Roberts, George Herzog (Hungarian American), Ida Halpern (Canadian), Frank Mitchell (Navajo), and Americans

Willard Rhodes, David McAllester, Alan Merriam, and Bruno Nettl. Ethnologists from Fletcher to McAllester (and beyond) demonstrated that music pervaded many aspects of North American Indian life, not just for work or ceremonial purposes, as had been observed by earlier writers. Music told stories, recounted personal experiences, taught lessons, and shaped character. It sometimes was codified into cyclic patterns of mythic symbolism, though more often than not it also remade itself from generation to generation by absorbing new influences (and continues to do so today).[17]

One of the first publications to take into account North American Indian music as part of the international array of representative folk cultures was, surprisingly, an 1890 compilation *National, Patriotic, and Typical Airs of All Lands,* prepared by John Philip Sousa for use by the U.S. Navy. The volume was designed to reflect the national character of diverse countries, including native America. Most of the anthology's Indian songs include words, and a few have descriptive footnotes that explain the song's source and its context. Among Sousa's collection is a Cherokee ball song transcribed by James Mooney. Having spent several years among the Cherokees in Oklahoma Territory, Mooney reported that the songs he heard were "always in the minor key [and] have a plaintive effect, even when the sentiment is cheerful." Although these are betting songs for use in games, Sousa provided for the first of them, "Híganúyahí," an accompaniment typical of the nineteenth-century war dance trope, including the old moresca rhythm and minor-mode chords. It was clear to the Indianists that much more sensitive and distinctive settings would need to be developed if Indian folk songs were to be taken seriously on a par with those of other cultures.[18]

The First Anthology of Omaha Indian Music

Alice Cunningham Fletcher (1838–1923) lived many years with the peoples of the Omaha reservation while maintaining close academic ties with Harvard's Peabody Museum. In her Omaha work, she had the assistance of Francis LaFlesche (1857–1932), one of the first American Indian ethnologists. Fletcher met LaFlesche during her first stay among the Omahas in 1881. That trip had been facilitated by Suzette LaFlesche Tibbles, Francis's sister, whom Fletcher had met in Boston during one of Suzette's eastern campaigns for the Indian Rights Association. Both Francis and Suzette had been raised in the progressive village established by their father Joseph ("Iron Eye"). In addition to learning traditional Omaha religion and ceremony, they had also been enrolled in the local Presbyterian Mission School. Francis had just accepted an appointment as a clerk and translator in the Office of Indian Affairs in Washington. He was on a summer trip home when he met "this remarkable woman" whose thoughts and expression "were more like a man." LaFlesche brought family and friends to visit Fletcher—who was then confined to bed with rheumatism—and the healing songs they sang for her made a deep and lasting impression. A friendship ensued in Washington in 1882 when Fletcher began her trips there to lobby for the Omahas. After a few political initiatives, the two collaborated on their study of Indian culture, and LaFlesche remained Fletcher's close friend for the rest of her life and her primary source of information on the Omaha peoples.[19]

LaFlesche also assisted Fletcher in collecting Indian songs. They did much of the transcribing in Washington during the winters, persuading Indians who were in the city for one reason or another to come and sing for them. George Miller, a young Omaha student at the Hampton Institute in Virginia, was a typical informant. He visited them in May 1888, and Fletcher reported to Francis Ward Putnam of the Peabody Museum that they had taken down eighteen songs in four days, adding to the thirty-seven they had already collected. By year's end they had accumulated some three hundred. The melodies of the songs were largely pentatonic, and in this sense they echoed some of the other traditions of American folk music, Appalachian songs, for example. For a few years, however, Fletcher seemed to be at a loss as to how to interpret the Indian transcriptions.

She took an interest in Omaha music only a year or two after Baker had visited the Carlisle Indian School in search of Indian music for his study. By the time Fletcher and LaFlesche had begun their transcriptions, the German theorist Carl Stumpf had published an article in a German musicological journal on problems of notating a dance song performed by Nuskilusta, a Bella Coola who was then in Europe with Carl Hagenbeck, a traveling showman. Stumpf had identified the use of quarter-tones in the singing of this Northwest Coast performer (as well as in the music of African groups also visiting Germany). In the spring of 1888 Franz Boas—who had worked with Stumpf in the preparation of the 1886 Bella Coola study—published his first article on the Kwakiutls, also of British Columbia. Although Boas focused on cultural description rather than musical detail, he included a few transcriptions of songs. Like Stumpf, he notated the melodies using Western-style key signatures and proposed the indication of a small ° over tones that were sung "a little lower" than notated and a small ˣ for those slightly higher. Younger ethnographers such as Otto Abraham and Erich von Hornbostel continued in this direction of experimenting with pitch notation, setting the stage for twentieth-century transcribers. Fletcher—who would later adhere to a diatonic theory (rooted in traditional Western scales) — must have been aware of the growing analytical controversy over pitch notation in Indian music.[20]

Feeling somewhat insecure about her technical knowledge of music, Fletcher sent one of the Omaha songs ("Hae-thu-ska Wa-an," later no. 21 in the 1893 collection) to John Fillmore in 1888. She not only sought his advice on how to analyze the song but also on how the tune might be expanded into a more elaborate musical statement, a distinctly "American" music. In the summer of 1890 Fillmore completed a short orchestral work: *Indian Fantasia No. 1,* a set of variations on the original "Hae-thu-ska" song he received from Fletcher. At the time, Fillmore was considering how to set the basic melodies of Fletcher and LaFlesche's collection in a diatonic setting, much like a jeweler might mount a gem in surrounding silver or gold. Before he had published any articles on his harmonic theories in the treatment of Indian music, however, he had already composed essentially the first truly iconic work of Indianism. On Fletcher's invitation, he developed his theories in his "Report on the Structural Peculiarities" of Omaha music, intended in part to justify his settings. With this substantial contribution to Fletcher's *Study of Omaha Indian Music,* Fillmore embarked on an official career in comparative musicology that would be terminated only by his premature death five years later. No existing document indicates that he ever composed another instrumental work on Indian themes. His harmonizations in this and other publications during the 1890s, however, constitute miniature compositions in themselves, and we will return to these in chapter 7.[21]

The process of collecting and notating Indian music grew increasingly controversial in the 1890s. Substantial competition arose between some of the ethnographers; one incident at the World's Columbian Exposition in 1893 pitted Gilman against Fletcher. Many less contentious ethnographers were forced to take sides, and music periodicals began to back one or another ethnographer. Beginning with such mainstream music journals as Chicago's *Music* magazine in the early 1890s, and continuing with *Musical America* and *Musical Courier,* many major music journals carried articles on Indian music alongside program announcements for performing artists such as Anton Seidl and Ignace Paderewski, reviews of concerts and opera, or advertisements for Steinway pianos. Such editorial practices would hardly have been imaginable forty years earlier.

Indians at the World's Fairs

In an age before permanent museums dedicated to natural history existed in America, the world's fairs were among the first major venues through which the general public encountered the results of studies by government agencies and ethnographic societies. The nineteenth-century world's fairs were grand-scale displays of culture and civilization. Housed in monumental edifices of classical architectural design on splendid grounds built and landscaped specifically for the purpose, the fairs displayed the collected evidence of art, science, and progress. Although designed to glorify the accomplishments of the entire human race, they were clearly rooted in principles of empire and social Darwinism and did not accord much value to non-European cultures. Representations of the North American Indians underwent several important changes from fair to fair. Most significant for their presentation of Indian music—or suppression of it, as the case may be—were the 1876 Centennial Exhibition in Philadelphia, the 1893 World's Columbian Exposition in Chicago, the 1898 Trans-Mississippi and International Exposition in Omaha, and the 1904 Louisiana Purchase Exposition in St. Louis.

The official commencement ceremonies of the 1876 Centennial Exposition in Philadelphia began not with the sounds of America, but with the American Centennial Overture, composed (hastily) for the occasion by Richard Wagner and conducted by Theodore Thomas. Historian Robert Rydell notes that, like the exhibition's displays of the progress of a hundred years, the ceremonies "emphasized national unity and America's destiny as God's chosen nation." As to the central conception underlying the Indian exhibit, "the Native American cultures and people belonged to the interminable wasteland of humanity's dark and stormy beginnings. The Indians' worth as human beings was determined by their usefulness as counterpoint to the unfolding progress of the ages." Many Indian artifacts were displayed, but, despite negotiations between the Smithsonian, the Commissioner of Indian Affairs, and the U.S. Congress, it was ultimately decided by the Secretary of the Interior that it would be indecent to permit live Indians to be on display at the fair.[22]

Seventeen years later, the World's Columbian Exposition in Chicago exceeded the Philadelphia fair in both size and scope. Nearly 28 million people attended (a number nearly half that of the population of the United States). Many visitors wrote with euphoria about the exposition. One of these, the critic and novelist William Dean Howells, saw it as a manifestation of what was good in American life and as an ennobling vision that Americans should strive to transform into reality. Ranking high in this utopian vision, after science and commerce, were art and music. Festival chorus, symphonic, chamber, and band concerts under William Tomlins, Theodore Thomas, Franz Kneisel, and John Philip Sousa, as well as guest soloists such as Paderewski and others, flooded the fairground pavilions no less than the modern electric lights that illuminated them. American novelist and critic Rupert Hughes called the Chicago Exposition "possibly the most important artistic event in our national history."[23]

Although the chief purpose of the exposition was to celebrate the Americas' "advancement" in the four hundred years since Columbus's discovery, all nations and peoples were to be represented. A small Indian delegation was included in the dedication ceremonies, and several tribal groups set up camp along the Midway Plaisance, a sideshow of live cultural entertainment (and amusement park) strategically placed in stark contrast to the edifices of the "White City," the latter filled with high-toned exhibitions of great Western art and demonstrations of scientific and technological progress. It was at this fair that many younger generations of Americans (of all origins) first heard music of the Eskimos, Ojibwes, and Navajos—not to mention that of Middle and Far Eastern peoples, particularly Turkish, Chinese, Javanese, and Samoan—who staged recurrent performances at stations along the midway. Moreover, thanks to Benjamin Gilman, who brought his graphophone to the fair, these ethnic performers made some of the earliest surviving recordings in America.[24]

The fair also hosted scholarly conventions (such as the history congress at which Turner read his "frontier thesis"). Within the Anthropological Pavilion itself, ethnologists held forums to discuss their research. Alice Fletcher delivered papers at three of the international congresses (music, anthropology, and religion), all of the papers drawing on her studies of North American Indians. In her music paper, she argued that Indian music was ordered, stable, easily transcribable, and based not on microtones—as Stumpf and Boas had previously suggested—but on the notes of Western scales (though these were often modified, she admitted, for expressive reasons).[25] John Fillmore, attending the exposition's music congress at the exposition, visited the lodge built at the exposition by a group of Kwakiutls from Vancouver Island. (Unlike the Indians on the midway, the Kwakiutls were given one of the controlled exhibits on the shores of the south lagoon.) Fillmore invited Duquayis (a Kwakiutl "chieftainess," he called her) to hear his attempts to render the music of her culture:

> [She] had not been willing to believe, at first, that any white man could sing the songs of the tribe correctly; but after I had taken her and her husband with the interpreter to a room in the Music Hall where there was a piano and had played and sung with the Indians for an hour some half dozen or more of the songs I had been collecting, she was evidently ready to acknowledge not only that the white man could master the Indian songs, but that the harmonized piano version was very delightful.[26]

Fillmore went on to explain how he had to convince Duquayis to sing one of her songs to him, the process involved in notating it, and his method of harmonizing the melody.

This was an unparalleled historical opportunity that could have only happened at this fair. For the first time in America, congresses devoted to the specialization of scholars were combined with actual exhibits and performances of world music. Scientific knowledge could be recalibrated against native performers' playing, singing, or dancing in one of the "live exhibits" presented in or near the Anthropological Pavilion or just a short distance away on the Midway Plaisance. The popular press, it should be noted, found most of the musical activities on the midway a source for amusement and cheap laughs.[27] Many musicians with an ethnological bent, however, took careful note of what they heard, among them Gilman, the music critic Henry Krehbiel (who published several remarkable articles on Indian music in the *New York Tribune*), and the young Frances Densmore.

Five years later, at the 1898 Trans-Mississippi and International Exposition in Omaha, the Smithsonian's Bureau of American Ethnology approved an Indian Congress, though this was clearly an attempt at salvage ethnology. Edward Rosewater, head of the exposition's department of publicity, was quoted in the *Omaha Bee* as saying that "this grand ethnological exhibit undoubtedly would be the last gathering of these tribes before the bronze sons of the forests and plains, who have resisted the encroachments of the white man, are gathered to the happy hunting ground." Rosewater, a Czech (who had befriended Dvořák in 1893), believed demand was high for an extensive exhibition illustrative of the life and customs "and decline of the aboriginal inhabitants of the Western Hemisphere." Scholars attending the fair, however, expressed disappointment at finding the bureau's proposed efforts for a living anthropological exhibition having degenerated into Wild West shows and sham Indian battles—gaudily advertised on huge poster boards and clearly designed to increase ticket sales. They were not the only ones who did not find the burnings at the stake, scalpings, and mutilations entertaining. Neither did President McKinley, according to the editor of a local newspaper. While the Indians pretended to destroy each other, McKinley appeared engrossed rather than amused in the spectacle, after which, the editor noted, he gave a "kindly greeting to the redmen."[28]

Despite the controversy over how the Indians could best be presented at the 1898 Omaha exposition, performances of Indian music were arranged in conjunction with a Music Congress. According to an advance notice in a May 1898 issue of *Musical Courier:* "Saturday, July 2, will be called 'Indian Music Day,' and will be devoted to an exposition of the results of original research in the music of the aborigines." The chairman's report on the fair noted that Fletcher, LaFlesche, and Fillmore spoke in the afternoon, accompanied by several Omahas who sang native songs for an audience composed largely of trained musicians. In a later publication, Fletcher commented that "this unique presentation not only demonstrated the scientific value of these aboriginal songs in the study of the development of music but [also] suggested their availability as themes, novel and characteristic, for the American composer."[29]

Fletcher's earlier suggestions that composers use Indian themes in their works had not been widely aired at the time of the 1893 exposition. But by 1898 she, Fillmore, and a few others had arranged a demonstration of just such a thing. The evening orchestra concert of July 2 was devoted to compositions "founded upon Indian themes," so the *Courier* reports, and included "the famous 'Indian Suite' recently composed by [Edward] MacDowell and a symphonic poem [*Hiawatha*] composed by Ern[e]st Kroeger of St. Louis." Aside from those in New York, Boston, or Chicago who may have already heard MacDowell's "Indian" Suite (1896), the Omaha Congress was probably the first occasion that scholars and ethnologists heard Indian tribal themes transformed into iconic concert works. (Much space would soon be given in press reports to Frederick Burton's cantata on *Hiawatha,* especially to the movement based on a Kwakiutl melody that he had borrowed from Krehbiel's transcription made at the 1893 Exposition. This startlingly original work—with its throbbing drum in three against the choral parts in two—was first performed in New York the month after "Indian Music Day" in Omaha and subsequently published.)[30]

Until the Omaha Music Congress in 1898, most transcriptions of Indian music could be found only in specialists' journals and bulletins, such as those published by the Bureau of Ethnology or the Peabody Institute. To correct this problem, Fletcher published a version of thirty songs in *Indian Story and Song from North America* (1900). The songs and the accompanying descriptive mythologies in this small volume were offered "in a more popular form," so that "the general public may share with the student the light shed by these untutored melodies upon the history of music."[31] Despite years of living among the Omahas, Fletcher could still write (in her preface, ix) that "these songs are like the wild flowers that have not yet come under the transforming hand of the gardener." The book circulated widely and remained one of the chief sources for composers of "Indian music" for the next two decades.

By the time of the 1904 Louisiana Purchase Exposition in St. Louis, the debate about whose versions of American Indian history and culture would be included could not be kept from coming to a head. As Robert A. Trennert has revealed, conflicts during the fair's planning stages between the ethnologists (who were most interested in "scientific" interpretations), the hucksters and entrepreneurs (who wished to make money from people's "morbid curiosity" about near-naked "savages"), and the assimilationists (such as Richard Pratt of the Carlisle Indian School, who on principle abhorred any attempt to resurrect the Indians' past life) largely succeeded in watering down any "live Indian exhibits" until they were little more than craft shows, even though the Louisiana Purchase Exposition featured, as the program book announced, "the most extensive anthropological department of any world's fair." Ironically, American Indians at the exposition from diverse tribal backgrounds—those, that is, that survived their harsh treatment and the lack of such simple amenities as clean water—succeeded in making good money from selling crafts. For the curiosity seekers, there was no limit to the voyeuristic opportunities at some of the other ethnic villages.[32]

In addition to reservation bands and other Indian performing groups, there were again adaptations of Indian music. One exposition orchestral concert at the Festival Hall under conductor Alfred Ernst featured several American compositions, among them *Dawn,* a new orchestral work by Arthur Farwell, the young New England composer, based on a tune from the Omaha collection. Another program indicates that Ernest Kroeger's *March of the Indian Phantoms* had been written expressly for the Festival Orchestra. The exposition band also played an adaptation of Carlos Troyer's fantastical *Ghost Dance of the Zuñi Indians.* In the San Francisco pavilion, an automated piano, which continuously played a roll of "Indian music" by Troyer, fascinated one local newspaper reporter who felt that this newfangled vehicle for the "melodies of poor Lo"—a character in a Bret Harte story—merited a feature story.[33]

"Indian Talks"

By 1904, what Fletcher had called the "wild flowers" of Indian song had already taken root. Fletcher's little published collection became the basis for a series of lecture-recitals given in cities and towns all across the country by Farwell, who had just returned from music studies in Germany and France. Farwell's series of lectures (with titles along the lines of "Music and Myth of the American Indians and Its Relation to American Composers") was popular and received wide and favorable attention in the press. In his early lecture-recitals (fig. 13) he generally featured his own adaptations, one of which was an item quoted on the program itself, the "Old Man's Love Song" from his *American Indian Melodies* of 1901). Increasingly, he included settings by others. At a lecture-recital given on 15 March 1906 at the Hall of the Twentieth Century Club in Chicago, Farwell began by playing three piano works by Carlos Troyer (*The Sunrise Call, The Coming of Montezuma,* and *The Great Rain Dance*). He followed this with a lecture-demonstration ("Examples of Mythological Expression in Indian Music") and concluded with a performance of *The Melodrama of Hiawatha* for narrator and piano by the Illinois-based composer

TWO LECTURE-RECITALS

I. MUSIC AND MYTH OF THE AMERICAN INDIANS
and its Relation to American Composition

SYNOPSIS:

PART I. The "Great Mystery." Gods, heroes and men. Music,—mythical, legendary and personal. Rendering of simple pianoforte transcriptions of traditional Indian songs, preceded by brief word-pictures of corresponding scenes from myths and legends to which they are related, as follows:

Elemental or Cosmic songs: The Approach of the Thunder God; Inketunga's Thunder Song.

Songs of Human Expression: The Old Man's Love Song; The Mother's Vow; Song of the Leader; Choral.

Songs of the Superhuman: Song to the Spirit; The Ghost Dance.

PART II. The present moment in the development of American music. The demand for music characteristic of America. The "Margin of the Un-German." Popular music. Music of Negroes, Indians and Cowboys. New Inventions of American Composers. Survey of contemporary work for American composition.

PART III. Presentation of original compositions in larger forms, developed from Indian melodies and myths.

Dawn.
"With the Dawn I seek thee."

Ichibuzzhi.
"The enemy comes and calls for you, Ichibuzzhi."

The Domain of Hurakan.
"Hurakan the mighty wind passed over the waters and called forth the earth."

Note. The above program is substantially the same as that given during the 1903-4 Western Tour, and is to be preferred as a general introduction to Indian Music. It is subject to change in accordance with the development of the work.

Figure 13. Program of a lecture-recital by Arthur Farwell, 1904. Farwell Collection, Sibley Music Library, Eastman School of Music.

Saidee Knowland Coe, who used Farwell's transcriptions of Fletcher's songs as thematic ideas for her dramatic accompaniment. Farwell's highly publicized and well-attended lectures at colleges, schools, churches, and clubs — as well as his friendships with composers and other artists along the way who supported his cause and who also believed in the persuasive power of American Indian music as a source for composition—quickly established his national reputation as an influential folklorist and composer.[34]

His lecture-recitals also spawned countless imitations by other performers, many of whom initially relied upon Fletcher and LaFlesche's transcriptions and Farwell's arrangements.[35] Harvey Worthington Loomis, a former pupil of Dvořák's at the National Conservatory, delivered many such talks, for which he created his own remarkable arrangements. His most documented appearance was the "Music of the North American Indian," a recital given with a small group of singers and musicians at Mendelssohn Hall in New York City on 27 April 1905. A reviewer wrote in the *Evening Sun* that the New York audience at first took the concert of Indian music as a joke, "laughing immoderately" while they "applauded with streaming eyes and aching sides." This was, after all, just about the time when vaudeville-style "Indian songs" were becoming wildly popular. But then slowly, "very slowly indeed, [the audience] perspired [*sic*] into a consciousness that here was one of the most interesting, most artistic, and most hopeful musical events of many seasons. [Loomis's] concert, to the elect, was epoch making." The piece that "reached everybody's hearts" was Loomis's *The Sun Worshippers,* his evocation of the American Southwest derived from Troyer's Zuni melody:

> As one woman's voice called from the footlights and another answered from the green room, while that curious artistic thing called "atmosphere" was whispered into the echoes by cello and piano tone colors in harmonic mauve and musical magenta, you forgot the footlights and the green room, you lost the satin gowns, the clawhammer coats, the black bulk of grand piano. This was no call of the wild with tame variations, but a highly idealized work of musical art.[36]

This review conveys some sense of what excited many American composers around the turn of the twentieth century: the possibilities for finding a music redolent of meaning in the American experience. *The Sun Worshippers* was probably also among the first "spatial performances" that used echo effects to imagine native America.[37]

Other "informances" to follow on Loomis's coattails were the "Indian Music Lectures" delivered by Troyer himself (1905–9); the all-Indian "American Music" concerts of Mrs. Lansing P. Wood (ca. 1914) with Charles T. Griffes at the piano; the "Indian Music Talks" by Pittsburgh-born music critic and composer Charles Wakefield Cadman (first with the tenor Paul Kennedy Harper in 1909–12, then, and more significantly, with the Cherokee-Creek mezzo-soprano Tsianina Redfeather in 1912–15); and "Songs, Stories, and Legends of the American Indian" by the music educator and arranger Thurlow

Lieurance (first with Princess Watahwasso, a Penobscot mezzo-soprano, then with his wife Edna Wooley in 1918–27). Troyer's sources were purportedly from Cushing's expeditions, but his presentations were dramatic invocations largely constructed to appeal to audiences' fanciful imaginations. (His published lecture reads like a scenario for a 1940s Hollywood escapist romance.) Cadman and Lieurance, like Frederick Burton before them, undertook fieldwork to procure their own "Indian music," although Cadman also relied heavily on the previous work of Fletcher and others.[38] Cadman's and Lieurance's series were also followed with interest by the major music periodicals, including *Musical America, Musical Courier,* the *Etude,* and the (Chicago) *Music News.*

Ethnologists younger than Fletcher apparently had similar expectations early in their careers for the flowering of Indian music in Western culture. Frances Densmore (1867–1957), for example, used Farwell's *Dawn* in 1903 to illustrate the application of Indian tunes to modern composition. In 1905 Natalie Curtis (1875–1921)—who, prior to her ethnological interests, had studied composition in Germany—experimented with harmonizations by making her own piano arrangements to corn-grinding songs of Laguna Pueblo. Cadman, Farwell, Curtis and others who lectured on behalf of Indian customs sometimes met with mixed response, even ridicule. Although President Theodore Roosevelt occasionally endorsed such works on or about American Indians—including Curtis's pathbreaking song collection *The Indians' Book* (1907)—his statements elsewhere made it clear that he viewed the Indians as the primary representatives of the antiprogressive principle in his vision of the West. He was merciless in his ridicule of the "foolish sentimentalists" who sought to protect and preserve the culture of reservation Indians. By the 1920s most ethnologists had discarded the idea that Indian music as a representative American folk culture should be incorporated into concert music. Although folk traditions later played a significant role in the classical music of Depression-era America, the two genres of folk and classical were increasingly seen as entirely distinct forms of cultural expression.[39]

At the close of the nineteenth century, the influences of both anthropology and popular culture stimulated composers to respond to progressivism's hold on the imagination, and Indian music seemed intrinsically a part of this response. The debates that ensued over the use of American Indian music often degenerated into arguments about whether so-called American music should absorb traits of Indian music in order to reflect the national character (if there ever was one such thing). Dvořák's visit to the Chicago Exposition in 1893 and his remarks on this subject sparked a controversy that provokes intriguing discussion even today. MacDowell's "Indian" Suite (1896), discussed in the next chapter, served as the central defining object of this debate, not only for its role in kindling much of the rhetorical fire but also for stimulating others to follow in its path.

6

The Nationalism Controversy: Quotation or Intonation?

In the 1890s, composers and music critics in the United States launched a debate about an idiomatic American concert music and its supposed roots in folk music. The debate—analogous to similar discussions in Bohemia, Norway, and Russia—considered the similarities between (principally) Native American, African American, and Anglo-American musics, even though many argued that dramatic differences in social context and meaning rendered the first of these an inassimilable exotic in contrast with the others. The notion of Indian music as a component of nationalism nevertheless persisted well into the twentieth century. It would seem that composers' attraction to such music suggests not nationalism—or at least not nationalism exclusively—but a powerful curiosity about difference and a sensibility toward seeking a musical language that would express degrees of otherness within American society. With this perspective in mind, I wish to examine some of the ideas debated by composers and critics at the turn of the twentieth century, especially those that specifically addressed the concept of what is "Indian," in order to uncover nuances of meaning beneath American expressions of musical nationalism. Several of Antonín Dvořák's American compositions, along with Edward MacDowell's "Indian" Suite, were central works in this debate.

Indian Music and American Music

Given every nineteenth-century schoolchild's familiarity with Indians' role in American history and in literary romances, it hardly seems unusual that many composers should weave musical fancy around an Indian legend or two. Unlike the sculptor Augustus Saint-Gaudens, who created a large marble study on a Hiawatha theme in 1872 and who later proclaimed Indian subjects "the youthful sin of every American artist," some composers returned repeatedly to Indian sources, especially in the late 1890s and early 1900s.[1] This might be explained as merely a naive romance with Indian lore were it not for the fact that American Indian subjects proliferated in American culture generally during these decades, a fact that cannot be overlooked in any discussion of the music. Indian subjects emerged in novels, plays, films, fashion, even graphic design. So-called "Indian music"—often short descriptive works—loomed fairly prominently as an aesthetic phenomenon. This music—unlike that based on New England revival hymns, and perhaps even more than that based on African American spirituals—presents thorny analytic and ethical problems. Understandably, the writings of more sociologically oriented music historians—Gilbert Chase and Bruno Nettl, for example—have expressed the injustices in the (mis)representations of one culture by another. Native American music, many ethnomusicologists have argued, is inherently incompatible with Western musical practices.

The complex notions that Indian musics could or should contribute to the formation of an American national style persisted for over thirty years. For much nineteenth-century instrumental music, national ideologies form the silent, often unacknowledged background to creative activity. "To select Indian tunes because they are useful is one thing," wrote John Tasker Howard at the end of this phase (1929). "To choose them for nationalistic purposes is a different matter entirely, for they are American in the geographic sense alone." What else truly defined the American nation, one might respond to Howard, if not the fact of different groups being thrown together, in part, by geography? Political debates about American nationalism have always hinged on this central tenet. Yet the complexity of the issues surrounding the borrowing of Indian music and their links with musical nationalism during the years of America's emergence as a world power have seldom been suggested. The use of Indian themes, particularly in concert music, was often seen as a blatant attempt to forge a uniquely American style that would parallel European models of nationalism. These ideas had long been discussed in American music circles, at least since the days of William Henry Fry and George Frederick

Bristow's direct encouragement. It was again nourished in the mid–1890s by Dvořák and his network of students at the National Conservatory in New York, some of whom explicitly advocated using American Indian music as one source for a distinctively American school of composition. (Dvořák's interest in native America, with all due respect to Saint-Gaudens, was hardly a "youthful sin.")[2]

Other composers and writers, though, have stressed (or stressed at the time) quite different motivations for incorporating native songs and dances. Charles Sanford Skilton, writing the entry on "American Indian music" for Oscar Thompson's *International Cyclopedia of Music and Musicians* in 1938, believed that the ritualistic practices of many North American Indian cultures were disappearing and could only be sustained through art. His essay began with studies of "aboriginal" music and dovetailed into composers' use of that music, as if the latter were an outgrowth (and even a logical continuation) of the former. Though his philosophy remained implicit, Skilton seemed to believe that the only living Indian music was that which had been transformed into character pieces, string quartets, and symphonic works.[3] The notion to salvage North American folklore by encasing it in Western-style concert music no doubt stemmed in part from similar attempts on the part of Europeans to increase the social status of their own native folk music. As more American Indians yielded to government-run schools, thereby assimilating into Western ideals of civilization, it seemed that their rituals and myths would eventually be forgotten. By aiming to capture the spirit of Indian life in musical composition, as others had tried to do in various genres—for example, Mary Austin with poetry and Edward Curtis in photography—American music suddenly acquired social and political urgency, thereby imparting a sense of higher purpose to the form as art.

Reacting to Indian music as a source for composition, some critics emphasized problems inherent in the use of borrowed folk song. For a paper on American music delivered in 1913—when musical Indianism was ubiquitous—Oscar Sonneck, first music librarian at the Library of Congress, argued that quality had nothing to do with the mere use of folk songs and that none of the compositions based on American Indian music had as yet attained what he called "high artistic value." "If the American composer's imagination is so poverty-stricken," Sonneck wrote, "that his salvation depends on mortgaging himself to Zunis, Apaches, Chippewas, etc., he might just as well stop composing." Sonneck qualified his objections, however, by admitting that "some very enjoyable and artistically highly successful experiments" had been accomplished using rhythms and melodies from Indian song.[4]

Sonneck didn't name any pieces, but by 1913 there were hundreds of works by composers from Boston to California based on Indian themes. While many critics and historians were lukewarm about the idea, they saw these experiments as part of a movement—an "Indianist movement," as Gilbert Chase labeled it. Writing some forty years after Sonneck, Chase linked all music based on Indian themes or subjects with nationalist ideologies and refuted, even more categorically than Sonneck, any lingering aesthetic achievement in this music, which he viewed as belonging to a transitory—thus extinct—phase of American musical development. According to Chase, attempts to create "representative American music" out of Indian material were based on a fallacy: "Indian tribal music was not part of the main stream of American culture. It was an interesting but essentially exotic branch that one could follow for a time as a digression, a diversion from the European heritage. But if followed to its source it led to a primitive culture that had nothing in common with prevailing norms and trends of American civilization."[5] Instead of "utilizing" Indian music (by which Chase probably meant quotation and development), twentieth-century composers were more likely to be interested in tribal music, if at all, more as a "manifestation of primitive cultural patterns" than as a source for a hypothetical musical nationalism.[6]

Dismissive views such as Sonneck's and Chase's held the dominant critical position in the first three quarters of the twentieth century. Dissenters, however, noted the use of Indian music as (affirmatively) anti-European and anti-Romantic. Writing only two years after Chase, cultural historian A. Irving Hallowell drew attention to what he interpreted as a conscious effort in the last decade of the nineteenth century to link the interest in Indian music not with nationalist ideologies but with the rising tide of European modernism: "Unlike the situation in Europe, there was no older tradition of folk music in America on which composers might draw. Following this, the 'modern' type of musical idiom began to gain ground and some American composers discovered that Indian music had anticipated some of the devices that were being exploited by composers of modern music. It was in this historical context that American composers turned to the Indians."[7]

Hallowell raised an interesting point. Some American native musics *did* use different pitch systems from Western music, though composers wouldn't try to incorporate these until the 1960s. As early as the 1880s, as noted previously, German musicologists had raised the question of how to notate the microtonal intervals heard in the music of visiting Bella Coolas, and nondiatonic scales were uniformly cited as a prominent feature of most North American indigenous musics. Moreover, many Indian styles used different metrical subdivisions for the singer and drum, and even Fillmore's 1893 settings incorporated polymeter (6/8 against 4/8, for example) to convey this quality. In Hallowell's view, some composers engaged in musical appropriation in order to create a fusion of two essentially different musical traditions. He saw a positive cultural force in this activity, whether or not such techniques would lead to a musical avant-garde. After highlighting Edward MacDowell's initial success with his "Indian" Suite—an oddly conservative example to be citing in 1957, but historically a significant impetus at the turn of the century—Hallowell added that an increasing number of American composers had made excursions to the western reservations. Thus "Indian themes were handled freely in the composition of original works; an excellent example of the principle of selective borrowing and adaptation of culture elements."[8]

Composers in the 1890s such as Dvořák, MacDowell, and Amy Beach, or lesser-knowns such as Frederick Burton or some of Dvořák's students—Henry Schoenefeld or Rubin Goldmark—did not go to reservations to be inspired to write Indian music. Nevertheless, they each found their way to Indian music—or Indian music found its way to them—in written sources or performing groups at world's fairs, touring medicine shows, or academic societies. Around 1898, however, this dynamic began to change, and reservation Indians (as well as the distinctive identities of specific tribal groups) took on greater significance for composers in search of American roots.

A Bohemian Catalyst

In 1893, the year of the Columbian Exposition and Turner's "frontier thesis," the idea that songs and dances of native American peoples should be snatched up by composers looking for American substance was not widely viewed or discussed. Only a handful of people had, by that time, experimented with Indian music quotation. Given his prestige in the classical music world, Dvořák proved to be a dominant catalyst for this movement. During his residence in the United States from 1892 to 1895, Dvořák taught at the National Conservatory of Music in New York and published several articles on the possibilities for a national style of music in America. His well-known and often quoted suggestion that American composers tap into "Negro" and "Indian" themes has so frequently been taken out of context that the issue needs sorting out, particularly in crucial matters of chronology and emphasis.

In fact Dvořák at first suggested only the use of African American music in his *New York Herald* article of 21 May 1893 (which appeared within days of the completion of his symphony "From the New World"). But on 15 December of that year, seven months later, he added Indian music as well (in the phrase that I italicize here): "Since I have been in this country I have been deeply interested in the national music of the Negroes *and the Indians*. The character, the very nature of a race is contained in its national music. For that reason my attention was at once turned in the direction of these native melodies."[9] We might read these three sentences today and wonder how they are connected. What does Dvořák mean by the term "national"? A white musician reading this in the 1890s might have assumed that the "national music" under consideration was that of the dominant society—a unified culture for America as a whole. But Dvořák mentions two separate racial categories, suggesting that *each* has its own *national* music. Perhaps this European composer thought of "nation" as a single racial entity, a common belief in the nineteenth century, though largely discredited today. (Even Sousa had organized his 1890 anthology of *National, Patriotic, and Typical Airs* by nation: Apache precedes Abyssinia, Cherokee precedes China, and Iroquois precedes Italy.) Perhaps Dvořák meant that it was the responsibility of any serious composer—speaking for himself, of course, but also by way of advice—to study the native music of one's country, whatever its ethnic roots. It was by steeping himself in his own region's ethnically complex Czech folk music, after all, that he had been able to free himself from the influence of his German and Austrian neighbors and find his own voice as a composer. It seemed logical, by extension, that the same thing was possible in the United States, that is, that the various "nationalities" (or ethnicities) that made up the country would be the ideal place for any American-born composer to turn. By the time Dvořák arrived in the United States, American Indians were largely a dispirited and defeated people with any sense of nationhood among them destroyed or at least temporarily suppressed. In the New York metropolitan version of America in which Dvořák lived, he encountered plenty of black people, including several among his students at the conservatory. But what happened in the seven months between the completion of the Ninth Symphony and the essay quoted above that broadened Dvořák's interests to include Indian music?

Between the appearance of the two *Herald* articles, Dvořák traveled through much of the heart of the eastern United States and ultimately ventured as far west as Omaha, Nebraska. He spent two summer months in a largely Czech community in Spillville, Iowa. There he saw three Kickapoo and Algonquin Indians (pitchmen Big Moon, John Fox, and John Deer) selling medicinal herbs and performing tribal dances at the local inn. He also composed two important works in Spillville: a string quartet (F Major, op. 96) and a string quintet (E♭ Major, op. 97). As John Clapham asserted, these exhibit "undeniable Indian influence," a point that Dvořák himself intimated in his writings.[10] In mid-August, he attended the World's Columbian Exposition in Chicago. At his hotel, he received a copy of Alice Fletcher's just-published *Study of Omaha Indian Music* (June 1893), sent to him by John Fillmore on behalf of the author.

Although Dvořák had heard Indian music before that time, he probably would not have had a previous opportunity to study a group of songs in transcription. He also saw and heard Kwakiutl Indians (and possibly Navajos and Iroquois) sing on the exposition's Midway Plaisance. During this same trip he visited the Minnehaha Falls near St. Paul, Minnesota, the spot where he supposedly jotted down the theme to the Larghetto of his Sonatina for Violin and Piano (op. 100), a theme that also exhibits "Indian" characteristics. In an effort to provide Dvořák with the proper atmosphere for his proposed *Hiawatha* opera, his patron Jeannette Thurber took him, in her words, "to see Buffalo Bill's Indians dance as a suggestion for the ballet."[11]

During a speech given in the Music Hall at the Chicago Exposition on 12 August ("Czech Day"), Dvořák could not have been more explicit in expressing his belief in a national musical style in the United States: "Every nation has its music. There is Italian, German, French, Bohemian, Russian; why not American music? The truth of this music depends upon its characteristics, its colour. I do not mean to take these melodies, plantation, Creole or Southern, and work them out as themes; that is not my plan. But I study certain melodies until I become thoroughly imbued with their characteristics."[12] By this point Dvořák would have had an opportunity to study the characteristics of at least one repertoire, the Omaha melodies in Fletcher's publication (colored by Fillmore's harmonizations, of course) and probably a few others as well, since he no doubt saw a copy of Sousa's widely distributed collection of national songs.

Despite these encounters with Indian song, however, Dvořák actually mentioned it very little in his statements about a national music. His only public reference to his own active interest in Indian music occurred in the single article quoted above (the only reference, that is, with the exception of a later instance in which he quotes the earlier article and proceeds to qualify it). Curiously, Dvořák had noted in 1892 that, while examining entries for the National Conservatory's composers' competition, he had occasionally come across a work expressing something other than the run-of-the-mill German style, something reflecting "another spirit, other thoughts, another colouring flash[ing] forth, in short, something Indian (something à la Bret Harte). I am very curious how things will develop."[13] Dvořák's reception of Fletcher's book in August 1893 is an important and often overlooked incident in discussions of the composer's position on a national American style. Only after he had been able to study the songs in print did he include Indian music in addition to African American as an alternative to Anglo-Saxon sources. The relatively disinterested opinion of this Bohemian nationalist provided an authoritative stamp of approval for younger composers interested in establishing a connection between Indian song and art music. (MacDowell, considered one of America's most gifted young stars in the field of classical composition, was one of these.)

The timing of Dvořák's exposure to American Indian music is important in another respect. As Michael Beckerman has pointed out, Dvořák incorporated some sketches for a planned *Hiawatha* opera into his symphony "From the New World."[14] Unfortunately, there has been a tendency to conflate this compositional activity with his remarks on Indian music. In fact, though, the symphony was complete in full score by 24 May 1893, whereas Dvořák did not see Indians perform in Iowa and Chicago nor receive the copy of Omaha songs until later that summer (though he probably would have heard some form of real or simulated "Indian music" in the Wild West show he saw that spring). By 1895 Dvořák had come to recognize the broad diversity of American musical experience, and in his famous *Harper's* article "Music in America" he expanded the national pool to include all sources of folk musics.

In this same essay Dvořák went on to say that "Since I came to this country . . . I have finished a couple of compositions in chamber music, which will be played by the Kneisel String Quartet of Boston. . . . They are both written upon the same lines as this Symphony and both breathe the same Indian spirit. One is a String Quartet in F major, and the other a Quintet in E-flat for two violins, two violas and violoncello." There has been some confusion over Dvořák's interest in Native American subject matter and his actual use of any Indian music. What did he mean by "breathing the Indian spirit"? Could this be accomplished by reading Washington Irving's *Tour of the Prairies,* Longfellow's *Hiawatha,* or Karl May's tales of Winnetou? Does an "Indian spirit" need a quotation—or, at least, direct imitation—of Indian music? We could also ask the same question regarding a perceived "Czech spirit" in some of Dvořák's other music. (Does a work need to have a Czech nationalist association such as words or a title, or quote a Czech folk song, to sound Czech?) Dvořák's American works, particularly the "New World" Symphony, the String Quintet, the Piano Suite, and the Larghetto movement of the Sonatina for Violin and Piano (the "canzonetta") have all been said to contain some evidence that Dvořák heard, responded positively to, and incorporated something of the spirit of Indian music. None of these works are labeled in any way to indicate a Native American content (although the canzonetta was later published under the title "Dvořák's Indian Lament," evidence to the fact that some performers and audiences *thought* it sounded Indian).

To address this thorny problem, we can find an important and underestimated model in Boris Asafiev's theory of intonation (*intonazia* in transliterated Russian). The theory was developed in the 1930s and 1940s as a means for explaining Socialist Realism in music. Yet Asafiev drew on procedures that had been in place well before that time, reaching all the way back to the early nineteenth century. The theory is defined, as Malcolm Brown has summarized it, as "any phonic manifestation of life or reality, perceived and understood (directly or metaphorically) as a carrier of meaning."[15] This admittedly broad definition encapsulates three categories of intonations. In the first category are the simplest and most direct associations, such as those that mimic identifiable sounds or characteristics or replicate natural phenomena. The second stems from association with other art forms, including the medium of language: poetry, painting, dance, or narrative programs can influence musical intonation. The third category includes those derived through purely musical reference—melodies, rhythms, motives, or characteristic turns of folk song, a style period, or even another composed work. Asafiev's categories of intonations, particularly the third, enable us to see how apparent sources of folk music can be absorbed into one's musical style so that even if the initial source is obscured, the essence remains—in effect, becoming part of the composer's language. (Or, as Dvořák phrased it, he studied the melodies until he himself became "thoroughly imbued with their character.") Theoretically, these types of intonations are difficult to prove, since they rest to some degree on connections made by the listener. But they *can* be illustrated by comparing the episode with surrounding passages, or with analogous passages in the composer's other works.

Beckerman has suggested comparing Dvořák's Piano Suite with the *Poetic Tone Pictures* for piano that precedes it in Dvořák's collected works. Beginning with the earlier work, "one passes from a world of virtuosity, chromaticism, ghoulishness, bacchanale, funeral marches, and weird recollections of the past to a clean, open space." If two works by the same composer written in different times and places can be shown to yield different stylistic intonations, might not different passages in the same work be compared for the same reason? For the slow movement of the "New World" Symphony, Beckerman has suggested three possible models in which the movement might reflect the influence of "Hiawatha's Wooing" from Longfellow: (1) reflecting merely the "mood" of the canto, (2) following the narrative details very closely, or (3) some middle ground between the two. He goes on to argue convincingly for the third model, using published and unpublished documents relating to Dvořák and to the writings of the composer's champion, music critic Henry Krehbiel. This interpretation makes sense, for such a model could be argued for many programmatic symphonies and suites from Liszt to Rimsky-Korsakov. Beckerman demonstrates, for example, how the middle section of the movement in C♯ minor depicts Hiawatha's and Minnehaha's long homeward trek, "a consonant and timeless journey through primeval America."[16]

Example 7. Dvořák, String Quintet in E♭ Major, op. 97 (1893), mvt. 4, mm. 33–36.

Since scholars have written extensively on Dvořák's musical style during his American years, I will only explore a few relevant examples here. Several marked passages occur in the String Quintet, a work written at Spillville in 1893 with no explicit "Indian" anchors. John Clapham has already noted the striking similarity between the Native American melody that Dvořák heard the medicine troupe sing at Spillville—and which was also transcribed by his traveling companion Jan Kovařík—with the second subject of the first movement. In an essay about this quintet, Jan Smaczny pursues this connection. But he does not cite—indeed, he probably would have thought it too speculative to do so—two features of the second movement: the rhythmic ostinato at the opening (♫♩♩♩|♩♩♫♩) and the shape and rhythm, if not the modal inflection, of the opening theme led by the first violin. Another example that Smaczny notes is the second subject of the fourth movement. This passage is not only pentatonic (ex. 7), but it consists of repeating descending arcs, it is harmonized in the minor mode, and Dvořák—like Burton in his Kwakiutl-based piece noted previously—uses an accompaniment of two against a melody in three. Smaczny concludes, however, that the passage's ancestry is completely European and can be traced back to the finales of two well-known piano trios, Schubert's E♭ Major (op. 100) and Smetana's G Minor (op. 15). I would argue differently. The influence of these two chamber works could certainly have been subliminal if Dvořák did not acknowledge them directly. But the composer's allusion to elements indigenous to some North American Indian groups—descending pentatonic melodies and, most important, melodies sung in an independent rhythm from the drum—would suggest that Dvořák imparted an American folk intonation, via Native American music, to this section of his quintet. (David Beveridge has also argued—quite persuasively—for Dvořák's distinctively American rather than European use of pentatonicism in his F-Major Quartet.) We can compare the second subject to the opening section of the movement, which is closer in tone to Dvořák's noted G♭-major *Humoresque,* graceful, coy, and not self-consciously ethnic in tone. With a few sustained half notes (each inflected by a grace note, an "exotic" Indian marker, as we have discussed), Dvořák introduces an entirely new character with this second theme. As Beckerman puts it, "the G-minor episode . . . takes us into another world, which for Dvořák would have been simply 'Indian.'" If Dvořák had wanted to set an example for his American students, wouldn't he have rather avoided obvious references to Viennese and Bohemian chamber works?[17]

In the Piano Suite of 1894, Dvořák similarly relies upon intonations of Indian music. The distinctive opening theme of the first movement, which returns cyclically in the last, is based on a descending pentatonic melody. As we have seen, this device alone is no marker for "Indian," least of all in Dvořák, who used pentatonic themes in his Czech music as well. But his iambic inflection of the melody (♪♩.) in measure 3—and in the parallel spot in measure 11—suggests the rhythm of northern Plains–style singing.[18] (MacDowell later draws on this same rhythmic inflection for his explicitly "Indian" music.) In the second movement Dvořák sets the C♯-minor melody in triplets against a duple figure in the left hand. This could of course also be a Czech influence, as the *Slavonic Dances* also contain this device and the melody here does not otherwise reflect Indian characteristics. But for the cadence in mm. 21–22 (identified in ex. 8), Dvořák repeats what he did in the Largo of the "New World" Symphony: he modifies the dominant seventh chord leading to the minor tonic by one note, a note that allows for the melody to contain a falling minor third. (In this case, the note is B falling to G♯, when in fact the note would have made more diatonic sense in Dvořák's normative style as an A♯.) This cadential falling third is not particularly endemic to European folk song (at least Western European folk song), and it must have been partly reflective of the "Indian spirit" that Dvořák wanted to breathe into his music. This same cadential adjustment appears in the third movement, where, as in the "New

Example 8. Dvořák, Suite for Piano, op. 98 (1894), mvt. 2.

World" Largo, Dvořák plays it first "straight"—with a falling second—and then again with the falling minor third (mm. 11–12 and mm. 15–16).

In the Western musical language, a drooping third cadence in minor has a mournful quality to it. (I would argue that the same holds true for this figure in a Native American context, at least in the modern world. In the 1994 PBS documentary *500 Nations,* the singer Chief Hawk Pope relied on this melodic cadence to underscore moments of great sadness and tragedy such as the Trail of Tears sequence.) Dvořák again used this cadence in the Larghetto of his Sonatina, although by then it had become a feature of his American style, turning up in several passages of a quiet, reflective nature. As late as 1910 Fritz Kreisler transcribed the single movement as "Indian Lament in G Minor" for violin and piano (as did Gaspar Cassadó for cello and piano in 1914), and he included his adaptation of the "Indian Lament" on his American tour of 1915 (and recorded it).[19] Perhaps Dvořák employed the pentatonic minor descent in the second measure and the cadential figure in the violin in the fourth measure to evoke an "Indian spirit" in the natural beauty of the North American landscape, but, if so, he never referred to the matter in words. In his American works Dvořák was not so much trying to imagine native America as he was drawing what he perceived of native America into his own style in order to "Americanize" it (a process that harks back to the practices of the eighteenth-century

Tammany societies and indeed even to the Boston Tea Party). Finally, another important intonation, discussed in chapter 4 (see example 4 there), is the "tonic-minor minor-seventh" chord (i^7) notable in the Scherzo movement of the "New World" Symphony. Many composers, both in classical and popular fields, drew on this sonority. The semantic richness of Dvořák's "Indian" intonations—or perhaps one should say their semantic ambiguity—illustrates why controversy raged around this component of American national music.[20]

Intonation in MacDowell's Suite

Just a little over half a year after Dvořák left America (in April 1895), the premiere of Edward MacDowell's Second Suite for orchestra, subtitled "Indian," revived the debate about Indian music and nationalism. MacDowell, a central figure in American music in the late 1890s, also served as a model for other composers. His popular and critical success with this suite, coupled with expectations surrounding his career as an emerging "nationalist" composer—when in fact he abhorred the idea—led others to improve on his model by seeking out new Indian sources on which to base their music. There was even some disagreement as to who had shown the way, Dvořák or MacDowell. Writers from the early part of the twentieth century are quick to acknowledge that MacDowell began his orchestral work on "indigenous folk music" before Dvořák publicized his opinions on such in the United States (i.e., that it was "just about finished" by September 1892—as he later noted—would have been prior to Dvořák's influence).[21]

The 1891 pencil sketch of the "Dirge" at the Boston Public Library, the earliest completed movement, conveys no information that it was composed as part of a larger work, let alone an "Indian" suite. Its tonal and harmonic language, in fact, resembles that of MacDowell's earlier symphonic poems rather than the later suite's self-consciously "Indian" inflections. Nevertheless, MacDowell did say in a much later interview (*San Francisco Chronicle,* 1903), that the "Indian" Suite reflected the results of his studies of Indian music and that the "Dirge" represented the lament of an Indian woman for her dead son. Musicologist Francis Brancaleone has made much of this claim, even going so far as to argue that MacDowell reused the Kiowa song supposedly quoted in the "Dirge" elsewhere in his non-Indian music. This is a fascinating hypothesis, but it requires that we believe that MacDowell found the Lydian-inflected 5–♯4–3–1 in his source for Indian music—Theodore Baker's *On the Music of the North American Indians* (1882)—rather than in dozens of other possible places, including many "exotic" works of the Russian nationalist composers whom MacDowell emulated. I believe Brancaleone's is a tenuous argument, for with the exception of those four notes, MacDowell uses nothing else from the Kiowa song (Baker XXIII). Nowhere does he say he took the melody for the "Dirge" from Baker. In fact he makes it a point in the same interview to state that the "Dirge" was not only his favorite of his works but entirely his own invention, a point recently stressed by Richard Crawford. It is more likely that MacDowell got the idea for an Indian suite following Dvořák's suggestions, since these views were widely aired and hotly debated in MacDowell's hometown of Boston, and then he constructed his other movements around the existing "Dirge."[22]

Little is known about the intent of this suite, aside from a few comments such as the one cited above, those in a short article by Henry Gilbert, MacDowell's pupil at the time (but written nearly twenty years later), some remarks by Mrs. MacDowell after her husband's death, and the brief labels in the score. (No account remains of its preview on two pianos by the Manuscript Society of New York). Again, Asafiev's theory of musical intonation proves useful in revealing how, in this influential work, MacDowell imagined native America. This suite, finished (and perhaps largely composed) in 1895, is often discussed within the context of musical nationalism, a topic crucial to defining America's sense of identity at the close of the nineteenth century. Ironically, however, MacDowell's musical syntax and narrative organization align this work with earlier depictions of the exotic, especially the "Indian war dances" of David, Wallace, Bristow, and others. It also shows familiarity with, or at least a shared aesthetic with, the *Hiawatha* works of Arthur Foote and Louis Coerne, both of whom used opulent harmonies and sonorities derived from Liszt and Wagner to evoke supernatural events in an allegorical setting. Some *Hiawatha* works also used horn-fifth calls, traditionally associated with hunting and pageantry, to summon abstract images of nature as the foundational and unifying source of all life. These musical elements, like the exotic "war dances" discussed in chapter 3, were projections onto Indian subject matter. Except for perhaps the imitation of drum rhythms in some of the war-dance features, they had nothing specifically to do with indigenous North American music.

On the other hand, MacDowell's music reveals the intonations of Indian music such as they were known to this white New England–born composer in the 1890s. First of all, he quotes (and develops) chants transcribed from native America. And yet the elements of his subject — a love scene before the battle, an Indian war, a mother's grief over her dead son, and the village festivities after the war — are deeply rooted in narrative paradigms of folklore. In this sense, MacDowell was more closely aligned with the primitivism of Rousseau than with existential primitivism, like his young friend Hamlin Garland, later author of *Book of the American Indian* (1925), who traveled out West in search of "Indianness." The subject matter of the suite is consistently handled as picturesque rather than empirical (compared with, say, Mahler's use of German *Wunderhorn* legends or Stravinsky's use of Russian folk songs). MacDowell remains the outsider, the observer, and he fails to find a point of connection with his subject. For this reason, this prominent work of musical nationalism in retrospect also emerges as a principal example of musical exoticism. The roots of the work's exoticism cannot be separated from any discussion about its borrowing and adaptation of American Indian music, since in the nineteenth century the exotic was entirely bound up with issues of authenticity.

MacDowell was born in New York and lived and studied in Paris (1876–78) and Germany (1878–88) before returning to the United States. As a virtuoso pianist-composer, he performed his own works throughout Europe and America. His greatest compositional influences were his teacher, Joachim Raff, and Franz Liszt, who championed his early works in Europe. His Boston years (1888–96) were the richest and most productive of his compositional life. By 1896 he had accepted an invitation to become Columbia University's first professor of music. (Hiring MacDowell was, in part, Columbia's answer to the success of the American composers' program at the National Conservatory.) In New York, where he thereafter made his home, MacDowell continued to compose, but he gave much of his attention to teaching with specific intent to "treat music historically and aesthetically as an element of liberal culture."[23] A cab injury in 1904, however, rendered him incapacitated until his death in 1908.

MacDowell's Suite No. 2 was first performed in public concert at the Metropolitan Opera House in New York on 23 January 1896 by the Boston Symphony under Emil Paur. It was generously and favorably reviewed. Theodore Baker was among those invited to this performance. He attended and afterward sent MacDowell an enthusiastic note. Interest in the suite quickly grew. The same performers gave several performances of the work in Boston's Music Hall; Theodore Thomas and the Chicago Symphony performed it in November 1897 at the Chicago Auditorium; Anton Seidl led the New York Philharmonic in the suite in January 1898; and in 1901 it was heard for the first time in London at a Queen's Hall Promenade Concert under Sir Henry Wood. This was a major international triumph by an American composer, perhaps the first of its kind.[24]

Numerous program notes and reviews exist, though I have not found these especially probative about the Indian content of the work. The only indications for each movement in the score itself are those of tempo and character. The moniker "Indian" is nowhere stated on the title page or at the head of the score. In a preface MacDowell suggested brief descriptive titles (those in italics below).

1. *Legend:* Not fast. With much dignity and character. [Then] Twice as fast. With decision.
2. *Love Song:* Not fast. Tenderly.
3. *In War-time:* With rough vigor, almost savagely. [Then] Slow. Tempo I.
4. *Dirge:* Dirge-like, mournfully.
5. *Village Festival:* Swift and light.

MacDowell excluded these labels from the printed programs for the New York and Boston concerts since he did not wish to suggest any precise "Indian" content of the suite; he left that to his listeners' imagination. The design of the work perhaps resembles more closely a symphony in five movements rather than a suite: the "Legend" being in quasi-sonata form; the "Love Song" being an inserted character piece; "In War-time" serving as a grotesque scherzo in 2/4 (Brahms's Fourth of 1885 had a scherzo in 2/4); a slow, elegiac fourth movement (presaging Mahler's Fifth of 1902); and a bright, dancelike finale. This grand-scale design brings with it, of course, the narrative potential and the philosophical implications of a late Romantic German symphony. Themes and motives take on a developmental life of their own, and their recurrence and transformation suggest to the listener that MacDowell's music conveys some kind of story. How does it do that, and how can analysis of this work bring the story into the foreground? These are questions that perhaps have no definitive answers. But *some* answers are well within the grasp of what we do know about this suite and what MacDowell's music implies by its character and design.

One aspect distinguishes this suite from other symphonic works of its time: it was said to be the first known orchestral work to incorporate Indian themes. Certainly this was true by the date of its first performance, taking into account such examples as Fillmore's *Indian Fantasia No. 1* (1890 but unpublished) and Burton's *Dance of Pau-Puk-Keewis* (presumably 1893, but not performed and published until 1898). For his Indian chants, MacDowell turned to Baker's thesis, his attention having been drawn to the work by Henry F. Gilbert, a student who in 1890 had been hired by Edward Curtis to transcribe Indian music from cylinders. "The thematic material of this work," MacDowell noted in the preface to the 1897 published score, "*has been suggested* for the most part by melodies of North American Indians" (italics mine). MacDowell's precise wording is crucial here. "Their occasional similarity to Northern European themes," MacDowell continued, "seems to the author a direct testimony in corroboration of Thorfinnkarlsefin's [*sic*] Saga." We'll return to

MacDowell's peculiar allusion later in this chapter. In the longer unpublished version of this note, however (in MacDowell's manuscript full score), the composer added: "The opening theme of No. 3, for instance, is very similar to the [presumably Russian] one made use of by Rimsky-Korsakov in the third movement of his symphony 'Antar.' "[25] (MacDowell was invoking an intonational model here: because the theme *sounded* Russian, he presumed that it was.)

MacDowell used seven known chants from Baker (table 4): two in movements 3 and 5 and one each in the others—if we count the debatable one in the "Dirge." Some of these chants also appear in other movements: the theme for the "Dirge" is introduced in the middle of the third movement and suggested in a fragment near the end of the last movement. No other explicit chants have ever been identified.

Can we assume that these themes would have been recognizable as "Indian" to an 1896 audience? Possibly the descending pentatonic melody played by the flute at the opening of the second movement, with its emphatic snapping iambic rhythms, might have been considered "folklike," at least, if not exactly American Indian. The flute would also have been heard as one of the few possible instruments in the symphony orchestra (beside the bass drum, tambourine, and gourd rattle) that resembles any native instrument. Would audiences in 1896 have been as startled then as they are today in the contrast between the first two themes at the opening of the third movement: the first sounding like an obviously European-derived modal folk song and the second like a cue for attacking Comanches in a film Western? If anything, obvious "Indianisms" such as this latter theme became known *through* MacDowell's work, given its popularity. Some in the original audience could probably recall having heard native music, but recognizing features of borrowed chants in an orchestral composition is another matter entirely. American composers in the 1890s were just beginning to experiment with folk melodies in any form, George Chadwick's works serving as exemplars in this area. (Certainly many American audiences would already have been familiar with the folk-based music of Smetana, Grieg, Tchaikovsky, and other Europeans. But the use of any American folk music—even Appalachian or that of black rural Mississippi—would have been limited to quotations in popular media such as variations and dances and not heard in more elaborate concert works.) Even analogous European composers such as Grieg or Elgar were more likely to imbue their works with the properties of folk song than merely to compose symphonic settings of well-known tunes. It was not, therefore, just the quotations from Baker's dissertation—the supposedly "authentic" Native American melodies—that made MacDowell's suite "Indian." Its Indianness (a "white man's Indianness" to paraphrase Robert Berkhofer) was the combined result

Table 4. Theodore Baker's Themes in Edward MacDowell's "Indian" Suite

MacDowell	Baker	
	page [origin]	transl/number
I—opening subject	60 [102]	II
II—principal theme	68 [118]	XVIII
III—opening two themes	75 [132]	XXXVIII and
	79 [140]	XLIII, 4
IV	70 [122]	XXIII
V	60 [104]	V
V	63 [108]	IX

Note: The Roman numerals correspond to the songs as outlined in chapter 5, note 10.

of (1) the adaptation of the themes, (2) MacDowell's distinctive harmonic progressions, and (3) the narrative structure of the music. All of these, of course, relied upon intonational procedures.

MacDowell never specified a narrative program. He opens the first movement with a loud call from three unison French horns, quoting the first few descending notes of an Iroquois harvest festival song. Baker noted that a harvest festival contained eighty-nine contiguous songs—of which this was the fourth—and that the festival had the character of a divine service. This particular song was always accompanied by a series of equally accented beats. MacDowell dispensed with the beats, but he imparted a sacred tone to the solo horn that quietly answers the opening cry as well as to the solemn restatement of the melody by the strings (not included in ex. 9). The composer asked that this slow introduction be played "with much dignity and character." A few dramatic crescendos on minor chords, some sharp cutaways in dynamics, and a trill on the dominant in the high violins build suspense as MacDowell prepares to introduce a faster tempo (ex. 9, part B). Here, the crisp, light-footed theme is original and modal. It is also surprisingly similar to that of the last movement of Dvořák's "New World" symphony, down to sharing the same key and same modal orientation (E-Hypodorian—the root on E but the melodic ambitus ranging from a fifth above to a fourth below).

MacDowell's use of modal melodies throughout this suite serves as a chief marker of the exotic, or at least of an "archaic" world (which often conveys a similar effect of exoticizing). He invariably couches these in a minor-mode context, as he does here. In this restless E-minor passage MacDowell builds tension between the decisiveness of the quietly surging, but sharply pointed, rhythmic melody (woodwind chords) and the expectation implied by the taut violin trills suspended above. The trills, used as an ominous pedal point,

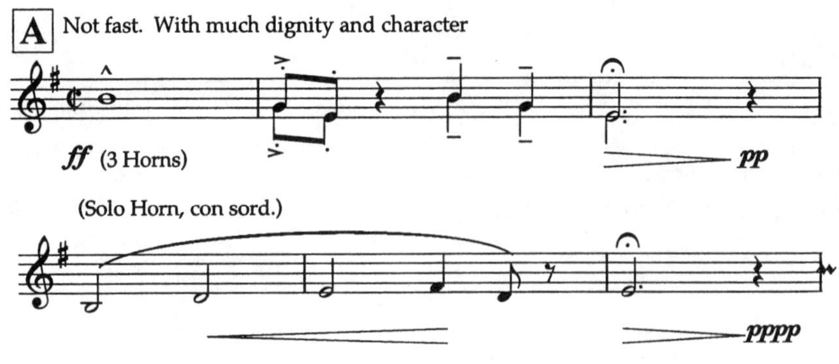

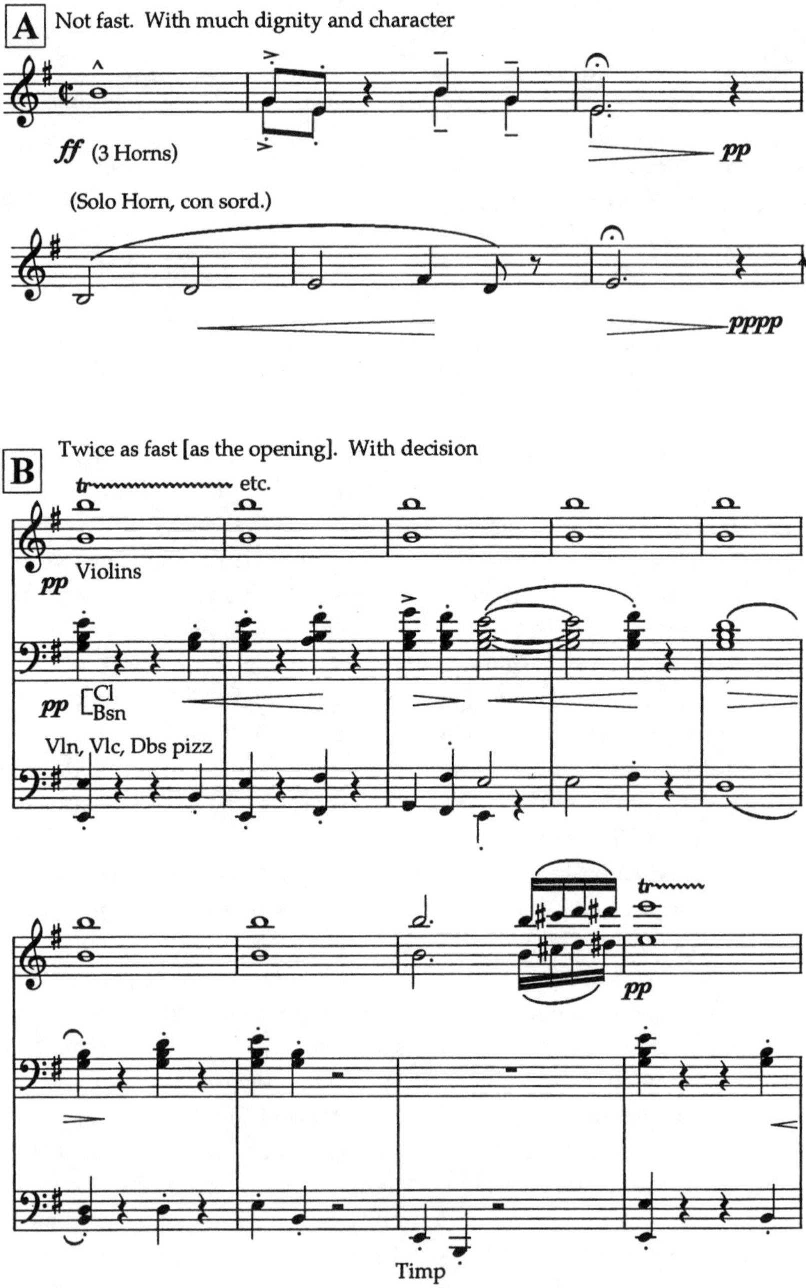

A
Not fast. With much dignity and character
ff (3 Horns)
pp
(Solo Horn, con sord.)
pppp
B
Twice as fast [as the opening]. With decision
tr etc.
pp Violins
pp Cl Bsn
Vln, Vlc, Dbs pizz
tr
pp
Timp

Example 9. Edward MacDowell, "Indian" Suite (1897), mvt. 1: opening horn call and beginning of the fast section.

tr
mf
Fl, Ob
p
Clar
3
(tr)
Hrn, Trp

suggest some impending danger. The opening three measures of the theme serve as a melodic cell for musical development later in this movement. As MacDowell whips up the excitement and sense of conflict—in what would be the bridge of the sonata form—he twice recalls the opening cry of the harvest song, but then dissolves the tension by melting into a lyrical theme for strings in C major.[26] Remaining true to his Germanic training, MacDowell derives his rhapsodic second theme from the first. As the theme builds, however, it takes on a vaguely "American" flavor redolent of Chadwick's style. The arrival point is reached gently; a lone flute plays what seems like a fragment of a melody, possibly even foreshadowing the character if not exactly the theme of the second movement. But the *agitato* character resumes, and a sense of conflict and even danger ensues, led by a curious three-note motive with a Lydian inflection. (In formal terms, this section would seem to be a collapsed development that leads directly back into the bridge section of the recapitulation.) As before, MacDowell twice recalls the opening cry of the harvest song and dissolves into the rhapsodic second theme. This time, though, the theme doesn't hold back as it did first, but instead pushes onward to the climax of the movement—a major-key restatement of the opening horn call. For just a few moments the call sounds heroic, but just as triumph is evoked it is almost immediately denied. With a forceful and sudden switch back to the minor, the movement ends on a tragic note.

The slow second movement is episodic in form, and it is here that MacDowell most reveals the influence of the Russian school. The gentle flute melody at the opening quotes an Iowa love song. Baker noted that young warriors sang this when out riding. In MacDowell it sounds more like a vehicle for courtship—perhaps a lover is playing the flute to seduce his beloved. The warm A-major tone of the opening yields to a more mysterious section in D minor. Eventually the love song returns, but it doesn't have the strength to stop the forward motion established in the middle section. The climax of the movement comes in two waves, the second only half a minute after the first. The passion of Tchaikovsky's symphonic music simmers beneath MacDowell's style here. Clearly some idea of a love relationship—if not an overt sexual act—is suggested in this movement. At last the flute returns in the manner of the opening, and the movement ends quietly, with a few almost halting phrases by the strings and winds.

The two D-minor themes at the opening of the third movement set the tone immediately—rhythmic, forceful, and driving (ex. 10). The subject is clearly war. MacDowell begins by quoting two songs from opposite coasts of the continent: the first considered by peoples on the eastern seaboard to be music of the spirits and sung only at important festivals, the second a boasting song

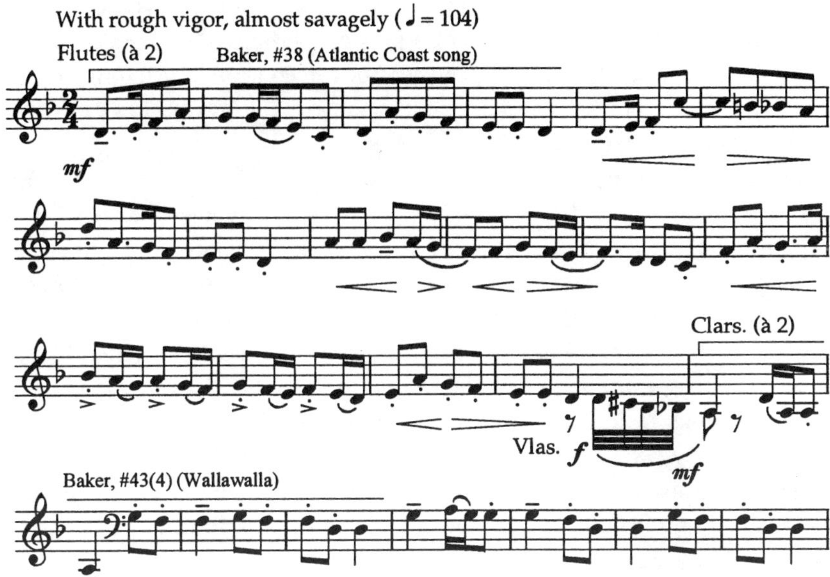

Example 10. MacDowell, "Indian" Suite, mvt. 3: opening.

from the Wallawallas (with the refrain "who would have feared such a human fear, truly!"). MacDowell uses these two melodies (one Dorian, the other tetratonic: D–F–G–A) like different characters in a drama, and the continual building up and falling back through the forward momentum paints vivid scenes of battle. When the high point of the conflict is reached (on a loud diminished chord), the conflict quickly subsides, leaving only the violas murmuring quietly on one note. Mysteriously, a mournful clarinet wails unaccompanied. (It plays the theme of the next movement, but exactly what MacDowell is foreshadowing is unclear.) The sense of conflict returns, and, using the two principal themes, MacDowell builds to a thrilling climax. The end, however, implies neither victory nor tragedy, just swift conclusion.

A quiet slow movement follows with a bell-like pedal in the winds. MacDowell presumably quotes a few notes from a Kiowa song of a mother to her absent son. Baker transcribed her words: "I have not seen him for a long time; there are many young men, but I love one, my son. When he comes back I shall see him; I lie awake every night until he comes; he will rejoice when he sees me again." MacDowell creates a long, winding melody from the few derived notes. The cellos and basses seem to be weeping with each phrase, while the violins and violas throb ominously on the same minor chord. It is difficult to hear this movement without bringing the imagination to bear on these quietly pulsing chords, against which the somber melody of the song sighs and droops. The regularity of the pulse suggests time passing, perhaps the ticking of a clock or, more appropriately, the plodding steps of someone making a long, weary journey. The movement ends with an offstage horn, as if the mother's song is heard only faintly in the distance.[27]

The last movement begins delicately yet joyfully. The first theme comes from a melody Baker labeled as "a song for the Iroquois women's dance." It is pentatonic (E–B–E–C♯–B–A–F♯–E) and rooted in the major mode. Although the basic tempo indication for the movement is "swift and light," MacDowell, perhaps imagining a celebratory dance, whips his orchestra into a flurry of activity, with driving, oscillating fourths in the bassoons, cellos, and double basses pumping wild energy into the rest of the ensemble. After a few minutes of this reveling, he introduces a more serious melody; Baker called it an Iroquois war song. MacDowell first presents it sternly, adding trills and chromatic inflections to create an aura of danger. As the tempo speeds up, one wonders if this will build into another conflict like the earlier movement's. Are we again at war? Suddenly, at the highest point, the bottom drops out and we expect disaster. For a moment MacDowell leaves us hanging in silence. But the piccolos joyfully begin the dancelike opening music, now faster and brighter. Gradually the rest of the orchestra joins in until the solemn opening theme of the first movement's introduction returns, now in major and gloriously harmonized. The work comes to a close with the horns seeming to call out "hurrahs" with their upward octave leaps and the rest of the ensemble responding enthusiastically in the brightly orchestrated final chords.[28]

Is there a hidden program here? The melodies may be Indian-derived, but is the story Indian? If there is, it may allude, like *Hiawatha,* to an imaginary native America steeped in an imaginary past. The Indian themes anchor the work in the geography of America, while lending it a degree of authenticity. In addition, several extramusical influences may have contributed to the suite's decidedly "Indian" allure for its turn-of-the-century listeners.

The first of these was a poetic source. William F. Apthorp, author of the 1896 program notes for the Boston Symphony, noted there that the suite's first movement had been suggested to the composer by a reading of "Miantowona," a poem by Thomas Bailey Aldrich. (MacDowell himself never mentioned this, as far as I have been able to determine.) The poem relates the origins of the water lily in a beautiful young Huron maiden who drowned herself for love. It has the flavor of a white man's campfire story. This may indeed have been its source, since Aldrich, a poet and magazine editor, did not travel much beyond the northeastern literary circles to which he was accustomed. First published in 1881, the poem probably came to MacDowell's attention after his return from Europe in 1888, when he began an aesthetic quest for American culture in literature and painting. Having tried his hand at one *Hiawatha* setting (in an uncompleted work), he may have been attracted to Aldrich's nostalgic vision of ancient America. Could the composer's mysterious theme in the first movement be a musical allusion to Aldrich's "In the pine-forest, / Guarded by shadows, / Lieth the haunted / Pond of the Red Men"? Or could the fourth movement derive from "Then, as the dirges / Rose from the village, / Miantowona / Stole from the mourners, / Stole through the cornfields, / Passed like a phantom / Into the shadows / Through the pine forest"? Aside from possibly a few conjectural allusions such as this, little if any of the content of Aldrich's "Miantowona" seems to have any consistent narrative presence in MacDowell's work. Along with the title "legend," these verbal descriptors do provide one clue: MacDowell was probably imagining a pre-Columbian America.[29]

The first-movement E-minor melody cited above, however, does bear distinctive harmonic and rhythmic traits that nevertheless might be identified as "Indian." Reinforced by block harmonies, the rhythm of the melody thrusts the accent onto the downbeat of each second bar, enforcing a stark rigidness. The final rhythmic cadence of each phrase—a sharply accented staccato iamb—evokes the sharp cadences of Algonquin words that MacDowell was likely to know from Longfellow ("wampum" or "Mishe-Mokwa"). This same theme emphasizes two nondiatonic intervals: the modal lowered seventh (D♮) and the raised fourth (written as a B♭). This short phrase (B–B♭–G), with its evocation of a Middle Eastern maqam, is actually a key motive in the entire suite, introduced nearly at the beginning as part of the principal theme (boxed in ex. 9, p. 201), and MacDowell repeatedly emphasizes the intrusive "foreignness" of its orientalist color by stressing the raised fourth. From its first appearance and thereafter, it functions as a decorative marker—like war paint identifying the face of a recurring character.

One of the most frequent of these devices in the suite is the use of modes, especially Dorian and Aeolian, with their flat thirds and lowered-seventh scale degrees. With the exception of Arthur Foote's use of modal harmony in his 1886 *Farewell of Hiawatha,* modality or modal allusion does not appear to have been a feature of "Indian" music written before the 1890s. MacDowell's use of modality in an Indian context, however, may well have been a major influence on later composers' Indian settings. Baker, of course, devoted considerable space in his thesis to a discussion of the modes of the "Ancients" (Greeks) and their similarity to the modal structures of Indian melodies. It is not difficult to see why this connection appealed to MacDowell, given his high regard for Russian and Scandinavian music. In these cultures, modal inflection served as an ethnic marker that defined their folk musics as different from western European. These melodies could be self-consciously borrowed or imitated in the West, of course, in which case they almost always alluded to a distant culture, or to Europe's own "ancient" Celtic culture. If Indians—as Dvořák and other composers of the 1890s began to argue—were indicative of the character of America, then MacDowell's exotic emphasis on modality here suggests a simultaneous articulation of the exotic and the national.[30]

This discussion of modality brings us to the second supposed literary/historical influence on the "Indian" Suite: the Norse reference to "Thorfinnkarlsefin" in MacDowell's preface. One "Northern" corroboration that MacDowell may have had in mind is detectable at the opening of the third movement ("In War Time"). The first of the two themes (played by two flutes in unison) is scalar, Aeolian, and not at all characteristically American Indian, whereas the second (played by two clarinets in unison) is pentatonic and exhibits instantly recognizable characteristics of Indian song. MacDowell assumed both themes to be equally Indian in origin—although in fact they were not—and the first of these, in line with his thesis, resembles "Northern European" (often defined as specifically Celtic) melody.

In 1880, while MacDowell was living in Germany, a nearly intact Icelandic seagoing vessel from the ninth century was discovered near Sandefjord, Norway. (It currently reposes in the Oslo Museum.) Although accounts of the Norse seamen were known to philologists and scholars of the thirteenth-century Scandinavian manuscripts, international interest began to accelerate following the discovery of the Viking ship. Translations and analyses of the sagas that dealt specifically with the Norse westward explorations were undertaken by Rasmus Anderson at the University of Chicago and Arthur Middleton Reeves at Oxford. Some of the original Icelandic and Norwegian sources were contradictory—no small wonder, since they were compiled a century or two after the events—and two men, Leif Eriksson and Thorfinn Karlsefni, were portrayed as potential first explorers. Only in the early twentieth century—with the research of scholars such as William Hovgaard, Geoffrey Gathorne-Hardy, and Edward Gray—did Leif Eriksson emerge as the first and principal of the Norse pioneers and Thorfinn lapse into relative obscurity. Some possibly confirming evidence of the Norse-Indian connection was found in several thirteenth-century maps that showed identifiable features on the North American coast from what is now Baffin Island down to Cape Cod. The manuscripts containing these maps (located mostly in Copenhagen) also detail the explorers' first contacts with the natives of North America—the "Skraelings"—in battles and trading.[31]

MacDowell was no doubt aware—if he had carefully read the text of Baker's thesis—that Baker had linked one of the songs to this earliest Norse-Indian encounter. Baker indicated that a certain tune had been sung for generations by the Atlantic coastal people, who had originally heard the song sung "in the air" many years before the arrival of the whites. Baker, who did not acknowledge his source, drew his information from a hymn collection of some thirty-five years earlier by Thomas Commuck, a Christian Narragansett. Baker inadvertently switched the information for the two songs, and the story surrounding the "Old Indian Hymn" now became attached to Commuck's original melody for "Shoshonee," the basis for the opening flute theme. (Like the British and New England tunesmiths who named their hymns after famous places, Commuck named his tunes after those of North American tribes.) The almost "Nordic" modality of "Shoshonee" neatly supported MacDowell's thesis that some Indian music may have been related or even derived from "Northern European themes," especially given MacDowell's relative lack of interest in Indian music but genuine love of Celtic culture. "In all my work," MacDowell is to have said, "there is the Celtic influence. I love its colour and meaning."[32]

In one of the dramatic episodes of the "In War-time" movement, the clarinet plays a few forceful phrases of "Shoshonee" while in counterpoint MacDowell maintains a galloping accompanying figure in the violas and cellos. This sharply accented three-note rhythm (♫♩), as we've discussed, comes directly from the war-dance trope. MacDowell eventually adds the descending pitches to it as well ($\hat{3}$–$\hat{2}$–$\hat{1}$ in minor). After a full statement of the "Shoshonee" theme, he veers off into chromatic variations, now led by the violas and cellos. Then the horns announce the second theme (the boasting song). MacDowell creates the dizzying frenzy of a warlike scene by combining an oscillating bass figure (on C♯–E, the familiar "hopping" minor thirds), slowly ascending trills in the violins, barking accents in the horns and trumpets, and swelling chromaticism in the lower strings and woodwinds.

A dramatic overview of the "Indian" Suite, then, might read into MacDowell's work the following "Indian saga" that traces the journey of a young brave to manhood (and one placed in a rather specific pre-Columbian time): The first movement depicts Indian life in the wilderness (with some poetic images drawn from Aldrich). Perhaps the protagonist—who utters the cry at the opening of the suite—leaves his familial home and sets off on a journey, encountering friends (the lyrical second themes), adventure, and danger along the way. But the friendship is cut off abruptly at the end of the movement, perhaps by tragedy. The second movement, with its tender flute melody and yearning strings, suggests that the protagonist woos a loved one (and probably succeeds). The rough third movement, with its two conflicting themes and exotic devices, clearly conveys war. But the explicitly different intonations of the two themes also suggest specific characters. The movement begins with two Norsemen setting foot on North American soil (two flutes). Two Indians observe and follow (two clarinets). As the themes interact, tension builds and war ensues. The events appear to be "told" from the protagonist's perspective. The swift and violent end implies thoughtless devastation of some kind. The fourth movement ("dirge-like") is said to depict a woman mourning for her son. Yet musically it strongly suggests instead a *waiting* mother, the heaviness of each phrase implying a sense of doom, but the steadily pulsing chords sounding unmistakably like slowly marching footsteps. As the theme of this movement was suggested already in the third (at the height of the battle, presumably), we could say that the warrior imagines his mother mourning his death, for during his long tread homeward he perhaps nearly does die. (He could also be burdened by the sorrow of having lost his comrades.) But in the final movement he returns home, and the whole village celebrates, beginning with a women's dance led by his mother. The bright tempo even seems to conform with Oliver LaFarge's description of a scalp dance: light and fast footwork, cheerful "and often beautiful" songs, and the "rapid beat" of a drum. Why the warlike passage in the middle of it? As the warrior jumps in to participate, his dance depicts his tale of war and conquest to his neighbors and family, boasting of his accomplishments and the slaying of the foreigners.

I am well aware that this interpretation does not comply with MacDowell's later comments about an Indian woman's lament for her dead son, nor with a jest he is supposed to have made the day after a performance: "killed the Indian again at Cambridge last night."[33] The above scenario is an attempt (highly personal, it's true) to accommodate the various spheres of influence in this work, as well as an exercise in intonational theory applied to a work with obvious programmatic and textual allusions. It may help us understand how MacDowell's music imagines native America, especially since this suite served as perhaps the most famous and well-known American orchestral work for at least twenty years after it was written.

When Henry Krehbiel reviewed Fletcher's *Study of Omaha Indian Music* in 1893, he gave no indication that Indian music might play a significant role in an American school of composition. But by the time of his review of MacDowell's "Indian" Suite, he served as a knowledgeable and influential voice. "There is one element of Indian music," Krehbiel wrote,

> of which effective use might have been made, which Professor MacDowell overlooked. This is their characteristic drumming. In much of the music of the Plains Indians and those of the Pacific coast cross rhythms are common, gener-

> ally three beats against four, but Iroquois songs are accompanied by a steady reiteration of time units, each preceded by an appoggiatura. Neither of these effects was utilized in the suite. Had they been, they might have added a national trait which would have appealed to the student of folksong, even if it would not have helped the ordinary listener to recognize the American element.

Krehbiel could have pointed out that Dvořák had already used cross rhythms in his string quintet, although without the label "Indian." Nevertheless, Krehbiel identified native America as the "American element," and he admired MacDowell's suite, even going to battle for him against the Boston skeptics who, in his words, "contend that there can be no American music, because there are no American melodies racy of the soil." In an article on the state of Indian music research two years later, he again drew attention to composers who had recently made use of Indian music in their compositions. As late as 1902 this adamant critic and scholar still held out hope that "when the right man comes [along] he may turn the characteristic features of Indian song to excellent account."[34]

Krehbiel may have ruled the roost in New York, but in Boston, Philip Hale served as the major critical force to be reckoned with, and he was decidedly against MacDowell's brand of American nationalism. Hale's 1896 review praised the suite's "rare beauty," but he did not hold back on the satire when it came to his New York colleague's support of such efforts:

> That Mr. MacDowell took some or all of his thematic material from North American Indians does not interest me in the slightest. I go to a concert to hear music, not to study or discuss folklore.
>
> Then these "Indian tunes." Might not some returned warrior avenge himself upon the white oppressor by inventing some melody on the spur of the moment? Somehow or other, I always associate Indian tunes with Mr. Krehbiel. [This was probably because of Krehbiel's five *Tribune* articles on the folk music that he heard at the World's Columbian Exposition in 1893.] I see him in close confab with a plug-hatted venerable chief, as they discuss folk songs over a jug of firewater. The phonograph is close at hand. The firewater begins to work, and old Three-Tones-in-His-Voice chirps like a cricket. "Did you ever hear this, my pale-faced brother? Listen to the Scotch snap." The phonograph records the wondrous melody. Another drink, another folk song, another burst of confidence to the phonograph. Why, the little jug is an anthology!
>
> Mr. MacDowell may take his themes where he pleases, from an intoxicated chief who weeps at the name of J. F. Cooper; from Brer Krehbiel and his fellow explorers; from a relative of George Catlin; or from the rich storehouse of Mr. de Koven. The question is: what does Mr. MacDowell do with the tunes after he takes them home?[35]

MacDowell himself, of course, had little to add on this point. Like Saint-Gaudens, MacDowell decided that creating large-scale works on Indian subjects was a youthful experiment he would not repeat.

During one of Hamlin Garland's visits with the MacDowells in 1896 (after the premiere of the "Indian" Suite), the young writer tried to demonstrate some of the Navajo and Ute songs that he had heard during his travels in Colorado and New Mexico. Garland hoped to interest MacDowell in traveling with him to the West the following year. But after hearing Garland sing to the accompaniment of his own drumming — with the lights turned down low and with Marian MacDowell's tambourine substituting for the drum — the composer is supposed to have gotten up, walked over to the piano, given his manuscript a flip, and said, "you make these things seem like milk and water." Although he began to study Fletcher's Omaha songs — as other composers were beginning to do — and would later incorporate some of these in two short piano works, MacDowell was not interested in the harsh realities of 1890s reservation life; his art found its safe haven in the ancient legends and — much to the regret of Philip Hale and other detractors — the evocative world of folklore.[36]

Both Dvořák and MacDowell experimented with ways to draw on American Indian music — either through quotation of themes or intonational devices — and both served as models for composers of art music who, against the rising tide of modernism and popular culture in the early twentieth century, longed to find the "spiritual soul of America." Of course, this soul could be found almost anywhere for an artist willing to look. But for some, like the young Arthur Farwell and the dozens of composers who were inspired by him, the Indian peoples were the only true Americans. It would be at least another generation before the United States government would demonstrate its recognition of that fact.

7

In Search of the Authentic: Musical Tribal Portraits, 1890–1911

During these two decades of rising progressive politics in America, "musical Indianism" continued a course of expansion, fueled to a large extent by the nationalism debates of the 1890s. It is obvious to us today that the peak of American musical nationalism was reached in the 1930s and 1940s, by which point African American and Anglo-American sources had replaced native America as a key source for nationalism. But interest in native America actually constituted the first major wave of "Dvořák's long American reach," as Adrienne Fried Block has called it, a wave that reached its apex about 1911. These two decades also evinced intensification in the rift between the classical arts and popular commercial-driven entertainment. The two were in fact deeply related in many areas, as a simple consideration of the career of John Philip Sousa or Victor Herbert would attest. The musical Indianism explored in this chapter—via instrumental character pieces that used quotation and served, in effect, as musical tribal portraits of native America—did not exist as mere nationalist marginalia. It exerted an influence on commercial entertainment no less than the reverse.

For example, in November 1911 Seattle photographer Edward Curtis produced a monumental tribute to native America entitled "The Vanishing Race" at Carnegie Hall in New York. This "lecture-entertainment," "picture-musicale," or "Indian picture-opera," as it was variously subtitled, opened before a distinguished audience of historians, anthropologists, photographers, cinematographers, and musicians. The evening entailed an unfolding display of photographs of North American Indians taken in the West and shown through magic lantern slides. Each thematic group of photographs, called "dissolving series," was accompanied by short orchestral character pieces (all by MacDowell's protégé Henry Gilbert) that were based on themes related to the subject matter of the photographs. Although the highly publicized "real Indian music" remained anonymous in the program, Gilbert's contributions had much to do with the evening's success. The reviews praised the music, describing its "barbaric chords and crashing rhythm" as "full of weird appeal that speaks in the red man's harmonies." Curtis's lecture-entertainments were subsequently mounted at the Belasco Theatre, at the Brooklyn Institute, at the Hippodrome, in various cities on a national tour during the winter of 1911–12, and on a transcontinental tour in 1912–13. Two musical excerpts were recorded by Columbia — again with no composer credited — but others were published under Gilbert's name as five *Indian Scenes* for piano and six *Indian Sketches*, symphonic "musical mood-pictures" that were performed by the Boston Symphony Orchestra in 1921 and by other orchestras.[1]

Gilbert's character pieces were not just quaint musical portraits of native America. The appropriation of Indian songs — in the language of cultural anthropology — suggests that these works (and others like them) had a deeper resonance than simply naive musical nationalism. Unlike Sousa or Herbert, whose "Indians" were completely indexical and purely meant to be entertaining, Gilbert and other musicians who fashioned character pieces after transcribed Indian music did so for at least two important reasons, neither of which could be tied to an imperialist nostalgia. It is true that the large number of Indian character pieces written during this time reflected the nation's growing recognition and use of its folklore. Like the music of hitherto marginalized European cultures that emerged with distinctive national voices in the nineteenth century, the Indian melodies that were transcribed in increasing numbers in the 1890s and early 1900s began to take on the aura of folk song, miniature chronicles of national consciousness. It became evident, however, that one principal reason for collecting folklore, as Alan Lomax would later famously put it, was to allow the voices of the voiceless to be heard in the greater society. Unlike the nationalist character pieces of Grieg, for example, Indian character pieces translated something of the experience of native America to the dominant society at a time when Indian songs and dances were officially under government suppression.

This suppression of Indian culture was linked, in the minds of many of the composers under discussion here, with the crisis of modernity. Given that music brought a spiritual dimension to so many aspects of Native American life, as the Indianists repeatedly emphasized, some non-Indian musicians turned to these translations as an expressive musical language in their search for alternatives to a culture increasingly driven by materialism and progressive politics. This retrenchment from modernity was in part a response to the spiritual turmoil of the late nineteenth century, a turmoil, to paraphrase T. J. Jackson Lears, that was evident in the cult of science and technical rationality and the worship of material progress. Those who spoke out on behalf of Indians and their cultures, as Helen Hunt Jackson had done a few decades before, were often derided. The use of Indian music was therefore both peculiarly conservative and subversive at the same time. Perhaps this is why so many of these composers met at first with such resistance and, as at Loomis's recital in New York, were greeted initially with laughter. Only in hindsight can we see that the discovery of native America at this time served as part of a quest for spiritual authenticity, much like the concurrent rise of interest in oriental religions or medieval mysticism. Composers who turned to Indian music as a source all faced the same problem: namely, how to establish a theoretical relationship between the melodies of Native American song—which are almost exclusively sung without any accompanying harmonic instruments—and Western music, which at this point in Euro-American history had reached a stage of considerable harmonic complexity.[2]

From about 1900 to World War I—concurrent with the rage for Tin Pan Alley "Indian songs" and "characteristics," which must be considered as a related but separate phenomenon—music publishers across the country produced dozens of descriptive instrumental character pieces. It was not always necessary for such works to directly quote Native American songs or dances. Many did. But some composers, like Victor Herbert or John Philip Sousa, were content to merely index features of Indian music in their character pieces. The Irish-born Herbert, for example, characterized three distinct racial and cultural groups of people in his *Pan Americana,* written for the 1901 Pan-American Exposition in Buffalo. *Pan Americana* had a minor-mode marchlike passage for Indians, a ragtime-based section for African Americans, and then a tango-based section for Latin Americans. Herbert's music for Indians drew on some of the war-dance features discussed earlier but also contained a pentatonic melody of his own devising. Similarly, Sousa's "The Red Man," in his suite of three pieces entitled *Dwellers in the Western World* (1910), also alluded to folk music traditions in the use of a pentatonic scale for one of its original melodies. By this time, of course, many popular American works of all stripes had been written using such five-note gapped scales (a trait evident as early as in minstrel songs of the 1830s). But certain distinctive uses of pentatonicism—a specific pentatonic mode composed only of minor thirds and whole steps, with the third gaps at the bottom and top (for example, C–E♭–F–G–B♭) combined with a diatonic minor-mode accompaniment as Sousa used it—remained a decidedly "Indian" trope well into the twentieth century. (In the first decade of the century, Bartók and Kodály, collecting folk songs in Hungary, labeled tunes in this particular pentatonic mode as "old Hungarian." The folk origins of this mode, as opposed to the specific features of how it was used, extend well beyond national, cultural, and linguistic borders.) In addition to composing a pentatonic melody in minor, Sousa drew on several other tropes of Indianism, demonstrating his fluency with their syntactic properties as well as his skill at adapting these for modern audiences. In effect, "The Red Man" was *perceived* by many to be authentically Indian because, aside from the general timbre of the concert band's instrumental forces and its toe-tapping beat, it has a distinctive referential character and doesn't sound like any of Sousa's other marches. And its title, of course, pointed listeners in the direction of native America.

Herbert and Sousa were two extraordinarily popular composers at the turn of the century, and it is perhaps not surprising that their fluency with this syntax was partly a manifestation of their keen compositional skills and their abilities to build huge international followings through popular middlebrow genres such as operettas and concert marches. Composers for whom music and social conscience were inseparable, however, chose to use the character piece—an instrumental genre usually for a single instrument (or perhaps a solo instrument with piano accompaniment)—as a vehicle for conveying the deeper expressive qualities of specific Indian experiences: the love song of an elderly Omaha man, for instance, or an Arapaho ghost dance. In this sense, the character piece became the haven for a new kind of national expression, one that—initially, at any rate—was intended to speak intimately to individual Americans rather than to large audiences at a sweep (although by 1911 they were also used for community pageants and films). These were iconic works, quoting native songs and dances. But they also developed their own lexicon of indexical features—one upon which mainstream popular composers such as Herbert and Sousa could draw.[3]

Fillmore's Settings of Indian "Folk Songs"

The lexical roots of the "Indian character piece" are found in John Fillmore's 1893 settings of Omaha songs, and so we must launch our theoretical investigation with these works. When Alice Fletcher approached Fillmore, then director of the Milwaukee School of Music, for help in analyzing her collection of songs, he already had an established reputation for his pedagogical works in music. Fillmore espoused the dualistic harmonic theories of Arthur von Oettingen and Hugo Riemann and adapted these to a practical theoretical basis for use in teaching. Fillmore criticized Stumpf's and Boas's use of microtonal notation. Instead, he observed that the Omaha repertory was clearly based on the acoustical principles of pentatonicism (as derived from the overtone series) and could be categorized as either major or minor-modal, depending on the orientation of their finals. Both types lacked the same scale degrees: the semitones that result in leading-tone progressions, B to C in C major, for example, or F to E in E-Phrygian. When Fillmore sought to harmonize an Omaha song, he could find no satisfactory scheme of known chords that would exclude the missing scale tones. (Bartók encountered the same problem in his earliest settings of Hungarian folk songs. In his case, leaning upon the example of Debussy, he devised new harmonies from the pentatonic folk material.) Fillmore also pointed out that while the songs he transcribed were sung in unison, he found that some Indians reacted with pleasure when he added what were rather traditional diatonic chords. Fletcher herself noted a similar reaction: "I first detected this feeling for harmony while rendering to the Indians their melodies upon an instrument; the song played as an unsupported solo did not satisfy my memory of their unison singing, and the music did not 'sound natural' to them, but when I added a simple harmony my ear was content and the Indians were satisfied."[4]

We have seen how Fillmore sought approval from within the Indian community for his rendering of an Omaha song. "I wished particularly to know," he wrote, going a step further than Fletcher, "whether the harmonies which seemed to me natural would prove satisfactory to Indian ears." Fillmore, of course, may have mistaken his native listeners' approval of his scientific experiments with the possibility that they wanted to please him. In the end, however, Fletcher published her controversial but highly influential study with Fillmore's harmonizations.

The settings of the ninety-three melodies in *A Study of Omaha Indian Music* can be categorized as follows:

- seventy-six melodies are set principally in major (only three of which end in keys unrelated to the tonic — neither subdominant nor dominant)
- three melodies begin in major and end in the relative minor
- three melodies begin in minor and end in the relative major
- seven melodies are set principally in minor
- four melodies are unaccompanied

This list shows that the Omaha melodies — at least those selected for the publication — leaned predominantly toward major tonalities. While closely adhering to their shape, Fillmore drew on research in physics and acoustics — relying on Helmholtz's theory of the overtone series—to support his observation that the Indian music he had studied indeed conformed with the same physical properties that governed Western music. Fillmore's mistake, if it can be interpreted that way in retrospect, was to subject these melodies—which did not always remain in one pentatonic mode—to a kind of rigid major-minor diatonicism. He was convinced that the Omahas sang their songs with a subconscious perception of harmonic relations that influenced the melodic succession of tones: "The result of the experiment was entirely satisfactory. The Indians were even delighted with the chords I had added to their song, showing that, notwithstanding the fact that they never make any attempt to sing in parts, they possess a latent sense of harmony, and this sense is precisely the same as ours. That is to say, the harmonic sense is innate in the human mind, is a natural constituent of universal human nature." After this apparent corroboration, he concluded that the melodies had to be guided by some imagined bass line, since shapes that outlined the minor triad—the A minor in A–C–D–E–G, for example—could not have been derived from the overtone series alone (the first minor third occurs quite high in the series and is therefore less "natural" than the major third).[5]

Fillmore also contended that the presence of pentatonic scales in the music of Indians suggested an as-yet-undeveloped harmonic sense. He equated the use of five-note gapped scales with "primitive peoples" even though, in the 1890s, the use of pentatonic melodies in classical composition was interpreted as a tonally progressive development. In France, for example, Debussy's well-known adoption of five-note scales from Javanese and other Asian cultures resulted in a dramatic style change for him. Fillmore, like Debussy (as well as Liszt and Saint-Saëns before him), approached pentatonic scales diatonically. Based on a study of Debussy's complete works, the Romanian ethnomusicologist Constantin Brailoiu categorized that composer's use of anhemitonic pentatonic scales (in other words, five-note scales with no semitones) according to five aspects or modes. This is the same classification used in Chinese theoretical treatises since the first century B.C.E. as well as by Helmholtz, although the German physicist numbered the modes differently. In her studies of American Indian music, Frances Densmore used Helmholtz's system, whereas eastern European ethnomusicologists such as Bartók or Brailoiu used the Chinese system. I follow the latter model, as it is today more common internationally. My application of these scales to the Western music in this book, like Brailoiu's analysis, assumes a diatonic background, and therefore the pitches are identified numerically by their positions relative to a seven-note diatonic mode. Many North American Indian repertoires do use pentatonic scales with semitones (as do some Japanese and Indonesian scales, for example). But with rare exceptions Western settings of American Indian music favor the anhemitonic pentatonic — perhaps because of its associations as a "universe of discourse" — and therefore all my further references to its five modes will follow the system shown in table 5.[6]

Most of the pentatonic modes — I, II, III, and IV — tend to sound major, while V — the one cited in the Herbert and Sousa works above — sounds minor. Fillmore referred to this mode as "minor-pentatonic," although theoretically any of these, it should be emphasized, could be given a major- or minor-mode context. Mode V also includes the "lowered seventh" (G) that requires a minor dominant (E-G-B), which in most Western contexts — even in a minor mode — inevitably sounds like a "color chord." Modes II, III, and IV tend to be used more in Asian representations, although when set to one of the diatonic modes they may convey both alterity and antiquity. From the 1890s well into the advent of sound film, almost any "Indian melody" — at least any chosen for adaptation by non-Indian composers — conformed to these modes.[7]

Most Indian musics, however, while pentatonically based, do not necessarily remain in one mode. Recognizing this feature, Fillmore identified the "keynote" of each mode as its major or minor quality; hence the keynote of mode II (using the notes in table 5 as an example), would, like mode I, also be a C. Densmore, however, writing some fifteen years later, determined keynote by such criteria as frequency, rhythmic stress, and final rather than relevance to a Western tonal center. (This is how I identify pentatonic modes in my analyses.) For his 1893 harmonizations of Omaha songs, Fillmore needed to resolve the problem of melodies migrating from one pentatonic mode to another (a mutational process that Brailoiu called, in French, *métabole*). Fillmore's handling of "metabolizing" Indian melodies has, perhaps, remained the most controversial aspect of his involvement. Nevertheless, his interest and adaptation of Indian music — regardless of his spurious contribution to ethnomusicology — induced what James C. McNutt called an "interdisciplinary awakening [to] Native American music" at the end of the nineteenth century.[8]

No. 72 from the 1893 collection, a war song, provides a clear illustration of this controversial approach (ex. 11). If we examine the melody by itself, we find that the first phrase (starting on C♯ and moving downward) is built on pentatonic mode IV in E (C♯–B–A–F♯–E), the second is on an implied mode II in B ([A]–F♯–E–C♯–B), the third on mode I in D (B–A–F♯–E–D), and the fourth on mode IV in A ([F♯]–E–D–B–A). Phrase two and four are melodic parallels, but their different finals (E and D) convey *métabole* and undermine a stable tonal center for the song. Until the introduction of the D, Western listeners are inclined to expect ultimate closure on B, not A. In his setting

Table 5. The Five Anhemitonic Pentatonic Modes
(Roots are underlined)

Mode	I	II	III	IV	V

Fillmore's "two types"	"Major" pentatonic				"Minor" pentatonic
Diatonic background	Ionian	Dorian	Phrygian	Mixolydian	Aeolian
Numerical orientation	1-2-3-5-6-(1)	2-3-5-6-1-(2)	3-5-6-1-2-(3)	5-6-1-2-3-(5)	6-1-2-3-5-(6)
Chinese equivalent	*gong*	*shang*	*jyue*	*zhi*	*yeu*
Helmholtz/Densmore	(3)	(4)	(5)	(1)	(2)

Example 11. *A Study of Omaha Indian Music* (1893), no. 72.

Fillmore tried to reconcile this disconcerting turn of events by adopting a modulating harmonization: A major to E major for the first two phrases, E major to D major for the last two phrases. The two major finals therefore each fall on the fifth of a different tonic. Fillmore's solution to the problem here and elsewhere was rooted in relatively traditional harmonic devices. Unlike Debussy, he rarely used pentatonically derived chords—for example, a major chord with an added sixth (C–E–G–A from mode I and E–G–A–C from mode II)—to bridge the different pentatonic modes.[9]

Example 12. *A Study of Omaha Indian Music* (1893), no. 45.

Yet Fillmore's settings do contain original harmonic touches. Fletcher and LaFlesche included twenty-six songs from the *Wa-Wan,* or pipe of fellowship ceremony. No. 45 ("Raising the Pipes") contains four phrases of unequal length (ex. 12). Each phrase begins lower than the preceding one and descends (except for the last phrase, which already begins at the base note and can fall no further). The first two phrases, written here in descending order, are in mode V (E♭–[C]–B♭–A♭–F), but missing the C). The third phrase, which begins with the missing C, is in mode IV ([E♭]–C–B♭–G–F) but is now missing the E♭. Fillmore's accompaniment is reminiscent of church hymnody—including even a Picardy third at the end—and perhaps he intended an intentional link between the sacred nature of the pipe ceremony and music for Christian worship. Here, however, he highlights a tonic ambiguity between these two pentatonic modes (V, which implies minor, and IV, which implies major). More important, he introduces a suggestive passing minor-seventh chord between the two (m. 16), creating a progression that will continue to resonate in

"Indian music" composed thereafter. The descending tenor-line A♭–G–F (mm. 15–17 and 25–27) results in a harmonic progression of D♭ major (VI) to a nostalgic-sounding G diminished with an added minor-seventh (ii^{6}_{5}) resolving solemnly to F minor (i). Though Fillmore himself did not overuse this progression (in chord notation: VI–ii^{6}_{5}–i), it became a common indexical feature in "Indian" character pieces and songs after this time.[10]

Fillmore also explored several unconventional methods for rhythmic notation. In one song that alternated freely between four and five beats to a measure, he used the key signature 5/4 (no. 6). He also used polymeters, as can be seen in no. 45, and even more daringly in no. 60, indicating 6/8 9/8 in the right hand against 4/8 6/8 in the left hand. Fillmore accented the pulsing bass chords as if the time signature read 2/4 3/4, however, in order to convey the effect of drumming (in the left hand) with the more rhythmically flexible voice of the vocal part (in the right hand).

In many of Fillmore's settings, a striking feature results merely from limitations in Western rhythmic notation. The campfire song of the Haethuska Society, for example (no. 11), fluctuates between two simple descending modes, [E]–C♯–B–A–F♯ and [A]–F♯–E–C♯–B. But Fillmore's rhythmic transcription is limited to combinations of quarter, eighth, and sixteenth notes over a pulsing eighth-note beat that, unlike no. 60 noted above, leads to a rigidification of the Indian melody (if performed as written):

Perhaps in an effort to capture the thunder of this warrior society's protector god, Fillmore had placed strong emphasis on the duple accent, especially in the third measure. Consequently, a stark, forceful quality emerges, given the notational limitations inherent in a system based on division exclusively by twos. The extant recordings Fletcher made of Omaha music in the 1890s demonstrate that the style of performance she heard, though marked with a strong vocal emphasis, was far more rhythmically supple. These settings could be compared with Walter Hoffman's 1885 transcription of Ojibwa Medicine Society songs. Hoffman strived for naturalism in rendering his informant's singing. The rhythms of Fillmore's notated transcriptions seem stark and unyielding by comparison.[11]

Several of these 1893 settings were reprinted in Fletcher's *Indian Story and Song* (1900), and this little volume of harmonized "Indian music" proved a frequent source for later composers in search of such melodies as the thematic basis for character pieces.[12] Moreover, rhythmic rigidity served as an indexical marker for a trope of primitive inflexibility and stoicism. Combined with the persistent syntax of war dances for which this throbbing music seemed apt, this trope carried over into many diverse musical genres, among them character pieces (Ernest R. Kroeger, "March of the Indian Phantoms," 1904; see table 6), cantatas (Hans Busch, *The Four Winds,* 1907), opera (Victor Herbert, *Natoma,* 1911), silent-film music (John Zamecnik, "Indian Attack," 1914), Wild West shows (Karl King, *The Passing of the Red Man,* ca. 1916), and ultimately Broadway musicals (Irving Berlin, *Annie Get Your Gun,* 1946).

MacDowell and the "Indian Character Piece"

Though most American Indian music is vocal, short instrumental works served as the ideal place for experimenting with Indian melodies. In these "songs without words," the essence of native America, it was believed, could be captured from its source in transcribed Indian song, and musicians, both professional and amateur, could relate these experiences through a musically acceptable translation. The piano miniature or character piece as developed in the early nineteenth century often served as the musical equivalent of an anecdote or poem. With a short work of relatively simple structure, a composer could tell a brief story or evoke a specific mood. Offering pianists at all levels a vehicle for poetic expression, the piano miniature became the refuge of the programmatic, of folk dances and legends, and of depictions of nature. Tchaikovsky's and Grieg's popular piano miniatures spawned hundreds of imitations by lesser-known composers in the late nineteenth century. Despite—or often thanks to—their overt nationalist characteristics, piano miniatures generally transcended national and continental boundaries.

Edward MacDowell largely owes his reputation to his piano miniatures. Indeed, he was often seen in his time as the first American to write successful artworks in a major European musical form. The best of these, like those of many eastern European composers, drew upon folk legend and fairy tales. The miniatures conjured a world that was or might have been and in this sense reflected, as Wilfred Mellers phrased it, "a boy's view of the American past."[13] One could easily argue that MacDowell's cultural naïveté—more than any privileged or detailed cultural knowledge—imparted candor and appeal to his music and led to its popularity.

MacDowell wrote only two "Indian" pieces in his sixteen sets of piano miniatures. (One other, an unfinished "Indian Melody," was found among his sketches.)[14] Both of these were written after his orchestral "Indian" Suite. They were composed at a time when MacDowell was attempting to reconcile his European musical training (which was progressive) with his love for American folklore and poetry (which was conservative). MacDowell must have tried to familiarize himself with the Fletcher-Fillmore publication, perhaps in the hopes of finding source material for further compositions. On one occasion in 1896, he played some of Fillmore's Omaha arrangements for Hamlin Garland. Garland agreed that the Fillmore arrangements did "suggest Indian music," but he found them distinctly whitewashed or "Sankeyized," as he put it. Garland was referring, of course, to the plain and straightforward harmonizations of Dwight Moody's evangelical hymns by Ira Sankey. These were ubiquitous in the United States after 1875, serving as standard editions for many gospel and Protestant sacred songs.

Clearly this was not what MacDowell was looking for. He discarded Fillmore's arrangements and instead went back to Baker, who had presented the chants monophonically. MacDowell's Indian character pieces are found in two of his most mature piano cycles, *Woodland Sketches* (1896) and *New England Idyls* (1901–2). Among the ten miniatures in *Woodland Sketches,* "From an Indian Lodge" and "A Deserted Farm" are the only slow, minor-mode works. "From an Indian Lodge," no. 5 of the set, is the more somber of these. Its stern, recitative-like introduction stands in marked contrast to "In Autumn," the playful and buoyant piece that precedes it. The cadential figure in mm. 6–7. with its diminished minor-seventh passing chord, resonates with echoes of Fillmore's dusky "Indian cadence," although MacDowell approaches it within an all-minor context (in chord notation: v^6–v^6–ii^6_5–i) instead of Fillmore's major-to-minor resolution (VI–ii^6_5–i). MacDowell thought of *Woodland Sketches* as framed by this indexical marker of Indianism. "From an Indian Lodge" concludes with these same somber chords, but more importantly they also return at the end of "Told at Sunset" to close the cycle (even though there is no specific "Indian" reference in the final work). The dark, bottom-heavy melody (mm. 10ff.) is firmly rooted in C minor, and the quiet but dry thud of open fifths in the bass, steadily pulsating on the second beat of each 3/4 measure, provides an austere subtext of timelessness and stoic resolve. MacDowell's indication of "mournfully" over the melody encourages a quality of lamentation in the hymnlike tune. Marian MacDowell wrote that her husband always felt that he should have called the work an "Indian Dirge," for that is what it really was: "a dirge for the death of a chieftain, or perhaps even a dirge symbolic of the passing of the race." These comments, published in 1910 after the composer's death, may suggest why characteristics such as stern, somber, and mournful are so apparent in this work. MacDowell, who was raised and educated in a liberal New York home, recognized the Indian crisis not only as a subject for poetry but also as a stain on the national conscience. Perhaps this sense of the larger tragedy is what MacDowell meant by "mournfully."[15]

The second Indian miniature, no. 6 of the ten *Idyls* (each prefaced with an original epigraph), is among MacDowell's last compositions. In marked contrast with the earlier work, the delicate "Indian Idyl" is in a major key. The epigraph reads:

> Alone by the wayward flame
> She weaves broad wampum skeins
> While afar through the summer night
> Sigh the wooing flutes' soft strains.

MacDowell used an original theme, as well as a Dakota "night song" he probably took either from Baker or from Sousa's 1890 publication (it occurs in both sources). In Baker it is no. 12, "Dakota Night-Song," a pentatonic mode IV serenade "sung by several young men who march with a drum through the village or camp." The opening of MacDowell's "Indian Idyl" in F major, unlike the solemn introduction to "From an Indian Lodge," is good-humored, even flirtatious, and is marked "lightly, naively." Simple yet elegant in expression, its similarities to Debussy's early *Bergamasque* miniatures are striking: the harmonic progressions, especially in the cadences, and the delicate "arabesque" playfulness of the melody.[16]

MacDowell again used a drumbeat imitation in the middle section of the "Indian Idyl," this time with far greater sophistication than in the "Indian" Suite. (Perhaps this was in response to Henry Krehbiel's criticism of the earlier piece.) Here again there are parallels with Debussy's aesthetic—more than with any single work. The effect of the open-fifth drumbeat imitation in the bass (see table 6) does not so much suggest young men strolling through a village and beating a drum as it does the dreamlike state of a young Indian woman, who hears the drum and flute only from a distance. The pentatonic "flute melody" is thickly harmonized, as if there were three or four flutes playing at different pitch levels simultaneously. The melody is set in triple meter (as it also appears in the Sousa source). The soft simulated drumbeat is anything but emotionless and rigid. Though gently reiterated every second beat—against the melody in three—the sustained open fifths provide a musettelike drone for the flowing melody above. A pedal E in the center of the texture (also in the left hand) softly reinforces an upper partial of the drone. Tender and coy, this setting of young men drumming and playing flutes seems filtered through the young woman's perception. Given the programmatic text, a performer (or listener) is more likely to interpret the piece in this light: perhaps a young man whom she secretly loves is among those she hears playing and singing in the distance. This short, delicate work, imbued with the atmosphere of a summer night, is less in MacDowell's romantic style than in an impressionistic one. In 1918 the American composer Charles Sanford Skilton, who wrote dozens of Indian-based works himself in the 1910s and 1920s, called MacDowell's "Indian Idyl" "perhaps the most perfectly conceived piece of Indian music ever written for the piano."[17]

MacDowell's mood pieces provided the ideal tone and genre for the next generation of American composers, who sometimes included an Indian subject or two within a set of musical Americana, though these compositions generally relied upon intonation rather than quotation. One of these, Ernest R. Kroeger of St. Louis, incorporated two Indian character pieces, "The Indian Lament," no. 7, and "Indian Air with Variations," no. 9, in his *American Character Sketches,* op. 53, for piano (1902).[18] Others to follow this practice were Eastwood Lane in *Five American Dances* (1919) and *Adirondack Sketches* (1922) and Marion Bauer in *From New Hampshire Woods* (1921). Music publishers such as White-Smith and Theodore Presser promoted sets of piano miniatures on Indian themes well into the 1920s. Composers interested more specifically in Indian subject matter, such as Arthur Farwell, Harvey Worthington Loomis, and Horace Alden Miller, had only to extend the Indian subject over the contents of an entire cycle. This may have been partly stimulated by the first publication of *New England Idyls,* in which G. C. Parker's cover design interpreted the New England of the title as referring to an era long past, specifically a "forest primeval" (in Longfellow's famous phrase) inhabited by flageolet-playing Indians.

Style and Ideology in Indian Musical Portraiture

The combined use of a program for both a character piece and a tribal melody, Kiowa or Dakota, implied that some composers in the early part of the twentieth century considered specific ethnic associations to be essential to the realism of their portrayal. This ideology was partly an extension of developments in poetry, art, and, most notably, photography, which, with the advent of periodicals such as *National Geographic,* seemed poised to eradicate all fanciful notions of savagery. "Each [of these] must be what it purports to be," wrote Edward Curtis in 1907 to accompany his remarkable photographic display of Native Americans. "A Sioux must be a Sioux and an Apache an Apache; in fact, every picture must be an ethnographic record."[19] Using stunning visual imagery, Curtis purported to illustrate what he saw, "not what one in the artist's studio presumes might exist." Thinking topographically, Curtis hoped his "ethnographic records" in vivid chiaroscuro would reflect the great national and cultural diversity of the many Indian nations.

Photographic portraits, like published transcriptions of tribal Indian music,

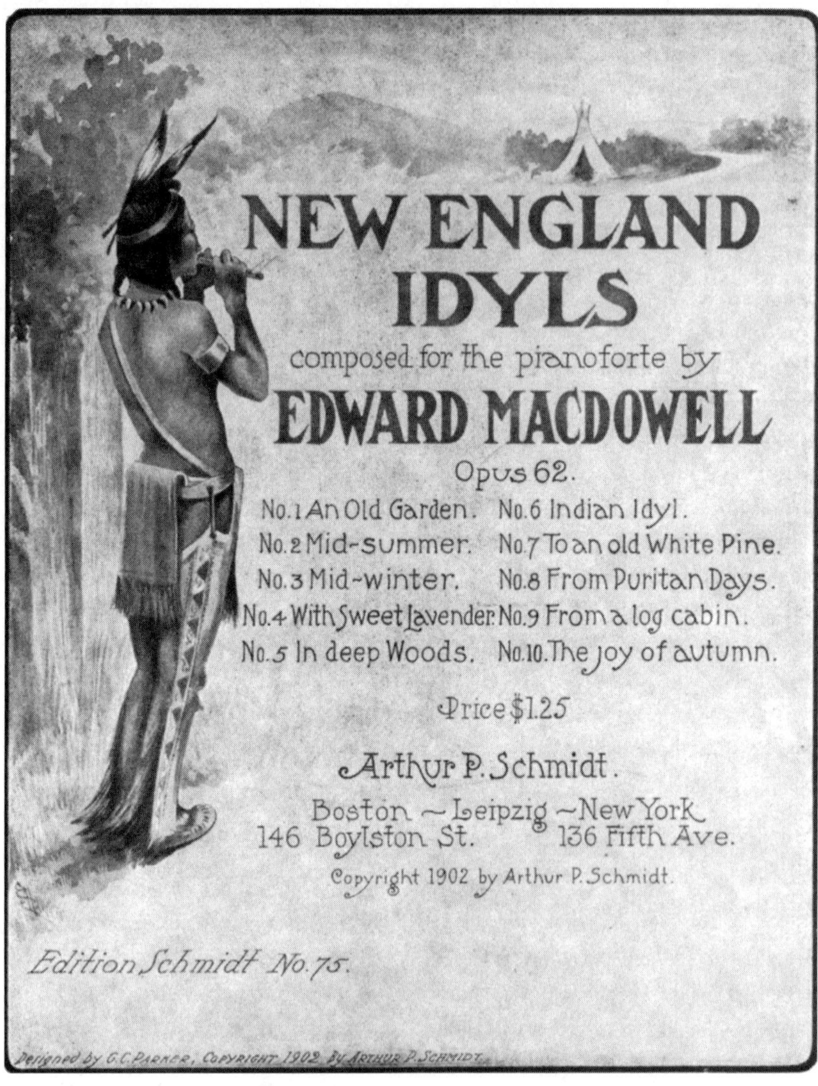

Figure 14. Original sheet music cover for Edward MacDowell's *New England Idyls* (Boston: Arthur P. Schmidt, 1902).

were slices of reality, answers to the romantic rendering of native America by many nineteenth-century painters. Yet photography, unlike an actual performance of Indian music (but like an instrumental character piece), is an artificial medium. It freezes images—sometimes very powerful and influential images—that are as much of the artist's making as they are reflections of the subjects in it. Its ability to convey is of course limited by what the photographer frames or chooses to emphasize. Variety is the greatest strength of Curtis's collections, particularly in his twenty-three-year publishing project entitled *The North American Indian.* Nevertheless, his determination to isolate authentic Indian cultures suggested a kind of imagined purity. Most efforts to define cultures as pure are deeply problematic from an anthropological perspective, even if they appear to succeed on a poetic level as art. Cultures are never entirely "authentic," notes anthropologist James Clifford, but rather contingent and subject to local reappropriation. In other words, ethnographic identity must always be understood as mixed, relational, and inventive. The racial and cultural purity that Curtis sought in his Indian portraits was first of all selective. He would often ask his male subjects, for example, to wear "traditional" costumes rather than their coveralls for his photographs, and his images rarely show Indian cultures as complex and adaptive.[20]

Carrying this analogy over into music, a transcribed Indian song notated by someone schooled in European musical practices differs from the actual performance of an Indian song in the same way that a photograph of an event differs from the event itself. Without knowledge about how to perform the song, its context, and allowances made for notational inaccuracies or compromises, the ink on paper fades to a pale substitution. This notated song is what we might call the first level of removal from a fully experiential cultural source.

In 1899 Krehbiel, a supporter of both Dvořák and MacDowell, prepared a survey of the scholarly literature on Indian music transcription. His resulting *New York Tribune* essay demonstrated his awareness of the complex (and sometimes ineffectual) processes involved in collecting and notating such music. He also drew attention to the number of American composers who had begun to adopt written transcriptions of Indian music "as thematic germs" for their own compositions. By 1899 Indian music had lost much of its earlier stigma. In fact it had developed a cachet, especially as adapted by composers. I would refer to adaptations such as MacDowell's character pieces as the second level of removal from an original musical source. Since the "folk melody" (or notated Indian song) is itself a mere lifeless "photo" once removed from the event, the composition is like a "portrait" of the musical photo. On the one hand, the composition reactivates the life of the notated melody (much as a documentary film that incorporates a photo might do), but, on the other, it adds a wholly imaginative dimension and crosses the threshold from life to art. Naturally, such musical portraiture fully engages the subjectivity of the artist, and each musical portrait, though it may use the same notated Indian themes as another work, results in a different interpretation of the subject it attempts to portray.

Musical portraiture similarly embodies constructs of native America that were based partly on source material (transcribed melodies) and partly on interpretation (the stylistic features of individual composers). Early twentieth-century composers, steeped in the notion that Indian cultures would soon vanish from the earth, felt it their right, if not their responsibility, to borrow what they saw as distinctive characteristics from Indian tribal musics. (Appendix 2 includes a selective list of such musical "tribal portraits," works that attempt to depict some particular aspect of a specific native American culture. The bulk of the tribal-specific compositions date from about 1903 to 1924, after which interest waned. For purposes of comparison, the list also includes important works that are largely indexical and do not feature specific tribal music. While this list is selective, it includes works produced by major music publishers, and I kept the overall proportion of findings roughly the same so as not to skew the data.) Following the recognition of the rhetorical power of pentatonicism in the 1890s, three new techniques that developed during this concentrated period contributed to the ongoing syntax in music that reflected native America—all of them in some way derived from folk cultures, though not necessarily American Indian cultures per se. These techniques encompassed (1) melodic parallelisms (also associated with primitivism, alterity, and orientalism); (2) modality (associated with ancientness as well as the sacred); and, less commonly, (3) dissonance (associated with the "rawness" of the primitive experience). Let's consider briefly the important roles of each of these with a few examples.

MELODIC PARALLELISM

It may be difficult to believe, but melodies stereotypically harmonized in parallel fourths or fifths, though ubiquitous in popular culture by the 1930s, were relatively uncommon at the beginning of the century. Westerners at this time would have had few opportunities to hear, for example, the sheng, a Chinese mouth organ that played melodies in parallel intervals such as fourths. Debussy and Ravel were familiar with it, of course, and imitated the effect in their later music. Puccini, though, was perhaps the first Western composer to use parallel fifths in *La bohème* (1896), where the fifths' "openness" symbolized the bleakness of winter. Melodies harmonized in parallel fourths first turn up in America—indeed, anywhere in modern Western composition, to my knowledge—in an Indian setting. These appeared as part of the remarkable (and much underrated) publishing venture of Arthur Farwell, who included a significant number of Indian character pieces in the early years of his Wa-Wan Press (Newton Center, Massachusetts, 1901–11).[21]

Particularly striking among the Indian items in the Wa-Wan series were those of Harvey Worthington Loomis. Exactly when Loomis wrote these is unknown, but Farwell published them in two installments as *Lyrics of the Red Man, Books 1 and* 2 (1903 and 1904). Loomis featured many of these works in his concerts, among them (as already noted) his much-publicized 1905 lecture-recital on Indian music in New York City. Though each of the character pieces was supposed to reflect some aspect of contemporary tribal Indian life, Loomis, who was no stranger to reaching beyond the borders of his style, created a distinctive Indian idiom all his own. Like his contemporary exoticists Granville Bantock in England and Charles Koechlin in France, he was steeped in orientalism and deeply immersed in Arabic and Chinese musical styles (as well as American Indian). In 1899 Witmark published Loomis's "Chinese Lullaby" (set to a verse by Edwin Starr Belknap), and as late as 1919 Oliver Ditson published "In Chinatown," a musical postcard from San Francisco. Works such the recitation *Sandalphon* and the opera *The Bey of Baba* reveal his fascination with the Middle East. One of Loomis's several dramatic pantomimes, *The Garden of Punchinello,* was even written for the Shah of Persia, Ahmad Shah Qujar, and in 1914 was performed in Tehran.[22]

To make the connection between Indian folksong and composition perfectly clear, Loomis (or Farwell, as editor) preceded each miniature with a musical epigraph of the original source melody from Fletcher and LaFlesche's *A Study of Omaha Indian Music.* Loomis's titles, like "Prayer to Wakonda," "Ripe Corn Dance," or "The Chattering Squaw," were clearly meant to stimulate performers' and listeners' imaginations. These were, at the very least, associations with specific aspects of modern Indian life, in contrast with, say, MacDowell's poetic titles. (As part of a lecture, of course, their Indian context would have been further clarified.) From a technical standpoint, they are more pianistically demanding than many other Indian character pieces. They are also stylistically different from anything that came before—indeed, from all previous Western instrumental music.

In "The Chattering Squaw," the work that caused such mirth among his New York audience, Loomis harmonized a pentatonic Cree melody in parallel fourths (table 6). While this feature might seem to us today to resemble some Tin Pan Alley Chinese stereotype, vaudeville songs about Asians at this time did not yet contain this particular feature. The parallel index entered the American popular song repertory sometime between 1903 and 1909, the same time that indexical Indian features began showing up in this venue.[23]

The accompaniment for "The Chattering Squaw" in the piano left hand is specified as imitating a large and small drum. The underlying rhythm is a persistent ♩ ♪𝄾. The original melody is basically in pentatonic mode V (here B♭–G–F–E♭–C), but it also contains nonpentatonic inflections: a D neighbor

Table 6. Melodic Parallel Motion in Three Indian Character Pieces, 1901–4

A. Edward MacDowell, "Indian Idyl" from *New England Idyls* (1901), middle section

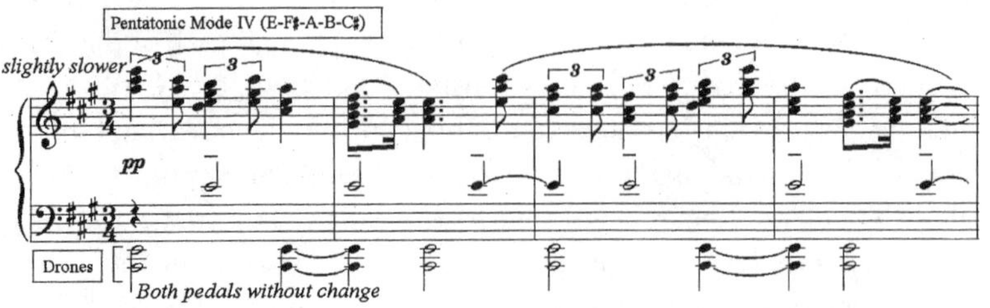

B. Ernest Kroeger, "March of the Indian Phantoms" (1904), beginning

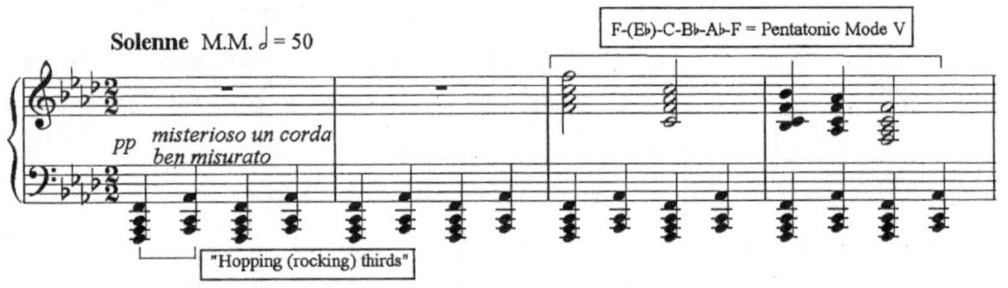

C. Harvey Worthington Loomis, "Chattering Squaw" from *Lyrics of the Red Man*, op. 76, book 2 (1904), mm. 3–10

tone above the high C and an A♭ passing tone between G and B♭. Loomis's parallelisms are actually quite sophisticated by comparison with the Tin Pan Alley parody of Chinese music, which is usually in strict parallel fourths. He keeps the A♭, for example, when the Cree melody reaches up to D, resulting in fourths that are sometimes perfect, sometimes tritone. The effect is odd but also shrill, which may have been intentional, given the nature of this droll song. In their use of melodic parallel fourths, Loomis's *Lyrics of the Red Man* are the earliest works to draw upon Far Eastern allusions to portray American Indians. Even Debussy, who used parallel fifths in the bass and inner voices, did not do so in the melody (in print anyway) until 1903 (in "Pagodes" from *Estampes*) and more overtly in 1905 (*La mer*) and 1910 (*Préludes*, Book 1). Indeed, Loomis's parallelisms in these Indian pieces seem to have been received as quite a novel effect. Critic Henry T. Finck's response implies that it was a new phenomenon to him as well. Instead of perceiving a connection with Asian music or anything by Debussy, however, Finck wrote that "The Chattering Squaw" was a work "in which consecutive fourths and fifths produce a cacophony reminding one of the medieval organum of Hucbald's day." We can presume that listeners in 1904 would have heard these melodic parallelisms as parody, as Far Eastern "oriental," or even—depending on their familiarity with music history—as neomedieval. In any case, a new trope had been added to musical Indianism.[24]

MODAL ACCOMPANIMENTS

Modality, on the other hand, had served as a distinctive colorist device in nineteenth-century Europe as a marker for the folk (as in Chopin's mazurkas) or for referencing older European church music (as in Liszt's oratorios). Western European composers also used modality for other purposes. Gounod and Respighi, for example, read late nineteenth-century treatises on sacred music by Niedermeyer, Bragers, Arnold, and others on how to provide accompaniments for, and thereby modernize, Gregorian chant. These scholars tried to reconcile the medieval Roman church modes with the normative practices of nineteenth-century major-minor harmony. The ancient Greek modes, from which the church modes were derived, were said to embody traits of character—Dorian for bravery, Phrygian for warlike, and so on—and it is well known that Plato believed strongly in their effect on human behavior. After several centuries of neglect, interest in the modes began to surge dramatically in the 1870s and early 1880s; this was largely due to influential composers such as Musorgsky (who found his national voice partly in old Russian Orthodox chants) and Debussy, who, significantly, had adopted the practice from Musorgsky. But in the early twentieth century, staunch nationalists like Vaughan Williams came to modality through a profound interest in regional folk music, much of which still retained the ancient modes. Moreover, pentatonic melodies could be mapped onto modal scales, as Bartók discovered around 1905. Pentatonic mode V, for example, could be set to Dorian, Phrygian, or Aeolian scales.

Modality was exceptional in nineteenth-century American orchestral and vocal music, showing up only in the "Indian" works of Arthur Foote and MacDowell. Yet by 1915, when Frederick Converse fashioned a sophisticated modal accompaniment as a solution for a migrating Cheyenne melody in *The Peace Pipe* (written for the Chautauqua Festival), modal settings of Indian music had become fairly common through tribal portraits and larger works. One obvious marker of modality, the lowered leading tone, "inevitably suggests antiquity," wrote the Iowa theorist and composer Horace Alden Miller in *New Harmonic Devices* (1930). Another particularly "Indian" device, according to Miller (who wrote quite a few Indian works himself), was the use of minor dominant chords (which of course incorporate the lowered leading tone). In a later study, *Modal Trends in Modern Music* (1941), Miller demonstrated how the harmonization of a Chippewa (Ojibwa) song could be accomplished without any dominant sevenths, relying solely on minor subdominants and other substitution chords. Miller even included examples of "Indian cadences" in his book. The lowered seventh figures prominently in many of these. One that Miller isolates as a particularly "interesting cadence" (B minor seventh to G major seventh) does have the uncommon effect of resolving to a dissonant chord. More important for our subject, however, the penultimate chord in this cadence (as well as the "minor dominant sevenths" that Miller highlights) is identical with the sonority of overlapping fifths in Dvořák's "New World" Scherzo (beginning in m. 5: E–B–G–D), which, as discussed in chapter 4, established a kind of primeval sound through modal suggestion.[25]

Natalie Curtis noted in 1913 that visiting European musicians such as Felix Mottl, Vasily Safonov, and Ferruccio Busoni, all of whom took "keen interest in our native music," found that Indian melodies needed a wider range of modal possibilities than simply major or minor accompaniments. The use of modes and other harmonic devices to avoid traditional harmonic associations has also been noted in the compositions of Amy Beach, not least in several works based on Indian themes, especially those of the Alaskan Inuit. Adrienne Fried Block has pointed out the expressive possibilities that Beach found in the use of folk music, particularly in her larger and more complicated forms. "Indian music," wrote Block, "provided her with themes of the utmost simplicity, almost without harmonic implications. In setting the theme Beach had to both simplify her harmonic style and find compositional means that allowed for development while not overwhelming the primitive themes."[26]

While composers such as Beach searched well into the 1920s for more effective ways to incorporate Indian themes (such as in the string quartet), modal harmony continued to offer an alternative to pure major-minor diatonicism, not only in Indianist music but also in works based on African American and Anglo-American spirituals and folk song, both of which retained many of the old modes. (We might ask why chromatic harmony, certainly another viable musical language in this post-Wagnerian age, was rarely used to invoke native America during this period. Given its fundamental connection to European musical modernism and expressionism, it may have been seen as too neurosis-laden or relating specifically to states of mind and therefore incompatible with the tropes of Indianism, which were either of the body and nature-based or of the soul and hence spirit-based.) Modality in Indian musical portraiture in the early twentieth century may have helped to infuse the works of MacDowell, Miller, Beach, Herbert, and even Sousa with a sense of authenticity (because of their ancientness). Perhaps because of its innate centuries-old characteristics, modality also served to deepen listeners' spiritual connection with the subject matter, regardless of how they may have felt about the contradictions between the nature of Indian music and the essentially Western medium of expression.

MODERNIST INFLUENCES

As editor of the Wa-Wan Press, Farwell wrote short essays to accompany each volume of this Americanist enterprise. In his introduction to volume 2, no. 12 (1903), he professed that he had arrived at nine "Articles of Faith" with which composers could turn to American Indian music, thereby finding the spiritual depth lacking in much contemporary classical music. At the same time, however, he had discovered "new motives and rhythms" in Indian music that were synchronous with modern sensibilities. He began with Fletcher's Omaha collection, of course, claiming that he had studied the songs as monophonic works, (i.e., without Fillmore's harmonizations). But when he set some of them himself in *American Indian Melodies* — his first character pieces — he rarely diverged from Fillmore's original harmonies. This may have been due largely to the fact that when he began setting Indian songs around 1900, there were no other models to follow, and his compositional style was still, as a young man, relatively undeveloped.[27]

The first of Farwell's *American Indian Melodies,* "The Approach of the Thunder God," could be compared with Fillmore's original setting to show that, with the exception of the added MacDowell-like "Indian" progression (iv^{6}–ii$^{6}_{5}$–i) in m. 9 and in the final cadence, Farwell makes only a few minor alterations in the accompaniment: some repeated notes and occasional smoother voice leading. Farwell's settings thereafter quickly grew more elaborate. Works such as *Dawn, Ichibuzzhi, The Domain of Hurakan* (all 1902), the first *Navajo War Dance* (1904 [later titled "No. 2" by John Kirkpatrick upon its belated publication in 1947]), and especially "Pawnee Horses" from the suite *From Mesa and Plain* (1905) are not just illustrations of how to harmonize an Indian melody; they are fully realized compositions that convey a solid compositional technique, an emotional depth, and a keen ability to convey the impression of place and experience in a quasi-narrative setting.[28]

Farwell was probably the first creative artist since George Catlin to draw existentially on American Indian subjects. He strove to escape the nineteenth-century's "imaginary Indian" and, like Edward Curtis, moved toward more realistic interpretations of living Indians and toward the representation of raw experience. His (actual) second *Navajo War Dance* for piano (1905) is particularly remarkable in its radical shift away from the more staid rhythmic and harmonic techniques of the previous generation of American composers. Dark and musically disjointed, its melodic inflections and rhythmic vigor reflect Farwell's encounters in the Southwest with Indian ritual music. He did not forget the thrill of excitement he first experienced from hearing two young Indian men sing Isleta Pueblo songs at the home of ethnologist and entrepreneur Charles Lummis in Los Angeles, nor the Navajo chanting and drumming he transcribed from Lummis's collection of cylinders. In 1909 he recalled the inception of the *Navajo War Dance*:

> It was at this time that I made my first really savage composition on Indian themes. . . . I had earlier inclined to the more pastoral songs and peace chorals, and folks reasoned naively that these could not represent the Indian, since the latter was a savage. Evidently I must reform and do something really Indian. The theme of the *Navajo War Dance* was something to make your blood curdle and your hair to stand on end.[29]

What was "blood curdling" about the work, however, was not any particular "savageness," but rather Farwell's experimentation with modernist techniques in harmony and rhythm in combination with the Navajo song. He peppered his accompaniment with nonfunctional dissonances and varied the length of successive phrases to avoid a sense of predictability. The first presentation of the theme, for example, cadences on the seventh measure, with an extra measure of repetition added to round off the phrase to eight. The next phrase cadences after only five measures, but Farwell adds a measure of interruption that seems imagistically evocative of a dancer's leap. After yet another extra measure (which sounds like imitations of vocal "yips"), a third phrase begins, though first with a one-measure false start. Played "with savage abandon," this phrase then proceeds to cadence unexpectedly on the sixth measure. The cadences are all on stark open fifths, but the harmonies that accompany the melodic phrases are quite pungent. Farwell also arrived at the solution—just about the same year as Bartók did—of setting a pentatonic melody to a nontraditional triad, one derived from the pentatonic mode of the source tune (in this case, C–D–G). He later adapted this piano work for the Westminster Choir in Princeton (*Four Songs on Indian Themes,* 1937). The eight-part a cappella choir sings triplets with Indian vocables: "*weh*-eh ah / *weh*-eh ah / *weh*-ah ha / *hi.*" In this revised version, the composer added even more dissonances and some new rhythmic features drawn from his experience of Navajo performers. The lower basses and altos hold firmly to a throbbing two (the drum) while the rest the chorus continues the triplets (the voices). In Navajo music, singers use freer rhythms, often in threes (which represents the spirit) against the regular patterns of the drumming (which represents the physical).

The Indian Character Piece in 1911

At this point, it may be useful to summarize some of the accumulating syntactical characteristics of the Indian character piece. John Fillmore first established a harmonic tradition for the genre by setting Indian songs in mostly major keys—rendering them rather like hymns—and used a modulating harmonization to accommodate the migrating pentatonic modes of the melodies. In addition to using polymeters, some of his more specialized harmonic devices involved the final falling on the fifth of the tonic and—in the rare occasion of minor cadences—the use of a specific progression ($\text{VI–ii}^{6}_{5}\text{–i}$).

MacDowell, in "From an Indian Lodge," expanded the "cadential Indian progressions" (to include $\text{v}^{6}\text{–iv}^{6}\text{–ii}^{6}_{5}\text{–i}$) and incorporated pulsing open fifths in the bass. In addition to adapting Fillmore's "modulating harmonization" and cadential figures, Farwell added dissonances to his Indian music to sharpen its intensity, and he varied the lengths of phrases partly in imitation of Native American improvisational styles. Loomis added melodic parallel fourths over persistent drumlike rhythms to create a new "oriental" trope, lending American Indian settings a distinctive Asian flavor. Meanwhile, the modality that all along had been an archetypal feature of the sacred and the spiritual in *Hiawatha* settings (by Foote and Coleridge-Taylor but also by others after 1900) challenged the older syntactical devices of savagery and established a kind of pseudospirituality available to all Indian character pieces.

We can now return to the Henry Gilbert character piece with which this chapter began. "By the Arrow," the first in the five *Indian Scenes,* was originally written, as previously noted, as part of "The Vanishing Race" musicale in 1911. "My greatest desire tonight," Curtis began his lecture, "is that each and every person here enter into the spirit of our evening with the Indians." Much later, after concluding a series of photographs taken on the shores of the

Example 13. Henry Gilbert, "By the Arrow" from *Indian Scenes* (New York: H. W. Gray, 1912), 4–5.

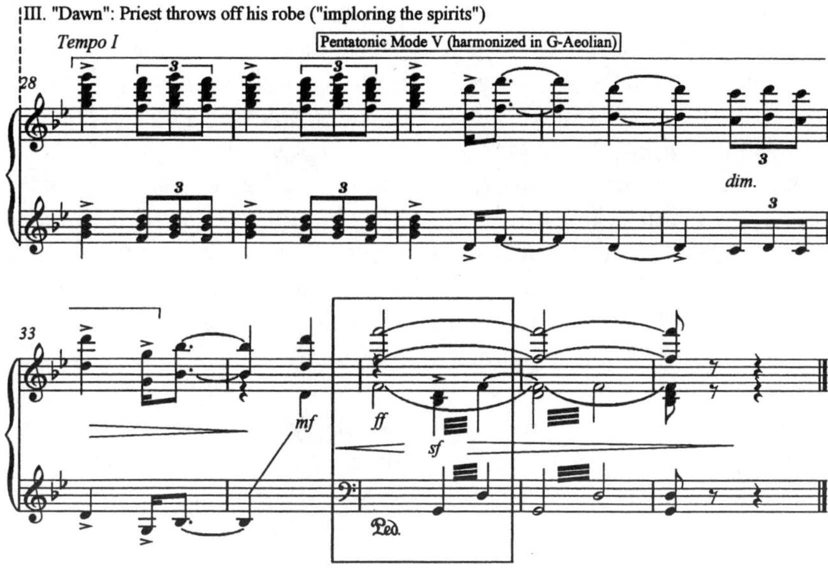

North Pacific, Curtis's slide show turned to the Puebloan peoples. His narration against a blank screen set the tone for the series of images to follow:

> "By the arrow I make my vow" is the thought in the coming dissolving view. In the first scene we have the striking figure of the priest against the sunlit sky, holding the arrow to the dying day. The theme of picture and music is the vigor of declaration and devotion. This sunset scene changes to one of our blanket-wrapped priest with arrow high held to the starlit sky, a powerful figure of invocation. Then creeps on gray dawn. As the sun appears our priest has again thrown off his robe, and stands imploring the spirits of the east and the newborn day.[30]

Curtis then fell silent as the orchestra took over and the dissolving series began. Gilbert's music served to bridge the lapses of time between the sunset, night, and dawn photos, unifying the images both emotionally and spiritually.

"By the Arrow" opens with resolve on a strongly reinforced unison Pueblo chant (the "sunset" photo). It uses only three-notes — G–F–D — and suggests a "minor" pentatonic (likely mode III, because D is set up as the tonic center). Gilbert avoids giving this melody a harmonic setting until it returns at the end (m. 28), where it now basks in a rich harmonization in G minor. Instead of ending on D, it moves downward through C to reach G, leading to a conclusive assertion of mode V (G–B♭–C–D–F) for the "dawn." Between the opening sunset, which fades on a sequence of whole-tone melodies, and the return of this rhythmically distinctive theme, the middle section (accompanying the "starlit" photo) is less melodic, more free-flowing, and more impressionistic in terms of vague motives and unstable keys. While the opening and closing melody clearly alludes to a firmly pentatonic world, the middle section (the "invocation") seems to float through a series of uncertain moods, marked only by the occasional iambic rhythm (the "Scottish snap," mm. 15 and 17) and the indexical open fifths in the bass (mm. 18–19). Gilbert suggests the coming dawn in the overlapping phrases as one image dissolves into another until a musical climax (*fortissimo*) is reached with the appearance of the sun and the final photo, which depicts the priest as a figure of great dignity, standing on a cliff and holding the arrow high against the natural beauty of the New Mexico desert.

Gilbert's *Indian Scenes* are little played today, and "By the Arrow" would probably not seem quite as effective in concert as, say, the character pieces of MacDowell or Farwell. In the history of American instrumental music that depicted "characters," however, it ranks high in importance because it was billed as "real Indian music" during its performances in Carnegie Hall and other important venues and was probably perceived as having been infused by such at the time. The features that are markers of the "ancient," notably the pentatonicism and octave doublings, and the harmonic features such as obscure or modulating tonal centers or modal suggestions (e.g., the natural seventh, rather than a leading tone, in m. 27), implied the "red man's harmonies" to white audiences in 1911. This was especially true when such features were combined syntactically, even though apart they may have suggested other origins or associations.

Most important, perhaps, the final powerful cadence as the priest implores the spirits of the newborn day could also not escape a long-standing Indian association. The final statement of the theme in m. 32, instead of resolving downward to G, goes up to F. This note, held against the thundering G-minor chord played by the full orchestra, results in a final climactic resolution on a minor dominant seventh (i^7), the same sonority previously noted in Dvořák's "New World" Symphony and one of the principal chords for "Indian cadences" cited in Miller's theoretical treatise. Here there is one crucial difference, however. Dvořák used this chord to build excitement and underpin the introduction of a new theme, while Miller used it as a true "modal dominant" that resolved to another chord. For Gilbert, this modal chord (which could imply Dorian, Phrygian, or Aeolian) served as an end in itself. Its effect here—as it increasingly became throughout its use in the early twentieth century—is one of ancientness, of darkness and mystery, but also of tragedy. As the priest greets the dawn in an ostensibly triumphant moment, the majestic Pueblo chant is overtaken by the shadow of lost grandeur — yet another device added to the long history of Indianist tropes.[31]

In this discussion of Indian character pieces, which essentially grew out of an ethnological interest in Indian culture and folklore, we have seen how each work had its own way of rendering an iconic "Indian portrait," even while some basic musical characteristics tended to recur from piece to piece. The apparent authentic qualities of these "Indian" works were later absorbed into larger instrumental forms, such as those of Busoni's elaborate *Indian Fantasy* (piano and orchestra, 1914); Charles Sanford Skilton's terse *Suite Primeval* (orchestra, 1916–21); Preston Ware Orem's amazing virtuoso showpiece, *American Indian Rhapsody* (piano, 1918, orchestrated by Sousa in 1919); Charles Tomlinson Griffes's poignant *Two Sketches for String Quartet on Indian Themes* (1919); Frederick Jacobi's modernist *Indian Dances* (orchestra, 1928); and Amy Beach's Inuit-inspired *Quartet for Strings in One Movement* (1929). By then, too, Latin American composers, among them Heitor Villa-Lobos, Manuel M. Ponce, José Rolón, Candelario Huízar, Carlos Chávez, and Silvestre Revueltas, had also begun to incorporate Indian songs or references into larger instrumental works. Among the most famous of these, perhaps, is Chávez's *Sinfonía India* (Mexico City, 1936), an orchestral work based on melodies collected from the Yaqui, Seri, Tohono O'odham, and other Mesoamerican Indians.

In the early twentieth century the Indian character piece thus emerged as a testimony to the fact that ethnographic knowledge about native America combined with modernist musical techniques could lead to a sense of authenticity in the creation of iconic representations. At the same time, however, many of these pieces also pointed to the possibility that even such hybrid representations would exist at a relatively greater distance from Indian people's experience. By 1911, the year of Curtis and Gilbert's "picture-musicale," the year when a new wave of operas with Indian characters began to reach the American stage, and about the time when film began its ascendancy as a dominant form of cultural expression, the standard theoretical components of music used to imagine native America had asserted their hegemony in the public sphere.

PART IV

Americans Again

8

"I'm an Indian Too": Playing Indian in Song and on Stage, 1900–1946

When a young Charles Wakefield Cadman embarked on his "Indian Music Talks" in 1909 with Tsianina Redfeather (Cherokee-Creek), the Cherokees were still recovering from the 1898 Curtis Act that first converted their reservation land into allotments and then, in 1906, into the state of Oklahoma. While in the first decade of the twentieth century many Indian people were struggling to make a place for themselves in American society (or to be left alone), romanticized Indians flourished in the arts. Not since the 1840s had there been such an astonishing proliferation of American Indian icons. How and why Indian subjects became extraordinarily commercial at a time when the political influence of Indians themselves was perhaps at its lowest point in history are questions that deserve more analysis than they have received. The enormous popularity of "Indian songs," rife with interracial flirtation and innuendo, was due at least partly to the gradual lifting of the Victorian veil of modesty after the turn of the century. But what exactly did Will Rossiter's music firm in Chicago hope to achieve in 1906 with "My Pretty Little Maid of Cherokee (I'd Like to Join Your Family)"? Or what purpose did anyone have in singing it? What kind of business did Newton Publishers (also in Chicago) hope to generate with "You're an Indian, He's an Indian, I'm an Indian too," a song popularized (also 1906) by vaudeville singer Stella Mayhew?[1] Or what did Rossiter's firm mean when it later sold "My Pretty Little

Indian Napanee" with the announcement that "it 'scalps' all other Indian songs"?

The backstory to the commercialization of native America during this decade includes the activities of groups such as the Indian Rights Association (formed in 1882 to encourage Indian assimilation), the territorial obsessions of the secretary of the interior, the meddling of the Office of Indian Affairs, and the government sale of allotments to Indian families, a plan partly devised in hopes that the federal government would thereby acquire any unassigned reservation land. The land runs in Oklahoma Territory that began in 1889, for example, culminated in the disastrous Supreme Court case *Lone Wolf v. Hitchcock* of 1901–3 (the years when Farwell began the Wa-Wan Press). (The Indian territories in Oklahoma around 1903—just about the time the "Indian songs" about reservations began to flood the sheet music industry—can be seen in map 3.) While Lone Wolf persisted in his appeals, the Office of Indian Affairs decided after the Supreme Court's first rejection of Kiowa-Cherokee claims that Indian consent was no longer needed to lease reservation lands and resources. With the humiliating Burke Act of 1906, Indians were forced to prove they were competent to manage their allotments; otherwise, they lost them. This law was the last straw for the Oklahoma Indians, the "final disposition . . . of the Five Civilized Tribes," as historian Francis Prucha has put it. In 1914 U.S. Secretary of the Interior Franklin Lane announced that the Cherokee Nation had officially ceased to exist. "It takes hold upon the imagination and the memory," he added, "[and] arouses dreams of the day when the Indian shall be wholly blended into our life, and at the same time draws the mind backward over the stumbling story of our relationship with him." After the Office of Indian Affairs' triumph over the Cherokees in 1906, the Standing Rock Sioux were next on the agenda. And so it continued.[2]

The year of the crucial Supreme Court decision, 1903, marked a turning point in Indian-white relations and raised new questions about the roles of American Indians in the nation. If Congress, following the Indian Rights Association, wanted the Indians to assimilate into American society (to "wholly blend"), how would white Americans deal with anxieties about Indians actually assimilating, especially at a time when laws against racial intermarriage were in effect in most states? Since "removal" was obviously no longer an option, would the United States be willing to absorb some 250,000 of its surviving Indian population? Could (or would) all Indians be assimilated? And what of white anxieties about past mistreatment of the Indian peoples, anxieties that no doubt still bubbled beneath the surface of many encounters? Efforts to eradicate the reservation system during a time of urban crowding and sharply rising immigration must have struck a chord that resonated deep

Map 3. Indian lands and allotments that were banded into the state of Oklahoma, 1885–1907. From Kenneth T. Jackson, ed., *Atlas of American History* (New York: Charles Scribner's Sons, 1943, rev. 1978), 176. Used by permission.

in society and perhaps even ran right to the heart of American identity. Indian characters and the worlds they supposedly inhabited adorned the covers of songs, but they also thrived as parodies in vaudeville and as serious characters in plays, silent film, and even on the opera stage. It was now acceptable—even fashionable—to fantasize being Indian, as "My Pretty Little Maid of Cherokee" seemed to assert.

For many Indians, living on the reservations increasingly meant being on the federal dole, while native languages and social traditions were constantly imperiled by government-run schools and Indian agencies seeking to transform tribal customs. And yet in popular American culture these spaces served as a fixed locus of idyllic romance. The lyrics and the dreamy music of "Indian love songs" provided urban Americans with a form of escape from the ills of the modern industrial city. It seemed relatively common, so the songs told us, for a white man to wander onto a reservation and fall in love with an Indian maiden. But such a mixed-race relationship could not easily be reconciled in the harsh light of early twentieth-century society. The only solution for the two lovers, it seemed, would be to remain on Indian soil.

American songs reflected a range of positions that were acceptable (or not) for Indian peoples to play in the future of America. One can't speak about the extraordinary popularity of Cadman's "From the Land of the Sky-Blue Water" (1909) or Rudolf Friml's "Indian Love Call" (1924) — both operetta-like in style — without also understanding how the war-dance trope entered the popular song market with such songs as "Navajo" (1903), "Big Indian Chief" (1904), or Gus Edwards's "Tammany" (1905), all of them featured in Broadway reviews. "Indian" sheet music — while the songs were not always of the same quality — sold as much for their richly colored covers as they did for the racy lyrics inside. Moreover, the genres of popular and "art" songs did not necessarily follow divergent paths. It would be shortsighted to discuss an operatic event such as the premiere of Victor Herbert's *Natoma* (1911) without understanding something of his librettist's connections with popular Indianism or with the elitist "grove plays" of the Northern California Bohemian Club. As in earlier decades of American history, serious efforts at "playing Indian" — for example, the Reservation Scene of Cadman's *Shanewis* (1918), an unusual experiment at both the Metropolitan Opera and the Hollywood Bowl — were parodied in song and onstage, leading to some of the most outlandish representations ever seen in Broadway reviews, musicals, and films, most memorable perhaps being those of *Whoopie!* and *Annie Get Your Gun.* Even a discussion of Robert Russell Bennett's orchestrations for the latter would be enhanced by knowing about Bennett's relationship with his first mentor Carl Busch, a noted Indian hobbyist. Many of the shared indexical (or "Indianesque") musical devices in these genres, as varied as they are, confirm that our present art-music/popular-music divide was not yet pronounced in the first half of the twentieth century, particularly regarding a subject matter as self-consciously "American" as that of North America's Indian peoples. When looking back on this period, it is important to recognize the dialectical relationship between these cultural genres, as well as the social and political circumstances that enabled them to flourish.

The Rage for "Indian Love Songs"

In 1899 an explorer for the Canadian Pacific Railway Company, L. O. Armstrong, founded the community of Desbarats in Ontario, Canada, and, with the endorsement of Longfellow's daughter, began to produce an outdoor *Hiawatha* play at Kensington Point along the banks of Lake Huron. He engaged his Ojibwa neighbors as actors who improvised, sang, and danced the story. For some atmospheric music Alice Longfellow recommended Frederick Burton, who the year before had conducted his *Hiawatha* cantata with the Yonkers (N.Y.) Choral Society and an orchestra of about thirty musicians. Burton responded by including some portions of his cantata but also by writing some new music based on Ojibwa songs that he learned while visiting the community. He hit on the solution of having the Ojibwas perform their own music at all diegetic moments in the play while a "hidden" chorus and orchestra of white performers would provide background music for the various pantomimes and scenes of pageantry. The performances ran several summers and attracted widely diverse audiences. In 1903 the *Hiawatha* play toured to several American and Canadian cities. For this run Burton wrote yet more music, including an overture, a funeral march, Hiawatha's "Death Song" (clearly a number requiring new text, since Hiawatha does not die in Longfellow), a set of variations on an Ojibwa song, and the lovely "My Bark Canoe," all of which he apparently derived while listening to native singers at Desbarats. Outdoor performances of the play continued for many years afterward, though Burton's romanticized background music was eventually dropped.[3]

When Burton included "My Bark Canoe" as one of his *Songs of the Ojibways* (1902), he was among the first to publish such vocal settings as art songs. A few years later he explained that he found the music of this northern Great Lakes tribe more beautiful, more conducive to "translation," than other North American Indian styles. It was the quality of the melodies themselves, he felt, and not the extramusical content that lent Indian music its special usefulness for composition. Hence it was not necessary for non-Indian listeners to know the legends behind the music. Burton also explained why he felt the need to cloak "My Bark Canoe" in Western harmonization. Though he admitted he would rather hear the tune sung in its natural environment, few white people, he lamented, would have the chance to hear it that way. Perhaps some would have had the politeness to listen to him render the song in the course of a lecture, Burton commented, but that could hardly compare to the number of times it was sung in public schools and concerts with its "pretty accompaniment":

> In these harmonized forms . . . it never fails to cause unbounded surprise that an Indian could have composed a melody so beautiful. Thus has it served well its first purpose in art, and incidentally it has been instrumental in awakening a sane human interest in the Indian and in inciting singers and hearers of the melody to the acquisition of some measure of truth about him to replace the ignorance and misinformation that fester in the average white man's mind with regard to him.

Whether this was Burton's original intent or not, the song demonstrated what he called "the common humanity of the red man." In its delicate and slightly nostalgic way, it carried a moral message and thereby sought to revise public opinion about the sentiment and creative spirit of Indian peoples.[4]

Burton published "My Bark Canoe" with the original Ojibwa text and with his own elaborated translation. He related how, sometime before the turn of the century, he transcribed what he happened to overhear in secret. The melody follows a migrating pentatonic pattern, beginning in mode V and modulating downward to mode IV:

E♭–F–E♭–C–B♭–A♭–F	5–6–5–3–2–1–$\underline{6}$ and
A♭–B♭–C–B♭–F–A♭–F–E♭	1–2–3–2–1–$\underline{6}$–$\underline{5}$

Burton set this tune to a delicate accompaniment that floats between tonic and subdominant; the occasional minor subdominant chord adds a wisp of melancholy. Yet the song's appeal was based on more than these simple features. It consists of three identical descending musical phrases, each with the same text. Translated, it reads simply: "I am out all night on the river." Later, when Burton gained the assistance of someone to help him with the Ojibwa verse, he was told it actually meant "I am out all night on the river seeking for my sweetheart." "Where is the word for sweetheart?" Burton asked. His Indian informant told him that it was not there, so Burton logically asked how one could know that a sweetheart was part of the story. "Why does a man keep awake all night when he want[s] to sleep?" was the rejoinder. "He might be hunting for deer, or something else to eat," Burton offered. "No, no! Only one reason," the Indian guide insisted. "We know that the man who made this song was looking for his sweetheart and we do not need the word."[5]

Leaning heavily upon this interpretation, Burton outfitted the tune with textual allusions to gliding canoes and nocturnal trysts. His setting, too, seems to suggest a romantic moonlit atmosphere. Burton concluded that, while "the Indian is content to sing his one line over and over again," the "paleface" must have some musical and textual variety. Hence the nature of this short love song. "My Bark Canoe" was the only piece from the Desbarats pageant to enjoy any life of its own. (Indeed, Julia and Ernest Seton included it in *Rhythm of the Redman,* a book that in the 1930s became an important addition to Boy Scout lore.) Meanwhile, as the *Hiawatha* play began to gain notoriety, Coleridge-Taylor's Victorian *Hiawatha* cantatas received their first American performances with choral societies in Boston, New York, Washington, Chicago, and elsewhere.

Coincidentally with "My Bark Canoe," John Philip Sousa had begun to perform a tune by Charles K. Daniels originally called "In Hiawatha: A Summer Idyll" (1901). The "Hiawatha" here was not Longfellow's or Coleridge-Taylor's protagonist or even that of the Canadian Ojibwa actors. It was the name of a small town in Kansas. Daniels's girlfriend lived in Hiawatha, and the rhythm of his piano piece was supposed to capture the rolling wheels of the train that often took him to that idyllic town. Daniels's tune began as a "characteristic," a romantic instrumental composed in a series of strains and a trio, and he probably played the song on the Peebles' parlor piano in an effort to woo their daughter, Ruth. He published the "idyll" with his own music company in St. Louis under the pseudonym "Neil Moret." In 1903 publisher Jerome Remick of Whitney-Warner in Detroit bought Daniels's tune for a reputed $10,000, according to ASCAP records, whereupon he added the genre designation of "intermezzo." As rights holder of the song, Remick thought an Indian subject would sell more copies, so he asked twenty-one-year-old James O'Dea, fresh from his success with the early Broadway extravaganza *The Wizard of Oz,* to add lyrics. Already growing in popularity as an instrumental, "Hiawatha (His Song to Minnehaha)" was sung in March 1903 in *Show Girl,* Seymour Rice's revue at the Detroit Opera House, and with the assistance of a Victor recording sung by Harry Macdonough, it proved an instant sensation. Even a reviewer in London wrote that "the bands [here] play it, the boys whistle it, hand organs grind it out, and the hawkers of pirated music sell it on the street." Sousa's rendering had already popularized the work as a bona fide march two-step—a novelty for the dance hall or review stage, not the parlor. Technically speaking, the song was not ragtime, as it lacked ragtime's requisite syncopations. But "Hiawatha" did have an infectious, easily counterfeited rhythmic device that O'Dea fitted to clever alliteration—"Oh the moon is all a*gleam* / on the *stream* where I *dream* / here of you my pretty *In*dian maid." As successful as this song was, there was nothing explicitly Indian about the music, nor did it feature any indexical Indianisms.[6]

Besides its catchy rhythm, another of its instantly memorable features was what Roger Hankins has called the "Indian theme": the refrain "I am your own, your Hiawatha brave," particularly the upbeat F–E–F (in F major) to G over the subdominant B♭ major, then F–E–D resolving to C over the tonic (or, in scale degrees, $\hat{1}$–$\underline{\hat{7}}$–$\hat{1}$–$\hat{2}$–$\hat{1}$–$\underline{\hat{7}}$–$\underline{\hat{6}}$–$\underline{\hat{5}}$). This polkalike passage isn't really an Indian theme, of course, but it turns up in such a significant number of popular "Indian" songs after "Hiawatha" that Hankins found it useful to label it as such.[7]

Moret's success with this song catapulted him into the role of publishing executive with Remick in New York, and "Hiawatha" itself sparked a host of imitations. Again, these were not ragtime songs but rather two-steps that duplicated the original's rolling-train rhythm and O'Dea's alliteration. Among the direct imitations were Vivian Grey's "Anona" (1903), Frederick Hager's "Laughing Water" (1903), Sadie Konisky's "A Wigwam Courtship" (1903), Theodore F. Morse's "Great Big Chickapoo Chief" (1904), Silvio Hein's "Pawnee" (1906), Charles Humfeld's "Red Moon" (1908), Johann C. Schmidt's "Moon-Bird" (1909), and Egbert Van Alstyne's "Golden Arrow" (1909). Although the covers of these songs seemed bent on outdoing one another with their colorful prairie vistas and fiery sunsets (fig. 15), the "Hiawatha" imitation pretty much ran its course with Percy Wenrich's "Silver Bell" (1910). On the other hand, Kerry Mills's "Red Wing" (1907) was probably the most long-lived song and dance piece to popularize this "Indian theme" refrain. Like many other popular American song composers in these decades, Daniels himself went on to compose several more "Indian" songs and instrumentals.[8]

As a genre unto itself, the instrumental characteristic has a long history, stretching back to "characteristic pieces" in theatrical productions of the early 1800s. In the first decade of the twentieth century, such works were used interchangeably for popular concerts, theatrical productions, and, beginning about 1910, for silent-film accompaniment. Indian characteristics also appeared under different rubrics. In the 1890s and early 1900s, the term "intermezzo" was used instead of rag to impart a sense of sophistication and to distinguish an instrumental from the naughtier genre. When, for example, Scott Joplin dedicated a rag to the woman he was going to marry, he called it an "Afro-American Intermezzo." Remick's intent with "Hiawatha" was probably to elevate its status. Perhaps because of their functional elasticity, a few "Indian intermezzos" were written in other countries as well. Herman Federoff's "Moja Indianka" was published in London in 1913, and then the following year in Baltimore as "My Indian Maid." (Its origins are presumably Slavic.) Of course, intermezzos—as the name implies—were sometimes used as entr'actes in stage productions; Theodore Bendix's intermezzo for *The Squaw Man,* produced by David Belasco in 1905, was one notable example. This theatrical practice was no doubt inspired by the famous operatic intermezzo from Mascagni's *Cavalleria rusticana* (1890), popularly adapted in America throughout the 1890s. But most Indian intermezzos were not theatrical. In 1910 in Bismarck, North Dakota, Sousa's band performed Rollin Bond's *Sacajawea: Indian Intermezzo,* a work commissioned for the dedication of a statue of the Shoshone heroine.[9]

As with instrumentals, several types of "Indian songs" were popular during this period. Art songs of the parlor and concert variety were stylistically related to the operetta genre, although not all originated on the stage. These were issued by classically oriented publishers—such as Farwell's Wa-Wan Press in Boston or Forster in Chicago—and ranged from songs based directly on Indian

Figure 15. Sheet music cover for Egbert Van Alstyne's "Golden Arrow" (1909). The Lester S. Levy Collection of Sheet Music, Special Collections, The Sheridan Libraries of the Johns Hopkins University.

sources, such as Burton's "My Bark Canoe" or Carlos Troyer's "Lover's Wooing" (1904), to freely imaginative tunes, such as Frederick Logan's "Pale Moon: An Indian Love Song" (1920). "Ragtime songs," popular from about 1903, usually meant words added to an instrumental; the opening or second strain became the verse, the trio the chorus. The proliferation of Indian "ragtime songs" during these years may well have been due partly to a desire to emulate Moret and O'Dea's success. At the same time, we should not overlook such coincidences as Coleridge-Taylor's visit to Washington in 1904 to conduct a complete *Hiawatha* in Constitution Hall with the expanded U.S. Marine Band, a performance that (given a black conductor on the podium) made quite a splash in the press. More importantly, however, the nation was experiencing social turmoil over the court decisions involving Indians and land rights. Just about the time of the Lone Wolf ruling, new features infiltrated the Indian "love songs," and these could not be attributed solely to the "Hiawatha" fashion.

Beginning with Sadie Konisky's "A Wigwam Courtship" and Egbert Van Alstyne's "Navajo" (both 1903), "Indian" songs gradually begin to reveal features of the nineteenth-century war-dance trope. Grace notes—long used as exotic inflections—turn up as end-of-phrase whoops in "Navajo," a song that also was the first of the "Indian songs" to use a pentatonic melody. In 1903 Marie Cahill inserted "Navajo" into the revue *Nancy Brown*. Her portrait on Remick's sheet-music cover helped to sell copies, and other singers took up the song, featuring delicate war-dance tropes in the verse and a mode III pentatonic chorus ("Na-va, Na-va, *my* Navajo"). A few golden-throated tenors such as Billy Murray and Harry Macdonough recorded it.

Not all the popular Indian songs were specifically written for Broadway revues, but many, like "Hiawatha" or "Navajo," received a boost when sung onstage. In Weber and Field's *English Daisy* of 1904, J. Rosamond Johnson's "Big Indian Chief" was noted as the hit of the show, even though the song—with its repeating "tom-tom" chords in the verse and mode IV pentatonic chorus—had nothing to do with the scenario, having originally been written as a variety number for the Mask and Wig, the University of Pennsylvania's thespian society. (The first line of the chorus ran "Big Chief love um little Kick-a-poo maiden, / Love um heap much too.") In Weber and Ziegfeld's *Higgledy-Piggledy,* also of 1904, composer Maurice Levi interpolated "Big Indian and His Little Maid" into this Americans-traveling-in-Europe farce. By 1904 "Indian songs" with a war-trope verse and a major-mode pentatonic chorus had become so fashionable that almost any opportunity to plug one seemed a good idea. (And it didn't hurt the expanding sheet music publishing industry either.) Moreover, the increasing surge of pentatonicism in popular music after 1904 may have received some impetus from the sensation surrounding the recent premiere of Puccini's *Madama Butterfly,* an operatic event with many ramifications in American drama and music.

The throbbing "tom-tom" fifths—also heard in *Butterfly* (act 3)—appeared in many Indian songs about this time. "A Wigwam Courtship" had used sustained pedal fifths (like a pastoral drone). In 1904 Louis Arden Schuch employed pulsing minor chords for "Idaho," and Theodore F. Morse used "rocking fifths" (as opposed to repeating fifths) in "Great Big Chickapoo Chief." Raymond A. Browne used a repeating tom-tom open-fifth trope for "On the War-Path: A Wild-West Two-Step" (also 1904). Though the tom-tom effect had occasionally appeared in nineteenth-century balletic *danses sauvages,* "On the War-Path" is the first such instance I have found in an American popular song.[10]

In 1905 Gus Edwards used the upwards octave leap in "Tammany: A Pale Face Pow-wow," repeating it insistently for effect (fig. 16). The song was originally written as a rallying cry for the New York political organization. (Other "Indian songs" were similarly written for clubs and societies.) "Tammany" was incorporated by comedian Jefferson DeAngelis in Sam Schubert's production of *Fantana,* for which, in his role as a valet posing as the Japanese ambassador, it had no specific connection. (Continuing a tradition begun as early as the appearance of the "Death Song" in Royall Tyler's *The Contrast* of 1787, this "Indian song" was fitted to the play simply because of its recent popularity.) In addition to the upward-octave leap, "Tammany" contains many war-dance characteristics. Hopping fifths, grace notes, and tom-tom effects accompany the verse ("Hiawatha was an Indian . . ."). The refrain ("Tammany") almost slips out of the war-dance trope, but the upward leaping octaves return with a vengeance in the final line, "Swamp 'em, Swamp 'em, get the 'wam-pum,' Tammany" (set to the same music as at the end of the instrumental introduction in fig. 16).

If Charles Daniels never intended any Indian allusions in his "Hiawatha," he certainly found himself swept up in the fashion by 1905. His "Silverheels Intermezzo," though an upbeat "Hiawatha"-style two-step, incorporates several new and interesting devices. The A strain features a mode V pentatonic melody (typically harmonized in minor) set here to a major-mode accompaniment. The effect is vaguely non-Western, but without any ethnic specificity. Then in the B strain comes the "savage" thrill: a plunging mode V pentatonic war-dance–style tune over an intricate rhythmic accompaniment in B minor. But all is well, as the trio cheerfully explores a migrating pentatonic melody over G major, with many prominent Es in the melody. Strange as it may seem given the pentatonic material, this added-sixth color (G–B–D–E as a chord) had not been emphasized in popular song before, and rarely, if at all, in Indian characteristic pieces. (MacDowell had hinted at it delicately in his "Indian Idyl" of 1901.) Daniels's intermezzo contains a topical variety that ranges from the minstrel-like exposition to the dramatic interruption of the throbbing B strain to an almost pastoral resolution in the trio. There is an element of

Figure 16. Gus Edwards, "Tammany" (1905). Historic American Sheet Music, 1850–1920, Duke University.

burlesque parody in Daniels's combination of these elements that almost escapes the listener, so masterful is his control of their fluidity.[11]

Burlesque also influenced the topics of many popular "Indian songs," almost all of which concerned love (and decidedly not, like the popular "Indian songs" of the 1840s, dead warriors or lost homelands). Usually the lovers were Indian, although sometimes the texts were racially vague, allowing for the possible interpretation of a white man wooing an Indian woman. Some others, such as Ted Snyder's "Ogalalla," sung in 1909 by the vaudevillian couple Mabel Hite and Mike Donlin, have the white man clearly speaking pidgin for the "benefit" of his Indian bride. In addition to poking fun at accented English and glorifying a childlike image of Indian life, Vincent Bryan's lyrics engaged a fake medicine-show dialect in the chorus:

(Verse) Many moons ago,
down in Mexico,
Out upon the Indian reservation,
Lived a redskin queen,
she was just eighteen,
Sweetest girl in all her dusky nation.
Riding from the north a cowboy came,
She met him and set his heart aflame,
Ev'ry night they'd ride
o'er the prairie wide,
While to explain his love he tried.

(Chorus) Ogalalla, Ogalalla,
Heap much lovee, you love me,
Soon we ride quick my tepee
Ogalalla, Ogalalla,
Big chief get sore, and he make much war,
But we go before,
If you be my squaw
My Ogalalla, follow me.[12]

The assonance and repetition of the word "Ogalalla"—set to the rhythm ♩. ♪♪♩. —served as an important hook for this song (much like O'Dea's "Hiawatha" alliteration). At the same time the lyrics evoked irresistibly delicious images: an escape to Mexico and cowboys sweeping young girls off their feet. But they also leaned heavily on verbal triggers already loaded with associations from dime-novel culture: words such as "redskin," "dusky," "big chief," and "squaw." Clearly, this minstrel-like song was not intended to poke fun at Indian life as much as it relied upon received ideas for a tale about courtship between a white man and an Indian woman (and the "much war" that would likely follow). If we dig a little deeper, however, we can also see that, for all its lampooning of Indian culture, the song laughs away the deep-seated taboo of miscegenation. Intermarriage between whites and Indians was technically legal (unlike for other racial combinations); Native American women had been marrying white men since colonial times, as many scholars have pointed out. But antimiscegenation sentiments lay at the core of many similar Tin Pan Alley songs. Unlike songs of the 1840s that served to distance Indians from dominant society, however, "Ogalalla" toyed with the idea that it was possible, even desirable, to "become Indian." The fake Indian speech, also found in other types of revue songs, masked the seriousness of the issues underlying such songs, many of them rooted in anxieties about racial assimilation. Surveys of popular songs of this period generally interpret the "Indian songs" as thwarted romance, with the lovers as both Indian.[13] But in many of these songs, racial identities are—purposefully, in my opinion—left vague, as with the "cowboy" in "Ogalalla."

If a song made no attempt to disguise a racial union, it rarely supported it. Peter S. Clark's "My Copper Colored Squaw" (St. Louis, 1909) is written from the point of view of the chief, who admonishes his daughter for loving a white man. Clark begins the song with melodramatic "horror chords"—emphatic diminished sevenths—that warn of the consequences of interracial union. As the "squaw's" father pronounces: "Big Chief heepee wild, / white man love him child, / squaw she make chief scalp her young white lover." (The cover, gentler than this, shows the daughter pleading with her father while the chief sternly orders her ranchman away.) Clark's song is practically a compendium of indexical Indian features, including octave leaps with grace notes and pentatonic melodies. It even opens with a simulated war dance in D minor over tom-tom fifths.

While cultural anxiety about Indian-white relations underlay many of the "Indian songs," the subjects were not always serious. The popularity of vaudeville in the United States (which continued well into the 1930s) demonstrated that a large number of Americans found great entertainment value in clichés and various cultural differences that could be milked for humorous effect. When, for example, American Indians enlisted to serve in the United States army during the Spanish-American war of 1898, they were welcomed by the federal government. But a prominent vaudeville song of 1918, Henry and Savino's "Indianola," ridiculed these valiant men even in the midst of a jingoistic call for American action against German imperialism: "Me hear cannon roar, Me help Yank win war, / Me much like to kill, Scalp old Kaiser Bill." The song's exclusively major-pentatonic melody in mode I (E♭–F–G–B♭–C) was paired with a driving two-step accompaniment. The upbeat tune, however, masked a dark undertone. Written from the point of view of a savage and simple-minded Indian, the song suggested that "Americans" could, during World War I no less, turn scalping "Indians" loose on their enemies (and the effect in Billy Murray's recording was quite hair-raising). Once again, popular culture revealed the darker sides of conflicted American values and attitudes.

It would be easy to conclude that popular songs written for the theater and dance hall were more pervasive, hence better known, than those such as "My Bark Canoe" written for the parlor and concert hall. In the first decade of the century, this was certainly true. Though Carlos Troyer—the German-born con artist who affixed wildly imaginative ritualistic descriptions of Indian life in the Southwest to his melodramatic fantasies—was lucky enough to have his songs cranked out on piano rolls at the 1904 St. Louis World's Fair, they were available mostly through "art music" publishers such as the Wa-Wan Press. Burton's and Troyer's songs reached a limited and somewhat rarified audience on the lecture circuit, compared with such popular hits as Mills's "Red Wing" (an "Indian Fable" with lyrics by Thruland Chattaway); Seymour Furth's "My Pocahontas" with lyrics by Edgar Selden and "introduced in Ziegfeld's Revue *Follies of 1907* at the Jardin de Paris"; or the previously mentioned "My Pretty Little Maid of Cherokee." But strangely enough, as I will explore later, two "art songs" by Charles Wakefield Cadman and Thurlow Lieurance, composers with an ethnomusicological bent, eventually surpassed almost every commercial "Indian song" in longevity, especially in their ability to adapt to the varied demands of the commercial market.

Music for Indians in Early Twentieth-Century Theater and Film

If 1903 was a signal year for the beginning of popular "Indian songs," 1905 marked the return of Indian characters to the center of the dramatic stage after many years in the shadows. The presence of Indians was essential to frontier drama, and, as Roger Hall has argued, the genre now became socially acceptable, which included a positive reception accorded by the critical establishment. The fear of "mixed bloods" that permeated popular song also provided dramatic fodder for theatrical productions and their filmic offshoots, with several important plays and films in the first twenty years of the century featuring prominent Indian characters. Since theater and film were closely interrelated in the first decades of the twentieth century, it is necessary to consider them together, as well as the music these media required.[14]

The first major Indian play of the century was William DeMille's *Strongheart,* which opened at New York's Hudson Theatre on 30 January 1905. Soangataha (Strongheart) leaves his Dakota tribe to attend Columbia University, where he makes his mark as an athlete. He falls in love with a sister of one of his teammates. Having been set up by a jealous schoolmate, however, he is wrongfully accused of passing the team's signals to a rival team. He is ultimately exonerated and wins the young woman's affections. But DeMille pushed the limits of white tolerance far enough. In the end he has Strongheart return to his people following the sudden death of his father, the tribe's chieftain, thereby giving up his girl. Though DeMille grappled with the ideas of assimilation and miscegenation, he thwarted the possibility of a genuine breakthrough. The play nevertheless offered a sympathetic portrait, perhaps the first, of a modern Indian male. Strongheart's sacrifice was an emotional one for audiences. Charles Daniels wrote a Strongheart song (1907), and the subject was still potent enough six years later when Albert Brown's song "Strongheart" stimulated many tear ducts in the *Passing Show of 1913*. The following year DeMille filmed *Strongheart* for Biograph (and remade it as *Braveheart* in 1925).

In contrast with DeMille's earnest treatment, a ludicrous (albeit consummated) interracial relationship ensued in Edwin Milton Royle's *The Squaw Man* (1905), a shameless plagiarism of *Madama Butterfly* (the first of many). Captain James Wynnegate, an aristocratic Englishman, buys a ranch in Wyoming, changes his name to Jim Carston, and marries an Indian woman named Nat-u-rich. When the man's former love comes to America to inform him of his inheritance, Nat-u-rich, who had earlier killed a man to save Jim's life, shoots herself so that Jim and their small son can be free to go to a new (and safer) world. Royle's plot actually makes better sense of the subject than does *Butterfly,* though his maudlin skills at writing dialogue severely date his play. *The Squaw Man* had music throughout, opening with Otto Langey's overture "Sounds of England" (1901) and featuring "A Hot Time in the Old Town Tonight" for the rise of the second-act curtain on Long Hoe's Saloon in Maverick. Theodore Bendix wrote most of the incidental music, including an intermezzo to convey the passing of time before the third-act setting of Jim and Nat-u-rich's ranch several years later. As an introduction to act 4, he composed "Nat-u-rich: Indian Idyll," an instrumental with a long passionate string melody in minor over quietly pulsing tom-tom fifths.[15] The trope is not strictly a war dance, as the music is elegiac in tone, but the throbbing underbeat confirms Nat-u-rich's primitive nature, one whose inflexibility allows her but one choice: death with honor. At the conclusion of her suicide, the orchestra—Puccini-like—rendered the "Indian Idyll" a final time. "Squaw man" was a derogative term, and while audiences may have wept real tears at Nat-u-rich's suicide speech, the play sent an unmistakable message that such marriages would naturally be fraught with cultural dissonance and irreconcilabilities.

The play was filmed no less than three times, all by Cecil B. DeMille, William's brother. The first of these (1914) starred actress Lillian St. Cyr (a Winnebago who adopted the moniker Princess Red Wing). In 1927 Rudolf Friml composed music for an operetta version entitled *The White Eagle,* which played briefly at New York's Casino Theatre. As Gerald Bordman has noted, its Indian heroine may have led Friml to hope he was working on another audience favorite like *Rose-Marie* (1924), but the show was a quick flop.

A positive theatrical response to miscegenation between whites and Indians came from the originator of *Butterfly* himself. In 1916 David Belasco produced George Scarborough's *Heart of Wetona.* The play was originally called *Oklahoma* and focused on problems of religious leaders in the new state. But Belasco changed some of the characters to Indians and the locale to a reservation. The story is an old-fashioned melodrama: Wetona, the daughter of a Comanche chief, is beloved of a young Indian agent but is seduced by a dissolute army officer. Wetona learns the truth about her no-good lover. Quannah, the chief, pursues the officer and kills him, while the agent manages to capture Wetona's heart. In 1919 director Sidney Franklin filmed *The Heart of Wetona* with the glamorous Norma Talmadge in the title role and several Native American actors in other roles. The film featured several Comanche chieftains as various characters, and Talmadge was made an honorary Comanche princess during the shooting. (*Moving Picture World* urged theater owners to play up the "Indian angle" when advertising this picture, even suggesting they add "an Indian touch" to their lobbies with a tepee and camp fire.)

Vaudevillian Archie Gottler wrote a title instrumental to ride the success of the film. Leo Feist published it with words added by Sidney Mitchell. The song began: "Far off on an Indian reservation, / lived a princess loved by all her nation."

Chorus
Heart of Wetona, I love you so,
I want to own you, so please don't go,
I've been so lonely, just for you only,
I never realized your eyes would haunt me so,
Please come away, dear, with me to stay, dear,
And our tomorrows from all sorrows will be free
Tho' you're an Indian Princess royal and true,
Boy of America is loyal to you,
Heart of Wetona, you were just made for me

By 1919, or so this song seemed to imply, interracial unions were more acceptable and could even be praised with rhapsodic music. *The Heart of*

Wetona also brought audiences to a modern reservation instead of depicting maladjusted Indians struggling in mainstream American society. On the reservation, Scarborough and Belasco's play argued, corruption and vice were not intrinsically inherent to Indian nature, and were usually perpetrated by U.S. military intervention.

Another serious play, which avoided the issue of miscegenation entirely, was Mary Austin's *The Arrow Maker* (1911), a tragedy about love and hubris set in the pre-Columbian Southwest. An ambitious young chieftain discards the affections of a female spirit doctor. When she withholds her counsel from his people in the face of attacks from a warring tribe, he kills her with a magic arrow she had given him for protection. Of Elliott Schenck's music for the production at the New Theatre, New York, only the *Indian Overture* remains. Scored for a large ensemble including a substantial percussion section with tom-toms and rattles, this was perhaps the first symphonic work on Indian themes since MacDowell's 1896 suite to acquire some lasting legitimacy in the concert hall. A few of its more important performances were by the Cincinnati Orchestra and St. Louis Symphony (1912), the Victor Herbert Orchestra (1919), the Boston Pops (1924), the Chautauqua Festival Orchestra (1932), and the Buffalo Philharmonic (1935). While Schenck drew on aspects of the war-dance trope (among them, minor-mode settings of pentatonic melodies over driving ostinato rhythms and grace notes ornamenting a string of repeated notes), the opening is majestic, with the throbbing tom-tom in 3/4 meter and violin and viola melodies in long, beautifully shaped arcs. The work builds in intensity to a frenzied conclusion. It is essentially a miniature symphonic poem that served to capture the spaciousness and mystery of the southwestern desert for its eastern urban audiences.[16]

Austin's play relied upon its mythological resonance and was not directed to those merely seeking escapism. While its subject had some literary influence over the next decade, most theater audiences did not seem interested in a realistic portrait of Indian life, past or present. Even opera, that most idealistic form of theater, seemed more fertile ground for escapist fantasies than works that took on serious issues pertaining to the American West. While *The Arrow Maker* ran in New York, composer Victor Herbert was fighting off journalists who wanted to know what "American" subject he had been contriving with producer Oscar Hammerstein. He and his librettist Joseph Redding managed to keep the subject a secret until *Natoma* finally went into rehearsal. The Irish-born Herbert was fascinated by nineteenth-century American culture and already had a long-standing association with Indian subjects. Over several years he had discarded many operatic possibilities before selecting Redding's Spanish California idea. One reject had been Belasco's *The Girl of the Golden West*

(1905), although it is uncertain whether Herbert knew about Puccini's almost simultaneous interest in the play. Puccini's opera beat *Natoma* to the American stage by about three months. (It premiered at the Metropolitan Opera on 10 December 1910.) Even though *La fanciulla del West* took place during the Gold Rush years, the opera included only two insignificant Indian characters. It was obvious to many that Puccini — even though he had quoted a few American tunes, even an "Indian" tune by Carlos Troyer — was not the composer to write an opera on an American subject. That responsibility fell squarely on the shoulders of Herbert, who in 1910 stood at the apex of his popularity with American audiences.[17]

Natoma was first produced in February 1911 at Philadelphia's Metropolitan Opera House and in New York three days later. It featured Mary Garden in the title role, and John McCormack, Lillian Grenville, and Hector Dufranne in supporting roles. Cleofonte Campanini conducted. The opera made headlines as far away as the *San Francisco Chronicle.* The sold-out Philadelphia and New York houses were filled with the cream of the crop of opera lovers and music critics. But *Natoma* failed to realize its promise as a "great American opera." Plans for European performances never materialized, although it ran successfully for three seasons and also toured to several American cities. Many critics found Herbert's score rich, colorful, and expressive and reserved their strongest criticisms for the libretto.[18]

Librettist Redding was a California lawyer and amateur composer. His theatrical experience had originated in the skits and "grove plays" of the Bohemian Club, an elite male social group of which he was a member and for which he contributed several plays of his own. The group, like the Tammany Societies of the eighteenth century, held "midsummer jinks" in their private forest enclave. One 1902 club announcement contained this note: "Under the perpetual green of our mystic woods, in the glow of our annual campfire, assemble for the great Midsummer Peace-pipe, on the sixteenth day of the Moon of August. Then shall be told you a story, in the music of Redding . . . and as once, in the Indian's tradition, the Evil Spirit was banished from the wigwams, so shall Care be slain in the forest and his ashes flung to the winds of Heaven." For a few blissful weeks each summer, these men shed the responsibilities of their jobs and families and headed to the forest to partake in the liberating experience of playing Indian.

Herbert's interest in Indian subjects may have been stimulated by a request he received in 1903 from Walter McClintock, a white man living among the Blackfeet (see map 2, chapter 3), to transcribe Blackfeet songs for non-Indian audiences. McClintock, originally a surveyor and photographer, had come to like the Indian peoples he met in the West, and he eventually decided to steep himself in Blackfeet culture in 1896 by going to live on the Montana reservation. Officially there to record privately the misdeeds of the white agency traders, he obtained wax cylinders in 1898 and spent the next five years recording stories and songs. Herbert wasn't interested in these cylinders, but he recommended instead a little-known young composer, Arthur Nevin. Nevin went to Montana in 1903 and, for several weeks, transcribed Blackfeet songs, although he didn't seem to share McClintock's enthusiasm for ethnology. One evening "while seated by the lodge fire," as McClintock put it, "I proposed to Arthur Nevin his composing an Indian opera, with a plot founded on the beautiful and romantic ideas of the Blackfeet legends, and with a stage setting depicting an Indian camp upon the prairies, with its picturesque lodges and the snowcapped Rocky Mountains for a background."[19]

Nevin went home and wrote his opera. With the help of McClintock's wealthy family, *Poia* received a concert performance in January 1907 by the Pittsburgh Symphony in Carnegie Hall (and was reviewed by the young Charles Cadman). It attracted considerable coverage in both the *Musical Courier* and *Musical America* for presumably being the first opera to deal expressly with Indian characters. (The presumption wasn't true, but some of the reviewers at the time had short memories when it came to America's musical history.) In April McClintock went to the White House to present some stereopticon pictures of Blackfeet camps to Theodore Roosevelt, and Nevin played excerpts from *Poia* on the piano (as Gilbert would later provide music for Curtis's 1911 picture-musicale). When McClintock, with the financial assistance of no less than Andrew Carnegie himself, took *Poia* to the Berlin Opera, it failed miserably, the weakness of the music being generally cited as the principal factor.[20]

Herbert and Redding, who had been inspired by this attempt but wished to avoid its pitfalls, decided that their opera would reflect a more historically diverse America. Natoma, a young woman in the 1820s from an unspecified tribe (though probably Ohlone), is a servant in the household of a rich Spanish family, whose daughter is engaged to a young American naval officer. The action takes place near the mission of Santa Cruz (see map 2). Natoma and the white officer fall in love, and this leads to Natoma's "savage nature" erupting in murder, for which she is mercifully consigned to the mission convent. Redding, who generally knew his California history, should have known that there were no convents in California before 1850. Missions, however, were often safe havens for Indian women, though most of the Catholic Spanish missions had been disbanded by civil decree by the early 1830s. For the Indians, this usually meant only a transfer from one master to another, since the Protestant Anglo-Americans who settled in Mexican California between 1833 and 1850 readily indentured most Indians. The change to American sovereignty did little to improve the Indians' situation. (Helen Hunt Jackson based her novel *Ramona* on some of these historical events.) Redding avoided this sensitive issue by situating his work in a pre-Anglo Mexican California, thereby displacing any culpability. At the same time, his account skirted dangerously close to another *Butterfly* adaptation though, as James Parakilas has pointed out, this was no typical "soldier and exotic" love story. "The racial difference between Yankee and Native American," Parakilas emphasizes, "is treated as so great that Natoma cannot even play the role of exotic to Paul. A representative of an intermediate race [the rich Spanish daughter] is needed for that role."[21]

The libretto describes the Indian heroine as the "last of her race." Her ancestor was the leader of a once-strong tribe whose descendants live in the mountains nearby. To evoke this ancient world, Herbert used a motive that clearly sounds like an Indian chant, but one that I have not been able to identify. The solemnity of the phrase—three sharply accented descending notes followed by an incisive thirty-second double-dotted eighth and supported above by tremolo strings—identifies Natoma's unyielding primitive nature:

The melody itself had already been quoted (or paraphrased) by Ernest Kroeger in his "March of the Indian Phantoms," a character piece played by the festival orchestra at the Louisiana Purchase Exposition in St. Louis in 1904 and circulated as an Ampico piano roll (see the opening of this work in chapter 7's table 6). It also resembles the Dakota "Song of the Dog Society" as collected by Natalie Curtis and published in her widely consulted *The Indians' Book* (1907), including the motive's reverse dotted rhythms. Moreover, it forms the basis for a "Tobacco Dance Song" recorded at the Crow reservation in Montana in 1910 by Thurlow Lieurance (and later quoted by him in his "Indian Suite" for piano). Because of its uncertain derivation, I will refer to it simply as the "ancestors' theme," particularly as it became well known through Herbert's use of it.[22]

Liner notes for *Natoma* call this motive her "theme of fate." A close study of the opera reveals that Herbert used the motive in very specific dramatic instances. In her first big aria, Natoma recounts how the spirits of the mountain and the waters long ago saved her people from starvation by bringing them abalone as a source of food. An amulet, a piece of abalone shell received from her father, symbolizes her people's survival. Herbert's music conveys a sense of majesty as she describes receiving this gift. But when the ancestors' theme makes its first appearance, Natoma reverts to the sternness of her ancient culture. Herbert's motive weaves its way through the score as a haunting reminiscence of authority, the voice of Natoma's ancestors urging her not to capitulate. In the end, however, its use is ironic: Natoma surrenders her amulet before entering the convent, and the ancestors' theme rings out threateningly and decisively. Herbert's use of this theme undermines Natoma's personal tragedy and emphasizes her resignation. But certainly on a deeper level the "fateful" implication exists that this outcome was inevitable.

One important colorist device of Herbert's opera was his continual use of the minor-seventh chord (F♯–A–C♯–E), a feature so prominently underscoring the title character that it would not be exaggerating to call it the "Natoma chord." This minor seventh as tonic can of course be traced at least as far back as the Scherzo of Dvořák's 1893 symphony (where it served another Indian context).[23] It was also used by Henry Gilbert for Curtis's "The Vanishing Race" to impart a sense of darkness and mystery—and also of tragedy and lost grandeur—to his "Indian" music. *Natoma* appeared in the same year as "The Vanishing Race" and shares many of the same racial ideologies. A conflict between "savagery" (the ancient cultures) and "civilization" (the modern one) complicates the identities of every Indian character: not only Natoma, but also her lost ancestors, her impoverished exiled relatives, and the various laconic, thieving, and otherwise shady "half-breeds." Among these is the disaffected Castro, half Spanish and half Indian, and therefore something of an outcast in both societies. When Mary Garden went onstage with Castro to enact the famous "Dagger Dance" at the climax of act 2, this was her chance to unleash all the primitive "savagery" that Herbert had coiled up tightly in his music.

The "Dagger Dance" theme (fig. 17) was supposedly based on a California Indian tune received from Redding. Again, I have not been able to locate a specific source for the tune (nor any reference to it in Redding's or Herbert's papers). The pervasive four-beat tom-tom, the minor-key setting of the tetratonic theme (even more primitive-sounding than a pentatonic one), the melody's downward motion, and its accented short-short-long rhythmic tail all confirm that Herbert was well versed in both the war-dance traditions of the nineteenth century as well as the popular songs and intermezzos of the previous decade. The four-note opening melody eventually opens out to pentatonic mode V ($\underline{6}$–1–2–3–5), identical with that used by Sousa the previous year in his "Red Man" from *Dwellers in the Western World*. Herbert's distinctive touch, however, lies in harmonizing the theme in parallel chords (mostly, though not all, minor), an effect that reinforces the idea of a solemn and steadfast ritual. The "Dagger Dance" vividly embodies a combination of

Figure 17. Victor Herbert, "Dagger Dance" from *Natoma* (G. Schirmer, 1911). The Lester S. Levy Collection of Sheet Music, Special Collections, The Sheridan Libraries of the Johns Hopkins University.

tropes: lost majesty (the preponderance of minor sevenths), oriental primitivism (the parallel chords), and warmongering (the throbbing tom-tom). The melody shifts midstream from pulling downward and rises up threateningly, an effect emphasized by the parallelism of the chords. Although the dance never speeds up, it builds a huge amount of tension, and at the climax Natoma breaks free and stabs Alvaro, the true villain.

The "Dagger Dance" became so popular that Herbert used it as an encore to his orchestra concerts and sometime afterward recorded it for the Victor label. He also adapted other music from the opera that was played by several major orchestras (for example, by the San Francisco Symphony, the Chicago Symphony at their "all American Concert" in 1913, and even as late as at the 1934 Century of Progress Exposition). Otto Langey arranged a *Grand Fantasia on "Natoma"* (Schirmer, 1911); this is an artfully designed tone poem that maintains the narrative thrust of the opera. Langey also prepared *Two Pieces from "Natoma"* for small orchestra (Schirmer, 1917) that included the "Dagger Dance" and an "Indian Invocation." These works served as prominent accompaniments for silent films with Indian characters. The "Dagger Dance" underscored "Indians on the warpath" or "majestic Indians of the Plains" tropes, while "Indian Invocation" underscored solemn or religious tropes. The former's four-beat tom-tom effect quickly became part of the musical language for other silent-film characteristics.[24]

The "Dagger Dance" also blended smoothly into popular culture. In the 1940s, for example, the Theodore Hamm Brewing Company of Milwaukee used the tune for its radio and then television jingles. It began:

> From the land of sky-blue waters [echo: "waters"]
> From the land of pines, lofty balsams
> Comes the beer refreshing,
> Hamm's the beer refreshing.

The words to the Hamm's jingle, while they do not explicitly mention Indian subjects, transport Herbert's music to the Lake Superior region, which is alluded to as a kind of "Indian country" ("the land of sky-blue waters"), and they imitate Injun English ("aged for many moons" in the second verse). The echo effect, not in Herbert, undoubtedly recalls the famous echo in Friml's 1924 "Indian Love Call." This commercial adaptation of Herbert's tune therefore drew upon several icons of early twentieth-century Indianism. As of the 1990s, advertisers for Hamm's beer in the western United States still used this jingle, although the visual image of an Indian paddling a gliding canoe down a river was dropped. The longevity of the "Dagger Dance" in American culture vividly illustrates that the irresistible allure created in sound and image in the early part of the century still feeds our fantasies of native America.[25]

Concert "Indian Songs"

The originator of "From the Land of the Sky-Blue Water" (1909), of course, was Charles Cadman. Few Americans were as voluble on the adaptation of Indian song. For at least a decade, he wrote tirelessly about the importance of studying and preserving Indian music and about rendering it in a more palatable Western guise, thereby keeping it in the public realm. Critical of the instrumental Indian character pieces of MacDowell and Farwell, Cadman suggested that the piano (or any combination of instruments) could not render the full range of possibilities inherent in Indian song. "The composer must study the related words," he later wrote in 1920. Indian music was essentially vocal, and its "idealization" in that form—as he put it—seemed more natural than in an instrumental form. Cadman was no doubt encouraged by Burton's sugary Indian parlor songs as well as by the songs published by the Wa-Wan Press and increasingly by such large publishers as Theodore Presser. The surge of interest in "Indian love songs" certainly had something to do with his choice of subject for "Sky-Blue Water."[26]

Cadman's journey toward native America actually began about 1907, when as a twenty-six-year-old composer and journalist in Pittsburgh he heard Nevin's *Poia*. Cadman and Tsianina Redfeather began including excerpts from *Poia* in their "Indian Music Talks." Until then, Cadman had expressed no special interest in adapting Indian music. Both he and freelance writer Nelle Richmond Eberhart, his lyricist, disliked "frivolous songs" such as Moret's "Hiawatha." Their answer to Tin Pan Alley Indianism began when Eberhart retrieved from her attic the Indian-inspired poetry written in her Nebraska days and Cadman offered to adorn her texts with "bona fide" Indian music. They knew, of course, that such music could be obtained at the library in the form of a recent publication (i.e., Fletcher's *Indian Story and Song*, 1900). For his adaptations, the largely self-taught Cadman sought out the advice of Emil Paur, who had conducted the premiere of MacDowell's "Indian" Suite in 1896 and who remained enthusiastic about what could be done with Indian themes.[27]

"From the Land of the Sky-Blue Water" became a best-seller for Cadman and his publishers White-Smith and was considered an ASCAP blue chip, the organization's highest classification, even as late as 1950.[28] The score to the original *Four Indian Tribal Melodies* informs us that "Sky-Blue Water" takes as its basis a chant from Fletcher's collections. Its pentatonic melody floats down from mode I to mode IV (6–5–3–2–1 to 3–2–1–$\underline{6}$–$\underline{5}$) and is rich in exotic implication, especially in its second phrase. At "they *brought* a captive maid," Cadman effectively conveys a sense of longing and even "faraway" dreaminess by using scale-degree 2 against IV$^6_4$ in the accompaniment (again the added sixth) and by ending on the root of pentatonic mode IV ($\underline{5}$ on "maid") instead of on the accompaniment's diatonic root. Cadman's persistent use of the "Scottish snap" rhythm in the accompaniment (in conjunction with its languid character) lends this melody a strangely affecting allure and sense of timelessness.

"Sky-Blue Water," like Cadman's earlier "At Dawning" (1906), became a remarkable example of crossover culture. The popular American operatic soprano Lillian Nordica frequently used it as an encore in her concert tours. Her performances of the work, and subsequent recordings by Alma Gluck, Louis Graveure, Florence Hinkle, Theo Karle, Mary Lewis, Jeanette MacDonald, Edith Mason, Alice Nielsen, Evan Williams, and Dame Maggie Teyte (as well as instrumental versions by Fritz Kreisler, Charles Milton, and André Kostelanetz), firmly established Cadman's international reputation as a composer of "Indian music," a perception that he was never quite able to alter. (Several prominent silent-film music collections include works by Cadman, attesting that his tuneful music served well as cinematic accompaniment.) Cadman's melody and his harmonic idealization was also transformed into fox-trot versions by band leaders such as Paul Whiteman (Victor, 1924) and Johnny Bothwell (Signature, 1946), and for swing band by Billy May (Capitol, 1952). "Sky-Blue Water" was also notably broadcast and recorded by Bing Crosby (for the *On the Air* radio show, 1937), who subsequently appeared singing it with the Andrews Sisters (1938).[29]

Other composers who were interested in Native American source material for concert songs used roughly the same approach. Thurlow Lieurance struck gold with "By the Waters of the Minnetonka" (written ca. 1912), even though he wrote many songs based on freely adapted Indian melodies. Keeping the sense of the original was, in his opinion, critical:

> When we remember that, as in Russia, the Indian has occupational songs for almost everything he does, the fund of material available for composition purposes is inexhaustible. It has always been my feeling that this material should not be dragged into musical composition where the purpose is more archeological than musical. Unless these themes can be idealized and presented in a way that does not destroy the original flavor, and unless the composer can see the beauties of them, he had better not attempt them. They must stand on their own musical merit or not at all.[30]

Example 14. Charles Wakefield Cadman, "From the Land of the Sky-Blue Water" from *Four American Indian Songs* (Boston: White-Smith, 1909).

Lieurance was born in 1878 and grew up near Pawnee Rock, Kansas, the son of a physician who, along with Lieurance's brother, provided medical services on the Crow and other reservations. During the Spanish-American War, he served as bandmaster of the 22nd Kansas Volunteer Infantry. Beginning in 1905 he was employed by the federal government to record American

Indian songs. This project ended when, on one of his trips, he was thrown from a wagon and subsequently lost the use of his legs. In 1918 he married Edna Wooley, a white woman brought up on a Sioux reservation. Until that point, Lieurance had spent many years with Watahwaso (Penobscot), a mezzo-soprano with whom he toured, giving informances about Indian music. His essay "The Musical Soul of the American Indian" reads today as one of the most sensitive writings of its time about Indian cultures by a white man.

Like Cadman, Lieurance developed a reputation as a tunesmith of "Indian songs" for use in parlor and concert. All his published songs were based on melodies he himself transcribed. Publisher Theodore Presser, which sensed a growing market for "Indian songs" of a serious nature, as opposed to ones that simply poked fun at Indian lovers, was impressed by Lieurance's magical touch with accompaniments. A Presser announcement from the 1920s indicates that the firm's catalog contained over thirty published songs based on Indian melodies "recorded and harmonized" by Lieurance. He is known to have written almost one hundred that appeared in countless instrumental and vocal arrangements. "Minnetonka" was far and above the most successful of these.[31]

Part of the song's allure was its story, here told by Lieurance in his own vivid (and musical) description for an orchestral performance at one of his "Indian Music Concerts":

> Many persons know the legend of Minnetonka—how the two lovers of the Sun and Moon clans of the Sioux Indians, loving against tribal law, fled to escape torture, and let themselves sink together into the waters of the lonely Northern lake. The silver ripples, it is told, mourn above them, and the winds bear the cry afar. But in the song they will arise from the depths of the lake for you; you will hear the steady and regular beat of their paddles, and see the diamond spray drip off in the moonlight as they pass, once again, in their ghost-canoe. A violin typifying the wind, if you choose, echoes the soft harmonies of the accompaniment, which rock to and fro on harp-chords, between the major key and its relative minor, in and out of that singular domain musicians know as the "added sixth" chord and its derivatives.[32]

Where did Lieurance get the idea for such a song? One October night in 1911, while in Montana, Lieurance was sitting with several members of the Crow, Cheyenne, and Sioux tribes. He had brought an Edison phonograph to record any songs he could get them to sing. One young Sioux—Sitting Eagle—sang a love song and also played it on his cedar flute. He also related the story about "Moon Deer" and "Sun Deer" and the tribal animosities that forbade them to marry. During their escape, they encountered Minnetonka ("round body of water" in Sioux). The lovers drowned themselves, Sitting Eagle related, rather than face capture by the enemy Cheyenne on the opposite side, and their song lives on in the waters of the lake. As Lieurance mulled over the haunting quality of the pentatonic tune Sitting Eagle played that night, he imagined it floating above a flurry of sixty-fourth-notes, just about the closest that music could come to an approximation of rippling waters. Lieurance attributed much of the popular success of this song to the original beauty of the Sioux melody and the idea of its simple yet descriptive accompaniment.

Like Cadman's Omaha tune, the Sioux melody also relied upon sharp iambic rhythms, and Lieurance made much of them, as every measure begins with one (ex.15). The dreamy accompaniment also creates an allusion of "far away and long ago," effectively conveying the sense that the song's story happened in ancient times. Lieurance was a veritable magician when it came to musical settings: his rippling effects seem to reflect moonlight on the waters. Moreover, the repeating F♯–E figure in the accompaniment — also emphasized in the violin-flute obbligato — has long-standing musical associations with lovers' sighs.[33]

During the years of its popularity, Lieurance's "By the Waters of the Minnetonka" had rich cultural resonances. Several important operatic singers popularized it, among them Frances Alda, Nelson Eddy, Mavis Bennett, and Ernestine Schumann-Heink. It was even recorded by Native American artists: Princess Watahwaso and Mohawk baritone Oskenonton (who was also a soloist in Coleridge-Taylor's *Hiawatha* at Royal Albert Hall and later in Cadman's opera *Shanewis*). Like "From the Land of the Sky-blue Water," it was also recorded by numerous instrumental and choral performers (among them André Kostelanetz, the Mormon Tabernacle Choir, the Cherniavsky Trio, and the Russian Folk Orchestra). Lieurance himself recorded a version on an Indian flute. A fox-trot adaptation. preserving Lieurance's luscious harmonies in mellow saxophones, was recorded as a dance number by Paul Whiteman in the early 1920s. "Minnetonka" even rivaled Ray Noble's "Cherokee" (1938) as an important jazz standard and was recorded in versions by Glenn Miller (1938), Tommy Dorsey (1940s), Bob Haggart (MGM, 1950), Charles Dorian (Kapp, 1956), and the Art Van Damme Jazz Quintet (Columbia, 1959).[34] It was also used for Ken Griffith's television show *67 Memory Lane* in 1955. Additionally, Lieurance's romance of two Indian lovers from warring tribes formed the basis for one of the early twentieth century's most enduring love songs, Friml's "Indian Love Call."

Another Operatic Experiment

Cadman, meanwhile, went on to write many more Indian songs, as well as other works based on Indian subjects. His 1918 opera, *The Robin Woman*

Example 15. Thurlow Lieurance, "By the Waters of the Minnetonka: An Indian Love Song" (Philadelphia: Theodore Presser, 1917).

(Shanewis), seemed then—and still does—a daring adventure for its time, given the turning point for the arts brought about by World War I. Cadman was motivated by at least three factors: his personal experiences with Indian peoples, his "idealizations" of Indian music, and his desire to reflect something of the nature of modern America, in which, in his opinion, native America played an important part. Tsianina Redfeather, who supplied Cadman with the scenario, didn't want to romanticize the past but preferred, like DeMille in *Strongheart,* to explore the role of American Indians in contemporary American life.

In the opera, Shanewis journeys from Oklahoma to Los Angeles to study singing. She is taken under the wing of a wealthy society woman, Mrs. Everton, whereupon she meets Lionel, an idealistic young man who falls in love with her. Unaware that Lionel is already engaged to Mrs. Everton's niece, Amy, a "Vassar girl," Shanewis brings Lionel to her reservation to test the honesty of his affections. Lionel's role remains static, for the plot in the reservation act revolves around the jealousy of Shanewis's brother Philip, his hotheaded friends, the sudden arrival of Amy and Mrs. Everton to rescue Lionel from his delusion, and Shanewis's painful realization of the impermeable class and racial divisions in American society. Though Cadman himself came from a background of wealth and relatively high social standing, his presumed homosexuality probably led him to sympathize with the outsider. Through Redfeather he learned about the complex lives of Indians who, when necessary, could adapt to prevailing American culture without having to abandon their own.[35]

After Victor Herbert's operatic failure, the search for another genuine American opera composer—as well as a wartime ban on all German music—may have led to the Metropolitan Opera's choice of *Shanewis,* even though Cadman and his team had conceived it for a less ostentatious venue in Denver. One caricature in the *New York Evening Mail* showed the composer leading his Indian singer by the hand from the reservation to the great city. The singers for all five principal roles, though led by the Italian conductor Roberto Moranzoni, were American-born and -trained. Contralto Sophie Braslau sang Shanewis, tenor Paul Althouse sang Lionel Rhodes, and Thomas Chalmers sang Philip Harjo (Har-Joe). Redfeather, though not invited to sing, was on hand to offer advice on matters Indian. Cadman, who did not trust the administration's staging of his work, involved himself in every rehearsal. The production was to appear "American" in every way, and he found it difficult to "make those foreigners understand that I fully expected to have my opera put on as I wanted it." Though reviewers were not as preoccupied with hailing a "great American opera" as they were for Herbert, *Shanewis* is in many ways a more credible example of that ephemeral species. The authors expressly wished to avoid the overly operatic and archaic use of language ("Bible English") that had pervaded *Natoma* and other recent American operas. Moreover, Cadman's home-grown and slightly eccentric musical language seemed more representative of an American sensibility than almost any operatic venture written in the generation or two before him. Cadman's eclectic musical background of marches, parlor songs, love ballads, and Presbyterian hymns—as well as his experience in writing school operettas and other educational works—resulted in a musical patchwork that seemed strangely apt for the subject.[36]

Cadman also admitted that he used "perhaps twenty genuine Red Indian themes" in his opera (though he acknowledges only six in the score's preface). Several of these appear in Shanewis's first two solos. When we first meet the title character, a young woman full of poetry and charm, she wears a beaded white "Alaskan caribou" dress. Accompanied by an onstage pianist (with the orchestra entering gradually), she begins with an incantation to spring and then sings a high-spirited Ojibwa canoe song. In the midst of an upper-class urban Los Angeles setting, she describes the Oklahoma countryside and remembers being a small girl sitting before the campfire and learning about the spring song of the robin woman, "an enchantress of a northern tribe." Using vivid nature imagery that harks back to Chateaubriand, Eberhart's lyrics invoke canoes on frozen lakes, southern winds melting fields of snow, fluttering birds, and leaping salmon. Despite Cadman's inexperience as an opera composer, his skills as a songwriter emerge with great vitality at this point. At the song's verselike opening, Cadman's harmonies and intervals suggest a primitive world: a minor-mode accompaniment, an inner descending chromatic line, a modal "Indian cadence," and open tom-tom fifths. He then turns to a less affected tonal language laced with delicate and folksy pentatonicism and melodies harmonized in parallel fourths, the latter a referent to archaism (or orientalism) he probably derived from Harvey Loomis's character pieces. In Cadman's hands, however, these devices seem remarkably integrated into a homogeneous style rather than markers for tropes of otherness. Moreover, the natural flow from one syntactic device to the next enhances the expressive flexibility of Cadman's musical language. The stylistic elasticity of a gay sensibility, as well as an elfin elusiveness, can be heard in nearly every measure. Though his style owed more to popular salon music than it did to anything remotely Indian, Cadman (with Eberhart and Redfeather) endeavored to present a more naturalistic portrait of a young Indian woman of the 1910s.[37]

At the same time, Shanewis's opening numbers may fall upon modern ears as sentimental, both in music and libretto. The character's statements seem too pure, too "correct" in observance of the polite social milieu, to be completely truthful. In the foreword to the published vocal score, Cadman writes that the first song was founded in part upon a Cheyenne melody recorded by Natalie Curtis (*The Indians' Book,* 180). Instead of calling "the birds of spring," however, the Cheyennes—according to Curtis—used this song to call "wood rats," a source of food, while taking turns on a tree swing. Cadman and Eberhart have drawn their Indian girl almost as a fairy creature, an idyllic woodland nymph summoned forth for the pleasure of high society. Yet Eberhart's text and Cadman's music at this moment strive for one common goal: to portray a young woman who is self-confident not in spite of, but because of her Indian background. Instead of appearing self-conscious, stoic, bewildered, resistant, intransigent, or any number of qualities usually superimposed upon Indian characters, she comes across as an ideal entertainer, one who knows how to use her voice to charm her audience and perform songs on topics that will please them.[38]

The reviews in New York were not generally favorable, although many praised Norman Bel Geddes's act 2 setting, especially its obvious break with conservative scenic design. Instead of showing an Oklahoma reservation as an escapist exotic fantasy with tepees and campfires, Bel Geddes depicted it as a contemporary scene with both native and Euro-American influences. As the curtain rises to Indian drumming, a powwow is in progress. Bel Geddes's backdrop of rolling farm country was enhanced with occasional patches of live oak and cottonwood trees. Encircling the camp was a canvas fence, over which could be seen the tops of tepees and improvised canvas shelters for the campers. The ceremonial dancers were in full regalia, while the spectators wore "holiday attire." Booths were decorated in red, white, and blue bunting and the stage was filled with automobiles as well as ponies pulling wagons full of Indian children. Ice cream, lemonade, and balloon vendors contributed to the festive, multicultural atmosphere. Redfeather's scenario had specified that the spectators be a diverse mix of whites, Indian full-bloods, and Indian half-breeds. In 1918 the reservation scene therefore depicted a liminal space that embodied both its Indian heritage and its "mainstream" American influences. By *Shanewis*'s performances the following season, *The Heart of Wetona* had opened in film houses across the nation, and the "Indian angle" played up by theater managers contributed to a heightened awareness of Indianism. At the close of World War I, these works seemed to remind Americans—a large number of whom were still steeped in their European ethnicities—that the roots of America were not those of Europe.

Shanewis was produced several times by small companies between 1919 and 1976, but its most elaborate production was in 1926 at the outdoor arena of the Hollywood Bowl in Los Angeles. The newly formed California Grand

Opera Company staged the opera to honor Cadman for his sixteen years of contribution to the city's cultural life. This time Cadman insisted on Redfeather for the title role, as well as Oskenonton for Harjo. Hundreds of extra performers reinforced the cast, and the two performances attracted some 40,000 spectators, according to the *Pacific Coast Musician* and other newspapers.[39] Cadman's venture had begun as a modest work of music theater in Denver. The Metropolitan burdened it with operatic pretensions that it perhaps could not justify. The Hollywood Bowl's further expansion of the reservation scene raised it to the level of an extravaganza. Cadman added more music, and White-Smith published a revised version of the score, a rare development in American opera of this—or any—period.

Near the end of act 2, scene 1, Cadman included a few remarkable touches that reveal his belief in American Indian music and his faith in their impact on American culture. Until this point, the music for the Indian participants and the white spectators have remained different in style. When the spectators begin packing up to leave, however, the white farmers echo the melody of the Indian sunset song as they prepare to return to work. Afterward, Shanewis holds Lionel back for "one more song," while four old Indian chiefs arrange themselves in the center of the stage to sing a ceremonial chant. Although the timpani and strings accompany them quietly from the orchestra, the chiefs shake rattles as they sing in falsetto from the "sayings of the ancient men" in the Osage language. Unlike many Western composers before him, Cadman approached his Indian characters not merely as an outsider; he believed in them. By insisting on Indian performers and enabling them to sing in Osage, Cadman offered a moment of genuine insight into Shanewis's Oklahoma, a truer, grittier place than the stage's usual romantic fantasy world.[40]

As Puccini often did in his later operas, Cadman foreshadows a tragic outcome in the first few measures of *Shanewis*'s orchestral prelude. He originally envisioned more of a "grand opera" ending to the story, namely, Shanewis's suicide. Had this been implemented, *Shanewis* might have emerged as little more than a pale imitation of *Madama Butterfly* or *The Squaw Man.* Instead, the hero Lionel dies, shot by Philip's poisoned arrow (a plot device borrowed from Mary Austin). Even though the authors tried to portray two cultures evenhandedly and to challenge the boundaries of white-Indian interaction, the opera's drama resolved in accordance with the prevailing social codes of the times. But *Shanewis* was more than just another problematic American opera. It was also a commentary on the multiplicity of cultural values in modern society. Although Lionel, a well-to-do white male, had already courted Amy, a privileged white female, according to the rules of their social class, he sees in Shanewis a woman with an irresistible blend of naive charm and exotic allure.

One reviewer of the Metropolitan production noted the designer's and director's special touch at the end of act 1. After all the guests had departed, their voices trailing off in the distance, Shanewis was left alone in the music room. It was after midnight, and she switched off the lights. The visual image that remained was "Shanewis, seen through the darkened room, alone on the porch in the moonlight, with the waters of the Pacific sparkling in the distance and an unseen chorus [heard] singing faintly far away."[41] There is an element of ecstasy and blissful triumph in this image: the vigilant Indian woman, once nearly banished from California along with her fathers and brothers, has now returned to conquer white society with her singing. And this image may well have lingered with audiences, long after the forced machinations of plot and character had been forgotten.

Playing Indian in the American Musical

Lionel was so enamored of Shanewis that he was willing to exchange his relative affluence for the unfamiliar world of the reservation. By the time that this operatic experiment had been performed at the Hollywood Bowl, a major new work of American musical theater had opened in New York and London: *Rose-Marie (A Romance of the Canadian Rockies).* The musical not only included several Indian characters but also the extraordinarily popular (and semioperatic) "Indian Love Call." *Rose-Marie* was first performed in September 1924 at the Imperial Theatre in New York with a book and lyrics by Otto Harbach and Oscar Hammerstein II, whose father had been instrumental in producing Herbert's *Natoma.* The music was a joint effort between the Bohemian-born Rudolf Friml (who composed the "Indian Love Call") and American-born Herbert Stothart (who composed some of the other songs and all of the extensive incidental music).

Often considered the first great musical of Broadway's golden years, *Rose-Marie* grossed more profits than any show before *Oklahoma!* The Broadway production featured Mary Ellis as Rose-Marie La Flamme, a singer at Lady Jane's, a small rustic hotel in Fond du Lac, Saskatchewan. Dennis King played Jim Kenyon, her beloved. The principal Indian characters were played by white actors: the hot-tempered gambler Black Eagle by Arthur Ludwig, and his wife Wanda by Pearl Regay. In 1928 MGM produced a silent version of *Rose-Marie* — with the young Joan Crawford in the title role — modifying several aspects of the plot, including dropping the central character of Black Eagle.[42] In 1936 MGM again produced *Rose-Marie,* this time with the operatically trained Jeanette MacDonald and Nelson Eddy. The two recorded the "Indian Love Call" at RCA Victor's studios with Nathaniel Shilkret leading the orchestra. In this form the song attained a life of its own, selling well over a million copies. In 1954 MGM remade *Rose Marie,* in which the "Indian Love Call" was blandly interpreted by Fernando Lamas and Ann Blyth. Meanwhile, Artie Shaw had made a hit recording of the song with vocals by Tony Pastor for the Bluebird label in 1938. (It was coupled with his all-time hit, Cole Porter's "Begin the Beguine.") "Indian Love Call" even sold over a million copies as performed by country singer Slim Whitman (Imperial, 1952).

Before Friml's famous tune there had been several other rhapsodic, operetta-style evocations of "Indian love," among them, "Pretty Little Rainbow" (1911), Lieurance's "Minnetonka" (published 1917), George Meyer's "Hiawatha's Melody of Love" (1920), Frederick Logan's "Pale Moon" (also 1920), not to mention Friml's own "Moon Dawn" (1923). Key elements in all these songs were a silvery moon and lovers meeting near a lake at evening. Logan's "Pale Moon" was such a popular tune by 1924 that Paul Whiteman included an orchestral version of it in his famous Town Hall concert that featured the premiere of Gershwin's *Rhapsody in Blue.* In fact, Indian love songs were so popular that year that publishers Denton and Haskins had J. McKenna add love lyrics to Christian Sinding's "Rustle of Spring," a semiclassical piano character piece, selling it as "Indian Love Moon."

The 1936 film version of *Rose-Marie* bore scant similarity to the earlier stage work, and both Indian characters were dropped (while the producers added another minor Indian character, Boniface, a lying, stealing half-breed). Only a few of the songs were retained, two of which were "Indian Love Call"—central to the plot of both play and film—and "Totem Tom Tom"—sung by Wanda in the play but staged in the film as an independent chorus number by choreographer Chester Hale. In the original Broadway version, the "Indian Love Call" served as a means for the two lovers, Rose-Marie La Flamme and Jim Kenyon, to communicate with one another. When Rose-Marie learns that Jim is accused of murdering Black Eagle over a land dispute, she warns him by singing the "Indian Love Call," an agreed-upon signal. The song, as she informed him earlier in act 1, was taught to her by the Indians when she was a little girl. "There's an old Indian story," she says in her Quebecois accent, about "lovers' rock" near her home. "When an Indian boy and Indian girl want for to make marriage, he would climb up hill and call down to her—and if, if she answered his call—dat means she tak' him for her man." Jim asks her to teach him the song, and she begins with a long descending phrase on "Ooh!" The refrain is in F major, but the call itself begins on the sixth above that (D) and ends with a distinctive chromatic slide from C down to A. Jim imitates her (echo fashion), and she continues to teach him how "echoes of sweet love notes gently fall." After an introduction of dreamy parallel chords that modulate to F minor, she then paints a nocturnal image to a haunting melody in the verse.

Friml evokes a peculiarly exotic flavor with a mélange of distinctive musical features. The rising C–D♮–E♮ of the yearning accompaniment leads to a dissonance with the F-minor seventh chord, adding an undertone of pain to this story. The melodic phrase on "When the lone lagoon stirs in the spring" (C–D♭–F–E♮–C) is a tetrachord from the so-called gypsy or Hungarian scale, Friml's eastern European way of hinting at the exotic. The unusual under-third cadential figure on "welcoming home some swany white wing" (G♯–A♮–*D*♭–F) leads to a cadence on an augmented chord (F–A–C♯), an unstable sonority used since the late nineteenth century for allure and mystery. Following "when the maiden moon, riding the sky" Friml elongates the harmonic ambiguity by filling out the augmented chord with a whole-tone scale, another early twentieth-century exotic marker. "This is the time . . . when love dreams to Indian maidens appear," Rose-Marie sings, her voice rising expansively to the notes of the "gypsy" scale, and "this is the song that they hear." As the melody melts into F major (with D, the added sixth), the refrain returns, this time a fuller statement of the love call: "When I'm calling you–ooo–ooo." In the play, the song functions not just as a love song but also as a signal. An "Indian song" thus serves to help Rose-Marie and Jim bring to justice an "Indian killer."

In the 1936 film, producer Hunt Stromberg, director W. S. Van Dyck, and their screenwriters changed several crucial aspects of the "Indian Love Call." Rose-Marie is now Marie de Flor, a famous Quebec opera singer, and Jim is Sergeant Bruce, a Royal Canadian Mounted Police officer. In this version Marie has come to the West to reach a small home in the woods where her brother is hiding after having accidentally killed a police officer. Unbeknownst to her, Sergeant Bruce is on her trail and therefore saves her from drowning in a lake. Marie has no choice but to camp with Bruce for the night. While they are talking, they hear mysterious singing from the opposite side of the lake—the refrain of the "Indian Love Call." Marie, who doesn't know about such things, is frightened. But Bruce tells her about "an old Indian legend" of two young Indian lovers caught between warring tribes. Though the lovers were killed, their spirits live on in these surroundings. Thus, not only are the roles reversed—Marie learns the song from Jim—but the context for the song itself is significantly changed. The Indian lovers are now dead, and their spirits haunt the lake. Between 1924 and 1936, Lieurance's popular "By the Waters of the Minnetonka" and its explicit Sioux tale of Romeo and Juliet style lovers must have had an effect on the three persons—Alice Duer Miller, Frances Goodrich, and Albert Hackett—who created the screenplay. It seems all the more unusual that the verse should have been cut, for its haunting accompaniment, with its underlying tone of anguish, was even more appropriate to the dead Indian lovers in the film version. The play suggests the idea that Indians pass their legends on to the white people. The film, except for the nocturnal totem dance, seems to suggest that Indians no longer occupy much of the land, but that it is nevertheless imbued with their loves, their pain, and their songs.

Friml's song does not draw much on standard tropes of musical Indianism. But these turn up in Stothart's music for Black Eagle and Wanda. In the original stage version, Rose-Marie does not have a brother; instead, Jim becomes embroiled in Black Eagle's murder, and it is he that Rose-Marie tries to save. Black Eagle is murdered by Wanda—his half-breed wife—and her lover, Hawley. Like most theatrical Indian half-breeds in the early twentieth century, Wanda is shown to be greedy, conniving, and otherwise morally corrupt. She dances lustily with all the boys in Lady Jane's Hotel, and the suggestion is that she's a slut. Stothart wrote a Wanda theme that is *molto misterioso*—parallel minor chords over a throbbing simulated tom-tom (not unlike Herbert's "Dagger Dance"). He uses this as a leitmotif in instances when Wanda is turning on her "alluring charms," as the book states it. During the cabin sequence, in which the murder takes place, the entire scene is played as a melodrama, spoken and pantomimed against continuous music. The Wanda theme figures prominently in this scene, although Stothart doesn't always score the theme in parallel harmonies, and he adapts the accompaniment to fit the growing complexity of the drama. He also composed a new theme for the Indians' "cabin in the woods." This theme, in contrast to the *misterioso* one, is to be played *molto maestoso*. The F♯-minor chord in the lower parts supports a pentatonic melody in the violins. The melody and its setting bear a remarkable similarity to the second movement of MacDowell's "Indian" Suite (as well as to the "Indian" works of Carl Busch and Victor Herbert); the music here is redolent with the tropes of lost grandeur—pentatonic melodies set to minor-seventh harmonies (Herbert's "Natoma chord"), Scottish-snap rhythms, phrases ending in sorrowful, drooping thirds, and repeating drone basses.

Unlike the operatic Natoma, however, or the bitter half-breed in that opera, Wanda is not always so droopy. Several days after the murder, she follows her lover to a pass in the mountains, stopping at the Totem Pole Lodge. There she whips up the hotel guests into the rousing "Totem Tom-Tom," a clever stage number written by both Friml and Stothart. It provides Wanda with her only song in the show and offers a big choral opportunity before the act I curtain. The scene is set just outside the lodge, with several totem poles standing along the back and the Canadian Rockies looming in the distance. "Long ago there used to be," Wanda sings, "a tribe of Indian smarties throwing their parties here." It's hard to imagine any mixed-race Indian in the 1920s joking about her ancestry in this way. But the sexy Wanda pulls it off, with the help of a group of men and women who are first mysteriously heard offstage singing a "semi-chant effect" and who then appear suddenly to form the corps for a big dance number featuring dancing girls in "totem dresses" who walk, hop, and roll to thudding tom-toms.

The number's effectiveness, however, perhaps lies less in the visual effects than in the melodic construction of the song's refrain. Wanda sings: "When my grand-pa, Chief Chickeekotem, / took grand-ma out to a totem, / Totem tom-tom, / Totem tom-tom." The rhythmically catchy melody is in pentatonic mode IV ($\underline{5}$–$\underline{6}$–1–2–3), but it also features a snakelike ascending and descending chromatic inner voice. Here Wanda is at her most alluring, not only rolling her hips suggestively but also fascinating the hotel guests with her knowledge of the mysterious rituals that supposedly occurred in this place. Chromatic inner voices have, since the early nineteenth century, often served to evoke lurid contexts such as orgies or pagan worship. This frisson of "savagery" aside, the song clearly has nothing to do with real totems; rather, it turns out to be an upbeat love song in the character of the popular Indian intermezzos. The satisfying melodic "correction" of pentatonic mode IV to mode I in the song's crucial cadence (on the words "Totem tom-tom")—$\underline{6}$–$\underline{5}$–$\underline{5}$–$\underline{5}$ to 2–1–1–1—brilliantly suggests an inherently American Indian aspect of the tune, while resolving it in accordance with Western practice. Friml and Stothart accomplished this with a certain snappy self-assurance that made this song and dance a crucial step in establishing the integrated production number as a staple of the Broadway musical. It's an infectious and delicious moment. Wanda's grandpa and grandma had a good time that night, and that's why, the song implies, she's here to tell the tale. The musical (and textual) evocation is also of something that happened long ago—a ritual that, with the Indians in the region dying out or intermarrying with white Canadians, is now only a memory.

Wanda does not exist in the 1936 film to lead the song. Instead Marie and Jim go to an Indian camp to find Boniface, and there a "totem ceremony" begins. The sequence was filmed at Lake Tahoe and featured a huge pole at the center of the dance, with several hundred smaller poles at various distances. According to the American Film Institute catalog (which cites the MGM campaign book as its source), the filming of this dance featured over seven hundred Indians from fifty different tribes. Since most of the dance was filmed in long shots, it is difficult to verify the truth of this audacious claim without examining any existing production records. Nevertheless, an attempt at "authenticity"—in this case the use of actual Native Americans—is always the first claim of exoticism. To its credit, the film at least suggested that Indians were a part of the present, even if they were mostly confined to their nighttime encampments.[43]

The "Indian Love Call," while it explored the idea of dead Indian lovers, avoided the issue of miscegenation so endemic to the previous decades, when composers and lyricists toyed with the notion of white males captivated by the romantic allure of Indian females. *Shanewis*'s reservation scene and the various popular songs about white men running off with Indian maidens — as well as Nesta Toumine's elaborate totem dance in *Rose-Marie* (if not also the huge corps de ballet employed in the annual British spectacles of Coleridge-Taylor's *Hiawatha*) — led to a parody of reservation romances and Indian production numbers in *Whoopee!* a musical comedy by William McGuire with music and lyrics by Walter Donaldson and Gus Kahn. The show opened on Broadway in 1928 at the New Amsterdam Theatre, home of Ziegfeld's famous *Follies.* Based on Owen David's *The Nervous Wreck,* it featured comedian Eddie Cantor as Henry Williams, a shy, upper-middle-class Jewish hypochondriac who moves to the West for his health. He offers a ride to the pretty Sally Morgan, who, unbeknownst to Henry, has left a note saying she is eloping to escape the romantic clutches of the local sheriff. Thinking that Henry is Sally's beloved, the sheriff angrily pursues the pair to the reservation. Sally is seeking her true beloved, the handsome half-breed Wanenis. Unlike most stage and film half-breeds, Wanenis is portrayed as a brave and honorable character. He comes to Henry and Sally's rescue when they are captured by Chief Black Eagle's scouts. The plot is resolved, Gilbert-and-Sullivan style, when it is revealed that Wanenis is not Indian at all but had been abandoned by a white family. Ziegfeld's most extravagant production number in the show was "The Song of the Setting Sun." According to Gerald Bordman:

> *Whoopee*'s Wild West locale thrilled Ziegfeld. No doubt he recalled all the times he played hookey as a boy to watch Buffalo Bill's entourage. Ziegfeld bedecked his beauties in feathers luxurious beyond an Indian's most colorful fantasies and then he brought the girls onstage riding real horses. He gave Joseph Urban free rein, and Urban created a series of brilliant sets, notably a re-creation in reds and rusts of the Grand Canyon.[44]

Samuel Goldwyn bought the film rights, and in 1930 Ziegfeld, with Busby Berkeley as choreographer, adapted *Whoopee!* in blazing two-tone Technicolor. As he had in the Broadway production, the Chilean-born orator and singer who went by the name Chief Caupolican played the role of Black Eagle and sang Gus Kahn's lyrics to "The Song of the Setting Sun" while standing atop a high precipice.[45]

The song is in the major mode (F), though the melody continually reaches

Example 16. Refrain from "Song of the Setting Sun" from *Whoopee!* (with some portions of the accompaniment removed). Lyrics by Gus Kahn, music by Walter Donaldson. Donaldson Publishing Co./Gilbert Keyes Publishing (ASCAP). All rights reserved. Used by permission.

up to the added sixth (D), by now a prominent feature in sentimental Indian love songs. The underlying harmony moves from F major to A minor on "mountain," a progression that suggests wistful melancholy, before winding its way chromatically down through G minor on "With the setting," then to C^7 and back to F major on "sun." The melody hardly ever strays from its mode I pentatonic framework except for chromatic descending passing tones on "With the setting" and later on "while you pray" and "yesterday." The descending chromatic inflection again alludes subtly to pagan worship.

The implication is that such rituals as songs to the setting sun are redolent of the past (reinforced also by lyrics like "Red Man, learn regretting") and do not represent the future of American Indians. This history of imagined native America has examined several accounts or depictions of rituals celebrating the rising sun among the Incas, Aztecs, Natchez, and others. This was a dominant image from the sixteenth to the early nineteenth centuries. The crucial interpretive shift to a twilight world of American Indians occurred at the end of Longfellow's *The Song of Hiawatha,* where the protagonist departed for all time into the glory of the sunset, an image, as we've discussed, that was captured in art as well as musical compositions. Like Hiawatha, *Whoopee*'s Chief Caupolican acknowledged the vanishing sun proudly and with raised arms against a richly hued sky, but his words allegorically—and unmistakably—referred to the end of the "Red Man's" dominion. (It may be my imagination, but it sounds as if the chief deliberately muffled these words, making them difficult to understand.)

The full production number consisted of four parts: (1) the "Song of the Setting Sun" at a slow, stately tempo, (2) a tom-tom dance at a suddenly faster tempo (with two concentric circles of dancing girls), (3) a stagy costume parade down a graded ramp at a majestic march tempo, and (4) a slower coda (assembly of the grand tableau). The tom-tom dance (no doubt partly a takeoff on the *Rose-Marie* tom-tom dance) incorporates the song's melody but also includes a new tune in minor mode and is rooted strongly in the tonic minor seventh (again, the "Natoma chord"). The new melody, like the "Dagger Dance" and Sousa's "Red Man," is rooted in pentatonic mode V ($\underline{6}$–1–2–3–5). Ray Heindorf vividly orchestrated the dance with snarling trombones, bright muted trumpets, mellow saxophones, and sparkling flutes and piccolos. Seen through bird's-eye-view camera angles, the "Indian girls" moved in highly organized kaleidoscopic patterns, a Berkeley trademark. For the headdresses and war bonnets in the amazing costume parade, as Richard Barrios has quipped, director Thornton Freeland and designer John Harkrider must have used every feather in California. While the glamour of Ziegfeld and Berkeley's stylish work would seem to parody Indian rituals, the music takes

Figure 18. Composite image from two frames of "The Song of the Setting Sun" from *Whoopee!* (Goldwyn, 1930).

itself quite seriously. Surprisingly moving, it embodies both majesty and a touch of melancholy, the latter made even more poignant when juxtaposed against the remarkable close-ups and smiling faces of the gorgeous Goldwyn girls.[46]

Broadway's Wild West

In contrast with Ziegfeld and Berkeley's production number, which showed Indian ritual as majestic and ennobled (if doomed to extinction), Indian ritual in the 1936 film *Rose-Marie* was wild, athletic, and a classic example of Hollywood kitsch run amok. In the film version, the dance more closely paralleled the primitive native dance in *King Kong* (1933) than the pageant Indians of *Whoopee!* After producing the original stage version of *Rose-Marie,* Rodgers and Hammerstein went on to write or produce several more musicals set in the West, most notably *Oklahoma!* (1943) and *Annie Get Your Gun* (1946). *Oklahoma!* opened a year after Copland's ballet *Rodeo,* in which the composer and choreographer Agnes de Mille imagined cowboys dancing on the prairie. Most cowboys—as nineteenth-century photographs of these rugged, often worn-down individuals clearly display—would hardly have been capable of the stylized exuberance that the ballet depicts. Copland seems to have captured instead the wild and enthusiastic frenzy of the homesteaders, such as those that made the Cherokee Strip run in 1893 or the "sooners" who burst into Kiowa and Comanche territories in 1901. Hammerstein's phrase in *Oklahoma!* "we know we belong to the land" could just as well have been "we know the land belongs to us."

Even the reservations no longer play a role in this imagined Oklahoma. The early twentieth-century plays and songs had determined the nearly invisible positions that would be acceptable for Native Americans in the art and entertainment of the mid-century United States. Congress believed it had settled matters with the Indian Citizenship Act in 1924, although it declined to extend the Bill of Rights to Indians living under tribal governments (and the Hopi and Iroquois nations declined citizenship). Indians as contemporary subjects in plays, popular songs, and films decreased dramatically after this point, almost disappearing altogether (or serving largely as faceless fodder in "shoot-'em-up" Westerns). During and after World War II, Indian characters were almost exclusively limited to their roles as historical figures. A musical such as *Annie Get Your Gun,* for example, set as it was in the late nineteenth century, required the use of Indians in telling its fanciful version of the Wild West.

Irving Berlin was considered a music theater composer of an older generation when, after the sudden death of Jerome Kern, Rodgers and Hammerstein turned to him in 1945 to write the music for an Annie Oakley musical based on a story proposed by Dorothy and Herbert Fields and designed as a vehicle for Ethel Merman. The real Annie (Phoebe Ann Moses), a legendary sharpshooter with Buffalo Bill's Wild West, had died in 1926 and left an autobiography, the source for her niece Anna Fern's *Missie: An Historical Biography of Annie Oakley.* Annie had joined Buffalo Bill in 1885, after she had already established her reputation as a markswoman in circus acts and the vaudeville circuit. In these shows Annie shot corks off bottles, the flames off candles, and the ashes off cigarettes. Her performance in an act with husband Frank Butler in St. Paul, Minnesota, so impressed Sitting Bull in 1884 that he adopted her, calling her "Watanya Cecilla" (Little Sure Shot). According to Oakley biographer Glenda Riley, Sitting Bull had lost a young daughter sometime earlier and grew very affectionate toward Annie during their days together in St. Paul. Annie also demonstrated high esteem for the Indian peoples she encountered. Many of the Indians traveling with Buffalo Bill trusted her, even going to her with problems or asking her to hold money for them. Buffalo Bill Cody also admired the Indian peoples, insisting throughout his career that those traveling with him be treated with utmost respect. They were, after all, the "principal feature" of the Wild West show, as he was fond of saying. Acting on Chief Standing Bear's counsel, Cody hired lawyers to bring Sioux grievances to the attention of President Theodore Roosevelt. Indeed, Cody hired Annie not solely because of her skills as a sharpshooter but also because of her status with Indians and her association with Sitting Bull, who consented to join the fair partly to remain close to Annie, though he was largely featured as an icon during the parades that preceded the shows themselves.[47]

For the stage version of *Annie Get Your Gun,* the authors shifted chronology and emphasis. Annie joins Cody's show as an unknown hick from a small town (she clearly takes pride in her backward ways in the song "Doin' What Comes Nat'rally.") Frank and Annie begin their romance while the show is on tour across America. Her sympathetic attitude toward the traveling Indians is only briefly suggested in one scene when they start a small fire in their car and she welcomes the whole troupe into her compartment. They set up shop, turning her car into an Indian encampment. Other than this one event, included primarily for its comic distortions of Indians' domestic practices, she demonstrates no special knowledge of them.

Sitting Bull sees Annie in the Wild West show—at the very show where she upstages Butler and temporarily incurs his jealousy and enmity—and the Sioux chief ("Mr. Bull") offers to adopt her. Confused over Frank's sudden disappearance, she is overwhelmed by two Indians who put a large ceremonial robe over her head, thus rendering her unable to see, while tom-toms begin offstage. At the entrance of "an Indian in full regalia" in front of the curtain, the scene shifts to the arena of the big tent where Sitting Bull has called together his tribe. Annie enters wearing "an Indian robe" and a band around her head. Sitting Bull is smoking a pipe. While a chorus of Indians sings quietly in the background, Sitting Bull utters a few phrases to Annie, who repeats them back to him. He raises a heavy necklace—"teeth of many bears"—and drops it around Annie's neck; she almost collapses from the weight. "Am I an Indian yit?" she asks. Sitting Bull puts a feather in her headband and says "Shh! Now!" At this point, Annie turns to the audience and sings "I'm an Indian Too." The song continues directly into a "tribal dance" in which Annie and Sitting Bull engage with all the Indians. The script notes that the dance should be performed for comedy as well as spectacle and that it should be an exhausting routine. When the number is over, Annie collapses, managing to pant "Do we always carry on thata way when we take in new members?" Aside from Sitting Bull's wise counsel later in the show that she should willfully lose a match to Butler ("keep missing and you win"), there is little other "Indian business," most of it contained in this one scene near the conclusion of act 1.

The Broadway show was a stunning success, sustaining Berlin's reputation as one of America's great song writers, fully able to reposition himself in the new postwar musical theater. *Annie Get Your Gun* appeared as a film in 1950, produced and directed by Arthur Freed and George Sidney. Filming began under Busby Berkeley's direction with Judy Garland in the title role. (Unused footage survives of Garland singing "I'm an Indian Too.") Berkeley was soon released from the project, however, presumably because his work was too "stagy," and Garland was also released due to her inability to keep up with a relentless filming schedule.[48] Ultimately, Betty Hutton sang and acted the role with a stilted Howard Keel as Frank Butler and J. Carrol Naish as Sitting Bull. The Indian encampment activities in Annie's compartment were slightly toned down, reportedly because MGM was warned by the Breen Office that the "Secretary of the Interior has gotten very Indian-minded and will raise hell about your showing the Indians lousing up the train."[49] The adoption scene, on the other hand, was ratcheted up for increased comic effect. While the adoption ceremony, the necklace, and the song "I'm an Indian Too" remain the same, Annie is presented to the tribe first and they engage in an exhausting and comic wild dance that has no discernible structure (i.e., they "behave like Indians"). Several times Annie escapes from the dance to inquire of Sitting Bull whether she is "an Indian yit." Twice Sitting Bull says "Not yet," and Annie is drawn back into the dance even more vigorously than before. Annie is clearly disoriented by the whole process. In both the play and the film, she is ignorant of all social graces. There was a strong negative reaction from those who had known Oakley and remembered her as a "distinguished lady," not the backward naïf portrayed in the musical. Nevertheless, the ritual of becoming an Indian offered Berlin an opportunity to dig deeply into the history of Indianesque tropes and create one of the most brilliantly crafted burlesque songs ever penned. Offensive or not, "I'm an Indian Too" embodies several influential American notions of native America. Rather than pretend that these stereotypes never existed, we should face them head on.

The original adoption ceremony began with a male in full regalia appearing before the curtain, singing a high-pitched chant ("Wataya, Wataya, Ayaprina").[50] As the scene opens, tom-toms begin offstage, followed by the orchestra playing a dance for the assembly of the Indians and the entrance of Sitting Bull. The music for this sequence is based on open fifths and repeated pentatonic gestures. The orchestration emphasizes the "ancient heritage" of the Indians by scoring all the open fifths for brass ("nobility"); their "savageness" is suggested by screeching woodwinds and high strings. The chorus of Indians begins the "ceremonial chant" (by Berlin) over a pastoral moresca rhythm (𝅗𝅥♩♩) on open fifths. The minor-mode pentatonicism of this melody (ex. 17) already suggests the tune of "I'm an Indian Too," which Annie appropriates once she has been officially "initiated."[51]

The lyrics of the adoption song revel in the assonance of several tribal names ("Navajo" and "Kickapoo") and parody the native tradition of name giving ("Hatchet Face" and "Falling Pants"). Berlin's lyrics are a veritable storehouse of Indian words already familiar to audiences from dime Western culture ("totem poles," "tomahawks," "moccasins," "wampum beads"). Berlin artfully spoofs the allegory of the commercial Indian love songs by having Annie

Example 17. Irving Berlin, "Ceremonial Chant" from *Annie Get Your Gun* (1946). Words and music by Irving Berlin. © 1946 by Irving Berlin. Copyright renewed. International copyright secured. All rights reserved.

imagine what it would be like to "hide away with Big Chief Hole-in-the-Ground" and have a "small papoose" of her own. (He even recalls "Indian summer," familiar from many prior musical treatments, Victor Herbert's only the most famous among them.) Though Annie has been brought to the ceremony against her will, she is now wholly engaged in "playing Indian," creating an imaginary life for herself that is rich with cultural resonance and accrued meaning.

Annie's inner Indian self inhabits a minor-key world and is accompanied by two ever-present musical companions: an open-fifth ostinato in the bass and a descending chromatic line in an inner voice (C–B–B♭–A–A♭–G, bracketed in ex. 18a). The first refrain ("Like the Seminole") opens with the suggestion of pentatonic mode V ($\hat{1}$–♭$\hat{3}$–$\hat{4}$–$\hat{5}$–[♭$\hat{7}$]). But the subsequent diatonic descent on "I'm an Indian too" ($\hat{5}$–$\hat{4}$–♭$\hat{3}$–$\hat{2}$–$\hat{1}$) reveals a modal orientation—Aeolian or natural minor—especially with the emphasis on the lowered seventh (B♭–C) on "A Sioux ooh-ooh!" (Moreover, the drawing out of the "ooh-ooh" from "Sioux" clearly points—subtly, but unmistakably—to Friml's love call, still popular in the 1940s.) The bridge slips easily into the relative major (ex. 18b). Berlin artfully colors the key of E♭ major with the familiarly "Indian" added sixth (C). He does this in several ways: by including it in the melody itself ("summer's day," mm. 27–28) and making it part of the accompaniment's C-minor chords and its regular alternation of the fifth and sixth scale degrees (B♭–C) in the middle voice. These alternating scale degrees provide an accompaniment feature that has come to be a trope of the West. They were a feature added in Kreisler's arrangement of Dvořák's "canzonetta," then in Langey's silent-film transcription ("Indian Lament"), and were incorporated in other film scores to suggest the binary clip-clop of horses' hooves and, by inference, the rumbling motion of wagon trains.

The melody of the bridge ("Some Indian summer's day") begins in pentatonic mode III on G (G–B♭–C–[E♭]) ($\hat{3}$–$\hat{5}$–$\hat{6}$–$\hat{1}$–$\hat{2}$) but then for "I may hide away" dissolves for one brief moment into a whole-tone scale, that most

Example 18. Berlin, "I'm an Indian Too" from *Annie Get Your Gun* (1946). Words and music by Irving Berlin. © 1946 by Irving Berlin. Copyright renewed. International copyright secured. All rights reserved. Reprinted by permission.

generic of early twentieth-century exoticisms, although by the 1940s it too had become part of Indian musical syntax.[52] In an interlude ("With my chief in his tepee, / we'll raise an Indian family") Berlin has Annie sing upward leaping octaves—a purposely awkward vocal device but a prominent feature in the nineteenth-century Indian war dances of Auguste Panseron, Hans Christian Lumbye, and others and, as we've noted, in Tin Pan Alley songs such as Gus Edwards's "Tammany." (We can look back even further to see this vocal device used in the eighteenth-century "Wampum Swampum.") As in "Tammany," the accompaniment is in major rather than minor, so war is not invoked. Taking all these features together, Irving Berlin, whether consciously or not, demonstrates more fluidity with the musical syntax and accumulated rhetoric of Indianism than any previous composer mentioned in this book. It would be difficult to find many musical devices of Indianism prominent in the late nineteenth and early twentieth centuries that Berlin does *not* use (the minor seventh for "lost majesty" being one of the few).

Unlike Cadman or Lieurance, Berlin had no personal experience with Indian life or Indian reservations. He was not claiming to be authentic in his portrayals. In the 1940s, unlike in the early nineteenth century, audiences no longer expected or wanted authenticity. What they sought was escapist diversion, and the most sophisticated entertainment needed to toy deliciously with the social codes of the day. "I'm an Indian Too" clearly did so, and stylishly, too, in a way that we perhaps have lost touch with today, having forgotten many of the references. At the same time, it dangerously reinforced many long-held misunderstandings about Native American peoples, not least of which was the notion that all it takes to "become Indian" is a name, a feather, and a wild ritual. Annie's adoption may have been based partly on history, but Berlin's song echoes with all the cultural resonance from earlier in the century when Indian reservations were portrayed as places of fantasy, when American anxieties about Indian assimilation were played out in song and onstage, and when ideas of relationships between Indians and whites could not be expressed without a tinge of naughtiness. We cannot hear this music today without an increased sensitivity to its hurtfulness to those who endured endless suffering merely for being "in the way." In one sense, Berlin's song laughingly brushed away any responsibility for presenting Indian exoticism in twentieth-century society. But clearly no other composer distilled the essence of America's Indian stereotypes to such a fine degree. Berlin's "Indian" music is so seductive that we may forget that it also obliges us to look long and hard at the way white Americans—not only in the first half of the twentieth century but since the beginning of this nation's history—both honored and defiled the Indian peoples, often simultaneously.

9

Underscoring Ancestry: Music for Native America in Film

"Pin your eyeballs, son, there's a redskin over that rock yonder!" shouts California Joe to George Armstrong Custer in the 1942 Warner Brothers film *They Died with Their Boots On.* As Custer's wife Libby replies apprehensively with "Indians?" we hear a throbbing tom-tom along with high unison woodwinds playing a short descending chromatic figure, a figure bookended by the interval of an augmented fourth. Clearly there is no musical ceremony or drumming taking place offscreen. Instead we see what California Joe sees: an Indian scout crouching atop a high hill. Before we have much time to interpret this image, however, Max Steiner's invisible orchestra interprets it for us. Not only tom-toms, but the descending chromatic figure and augmented fourths have long carried specific connotations for concert-, theater-, and filmgoing audiences. Was this veteran film composer resorting to overdone and outworn musical stereotyping here? Yes, in a way. But a closer look at Steiner's music for this film reveals that his musical portrayal of the Sioux, especially of Chief Crazy Horse, is more complicated than a simple dismissal of "stereotyping" would suggest. What are the stereotypes implied in the moment described? Is the music pitched to our reaction as spectators, or does it reflect the point of view of California Joe and, by transference, General Custer, who, in this version of history, is experiencing his first encounter with the northern Plains tribe? As Raoul Walsh's film unfolds, Custer is shown to gain significant (if guarded) respect for the Sioux, at least for their determination as resistance fighters. Steiner's score adds a running musical commentary to the film that sometimes substitutes for the impartial voice of an external narrator and at other times assumes a particular character's point of view. Like the theatrical "Indianesque" music of Victor Herbert or Irving Berlin, Steiner's score relies on devices embodying complex layers of meaning that had accrued over decades—if not centuries—although he combined them in ways wholly personal. Because Steiner was such a dominant figure in Hollywood in the 1930s and 1940s, the style of film accompaniment that he helped create for Warner Brothers set the standard for other studios and composers. For this reason, he is central to any discussion of American film music. At the same time, many social developments throughout the middle and late twentieth century, particularly Indians' cultural reemergence and the pan-Indian movement—not to mention the co-opting of some of these ideals by popular culture gurus and the increasing youth of Hollywood's target audience—led to more diverse approaches to underscoring Indian characters in the cinema, particularly after the late 1960s.

While film music builds on established methods of dramatic accompaniment, it is also a developing art form in which composers draw continually on current musical styles and technical developments in sound production. Though some reviewers may speak of "movie Indians" or of "stereotypical Indian music," Westerns in fact have offered a variety of Indian characters and music depicting them. Even a cursory glance at Michael Hilger's survey of films about American Indians will convey the breadth of this subject matter. No comparable survey for the music in these films exists, however. While there have recently been some excellent detailed dramatic analyses and critiques by John E. O'Connor, Phil Lucas, Steven M. Leuthold, Jacqueline Kilpatrick, Ward Churchill, and others concerning Indian portrayals in Westerns, little has been published about the music for Indians in the narrative cinema. Perhaps most film scholars have assumed the subject to be fairly uncomplicated. Claudia Gorbman is one exception. Comparing three Hollywood Westerns—one each from 1950, 1970, and 1990—she has demonstrated significant differences in the way Indian characters were conveyed in sound over this forty-year period. Few nonmusicians who have written about Westerns or Indian characters in film have paid similar attention to the music and what it contributes. Perhaps they cannot be faulted for this; as Gorbman elegantly puts it, "film music is like the medium of a dream, forgotten in the waking state." Thus entire books, excellent though they may be, have been written about celluloid Indians with almost no mention of the musical soundtrack, unless, of course, it accompanies particular dances or ceremonies enacted on-screen. But surely David Raksin's modernist musical commentary in *Apache* (1954) or John Barry's lush underscoring in *Dances with Wolves* (1990) affects how we read the Indian characters in these films and to what degree we interpret the situations emotionally and intellectually.[1]

Since it would be impractical to attempt a comprehensive survey of this fascinating yet vast repertoire within one chapter, I have therefore chosen, as I have throughout this book, to focus on one or two dominant themes or questions that seem pervasive in the genres and periods in question. One of these themes is how music sometimes subverts the standard stereotypes (or, as I prefer to call them in dramatic media, archetypes) of Native Americans as depicted on-screen through actions and words. In the example cited above, California Joe—an old-timer who regards "Injuns" basically with suspicion and contempt—determines the point of view. Hence the music we hear for the Indians' first appearance signals "danger." Music is often used in the cinema to characterize, particularly since information about an individual or group must often be conveyed quickly through a few establishing shots. Moreover, it can supply additional information not provided on-screen. Through music a character can be portrayed, almost instantaneously, as depraved or virtuous, friendly or hostile, foreign or native.[2]

Yet Steiner's music for *They Died with Their Boots On* suggests other things as well, one of which is the ancientness of the people in question. This second and more specific idea relies on music to reinforce an implied connection between the antiquity of the continent and Indian ancestry, since such a concept can only be partly conveyed by visual images. These people are of very old stock, the music often implies. This is a crucial linchpin for our understanding of why, and how, Native American characters have been portrayed in some of the ways they have been. As demonstrated throughout this book, music can be used to underscore a sense of remoteness or timelessness. An important dimension of Indian traditions is the expression of close ties to and respect for the land. Sometimes a musical commentary about "ancientness" is made explicit by dialogue: a character may refer to the burial grounds of his or her ancestors, thereby establishing an explicit connection between individuals and the space they inhabit. At other times this connection is made solely through music.

How and why the evocation of ancestry came to play such an important role in Hollywood film can partly be explained as a reaction to an earlier notion of Native American cultures as "vanishing." Most recent film scholars note the persistent stereotypes of Indians and occasionally mention the "stereotypical music" that accompanies them. But underlying Hollywood's reconstitution of often narrowly defined Indian characters—or perhaps as a consequence of it—some composers have used music to add new layers of meaning to the situations depicted on-screen. One of these is the implication of "authenticity" through ancient lineage, an important and often overlooked aspect that I will explore in more detail later. This layer of meaning (created through music) is a quality that film theorist Michel Chion would categorize as "added value." While Hollywood's Indians, particularly those from the 1930s to the 1970s, may rarely speak or act in ways recognizable to most Native Americans, a film's musical underscoring can convey psychological and emotional information that supplements—indeed, influences—our understanding of these characters. In Ward Churchill's otherwise excellent analysis of *Black Robe* (1991), he notes that composer Georges Delerue's "superbly understated ensemble . . . works with subtle efficiency to bind the whole package together." In other words, everything is already there in the film; the music is just the wrapping. I prefer to examine how music can be used to represent aspects of native America that may not be evident in the dialogue and visuals alone. Films such as *Black Robe* notwithstanding, plots in Western cinema (especially Hollywood cinema) are often scripted and directed according to a set of values that has almost always been understood as reflecting those of a loyal mainstream audience.[3]

Indian Archetypes and Music for Hollywood Westerns

Critics of Native American representation in film have often provided examples of stereotypes, each somewhat different, but with most originating well before the advent of the cinema.[4] In their panoptic essay on "The Indian in the Movies," Michael T. Marsden and Jack Nachbar identified three overarching dramatic stereotypes of Indians that, though undergoing some variation from time to time, remained essentially intact in American cinema until the 1980s (and, it could be argued, beyond). The first is the Pocahontas figure: the sentimental Indian woman who comes to the aid of her white brethren, often at the risk or sacrifice of her own life. Marsden and Nachbar trace this archetype back to John Bray's 1808 stage melodrama *The Indian Princess.* The second is what the authors have called the "Noble Anachronism," a type first established in the frontier novels of Cooper: this Indian is characterized by a high degree of natural virtue made more poignant by the audience's knowledge that he is doomed by an oncoming white culture not compatible with his admirable but primitive mode of living. The third dramatic stereotype is the "Savage Reactionary," whose attributes stem from the dime novel and action melodrama. He is a killer because he detests the manifest advancement of white culture and is a victim of his own primal impulses. In the classic Western, as Marsden and Nachbar put it, the Savage Reactionary "must be annihilated for the good of civilization."[5]

To some extent, Marsden and Nachbar demonstrate that these character types, though they exclude much of actual Native American experience, have been resilient enough dramatically to survive constantly varied treatment throughout more than seventy-five years of cinema. Like archetypes in classical mythology, the Pocahontas figure, the Noble Anachronism, and the Savage Reactionary have stimulated countless stories created about them, although it can be argued that they serve one larger narrative: the territorial expansion and economic development of the United States. The music used to tell these various stories hasn't always conformed to pure archetypes, however, and occasionally has even blurred the distinctions between them. In the first decades of the twentieth century, music for silent Westerns generally (though not always) reinforced the central tenets of these Indian archetypes. This is perhaps not surprising, since much of the so-called stock music used to accompany silent films was usually derived from the indexical figures developed in the nineteenth century within the contexts of musical nationalism and exoticism.

One surviving collection (now at UCLA) that was assembled by Louis B. Schnauber as music director for several theaters in Omaha between 1910 and 1927 contains many published "Indian" pieces used as film accompaniments. Charles K. Herbert's "Indian War Dance No. 19" (1916) was recommended "for fight scenes," and Gaston Borch's "Indian War-Song" (1919) was used at the title card "Courageous Little Families" (presumably a white settler's family under attack by Savage Reactionaries). Some items, such as Sol Levy's "Indian Mysterioso" (1918), were categorized for general use where appropriate, while a selection such as J. S. Zamecnik's "Indian Dawn" (1924) was intended to suggest Sioux territory somewhere "in the Black Hills."

Since most major film theaters between 1913 and about 1930 had their own libraries of pieces categorized by mood, character, and ethnicity (or "nationality"), a large number of such "Indian" works could be found in almost every collection. For example, the Capitol Theatre Orchestra Library of New York City (now at the Eastman School of Music) contains almost thirty "Indian characteristics" for silent film. William Axt's "Indian Orgy" (1924) could serve "for Indian gatherings, uprisings, dances, and festivals." Otto Langey's "Indian Agitato" (1918) was recommended to suggest "dramatic excitement for Indian emotional scenes, rivalry, jealousy, expectancy, apprehension, etc." Both of these works drew heavily on the war-dance tropes developed in the middle to late nineteenth century, whereas a piece such as M. L. Lake's "Indian Love Song" (1914, also from the Capitol Library) derived more from the Dvořák-MacDowell intonations of the pastoral Indian, which Lake undergirded with a gentle moresca rhythm. Studio-issued "mood" books for silent-film accompaniment, such as those by Sam Fox or Erno Rapée, also contained several "Indian" characteristics. Copies of works such as these remained in the libraries of film studios and were used by music supervisors as stock filler well into the sound era.[6]

Some early silent films even boasted complete orchestral accompaniments based on the transcriptions and adaptations of Indian song in character pieces (as in Gilbert's "By the Arrow"). Two films from 1913—*Hiawatha: The Indian Passion Play* (F. E. Moore) and *The Cheyenne Massacre* (Kalem)—were distributed with specially prepared scores, a new experiment at the time. *Hiawatha*'s score was even advertised in film trade magazines as consisting of genuine Ojibwa music.[7] Much of this "Indian music" was of course culled from Burton's *American Primitive Music,* as well as other Indianist sources. Moreover, not all theaters used the prescribed music, which is probably why cue sheets rather than special scores remained the norm during the silent period. In one of his weekly "Music for the Picture" essays for *Moving Picture World,* Clarence Sinn reported that R. J. Bessette, music director for the Crown Theatre in Hartford, Connecticut, decided not to use the special score sent for *The Cheyenne Massacre* but to compile his own music based on the theater library's holdings. In the film, Swift Bear and the Cheyennes are plotting an attack on Fort Bryson, a frontier post. Thanks to Indian scouts, the Cheyennes are warned about a command of soldiers sent to quell their rebellion. They overtake the soldiers, killing most of them. For this cue, titled "Vengeance of the Red Men," the music director had his tiny ensemble play "Big Chief Battle-Axe," Thomas Allen's popular dance novelty (and later jazz standard) of 1907. This number continued into the following sequence at the fort, where General Foster gets word about the attack. His attempts to telegraph for help are thwarted when Swift Bear cuts the wires. Bessette's choice of accompaniment for this sequence illustrates that popular music played an important role in film music from its early days and also demonstrates the flexibility of musical underscoring for Indians during the silent period. Instead of using a typical "Indian agitato" for this fight sequence, Bessette chose a light touch of mock heroism. The verse of "Big Chief Battle-Axe" incorporates many war-dance tropes, including tom-tom effects, octave leaps with grace notes, and "yip, yip, yips" for the musicians to shout. While these elements added excitement and immediacy as the Cheyennes gained the upper hand in their attack upon the fort, they also served to characterize Swift Bear as a bona fide Savage Reactionary—something the film itself did not specifically convey.[8]

In *Sundown* (First National Pictures), a full-length Western of 1924, Indians played only a minor role as nameless figures in a small midwestern town in the late nineteenth century. In preparing the cue sheet for the film's accompaniment (fig. 19), directors Harry Hoyt and Laurence Trimble and music compiler James C. Bradford assigned a dancelike novelty (cue 5, "Tehama" by Chauncey Haines) for a pair of Indians who head into town to use the general store. "Oh look, Indians," says one of the ranchers to the other, and this signals music cue 5. Yet for the first shot of the film, the cue sheet recommends the ancestors' theme from Victor Herbert's *Natoma,* a sharply descending pentatonic motive — actually tetratonic (only four notes) — that appears throughout the opera whenever Natoma refers to her people. As I argued in the last chapter, the current musical divide between classical and popular genres was not fully evident in the first half of the twentieth century. An operatic work like *Natoma* could and did have an impact on popular music and the cinema. Otto Langey's arrangements of excerpts were common accompaniments for film scores involving Indian characters, and his "*Natoma* Selections" began and ended with a powerful statement of the ancestors' theme. The plot of *Sundown* involves homesteaders who are forced to leave their property and who join a group of cattlemen heading for Mexico. Although Indians do not appear in the opening shot, the cue sheet recommends Herbert's stern and forceful theme, no doubt to suggest their presence — or the spirit of their presence — in the opening vista of the American prairie. The unthreatening "real Indians" in the film no longer have anything to do with the "ancient Indians" that once occupied this land but whose presence, in 1924, could still be invoked solely through music.

With the development of film soundtracks (and the speaker systems to project them), accompanying music of course no longer remained a matter of choice, as it had largely been before 1928. The archetypal figures in early cinema had been to some extent tempered by the fact that Native American actors played many of the lead Indian characters, a practice gradually overturned by film studios in the late 1920s and early 1930s. Films that dealt with issues of love and courtship, between Indians and whites as well as among members of the same tribe, fell out of favor. The Motion Picture Production Code of 1930 expressly forbade the depiction of miscegenation (although technically the code defined it as relationships between white and black races). To satisfy the Hays Office and to avoid offending large conservative constituencies, studio heads began censoring attempts to film any physical contact between persons of different races. This practice led to a fifty-year tradition of white actors playing Indians, particularly in roles that required romance with a non-Indian character. Those Native American actors who were still used in the 1930s and 1940s were cast principally as chieftains or father figures, like Two Hawks and Last Elk in *The Miracle Rider* (1935), White Horse in *Stagecoach* (1939), and John Big Tree in *Western Union* (1941). The fact that many

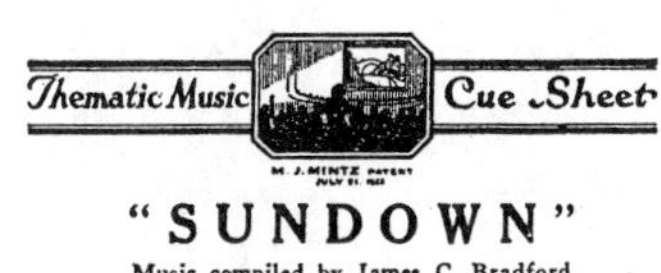

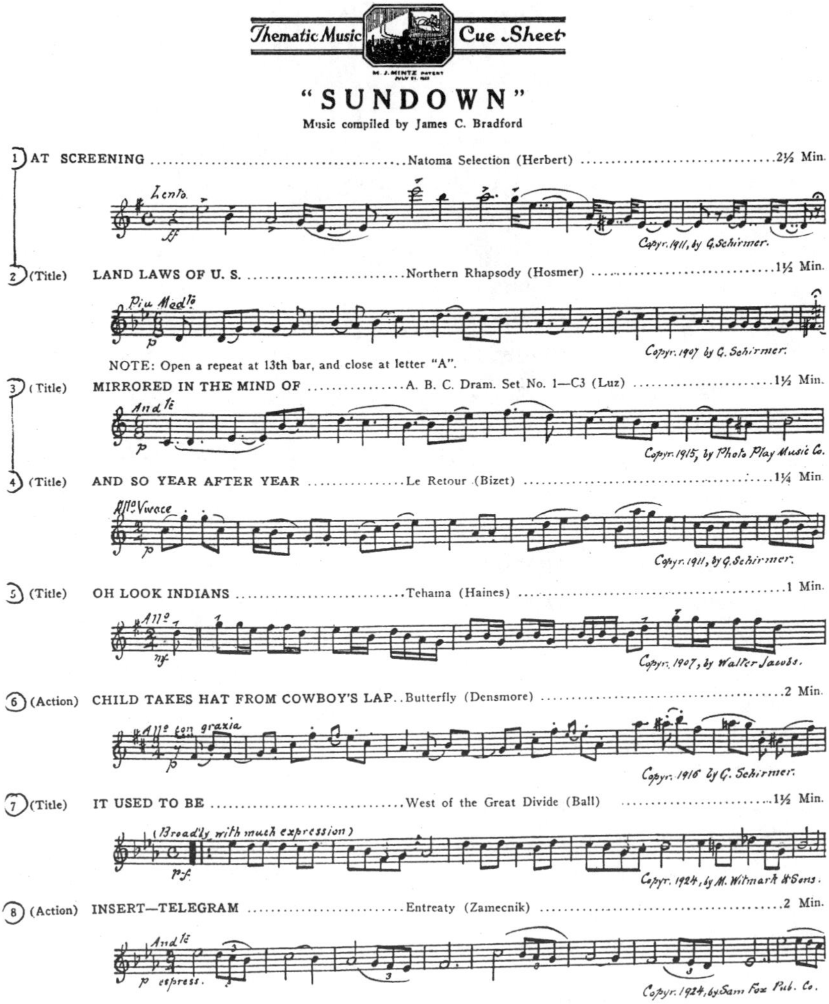
Thematic Music Cue Sheet
M. J. MINTZ PATENT
"SUNDOWN"
Music compiled by James C. Bradford
1 AT SCREENING ....Natoma Selection (Herbert) ....2½ Min.
Lento
Copyr. 1911, by G. Schirmer.
2 (Title) LAND LAWS OF U. S. ....Northern Rhapsody (Hosmer) ....1½ Min.
Piu Modto
Copyr. 1907 by G. Schirmer.
NOTE: Open a repeat at 13th bar, and close at letter "A".
3 (Title) MIRRORED IN THE MIND OF ....A. B. C. Dram. Set No. 1—C3 (Luz) ....1½ Min.
Andte
Copyr. 1915, by Photo Play Music Co.
4 (Title) AND SO YEAR AFTER YEAR ....Le Retour (Bizet) ....1¼ Min.
Allo Vivace
Copyr. 1911, by G. Schirmer.
5 (Title) OH LOOK INDIANS ....Tehama (Haines) ....1 Min.
Allo
Copyr. 1907, by Walter Jacobs.
6 (Action) CHILD TAKES HAT FROM COWBOY'S LAP..Butterfly (Densmore) ....2 Min.
Allo con grazia
Copyr. 1916 by G. Schirmer.
7 (Title) IT USED TO BE ....West of the Great Divide (Ball) ....1½ Min.
(Broadly with much expression)
Copyr. 1924, by M. Witmark & Sons.
8 (Action) INSERT—TELEGRAM ....Entreaty (Zamecnik) ....2 Min.
Andte
p espress.
Copyr. 1924, by Sam Fox Pub. Co.

Figure 19. First page of the cue sheet for *Sundown* (Sam Fox Pub. Co., 1924). John Ward Collection, Harvard Theatre Collection, Houghton Library. Used by permission.

"Indians" in Hollywood films were now generally white actors with some Native American or Mexican American actors mixed in may have provided another reason why musical underscoring during these years drew so heavily on the standard tropes of nineteenth-century Indianism. Without music that carried the weight of self-evidence, audiences would have been more likely to question the multiple ethnicities of the performers or the absurdity of simply darkening white actors' faces to make them appear Indian.

Throughout the 1930s, Hollywood studio composers developed a kind of musical "war paint" that not only masked the ethnic differences between actors playing Indian but also effectively increased the audience's perception of difference between those playing Indian and those playing white. By the time of John Ford's *Stagecoach,* a tradition of using stock characteristic music to underscore ethnicity was standard practice (in addition to the use of traditional mood and melodramatic music). The score for *Stagecoach* was composed and compiled by no less than six people: Louis Gruenberg, Richard Hageman, Frank Harling, John Leipold, Leo Shuken, and Gerard Carbonara, the latter perhaps the most outstanding contributor among them although he is not even listed in the credits. Carbonara, born in 1886, began to compose for the Paramount and First National studios in 1928, but his first Western subjects date from 1936. More important, he was among the earliest of studio composers to impart to these films a "Western" color, a technique derived partly from the intonation of American folk and cowboy songs—a style often credited largely to Aaron Copland—and partly from a desire to replicate in broad musical strokes the powerful impression created by the immutable western landscape. Carbonara studied at the National Conservatory in New York (ca. 1906), where Dvořák's influence still remained strong. Later, as a young conductor of opera and symphony in Italy, he was deeply influenced by recent developments in Italian music, notably by such symphonic works as Ottorino Respighi's *The Pines of Rome* (1924), a descriptive suite also popularized in America by Toscanini and others after 1926. In the suite's "The Pines Near a Catacomb," Respighi suggested the ancientness of the Roman tombs by doubling the chantlike melody at the fourth or fifth in imitation of an ancient organum style, even though organum was a development in medieval sacred music and had no known connection with ancient Roman music. (Miklós Rózsa would later use the same device for his scores to Roman epics in the 1950s.) Carbonara was thus an important link between European composers such as Respighi and the sound of the 1940s Western, especially in his mix of modality and parallelisms and his ability to suggest "ancientness" through music.[9]

One does not hear this ancientness, for example, in George Antheil's music for DeMille's *The Plainsman* (Paramount, 1936). In fact a *Variety* reviewer in 1937 criticized the score, calling it "unauthentic" and lacking in color.[10] By 1937, it would seem, audiences had already come to expect a tone of authenticity in the accompanying soundtrack. What might this have been? None of the Hollywood films of the 1930s or 1940s, to my knowledge, allowed Native Americans to create their own music, so the concept of musical "authenticity" must have meant something different than what it implies today. Since Hollywood specialized in creating imagined worlds, anything that might dispel the fantasy—particularly intrusive music—would generally be eliminated in favor of music that lulled the viewers into a susceptible frame of mind (and aimed to keep them there). With this in mind, "authentic" then could be translated as "supportive of the visual impression and emotional content of the film." A bit of nostalgia might also be useful, but the music of the 1940s and '50s Westerns rarely suggested urbanity, only the spaciousness and fecundity of the pioneer experience.

Following in Carbonara's footsteps, several composers specialized in thus authenticating Hollywood's Wild West by providing sonorous, folk-inspired (though always symphonic) scores, among them Raoul Kraushaar, Mischa Bakaleinikoff, Dimitri Tiomkin, Elmer Bernstein, David Buttolph, Hugo Friedhofer, Leigh Harline, Jimmie Haskell, William Lava, John Leipold, Alfred Newman, Hugo Riesenfeld, Frank Sanucci, Frank Skinner, Max Steiner, Herbert Stothart, and Victor Young. Especially productive (and perhaps most influential in establishing the sound of the Western in the 1940s and into the 1950s) were Hans Salter, Lee Zahler, and Paul Sawtell, who were prolific in the field of B films generally. Zahler, the only American-born of the three, composed, compiled, and arranged film scores under the general title of music director for some 133 films in the 1930s and '40s. Salter began scoring for films in his native Austria; in Hollywood he contributed mostly stock and uncredited music for over 400 films from 1938 to 1967. The Polish-born Sawtell wrote scores and contributed stock music for over 480 films from 1939 to 1973. Along with these three, William Lava similarly wrote and contributed music for some 360 films, many of them Westerns, from 1937 to about 1970. Much of this hasty "composition" was probably the result of studio compilation techniques rather than of creating original works; these composers are credited in the American Film Institute catalogue most often for their contributions of stock music to films.

The American-born but European-trained David Buttolph, who prepared several hundred Hollywood studio scores between 1933 and 1964, also composed and arranged for dozens of Westerns. His 1941 score for Fritz Lang's *Western Union* (Twentieth Century Fox) typifies the approach during these years. As Zane Grey's original novel tells it, this agency is struggling to install the first telegraph wire across Nebraska during the years of the Civil War. Its biggest problem stems not from any credible resistance by the Sioux, who are generally portrayed as drunken fools throughout the film, but from a group of Confederate renegades who disguise themselves as Indians and keep attacking the federal outposts. At first, both the real Indians and the pretend Indians receive the same music, as viewers are not supposed to realize that the Sioux are simply the pawns of Confederate malcontents. The "Indian" motive consists of eight notes:

The generic treatment to which Buttolph subjects this tetratonic motive is typical of the faceless Indians who attacked in Hollywood films. The motive itself consists of just enough notes to function as a recognizable gapped melody that effectively conveys the presence of exotic others. Like the examples we have examined earlier in concert music (notably the opening of MacDowell's "Indian" Suite) the motive suggests a hunting call: its rhythms, particularly as they are played, are sharp, rigid, and unyielding. The crisp iambic rhythms—the old Scottish-snap effect—are crucial markers of Indianness. As in Respighi's *The Pines of Rome* and in Carbonara's *Stagecoach* music, the melody is doubled in parallel fourths, conveying here the "ancientness" of the Sioux. It is also accompanied by a throbbing drumbeat in two with the same rhythm doubled in the cellos and basses, which drone in open fifths. In one context, this music might convey a certain heroic defiance. But given the on-screen treatment of these painfully absurd movie Indians, it is difficult to hear Buttolph's music as adding much "authenticity," as was no doubt intended. Perhaps in 1941, when many audiences in the growing American suburbs were used to seeing Indians portrayed as wild animals with no substantive culture of their own, it was dramatically useful for the music to underscore their apparent harmlessness with at least the threat of danger. Buttolph repeated this formula for John Ford's *My Darling Clementine* (1946) and for other films with genuinely bloodthirsty Indians.

Music for Custer, Crazy Horse, and the Sioux on the Silver Screen

From this prevailing studio practice, in which again no less than six composers contributed to a film such as *Winners of the West* (Universal, 1940), emerged *They Died with Their Boots On* (Warners, 1942) with an original score almost entirely by Max Steiner, who then headed the music department at Warner Brothers. The "they" in the title was of course the Seventh Army Cavalry under George Armstrong Custer. The battle was that of the Little Big Horn (1876), in which some four thousand Sioux under Chief Crazy Horse wiped out the 265 men of Custer's division as well as the general himself. The original Custer was, like William Henry Harrison and Andrew

Jackson, an Indian fighter who tried to build his political reputation by staging "Indian wars." In Walsh's version, history is pretty much left in the dust. This wartime film naturally portrayed Custer as a prototype American hero—just, good, kind, a bit awkward socially (especially with women and his commanding officers), but fearless against bullies of all stripes. Errol Flynn, who always looked dashing in a uniform, was ideally cast for this Hollywood image of the hero general.

The Vienna-born Max Steiner, already a twelve-year veteran composer at Warner Brothers, wrote a sturdy, upward-striving motive for Custer, one we hear immediately in the opening titles of the film. The rhythm is that of a restrained quickstep (6/8), a bit lanky but determined in its steady gait. The motive is almost always played by the trumpets and trombones—linking heroism with the brass of royalty—and is infused with some warmth from the strings, which add an element of human vulnerability. Throughout the film, Steiner uses the brass motive as Custer's identifying theme, reminding the audience of his innately heroic character. We hear it particularly when the general is acting decisively and even when he is shown deliberating, for it informs us that the Hollywood Custer will deliberate fairly, justly, nobly. A second tune in the film also associated with Custer, or rather with his post as general of the Seventh Cavalry, is the Irish tune "Garry Owen," the actual Custer's favorite song (and still used for the Seventh Cavalry today). The film draws particular attention to this song. Custer first hears an Irish soldier singing it in a saloon. He is immediately captivated by its spirited lilt and requests that it be played for his cavalry's military exercises. After presenting the tune in several on-screen versions, Steiner then renders it heroically as part of the nondiegetic soundtrack. With the full studio orchestra blaring out a rousing version of "Garry Owen," we see Custer's army riding off to battle. Superimposed over this are the words, "And so was born the immortal Seventh U.S. Cavalry which cleared the plains for a ruthlessly advancing civilization that spelled doom to the red race." As the image dissolves from Custer's men to long shots of individual Sioux warriors wreaking havoc on settlers, Steiner switches abruptly to his Indian music, the high chromatic descending scales mentioned at the outset of this chapter. (Steiner described this music as "Sioux" in the cue sheet for this sequence, next to the titles "Garry Owen," "charge" and "bugle call.")[11]

The first time we heard this "Sioux" music, of course, was on Custer's journey by wagon from Bismarck to Fort Lincoln, when California Joe first pointed out the Indian scouts. At that point, we saw (and heard) these scouts as Joe perceived them: as a dangerous threat. By recalling this music nearly each time the Sioux appear on-screen—now as Savage Reactionaries—Steiner limits our understanding of this tribe to little more than generic warmongers. (If you close your eyes, you might even imagine Cossack barbarians.) In one montage the Sioux attack white settlers with hatchets and shoot soldiers with arrows. When Walsh finally shows them in retreat during a harsh winter storm—fleeing the determination of Custer's cavalry and therefore no longer Savage Reactionaries—Steiner again plays the Sioux motive, a bit slowed down and beleaguered perhaps, but still embodying the exotic flare and threatening chromaticism of the original. As California Joe described these enemies: "Injuns is too ignorant to fight right, they fight wrong every time; that's why the soldiers always get licked. To lick an Injun you gotta fight 'em like an Injun."

Perhaps this is why Steiner modifies his Indian music once Crazy Horse enters the film. By slowing down the original Sioux music, reducing the orchestration, and extending the "danger" motive into a full-fledged melody, Steiner turns what was generic "Sioux music" into music that characterizes one individual. Crazy Horse makes his first on-screen appearance during the initial attack on Custer's wagon train where the general, in a sudden display of innate Indianness, overpowers him and tackles him to the ground. True to Hollywood practice, the youthful Crazy Horse was played by Mexican-born American actor Anthony Quinn (who, unknown to most viewers, was part Tarahumara). Custer promises to protect the young chieftain, for it is evident when they arrive at the fort that the soldiers are determined to hang him. The general keeps his word and instead has the chief impounded in the guardhouse to "let him cool off his heels for forty days." Custer then encounters the lax rules of the fort with disapproval, and he immediately begins to take charge. "What are all these Indians doing inside the fort?" he asks California. "Trading for rifles" is the answer. Meanwhile, Crazy Horse—to the accompaniment of his music—is being led to the guardhouse and secretly exchanges signals with one of the fort Indians. A few minutes later the Indian helps Crazy Horse to escape, which effectively proves Custer right in his assessment of the fort's poor management.

The guardhouse sequence is laid out in example 19. I've consolidated Hugo Friedhofer's orchestration into one line, putting in as much detail as is possible while still allowing space for dialogue and visual cues. The most notable feature is the persistent tom-tom (doubled by finger cymbals), accented in groups of two, not four. This ostinato continues throughout the entire sequence, from the moment Crazy Horse is led forward until his escape several minutes later. The allusion is clearly to native drumming, but here it also works psychologically to create some expectation that the Indian chieftain may outsmart his captors. The ominous effect of the throbbing ONE-two-ONE-two-ONE-two-ONE-two suggests a heartbeat, and the deliberate tempo builds an extraordinary amount of tension. The persistent throbbing is iconic, in that most listeners will associate it with tribal drumming, but it also physical, in that it draws the listener to participate in the mounting stress, not just deduce it from the events on-screen. The alto flute slowly and solemnly intones the longer version of the "Sioux" motive. The opening phrase (the "danger" motive) includes features from the war-dance and pagan tropes, particularly grace-note ornaments and sliding chromatic passing tones. Here the tone is more subdued. In addition to the grace notes and chromatic inflections, Steiner creates a migrating modal tune, its basic outlines being (from high to low): F–E–slithering down chromatically to B; B (grace-note inflected) –B–G–F♯–B; and then B–B–G♯–F♯–G♯–D♯/E♭–D♭–E♭–D♭–B♮–A–B (ending on B against the persistent timpani throbbing on F and C). The original Sioux music, animalistic and wild, here creates a sense of mystery surrounding Crazy Horse. Steiner draws on some Plains Indian practices: a downward pentatonic melody that migrates from one tonal center to another. The concluding whole-tone phrase, constructed, it would seem, to invoke the exotic, brings the melody back to its starting pitch (B).

Curiously, Steiner jotted on his manuscript sketch (now at Brigham Young University), that this tune stems from an "authentic Indian melody" that had been sung to him by an Indian chief.[12] (Unless this information were to be confirmed by the chief in question, however, I am inclined to be skeptical, given the uses to which such claims have been put, as illustrated throughout this book.) Using flute and drums alone, this is the closest this score comes to anything that sounds indigenously Native American. Within the context of this film, Crazy Horse is thereby authenticated as a "real Indian"—a rebel and a fighter—and therefore Custer's only legitimate opponent.

In the context of the conflict between the Sioux and the cavalry soldiers, Steiner uses another motive, one easy to miss on first viewing the film:

Except for a slight variation in rhythm, this motive is identical to the ancestors' theme in Herbert's *Natoma,* known in the industry from the versions prepared by Langey and used in silent films (as in the *Sundown* example). Perhaps Steiner knew the opera, or perhaps he found a copy of Langey's version in the Warner Music Archives. (Or perhaps *this* was the "authentic" melody sung to him.)

Molto moderato (misterioso)

Soldiers: "Crazy Horse! String him up!"

2 Timp, 2 Tom-toms, Finger cymbals

(cont.underneath melody)

Alto flute

Crazy Horse: "You give word, Long Hair, no rope..."

Custer: "I keep my word... Take him to the guardhouse."

"And see that he's well-treated."

"California, what are all those Indians doing inside the fort?"

California: "Trading for rifles."

Custer: "Rifles!?"

(Conversation between California and Custer about his joining the army.)

(Timp/Tom-toms)

(cont.)

Clar.

(Cut to guardhouse.)

Example 19. Max Steiner, "Reel 9, Part 1" from *They Died with Their Boots On* (1942). Courtesy of the Warner Brothers Archive, University of Southern California, Los Angeles.

(Crazy Horse is being let by several officers. Fort Indian quietly observes)

(Cut to Crazy Horse. Serious look as he conveys wordless message to fort Indian.)

Although the Warner Brothers cue sheet offers no special name for this prominent theme, it seems to me to function as an alternative Sioux motive, the earlier music having been developed largely around the character of Crazy Horse. The theme first appears, played by all the woodwinds and doubled by the celesta (a "magical" effect), when California Joe is inadvertently discovered to the expectant father of an Indian child. Its most important and powerful appearance, however, played by the full brass with thunderous timpani, accompanies Crazy Horse's meeting with Custer, a truce sequence in which the two discuss the protection of the sacred Black Hills. In the interlude that follows, a document flashes before the screen—"A Treaty between the United States of America and the Sioux Nation of Indians." As the camera zooms in on this title, the orchestra blares out "America" but then, even louder, the "ancestor" motive. For a time, Steiner seems to imply, these two "nations" are on equal footing.

With Errol Flynn and Anthony Quinn both cutting smart figures, and with Steiner's rousing score, *They Died with Their Boots On* is first-class entertainment. But for native peoples, and for anyone else with an awareness of America's historical treatment of them, it is only possible to enjoy this film as a guilty pleasure.

Entering Apache Territory

The Sioux, with their picturesque tepee villages and chieftains in large war bonnets, offered Hollywood films—as they had earlier for Buffalo Bill's Wild West—the most elaborate opportunity for Indian props and costumes (courtesy since 1912 of the Western Costume Company). But despite popular actors such as Quinn or Victor Mature playing the victorious Oglala warrior—the latter in George Sherman's self-consciously pro-Indian *Chief Crazy Horse* (1955)—the greatest fighters in Hollywood Westerns were far and away the Apaches. Even just this tribal name, when shouted in a film by a settler, could raise hairs among a 1950s audience. Ever since *les apaches,* a defiant group of disgruntled European adolescents, began to infest Parisian nightclubs after 1902, "Apaches" remained a symbol throughout the Western cultural world for the untamed (and perhaps untamable) warrior.[13] The actual nomadic Athabascan tribes of the region that is now west Texas, New Mexico, and Arizona were noted for their warlike disposition and fierce opposition to European colonizers, at least from the time Spanish explorers first wrote about *apiches* until the capture of Geronimo in 1886. They were certainly among the most staunchly defiant native peoples of the entire continent and therefore provided significant dramatic potential for Hollywood.

Beginning with *Valley of the Sun* (1942, RKO) and *Apache Trail* (1943, MGM), reviewers noted that the Indian uprisings depicted in these films were already timeworn subjects, best suited as diverting entertainment for youngsters. Little did these writers know that dozens of mainstream films depicting confrontations between settlers, soldiers, and Apaches would be produced in Hollywood over the next twenty-five years. Only the Sioux approached the Apaches in sheer numbers of films. Clearly these two large tribal groups appeared to have "put up the best fight" in the struggle for the West, and hence they provided the crucial source of external conflict necessary for all good action drama.[14]

Table 7 lists some of the better-crafted films of this genre. From this representative sampling I will focus a bit more closely on four of these (indicated with an asterisk), which I chose to demonstrate not how they replicated patterns but rather how they sometimes subverted expectations.

As shooting on location became increasingly attractive, especially with color film, it seemed obvious that the beauties of the American Southwest would offer extraordinary natural backdrops for breathtaking views and unusual shot composition (vividly employed, for example, by John Ford). Such settings also afforded composers a chance to draw not only on Native American sources (or "Indianesque" adaptations of Indian music), but also on a newly developing trope that signified, or rather came to signify, the West. While the "Americanism" that is most pronounced in the late–1930s classical music of Copland, Virgil Thomson, Elie Siegmeister, and other younger composers seems self-evident, its sources still await thorough exploration. It is possible to detect these resonances already in 1911 with Lieurance's "By the Waters of the Minnetonka" and in a 1927 Broadway number such as Walter Donaldson's "The Song of the Setting Sun." What is freshest in the late 1930s Americanists is a Stravinskian neoclassical influence: sparse texture and instrumentation; melodic and harmonic emphasis on seconds, fourths, and flatted sevenths as opposed to thirds, fifths, and sixths; and snappier, dancelike rhythms. This influence was of course injected into Hollywood film partly by Copland himself and was quickly imitated by others, Friedhofer and Salter among them. In addition to neoclassicism, the most noticeable trait of the new "musical Americanism" was its quotation of recognizable rural American folk music (which *did* use thirds, fifths, and sixths). By the 1950s the idea of "Western" music—music that quoted a pentatonic tune such as "The Lone Prairie" and other cowboy songs—was a standard film-scoring device, the "folklore" of white rural America serving as its principal source.[15]

Typical of this practice was Hans Salter's music for *Walk the Proud Land.* Salter's main title for the film repeats a process that harks back to *Sundown.* With a shot of the western Nebraska countryside, slightly more mountainous than in reality, we hear an indexically "Indian" horn fanfare, an attention-getting opener. This device immediately alerts viewers to the external danger —the Apaches—and their prominence in the film. When the actual title appears, however, the music changes to "Western" in tone—that is, the West of the white settlers as implied by the intonation of rural American folk songs.[16] In accompanying the interracial love scenes, Salter lays on the indexical features thickly, perhaps to distract audiences from pondering too closely the fact that Anne Bancroft is not actually an Apache woman (a goal more attainable at a time when the young actress was not so well known).

Later in the film, at an Indian ceremony held to entertain a visiting general, Hollywood actors simulate Apache singing and dancing with results that would provoke hilarity from most audiences today. "All of these dances have some sort of meaning, is that so?" asks the apparently clueless general of Indian agent John Clum. The question seems absurd, although a general of the 1870s might not be expected to know such things. The "war dance" in *Walk the Proud Land,* however, as entertaining as it might be, is virtually unrecognizable as anything meaningfully Indian. As with the artisans at the Philadelphia theater in 1817 (for the "Ludicrous Ceremonies" in Barker's *The Armourer's Escape*), depicting a world that would seem as exotic as possible

Table 7. Apaches in Selected Hollywood Films, 1948–65

Title	Year/Studio	Director	Music
Fort Apache	1948, RKO	John Ford	Richard Hageman
Apache Chief	1949, Lippert	Frank MacDonald	Albert Glasser
**Broken Arrow*	1950, Twentieth Century Fox	Delmer Daves	Hugo Friedhofer
Rio Grande	1950, Republic	John Ford	Dale Evans, Stan Jones, Tex Owen, Victoy Young
Apache Drums	1951, Universal	Hugo Fregonese	Hans Salter
Battle at Apache Pass	1952, Universal	George Sherman	Hans Salter
Arrowhead	1953, Paramount	Charles Marquis Warren	Paul Sawtell
Conquest of Cochise	1953, Paramount	William Castle	Mischa Bakaleinikoff (uncredited), Irving Gertz, Paul Mertz
Stand at Apache River	1953, Universal	Lee Sholem	Frank Skinner
**Apache*	1954, MGM and United Artists	Robert Aldrich	David Raksin
Fort Yuma	1955, United Artists	Lesley Selander	Paul Dunlap
The Man from Laramie	1955, Columbia	Anthony Mann	George Duning (with title song by Lester Lee)
**Walk the Proud Land*	1956, Universal	Jesse Hibbs	Hans Salter (with Joseph Gershensen as "music advisor")
Apache Territory	1957, Columbia	Ray Nazarro	Mischa Bakaleinikoff, George Duning, Henry Vars (all uncredited)
Apache Warrior	1957, Twentieth Century Fox	Elmo Williams	Paul Dunlap
Fort Massacre	1958, United Artists	Joseph M. Newman	Marlin Skiles
Sergeant Rutledge	1960, Warner	John Ford	Howard Jackson (with song by Mack David and Jerry Livingston)
Geronimo	1962, MGM and United Artists	Arnold Laven	Hugo Friedhofer
A Distant Trumpet	1964, Warner	Raoul Walsh	Max Steiner

Table 7 Continued

Title	Year/Studio	Director	Music
**Rio Conchos*	1964, Twentieth Century Fox	Gordon Douglas	Jerry Goldsmith
Apache Rifles	1964, Twentieth Century Fox	William Witney	Sid Sidney
Apache Uprising	1965, Paramount	R. G. Springsteen	Jimmie Haskell

*Films discussed in this chapter's text.

to the audience—while at the same time strongly conveying the *impression* of authenticity—was more exciting theatrically (and therefore cinematically) than trying to adhere to anything remotely authentic. The entire sequence in *Walk the Proud Land* makes more sense when we realize that the actual John Clum in 1876 took Apaches to theaters in St. Louis and other cities to perform Wild West skits, stunts, and war dances. The impulse to simulate Apache singing, whooping, and dancing in this film (or rather to *outdo* them) owes its impetus to John Durang, who, as we've described, entertained audiences in 1797 with his own exaggerated versions of Indian dances.[17]

A more original and inspired approach to an imagined (if more believable) Apache world was *Broken Arrow* (Twentieth Century Fox, 1950), a film that many have cited as a turning point away from Hollywood's persistent vilification of American Indians. Though this film preceded *Walk the Proud Land,* its dance sequence, a prelude to the puberty ceremony of Sonseeahray, the young female lead, is an actual Chiricahua Apache dance, filmed at the White River Reservation. In *Broken Arrow,* Tom Jeffords (a white scout played by James Stewart) goes to meet with Cochise (Jeff Chandler) to discuss letting American mail riders pass safely through Apache territory. In order to accomplish this dangerous meeting, Jeffords learns Cochise's language and visits his stronghold deep in Apache territory. Once Jeffords's presence is accepted, he witnesses this ceremony. He ascertains the importance of the dance and asks about it. Cochise tells him that it involves the spirits of good and evil. Not everyone can do this dance, "for if done incorrectly, the spirits would be displeased." Five masked dancers with elaborately painted headdresses drive away evil spirits while doing a winding dance to an Apache chant. Young women form a straight line and move solemnly toward and away from the maskers, as if provoking and then recoiling from the spirits. Although the sequence lasts for less than a minute, it is one of the rare moments in Hollywood film when native culture is allowed to speak for itself.

Hugo Friedhofer's orchestral underscoring contributes to one of *Broken Arrow*'s most spectacular sequences, Jeffords's first journey into Cochise's territory. With the help of smoke signals from an Apache friend and his newly acquired language skills, he makes the long trek by horseback through the perilous countryside, well aware that he could be ambushed at any moment. Surprisingly, the Apache scouts allow him to pass without incident. The climax of the sequence is his arrival at a magnificent encampment of Apache wickiups, nestled peacefully but majestically in the mountains. Friedhofer's music for this cue ("Tucson and Cochise") begins quietly and draws on many indexical features—a motive in the pentatonic minor ("Apache theme 1"), Scottish snaps in the rhythm, opens fifths in the basses, and so on—and yet he fills the score with a growing sense of wonder, mystery, and even awe. There is a hint of Natoma's "Dagger Dance" in this music—the danger, the sternness, the rigidity—but mostly Friedhofer uses these features not to characterize the Apaches but rather to convey Jeffords's sense of the unknown. Friedhofer demonstrates his skill as a musical narrator by alternating between Copland-esque intonations of the American West and standard suspense devices to build an extraordinary amount of tension over this five-minute sequence. As Jeffords ventures further into territory never (or presumably never) penetrated by a white man, the intensity builds. The rhythmic underpinning for the "Apache theme" doesn't just mindlessly repeat one-two, one-two, but is more intricate. The long melodies and sharply punctuating brass and timpani work in counterpoint to the stealthily moving scouts, who wordlessly communicate by using mirrors to flash signals, alerting one other to the arriving stranger. "I knew then," Jeffords narrates in a voice-over, "that Cochise had allowed me to enter." Friedhofer's music doesn't limit our understanding of Cochise's stronghold by narrowly defining the Apaches. It works, as does all good film music, to arouse our interest in wanting to know more (an interest partly fulfilled by the dance). Writing about this film, Ward Churchill (Keetoowah Cherokee) has criticized Delmer Daves's Apaches and the director's "Kiplingesque parody" of Cochise. He has little patience with those who have found *Broken Arrow* moving and sensitive. Like other writers whose principal concern is plot and character, however, Churchill has perhaps forgotten the role that music plays in an audience's emotional response to film.[18]

Unlike the concessionary Cochise—the object of Jeffords's encounter (and Churchill's criticisms)—the protagonist of Robert Aldrich's *Apache* is Massai, the resistance Indian who several times eluded capture by the U.S. Army. Composer David Raksin's task of characterizing this Savage Reactionary was a challenging one, as Burt Lancaster was already well known to filmgoers by the time he undertook the role. Raksin's theme for the hotheaded rebel, announced at the outset of the film's credits and played in unison by four unaccompanied horns—a recurring device—suggests noble defiance. It also sounds like it could be an Apache song, even if the tune is not in fact original. In general, however, Raksin's terse, modernist, and somewhat coolly neoclassical underscoring for this film works to distance the listener, to position the audience in a slightly alienating environment. Although the film employs many accrued stereotypes of Apaches, the score—by a renegade composer trying to work against the normative practices of Hollywood—functions symbolically to distinguish its independent-thinking Indian protagonist.

Further change toward breaking down the musical reinforcement of archetypes came about with a new generation of conservatory-trained neoclassicists in the early 1960s: Leonard Rosenman (*The Outsider,* 1961), Elmer Bernstein (*Comancheros,* 1961), Alex North (*Cheyenne Autumn,* 1964), and especially Jerry Goldsmith (*Rio Conchos,* 1964). Gordon Douglas's *Rio Conchos* (Twentieth Century Fox) was based on a novel by Clair Huffaker and was set in the post–Civil War Southwest. The plot brings together several unusual characters who must travel in the same wagon: a white captain and a black sergeant on a trade mission to Mexico, a white Indian-hater out for revenge, an escaped Mexican prisoner who has volunteered for the promise of freedom, and, eventually, a young Apache woman, caught by the men and carted along for her presumed knowledge of the territory. Goldsmith, one of the most original voices working in Hollywood in the 1960s, wrote an eclectic and imaginative score for this off-color Western. While drawing on some of the established traits of musical Indianism, his underscoring for "Sally," the name given to the Apache woman, and Bloodshirt, a battle-scarred rebel, demonstrate an intriguing sensitivity to issues of race, ethnicity, and culture.

Once again, the score reveals the skill with which an experienced and gifted composer can valorize characters or a character's point of view through music. Some of Goldsmith's cues were influenced by popular styles, which lends this Western a more contemporary feel. For Sally and Bloodshirt, however, he devised what is clearly an "Apache" motive. Given that it is an essentializing marker for Indianness, the motive is surprisingly subtle and sparingly used. It is first heard when, after a gunfight with Mexican bandits, a lone woman comes running down a hill with a gun, shooting at the intruders. Captain Haven grabs her and pins her to the ground. At the close-up of her ochre-colored face (fig. 20), Lassiter, the Indian hater, shouts "Apache!" Goldsmith's long-breathed Apache motive soars offscreen, played by horns and lower woodwinds like some dark-hued rebel fanfare. (The motive, in a slightly varied form, is bracketed in ex. 20.) This pentatonic motive does not just confirm what we see; it serves partly to convince us that Wende Wagner, a 1960s

Figure 20. Actress Wende Wagner as herself and as "Sally," the Apache woman in *Rio Conchos* (Twentieth Century Fox, 1964).

bombshell actress, is actually a fighting Apache. Wagner's mixed French, German, and Hawaiian ethnicity was the closest postwar Hollywood had yet come to having an Indian woman play the role. The close-up of her slightly exotic features (exotic, that is, for early 1960s Hollywood) obviates the need for heavy-handed musical indexing, and the Apache fanfare communicates as much to viewers, if not more, about her character and spirit as it does about her race.

Goldsmith uses this motive only three times after that. The first of these is when Captain Haven sees smoke billowing out from behind a nearby hill—Apache signals along the Rio Grande. It next appears when the taciturn Sally quietly mourns the death of a baby she had been nursing. It occurs a third time at the turning point of the film, when Lassiter accidentally comes face to face with Bloodshirt. In the first instance, we don't see the Indians, only the smoke. Until Sally's entrance, Goldsmith had used guitar and maracas (very delicately) along with standard strings to convey both a taste of the Spanish Southwest and a hint of the party's ethnic diversity. With Sally as captive, however, and a cut to the smoke rising, the "Apache" fragment is unmistakable as a unison statement in the cellos, basses, bass clarinet, and four horns (with wood mutes).[19] Curiously, neither the motive's pentatonic content alone (mode V), its melodic and rhythmic shape (with an emphasis on fourth intervals), nor its unusual instrumental timbre signals "Indian." Heard apart from the film, one might not necessarily imagine Indians, although this music definitely implies otherness of some kind. The theme even resembles Rózsa's "Roman" style used a few years before for *Ben-Hur* (1959). For his Apache smoke signals Goldsmith, like Rózsa, combines elements that are suggestive of ancientness and an exotic otherness, although in this instance he avoids the now-standard open fifths or melodic parallel fourths.

One of the most unusual cues in the film occurs during Sally's lament. At one point on their journey, the party comes across a white family's ranch that has recently been raided and ransacked by Apaches. The husband has been killed and the unseen wife, just barely alive, lies moaning in agony on the bed (suggesting that she has been left for dead). Lassiter has no choice but to end her agony with a bullet from his rifle. The shot startles a sleeping baby. Sally takes the crying, blood-spattered child in her arms and tries to nurse it back to health. Later that evening, as Sally sits by a campfire that brightly illuminates her golden face, she rocks slowly and begins to chant quietly, realizing that the baby has died.

Quietly, unobtrusively, Goldsmith here brings in a few muted strings in unison and then a gentle flurry in an unusual combination of instruments—vibraphone, celesta, and a gamelan instrument, as well as delicate punctuation

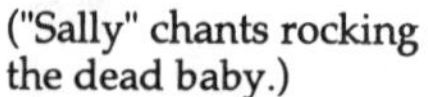

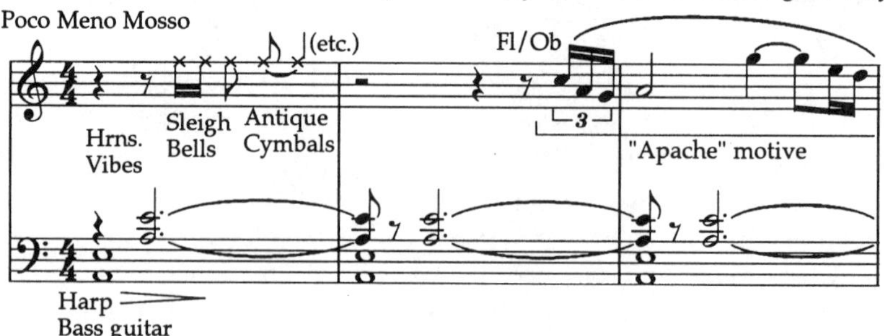

Example 20. Jerry Goldsmith, "Lonely Indian" from *Rio Conchos* (1964). Courtesy of the Margaret Herrick Library, Academy of Motion Picture Arts and Sciences, Beverly Hills.

(Haven hands the baby to Sgt. Franklin. Sally looks up at Haven. They seem to

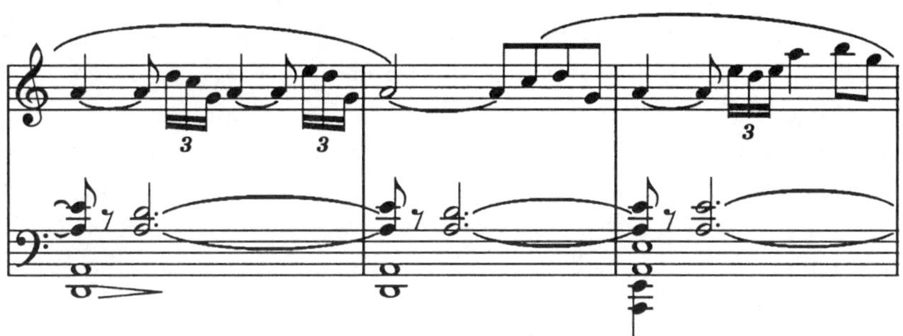

have an understanding.)

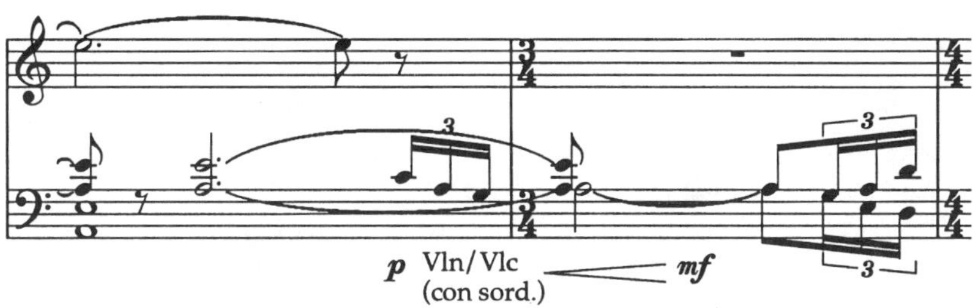

Haven: "Maybe she'll tell us now." (Rodriguez laughs cynically.)

by tree bells and a jaw bone. Again, if one heard this music apart from the image, one might more likely imagine a film set in the Far East rather than the American Southwest. Goldsmith is thus playing against type here: while the young Apache girl chants quietly, the music encourages audiences to reinterpret her role among these men. On the one hand, the aural allusion can be heard as an invocation of an ancient connection between the Apache peoples and the tribal societies on the east coast of Asia. It can also be heard as an imaginative placement of Sally within the "new West," a place where the Asian influence has always been more strongly felt than in the American East. When the men realize that the baby is dead and Sally reluctantly gives up the child's body, strings enter on sustained open fifths (for the first time in the score). Their quiet drone is punctuated delicately by guitar, harp, and antique cymbals. A flute and oboe now spin out a variation of the Apache motive into a full-blown melody—remaining firmly in the fifth pentatonic mode—over the sustained open fifths.[20]

Dramatically, this is a confusing episode in the film. No clear reason for Sally's empathy with the white baby has been established. Is her reaction simply a maternal one? The music cue, entitled "Lonely Indian" in the composer's score, draws on many of the obvious features of "Indian laments." At the same time, the underscore interprets, at least emotionally, and astute listeners can discern the music's delicate characterizing features. The young Apache girl, a Savage Reactionary when we first meet her, has made her peace with the white people, and the death of this innocent rescued child symbolizes, first for her, and then for us, the endless cycle of revenge and retribution. Her mourning is a turning point that transforms her, albeit reluctantly, into a Pocahontas archetype; near the end of the film she rescues some of the men during their brief respite from Blackshirt's tortures.

Goldsmith brought a modern sound and an eclecticism, not to mention extraordinary sympathy and intimacy, to this moment. The celluloid Apaches in *Rio Conchos,* although still "reel Indians," have come a long way since the days when whooping Savage Reactionaries simply lent films some action by chasing after stagecoaches to agitated music.

The Impact of World Music, New Technologies, and the Art/Popular Divide

Goldsmith's use of gamelan instruments in a 1964 Western suggests a change of attitude toward expanding the standard Hollywood studio orchestra and including non-Western sounds. Throughout the 1960s there was an increasing use of diverse musical styles—not just jazz and classical modernism (both of which found their way into Hollywood in the 1950s) but also non-Western folk and traditional music as well as contemporary popular genres. In the late '60s it became trendy to use pop music to alleviate the stodginess of the traditional Western (as in *Butch Cassidy and the Sundance Kid*), even in those Westerns that focused on Indian subject matter. Prominent pop musicians provided hip soundtracks for several mainstream films with significant Indian content—for example, Quincy Jones for *MacKenna's Gold* (1968), Dave Grusin for *Tell Them Willie Boy Is Here* (1969), Marvin Hamlisch for *Flap* (1970), and John Hammond for *Little Big Man* (also 1970).

By this time, of course, Native Americans themselves—not just representations of them—were emerging once again on the American political and cultural maps. In the 1960s the National Indian Youth Council inspired new hope among native peoples, some of which was expressed through "Red Power" activism. The American Indian Movement, a nationwide organization, began to receive wide media attention. One method through which Indians across the nation gained strength and asserted their identity was by means of music and dancing festivals. While the musical style of these pan-Indian powwows was predominantly that of Plains Indians, the high-pitched singing and drumming was fast becoming a kind of national style of Indian music.[21] The increasing availability of Indian music through recordings and live performances coincided with another nationwide surge of interest in folk music, and some Indian musicians became aligned with the counterculture movement.

Beginning about 1966 with the founding of the Indian Actors Guild, Native Americans themselves began to participate directly in filmed portrayals of Indians. Their inclusion helped to dilute the three cinematic archetypes of Indians, and music continued to play an increasingly important role in lending nuance to the ways native America was conveyed. Some age-old misconceptions persisted, however, since it was still usually non-Indians who, in Hollywood mainstream cinema, determined films' subject matter and approach.[22]

One egregious case was *A Man Called Horse* (1970), a somber film that, despite a heavy-handed attempt at ethnographic accuracy and a cast that included Indian actors such as Eddie Little Sky and Iron Eyes Cody in leading roles, created yet another fanciful, disturbing travesty of native America. Its outrageous depiction of the Lakota ceremony of the Sun Vow stemmed partly from an exaggerated interpretation of sources such as Catlin's paintings and seemed to strive largely for shock value. Much of the film resembles the wish fulfillment of a boy scout: a Euro-American protagonist is captured by members of the Lakota tribe and then, after being tortured, "out-Indians" the Indians by becoming a warrior, winning a princess bride, and ascending to the role of a chieftain. Surprisingly, composer Leonard Rosenman, using principally a small studio ensemble and a modernist idiom, was able—in one scene anyway—to bring a human touch to the Lakotas, who are otherwise depicted as little more than self-interested savages. Rosenman's most compelling music is for what I call the "transformation through acculturation" montage, a pivotal sequence during which Horse takes the first steps toward "becoming a Lakota." As Claudia Gorbman observes, this was the first time that a relationship was drawn between on-screen chanting and drumming and a film's background score. While Horse is shown developing his warrior skills, the Lakota men and women sing in a traditional style with mixed words and vocables to the beat of a drum. Rosenman's music enters over this ensemble with a string crescendo that leads into a rhythmic ostinato (in 3/4), while the traditional Lakota singing morphs into a Westernized studio chorus (in a style akin to Farwell's 1937 choral "Navajo War Dance") that draws on key features of the singing and drumming. As Gorbman puts it, "Rosenman's score *translates* the Indian music" for non-Indians. This clever bit of artfulness puts viewers into a frame of mind to understand partly what is being communicated in the native music-making experience. As Horse presumably becomes more visibly "Indian," the native singing takes on a more familiar caste for non-Indian audiences. (It can also be argued that this music is going on in Horse's mind, the musical transformation as a metaphor for his cultural journey.)

The approach to music for *Little Big Man,* a more widely acclaimed film from the same year, could hardly be more different. To begin with, Arthur Penn's direction reflected Hollywood's changing aesthetics. The film's recreation of the Washita River massacre by Custer in 1868 was an attempt, in part, to reverse the Savage Reactionary archetype by portraying the white soldiers as the true savages. As many have noted, the film was also an allegory for the Vietnam War, the bloodbath at the film's climax pointedly symbolic of America's treatment of the Vietnamese. John Hammond, a blues musician, provided music that went against most of the established norms of Hollywood. There is no music for "the Indians" per se. The only nondiegetic music in the film is that of a solo harmonica used to characterize Jack Crabb (played by Dustin Hoffman), the hapless white protagonist who despite his perilous predicaments we know will survive, since he narrates the story. The harmonica consistently underscores Jack's point of view. Native America is seen through Jack's eyes, and the harmonica serves as his slightly humorous interpretation of events and the somewhat absurd circumstances in which he often finds himself. Since he is adopted by the Cheyennes ("human beings"), he is the vehicle by which we come to identify with their circumstances and way of life. Hammond's lonely harmonica for Crabb, rather than any underscoring for the

Cheyennes or their enemies, the Pawnees, marks a shift in aesthetics that lasted for a decade or more. Hollywood producers grew skeptical of emotive film scoring. Music used expressly to imagine native America during these years would have probably seemed to most directors (and, no doubt, to audiences as well) as unduly manipulative. By 1970 the notion of music drawing on an essentially Western rhetorical style to characterize race or nationhood seemed increasingly in bad taste.

The musical underscoring, for example, in Keith Merrill's two sympathetic portrayals of Indian life, *Three Warriors* (Fantasy Film, 1977) and *Windwalker* (Pacific International, 1980), avoids characterizing in any obvious manner. A standard orchestra (much muted and subdued) serves only the limited melodramatic functions of mood, action, and suspense, and in this way composer Merrill Jenson's approach typified a newer Hollywood aesthetic: mood and action music was acceptable in a film's dramatic moments but should not draw too much attention to itself. Like *Little Big Man, Windwalker* is set in a Cheyenne world, this time in the eighteenth century. The young protagonist woos his future wife, Tashina, by playing an Indian flute, its solitary but steady tone echoing throughout the forest. Thereafter the sound of the flute—along with echo effects, additional flutes, harp, and occasionally quiet sustained strings—serves to underscore their courtship and the stages of their marriage. Jenson's melodies are lyrical but not memorable, unsentimental in an angular modernist way, neither consistently diatonic/modal nor pentatonic. It is the closely miked sound of the breathy wooden flute itself—and its associations with nature and Indian courtship—rather than pitches or specific musical gestures that linked this film with the New Age aesthetics of the 1980s.

To some extent, this sound had already been developed in the 1960s by Ennio Morricone at Italy's RCA Studios. For *Navajo Joe* (1966), Morricone combined voice and twangy electric guitar (as for his "spaghetti Westerns") with skin-head drum and an ambient mix to convey an impression of the West's open spaces. This sound was almost a cliché by the time of *Powwow Highway* (1988), a film popular in some parts of the Indian community for its approach to native bonding and to confronting societal stereotypes. This film presented important musical images of native America not just by including portions of an actual powwow filmed at the Pine Ridge Reservation but also because of Barry Goldberg's blend of synthesized and acoustic music, used to convey the transformation of the (actual) Indian protagonist. Gary Farmer (Cayuga) plays Philbert Bono, a character in search of his Cheyenne roots who embarks on an urgent mission to bring a friend to New Mexico but instead makes a detour to find Sweet Butte in the Black Hills, a holy place where generations ago—we learn in the film if we did not know it already—Light

Cloud experienced his vision for the Cheyenne people. Seated under an abandoned shelter, Philbert closes his eyes as a deep, sustained synth drone gradually eases up in volume. Philbert breathes, smiles, and begins his vision. Sampled strings enter in open fifths as the camera closes in on his radiant face. Higher strings enter on open fifths (continuously sustained on the nonbreathing synthesizer), and a flute begins a gentle melody as the sequence cuts to an eagle soaring in flight. A sudden heavy drum stroke interrupts with a sharp visual cut to Light Cloud, who approaches mystically, holding out a sacred arrow. While the flute hovers over the sustained strings (which begin to fill out the synth background more pentatonically), Light Cloud approaches the offscreen Philbert. The music fades as the camera tracks left to Philbert's face, still in a trance. It disappears completely only when he awakens to find not a man but a coyote in front of him. ("Light Cloud?" Philbert inquires gently.) Reaching the top of the butte, Philbert leaves an offering (a precious bar of chocolate), whereupon his spiritual journey toward becoming a warrior has begun. The drums begin again but now blend into a slow rock beat with a synth background (ambient and pentatonic, but not strictly anhemitonic). As the camera lingers dreamily throughout a slow panorama of the vast South Dakota landscape, we hear the high, raspy voice of Robbie Robertson (Mohawk), which serves thereafter as a kind of leitmotif for Philbert's calling.[23]

Powwow Highway's strength was its depiction of a living connection between old native ways and the modern world, and its combination of spirit-based and popular music symbolized the polyphony of modern Indian life. In the late 1980s, however, United States culture entered a triumphalist phase at the end of the Cold War, and the great success of several rather cardboard heroic epics—with elaborate symphonic scores by John Williams and others—led to a return to some of the manipulative techniques of classical Hollywood practice. By *Dances with Wolves* (1990), lush neoromantic underscoring, particularly in films with a historical setting, was back in vogue. As Gorbman puts it, more generously, John Barry's *Wolves* score "is replete with beautiful themes that bestow narrative clarity and emotional force on the story."[24] The music also bathes the Lakota people (and the North Dakota landscapes) in such luscious sounds that viewers cannot help but empathize with these characters, despite what doubts audience members may harbor regarding the truthfulness of the historical background.

Perhaps because of the success of *Dances with Wolves,* the Canadian film *Black Robe* (1991) also employed a lush symphonic score. This was largely the work of composer Georges Delerue, scoring the last film in his long career. The story takes place in New France in the seventeenth century, and Delerue seems to have modeled his "journey theme"—a moving chorale for strings that underscores both the unspoiled beauty of the St. Lawrence region and the religious fervor of the Jesuits — on a seventeenth-century Calvinist hymn. The score's effectiveness was enhanced enormously by the quality of the recording and its sonic depth of field. The influence of "spatial" or "ambient" music in the 1970s and advancements in recording and mixing techniques in the 1980s enabled engineers Phil Judd and Gary Wilkins to employ a sonic picture that far exceeded the dimensions of the image itself. A single woodwind — amplified and played back with reverb through a multispeaker system — could fill a theater, as it did in Morricone's mournful tune for Father Gabriel's oboe in *The Mission* (1986). In the last two decades of the twentieth century, it became increasingly difficult to speak about a film's musical score as separate from its overall "sound design," so crucial were the roles that the sound engineer, the multitrack mixing board, and the film's sonic space now played in the effectiveness of the soundtrack. When in *Black Robe* the camera moves between three different locations, each with its different music — Jesuit a cappella chanting, Quebecois villagers with their pipes and tabors, and Huron singing and drumming — the spatial effect of the recording, even more than the visuals, envelops the audience in a seventeenth-century colonial world. One need no longer imagine the native American past, it seems, when the sounds of cinema can virtually transport us to such a time and place.

Historicism of the 1990s: Representing Ancient America Again

For most of the history of sound pictures until the early 1990s, the major context for American Indians was fictionalized history that essentially took place during the Western wars (ca. 1860s–1890). (There were a few rare exceptions: films about the colonial period, and in the 1970s and 1980s about modern Indians.) By the early 1990s Native American cinema had come of age, particularly as the market for independent films grew. Hollywood, however, took little notice. Reflecting the advent of the quincentenary of the early European-Indian encounters, the focus in mainstream cinema reverted to the early years of conquest and the Discovery of the Americas. In addition to *Black Robe* there was *1492: Conquest of Paradise* (1992), *The Last of the Mohicans* (1992), Disney's *Pocahontas* (1995), and several documentaries for television, including *500 Nations* (1994), perhaps the most far-reaching among them. Music was not only more present (hence more persuasive) in the viewing/listening experience, but it was also separately marketed as soundtrack recordings, designed to have some listening appeal apart from the films for which it was created.

Due to the technical polish of these films, audiences—particularly younger audiences—may be more easily seduced into accepting the fanciful worlds they create. Once again, questions of authenticity loom large, not just in elements of plot but also in choice of music. *The Last of the Mohicans* was directed by Michael Mann of *Miami Vice* fame, and it seemed as if he often confused the second project with the first. The film bears only the palest resemblance to Cooper's original novel, itself a fanciful retelling of the French and Indian Wars. In deromanticizing and reimagining an already fictionalized eighteenth-century American world, Mann pumps so much testosterone into the plot that his cinema of muscularity obscures most of the essential truths of the original. The music by Trevor Jones and Randy Edelman is largely overbearing and blatantly manipulative, occasionally adding the usual glamorous strain of 1990s-style triumphalist heroism (with a big, soaring melody for the tough young protagonist) and even a thematic love song. A "frontier rock video," one viewer called this film.[25]

The Last of the Mohicans may have been *Dances with Wolves* on steroids, but the box-office success and heroized subject matter of these films were typical of a trend that had been seen before. Indeed, each final decade of the last four centuries brought about a resurgence of interest in Indian subjects in Western culture. Perhaps the coincidence with anniversaries of 1492 may be more significant than we realize. The first operas about the Discovery were composed in the late seventeenth century, and a vast number of plays about the New World (and particularly Pizarro's conquest of Peru) were written in the late eighteenth century. Americans in 1892–93 witnessed the compelling Native American presence in national commemorative events such as the World's Columbian Exposition in Chicago. That year also served as a turning point in America's interest in folk music (including North American Indian music), stimulating a debate among composers and critics that lasted some ten or more years (and with reverberations far beyond that). The reawakening of cultural historicism in the 1990s, if it can be called that, similarly resulted in many mainstream films about America's colonial past (not to mention books, articles, plays, and even operas)—in effect, a return to "ancient America."

Of all the films and television specials about Columbus's first voyage released in 1992, Ridley Scott's *1492: Conquest of Paradise* (Paramount/Touchstone) was unquestionably the most remarkable attempt to capture a moment when the fabric of ancient America was indelibly pierced. The film also intelligently explored some of the political dimensions of the journey. Reviews of this beautifully made film were mixed. Like the characters of Dunbar in *Dances with Wolves* and Hawkeye in *The Last of the Mohicans,* Columbus here seemed to be more a man of the 1990s than anything close to the historical figure. As

Jacqueline Kilpatrick has written, "the failure of the film . . . is that Scott tries to walk a razor's edge between depicting the national myth and revising that myth. The result is that no one is particularly pleased."[26]

Greek-born composer "Vangelis" (birth name Evangelos Odysseus Papathanassiou) created the largely synthesized score for the film. One of the most powerful scenes in the film — and well it should be — is the arrival in the New World. The sequence, which begins when the Spaniards sight land for the first time and continues to their setting foot on the islands of Hispaniola, is visually told entirely from the Spanish perspective. We have not yet met the Taino peoples, nor has the camera been situated in the Western Hemisphere before Columbus's arrival. But Vangelis decided to compose something that told a larger story, more than just the Spanish point of view. If he had supported only the latter, the score would probably have exhibited unqualified excitement, awe, even joy and relief — and there is certainly plenty of awe. Instead Vangelis adds his own metanarrative to the unfolding events, related in slow motion. This is a decisive and irreversible moment, the music tells us. The voices chanting deliriously in Latin suggest the unrelenting power of the Roman Catholic Church, pushing Columbus's tiny ships like a mighty unseen hand onto the islands. Columbus may think he's here to discover a trade route to the Indies, but there are larger political and religious issues surrounding his mission than he is yet able to intimate. Most audiences are aware of this history, of course, but the political subtext can actually be *heard*, transformed metaphorically into Vangelis's slow, ominous, and powerful crescendo.

All the films discussed so far in this chapter have been mainstream narrative films, and one presumes that viewers enters into such an experience with some expectation that what they see (if not also hear) will in part be fantasy. This is not true of documentaries, in which audiences particularly expect to hear facts and to see visual evidence to back these up. It is true that some sections of narrative Westerns have had a documentary feel to them. The white protagonists in *Broken Arrow* and *Walk the Proud Land* introduce these films with voice-overs that inform viewers that the stories are based on actual accounts and real people, and *A Man Called Horse* begins with a title card (in bold lettering) that alerts audiences to "the most authentic description of American Indian life ever filmed." But documentaries filmed by native peoples for alternative rather than network television stations have set a new standard. In films such as *Imagining Indians* or *Surviving Columbus: The Pueblo Peoples* (both 1992), the tables are turned. One expects to hear (and is rewarded with) an Indian perspective, with native peoples making their own music.

The stakes are raised, however, when an expensive network documentary intends to reach a wide network audience. Such was the case with *500 Nations*

(1994), a television miniseries directed by Jack Leustig and first aired in eight parts by CBS. The first episode begins with the massacre at Wounded Knee and then backtracks to the ancient civilizations of the Americas. Episode two is devoted to the Aztec Empire, and episode three focuses on the impact of Spanish expansion and exploration of the Caribbean and American Southeast. The music for the documentary was prepared by Peter Buffett with contributions from, among other native performers, Douglas Spotted Eagle on flute and David Arkenstone on guitar. Buffett, originally from Omaha, Nebraska, already had a history of writing music for and about native America. He had contributed the fire dance sequence to *Dances with Wolves* (although the rest of the score was by Barry). In 1991 he had produced an album entitled *Yonnondio,* an Iroquois term meaning "lament." Like Laurie Anderson, whose "Hiawatha" from *Strange Angels* (1989) layered samples of Native American singing with rock music to create a multivalent Indian universe, Buffett composed his music in a studio, using both sampled and electronically designed sounds. He created the score for *500 Nations* on the Synclavier digital music system, weaving electronic sounds around the acoustic performances.

Buffett likes to think of his music (perhaps not so differently from some earlier figures we've seen in this book) as an example of what new amalgams could be created if native music and Western music were blended together, much like jazz, rhythm-and-blues, and rock developed out of combining idioms.[27] Since the noninterview parts of the *500 Nations* documentary relied upon still images or movement through computer-generated spaces, music was necessary to involve the viewer emotionally. Buffett's tasks, like those of any film composer, were to find the emotional pitch of each sequence, compose appropriately atmospheric music, and then keep the music out of the way of the individual narrators, while still working to maintain continuity and sustain viewer interest. In some cases, as in the Columbus sequence, Buffett used modern sounds: electric guitar riffs and a rock beat accompany Columbus's orders to his soldiers to force the Tainos to dig for gold. Though wildly anachronistic, this music follows the traditions we have been exploring: it uses the sounds of contemporary music—speaking the lingua franca of a modern audience—to tell an ancient story. In the documentary, of course, this encounter is told as if from a native perspective, though it is not necessarily any less imaginary in evoking the native experience. In this sense, music for documentaries—with the exception of music that is performed on-screen as part of the account—is not different from music for narrative film. It functions in identical ways. It heightens our awareness, creates the right mood for the sequence to follow, and contributes characterization and point of view to any filmic moment it accompanies.

We can see how this works by examining one short sequence. The conclusion of part one focuses on the Mayas, whose civilization existed in Central America from sometime B.C.E. until the last independent Maya kingdom fell to the Spaniards in 1697. There were at least two earlier narrative films concerning these peoples with music by major composers: Silvestre Revueltas scored *La noche de los mayas* (Mexico, 1939), and Elmer Bernstein scored *Kings of the Sun* (1963), though both of these films dealt with the Maya kingdoms that overlapped with the Spanish invasion. The Maya world of *500 Nations* is perhaps the most "ancient" America ever to be depicted in image and sound. How does one respond to this task when virtually nothing is known about ancient Maya music making except descriptions of conch-shell trumpets and wooden drums and scant knowledge about instruments from the later period that have survived into present-day Guatemala, instruments such as palitos, ocarinas, kayum drums, and the triple flute? Buffett's choice was to rely for color on the modern flute and drumlike instruments indigenous to the folk cultures of Central America, but to couch these within an electronic simulation of a full orchestra to fulfill the functional needs of a music soundtrack (particularly those of establishing time and perspective). In addition, he layered the score with contemporary sounds and musical styles so that the film would speak to a modern audience.[28]

For the three-minute Maya segment, director Leustig focuses on the rise and fall of the city of Palenque, ca. 600–800 C.E. He begins with the archaeological evidence. The remains of a pyramid built for emperor Pacal the Great had been overrun by the jungle for twelve centuries before it was discovered in 1949. After several location shots of the dense Guatemalan forest and fast-running rivulets, Leustig uses a timeline to chart the historic population growth in this highly agricultural region while a narrator supplies the details. With a dissolve to a computer-generated image of a courtyard in the royal apartments as they might have looked around 650, Buffett's music begins. Evoking an ancient world coming back to life, an Indian flute enters quietly, playing a pentatonic melody that is inflected by breathy tones that fall away from the pitches (as the flute player "bends" the flute away from his lips). Below this, two slightly differently pitched skinhead drums begin a syncopated rhythm. The flute plays the first of three long phrases. The first phrase of music accompanies us from the courtyard to the door of the apartments and takes us through it. The second phrase begins as we see the hallway, the carpets on the floor, a jug, and artwork hanging high on steeply sloped ceilings. The camera continues on its simulated journey into an adjoining room, revealing a table against the wall and a pictograph mounted above it. "Art, mathematics, astronomy, architecture, priesthood, and royalty all flourished," relates the narrator as the drum rhythms become increasingly more complicated. The third melodic phrase, now much higher, begins when we are fully in the second room. As we move toward the table with its two bowls, the third phrase culminates with the entrance of sustained open fifths over several octaves. In the distance, over these fifths, one can hear a high woodblock (the chirping of insects?) and a fleeting glissando (an exotic bird call?). The flute begins a fourth phrase at the dissolve to a reverse shot from the table, looking out toward an opening in the wall to a large open square below. But just as the phrase begins, it is sharply interrupted by two upwardly moving parallel fifths (the first on the lowered seventh, the second on the tonic), the musical high point of this sequence. As this sustained drone fifth continues, accompanied by the intricate drumming, the camera takes us out through the opening, where we obtain a view of the distant temple and many colorfully dressed people moving toward it. "By the mid 700s at Palenque alone," the narrator continues, "the sons of Pacal ruled over 200,000 Maya, living in regional communities of farmers, weavers, stonemasons, and feather workers." Buffett captures, or rather reinforces, the sumptuousness of the royal interiors and the stateliness of the moving crowds below by conveying an increasing luxuriousness in the music. At this climactic visual moment—suggesting an apex in the Maya civilization—the flute melody, drums, simulated strings and woodwinds, and distantly miked percussion all work together in counterpoint (and sonic depth) to suggest a vast place of harmony, tranquility, efficiency, and, above all, great beauty.

Even a documentary about native America—involving a fairly reliable telling of known events—must engage the viewer's imagination in re-creating its culturally remote peoples and places, and it therefore relies on music to do so. Buffett's underscoring for the Maya sequence sounds fresh, contemporary, and original even if he draws on an indexical musical language, including parallel melodic fifths, lowered sevenths, and open fifth drones, to suggest an ancient world.[29]

In contrast with the films in this chapter, *Smoke Signals* (1998), a mainstream film produced, directed, and scored entirely by Native Americans, didn't need to imagine Indian worlds. Director Chris Eyre based the film on stories from Sherman Alexie's *The Lone Ranger and Tonto Fistfight in Heaven.* Victor and Thomas, two young men from the Coeur d'Alene reservation in Idaho travel by bus to Arizona to settle the affairs of Victor's recently deceased father. While the bus makes a stop, Victor convinces Thomas that it is time for a makeover: the wide-eyed optimist needs to let his hair down, lose the glasses, tie, and vest he always wears, and shed his silly grin. Trusting in his friend,

Thomas emerges from the bus stop to a rock beat (music by B. C. Smith), having transformed himself into a "super Injun." But when the two return to their seats, they find them taken by two burly white rancher types. "Excuse me," Thomas asks politely, "those are our seats." "These *were* your seats, you mean," the biggest guy snarls. After a few more exchanges it quickly appears that Thomas's new look isn't going to gain him any more respect and that the two young men have no choice but to move to the back of the bus. "The cowboys always win," Thomas comments grudgingly, beginning an argument with his friend Victor, who loudly disagrees. Underscoring their conversation is a small but full-throated choir of Indian singers (the group Ulali). The uplifting voices are undeniably Native American, but one needs to listen closely to realize that they are singing a harmonized adaptation of "Garry Owen," which suggests to informed listeners that for most American Indians, even today, memories of that victorious battle with Custer are never far away. At the same time, the harmonized version suggests that Native Americans have the right to take the tune, adapt it, and sing it heroically as a kind of war trophy. After all, Custer was the one U.S. general decisively defeated, and this victory never grows stale.

Meanwhile, Victor has decided that Hollywood's favorite cowboy, John Wayne, wasn't such a flawless hero. Something must have been wrong with his teeth, since he never showed them when he smiled. Using his leg for a drum, Victor launches into a solo song about John Wayne's teeth ("are they plastic, are they steel?"). The other passengers look around with puzzled expressions. As an external pan shot captures the bus heading through the desert, Victor's singing of the John Wayne song on the soundtrack dovetails into a voice-over of the Eaglebear Singers, who "translate" Victor's song into Native American style: sung vocables over the beating of a skinhead drum. It is a delicious moment, and a precious gift of insight to those of us who are non-Indian.

Smoke Signals is not just a film about Native Americans; it is also a critique of the way dominant American society has viewed the First Peoples of the Americas. While Europeans and white Americans tended to define Indians within their cultures — and music — as relatively static and unchanging, Native Americans themselves have always been absorbing ideas from other cultures — even mocking them in their songs. Those Euro-Americans who have fashioned music for film rarely, if ever, credited American Indians with such inventiveness and resilience. Instead they have followed indexical practices that had begun long before them.

Conclusion

By way of concluding this overview of some four hundred and fifty years of music, we should return to a few of the questions raised in the introduction, perhaps rephrased now with greater nuance in the light of historical perspective. To what degree is it possible to interpret the peoples and cultures of native America — or any peoples — through musical expression? What role does context play in the way we hear music (especially given music's allusive nature)? What can we say now about the "collective storehouse" of indexical features — some might call them musical clichés — that have been mixed and matched to tell stories (most often non-Indian stories) about native America?

Visual and literary images have maintained stereotypes of native America throughout much of United States history, particularly since they were often symbols that reinforced the concept of Manifest Destiny. But the Indians of the Americas also came to represent for the world over, almost from the moment of contact, an awareness that values that were ancient in human civilization were still a part of the modern world. This realization was at first met with wonder and amazement, then with diplomacy (both successful and failed), then with the strategic conquest of land and resources, then with activism to protect the erosion of these values by means of Western engines of "progress," and finally with increasing recognition for American Indians' long-standing position and influence in the world. Music, which reflected multiple layers of meaning during all these phases, served as one of the most complex barometers of temperament. Much of this music functioned like a language that engaged the ideologies of its time in a fascinating discourse.

Boundaries between art and reality are often occupied by ideologies. Because its symbolic language is less specific than those of the literary or visual arts, music can be a powerful and persuasive tool for manipulation. After all, composers such as Rameau, Bishop, Stoepel, Sousa, Herbert, Berlin, and Steiner did in fact manipulate their audiences through their use of "Indian" music. But unlike citizens in totalitarian regimes that have used symbol-laden messages to control social behavior, the audiences for "Indian" music came to opera houses, concert halls, and movie theaters expecting to find pleasure in being manipulated. This is an important and sometimes overlooked consideration for why art often embodies ideologies at odds with those of the societies that support it.

To what degree, then, does pleasure factor in the proliferation of musical stereotypes—pleasure in musical sounds and the recognition of recurring tropes and ideological patterns? The answer to this last question, though only suggested rather than stated throughout this book, is obviously a great deal. In the years that I have spent looking and listening to all of this "Indian" music, I admit that much of it has struck me as quite seductive, and I have refused to dismiss any musical expression as simply a cliché. I realize that my comments about such works at "The Song of the Setting Sun" or "I'm an Indian Too" may convey a certain amazement at the fluidity with which various composers used a highly specific musical terminology, not to mention their incredible persuasiveness in evoking imaginary worlds. At the same time, this book is not an attempt to resuscitate such misleading representations of native America. My goal has been to provoke readers into thinking more subtly about the language of musical stereotypes and their complex chain of influences. It is all too easy to think in red and white. But we live in a shaded world, where our understanding of one another is at best only partial. As it became clear to me in writing this book, racial and ethnic stereotypes, though always limiting, have historically taken new forms rather than fading away. Focusing the broader cultural discourse on the details of stereotypes, as I have done here with music, may help to limit their destructive influences on people.

Other writers may go on to pursue "Indianism" in more recent popular music, especially given the attempt by many recording companies to bring traditional native songs into the present "with the addition of contemporary instrumentation," as one label puts it. Clearly these adapted songs evoke native America in their own ways. It would also be important to explore further the roles that Indians themselves have played in overturning some of the stereotypes in the twentieth century, both in popular music (for example, by Buffy Sainte-Marie, Jay Begaye, Bill Miller, Robbie Robertson, Cher, or the group Young Bird) and concert music (by composers such as Luis Ballard or Brent Michael Davids), as well as in the work of many Canadian and Central and South American musicians. I wanted this book to provide the historical, cultural, and analytical background with which analyses of these works can be undertaken. I hope others will follow through.

Censoring a stereotype—even one based in sound—does not make it disappear. But putting a frame around it, consciously acknowledging its borders, and addressing its history at least helps us to understand why such stereotypes exist in the first place, and perhaps even to recognize, when we next encounter them, their effects on us and on society as a whole.

Appendix 1
Forty-nine Parlor Indian Songs and Ten Parlor Instrumental Works, 1802–1860s, Arranged Chronologically

Composer	Title	Year/Place	Key	Meter
Thorley, Thomas	"Poor Eliza, or The Indian Captive"	1802, London	F major	6/8
Bishop, Henry	"Yes, 'tis the Indian Drum"	1823, London+	B♭ major • G minor	4/4
Maddison, George W.	"The American Lake Song"	1825, London	G major	6/8
Gladstanes, J. C.	"The Indian. Glee for Three Voices"	1830, London	A major	4/4
Machold, G.	"The Indian Girl"	1830s, New York	A♭ major	2/2
Horn, Charles E.	"The American Indian Girl"	1835, New York*	F major	3/4
Russell, Henry	"The Indian Hunter"	1837, New York	G major	6/8
"An Eminent Professor"	*Metamora* "Grand March" (instrumental)	1840, New York*	D major	4/4
Russell, Henry	"The Chieftain's Daughter"	1841, New York+	B♭ major	4/4
Russell, Henry	"The Soldier and His Bride"	1841, New York+	A♭ major	6/8
Knight, A. F.	"The Song of the Red Man," from *The Indians*	1843, Boston+	C major	6/8
Lull, L. A.	"On-Ka-Hye Waltz," from *The Indians* (instrumental)	1843, Boston+	B♭ major	3/4
Knaebel, S., arr.	"King Philip Quick Step" (instrumental)	1843, Boston+	C major	6/8
Romani, F.	"The Indian Bride's Farewell, Ballad"	1844, Baltimore*	F major	3/4
Owen, Robert Dale	"'Tis Home Where'er the Heart Is," from the drama *Pocohontas*	1844, Baltimore+	E♭ major	4/4
Sullivan, Mrs. M. D.	"The Blue Juniata"	1844, Boston+	F major	2/4

Composer	Title	Year/Place	Key	Meter
Saroni, Herrman S.	"The Pequot Brave"	1844, New York*	• C minor	4/4
Brown, Francis H.	"The Indian and His Bride"	1844, New York*	E♭ major	3/4
Philipps, Henry	"The Huron's Prayer"	1845, New York*	• C minor	4/4
Woodbury, Isaac B.	"The Indian's Prayer"	1846, Boston*	D major	3/4
Baker, Benjamin F.	"The Death of Osceola"	1846, Boston+	E major	6/8
Dempster, William R.	"The Song of the Indian Hunter"	1846, Boston+	G major	4/4
Heinrich, Anthony Philip (with William V. Wallace, poem)	"Ne-La-Me. Romanza Indiana." No. 2 from *Breezes from the Wild Wood*	1846, New York*	E♭ major	4/4
Barrus, H. G.	"*Montezuma* Grand March" (instrumental)	1847, Boston*	G major	4/4
Crosby, L. V. H.	"The Lone Old Indian"	1847, Boston*	D major	6/8
Lee, George Alexander	"The Wild Free Wind"	1847, London+	E♭ major	6/8
Berg, Albert W.	"La Belle Indienne, Valse Brillante"	1847, New York*	F major	3/4
Saroni, Herrman S.	"Speed Away! (A Song Founded on a Beautiful Indian Superstition)"	1847, New York*	F major	12/8
Jacob (of the Orpheans)	"The Indian Girl's Lament on the Banks of the Kennebec"	1847, New York+	E♭ major	2/4
Howard, Frank	"The Indian's Dream"	1848, Boston*	B♭ major	4/4
Dempster, William R.	"The Dark Eye Has Left Us." Song of Indian Women, from *The Bridal of Pennacook*	1848, Boston+	A♭ major	3/4
Pond, Auguste H.	"The Indian Bride's Farewell"	1848, Cincinnati*	F major	3/4
Gibson, J. N.	"The Red Man's Chant"	1849, Boston+	D major	4/4
Heinrich, Anthony Philip	"Indian Carnival" (instrumental)	1849, New York*	G major	3/4
Lover, Samuel	"Give Me My Arrows and Give Me My Bow"	1849, New York*	E♭ major	4/4
Blessner, Gustave	*Montezuma* "Grand Heroic March" (instrumental)	1849, Philadelphia*	F major	2/4
Lenschow, C.	"Indian Polka" (instrumental)	1849, Philadelphia*	F major	2/4
Allen, G. N.	"The Young Indian Girl"	1850, Boston	E♭ major	4/4
Martin, George H.	"The Grave of Uncas"	1850, Boston*	E♭ major	3/4
Pike, Marshall S.	"The Indian Warrior's Grave"	1850, Boston*	E♭ major	4/4
White, Edward L.	"The Sachem's Daughter"	1850, Boston*	E♭ major	3/4
Bohannan, G. H.	"The Hunter's Bride"	1850, New York+	F major	6/8
Heffernan, W. J.	"The Indian's Song of Peace"	1851, Louisville*	A major	6/8
Hewitt, John Hill	"The Indian Polka" (instrumental)	1852, Baltimore+	• A minor	4/4
Magruder, James E.	"The Indian Captive, or The Absent Lover"	1854, Baltimore*	A major	3/4
Converse, Charlie C.	"Wake! Oh, My Forest-Flower! An Indian Serenade"	1854, Petersburg, Va.*	G major	6/8

Composer	Title	Year/Place	Key	Meter
Clark, James G.	"The Indian Mother's Lullaby"	1855, Boston*	G major	3/8
Hosmer, E.	"Dark-Eyed Ulalee, or, Indian Maiden of Echo Lake"	1855, Boston*	F major	6/8
Hubbard, J. Maurice	"The Maid of Cherokee"	1855, New York*	G major	2/4
Wood, T.	"They Are Gone! They Are Gone! Or, The Red Man's Requiem"	1855, New York*	E♭ major	3/4
Woolcott, Francis	"Wenona of the Wave," from *Songs of the Prairies*	1855, St. Louis	G major	4/4
Woolcott, Francis	"Ka-Loo-Lah, or The War Path," from *Songs of the Prairies*	1855, St. Louis*	F major	4/4
Peticolas, C. L.	"Hiawatha Polka" (instrumental)	1856, Boston*	E♭ major • C minor	2/4
Hawthorne, Alice	"Hiawatha Polka" (instrumental)	1856, Philadelphia*	G major	4/4
Schrivall, Frederick R.	"The Indian Girl's Lament"	1856, unknown	F major	2/4
Schrivall, Frederick R.	"The Indian Hunter's Serenade"	1856, unknown	A major	6/8
Hosmer, E. A.	"Indian Girl's Song"	1859, Boston*	G major	4/4
Winner, Septimus	"Ten Little Injuns"	1860, Boston+	G major	4/4
Glover, Stephen	"The Indian Hunter's Bride"	1869, London+	G major	6/8

• indicates song (or substantial section) in a minor mode
* included in *Music for the Nation, 1820–1860*
+ included in *Lester S. Levy Collection*

Appendix 2
Selected List of Instrumental Character Pieces (Musical Tribal Portraits)

Date	Composer and Work	Native Musical Source
1901	Farwell, Arthur. *American Indian Melodies* (piano)	Omaha
1902	Farwell, Arthur. "Dawn" (piano)	Omaha
	Farwell, Arthur. "The Domain of Hurakan" (piano)	Vancouver, Pawnee, Navajo
	Farwell, Arthur. "Ichibuzzi" (piano)	Omaha
	Kroeger, Ernest. "Indian Lament" and "Indian Air" from *Ten American Character Sketches* (piano)	Unknown
	MacDowell, Edward. "Indian Idyl" from *New England Idyls* (piano)	Dakota
1903	Loomis, Harvey W. *Lyrics of the Red Man* (piano), Book 1	Omaha, Cree
1904	Farwell, Arthur. "Ghost Dance of the Zuñis" (piano), Wa-Wan Press, vol. 3, no. 20.	Zuni
	Farwell, Arthur. "Navajo War Dance" (piano)	Navajo
	Farwell, Arthur. "Toward the Dream" (piano)	Unknown

Date	Composer and Work	Native Musical Source
	Kroeger, Ernest. "March of the Indian Phantoms" (orchestra)	Unknown
	Loomis, Harvey W. *Lyrics of the Red Man* (piano), Book 2	Omaha
1905	Busch, Carl. "Variations and Fugue on an Omaha Indian Theme" (string orch.)	Omaha
	Farwell, Arthur. "From Mesa and Plain" (piano)	Navajo, Pawnee
	Farwell, Arthur. "Impressions of the Wa-Wan Ceremony of the Omahas," op. 21 (piano)	Omaha
1906	Beach, Mrs. H. H. A. "Eskimos" (piano)	Inuit
1907	Troyer, Carlos. "Kiowa-Apache War Dance" (piano)	Kiowa-Apache
1909	Burton, Frederick R. *American Primitive Music* (piano)	Ojibwa
	Cadman, Charles W. "To a Vanishing Race" from *Three Moods for Piano*	Omaha
1910	Miller, Horace A. *Melodic Views of Indian Life* (piano)	Ojibwa, Arapaho, Caddo, Kiowa, Paiute
1911	Sousa, John Philip. "The Red Man" from *Dwellers in the Western World* (band)	None
	Speck, Frank G. "Ceremonial Songs of the Creek and Yuchi Indians" (piano)	Creek, Yuchi
1912	Cadman, Charles W. *Idealized Indian Themes* (piano)	Omaha
	Gilbert, Henry. *Indian Scenes* (piano)	Pueblo, Kutenai
1913	Burleigh, Cecil. *Five Indian Sketches* (violin and piano)	Unknown
	Troyer, Carlos. "Zunian Clown Dance (Kor-kok-shi)" (piano)	Zuni
1914	Burleigh, Cecil. "Ghost Dance" (violin and piano)	Sioux
	Busoni, Ferruccio. *Indian Fantasy* (piano and orchestra)	Mixed: Hopi, Laguna, Acoma, Pima, Kwakiutl
	Grunn, Homer. "Hopi Indian Dance" (orchestra)	Hopi
	Hammer, Heinrich. *American Indian Rhapsody: Sioux Indian Sun Dance* (orchestra)	Sioux
	Lieurance, Thurlow. *Indian Suite* (piano)	Gros Ventres, Sioux, Crow

Date	Composer and Work	Native Musical Source
1915	Busoni, Ferruccio. *Indian Diary*, Book 1: "Four Piano Studies" (piano)	Hopi, Cheyenne, Laguna, Pima, Wabanaki
	Skilton, Charles S. *Two Indian Dances* (piano)	Chinook, Cheyenne
1916	Eames, Henry P. *The Sacred Tree of the Omahas* (pageant)	Omaha
1917	Cadman, Charles W. *Thunderbird* Suite (piano)	Blackfoot, Omaha, Pueblo
	Grunn, Homer. "Zuni Impressions" (orchestra)	Zuni
	Miller, Horace A. "Four Indian Themes" (piano)	Cheyenne
	Otterström, Thorvald. *Musical Pictures of Chippewa Indian Life* (piano)	Ojibwa
1918	Busch, Carl. *Four Indian Tribal Melodies,* or *Indian Suite* (string orch.)	Ojibwa
	Carpenter, John Alden. "Little Indian" from *Two Pieces for Piano* (piano)	None
1919	Lane, Eastwood. "The Powwow (An Indian Reminiscence)" from *Five American Dances* (piano)	None
	Griffes, Charles Tomlinson. *Two Sketches Based on Indian Themes* (string quartet)	Iroquois
	Lieurance, Thurlow. "Ghost Dance" (piano)	Menominee
	Skilton, Charles S. *Three Indian Sketches* (piano)	Kickapoo, Sioux, Winnebago
1920	Lieurance, Thurlow. *Sioux Scalp Dance* (piano)	Sioux
1921	Burlin, Natalie Curtis. "American Indian Dances" (piano)	Unknown
	Gilbert, Henry. *Indian Sketches* (orchestra)	Zuni, Apache, Pueblo, Kutenai
	Rea, Florence. "Yakima: Indian Story" (piano)	Yakima
	Skilton, Charles. "War Dance" (string quartet)	Cheyenne
	Strickland, Lily. *Two Cherokee Indian Dances* (piano)	Cherokee
1922	Beach, Mrs. H. H. A. *From Blackbird Hills: An Omaha Tribal Dance,* op. 83 (piano)	Omaha

Date	Composer and Work	Native Musical Source
	Busch, Carl. *Indian Rhapsody* (orchestra, adapted from 1905 work)	Omaha
	Lane, Eastwood. "A Dirge for Jo Indian" from *Adirondack Sketches* (piano)	None
	Kinscella, Hazel. "Scalp Dance" (orchestra)	Sioux
	Read, Angelo. *Indian Legends*: "The Calumet of Peace" and "Tirawa's Vengeance" (piano)	Pawnee
	Skilton, Charles. *Shawnee Indian Hunting Dance* (orchestra)	Shawnee
1924	Cardin, Frederick (Pejawah). *Cree War Dance* (violin and piano)	Cree
	Lieurance, Thurlow. *Ghost Pipes* (violin and piano)	Sioux
	Stringfield, Lamar. *Indian Sketches* (flute and string quartet)	Cherokee
1925	Stringfield, Lamar. "Squaw Dance" (orchestra)	Cherokee
1927	Fairchild, Blair. *Some Indian Songs and Dances* (piano)	Lakota Sioux
1928	Jacobi, Frederick. *Indian Dances* (orchestra)	Unknown
	Skilton, Charles. "Kickapoo Social Dance" (piano)	Kickapoo
1931	Gaul, Harvey. "From an Indian Long House" (suite for string orch. and Indian percussion instr.)	Seneca and Tuscarora
1932	Busch, Carl. "A Chippewa Lament" (symphonic band)	Ojibwa
1933	Philipp, Isidore. "Ghost Dance" (piano)	Menominee
	Philipp, Isidore. "Prayer to the Rain God" (piano)	Crow
1935	Miller, Horace A. *Three Pieces from the Indian World* (organ)	Mandan, Papago
	Gould, Morton. "Indian Nocturne: Americana, Mood Sketches No. 2" (piano)	None
1937	Burke, Carleton. *Symphony Iroquoian* (symphonic poem for orchestra)	Iroquois
1938	Cowell, Henry. *Amerind Suite* (piano)	Unknown
1942	Castelnuovo-Tedesco, Mario. *Indian Songs and Dances* (orchestra)	Zuni, Navajo

Date	Composer and Work	Native Musical Source
	Kaufmann, Walter. *Six Indian Miniatures* (orchestra)	Unknown
1945	McPhee, Colin. *Iroquois Dances* (small orchestra)	Iroquois
1946	De Lamarter, Eric. "From the Long Room of the Sea" (organ)	Ojibwa
1949	Jacobi, Frederick. "Yebiche: Variations on an American Indian Theme" (orchestra)	Navajo

This listing does not include texted works such as art or popular songs, operas, or *Hiawatha* settings.

Notes

Short titles are used for those works included in the bibliography. Sources frequently cited have been identified by the following abbreviations:

DeVincent	Sam DeVincent Collection of American Sheet Music. Lilly Library, Indiana University, Bloomington, Indiana.
LEVY	Lester S. Levy Collection of American Sheet Music. Special collection at the Milton S. Eisenhower Library, Johns Hopkins University, Baltimore, Maryland. Available online at http://levysheetmusic.mse.jhu.edu.
MftN	Music for the Nation: 1820–1860 and 1879–1885. Sheet music collection at the Library of Congress, Washington, D.C. American Memory series. Available online at http://memory.loc.gov/ammem/smhtml/smhome.html.
WAIM	Victoria Lindsay Levine, *Writing American Indian Music: Historic Transcriptions, Notations, and Arrangements.* Vol. 11, *Music in the United States of America.* Middleton, Wis.: Published for the American Musicological Society by A-R Editions, 2002.

Introduction: A Language for Imagining Native America

1. There isn't space in this book to discuss all the classically oriented works composed on Indian themes after about 1911, and there were indeed hundreds if not thousands of such works composed in America alone. For excellent critical and detailed analyses of some of these, see Browner, "Transposing Cultures."

2. Anderson, *Imagined Communities,* 6. On the "ambivalent margin of the nation-space," see Bhabha, *Nation and Narration,* 4.

3. On the representation of African Americans in early nineteenth-century minstrelsy, see chap. 1 in Lott, *Love and Theft,* 15–37. On the splintering of culture in America, see "Order, Hierarchy, and Culture" in Levine, *Highbrow/Lowbrow,* 171–242.

4. The *Evangeline* cast (including "Lo") is cited in Root, *American Popular Stage Music,* 148–50.

5. Thomas Nast's 1872 cartoon is reproduced in Dippie, *The Vanishing American,* plates between pages 138 and 139.

6. Said, *Orientalism,* 21. On orientalist literature in music, see, for example, Mary Hunter and Eric Rice on *alla turca* exoticism in Mozart and Beethoven; Roger Fiske on Scotland as a European exotic; Ralph Locke on Middle-Eastern orientalism; Jonathan Bellman on the Rom; Jann Pasler on India; Eric Lott on American minstrelsy; Carol Hess on De Falla; Carol Oja on Colin McPhee; Mervyn Cooke on the gamelan in Britten; William Ashbrook and Harold Powers on chinoiserie in Puccini; Richard Taruskin on the concept of *nega* in Russian orientalism; W. Anthony Sheppard on Japanese exoticism in Hollywood cinema; and at least two collections of essays to date: Bellman, ed., *The Exotic in Western Music,* and Born and Hesmondhalgh, *Western Music and Its Others.* For details and a more complete list, see Locke, "Exoticism," in the *New Grove Dictionary of Music and Musicians.*

7. Art history, on the other hand, has identified a school of orientalism. Core writings in this field are Philippe Jullian, *The Orientalists: European Painters of Eastern Scenes* (Oxford: Phaidon, 1977) as well as Linda Nochlin's "The Imaginary Orient" in her *Politics of Vision: Essays on Nineteenth-Century Art and Society* (New York: Harper and Row, 1989).

8. James Parakilas has observed that Russian musicians' interest in Spain was different from that of the French, who exoticized their neighbors. For Russian musicians, Parakilas argues, the representation of Spain "meant finding a mirror of their own cultural situation in the corner of Europe most different from themselves." See Parakilas, "How Spain Got a Soul," 138.

9. Dahlhaus, *Nineteenth-Century Music,* 304–6; Bartók quoted in Fassett, *Naked Face of Genius,* 331; Whaples, *Exoticism in Dramatic Music,* introduction, 1–12.

10. On hip-hop musicians' sampling of non-Western music, see Hesmondhalgh, "International Times: Fusions, Exoticism, and Antiracism in Electronic Dance Music" in Born and Hesmondhalgh, *Western Music and Its Others,* 293.

11. Michael Spitzer explores connections between "cognitive metaphors" and "poetic metaphors" in *Metaphor and Musical Thought,* 54–91. See also Tagg and Clarida, *Ten Little Title Tunes,* for such helpful terms as "constructional" and "receptional" as ways to discuss music's ability to connote or denote.

12. In his essay on musical rhetoric, Patrick McCreless writes "what the late eighteenth century tended to call rhetoric gradually began to be subsumed under what the nineteenth century called structure, to the point that musical rhetoric disappeared altogether." See McCreless, "Music and Rhetoric," 872. This may be true if we are speaking principally about the theoretical traditions of Germanic concert music. It seems to me, however, that rhetorical language was still a viable expressive principle in music directed toward the rising middle classes.

13. Browner, "Transposing Cultures," 15–19. The work of semioticians such as Louis

Hjelmslev, Roland Barthes, Claude Lévi-Strauss, and Roman Jakobson, and of musical semioticians Raymond Monelle, Eero Tarasti, Robert Hatten, Philip Tagg, and Marta Grabocz, has provided helpful tools for unraveling musical languages of nationalism and exoticism. See also Turino, "Signs of the Imagination," for a concise overview of semiotics as relevant to music.

Chapter 1: Noble Savagery in European Court Entertainments, 1550–1760

1. The engraving of the *Timbalier et Trompette Ameriquains* [*sic*] from the 1662 carrousel can be seen in Isherwood, *Service of the King,* 262.

2. Manuscript of *Flore* in the Philidor Collection, Bibliothèque National, Paris. "Indiens" in works such as Lully's *Ballet des muses* (1666) refer to East Indians. The subject matter of the ballet generally makes this clear. In any case, "Américains" is usually the seventeenth-century French word for American Indians.

3. Ramón Pane, "Escritura de la antiguedad de los indios," a manuscript not printed until 1892 (cited in Stevenson, "Written Sources," 1). Irving Rouse's otherwise excellent *Tainos* doesn't mention anything about music other than "singing, drumming, and rattling" (15). Todorov, *Conquest of America,* 203, cites the criticism of Diego Durán (*Historia de las Indias . . .*, 1578), who blames the early Spanish evangelists for attempting to erase much of Aztec culture.

4. Pedro de Castañeda's accounts are quoted in George P. Hammond and Agapito Rey, eds. and trans., *Narratives of the Coronado Expedition, 1540–1542* (Albuquerque: University of New Mexico Press, 1940) and cited in Stevenson, "Written Sources," 4. De la Vega's experience is recounted in Stevenson, "Written Sources," 5.

5. Cited in Stevenson, "English Sources," 400–403.

6. J. de Léry, *Histoire d'un voyage fait en la terre du Brésil,* 3rd ed. (1585). Music cited (with harmonization) in Savage, "Rameau's American Dancers," 448. Stephen Greenblatt argues that Léry recognized the transgressive power of such singing to resist capture in writing. See the discussion of Léry and evaluation of modern interpreters in Tomlinson, "Ideologies of Aztec Song," 374. On the Tupinambá visit to Paris in 1613, see Hemming, *Red Gold,* 206. Lescarbot's Micmac song is in facsimile in *WAIM,* 3.

7. The anonymous Huron account was published as *Relation de ce qui s'est passé . . . en la Nouvelle France és années 1657 et 1658* (cited in Savage, "Rameau's American Dancers," 446). Dablon is cited in Stevenson, "Written Sources," 32, fn. 74. A facsimile of Iroquois song is available in *WAIM,* 7.

8. Mersenne's "Chanson Canadoise" is in facsimile in *WAIM,* 6. The Onondaga greeting is cited in Stevenson, "Written Sources," 32, fn. 74. By the eighteenth century, transcriptions by the Sulpician order published by the Abbé Prévost contain diatonic melodies and raised leading tones. Transcriptions in Stevenson, "Written Sources," 22.

9. The account of Aztecs at Charles's court is in Savage, "Rameau's American Dancers" (whose source is Stevenson, *Music in Aztec and Inca Territory*), 445. Weiditz's sketch is reproduced and discussed in Stedman, *Shadows of the Indian,* 8 and 253–54.

10. J. Smith, "Close Encounters," 17–19.

11. On the French "Brazilian village," see Wintroub, "Civilizing the Savage." See also the account in Hemming, *Red Gold,* 12–13. Description of the *Ballet de la reine* appears

in De la Laurencie, "America in the French Music," 286, and in Stevenson, "Written Sources," 21. In *L'art du ballet de cour en France,* McGowan calls this a *Ballet à la Royne.* Manuscript musical sources are at the Bibliothèque nationale, Paris; they are by Michel Henry (Ms. Fr. 24357) and published by Michael Praetorius (*Terpsichore, Works* vol. XV, no. 263), by R. Ballard (*Recueil d'airs de luths,* f. 17), and by G. Bataille (*Airs de differents autheurs mis en tablature,* 1609, ff. 5–7).

12. Malherbe's account of the Tupinambá is in *Oeuvres,* vol. 3, 297, cited in Savage, "Rameau's American Dancers," 447. An essential feature of the branle was that it was performed by a group of people in a circle. Says Randle Cotgrave's *Dictionarie of the French and English Tongues* (1611): "a brawle . . . wherein many holding by the hands sometimes in a ring, and otherwhiles at length, move all together." Whaples discusses Gaultier in *Exoticism in Dramatic Music,* 208. I consulted with lutenist Paul Odette, who confirmed that it is not known which, if any, of Gaultier's surviving sarabandes is the one commissioned by Malherbe.

13. The *New Grove* entry on "Hurdy-gurdy" says the instrument first appeared at the French court in 1661 in a Lully ballet. Clearly, it had been used in the *ballet de cour* before that time. The most comprehensive study of the instrument is Leppert, *Arcadia at Versailles* (1978).

14. The "Branle de Bresse" is from the *Traite de Musette de Borjon* (1672) and was transcribed in *Les spectacles à travers les âges: Musique, danse* (Paris: Aux Éditions du Cygne, 1932), vol. 1, 281. The libretto for the *Grand Bal de la douairière* is published in Lacroix, *Ballets et mascarades de cour,* vol. 3. No specification to music or types of dances is included. On the *Grand Bal,* see McGowan, *L'art du ballet de cours,* 149–53. See also "The Amerindian in French Humanist and Burlesque Court Ballets," app. 4 in Franko, *Dance as Text,* 186–90. An account of the ballet that followed can be found in De la Laurencie, "America in the French Music," 286 and Stevenson, "Written Sources," 21. Another illustration shows several dancers representing the "peoples and costumes of America." Following a llama, they play musettes and crotales. See illustration in Christout, *Le ballet de cour au XVIIe siècle,* 138.

15. The music for the Richelieu ballet is preserved in the Philidor Collection at the Paris Conservatory. De la Laurencie quotes a musical example in "America in the French Music," 289. On the moresca, see Sachs, *World History of the Dance,* 333–39.

16. The description of "Jacques" is quoted from a Dutch exhibition catalogue by Roelof van Gelder (Amsterdam, 1982) and was cited by Hamell in "Mohawks Abroad," 189. Hemming describes the Tapuia in the Hague in *Red Gold,* 290–91.

17. Constance Rourke noted the influence of European woodcuts and a preoccupation of the heathen savage in early views of America. See Rourke, *The Roots of American Culture,* 60. Liebersohn discusses the continued use of the term *sauvage* in *Aristocratic Encounters,* 13, n. 1.

18. Stevenson, *Music in Mexico,* 52f. See also Spiess, "Church Music in Seventeenth-Century New Mexico."

19. Sagard's four-part arrangement is available in facsimile in *WAIM,* 4–5, as is Rousseau's transcription of Mersenne, 11–12.

20. Blanning describes Louis XIV dancing as Apollo in *The Culture of Power,* 34.

21. Occasionally, "Indiens" appearing in such works as Lully's *Ballet des Muses* (1666)

refer to East Indians. The subject matter of the libretto generally makes this clear. Most of the time, "Américains" is usually the word for American Indians. For more on the political associations of the ballet *Le temple de la paix,* see Isherwood, *Service of the King,* 279–80.

22. Greenblatt, *Marvelous Possessions,* 16–23.

23. The manuscript full score of *Il Colombo* exists at the British Library, a gift of Domenico Dragonetti. Unfortunately, neither the opening sinfonia nor the *ballet des nations* that concluded the work are contained in this manuscript. Pasquini's ballet—if in fact it *was* by Pasquini—must be presumed to be lost. Viale Ferrero's study of this opera in relation to the Ottobone family (1988) is cited in Maehder's "Representation of the 'Discovery'" without bibliographical information. The love intrigues in *Il Colombo* are contrived: Ginacra, the fictional king of the Indians, falls in love with Columbus's wife, while the discoverer's son falls in love with Ginacra's daughter.

24. *The Indian Queen* dramatized a conflict between the Incas and the Aztecs before the invasion of the Spaniards. In this highly fictional account, Moctezuma is an Inca who defected to the enemy after realizing that the queen of the Mexicans is a pretender and upon learning that his mother is the rightful queen. (Perhaps Moctezuma's defection justified his deposition in the sequel.) *The Indian Emperor* therefore focused on Cortés's encounter with Moctezuma. Several decades before Dryden's *Indian Queen,* Willaim Davenant had written and composed *Cruelty of the Spaniards in Peru,* a pictorial ballet in six entrées. The music is lost, but details about the text and performance can be found in Haun, *Libretti of Restoration Opera,* 73–83. On the allegorical use of key and mode in late sixteenth-century British theatrical music, see Price, *Henry Purcell,* 21–26.

25. Purcell died prematurely in 1695. His brother Daniel Purcell wrote a final masque to complete *The Indian Queen,* presumably for the first full performance. See Pinnock, "Play into Opera."

26. Price, *Henry Purcell,* 797–98.

27. It may be argued that the score's excessive chromaticism could be interpreted as an exotic device, but I will not do so here. See Price, *Henry Purcell,* 797–98.

28. Whaples has noted that the Conjurer's Song "follows a pattern of incantations and ritual scenes, which contributed so much exotic atmosphere to Baroque and Classical opera [and] constitute a genre with its own style; and these are independent of the time and place of the action" (*Exoticism in Dramatic Music,* 226).

29. See Nettl, "The Moresca."

30. Dablon (1670) added that "this was done so well—with slow and measured steps, and the rhythmic sound of the voices and drums—that it might pass for a very fine Entry of a Ballet in France." See Stevenson, "Written Sources," 21.

31. See Sven Hansell, "Mythological Subjects in Opera Seria" in Collins and Kirk, *Opera and Vivaldi,* 50. The fact that no music from this opera was known to exist did not stop Jean-Claude Malgoire from creating a "reconstruction" and recording it in 1992. Nowhere in his program notes does Malgoire detail the sources of his Vivaldian "pastiche."

32. *The Indian Emperor* is quoted several times in Voltaire's notebooks, according to Besterman, *Voltaire,* 187, fn. 4.

33. Voltaire set *Alzire* in Lima, Peru, although Montezuma and his daughter come

"from another part" of the region. He never uses the term "Inca," so I have taken the liberty of assuming that Montezuma and Alzire are here displaced Aztecs. The problem of religion that preoccupied Voltaire may have been one that also interested Verdi a century later, as his *Alzira* is based roughly on Voltaire's play.

34. Ernest Helm argued that the plot of Graun's *Montezuma* was partly modeled after Voltaire's *Alzire.* See Helm, *Frederick the Great,* 67–70. Frederick adored *Alzire* and recognized that Christianity, ill understood and guided by false zeal, "renders men more barbarous and more cruel than paganism itself." (Parton, *Life of Voltaire,* vol. 1, 345.) For more on the relationship between Frederick and Voltaire, see Blanning, *Culture of Power,* 219.

35. Around the turn of the eighteenth century, many German music theorists recognized and categorized types of musical affects as well as the affective connotations of musical rhetoric. See especially the theoretical treatises of Werckmeister, Mattheson, Marpurg, Scheibe, and Quantz.

36. See Whaples, *Exoticism in Dramatic Music,* 232–33, for discussion and example.

37. J.-B. Dubos, *Réflexions critiques sur la poésie et sur la peinture* (Paris, 1719). Translation of excerpted passage is from Anthony, *French Baroque Music,* 45.

38. The letter is quoted in Girdlestone, *Jean-Philippe Rameau,* and translated by Savage in "Rameau's American Dancers," 444. "Les sauvages" was published in Rameau's *Nouvelles suites de pièces de clavecin* (1728).

39. This summary is paraphrased from Roger Savage's translation of the account. See "Rameau's American Dancers," 446.

40. Allouez is quoted in Laubin, *Indian Dances,* 233. Lafitau's quotation is from *Jesuit Relations,* vol. 59, 129, and cited in Stevenson, "Written Sources," 21.

41. Savage, "Rameau's American Dancers," 449.

42. According to Charles Dill, "*Les Incas* is the only entrée to move beyond romantic dalliance, the standard subject of opera-ballet, to the more serious issues of honor, loyalty, and commitment. We see this range in the opening scene, where the Spanish conqueror Carlos within a single statement challenges the patriotism, religious devotion, and sincerity of his lover, the Incan princess Phani-Palla." Dill, *Monstrous Opera,* 22.

43. Dill, *Monstrous Opera,* 21.

44. Whaples, *Exoticism in Dramatic Music,* 242–43.

45. Louis Hennepin, *New Discovery of a Vast Country in America,* 2nd ed. (London: Printed for M. Bentley, J. Tonson, H. Bonwick, T. Goodwin, and S. Manship, 1698), vol. 2, 653–56.

46. All quotes from the libretto are in James O. Wooton's translation from liner notes accompanying the recording by Les Arts Florissants (Harmonia Mundi France HMC 901367.69).

47. Hennepin, *New Discovery,* vol. 1, 168.

48. The first known source for the word *chacona* is a 1598 Mexican poem by Mateo Rosas de Oquendo. See Hudson, *Passacaglio* [*sic*] *and Ciaccona,* 4.

49. Gaspare Spontini, *Fernand Cortez, ou La conquête du Mexique* (Théâtre de l'Académie Impériale de Musique, Paris, 1809). In addition to using a full complement of percussion instruments in the pit, Spontini had onstage dancers play Mexican *ayacachtli* (gourd or pottery rattles) as well as tambourines and cymbals. For additional operas from

Spontini through Glass, see Jürgen Maehder, who provides a list of works in "Representation of the 'Discovery.' " On the background to Verdi's *Alzira,* see Budden, *Operas of Verdi,* vol. 1, 225–42.

Chapter 2: Death, Defiance, and Diplomacy, 1710–1808

1. The John White quotation is cited in Stedman's "Literary and Historical Chronology" in *Shadows of the Indian,* 254. Strachey's 1609 letter on Virginia reports that "in some parte of the country they have yearely a Sacrifice of Children," citing in one instance "fifteen of the properest young boys betweene 10 and 15 years of age." See a description of this eyewitness account of child sacrifice in Stevenson, "English Sources," 401. On the confusion between "good" and "bad" Indians in early New England, see Lepore, *Name of War,* 156–58.

2. Hubbard is quoted in Stedman, *Shadows of the Indian,* 254. An account of the French-Iroquois massacres can be found in Moogk, *La Nouvelle France,* 256. For a fascinating analysis of the behavior of the New England Puritans toward the Narragansetts (and vice versa), see Lepore, *The Name of War,* 14–18.

3. Swift's decry appeared on 28 Apr. 1711 in *Journal to Stella.* Hamell notes Swift's use of the term "Mohawks" in "Mohawks Abroad," 189. On the sachem song and dance, see Bond, *Queen Anne's American Kings,* 51. Yee-Neen-Ho-Ga-Prow returned in 1740 to be received by George II. Sa-Ga-Yean-Qua-Prah-Ton was Joseph Brant's grandfather.

4. In an *Essay upon the Present State of the Theatre in France, England and Italy* (1760), the anonymous author states that "nothing can be more ingenious than the pieces composed in the Italian taste by M. de Marivaux and M. de Lisle: the *Harlequin Sauvage* of the latter is a character that shews a most admirable creative genius in the author." I have not been able to find any surviving music from this Harlequinade. See also Jones, *Native Americans,* 15. An advertisement describing the "dance of Indians" appeared in the *London Daily Post* (1744). I am grateful to Simon During for this information.

5. Liebersohn, *Aristocratic Encounters,* 30.

6. On Hyam Myers, see Hamell, "Mohawks Abroad," 176–77. On Sychnecta, see Foreman, *Indians Abroad, 1493–1938,* 83.

7. A copy of Sayer's engraving at the Huntington Library, Los Angeles, California, shows the date 1772 (call no. 437733). A copy of Claggert's comic tunes is available at the British Library.

8. Special thanks to Simon During for sending me these verses. See additional verses in Pratt, "Reynolds' 'King,'" 145.

9. On Howard, see Foreman, *Indians Abroad,* 87. Pratt's comment is from "Reynolds' 'King of the Cherokees,' " 145. A facsimile of the Howard broadside, with headpiece, is in LEVY.

10. Hoig, *Cherokees and Their Chiefs,* 49. There is virtually no biographical information on Samuel Boyce in published sources. It is difficult to tell where he was in 1765.

11. See Ratner on the march as a style topic in *Classic Music,* 16.

12. Temporal analysis according to Salisbury, "The Indians' Old World: Native Americans and the Coming of Europeans," 438–49. Priber, a "German intellectual" who had learned the Cherokee language and married into a Cherokee family, encouraged the

Cherokees to stick closely with other Indian tribes and learn to rely less on the Europeans. For this, South Carolina had him arrested in 1743, and he died in prison a year later.

13. Lafitau, *Mœurs des sauvages américains*, vol. 2, 283–84.

14. Lafitau, *Mœurs des sauvages américains,* vol. 2, 194.

15. A. H. Hunter, *Poems,* 80.

16. Stevenson, 17. Whaples (212) says that the "chanson" is actually a confusion of two of DeBry's Tupi melodies, the bird song and the dance. Facsimiles of Picquet and Rousseau's transcriptions are included in *WAIM,* 10–11.

17. Ritson, *Scotish Songs*, vol. 2, 261–62. See Koegel, "Indian Chief," 459, for account of Ritson's research.

18. See facsimile in *Die Musik in Geschichte und Gegenwart* (Kassel: Bärenreiter-Verlag, 1952), vol. 2, col. 1001.

19. See A. P. Brown, "Musical Settings of Anne Hunter's Poetry," 46–48. The earliest known printings of the "Death Song" are undated. One of them is that included here from "Nine Canzonetts for Two Voices; and Six Airs *with an Accompanyment for the Piano-Forte by A Lady.* ["Mrs. Hunter" later added in pen] *To which is added* The Death Song *of the Cherokee Indians. (Now First Published by the Author),*" London: Longman and Broderip, n.d. The undated print has been inscribed 1783. The song first appeared in print in the United States (also anonymously) in two newspapers in 1785, *Charleston Evening Gazette* (Charleston, S.C.) on 20 Sept. and *Massachusetts Spy* (Worcester, Mass.) on 22 Sept., and in book form as "The Indian Chief" in Andrew Adgate's *The Philadelphia Songster, Part I. Being a Collection of Choice Songs* (Philadelphia: John M'Culloch, 1789), 8. See facsimile of the 1789 edition in *WAIM,* 215. Surprisingly, the song also appeared as early as 1783 in a Rhode Island manuscript copybook; see Koegel, "Indian Chief." The poem was also printed in the United States in 1787 in the January issue of the *American Museum,* where it is credited to the American poet Philip Freneau; see Jones, *Death Song,* 98. The name "Turner," however, also occurs in association with "The Death Song" in a 1791 Edinburgh weekly newspaper citation; see Brown, "Musical Settings," 47.

20. See Koegel's list in "Indian Chief," 462–68.

21. Koegel, "Indian Chief," 453–54.

22. Marrocco and Gleason, *Music in America,* 213.

23. According to Jones (*Native Americans,* 1–2), European theater producers in the eighteenth century found American Indians useful in contemporary drama for three reasons: (1) as a surefire audience lure; (2) as a righteous noble savage cudgel to beat fellow Europeans for their foibles and sins; and(3) as a propaganda device at times when national unity was necessary.

24. Fiske devotes several pages to a discussion of *Inkle and Yarico;* see *English Theatre Music,* 476–80. The one "American tune" specified in the libretto is not in the score and remains unidentified.

25. Dibdin wrote other "Indian" songs for his "table entertainments," among them, "Dear Yanko, Say" (*The Oddities,* 1789). This song appeared in *Venice Preserved* at Covent Garden in 1790. For a list of non-Hunterian death songs, see the list of eight titles in Koegel, "Indian Chief," 479.

26. Note that some references give the year as 1783, though these are likely based on a

single erroneous source. 1792 is confirmed as the original year of authorship, but the title elsewhere is *Columbus; or A World Discovered.* The play opened in Baltimore in 1801, in Boston in 1802, and in Charleston in 1807 and was produced in America well into the 1810s.

27. Franz Xaver Gerl, "Trauergesang" from *Die Spanier in Peru* (Brünn, 28 Feb. 1796).

28. The quotation is from Leon Vallée, *Bibliographie des bibliographies,* translated at http://regencycafe.tripod.com/marmontel.html (accessed 10 Nov. 2002). The last edition of this work was published in 1818 before a recent 1990s edition in French. Marmontel's *Les Incas* was published in translation in England in 1777, the same year it appeared in France.

29. The composers for the *Columbus* productions are cited in Porter, *With an Air Debonair,* 74; Porter also quotes the Philadelphia review, 144.

30. See Whaples, *Exoticism in Dramatic Music,* 65–172.

31. Since music played an intrinsic role in spoken theater of the early nineteenth century, we may assume that similar "Indian" music was incorporated for the increasing number of plays involving Indians in the 1830s and 1840s. Because little research has been done to uncover the types of theater music composed during this period, however, no representative samples from this period could be located to cite here.

32. See Porter, *With an Air Debonair,* 408. The song texts are available in Frank Pierce Hill, *American Plays Printed 1714–1830* (New York, 1905; Readex Microprint). There is a song for voice and keyboard by Hewitt entitled "The Wampum Belt" (published New York, 1797), but this is apparently unrelated to *Tammany;* see the reprint with an introductory essay by John W. Wagner in "James Hewitt: Selected Compositions," *Recent Researches in American Music* 12 (1980): 43.

33. Deloria, *Playing Indian,* 12.

34. Deloria, *Playing Indian,* 17–18. My investigation into Tammany sources has failed to turn up satisfactory answers for any of these questions.

35. Jones, *Native Americans,* 17–18.

36. According to Odell's *Annals,* vol. 1, 289, "Peter" danced the Indian War Dance in New York on 24 Jan. 1791 in Indian dress ("in complete armour"), with no location given. It appears that such occurrences as "Peter's" and Durang's Indian dancing were rare before the 1790s in America, but increased after the appearances of American Indian dancers. Simon During referred me to an ad in the *London Times* (18 June 1795) that observed two native Indians from the "Cataubo Nation" exhibiting "exercises and feats of dexterity with bow, tomahawk, etc. at Sadler's Wells" and then as part of a ballet called *The Ambuscade.* A "Grand Indian Dance" was subsequently appended to *Inkle and Yariko* in 1797 (as noted previously).

37. Cited in Fenner, *Opera in London,* 413.

38. There is a substantial bibliography on Sheridan's *Pizarro,* given its central role in British theatrical history. I recommend two key discussions of the play that are contained within larger works: Ranger, *Gothic Drama,* 126–138, and O'Toole, *Life of Richard Brinsley Sheridan,* 345–355. Michael Kelly's score, like those for early melodrama at Covent Garden and Drury Lane, was published. The numbers included, however, are only what would later be called the incidental music—the songs and stage music. Any melodramatic underscoring that was used for dialogue sequences has not survived. See

the reprint of this score, edited with an introduction by Stoddard Lincoln (New York: Da Capo Press, 1979). Dussek's published overture and "Characteristic Pieces" and Thomas Simpson Cooke's overture for the Dublin production of 1800 both survive, with copies in the British Library. A manuscript full score and eight parts (with music different from Kelly's) survive in the Drury Lane Archive, British Library, for an unidentified nineteenth-century production of *Pizarro*. There is also "The Favorite march in Pizzarro [*sic*]" dated 1803 and composed by James Hewitt, presumably for the first New York production. A copy of this march is available at the Harry Ransom Humanities Research Center at the University of Texas, Austin; the library's record says that the march is by Kelly, but this cannot be correct as it does not appear anywhere in Kelly's score. I have not been able to determine from the nature of the march where in the play it would have been used, and so I have not referred to it in detail in this chapter.

39. The noted actors Dorothea Jordan and John Philip Kemble played Cora and Rolla at the premiere, although the principal Rolla of the early nineteenth century was Edmund Kean.

40. George III's opinion as told to Lord Harcourt is cited in O'Toole, *Richard Brinsley Sheridan,* 351. Kelly's account appears in his *Reminiscences,* vol. 2, 148. Samuel French's catalog appears in Wentworth Hogg, *Guide to Plays; or Manager's Companion* (London: Samuel French, 1882). None of the *Pizarro* music advertised for hire has been located.

41. The *Anti-Jacobin Review and Magazine,* 1798; cited in O'Toole, *Richard Brinsley Sheridan,* 345.

42. Ranger, *Gothic Drama,* 126. Rowell's comments are in *Victorian Theatre, 1792–1914: A Survey,* 2nd ed. (Cambridge: Cambridge University Press, 1978), 44.

43. Playbill for *Pizarro,* Princess Theatre, London, 1 Sept. 1856; notes by Charles Kean, manager.

44. Hewitt's contribution to *Pizarro* is observed in Porter, *With an Air Debonair,* 479. This production opened March 26; a review—"Crito's notice"—appears in Odell's *Annals,* vol. 2, 85–87. Brief plot descriptions of various short-lived operatic works inspired by Marmontel's *Incas* between the 1780s and the twentieth century can be found in Frederick H. Martens, *A Thousand and One Nights of Opera* (1926). Martens includes Cordeille's *Pizarre* (Paris, 1785), Méhul's *Cora* (Paris, 1791), Cimarosa's *La vergine del sole* (St. Petersburg, 1791), Alessandro Rolla's *Pizarro, o la conquista del Peru* (Milan, 1807), and Henry Rowe Bishop's *Virgin of the Sun* (London, 1812).

45. Scheckel, *Insistence of the Indian,* 50–51.

46. See Hitchcock, "An Early American Melodrama," for more information about Bray's music for Barker's play. Hitchcock also edited a reprint edition of the musical score (Da Capo Press, 1972).

Chapter 3: Imagining the Frontier, 1795–1860

1. Cited in Stewart, *Adventures and Sufferings,* 182.

2. I have not been able to find out much about Lefolle, except that he gave a series of concerts in Boston in 1816. He is listed in the *Philadelphia Directory & Stranger's Guide for 1825* as "Leader of the Band of the New Theatre" (on Chestnut Street).

3. The Cherokees had already suffered a lethal attack of smallpox in 1738 that report-

edly "wiped out an estimated half the Cherokee." See Hoig, *Cherokees,* 54. The inoculation was first used in England in 1721 but apparently wasn't available to help the Cherokee people.

4. Liebersohn, *Aristocratic Encounters,* 3.

5. The original music for *Paul et Virginie* was by Joseph Mazzinghi (published London: G. Goulding, 1795) and was written for the English production of the well-known play based on Bernardin de Saint-Pierre's 1787 romance *Paul et Virginie, et l'Arcadie.* This novel is set on the volcanic island of Mauritius off the coast of Madagascar. Anything "Indian" associated with this work was probably just generic *sauvagerie.* F. LeSueur produced an opera on *Paul et Virginie* at the Theatre Feydeau in 1793. Famous in each production was the shipwreck near the end, in which Virginie was killed.

6. Surprisingly, Susan Youens (and others before her who have written about this song) never mentions the Kotzebue *Pizarro* connection. See Youens, *Schubert's Poets,* 40–41. Since the play was popular in the 1790s, however, when Bamberg was already quite mature, and since operatic models were crucial to the formation of Viennese song before 1815, as Youens notes (p. 3), all evidence points to the fact that the subject of this song is the Peruvian Cora. The song can be found in the old Schubert critical edition (*Lieder,* vol. 3, p. 50) and in *F. Schubert: Neue Ausgabe,* vol. 9.

7. Henry Saxe Wyndham (*Covent Garden,* vol. 1, 29) observed that the song was still sung even "at the present day" (1908).

8. See Hunter, "The *Alla Turca* Style," 44–47, 49. Eric Rice also provides a helpful topography of the interplay between these two categories in *mehter*-inspired Western music ("Representations of Janissary Music").

9. David Brown, *Mikhail Glinka: A Biographical and Critical Study* (London: Oxford University Press, 1974), 276.

10. Some of the chroniclers of the new frontier were John Bradbury, *Travels in the Interior of America, 1809–11;* Meriwether Lewis, *History of the Expedition under the Command of Captains Lewis and Clark, 1804–6* (Lewis and Clark, with the assistance of the guide Sacagawea, charted a northward path all the way to the Pacific); Edwin James, *Accounts of S. H. Long's Expedition . . . 1819–32;* and Maximilian, Prince of Wied, *Travels in the Interior of North America, 1832–34.*

11. Carver's account of Plains war dancing is in his *Travels,* 266–83. Mathews (*The Osages,* 356–57) cites some of the Osage party as Traveling Rain, White Hair, Big Soldier, Beautiful Bird, and Makes-Tracks-Far-Away.

12. "The War Dance No War Whoop: Being a Reply to a Letter from George Dashiell" (Baltimore: privately printed, 1804), 8–12. This essay includes letters reprinted from *The American, Plain Truth,* and *The Federal Gazette.* See also "The War Dance, No War Whoop, No. 2." Both are available in *Early American Imprints,* 2nd series, no. 7691.

13. Odell's *Annals,* vol. 2, 211, reports that the New York appearance occurred 13 Aug. 1804.

14. McKenney and Hall, *History of the Indian Tribes* (Atlas volume), 3–4. Cited in Laubin, *Indian Dances,* 138–51.

15. LaFarge, *Pictorial History,* 100.

16. Durang, *Memoir,* 79–80.

17. I have not found any management records relating to the details of this perfor-

mance in Philadelphia. I hope someone will discover these someday, as they may reveal a great deal about the relationship between the white theatrical agency and the Indians who were hired as performers.

18. Bank, *Theatre Culture in America,* 67. See Odell's *Annals,* vol. 3, passim, for more instances of Indian dancers.

19. Koegel, "Indian Chief," 497.

20. Duden, *Report on a Journey,* 87–88.

21. Irving, "Traits of Indian Character," 275–76.

22. The Emerson quotation is cited in Lepore, *The Name of War,* 206.

23. Catlin, *Notes of Eight Years' Travel,* vol. 1, 62.

24. The Pawnees at the president's house were described in William Faux [British], *Memorable Days in America,* cited in Laubin, *Indian Dances,* 37. *King Shotaway* is mentioned in Eileen Southern, *The Music of Black Americans: A History,* 3rd ed. (New York: Norton, 1997), 120. Odell's *Annals* is the source for most of the theatrical information in this paragraph; the "Grand Battle of Susquehannah" is cited in vol. 3, 71.

25. The war dance at President Monroe's is mentioned in Bank, *Theatre Culture in America,* 61; the source cited is Herman J. Viola, *The Indian Legacy of Charles Bird King* (Washington, D.C.: Smithsonian Institution Press, 1976), 22–43. Most of the theatrical music for the early part of the nineteenth century in America has disappeared. It is unfortunate that no music survives for Mordecai Noah's *She Would Be a Soldier, or The Plains of Chippewa* (Park Theatre, 1819), a play that featured a defeated chieftain who bore a remarkable resemblance to the recently defeated Tecumseh. There is no surviving music for any of the other plays of the early part of the nineteenth century that featured songs or incidental music for Indian characters, among them George Custis's *Indian Prophecy* (Philadelphia, 1825), John August Stone's *Metamora, or the Last of the Wampanoags* (1829), Custis's *Pocahontas, or the Settlers of Virginia* (1830), or Richard Emmons's *Tecumseh, or the Battle of the Thames* (Philadelphia, 1836).

26. See Scheckel, *Insistence of the Indian,* 58–69, and Bank, *Theatre Culture in America,* 67.

27. Cited in Keiser, *The Indian in American Literature,* 191.

28. A facsimile of "The American Indian Girl" is included in MftN.

29. Finson, "The Romantic Savage," 243.

30. Herder is quoted in Friedrich Blume, *Classic and Romantic Music: A Comprehensive Survey,* trans. M. D. Herter Norton (New York: Norton, 1970), 20–21. No source citation is given there or in the original *Musik in Geschichte und Gegenwart* article.

31. Arroyo de la Cuesta is cited in Stevenson, "Early Sources," 11–12. A facsimile of his transcriptions is included in *WAIM,* 17–18. Throughout this book, the designations "Chippewa" and "Ojibwe" refer to the same Great Lakes tribe. Schoolcraft's transcription is in his *Historical and Statistical Information,* 562. A transcription by Stephen H. Long among Dakota singers in 1823 and published two years later predates Schoolcraft's by several decades. Facsimiles of both of these appear in *WAIM:* Long's "Dog Dance of the Sioux" (p. 20) and Schoolcraft's "War Song of the Chippewas" (p. 24).

32. Quotes are from Halpin. See Catlin's *Letters and Notes,* ix and vii.

33. The Caledonian ball is mentioned in *Catlin's Notes, or Eight Years' Travels,* vol. 1, 70f., as is the quote from the London *Morning Post* (vol. 1, 211).

34. For an account from the Indians' perspective, see Christopher Mulvey, "Among the Sag-a-noshes: Ojibwa and Iowa Indians with George Catlin in Europe, 1843–1848" in Christian F. Feest, ed., *Indians and Europe,* 253–75. Not all of the Indians survived to make it home. British children's war whoops are mentioned in *Catlin's Notes,* vol. 1, 99. On the Indian Gallery in Paris, see Halpin in Catlin's *Letters and Notes,* xi; Stedman, *Shadows of the Indian,* 257; *Catlin's Notes,* vol. 1, 95; and Mulvey, "Among the Sag-a-noshes," 253.

35. *Catlin's Notes,* vol. 1, 138.

36. See John Hill Hewitt's account of meeting "Father Heinrich," introducing him to President Tyler, and Heinrich's embarrassing performance in the president's parlor, in "Fiasco in the White House" from *Shadows on the Wall* (1877), excerpted in Jacques Barzun, ed., *Pleasures of Music: A Reader's Choice of Great Writing about Music and Musicians from Cellini to Bernard Shaw* (New York: Viking Press, 1951), 328–31. The most comprehensive account of Heinrich's activities in America is Upton's *Anthony Philip Heinrich.* A fascinating study of Heinrich ("Log Cabin Composer") can also be found in Broyles, *Mavericks,* 39–68.

37. One of Heinrich's elaborate "Indian" piano works that is currently available is the two-part fantasy *The Indian Carnival: Toccata,* and *The Festival of the Dead and the Cries of Souls* ("a 'Bacchanale' among the North American Indians"). A facsimile of Heinrich's privately published score was recently included in Schleifer, *Three Centuries,* vol. 3, 266–77. When Oscar Sonneck cataloged Heinrich's music for the Library of Congress in 1917, he noted that Heinrich was "probably the first composer to utilize Indian themes." Others have referred to Heinrich in this same way, but it should be emphasized that they, like Sonneck, invoked the idea of "Indian themes" only in terms of subject matter. No actual native sources have been found in Heinrich's music.

38. See Maust, "American Indian," 310. The only one of Heinrich's orchestral works based on Indian subjects that was performed in his lifetime was the *Indian War Council: Gran Concerto Bellico, a Grand Heroic Divertissement for 41 Instrumental Parts* (unpublished, but performed in Boston, 1846). The work is a musical portrait of the chief Tecumseh, and the performance was accompanied by an extensive descriptive program. Inexplicably, the aptly titled *Manitou Mysteries* bears no program, though it does contain such oddities as a "minuetto" movement. For a copy of the program, see Upton, *Anthony Philip Heinrich,* 196–97. The score is at the Library of Congress. No source suggests that Heinrich wrote this music for Emmons's play, which I offer only as a logical assumption. Heinrich served as a violinist at Philadelphia's Southwark Theatre in 1814, and he provided music for at least one play, Labasse's production of *La belle Peruvienne* (New York, 1822), a likely adaptation of Goldoni's *La Peruviana* (1754). According to John Rowe Parker, Heinrich contributed much of the music to this work, some of which later went into his *Dawning of Kentucky.* See Broyles, *Mavericks,* 59.

39. Dwight's review appeared in *The Harbinger* 5 (11 Sept. 1847): 224; quoted in Upton, *Anthony Philip Heinrich,* 200–01.

40. A copy of Heinrich's letter appears in the Heinrich scrapbook at the Library of Congress, 517; cited in Upton, *Anthony Philip Heinrich,* 203. Heinrich continued with a dig at Dwight: "Had my instrumental works been properly performed in Boston, they would possibly have acted quite otherwise upon the Yankee notions, or upon the Musical

Philosopher of the placid Brook Farm, where no cymbals or the rolling of drums disturb the music of Nature, except perhaps the many peals of the gong for their social frugal dinners."

41. This work is no. 4 in *Presentazioni Musicali: Four Fantasies for the Voice and Pianoforte.*

42. Russell, *Cheer! Boys, Cheer!* 159–73.

43. Hamm, *Yesterdays,* 176–84, 219.

44. Many of these songs can be found in MftN or in LEVY.

45. On the Hutchinson Family, see Cockrell, *Excelsior,* 137, 228, 399, and passim, as well as Hutchinson's *Story.* The account of Sam Houston's daughter is in a booklet by Daniel Agnew entitled *Kaskakunk, or Kuskuskee, The Great Delaware Town on the Big Beaver River* (Pittsburgh: Myers, Shinkle & Co., 1894).

46. Finson, "The Romantic Savage," 269.

47. See chap. 9 for a discussion of a quickstep used to inspire a Hollywood General Custer in his battling of the Indians in *They Died with Their Boots On.*

48. *The Indian War Hoop* suggests, for the first time in Western composition, an attempt to depict what Robert Stevenson has called "unalloyed aboriginal song." See Stevenson, "Written Sources," 25.

49. Foreman, *Indians Abroad,* 132–46.

50. Mathews, *The Osages,* 544–55. Mathews doesn't cite a specific source for this information.

51. Paul Le Jeune first wrote about the chichiguoan in *Relation de ce qui s'est passé en la Nouvelle France* (1635). "They do not strike it, as do our Europeans," he wrote, "but they turn and shake it, to make the stones rattle inside." Cited in Whaples, *Exoticism in Dramatic Music,* 363–64.

52. As Marta Grabócz has demonstrated, nineteenth-century composers relied upon basic semantic units (which she calls *semes*) singly or in combination, the intent often to convey identity or narrativity in music. For more on musical syntax and musical intonation in the stylistic context of one composer (Liszt), see Grabócz, "The Role of Semiotical Terminology," 196–218.

53. Hagan, *Félicien David,* 120–21.

54. A copy of Hewitt's "Indian Polka" is available in LEVY.

55. Much of Lumbye's music, including the ballet, was lost in a fire. Orchestral musicians, apparently out of love for the composer, reconstructed some of the most popular works from surviving parts and "from memory." See the liner notes by Svend Erik Sorenson to *"The Strauss of the North": More Galops, Marches, and Dances* (Unicorn-Kanchara DKP-CD 9143). The text for the vaudeville/ballet *Fjernt fra Danmark* was published without music in 1860. It also included compositions by Gottschalk. Lumbye's music for this "war dance" was included on the above-mentioned recording, performed by the Odense Symphony Orchestra with Peter Guth, conductor. Whether the tambourine was added in the reconstruction is not clear.

Chapter 4: "In the Glory of the Sunset"

1. First quote from Buell, introduction to *Selected Poems,* xxix. See a more recent edition of *Hiawatha* in McClatchy, ed., *Henry Wadsworth Longfellow.* The idea of the noble

savage as reminder is paraphrased from Judith Elise Braun, who discusses nineteenth-century whites' opinions of Indians in "North American Indian Exhibits," 8–9.

2. From an unsigned review in *The Knickerbocker,* vol. 46 (1855): 630.

3. The similarity of poetic rhythm and narrative style between *The Song of Hiawatha* and the *Kalevala* may best be seen in early English translations of the Finnish epic. See, for example, W. F. Kirby's translation for Everyman's Library (London: Dent, n.d. [ca. 1907]).

4. Kennedy, *Henry W. Longfellow,* 85. A complete list of musical settings derived from *Hiawatha* would be too extensive to list here. See "Longfellow" in Hovland, *Musical Settings,* 177–245, as well as additional *Hiawatha* titles missed by Hovland in Pisani, *Exotic Sounds,* 158 and 202–203.

5. The text of *The Song of Hiawatha* is now available complete online at several Web sites.

6. Dorson, *Folklore and Fakelore,* 6. Roy Harvey Pearce wrote that Longfellow "saw how the mass of Indian legends which Schoolcraft was collecting depicted noble savages out of time, and offered, if treated right, a kind of primitive example of the very progress which had done them in." See Pearce, *Savages of America,* 192.

7. Various forthcoming performances were mentioned in Dwight's *Journal,* vol. 14, no. 4 (23 Oct. 1858): 240, in the New York *Evening Post* (n.d., 1858), and in the New York *Musical World,* vol. 20, no. 5 (31 July 1858): 482. Krohn, in *A Century of Missouri Music,* 16, writes—erroneously perhaps—that the cantata was written for eight voices, chorus, and orchestra, and "was produced at St. Louis several times in the year 1860." The [undated] program, presumably from the first performance, published by E. P. Studley in St. Louis, 1858, may be found at the Missouri Historical Society and the Minnesota Historical Society. The program includes Karst's complete libretto. The music for both the Karst and Miquel pieces is now lost. As Miquel died in 1857, his *Tone-Paintings of the Far West* must have been composed before that time. The individual movements were titled: I. "Buffalo Hunt." Fanfare for Orchestra; II. "Lullaby"; III. "The Fireflies." Caprice; and IV. "The First Steamboat." (In the late 1850s, there was already a steamship called the *Hiawatha.*) Biographical information on Emile Karst may be found in Stevens, *St. Louis,* 716, as well as in a clippings file at the Missouri Historical Society Archives.

8. See the footnote appended to the description of the "Black-Robe Chief" in the original edition. Longfellow's source was Jacques Marquette's *Voyage et découvertes de quelques pays et nations de l'Amérique Septentrionale* (Paris: E. Michallet, 1681), section V.

9. Copies of Stoepel's *Hiawatha* Symphony can be found at the Library of Congress, the Music Collection of the New York Public Library, Houghton Library at Harvard University, the Boston Public Library, and the British Library. A microfilm is available through Vanderbilt University Library.

10. *New York Times* (22 Feb. 1859): 4.

11. Among Heron's most famous roles were Marguerite Gauthier in her own translation of Dumas's *La dame aux camélias* and Nancy in *Oliver Twist.* The information on Stoepel's life has been culled from several scattered sources. Among the more substantive are "An Old Musician Dead," obituary, *New York Times* (2 Oct. 1887): 16; a post-mortem set of additions to the obituary, *New York Times* (9 Oct. 1887): 14; James A. Browne, "Correspondence: R. Stoepel," (London) *Monthly Musical Record* 37 (1 May

1907): 104; and Odell, *Annals of the New York Stage,* passim. For more detailed information on Stoepel's theatrical career, see Pisani, *Music in the Theatre: The Melo-Dramatic Tradition in Nineteenth-Century London and New York* (University of Iowa Press, forthcoming).

12. Stoepel probably began work on *Hiawatha* between 1856 and 1857, about the time that he had undertaken conducting a series of choral-orchestral promenade concerts at the New York Academy of Music, and not, as one writer in the *New York Times* later alleged, as original incidental music to Walcot's *Hiawatha, or, Ardent Spirits and Laughing Water,* the burlesque mentioned earlier for which Stoepel had led the orchestra at Wallack's Theatre in one of its revivals. See the obituary additions, *New York Times* (9 Oct. 1887): 14.

13. In the only surviving music for an unknown British production of *The Octoroon* (in the Drury Lane Collection of music manuscripts, British Library), Wahnotee is not musically characterized.

14. The Stoepel letters of the Longfellow-Stoepel correspondence are at Houghton Library, Harvard University, and have not been published. Longfellow's letters to Stoepel have never been found.

15. Tompkins, *History of the Boston Theatre,* 43.

16. John Sullivan Dwight in *Dwight's Journal* 14, no. 16 (15 Jan. 1859): 335.

17. Ibid.

18. The first quotation is from an unsigned review in the *New York Evening Post* (11 Jan. 1859): 2. New York's *Musical World* critic Richard Storrs Willis related that "Mr. Longfellow was immensely interested [in Stoepel's *Hiawatha*] and attended all the rehearsals and readings." *Musical World* 21, no. 4: 52. Longfellow's 8 Jan. 1859 entry appears in S. Longfellow, *Henry Wadsworth Longfellow,* vol. 2, 368.

19. New York's *Spirit of the Times* (5 Mar. 1859): 217.

20. Re the 1861 performance: See the [London] *Musical World,* vol. 39, no. 7 (16 Feb. 1861): 109, and an anonymous foreign correspondent's "The Diarist in London: Light Reading for Hot Weather,"*Dwight's Journal* 19 (27 July 1861): 130–32. Two years after *Hiawatha*, another work on an American Indian subject, William Vincent Wallace's *The Desert Flower* (1863), would be given at Convent Garden. Perhaps Wallace, who married Stoepel's sister and spent some years in America, was stimulated by *Hiawatha* (as well as *The Green Bushes*) in his setting of an idyllic tale of Indian-white encounters in the New World.

Re the 1863 performance: See *Spirit of the Times* (21 Nov. 1863), unpaginated clipping in the extra-illustrated volume for Matilda Heron, Harvard Theater Collection, Houghton Library, Harvard University. The singers for the 1863 performance were J. M. Mott, mezzo soprano, W. Castle, tenor, and S. C. Campbell, baritone.

Re the score: William Hall's published vocal score seems to be the only surviving music from *Hiawatha.* So far, my attempts to locate a full score and a set of parts have been unsuccessful.

Re the dedication: I have been unable to trace any connection between Gottschalk and Stoepel. Perhaps Gottschalk had been one of those whom Stoepel identified as having offered "flattering opinion," but it would have had to have been around the time of the revival and not the first performances in 1859. Gottschalk was in Puerto Rico from July

1857 to July 1858 and then was off to Venezuela, Martinique, and elsewhere, not to return to New York—or indeed anywhere in the United States—until February 1862.

21. *Boston Courier* (13 Jan. 1859), repr. in *Dwight's Journal* 14, no. 17 (22 Jan. 1859): 338–40; *Dwight's Journal* 14, no. 16 (15 Jan. 1859): 334–35.

22. Unfortunately, we can't compare Stoepel's *Hiawatha* with a similar work written at the same time, Edward Sobolewski's *Mohega, the Flower of the Forest* (1859, Milwaukee). The opera dealt with a Pocahontas–John Smith type of love affair, but the score has disappeared.

23. Dwight in *Dwight's Journal* 14, no. 16 (15 Jan. 1859): 334; unsigned review in the *Boston Courier* (13 Jan. 1859), repr. in *Dwight's Journal* 14, no. 17 (22 Jan. 1859): 338; and probably the music critic Henry C. Watson in *Leslie's Illustrated* (22 Jan. 1859): 120.

24. *Dwight's Journal* 14, no. 16 (15 Jan. 1859): 334.

25. Charles Seymour, *New York Times* (22 Feb. 1859): 4

26. The pentatonicism was perhaps what led one reviewer to describe the movement as "more Scotch than Indian"; see "Dramatic Feuilleton: Academy of Music" in *The* [New York] *Saturday Press,* 26 Feb. 1859. Stoepel was the first to capture a quality that I refer to in later chapters as "ancestral," and the same four-note melody would much later be used by MacDowell, Victor Herbert, and many others to convey this quality.

27. Author identified only as a "Stray Musician in Modern Athens," *Dwight's Journal* 14, no. 16 (15 Jan. 1859): 334.

28. It was easy to measure genuine audience appreciation. The audience simply applauded until the performers repeated the number. Reviewers often noted such replayings. In addition, a movement might be "encored" more than once. One positive byproduct was that the audience gained a greater familiarity with the music. A drawback, of course, was that concerts became too long.

29. The "jig-like" quote appeared in *Dwight's Journal* 14, no. 16 (15 Jan. 1859): 334–35. The anonymous response was published in *Dwight's Journal* 14, no. 18 (29 Jan. 1859): 350–51.

30. Willis's review of the New York performance appeared in the New York *Musical World* 21, no. 9 (26 Feb. 1859): 131.

31. "The Diarist in London," 130–32.

32. Fry comments in the *New York Tribune* are quoted in "*Israel in Egypt* Again," *Dwight's Journal* 14, no. 23 (5 Mar. 1859): 391.

33. See the review of Longfellow's *Hiawatha* in the *Saturday Review* (10 Nov. 1855): 34.

34. This information was derived from notes found in MacDowell's "Sketch Book, April 22, 1887" at the MacDowell Colony. See Lowens, *New York Years of Edward MacDowell,* 55.

35. The Bostonians' responses were primarily to Dvořák's discussion of "Negro melodies." See Block, "Boston Talks Back to Dvořák," 10–15.

36. Of the ninety-page full score in the Archives of the Delius Trust, London, pp. 4–17 and 46–53 are missing. Delius himself may well have borrowed the missing pages himself to incorporate sections of the music (or even the pages themselves) into other compositions. An excerpt from Delius's *Hiawatha* appears in Fenby, *Delius,* 40, and a facsimile of the first page of the ms. score is included in Lowe, *Frederick Delius,* 16. Beecham is

quoted in Lowe, *Frederick Delius,* 36–37. On the documentary, see Threlfall, *Catalogue,* 126. Threlfall notes (in his *Supplementary Catalogue,* 1986, p. 70) that Delius's *Hiawatha* was transcribed and (in part) transposed for Norwegian television by Andrew J. Boyle and recorded in Oslo in 1983.

37. See, for example, Clapham, "Dvořák and the American Indian." Following the lead of other Dvořák scholars such as Sourek, Sychra, and Clapham, Michael Beckerman has written extensively about these connections; see the bibliography. On the idea for Dvořák's *Hiawatha* opera, see Thurber, "Dvořák as I Knew Him." See also Beckerman's study of Dvořák's *Hiawatha* sketches in his *New Worlds of Dvořák,* 66–76.

38. Kovařík's 1927 letter to Otakar Sourek is cited in Beckerman, "Dvořák's 'New World' Largo," 36. Also see Beckerman, *New Worlds of Dvořák,* 25–39. Hepokoski suggests that the Largo is a complete picture of canto 20, "The Famine," but that Dvořák delayed Minnehaha's death until the symphony's fourth movement; see Hepokoski, "Culture Clash." This argument seems difficult to support.

39. To understand Dvořák's sensitivity to the work's ethnic associations, compare the two versions of the C♯ minor theme in the second movement (*poco meno mosso*)—the one in the printed score (revised?) and that in Krehbiel's article (original?). The latter has a melodic cadence commonly associated with "Indian" themes; the "Scottish snap" of the former (possibly a revision) exhibits a more international flavor.

40. An interpretation of this Scherzo as a *mélodrame* with Longfellow's text can be heard on the CD accompanying Beckerman's *New Worlds of Dvořák.*

41. *Scenes from the "Song of Hiawatha"* (three cantatas for soli, chorus, and orchestra): part 1 (op. 30, no. 1), *Hiawatha's Wedding Feast* (London: Novello, 1898); part 2 (op. 30, no. 2), *The Death of Minnehaha* (London: Novello, 1899); and part 3 (op. 30, no. 4), *Hiawatha's Departure* (London: Novello, 1900). The *Overture to the Song of Hiawatha* (op. 30, no. 3), composed in 1899, is based on an African American spiritual and is not related thematically to the three Hiawatha cantatas. It was intended to be played between parts 2 and 3, according to Tortolano, *Samuel Coleridge-Taylor,* 44. On the ballet, see Tortolano, 292.

42. "I am always a champion of Dvořák," Coleridge-Taylor wrote in the last year of his life; see Berwick Sayers, *Samuel Coleridge-Taylor,* 71. On the similarities to MacDowell's "Indian" Suite, compare especially *Hiawatha's Wedding Feast,* vocal score, p. 20, mm. 1–2, with MacDowell's suite, 1st movement, mm. 22–23. Coleridge-Taylor's publisher sent him a copy of Cowen's song ca. 1898, and received the reply: "Evidently Onaway's lover in Mr. Cowen's conception is a very different—and less sentimental, less languid—person from mine." Quoted in Berwick Sayers, *Samuel Coleridge-Taylor,* 67.

43. On the importance of the Gounod influence, see Nigel Burton, "Oratorios and Cantatas," chap. 10 in Temperley, *Romantic Age: 1800–1914,* 228–29, and passim by other authors in the volume: 13, 115, 154, 181, 199, 200–201, 226, and 332.

44. Berwick Sayers, *Samuel Coleridge-Taylor,* 108, 120, and 144.

45. Some sources say 2,000 people attended. The 1,500 figure is from Tortolano, though "nearly 3,000 people were turned away" at the public rehearsal. Tortolano, *Samuel Coleridge-Taylor,* 32.

46. Berwick Sayers, *Samuel Coleridge-Taylor,* 161–62. Constitution Hall ("Convention Hall") is the same space in which, in 1939, Marian Anderson was not permitted to

sing because of her African ancestry. This coincidence reminds us that racial tolerance in America has experienced many cycles rather than following a steady upward growth.

47. See Booker T. Washington's preface to Coleridge-Taylor's *Twenty-Four Negro Melodies Transcribed for the Piano* (Boston: Oliver Ditson, 1905). The "thirteenth [*Hiawatha*] performance" is cited in Berwick Sayers, *Samuel Coleridge-Taylor,* 200. The Chicago performance was reviewed by W. S. B. Matthews in the Chicago-based *Music* 20 (1901): 32; he erroneously refers to *Hiawatha's Wedding Feast* as "Hiawatha's Wooing."

48. The series of three-note sequences actually employs the pitches in a full seven-note scale (Aeolian mode) and are not strictly pentatonic.

49. Chap. 7 discusses the use of pentatonicism in Indian settings at the turn of the twentieth century.

50. One might also describe this style as an artful combination of the standard methods of duet construction inherited from Italian operatic traditions: "similar" duets, in which the second character repeats the music of the first, and "dissimilar" ones, in which the second offers contrasting music. See Budden, *Operas of Verdi,* vol. 1, 17–18.

51. Statistics on performances are included in Tortolano, *Samuel Coleridge-Taylor,* 31. A review of the 1924 *Hiawatha* by "H. F." appeared in the *Musical Times* (1 June 1924): 551. For a summary of the cast changes and modifications made in Fairbairn's stagings from year to year, see Self, *Hiawatha Man,* 270–72. Oskenonton's participation is observed in Taylor, "Indian Hobbyist Movement," 563.

52. R[eginald] Nettel's *Music in the Five Towns,* n.p., is quoted at length by the composer's daughter in A. Coleridge-Taylor, *Heritage,* 39.

Chapter 5: Ethnographic Encounters

1. Greeley "The Plains," 92.

2. For background on the Indian-white conflict behind the Indian wars of the nineteenth century, see McNickle, *They Came Here First,* chap. 1.

3. Rosaldo, *Culture and Truth,* 71–72, and Pearce, *Savages of America,* 129.

4. In his argumentative but highly influential scientific examination of social phenomena, Spencer applied Charles Darwin's theory of the evolution of biological species to that of human society. His earliest writings on this subject actually preceded those of Darwin. He later changed his original opinion of inherited abilities to concur with Darwin's findings of natural selection and is known for coining the term "survival of the fittest" (in *The Principles of Biology,* vol. 1, 1864). Morgan (in *The League of the Iroquois,* 1851, and *Systems of Consanguinity and Affinity of the Human Family,* 1870) pioneered the study of kinship systems, and his distinctions between primitive society and civil society and his materialist theory of cultural evolution in terms of technology influenced Marx and Engels. Morgan's historical inquiries eventually culminated in his 1877 theory of social evolution (*Ancient Society*), a crucial element in the early stages of the disciplines of anthropology and sociology.

5. American Indians were regularly featured as exotic attractions in circuses at the turn of the century. One section in E. T. Paull's sheet music for *The Circus Parade* (1904) is designated the "*Grand Entre* (Cossacks, Indians, Elephants, Camels, etc.)." See the facsimile in Schleifer, *Three Centuries,* vol. 2. On Cody's use of music in the Wild West

shows, see Masterson, *Sounds of the Frontier,* especially 108–89. Masterson provides a measure-by-measure analysis (179–88) of Karl King's *Passing of the Red Man: Indian Characteristic* (Oskaloosa, Iowa: C. L. Barnhouse, 1916), written for Cody during his last years as a showman. King composed this work too late, however, to be influential on most of the music discussed in the next two chapters. The cornet part of King's piece is reprinted in Masterson's appendix 3 (319). On the dime novel, see Berkhofer, *White Man's Indian,* 97–99. Some examples of this type of popular novel, which catered to tastes for the stereotyped Indian, are Ann Sophia Winterbotham's *Malaeska, the Indian Wife of the White Hunter* and Edward S. Ellis's *Seth Jones, or, The Captive of the Frontier.*

6. Slotkin, *Gunfighter Nation,* 22. America would continue to explore other real and imaginary frontiers throughout the twentieth century, Slotkin argues (56).

7. Turner, "Significance of the Frontier."

8. *Journal of American Folklore* 1, no. 1 (Apr.–June 1888): 5. The four other categories of "fast-vanishing" folklore were relics of old English (ballads, superstitions, etc.); Southern Black; French Canadian; and Mexican.

9. Ibid., 6.

10. Origins of the forty-three songs in Baker's dissertation, using Baker's original Roman numbering: Songs I–X, Notated from "one of the most skilled singers" following a harvest festival in a Seneca village in western New York; Songs XI–XXXII, Collected during a visit to the "School for Indian Youth" at Carlisle, Pennsylvania; Song XXXIII, From Schoolcraft, vol. 5; Songs XXXIV–XXXVIII, From T. W. Chittenden of Appleton, Wisconsin; Chittenden, who transcribed the songs, then sent them to Baker; Songs in No. XXXIX, From M. Eels, Washington Territory [Eels had already published twenty-four Indian tunes in *American Antiquarian* 1 (1878–79): 49–53.]; Song XL, From Keating, vol. 1; Song XLI, Unspecified source; Songs XLII, From Wilkes, vol. 4, 200; Songs in No. XLIII, First two from R. H. Hamilton, Vancouver (transcribed at Baker's request); second two from Rev. T. L. Riggs, Dakota Territory. In addition to the forty-three songs, Baker's dissertation includes a critical analysis of their melodic and harmonic structures; Baker based this analysis on only the first thirty-two songs, those that he himself had heard and transcribed.

11. See Adler, "Umfang, Methode und Ziel."

12. The circumstances for the dictation of Indian music varied considerably, as did the degree of Westernization, for some of the informants (Mark, *Stranger in Her Native Land,* 221). As Mark has observed (240), the early ethnologists pioneered the methodology of "dual vision," the ability to look at another society from within and without, sympathetically and analytically. Before "participant observation" acquired the status of a discipline in anthropology, "it was invented by Alice Fletcher among the Omahas, Frank Cushing among the Zunis, and Franz Boas among the Eskimos and Kwakiutls." For more on Indianist ethnographers, see the examples and biographical information in *WAIM.* For their publications, see Bonnerjea, *Index to Bulletins.*

13. Fletcher and LaFlesche, *Study of Omaha Indian Music;* pages 59–77 consist of Fillmore's "Report on the Structural Peculiarities of the Music."

14. Powers identifies the North American hobbyist movement as having begun around

1900 and links it with Ernest Seton and the founding of the Boy Scouts, but the practice of collecting Indian artifacts, exploring Native American customs and folklore, and dressing in tribal garb already existed as a protohobby in the early nineteenth century for Americans such as Henry Rowe Schoolcraft and Lewis Henry Morgan, who developed participatory interests in Indian lore decades before ethnography had been established as a systematic discipline. Powers sees the publications of hobbyists in the twentieth century, their later contributions about Indian folklore to mainstream publications such as *Boys' Life,* and their enactment of powwows to be partly responsible for the resurgence in the 1960s of powwows among many indigenous groups of North America, a phenomenon that anthropologists have linked with the "pan-Indian" movement. See Powers, "Indian Hobbyist Movement," 558. Edward E. Ayer (1841–1927) was also the first president of Chicago's Field Museum of Natural History from 1893 to 1899; see *Dictionary of American Biography* (New York: Scribner, 1928–58), vol. 1, 448–49.

15. Troyer called the Zuni "the cliff dwellers of the Southwest"; see *Musical Courier* 37 (4 July 1898): [27] as well as the "Carlos Troyer" entry in *The New Grove Dictionary of American Music,* eds. H. Wiley Hitchock and Stanley Sadie (New York: Grove's Dictionaries of Music, 1986). Apparently Troyer had previously traveled in Brazil and collected tribal songs that were honorably recognized by the Brazilian government. His Zuni music exhibits virtually no trace of indigenous elements. Charles Lummis, the famed Southwest photographer, questioned the veracity of Troyer's accounts, and Frederick W. Hodge, director of the Southwest Museum in Los Angeles from 1932 to 1955, called Troyer "an old faker; he never lived among any Indians" (cited in Farwell, *Wanderjahre of a Revolutionist,* 113, n. 7). The Frank Hamilton Cushing collection in the Southwest Museum contains nothing to verify that Troyer ever traveled with Cushing. Since it is unlikely that he would have made the perilous journey into the Zuni territory, he probably crafted his musical settings from melodies that Cushing gave him afterward. Charles W. Cadman, on the other hand, wrote that Troyer, who was "not satisfied" with the task of interpreting Cushing's songs, "himself made a prolonged visit to this tribe and obtained their traditional lore"; see Cadman's introduction to Troyer, *Indian Music Lecture,* v. While Fillmore already had at least one work based on Omaha Indian themes in manuscript (1890), Troyer's *Two Zuñi Songs* of 1893 (dedicated to Cushing) are the first known published compositions said to be based on traditional tribal Indian music. Barbara Tedlock, a more recent scholar of Zuni music, gives more credit to Troyer; see her "Songs of the Zuni."

16. On Ediphones and graphophones as tools of transcription, see Mark, *Stranger in Her Native Land,* 231. Cushing's account can be found in "My Adventures in Zuñi." Among others, music critic W. J. Henderson noted in 1887 the shortcomings of "modern musical notation" in his efforts to notate the songs of birds ("The Sportsman's Music," *Century* 34, no. 3 [July 1887]: 417). As the discussion of Indian music intensified over the course of the twentieth century, criticisms were leveled at the early Indian researchers. Nina Marchetti Archabal argues that Frances Densmore's academic background in western European art music actually hindered her efforts to achieve accurate transcriptions ("Frances Densmore," 94–115). Also see *WAIM* for representative examples of some period transcriptions. Fletcher described her experience with recordings in "Indian Songs

and Music," 90. These wax cylinders are now at the American Folklife Center, Library of Congress and many are also available online, along with the rest of her collection, at http://memory.loc.gov/ammem/omhhtml/omhhome.html.

17. In 1965 Bruno Nettl observed that studies of Indian musics in North America (north of Mexico) constituted six main areas. He grouped the musical traditions by region as follows: (1) the Northwest Coast–Eskimo area (2) the California-Yuman area; (3) the Great Basin of Nevada, Utah, and northern interior California; (4) Athabascan (including Navaho and Apache); (5) Plains-Pueblo (Plains: Blackfoot, Crow, Dakota, Comanche, Kiowa; Pueblo: Hopi, Zuni, Taos); and (6) eastern United States and southern Canada. Nettl noted that his distinctions between regions were statistical "in that they depend on the frequency of a given trait rather than its simple presence or absence." See Nettl, "The American Indians," 156–62.

18. Mooney is quoted in Sousa, *National, Patriotic, and Topical Airs,* 59. For more on Mooney's Cherokee transcriptions, see his "Cherokee Ball Play." "Híganúyahí" is available in facsimile in *WAIM,* 34–35 and 247–48.

19. See Ramsey, "Francis LaFlesche." LaFlesche's comments—from his private papers—are cited in Mark, *Stranger in Her Native Land,* 47.

20. On quarter-tones see Stumpf, "Lieder der Bellakula." About 1885, according to Henry Krehbiel ("Folk-Music in Chicago, I"), Hagenbeck of Hamburg (later a traveling showman dealing with trained animals) brought nine Bella Coola to Germany, where they entertained with their songs and dances. A facsimile of Nuskilusta's song is in *WAIM,* 53–54. On notational symbols, see Boas, "On Certain Songs and Dances," 50.

21. In a later article Fillmore cited the song and indicated it was the one originally submitted to him; see John C. Fillmore, "A Study of Indian Music," *Century Magazine* 47, no. 4 (Feb. 1894): 616. Fillmore's manuscript of the *Indian Fantasia* is at the Library of Congress (copyrighted 30 July 1890). On Fletcher, Mark recalls an incident recorded in Sidney Lanier's diary from 1873 in which the ethnologist approached the flutist after one of his concerts. She was overwhelmed by two of his compositions that quoted birdsong of his native Georgia. She informed Lanier that "he must become the founder of a truly American music." Though we may never know all the reasons, it is tempting to deduce from this early encounter that Alice Fletcher's initial motivation for studying Indian culture was probably at least partly fueled by her desire to find an indigenous source for American music. See Mark, *Stranger in Her Native Land,* 16–17.

22. Quotes are from Rydell, *All the World's a Fair,* 15–16, 25. See also Braun, "North American Indian Exhibits," 26–39.

23. Howells's comments are in "Letters from an Altrurian Traveller," *Cosmopolitan Magazine* 16 (1893), cited in Rydell, 40. The bibliography regarding musical events at the fair is too substantial to summarize here; an overview may be found in Guion, "From Yankee Doodle," 81–96. The Hughes quotation is from his *Contemporary American Composers,* 376.

24. For more on the individual cultures represented in the 1893 midway, see Badger, *Great American Fair.* For a critical analysis of the fair as a turning point in American cultural history, see Trachtenberg, *Incorporation of America,* 208–34. For a catalog of surviving cylinders in the Benjamin Ives Gilman Collection relating to the fair, see Lee, *Early Anthologies.*

25. Mark, *Stranger in Her Native Land,* 235–36. Fletcher's paper was later published in both *Music* and *Music Review* ("Music as Found in Certain North American Indian Tribes"). Benjamin Ives Gilman and others disagreed with her on many of her conclusions.

26. Fillmore, "Woman's Song," 285.

27. Guion offers a sampling of comments in "From Yankee Doodle," 92–96.

28. Rosewater, originally quoted in the *Omaha Bee,* is cited in Rydell, *All the World's a Fair,* 111 fn. (On Dvořák's visit to Omaha in 1893 to see Rosewater, see letter in Tibbetts, *Dvořák in America,* 399.) James Mooney, the representative for the Bureau of American Ethnology, was one of those to express great disappointment at the exposition's commercialization (Rydell, 117). McKinley anecdote, described in the *Omaha Bee,* is cited in Rydell, 122.

29. Fletcher, *Indian Story and Song,* vii.

30. See "National Congress of Musicians: Omaha (I)," 27. Homer Moore was the chair of the congress, and the others on the executive committee were Louis C. Elson (Boston), William H. Sherwood (Chicago), Adolph Foerster (Pittsburgh), Ernest R. Kroeger (St. Louis), and John C. Fillmore (Claremont, California). On Krehbiel's transcription, see his "Folk-Music in Chicago, II." Burton wrote in his posthumously published *American Primitive Music* (1909), 190: "The 'Dance of Pau-Puk-Keewis' . . . was written years before I had become an enthusiast in our primitive music. For the limited purpose it was designed to serve, the Indian theme was decidedly useful, and development was spontaneous." Burton does not give many dates, so it is difficult to pinpoint exactly when he "had become an enthusiast." However, he does provide a clue in one passage from *American Primitive Music* that his consideration of Fletcher's publication and his own use of a Kwakiutl tune occurred at roughly the same time: "My attitude years ago toward the Omaha songs collected by Miss Fletcher [1893] was doubtless that of many another musician who examined them. Most of them repelled me by their manifest crudity. I saw and felt the rudiments of form in some of them, but they impressed me as incomplete and dull, considered as tunes, and wholly barren of suggestion. I was eager to find thematic material in them and could not do so. My eagerness may be fully appreciated when I explain that I was then at work on the composition of 'Hiawatha,' and that I wished to give the music a distinctively American color if I could. The best I could do was to use a Kwakiutl song as a theme for the Dance of Paupukkeewis in which I aimed frankly not at beauty but at something bizarre and barbaric" (18–19).

31. Fletcher, *Indian Story and Song,* viii.

32. Information about the fair as a whole can be found in Rydell, 155–83. How North American Indians were to be presented at the fair has been examined by Trennert, "Resurrection of Native Arts and Crafts"; it is evident from this account that "political correctness" did not originate in the 1960s and '70s. For some insight into how one tribal group of Indians felt about "living in full view of the public," see Nancy J. Parezo and John W. Troutman, "The 'Shy' Cocopa Go to the Fair" (in Meyer and Royer, *Selling the Indian,* 3–43).

33. The orchestral version of Farwell's *Dawn* is based on the piano character piece of the same title (Newton Center, Mass.: Wa-Wan Press 1, no. 4, 1902). "Lo" is cited in Edwards, "Indian Tunes at Exposition." Some of the other works noted were *Zuñi Cradle*

Song and *Lover's Wooing*. Concerts were scheduled daily in several locations throughout the grounds proper, although the more high-minded of these did not draw the expected crowds. The music bureaus for future fairs were therefore advised to schedule more judiciously. After all, people had traveled great distances to see the exhibits, not to sit through concerts, despite the eminent reputation of the guest artists. Expense records of the 1904 fair in St. Louis show attendance to have been much higher at the relatively smaller number of scheduled musical events. There has yet been no study of musical activities at this fair. My information is drawn from "The Work of the Bureau of Music," a typescript courtesy of the Missouri Historical Society.

34. The Coe work (written in 1903) was published in Chicago by Clayton F. Summy in 1905. For a discussion of this work, see L. M., "Melodrama of *Hiawatha*." Some of Farwell's friends and advocates were composers Arne Oldberg, Arthur Shepherd, Ernest Kroeger, Carl Busch, Carlos Troyer, Henry Gilbert, Charles Tomlinson Griffes, Harvey Worthington Loomis, Frederic Ayers, Gena Branscombe, Lawrence Gilman, the singer David Bispham, and poet Kahlil Gibran. See Culbertson, *He Heard American Singing*.

35. Other "lecture-recitalists" in the first decade who used Fletcher's and Farwell's Indian music were baritone Walter Bentley Ball ("Folk Songs of America"), Mrs. Frederick (Eugenia) Crowe ("Illustrated Lecture"), Rita Brezée Rich ("Folk Songs in Costume"), and Rev. and Mrs. William Brewster Humphrey ("An Hour with North American Indians"). Dozens of nonlecturing vocal recitalists, among them the eminent singer-actor David Bispham, used Indian music on their concerts, and many of them sent Farwell copies of their programs; see Farwell, Scrapbook. Even Native Americans became involved in the lecture-recital circuit. On Floating Cloud's performances from 1913–15, see "An Indian Girl's Success," in *New England Conservatory Magazine-Review* 5, no. 3 (Mar. 1915): 145.

36. Unidentified reviewer, *New York Evening Sun* (28 Apr. 1904); clipping in Farwell, Scrapbook.

37. The "Indian echo" played a large role in twentieth-century popular song, as discussed in chap. 8.

38. So did other composers. Arthur Nevin, the lesser-known brother of composer Ethelbert Nevin, was one of these; for information on his research trips with his friend Walter McClintock in 1903–4 and the use of fieldwork for music composition, see his "Two Summers" and McClintock, "Illustrated Lecture." For more on Cadman's fieldwork among the Omahas in the company of Fletcher's collaborator, Francis LaFlesche, in 1910, see Perison, *Charles Wakefield Cadman*, 98–99, and Cadman's own "Anent That Injun Music." Lieurance had close ties to the Crow Reservation through his brother, who was a physician there, and was employed by the U.S. government from 1905 to make recordings of music of several Indian tribes; see "Lieurance Recognized Authority" and "Lieurance, Thurlow" in *National Cyclopaedia of American Biography* 51:638.

39. Curtis's lectures are noted in Archabal, "Frances Densmore," 98. Her acorn-grinding songs appear in Curtis, *Songs of Ancient America* (New York: Schirmer, 1905). She studied with Ferruccio Busoni in Berlin and with Julius Kniese in Bayreuth. I have not been able to locate the source in which Densmore said it was Cosima Wagner who had urged her to study the music of the American Indians. Roosevelt sent a supporting letter to Curtis for the publication of her *Indians' Book* (1907) and also wrote the foreword to

Edward Curtis's *The North American Indian* (1907–30). His ridicule, however, is observed in Slotkin, *Gunfighter Nation,* 40.

Chapter 6: The Nationalism Controversy

1. Saint-Gaudens's comment is cited in Dippie, *Vanishing American,* 216.

2. Howard's quotation is from *Our American Music,* 415. Among scholars who have written recent articles of special insight into musical Indianism are Block, "Amy Beach's Music on Native American Themes"; Browner, "Breathing the Indian Spirit"; Chase, "'Indianist' Movement"; Levy, "In the Glory of the Sunset"; McNutt, "John Comfort Fillmore"; Smith, "American Indian Music"; and Tawa, "The Pursuit of National Music." Three significant monographs on the subject are Briggs, "North American Indian as Depicted in Musical Compositions"; Browner, *Transposing Cultures;* and Osman, *American "Indianist" Composers.* On European musical nationalism, see Wiora, "Of Art Music and Cultural Classes." Barbara A. Zuck has shown how the desire for "an American school of composition" grew in the 1870s and 1880s in the early days of the Music Teachers National Association, in Frank Van der Stucken's "novelty concerts" at Steinway Hall, and in the formation of the manuscript societies; see her *History of Musical Americanism,* 41–53. The forms that musical nationalism later took after Dvořák's American residence have been simplified and neatly sequenced by Adrienne Fried Block. Expanding upon Hugo Leichtentritt's concept of a "first wave of Americanism," Block notes that "three overlapping waves of consciously nationalist art music arose in America. Each was dependent on the availability in print, in performance, and on recordings of a specific folk or traditional repertory. The first wave of art music was based on Native American music, the second on traditional Black music, and the third—one that Dvořák did not foresee but that nevertheless was inspired through his students—on Anglo-American music." See Block, "Dvořák's Long American Reach," 53.

3. See also Skilton's "Realism," 112–13.

4. According to *Merriam-Webster's Ninth New Collegiate Dictionary* (1984), the term "folk song" entered the English language in 1870.

5. Chase, *America's Music,* 400–401.

6. Ibid., 401.

7. Hallowell, "Impact of the American Indian," 126.

8. See Stumpf, "Lieder der Bellakula-Indianer," and Hallowell, "Impact of the American Indian," 127.

9. From Dvořák, "Dvořák on His New Work." By "native melodies," Dvořák seems to use the term as his contemporaries did, referring inclusively to all culture *native* to America, not in the restrictive sense of Native Americans that the word has today. The earlier *New York* Herald article (21 May), may not have been in fact by Dvořák but rather by Henry Krehbiel; see Tibbetts, *Dvořák in America,* 16.

10. On Dvořák in Spillville, see Spector, "Dvořák's American Period," 8, and Tibbetts, "Dvorak's Spillville Summer," 90–91. Dvořák's "usual place . . . in the front row" was apparently also confirmed by the composer's son, Otakar Dvořák, to John Clapham; see Clapham, "Dvořák and the American Indian," 117. In his memoirs (*Antonín Dvořák,* 23), Otakar recalled that his father persuaded Big Moon and some others "to perform

some Indian dances and songs for us. The program was very nice, and people came to see the Indians perform." After the performance, Dvořák received three photos from the Indians; he kept the photos in his studio until his death. The quintet theme is probably that jotted down at Spillville by his friend Josef Jan Kovařík; see Clapham, "Dvořák and the American Indian," 119.

11. On Dvořák in Chicago, see an unpublished letter from Fillmore to Dvořák (11 Aug. 1893) indicating that he and Fletcher had sent the composer a copy of their *Study;* cited in Clapham, "Dvořák and the American Indian," 118. In the article cited earlier, Dvořák referred to Fillmore only as "a friend": "[I] carefully studied a certain number of Indian melodies which a friend gave me, and became thoroughly imbued with their characteristics—with their spirit, in fact" ("Dvořák on His New Work," 363). Clapham believed that this anonymous friend was Krehbiel. This confusion may have come about because Dvořák himself later admitted the influence of said friend's Indian themes on his "New World" Symphony, even though he had completed the full score on 24 May 1893, three months before the Fletcher/Fillmore contact. Clapham—who spent a great deal of time and ink trying to trace the actual content and source of Native American influence on Dvořák's works—was inclined to believe that the transcriptions of three Iroquois songs in Krehbiel's hand (and found among Dvořák's papers) were the songs to which Dvořák referred. However, Clapham probably knew little of the history behind Fletcher's contact with American composers and her plan for a national school. Dvořák would have had no reason not to identify Krehbiel by name. An editor's comment in a newspaper interview that Dvořák had "made a serious study of the national music of this continent as exemplified in the native melodies of the negro and Indian races" ("Dr. Dvořák's Great Symphony," *New York Herald,* 15 Dec. 1893) has been understood to mean that Dvořák himself undertook the study. Now that we have access to Fillmore's letter and know that Dvořák received a copy of the Fletcher/Fillmore collection, we can suspect that Dvořák's "serious study" consisted of working with their book (and perhaps a few other published sources), not in doing original fieldwork. The St. Paul trip is mentioned in Tibbetts, *Dvořák in America,* 16–17. For an artistic rendering of what Dvořák would have seen, see W. H. Gibson's *Falls of Minnehaha,* engraved by W. H. Morse in a late nineteenth-century edition of *The Poetical Works of Henry Wadsworth Longfellow, Illustrated* (Boston: Houghton Mifflin, 1879), vol. 1, 253. Thurber recalls the Wild West show in "Dvořák as I Knew Him," 382.

12. Speech given at the Music Hall on 12 May 1893 and printed the following day in the *Chicago Tribune* as "For National Music" (13 Aug. 1893).

13. The quotation is from a letter of Dvořák to Mr. and Mrs. Hlavka in Prague, 27 Dec. 1892, repr. in Tibbetts, *Dvořák in America,* 389–91. Bret Harte was known in the 1860s for his short stories dealing with the years of the gold rush. After his American career flagged in the late 1870s, he became consul in Germany and Scotland and was a favorite in European literary circles.

14. See Beckerman, *New Worlds of Dvořák,* 66–76.

15. Brown, "Soviet Russian Concepts of 'Intonazia,'" 559. For more on "intonation," see Zak, "Asaf'ev's Theory."

16. Beckerman's remarks on the Piano Suite and *Poetic Tone Pictures* are in his *New*

Worlds of Dvořák, 156. His comment on the slow movement is from "Dvořák's 'New World' Largo," 42.

17. Smaczny, "E-flat major String Quintet," 240; Beveridge, "Sophisticated Primitivism"; and Beckerman, *New Worlds of Dvořák,* 149.

18. It is true that this same gesture is commonly found in some eastern European folk musics, notably Magyar, Slovak, and Czech.

19. Kreisler's adaptation was published as the "Indianisches Lamento" (Berlin: Simrock, 1910). The original Dvořák movement had already been called the "Indian canzonetta," having been published in 1894 by Simrock separately as op. 100, no. 2, apparently without the composer's authorization.

20. The tonic-minor minor-seventh chord (i^7) is modally ambiguous, especially in an Indian context. Dvořák's "New World" minor seventh is spelled E–G–B–D. This can be a tonic chord in E-natural minor (or in any of the three ancient European modes: Aeolian, Dorian, and Phrygian). It can also be derived, and therefore used with, the so-called minor pentatonic scale: E–G–A–B–D. The chord's harmonic ambiguity may have been part of its allure.

21. Currier, "Edward MacDowell," 17–51. Henry Krehbiel recalled in 1897 that the suite was the result of a conversation in Boston "four or five years ago" ("Music at Worcester"). MacDowell himself referred in journal articles and other writings of 1894 and 1895 simply to his "suite," and it's clear from the musical details that he means the first and not the "Indian" suite. Moreover, the conclusion of the Second Suite resembles the ending of Dvořák's symphony. It is unlikely that the modeling would have occurred in the other direction. See my essay, "Issues of Chronology Surrounding the Composition of MacDowell's 'Indian Suite' (1891–1896)," app. D in *Exotic Sounds,* 573–75.

22. The manuscript of the "Dirge" (at the Boston Public Library) is the only extant sketch of the suite dating from 1891. It may have been composed originally with some other intent in mind. MacDowell's interview, "America's Leading Composer Is Here," appeared in the *San Francisco Chronicle* (3 Jan. 1903): 14. See Brancaleone on the Kiowa song in "Edward MacDowell," 359–81. Richard Crawford's recent analysis of MacDowell's nationalism offers some of the most penetrating insights into this composer's work and philosophy; see his "Edward MacDowell," esp. 551–60. Crawford also synthesizes many of the writings concerning MacDowell's use of Indian themes.

23. MacDowell's program of instruction is quoted in the preface to his *Critical and Historical Essays,* iii.

24. Margery Lowens cites Baker's acceptance of MacDowell's invitation in *New York Years,* 69, fn. 275; see also Levy, *Edward MacDowell,* 134, n. 80. Paur conducted the suite from MacDowell's manuscript, and the score was published the following year in Germany by Breitkopf and Härtel.

25. MacDowell's remarks were cited in the Boston Symphony program notes by William F. Apthorp.

26. Orchestral score, 13, rehearsal letter E.

27. Crawford provides a concise overview of the "Indian" Suite and a close reading of its fourth movement in "Edward MacDowell," 551–55. MacDowell composed the "Dirge" in 1891, a few years before the rest of the suite. The oft-cited relationship of its

principal theme to a Kiowa melody in Baker's thesis, although noted even in MacDowell's time, has always seemed to me tenuous at best. Francis Brancaleone has built an even more elaborate argument on this relationship, and he extends the connection to many of MacDowell's other works; see his "Edward MacDowell and Indian Motives," 366–67. If one is not fully convinced of the Kiowa derivation of the falling minor-second/augmented-fourth motive in the "Dirge," however, his whole argument of MacDowell's use of that theme in other works collapses.

28. For an interesting interpretation of MacDowell's style using the methods of Jan LaRue, see Sorce, *Investigation of Compositional Techniques.* The "Women's Dance Song" from Baker is available in facsimile in *WAIM,* 44–45.

29. See the discussion of "Miantowona" in Samuels, *Thomas Bailey Aldrich.* The mood and content of the piano miniature "To A Water-Lily" in the set *Woodland Sketches* (1896) does not seem to reflect the influence of Aldrich's poem, either.

30. For Baker on modes of the "Ancients," see *Über die Musik,* 76–77. MacDowell does not include mode (other than the "oriental" type of augmented seconds and diminished thirds) in his classification of national music features; see MacDowell, "Folk Song," 151–53. Nordic musical identity would later be taken up with gusto by Percy Grainger and Henry Cowell, among others. For a study of Grainger's writings on Nordic characteristics in music and his belief that "Nordic music is the voice of the wide open spaces [and] the soul of virgin nature made manifest," see Ross, "Percy Grainger's Nordic Revolt," 53–65. For Cowell's strong early interest in Celtic music (as well as his correspondence with Grainger), see Lichtenwanger, *Music of Henry Cowell,* 1–30 passim.

31. See Hovgaard, *Voyages of the Norsemen,* Gathorne-Hardy, trans., *Norse Discoverers of America,* and Gray, *Leif Eriksson.* It should be mentioned that Henry Gilbert, twenty years after his studies with MacDowell, also noted Thorfinn Karlsefni's secondary historical position in "Personal Recollections of Edward MacDowell," 497.

32. Baker quotes the tune in *Über die Musik,* 40. The mistaken identity between the "Old Indian Hymn" and SHOSHONEE has already been noted by Robert Stevenson in "English Sources," 412–14. In the preface to his *Indian Melodies,* Commuck made it clear that his collection was a business venture, but also that by striving toward Christian civilization he hoped to counter the prejudice of "enlightened American people" against Indians. Oddly, MacDowell calls SHOSHONEE a "Russian tune" in his folk music essay; see *Critical and Historical Essays,* 153. MacDowell's love of the Celtic is quoted in Gilman, *Edward MacDowell,* 136.

33. Recalled in Currier, "Edward MacDowell," 37.

34. Krehbiel's three quotations are from "Music of the Omahas," "Music at Worcester," and "Folk-Music Studies: Songs of the American Indians," *New York Tribune* (Illustrated Supplement, 8 Oct. 1899): 15. For a summary of the nationalist views of the "wise men of Boston" (which included one woman), see Block, "Boston Talks Back to Dvořák." Given Krehbiel's interest in the Indian element of MacDowell's suite, it is surprising to note that in October 1896—almost a year before the Worcester review but eight months after the suite's premiere—Krehbiel did not seem to be aware of the Indian connection, or if he was, he never mentioned it in his discussion of the work for a three-column article on MacDowell; see *New York Daily Tribune* (11 Oct. 1896), II:3. Krehbiel's "right man" comment is from his "Indian Melodies" article.

35. Hale, "MacDowell's Suite," 23. I have been trying to locate Reginald de Koven's "rich storehouse" of themes of which Hale speaks but have had no luck. His "Indian Love Song" (Schirmer, 1891) is based on a Hindu poem. De Koven scholar Orly Krasner noted (in a conversation with the author) that criticism was often leveled at de Koven for borrowing folk tunes from other cultures, but she was unaware that he himself had ever collected Indian melodies. Based on views he expressed in an 1895 article entitled "Nationality in Music and the American Composer," it is doubtful whether de Koven would have been sympathetic to MacDowell's (or anybody else's) use of Indian music. Here he wrote: "The Indian melodies represent a dying race, whose influence upon or even connection with this country as a nation has long since passed away"; see Seidl, *Music in the Modern World,* vol. 1, 192.

36. The "milk and water" quotation appears in Garland, *Roadside Meetings,* 322. In his prefatory notes to *Über die Musik* (40–41), Baker provided an example of how this "Harvest Song," which MacDowell used as his cyclical motto, would be performed in context, drumbeat and all. MacDowell therefore had clear access to at least a "written model" had he wished to take a more authentic approach (as had Frederick Russell Burton in his *Dance of Pau-Puk-Keewis,* written sometime between 1893 and its publication in 1898). MacDowell's lectures from Columbia University, however, reveal his more realistic approach to cultural differences in European music, especially in that of the ancient world and the folk song traditions of Asia; see his *Critical and History Essays,* 1–90.

Chapter 7: In Search of the Authentic, 1890–1911

1. The information on Curtis's venture comes from Gidley, " 'The Vanishing Race.' " Sales of Curtis's photographic book series, *The North American Indian,* no doubt benefited enormously from his live presentations. The incidental music to Curtis's "The Vanishing Race," played by "Prince's Orchestra," was recorded ca. 1915 and released as Columbia record number A-4347 (cited in Gidley, " 'The Vanishing Race,' " 85, fn. 30). Excerpts from Gilbert's score and the images from "The Kutenai of the Lakes" are available online at http://xroads.virginia.edu/~MA02/daniels/curtis/musicale.html (Web site created by Valerie Daniels, June 2002; accessed 30 Mar. 2004). Upon transcribing Indian songs from cylinders and editing them for Curtis's *The North American Indian,* Gilbert began to take an interest in them as a source for composition. Ultimately, however, he found most of the "barbaric chants" little more than "potent suggestions pointing in the direction of an unexplored domain of musical color"; see Gilbert, "Indian Sketches."

2. On the quest for spiritual authenticity at the turn of the twentieth century, see T. Jackson Lears, *No Place of Grace: Antimodernism and the Transformation of American Culture, 1880–1920* (New York: Pantheon Books, 1981). A few of the distinguished (and amazingly varied) "antimodernists" discussed in Lears's study are social reformer Jane Addams, journalists Van Wyck Brooks and Lafcadio Hearn, philosopher George Santayana, astronomer Percival Lowell, psychologist Stanley Hall, poets Longfellow and Louise Guiney, professors Brander Matthews and Charles Eliot Norton, and novelists Samuel Clemens (Mark Twain), Frank Norris, and Edith Wharton.

3. For a concise critical discussion of iconic settings after about 1890, see Browner,

"Breathing the Indian Spirit." This is insufficient space here to discuss the use of Indian character pieces in the American pageant movement; see Prevots, *American Pageantry,* 153–72, and Pisani, "Indian Music Debate."

4. Fillmore's pedagogical works were *A History of Pianoforte Music* (1883) and *New Lessons in Harmony* (1887). On Fillmore and dualism, see Devore, "Nineteenth-Century Harmonic Dualism." Fletcher's quotation is from Fletcher and LaFlesche, *Study of Omaha Indian Music,* 10.

5. Fillmore's quotation is from Fletcher and LaFlesche, *Study of Omaha Indian Music,* 617. On the bass line, see Fillmore, "Report on the Structural Peculiarities of the Music," 63.

6. Brailoiu, "Pentatony in Debussy's Music." For a recent discussion of pentatonicism in traditional music, see Simha Arom in *Musicæ Scientiæ* 1, no. 2 (Autumn 1997). *Musicæ Scientiæ* subsequently published a discussion forum of ethnomusicologists led by Arom on pentatonicism in African musics. The question of pentatonicism as a "universe of discourse" still persists.

7. In table 5 I have substituted $\underline{5}$ and $\underline{6}$ for Brailoiu's V and VI to avoid confusion, since the roman numerals are labels for chords. See Brailoiu's "Pentatony in Debussy's Music." To point out one of the possible confusing relationships in the table, mode IV is related to mode I in that it is often used as a plagal version of it (they approach the root in the same way and are sometimes both used in one melody). Similarly, mode III is a plagal version of mode V. Finals, however, could either be on 1 or on the first note of a mode. Hence mode V could sometimes be rooted on $\underline{6}$ and would therefore sound minor. On theoretical approaches to pentatonicism in Western art music, see Day-O'Connell, *Pentatonicism in Nineteenth-Century Music,* as well as the significant bibliography under "pentatonic" in the *New Grove Dictionary of Music and Musicians,* 2nd ed.

8. McNutt, "Reply to Pantaleoni," 229.

9. A similar problem arose in France during the chant revival in the late nineteenth century around the need for church organists to be able to provide harmonic accompaniments for modally modulating chant melodies. The most prominent method in this field was that of Louis Niedermeyer, systematized in his *Traité théorique et pratique de l'accompagnement du plain-chant* (Paris: Heugel, 1876).

10. See also my extensive discussion of Converse's *Peace Pipe* (1915) in chap. 8 of *Exotic Sounds,* 251–69, and in Pisani, "I'm an Indian Too."

11. According to Fletcher, the words of no. 11 imply that the warrior is weary, waiting for the time when he shall go forth to fight under the shadow or protection of Thunder, the god of war. The music is supposed to express the eagerness of the warrior and suggests the tremulous movement of leaves just before a thunderstorm. See Fletcher and LaFlesche, *Study of Omaha Indian Music,* 26. Fletcher's cylinders may be found in Lee, *Early Anthologies,* and also online at http://memory.loc.gov/ammem/omhhtml/omhhome.html (accessed 5 May 2004). See *WAIM,* 163–71, for a facsimile of Hoffman's transcription of Sigkas'sige's song.

12. Fillmore's texted settings also inspired a genre of "Indian" songs for voice and piano. The parlor songs of Frederick Burton, Carlos Troyer, Charles Wakefield Cadman, Thurlow Lieurance, and others originated from a somewhat different set of conditions.

13. Wilfred Mellers, *Music in a New Found Land: Themes and Developments in the History of American Music* (1965), 2nd ed. rev. (London: Faber and Faber, 1987), 27.

14. The unfinished work was accompanied by one of MacDowell's own poems "Autumn Went Wooing" and is presumably based on an Indian melody (possibly from Fletcher). The poem was reprinted in Edward MacDowell, *Verses* (Boston: Arthur P. Schmidt, 1908), 7. In addition to MacDowell's two completed Indian character pieces, however, other later works suggest the possible influence of his Indian studies. See the fourth movement of Sonata No. 2 in G Minor ("Sonata Eroica"), op. 51 (1894–95), and "To an Old White Pine" in *New England Idyls,* op. 62 (1901–2).

15. Francis Brancaleone has convincingly shown the origins of MacDowell's introduction in Baker's no. 52, nos. 1 and 2; see his "Edward MacDowell," 362 and 365. The principal theme, used at "mournfully," comes from Baker's no. 37, p. 132. The "Song of the Brotherton Indians" and MacDowell's "From an Indian Lodge" are in facsimile in *WAIM,* 264–66. As noted previously, MacDowell had studied Fillmore's settings of Fletcher and LaFlesche's melodies; see Hamlin Garland's account of finding the volume on MacDowell's piano in 1896 in *Roadside Meetings,* 321. Marian MacDowell's comments appear in her *Random Notes,* 12.

16. Debussy composed his *Suite bergamasque* in the early 1890s, but it was not published until 1905 and MacDowell could not have known it. The "Indian Idyl" also bears resemblance to a later Debussy piece on a Scottish subject, "La fille aux cheveux de lin" (*Préludes,* Book 1, 1910).

17. Skilton, "Realism in Indian Music," 109.

18. Kroeger's "March of the Indian Phantoms" of 1904 proved influential for its distinctive indexical features; Herbert in particular imitated it as a principal motive in his opera *Natoma.*

19. Edward S. Curtis, "North American Indians," *National Geographic* 18, no. 7 (July 1907): 483.

20. Clifford, *Predicament of Culture,* 10. On Curtis's methods of composing his photographs, see Lyman, *Vanishing Race and Other Illusions.*

21. Puccini used melodic parallelisms as early as *Edgar* (1889), but not fourths or fifths. Act 2 of *La bohème* opens in a festive mood with parallel triad chords. It can be argued that the parallel fifths at the opening of act 3 shadow the earlier parallels and symbolize the fact that the warmth of love has turned to ice. The last "Indian" set in the Wa-Wan Press series appeared in 1906; two short piano miniatures by Carlos Troyer appeared in separate issues the following year and were its final Indianist works.

22. Henry T. Finck wrote that Loomis's reputation rested on his songs; see Finck, *My Adventures in the Golden Age of Music* (New York: Funk and Wagnalls, 1926), 275. A short assessment of the first half of Loomis's career can be found in *The Musiclover's Calendar* 2 (1906): 73–75. Several of Loomis's dramatic pantomimes were produced by the Academy of Dramatic Arts in New York. The majority of his works can be found in the Loomis Collection in the Music Division of the Library of Congress. The manuscript score of *The Garden of Punchinello,* with the original scenario by Kendall Banning, is at Dartmouth College Library.

23. My assessment is based on the songs published between 1900 and 1920 on Asian

subjects in the online MftN aand LEVY databases. Angelo Read, the Canadian composer and conductor, illustrated melodic similarities between "Indian music" and "Asiatic music" in "The North American Indian and Music" (*Musical America,* 13 July 1907). Such ideas, expressed elsewhere during this period, were aligned with those of Francis E. Leupp, Theodore Roosevelt's commissioner of Indian Affairs, and other "race fusionists," as they were called. It is not possible to determine exactly when American sheet music publishers began to issue popular songs that depicted Asian subjects. For more on this early twentieth-century repertory, see Tsou, "Gendering Race," and Lancefield, *Hearing Orientality.* Other American composers of this time who took an interest in Asian subjects were Edgar Stillman Kelley ("Aladdin" Suite, 1892), Charles Tomlinson Griffes (*Sho-Jo,* 1917), and Henry Eichheim (*Oriental Impressions,* 1928).

24. Finck's comment on Hucbald appears in "What Is American Music?" 12. Other composers of serious instrumental character pieces after Loomis adopted this dichotomous "medieval"/"oriental" technique for their "Indian" music. Notable among them, perhaps, was Blair Fairchild in his *Some Indian Songs and Dances* (1927). Fairchild's adaptation of Indian themes in an orientalist light clearly related to his general interests; many of his other compositions were inspired by the Middle and Far East. I have been unable to find an example of Loomis's technique in any music from the preceding three decades, as opposed to other parallel harmonic progressions—such as those involving full triads—that can readily be found elsewhere in nineteenth-century music.

25. John Vincent (*The Diatonic Modes in Modern Music,* 71) has found the III^7–i cadence (but without the added seventh in the III chord) in the slow movement of Dvořák's "New World" Symphony, the second act of *Rusalka,* Sibelius's First Symphony, and Ravel's *L'heure espagnole,* among others, where he notes that "the blandness of the III to i close offers grateful relief from the directness of the classical V–i cadence which in many cases [i.e., illustrated by the examples provided] would be too severe or too brusque."

The role of modality in American music has an interesting backstory. In her famous essay "The Roots of American Culture" (188–89), Constance Rourke pointed out that New England in the early nineteenth century (which at the time represented a microcosm of American sophistication) turned its back on the emerging, and essentially rural, shape-note singing, which used modal harmonies. Its approach was considered unsophisticated and primitive. Because it was used in England long before the sixteenth century, "it belonged to an order of feeling antedating the complexly intellectual religious thought belonging to the Puritans; and this may be the true reason why, even with the lead of Billings, even with the inheritance of ballads and glees and catches cast in these older forms, shape-note religious song, which for many years used mainly the pentatonic or hexatonic scale, did not take firm root in New England."

26. The Curtis quotation is from "Perpetuating of Indian Art," 631. The Block quotation is from "Amy Beach's Music on Native American Themes," 162. See also Block, "Amy Beach's Quartet on Inuit Themes."

27. Farwell, who had prepared his 1900 lectures for Cornell University largely from August Wilhelm Ambros's *Geschichte der Musik,* was no doubt well aware of Ambros's earlier "harmonizations" for some non-Western monodic melodies in his book, for example, the Chinese songs.

28. All of these pieces are reproduced from original editions in Vera Brodsky Lawrence, ed., *The Wa-Wan Press, 1901–1911,* vols. 1, 2, and 4 (New York: Arno Press, 1970).

29. Farwell, "Second Trip West," in *Wanderjahre,* 123. This *Navajo War Dance,* from *From Mesa and Plain: Indian, Cowboy, and Negro Sketches,* five works for piano (Wa-Wan Press 4, no. 28, 1905) was actually the second such titled work Farwell wrote. An earlier unpublished *Navajo War Dance* (1904) was edited by John Kirkpatrick in 1940 and later published (somewhat confusingly) as *Navajo War Dance No. 2* (Music Press, 1947).

30. Mick Gidley provides the transcript for one of Curtis's lectures as an appendix to his article "The Vanishing Race," 75–87. Douglas Seefeld of the University of Virginia has made one set of images along with Gilbert's music available on the Web at http://xroads.virginia.edu/~MA02/daniels/curtis/musicale/Kutenai.html.

31. One of the examples in Miller's book, Butterfly's final "Tu, tu, piccolo Iddio" from Puccini's *Madama Butterfly* (1904), illustrates the overwhelming sense of tragic realization in the minor V^7 (a "modal dominant") that forms the powerful climax to that aria. Victor Herbert also used this chord for the title character in *Natoma* (1911).

Chapter 8: "I'm an Indian Too," 1900–1946

1. A copy of Newton Publishers' "You're an Indian" is included in DeVincent.

2. See Prucha, *Great Father,* 295–309.

3. An unsigned and rather noncommittal review of Burton's *Hiawatha* cantata in Yonkers appeared in the *New York Times* (29 Aug. 1898): 7, col. 5. See also Burton, "Hiawatha, the Indian Musical-Play"; Burton, "Songs of the Ojibways"; an unsigned review of the Debarats *Hiawatha* play reprinted from the *Boston Transcript* (in *Musical Courier* 45 [1902]: 33); and Hale, "Hiawatha Played by Real Indians."

4. In 1909 Burton published some of the *Hiawatha* vocal excerpts in a collection whose title, *American Primitive Music,* seemed to imply that the songs were more Indian than Burton. Burton describes his first encounter with Ojibwa music on p. 19. His quotation appears on pp. 178–79. Some of the songs from *Hiawatha,* as Gilbert Chase noted, served as pretty but trifling additions to the art song repertory; Chase wrote that Burton had found among the Ojibwa "a number of attractive tunes, such as 'My Bark Canoe' and 'The Lake Sheen,' which, harmonized and provided with stylized piano accompaniments, caused these songs to become widely and favorably known." See Chase, *America's Music,* 411. Several versions of "My Bark Canoe" are available in facsimile in *WAIM,* 60–64.

5. Burton recounts his experience in translating "My Bark Canoe" in *American Primitive Music,* 151.

6. I am grateful to Nan Bostick, Charles K. Daniels's granddaughter, for helpful information on her grandfather's success with this song. I have also found at least two march two-steps on Indian subjects that preceded Daniels's "Hiawatha" (Fred Stone's "The Indian" [Detroit, 1895] and A. E. B. Leonard's "Wigwam Dance" [New York, 1896]), as well as one song that preceded it as a popular vocal piece: Max Hoffmann's "Eulah! Eulah! (My Indian Maid)" (New York, 1902). I have not been able to examine these works—all at the British Library—for their associations. They are probably vaudeville

songs or burlesques, like the music for *Wanita,* Ralph Baldwin's 1892 amateur light opera.

7. Hankins, "Sounds Familiar," 5.

8. Most of the songs mentioned here can be found in LEVY.

9. Special thanks to Edward Berlin for helpful information on the genre of the popular intermezzo (personal communication, July 2001). The lyrics in the British publication of "Moja Indianka" were adapted by Everett J. Evans. I have been unable to trace this song to an earlier origin. It is possible that it was directed at a Russian community in the United States and served, in effect, as a parodistic means of "Americanizing" these immigrants.

10. Frederick Cowen's *Indian Rhapsody* of 1903 was played by the Pittsburgh Symphony in that year and used tom-tom fifths in the bass combined with minor-mode melodies. The work was not published until 1904, however.

11. Daniels's "Silverheels Intermezzo" is included in LEVY.

12. Snyders's "Ogalalla" is included in LEVY.

13. See, for example, Schafer and Riedel, *Art of Ragtime,* 112–129.

14. Hall, *Performing the American Frontier,* 15.

15. The orchestra parts for all the music for *The Squaw Man* are available at the New York Public Library Research Division in the David Belasco collection of incidental music, available on microfilm reel 64. These parts were used for revivals of the play as late as 1918 and for productions as far away as Wheeling, West Virginia.

16. The full score for Elliott Schenk's *Indian Overture* is in the Fleischer Collection of the Free Library of Philadelphia.

17. The *Natoma* secret was apparently the result of an agreement with Oscar Hammerstein, who originally planned to produce the opera with his company; see "Look-a-Here What Joe Redding Has Done," *San Francisco Chronicle* (9 Sept. 1909), unpaginated clipping from the Redding papers, Bancroft Library, University of California, Berkeley. On Puccini's use of an "Indian melody" by Troyer, see Atlas, "Belasco and Puccini."

18. See "'Natoma' Scores One More Triumph," *San Francisco Chronicle* (9 Mar. 1911). Edward Waters (in *Victor Herbert,* 379) wrote that "Less than a week before the first performance a feature newspaper . . . called Herbert the man of the hour, referred to him as a symbol of patriotism and democratic life, [and] claimed that he was to American music what Emerson and Whitman were to American literature [Agnes Hogan, *Philadelphia Record* (19 Feb. 1911): sec. 4, p. 5]. . . . It was absolutely impossible for any work of art to be as great, as wonderful, as significant as the four-year-long build up would have it; but the advance enthusiasts threw caution to the winds as they prepared the country for the phenomenal day. Neither Herbert nor Redding was responsible for these conditions; they were simply victims of well-meaning admirers and a national psychosis." Waters's biography of Herbert has a full chapter on *Natoma,* but his discussion is restricted to the opera's composition history and first performances. At least five excerpts from *Natoma* were recorded under Herbert's supervision. Unfortunately, none of Natoma's music as sung by Mary Garden was included. For all five excerpts, including the "Dagger Dance" conducted by Herbert himself, see *Music of Victor Herbert* (Smithsonian American Musical Theater Series), RCA 3–LP album (R 017), DPM 30366 (1986).

19. Smith, "Among the Blackfeet," 69–70, and McClintock, "Arthur Nevin," 9.

20. At least one opera based on Cooper's *The Last of the Mohicans* had been performed on a European stage before *Poia*: Franz Richard Genée's *Die letzten Mohicaner,* libretto by F. Zell (Vienna, 1878). Another that followed *Poia* was Paul Hastings Allen's *L'ultimo dei mohicani,* libretto by Zangarini (Florence, 1916). The most inclusive study of these operas is Briggs, "North American Indian as Depicted in Musical Compositions."

21. Parakilas, "The Soldier and the Exotic," 55–59. Information on the California missions is drawn from Weber, *Mexican Frontier,* 60, and Cook, *California Indian and White Civilization,* 255–361.

22. The source for Kroeger's "March of the Indian Phantoms" is unknown, although this is one of several works he wrote on "Indian themes." According to Curtis's *Indians' Book* (50 and 69–70), dog soldiers, like the bagpipers of Scottish and other cultures, were to stand their ground even unto death "for death is nothing, and pain is nothing; but cowardice is a crime, and disgrace is the greatest punishment." (In a similar vein, see a Sioux song attributed to Sitting Bull published in Densmore, *American Indians and Their Music,* 83.) On the "Tobacco Dance Song," Lieurance observed in his "Descriptive Notes" to the published score that "this song was recorded on the Crow reservation at the Reno Lodge, just below the Custer battlefield during the Indian dances at Christmas time, 1910"; see *Indian Suite* (Philadephia: Theodore Presser, 1914).

23. Dvořák's chord, as noted in chap. 4, is spelled as an E-minor seventh (E–G–B–D) and functions as a sustained pedal accompaniment to the principal theme. He therefore treats the D not as a dissonant seventh longing for resolution, but rather as a color note added to an otherwise stable tonality. He uses the minor seventh in its more usual function in the third theme of the first movement and in the first theme of the fourth movement.

24. Langey's *Grand Fantasia on "Natoma"* has been recently recorded in Rochester by Donald Hunsberger and the Eastman-Dryden Orchestra, as well as in Bratislava by the Slovak Radio Orchestra.

25. I am grateful to the advertising department of Pabst in Milwaukee (who purchased Theodore Hamm Brewing from Olympia in 1982) for permission to reprint the text to this jingle. The sheet music is undated and bears no author or copyright, but the staff at Pabst suspects that it originated "sometime in the Fifties."

26. Cadman, "The American Indian's Music Idealized," 659. Cadman remained undaunted by criticism of his adaptations and no doubt felt that he was doing a good thing for Indian music by "idealizing" it. "You may," he wrote his critics, "find an educated Indian in the United States here and there who may not be in sympathy with the movement to preserve his native tunes, or with the idea of idealizing and harmonizing them, but my experience in the work has convinced me that eighty per cent of 'musical Indians' are pleased when the white man objectifies his songs and makes them understandable and perhaps more enjoyable to the white man's ears through the medium of the white man's musical medicine." What criteria Cadman used to establish the "musical" from the non-musical Indian he does not say. See Cadman, "In Defense of Idealization," an essay printed in the score of his *Thunderbird,* a piano suite arranged from incidental music to the drama of the same name by Norman Bel Geddes (Boston: White-Smith, 1917). At the Wa-Wan Press, Farwell rejected Cadman's "From the Land of the Sky-blue Water," along

with the rest of the *Four American Indian Songs,* before White-Smith published them. A copy of song is included in *WAIM,* 255–58.

27. One of the "Indian Music Talks" programs is reprinted in Perison, *Charles Wakefield Cadman,* 443. Cadman and Eberhart's working relationship is told in "The Pennsylvanians," an unpublished story, 1911 (cited in Wu, *Constance Eberhart,* 14) as is Cadman's encounter with Emil Paur (16). Alice Fletcher responded quickly and warmly to Cadman's request for permission to use her transcribed songs; see Perison, *Cadman,* 66–67.

28. Robert M. Yoder noted the commercial success of "Sky-blue Water" in "Tin-Pan Alley's Wonderful Monopoly."

29. See Oja, *American Music Recordings,* 42–43. Recordings of arrangements have been verified from existing Library of Congress listings.

30. Lieurance, "Beauties in the Music."

31. Lieurance in *WAIM,* 259–64. For a history of "By the Waters of the Minnetonka," see Lieurance, "Stories of Famous Concert Songs."

32. "Indian Music Concert" program (1921) used for concerts in Washington, D.C. (Masonic Auditorium), San Antonio (Beethoven Hall), Fort Worth (First Baptist Church), Dallas (City Temple), and other cities; from the Lieurance collection, State Historical Society of Iowa, Historical Division of the Department of Cultural Affairs.

33. The $\hat{6}$–$\hat{5}$ pattern in the accompaniment is perhaps best known in Western music as the "sighing" in Tchaikovsky's love theme for his *Romeo and Juliet* overture. Dvořák later used it in the second movement of his violin Sonatina (1893), which, as already noted, he wrote while visiting the Minnehaha Falls near St. Paul and which Simrock published in 1894 as Dvořák's "Indian Canzonetta." (Also known as the "Indian Lament," this work was popularized in the early 1900s by Fritz Kriesler, who recorded it for RCA Victor. It was even arranged by Otto Langey in 1918 as an "Indian" piece for silent-film accompaniment.)

34. Oja, *American Music Recordings,* 201–2. Recordings of arrangements have been verified through an Online Computer Library Center search.

35. Though this operatic representation of early twentieth-century society may at times seem glib, *Shanewis*'s unusual subject matter led Cadman, Eberhart, and Redfeather to pioneer some techniques that would later be adopted by George Gershwin and Virgil Thomson in their consciously styled American operas. In the late 1910s and early 1920s, nearly every serious musician in the United States would have heard of the *Shanewis* operatic experiment, even if they did not know the opera itself. *Shanewis*'s possible influence on Gershwin and Thomson merits a separate study. Whether either heard or studied the work is not known; they were both in their late teens when it premiered. They certainly would have seen the published vocal score (with its distinctive cover) after 1918, as most serious music shops in America carried a copy.

36. General manager Giulio Gatti-Casazza was pressured by the Metropolitan Opera's board of directors to cancel performances of all operas by German composers in the upcoming 1917–18 season. He then sent requests for submissions to American composers, Cadman among them; see Perison, *Cadman,* 189–97. The Met produced *Shanewis* five times that season and twice again in 1919. On *Shanewis*'s performance history, see

Perison, "The *Indian* Operas." Relatively little has been written on this opera though, like *Natoma,* it is regularly cited in major surveys of American music. Unlike *Natoma,* it has received several performances since its premiere, including one by the Central City Opera Company in 1979. Cadman describes operatic "foreigners" in a letter to Francis La-Flesche dated 29 Dec. 1917 (LaFlesche Family Collection, Nebraska State Historical Society, and cited in Perison, *Cadman,* 191). "Bible English" librettos are discussed in letters written later from Cadman to Eberhart, 9 Sept. 1937 and 17 Sept. 1937 (in the Constance Eberhart collection, Music Division, New York Public Library, and cited also in Perison, *Cadman,* 332). Some of the culprits of operatic "Bible English" included Frederick Converse's *Sacrifice* (1911) and Cadman's own *Daoma* (unfinished).

37. Cadman's "twenty genuine . . . themes" statement is cited in Perison, *Cadman,* 182. Cadman's lifelong interest in cultural diversity reinforced the sincerity of his purpose in "idealizing" Indian melodies as a means for incorporating them into what has been called his American ballad style. "[Cadman's] ingenuous ballad style," writes Perison, "adequate as it was for his numerous ballads, was too static and too shallow to succeed on the operatic stage. . . . As a whole Cadman's operas, both Indian and non-Indian, must be regarded less as significant contributions to the development of American opera than as monuments to the lofty but frustrated aspirations of a gifted composer of popular ballads" (Perison, "Indian Operas," 48). Cadman's idiosyncratic and eclectic style of expression can also be seen in his letters, many of which switch abruptly from topic to topic. These, as well as the majority of his scores and manuscripts, can be found at the Pattee Library, Pennsylvania State University.

38. Cadman took Shanewis's second song quite literally from Burton, harmonization and all ("Her Shadow," *American Primitive Music,* part 2, 29–31). The pentatonic melody was not altered from Burton's original, and Cadman retained Burton's simple, diatonic strophic setting. Remarkably similar in tone and meaning to "My Bark Canoe," the song tells of a young man who paddles his canoe quietly along a river's wooded bank, where he suspects that his shy sweetheart is hiding.

39. See "40,000 Witness 'Shanewis,'" and "Fifth Summer Season at Hollywood Bowl."

40. The source of the Osage songs is LaFlesche (later published in "The Osage Tribe"). Cadman's procedure departed from operas that used onstage music before that time (such as the "gypsies" in *La traviata,* for example).

41. Unsigned review, *Musical Courier* 76, no. 13 (28 Mar. 1918): 5.

42. The most famous historical Black Eagle was a Nez Perce who traveled to St. Louis in search of Christian teachings and died there in 1831. The character in *Rose-Marie* would seem to be no relation, since the name frequently cropped up in early films and theatrical works.

43. The clipping file on *Rose-Marie* at the Academy of Motion Picture Arts and Sciences notes dozens of Indian dancers and extras but provides no personal details.

44. Boardman, *American Musical Theatre,* 446.

45. Chief Caupolican was a noted speaker on the Chautauqua circuit and was also an operatically trained singer. He sang the title role in Karel Weis's *The Polish Jew* at the Metropolitan Opera in 1921.

46. On the film version of *Whoopee!* see Barrios, *Song in the Dark,* 241–44.

47. This iconic use of Indian chiefs had been practiced, as we've noted, at least since the days when Black Hawk was paraded with the U.S. military after the Sauk Wars of the early 1830s.

48. Information on the making of the film adaptation can be found in "Bull's Eye! MGM Annie Get Your Gun Hits the Home Screen" by Bert Fink, printed in the Fall 2000 issue of *Happy Talk: News of the Rodgers and Hammerstein Organization,* posted online at www.rnh.com.

49. *American Film Institute Catalog of Motion Pictures Produced in the United States, Feature Films, 1941–1950,* s.v. "Annie Get Your Gun."

50. The "Wataya" chant is strikingly similar to the orchestral prelude that opens the reservation scene in act 2 of *Shanewis.*

51. During the years of *Annie Get Your Gun,* Berlin worked with Helmy Kresa on his songs. According to Bruce Pomahac, director of music at the Rodgers and Hammerstein Library, New York, Berlin played through his songs several times for Kresa, who served as Berlin's stenographer, not adding anything of his own. Neither Edward Jablonski nor Michael Freedland—two of Berlin's principal biographers—suggests that Kresa's role was anything other than transcriber of Berlin's dictation. (Philip Furia, another important biographer, does not mention Kresa.) Since the manuscripts of these songs are in Kresa's hand, there is probably no way that this information could ever be verified. I have inquired whether anything was added to Berlin's songs by the first orchestrator, Philip Lang, or by Robert Russell Bennett, who took over from Lang; neither Lang nor Bennett is known to have added harmonies or countermelodies to Berlin's songs. (Only a careful perusal of all manuscript sources can lead to any definitive answers to these questions. That task is beyond the scope of the research for this book.) The 1999 Broadway revival version was reorchestrated by Bruce Coughlin. The choreography of the original 1946 version was by Helen Tamiris. The author of the original dance arrangements is unknown. This is the version printed in the 1947 vocal score. Bennett's role in the orchestration of the dance music may also be difficult to ascribe. Certainly the instrumental colors—heard on the studio reconstruction recorded by John McGlinn for EMI Classics, 1991—reflect a familiarity with the "Indian idiom" of Bennett's teacher Carl Busch, as well as of Victor Herbert. The elaborate dance numbers in the 1967 revised vocal score, by Richard De Benedictus, were used in the 1966 revival. In this score—the one currently available for productions of *Annie Get Your Gun*—Kresa is credited with the "piano arrangements."

52. Again, Berlin reveals his familiarity with the full panorama of indexical Indian devices. In his *American Indian Fantasie* (organ, 1920; cello and orchestra, 1929), Charles Sanford Skilton, an ardent Indianist, used the whole-tone scale as a harmonic coloring device. This became his hallmark technique, also evident in his orchestral *Suite Primeval* ("on Tribal Indian Melodies," 1921), a work widely performed by major orchestras in the 1920s and in various versions for band and theater orchestra. The addition of the whole-tone scale to the tropes of musical Indianism occurred almost at the point when compositions with Indian themes began to decrease rapidly. Nonetheless, for some 1940s listeners, "I will run away . . ." (in Berlin's song) may well have been heard as a parody of Skilton's association of whole-tone scales with Indian music. (In 1942 composer Max Steiner also used a whole-tone scale in his musical characterization of Crazy Horse in the film *They Died with Their Boots On.*)

Chapter 9: Underscoring Ancestry

1. Two important critiques of Native American characters in film are Phil Lucas's *Images of Indians,* a native-produced documentary filmed for KCTS-TV in Seattle, and Steven M. Leuthold's "Native American Responses to the Western." For an excellent discussion of the music for Indian characters in sound cinema, see Gorbman, "Scoring the Indian." Gorbman's quote on film music as a dream appears on p. 234.

2. For a detailed list of the principal functions of music in film, see my essay "Teaching Film Music in the Undergraduate Liberal Arts Curriculum" in Warren Sherk and Claudia Gorbman, eds., *Film Music II* (Los Angeles: Film Music Society, 2004), 222–23.

3. Chion, *Audio-Vision: Sound on Film* (New York: Columbia University Press, 1994), 8–9; Churchill, *Fantasies of the Master Race,* 225.

4. Friar and Friar list dozens of categories in their appendix. Most of these, such as drunken Indians, turncoats (Indians who help whites against their own), and "Indian woman loves white man" seem more to be recurring topics than stereotypes. See Friar and Friar, *The Only Good Indian,* 285–23. Churchill's categories of stereotypes are broader and phrased as if from a white perspective. He offers about eleven: Indians as creatures of a particular time; Creatures of a particular place; Seen one Indian, seen 'em all; Peoples without culture; The only good Indian . . . ; Voices of the voiceless; Those cavaliers in buckskin; Ravages by savages; Lust in the dust; Cowboys and . . . ; and The song remains the same. See Churchill, *Fantasies of the Master Race,* 167–206.

5. Marsden and Nachbar identify the three primary stereotypes in "The Indian in the Movies," 609. The rest of their essay is divided into chronological periods, 1903–1913, 1913–1950, 1950–1975, and 1976–1987, in which the authors demonstrate how these stereotypes were flexible enough to withstand varied treatment.

6. Otto Langey's "Indian Agitato" was also published, along with other "Indian" works, in Rapée, *Motion Picture Moods,* 367. Other collections containing "Indian" pieces for silent film (and listed in the bibliography) were those by J. S. Zamecnik (1913), Lyle C. True (1914), Edith Land and George West (1920), George W. Beynon (1921), and Erno Rapée (1925).

7. Marks, *Music and the Silent Film,* 191. Various issues of *Moving Picture World* throughout March 1913 mention music in addition to other "authentic" aspects of Moore's *Hiawatha,* as well as his use of 150 "full-blooded Indians."

8. Clarence E. Sinn, "Music for the Picture," *Moving Picture World* (7 June 1913): 1020. The use of popular "Indian" songs was not uncommon. Studios even worked them into the cue sheets. An instrumental version of a song such as Henry Sawyer and Jeff Branen's "Os-ka-loo-sa-loo" (1906) proved one standard in early silent-film cue sheets, perhaps because of its many atmospherically "Indianesque" features.

9. Melodic parallelisms were introduced as a feature of Indianism, as described in chap. 7, by Harvey Loomis in his "Lyrics of the Red Man" in 1903 and 1904. The "ancient" parallelisms in *The Pines of Rome* can be seen in the Ricordi miniature score, pp. 34–35.

10. *Plainsman* review (13 Jan. 1937), repr. in *Variety Film Reviews,* vol. 5.

11. The full score for *The Died with Their Boots On* is in the Steiner Collection at the University of Southern California, Los Angeles.

12. Steiner's note was first observed by Bill Rosar and mentioned in his "Movie Indian

Music and Film Music Convention," 76. I am grateful to Mr. Rosar for sending me a copy of his unpublished paper. It should perhaps also be pointed out that musical "Indianism" in the classical sphere reached its apex by the 1920s, and by the 1940s had fallen off dramatically. In fact it was then considered rather old-fashioned and somewhat tasteless for an American to compose anything for the concert hall "on Indian themes" or on an American Indian subject. Meanwhile, the movie Westerns perpetuated many of the Indianisms developed in classical music (and furthered by leading figures such as Steiner, who purported to ground his "Indian music" in supposed Indian melodies).

13. A whole subculture sprang up in France in the early twentieth century around *apaches* (see Haine, "The Development of Leisure"). In the famous *L'amour de l'apache* at the Moulin Rouge in 1908, pantomimist G. Molasso introduced the "Apache dance" to an arrangement of musical motives from Offenbach. In a later Hollywood musical, *Love Me Tonight* (1932), Rodgers and Hart created a song about these bohemians with "The Poor Apache." The "Indian" in the title refers not to the Southwestern tribe but to the *apaches* in turn-of-the-century Parisian Moulin Rouge culture. The original craze sparked many other "Apache dances," including one for the British film star Ivor Novello.

14. Compare subject matter listed in Friar and Friar, *The Only Good Indian,* 285–323. Although their list ends ca. 1970, their count begins in 1910. For all American films with Indian characters made between 1910 and 1970, the Apaches lead as subjects, with the Sioux a close second. Comanches come in third by some distance.

15. Beth Levy's dissertation, *Frontier Figures,* partly explores this topic.

16. This pattern can be found throughout many Westerns of the 1950s. In *Arrowhead* (1953), for example, the film begins newsreel-style with a long title card listing the generals who fought against the Western tribes; this listing is accompanied by military bugle calls. Then Paul Sawtell's main titles begin with heavy-handed "Indian" music (pentatonic and modal) over a shot of Apaches on horseback, dovetailing into heroic symphonic music (major) for the remainder of the credits, as if affirming that white heroes saved the West from the "savages."

17. See Friar and Friar, *The Only Good Indian,* 57–59. The Friars also include a playbill from one of the programs.

18. On details of Friedhofer's score, see Bill Rosar's liner notes for the Brigham Young Film Archives remastering of original recorded tracks from *Broken Arrow* (FMA-HF105, 1999). Churchill's comments appear in *Fantasies of the Master Race,* 180–82 and fn. 80.

19. Jerry Goldsmith's manuscript score for *Rio Conchos* is at the Margaret Herrick Research Library, Academy of Motion Picture Arts and Sciences, Beverly Hills.

20. It should be added that little of this detail can be heard in the video release's soundtrack for this film. I have not seen a print of *Rio Conchos* shown in a theater that would play the original mono tracks stereophonically, as Goldsmith no doubt intended during the mixing of this sequence.

21. See especially Browner, *Heartbeat of the People,* and Powers, *Plains Indian Musical Performance.*

22. In 1966 veteran Indian actor Jay Silverheels spearheaded the formation of two Los Angeles groups, the Indian Actors Guild and the Indian Actors Workshop, to teach acting skills to Indian performers and to promote the use of native people in native roles. See Marsden and Nachbar, "The Indian in the Movies," 614.

23. In Maggie Jaffe's review of this film, she notes that Light Cloud appears "in the shape of a coyote, an animal of great cunning and endurance, also revered as a trickster." See Maggie Jaffe, "The Peace Pipe in *Powwow Highway*," *Rag Baby Online Magazine*, June 18, 1999, http://www.countryjoe.com/ragbaby/magazine/19990618c.htm (accessed May 2004).

24. Gorbman, "Scoring the Indian," 248.

25. This comment is from an online review at amazon.com by Kenton Larsen of Winnipeg, Manitoba, http://www.amazon.com/gp/product/customer-reviews/B00062XM7/ref=cm_7rev_7next/102-3676250-0949753?%5Fencoding=UTF8&customer-reviews.sort%5Fby=-SubmissionDate&n=404272&customer-reviews.start=141&me=ATVPDKIKX0DER (accessed 26 Jan. 2002).

26. Kilpatrick, *Celluloid Indians*, 131.

27. Special thanks to Peter Buffett for sharing details of his scoring experience with me (personal communication, Oct. 2002).

28. Details on Maya culture and history—but virtually nothing on music except for a few instruments that are mentioned—can be found in Schele and Freidel, *Forest of Kings*.

29. The soundtrack album produced in conjunction with the video—but separately mixed—offers "Maya" as well as seventeen other cues. For some unknown reason a prominent and annoying rap beat has been added to several of these cues, perhaps in an effort to increase the salability of the album. On this unlikely ground, the sounds of late twentieth-century urban rap and the early modern primitivist rhetoric adapted for ancient America meet.

Bibliography

Aaron, Daniel. Introduction to *The Song of Hiawatha,* by Henry Wadsworth Longfellow. London: J. M. Dent, 1992.

Adair, James. *History of the American Indians.* [1775]. Reprint, New York: Promontory Press, 1930.

Adler, Guido. "Umfang, Methode und Ziel der Musikwissenschaft" (Scope, Methods and Goals in Musicology). *Vierteljahrsschrift für Musikwissenschaft* 1 (1885): 5–20.

Albrecht, Adalbert. "Indianische Musik." *Die Zeit* 39 (1904): 57–58.

Aldrich, Richard. Review of *Natoma. New York Times* (26 Feb. 1911).

Aldrich, Thomas Bailey. *Miantowona.* Originally published in *Friar Jerome's Beautiful Book, and Other Poems,* 1881. Reprinted in *The Poems of Thomas Bailey Aldrich,* 90–97. Boston and New York: Houghton, Mifflin, 1897.

Aleiss, Angela. "A Race Divided: The Indian Westerns of John Ford." *American Indian Culture and Research Journal* 18, no. 3 (1994): 167–86.

———. "Race in Contemporary American Cinema: Part 4—Native Americans: The Surprising Silents." *Cineaste* 21, no. 3 (Summer 1995): 34–38.

Alger, William Rounseville. *Life of Edwin Forrest: American Tragedian.* London and Philadelphia: Lippincott, 1877.

A. M. "How an Italian Composer Came to Create the First 'All-Indian' Opera (On Bimboni's *Winona*)." *Musical America* 27, no. 25 (20 Apr. 1918): 21.

Amacher, Richard E. "Behind the Curtain with the Noble Savage: Stage Management of Indian Plays, 1825–1860." *Theatre Survey* 7, no. 2 (Nov. 1966): 101–14.

American Memory: Historic American Sheet Music, 1850–1920. Sheet music collection at Duke University, Special Collections Library. Online at http://memory.loc.gov/ammem/award97/ncdhtml/hasmhome.html.

American Memory: Music for the Nation. American sheet music from the Library of Congress, 1820–1860 and 1870–1885. Online at http://memory.loc.gov/ammem/smhtml/smhome.html.

Anderson, Benedict. *Imagined Communities.* London: Verso, 1983.

Anderson, Donna K. *Charles T. Griffes: A Life in Music.* Washington, D.C.: Smithsonian Institution Press, 1993.

Anderson, Rasmus Bjorn. *America Not Discovered by Columbus.* Chicago: S. C. Griggs, 1883.

Anthony, James R. *French Baroque Music from Beaujoyeulx to Rameau.* Rev. ed. Portland, Ore.: Amadeus Press, 1997.

Apess, William. *A Son of the Forest.* [1829]. Amherst: University of Massachusetts Press, 1997.

Appleford, Robert. "Coming Out from Behind the Rocks: Constructs of the Indian in Recent U.S. and Canadian Cinema." *American Indian Culture and Research Journal* 19, no. 1 (1995): 97–118.

Archabal, Nina Marchetti. "Frances Densmore: Pioneer in the Study of American Indian Music." *Women of Minnesota: Selected Biographical Essays,* 94–115. St. Paul: Minnesota Historical Society, 1977.

Armstrong, William. "The American Indian Legend in Music." *Music* 16, no. 2 (July 1899): 119–24.

Asafiev, Boris. *Musical Form as Process.* [1930]. Trans. with commentary by J. R. Tull. Ph.D. diss., Ohio State University, 1977.

Atlas, Allan W. "Belasco and Puccini: 'Old Dog Tray' and the Zuni Indians." *Musical Quarterly* 75, no. 3 (Fall 1991): 378–88.

Austin, Mary. *The American Rhythm: Studies and Reëxpressions of Amerindian Songs.* Orig. ed., 1923; 2nd enlarged ed., 1930. Reprint, New York: Cooper Square, 1970.

Avery, Emmett L., Charles Beecher Hogan, William Van Lennep, Arthur H. Scouten, and George Winchester Stone Jr. *The London Stage, 1660–1800: A Calendar of Plays. . . .* 11 vols. Carbondale: Southern University Illinois Press, 1968.

Badger, R. Reid. *The Great American Fair: The World's Columbian Exposition and American Culture.* Chicago: Nelson Hall, 1979.

Baird, Robert. "Going Indian: Discovery, Adoption, and Renaming Toward a 'True American,' from *Deerslayer* to *Dances with Wolves.*" In *Dressing in Feathers: The Construction of the Indian in American Popular Culture,* edited by S. Elizabeth Bird, 195–209. Boulder, Colo.: Westview Press, 1996.

Baker, Theodore. *Über die Musik der nordamerikanischen Wilden.* Ph.D. diss., University of Leipzig, 1881. Translated by Ann Buckley as *On the Music of the North American Indians.* The Netherlands: Frits Knuf, 1976. Reprint, New York: Da Capo Press, 1977.

Bank, Rosemarie K. *Theatre Culture in America, 1825–1860.* New York: Cambridge University Press, 1997.

Barbeau, M. "Asiatic Survivals in Indian Songs." *Musical Quarterly* 20 (Jan. 1934): 107–16.

Barnum, P. T. *Struggles and Triumphs, or, Forty Years' Recollections of P. T. Barnum.* [1871]. Reprint, New York: Macmillan, 1930.

Barrios, Richard. *A Song in the Dark: The Birth of the Musical Film.* New York: Oxford University Press, 1995.

Barthes, Roland. *Image, Music, Text.* [1964]. Translated by Stephen Heath. New York: Hill and Wang, 1977.

——. *Mythologies.* [1957]. New York: Hill and Wang, 1972.

Bataille, Gretchen, ed. *Native American Representations: First Encounters, Distorted Images, and Literary Appropriations.* Lincoln: University of Nebraska Press, 2001.

Bataille, Gretchen, and Charles Silet, eds. *The Pretend Indian: Images of Native Americans in the Movies.* Ames: Iowa State University Press, 1980.

Bauer, Marion. "French Folk Music." In *International Cyclopedia of Music and Musicians,* edited by Robert Sabin. 9th ed. New York: Dodd, Mead, 1964.

Bauman, Thomas. "Montezuma." In *The New Grove Dictionary of Opera,* vol. 3, edited by Stanley Sadie. New York: Grove's Dictionaries of Music, 1992.

Beaumont, Antony. *Busoni the Composer.* London: Faber and Faber, 1985.

Beckerman, Michael. "The Dance of Pau-Puk-Keewis, the Song of Chibiabos, and the Story of Iagoo: Reflections on Dvořák's 'New World' Scherzo." In *Dvořák in America,* edited by John C. Tibbetts, 210–27.

——. "Dvořák's 'New World' Largo and *The Song of Hiawatha.*" *Nineteenth-Century Music* 16 (Summer 1992): 35–48.

——. "Henry Krehbiel, Antonín Dvořák, and the Symphony 'From the New World.'" *Notes: Quarterly Journal of the Music Library Association* 29, no. 2 (Dec. 1992): 447–73.

——. *New Worlds of Dvořák: Searching in America for the Composer's Inner Life.* New York: Norton, 2003.

Beecham, Sir Thomas. *Frederick Delius.* New York: Alfred A. Knopf, 1960.

Bellman, Jonathan. *The Exotic in Western Music.* Boston: Northeastern University Press, 1996.

——. *The* Style Hongrois *in the Music of Western Europe.* Boston: Northeastern University Press, 1993.

Benn, Carl. *Iroquois in the War of 1812.* Toronto: University of Toronto Press, 1998.

Berkhofer, Robert F. "White Conceptions of Indians." In *History of Indian-White Relations,* edited by Wilcomb E. Washburn, 522–47. Vol. 4, *Handbook of North American Indians,* edited by William C. Sturtevant. Washington, D.C.: Smithsonian Institution, 1988.

——. *The White Man's Indian: Images of the American Indian from Columbus to the Present.* New York: Random House, 1978.

Berwick Sayers, *W. C. Samuel Coleridge-Taylor, Musician: His Life and Letters.* London: Cassel, 1915.

Besterman, Theodore. *Voltaire.* New York: Harcourt, Brace, and World, 1969.

Beveridge, David. "Sophisticated Primitivism: the Significance of Pentatonicism in Dvořák's 'American' Quartet." *Current Musicology* 23 (1977): 25–36.

Beynon, George W. *Musical Presentation of Motion Pictures.* New York: Schirmer, 1921.

Bhabha, Homi. *Nation and Narration.* London: Routledge, 1990.

"Bibliography of Music and Books, Founded on Indian Themes and Subjects, with List of Phonograph Records." *Etude* 38 (1920): 667–68.

Bieder, Robert E. *Science Encounters the Indian, 1820–1880: The Early Years of American Ethnology.* Norman: University of Oklahoma Press, 1986.

Bierley, Paul E. *John Philip Sousa: American Phenomenon.* New York: Appleton-Century-Crofts, 1973.

"Biography of Princess Tsianina Redfeather." *Music News* 15 (31 Aug. 1923): 9.

Black, Liza Elizabeth. *Looking at Indians: American Indians in Movies, 1941–1960.* Ph.D. diss., University of Washington, 1999.

Blanning, T. C. W. *The Culture of Power and the Power of Culture: Old Regime Europe, 1660–1789.* London: Oxford University Press, 2002.

Block, Adrienne Fried. "Amy Beach's Music on Native American Themes." *American Music* 8, no. 2 (Summer 1990): 141–66.

——. "Amy Beach's Quartet on Inuit Themes: Toward a Modernist Style." In Amy Beach, *Quartet for Strings in One Movement,* Op. 89 (*Recent Researches in American Music,* Vol. 23), edited by Adrienne Fried Block. Madison, Wis.: A-R Editions, 1994.

——. "Boston Talks Back to Dvořák." *ISAM Newsletter* 18, no. 2 (May 1989): 10–15.

——. "Dvořák, Beach, and American Music." In *A Celebration of American Music: Words and Music in Honor of H. Wiley Hitchcock,* edited by Richard Crawford, R. Allen Lott, and Carol J. Oja, 256–80. Ann Arbor: University of Michigan Press, 1990.

——. "Dvořák's Long American Reach." In *Dvořák in America,* edited by John C. Tibbetts, 157–81.

Boas, Franz. "On Certain Songs and Dances of the Kwakiutl of British Columbia." *Journal of American Folklore* 1, no. 1 (Apr.–June 1888).

Bond, Richmond P. *Queen Anne's American Kings.* Oxford: Clarendon Press, 1952.

Bonnerjea, Biren. *Index to Bulletins 1–100 of the Bureau of American Ethnology; with Index to Contributions to North American Ethnology, Introductions and Miscellaneous Publications.* Bureau of American Ethnology, Bulletin No. 178. Washington, D.C.: Smithsonian Institution, 1963.

Boorsch, Suzanne. "America in Festival Presentations." In *First Images of America,* edited by F. Chiappelli, 503–15. Berkeley: University of California Press, 1976.

Bordewich, Fergus M. *Killing the White Man's Indian: Reinventing Native Americans at the End of the Twentieth Century.* New York: Doubleday, 1996.

Bordman, Gerald. *American Musical Theatre: A Chronicle.* 2nd ed. New York: Oxford University Press, 1992.

Born, Georgina, and David Hesmondhalgh, eds. *Western Music and Its Others: Difference, Representation, and Appropriation in Music.* Berkeley: University of California Press, 2000.

Borroff, Edith. *American Operas: A Checklist.* Edited by J. Bunker Clark. Warren, Mich.: Harmonie Park Press, 1992.

Boyle, David. "Iroquois Music." *Ontario Archaeological Museum Report* (898): 143–56.

Bradbury, John. *Travels in the Interior of America, 1809–11.* Reprinted in Reuben G. Thwaites, *Early Western Travels, 1748–1846,* vol. 5. Cleveland: Arthur H. Clark, 1906.

Brailoiu, Constantin. "Pentatony in Debussy's Music." In *Studia memoriae Belae Bartók sacra,* edited by B. Rajeczky and L. Vargyas, 377–418. 3rd ed., translated. London: Boosey and Hawkes, 1958.

——. *Problems of Ethnomusicology.* Cambridge: Cambridge University Press, 1984.

Brancaleone, Francis. "Edward MacDowell and Indian Motives." *American Music* 7 (Winter 1989): 359–81.

——. *The Short Piano Works of Edward MacDowell.* Ph.D. diss., City University of New York, 1982.

Braun, Judy Elise. "The North American Indian Exhibits at the 1876 and 1893 World Expositions: The Influence of Scientific Thought on Popular Attitudes." Master's thesis, George Washington University, 1975.

Bray, John. *The Indian Princess,* with an introduction by H. Wiley Hitchcock. New York: Da Capo Press, 1972.

Briggs, Harold. "Indians! A Whole Movement of Native Opera Romanticized the American Savage." *Opera News* 40, no. 23 (June 1976): 22–51.

——. "The North American Indian as Depicted in Musical Compositions, Culminating with American 'Indianist' Operas of the Early Twentieth Century: 1900–1930." Master's thesis, Indiana University, 1977.

Broekhoven, J. van. "On *Natoma.*" *Musical Observer* 5, no. 3 (1911): 6–10.

Brown, A. Peter. "Musical Settings of Anne Hunter's Poetry: From National Song to Canzonetta." *Journal of the American Musicological Society* 46, no. 1 (Spring 1994): 46–48.

Brown, Malcolm H. "The Soviet Russian Concepts of 'Intonazia' and 'Musical Imagery.'" *Musical Quarterly* 60, no. 4 (Oct. 1974): 557–67.

Browner, Tara. "'Breathing the Indian Spirit': Thoughts on Musical Borrowing and the 'Indianist' Movement in American Music." *American Music* 15, no. 3 (Fall 1997): 265–84.

——. *Heartbeat of the People: Music and Dance of the Northern Pow-Wow.* Urbana: University of Illinois Press, 2002.

——. *Transposing Cultures: The Appropriation of Native North American Musics, 1890–1990.* Ph.D. diss., University of Michigan, 1995.

Broyles, Michael. *Mavericks and Other Traditions in American Music.* New Haven, Conn.: Yale University Press, 2004.

Budden, Julian. *The Operas of Verdi.* 3 vols. New York: Oxford University Press, 1973–78.

Buell, Lawrence. Introduction to *Selected Poems of Henry Wadsworth Longfellow.* New York: Penguin Books, 1988.

Burlin, Natalie Curtis. *See* Curtis, Natalie.

Burton, Frederick R. American Primitive Music, with Especial Attention to the Songs of the Ojibways. New York: Moffat, Yard, 1909.

——. "The Civilizing of Indian Music." *Southern Workman* [Hampton, Va.] 36 (1907): 305–10.

——. "Hiawatha, the Indian Musical-Play." *Concert-Goer* (29 Nov. 1902): 7–9.

——. "In Defense of Idealization." Introduction to *Thunderbird,* piano suite arranged from Cadman's incidental music for Norman Bel Geddes's play. Boston: White-Smith, 1917.

———. "Songs of the Ojibways." *Concert-Goer* (6 Dec. 1902): 8–9.

Busch, Carl. "A Chant from the Great Plains." *Etude* 47 (Feb. 1929): 105, 131.

Cadman, Charles Wakefield. "The American Indian's Music Idealized." *Etude* 38, no. 10 (Oct. 1920), 659. (An article revised from his earlier "The Idealization of Indian Music," *Musical Quarterly* 1 [July 1915]: 387–96.)

———. "Anent That Injun Music." *Musical Courier* 60, no. 15 (1910): 39.

"Cadman and Princess Tsianina at [Chicago] Playhouse." *Music News* 13 (28 Oct. 1915): 7.

"Cadman and Tsianina [at the Panama-California Exposition]." *Music News* 7 (30 July 1915): 21.

Cady, Calvin B. Review of A. Fletcher's *A Study of Omaha Indian Music. Music Review* 3 (1893): 53–57.

Carver, Jonathan. *Travels through the Interior Parts of North America, 1766, 1767, 1768*. London: Printed by J. Walter, 1778.

Castro, Michael. *Interpreting the Indian: Twentieth-Century Poets and the Native American.* Albuquerque: University of New Mexico Press, 1983.

Catlin, George. *Catlin's Notes, or Eight Years' Travels and Residence in Europe with the North American Indian Collection.* 2 vols. 3rd ed. London: Published by the author, 1848.

———. *Letters and Notes on the Manners, Customs, and Condition of the North American Indians. Written During Eight Years Travel among the Wildest Tribes. . . .* London: David Bogue, 1844.

Champagne, Duane, ed. The Native North American Almanac: *A Reference Work on Native North Americans in the United States and Canada.* Detroit: Gale Research, 1994.

Chase, Gilbert. *America's Music.* New York: McGraw-Hill, 1955.

———. "The 'Indianist' Movement in American Music." Liner notes for New World Records no. 213, 1977.

Chateaubriand, François-René, vicomte de. *Atala, or The Love and Constancy of Two Savages in the Desert.* [1801]. Facsimile of the 1st English ed. Boston: Printed by David Carlisle for Caleb Bingham, 1802.

"Chicago Opera to Produce *Natoma,* Herbert's First Serious Opera; Composer Discusses His Work." *New York Times* (10 Oct. 1910) 9:1.

Christout, Marie-Françoise. *Le ballet de cour au XVIIe siècle.* Genève: Éditions Minkoff, 1987.

Churchill, Ward. *Fantasies of the Master Race: Literature, Cinema, and the Colonization of American Indians.* 2nd ed., rev. San Francisco: City Lights Books, 1998.

Churchill, Ward, Norbert Hill, and Mary Ann Hill. "Media Stereotyping and Native Response: An Historical Overview." *Indian Historian* 11, no. 4 (1978): 45–56, 63.

Cipolla, Wilma Reid. *A Catalog of the Works of Arthur Foote, 1853–1937.* Detroit: Published for the College Music Society by Information Coordinators, 1980.

Clapham, John. "Dvořák and the American Indian." *Musical Times* 107, no. 1484 (Oct. 1966): 863–67. Reprinted in *Dvořák in America,* edited by John C. Tibbetts, 113–22.

Clark, Blue. *Lone Wolf v. Hitchcock: Treaty Rights and Indian Law at the End of the Nineteenth Century.* Lincoln: University of Nebraska Press, 1994.

Clark, J. Bunker. "Anthony Philip Heinrich: A Bohemian Predecessor to Dvořák in the Wilds of America." In *Dvořák in America,* edited by John C. Tibbetts, 20–26.

Clifford, James. *The Predicament of Culture: Twentieth-Century Ethnography, Literature, and Art.* Cambridge, Mass.: Harvard University Press, 1988.

Clifton, James A., ed. *The Invented Indian: Cultural Fictions and Government Policies.* New Brunswick, N.J.: Transaction Publishers, 1990.

Cockrell, Dale, ed. Excelsior: Journals of the Hutchinson Family Singers, 1842–1846. Stuyvesant, N.Y.: Pendragon Press, 1989.

Cohen, Aaron I. *International Encyclopedia of Women Composers.* 2nd ed. New York: Books and Music, 1987.

Cole, Malcolm S. "Peter Winter's *Das unterbrochene Opferfest:* Fact, Fantasy, and Performance Practice in Post-Josephinian Vienna." In *Music in Performance and Society: Essays in Honor of Roland Jackson,* edited by Malcolm Cole and John Koegel, 291–324. Warren, Mich.: Harmonie Park Press, 1997.

Cole, Rossetter. "Musical Inspirations from Longfellow." Paper read at the Chicago Literary Club, 1903. 28-page typescript at the Newberry Library, Chicago.

Coleridge-Taylor, Avril. *The Heritage of Samuel Coleridge-Taylor.* London: Dennis Dobson, 1979.

Collins, Michael, and Elise K. Kirk. *Opera and Vivaldi.* Austin: University of Texas Press, 1984.

Cone, Edward T. *The Composer's Voice.* Berkeley: University of California Press, 1974.

Conrad, Rudolf. "Mutual Fascination: Indians in Dresden and Leipzig." In *Indians and Europe,* edited by Christian F. Feest, 455–74.

Cook, Sherburne F. *The Conflict between the California Indian and White Civilization.* Berkeley: University of California Press, 1976.

Cooke, Deryck. *The Language of Music.* London: Oxford University Press, 1959.

Cracroft, Richard. "The American West of Karl May." Master's thesis, University of Utah, Salt Lake City, 1963.

Crawford, Richard. *America's Musical Life.* New York: Norton, 2001.

———. "Edward MacDowell: Musical Nationalism and an American Tone Poet." *Journal of the American Musicological Society* 49, no. 3 (Fall 1996): 528–60.

Crompton, Samuel Willard, ed. *Illustrated Atlas of Native American History.* Edison, N.J.: Chartwell Books, 1999.

Cronyn, George W., ed. *The Path on the Rainbow: An Anthology of Songs and Chants from the Indians of North America.* New York: Boni and Liveright, 1918.

Culbertson, Evelyn Davis. *He Heard America Singing: Arthur Farwell, Composer and Crusading Music Educator.* Metuchen, N.J.: Scarecrow Press, 1992.

Currier, T. P. "Edward MacDowell as I Knew Him." *Musical Quarterly* 1 (Jan. 1915): 17–51.

Curtis, Edward S. "North American Indians." *National Geographic* 18, no. 7 (July 1907): 469–84.

Curtis, Natalie [Natalie Curtis Burlin]. "An American Indian Composer." *Harper's Magazine* 107 (1903): 626–32. [Contains music of the Hopi Indians.]

———. "Busoni's Indian Fantasy." *Southern Workman* 44, no. 10 (Oct. 1915): 538–44.

———. "Folksong and the American Indian." *Southern Workman* 44, no. 9 (1915): 475–80.

——. "Indian Cradle Songs." *Musical Quarterly* 7 (Oct. 1921): 549–58.

——. *The Indians' Book*. [1907]. Reprint, New York: Dover, 1968.

——. "The Perpetuating of Indian Art." *Outlook* (22 Nov. 1913): 620–32.

——. "A Plea for Our Native Art." *Musical Quarterly* 6, no. 2 (Apr. 1920): 175–78.

——. "Recording for Posterity the Music of Primitive Humanity." *Musical America* 35, no. 21 (21 Mar. 1922): 3, 38.

——. "Two Corn-Grinding Songs." *Craftsman* 7 (1904–5): 35–41.

Cushing, Frank Hamilton. "My Adventures in Zuñi." Originally in *Century* magazine. Reprint, Santa Fe: Peripatetic Press, 1941.

Dahlhaus, Carl. *Nineteenth-Century Music*. Translated by J. Bradford Robinson. Berkeley: University of California Press, 1989.

Danly, Linda. "Hugo Friedhofer's Westerns." *Cue Sheet* 11, no. 2 (Apr. 1995): 19–24.

Davison, Sister Mary Veronica. *American Music Periodicals, 1853–1899*. Ph.D. diss., University of Minnesota, 1973.

Day-O'Connell, Jeremy. "Pentatonic." In *The New Grove Dictionary of Music and Musicians*, edited by Stanley Sadie. New York: Grove's Dictionaries, 2000.

——. *Pentatonicism in Nineteenth-Century Music*. Ph.D. diss., Cornell University, 2001.

——. "The Rise of $\hat{6}$ in the Nineteenth Century." *Music Theory Spectrum* 24, no. 1 (Spring 2002): 35–67.

De la Laurencie, Lionel. "America in the French Music of the Seventeenth and Eighteenth Centuries." *Musical Quarterly* 7, no. 2 (Apr. 1921): 284–302.

Deloria, Philip J. *Indians in Unexpected Places*. Lawrence: University Press of Kansas, 2004.

——. *Playing Indian*. New Haven, Conn.: Yale University Press, 1998.

Densmore, Frances. *The American Indians and Their Music*. [1926]. Reprint, New York: Johnson, 1970.

——. "Four Saints and Some American Indian Music." *Musical America* 54, no. 13 (Aug. 1934): 12.

——. "How the Indian Seeks Power through Dream Music." *Musical America* 46 (11 June 1927): 3, 20.

——. "Study of Indian Music." *Musical Quarterly* 1 (Apr. 1915): 187–97.

——. "The Study of Indian Music in the Nineteenth Century." *American Anthropologist* 29 (1927): 77–86.

——. "Use of Indian Music." *Musical America* 73, no. 5 (1 Apr. 1953): 15.

Devore, Richard. "Nineteenth-Century Harmonic Dualism in the United States." *Theoria* 2 (1987): 85–100.

Dill, Charles. *Monstrous Opera: Rameau and the Tragic Tradition*. Princeton, N.J.: Princeton University Press, 1998.

Dippie, Brian W. *The Vanishing American: White Attitudes and American Indian Policy in the Nineteenth Century*. Middletown, Conn.: Wesleyan University Press, 1982.

Domhoff, G. William. *The Bohemian Grove and Other Retreats: A Study in Ruling Class Cohesiveness*. New York: Harper and Row, 1974.

Dorson, Richard M. *Folklore and Fakelore: Essays toward a Discipline of Folk Studies*. Cambridge, Mass.: Harvard University Press, 1976.

Duden, Gottfried. *Report on a Journey to the Western States of North America and a Stay of Several Years along the Missouri (During the Years 1824, '25, '26, and 1827).* [1829]. Translated by George H. Kellner, Elsa Nagel, Adolph E. Schroeder, and W. M. Senner. Columbia: State Historical Society of Missouri and University of Missouri Press, 1980.

Durang, Charles. *The Philadelphia Stage, 1749–1821.* Published serially in the *Philadelphia Sunday Dispatch* (beginning 7 May 1854). [Copy of extra-illustrated edition in the Harvard Theatre Collection. Also available on microfilm.]

Durang, John. *The Memoir of John Durang, American Actor, 1785–1816,* edited by Alan S. Downer. Pittsburgh: Published for the Historical Society of York County and for the American Society for Theatre Research by the University of Pittsburgh Press, 1966.

During, Simon. *Modern Enchantments.* Cambridge, Mass.: Harvard University Press, 2002.

Dvořák, Antonin. "Dvořák on His New Work." *New York Herald* (15 Dec. 1893). Reprinted in *Dvořák in America,* edited by John C. Tibbetts, 363.

——. "Music in America." *Harper's New Monthly Magazine* (Feb. 1895). Reprinted in *Dvořák in America,* edited by John C. Tibbetts, 370–80.

Dvořák, Otakar. *Antonín Dvořák, My Father.* Translated by Miroslav Nemec. Edited by Paul J. Polansky. Spillville, Iowa: Czech Historical Research Center, 1993.

Dwight, John Sullivan, ed. *Dwight's Journal of Music.* Boston, 1852–81. Reprint, New York: Johnson Reprint Corp., 1968.

Eals, Myron. "Indian Music." *American Antiquarian* [Chicago] 1 (1878–79): 249–53. [Contains 24 tunes.]

Edwards, Paul. "Indian Tunes at Exposition: Melodies of Poor Lo, Written by Californian, Give Public a Musical Treat." Unidentified clipping (20 Aug. 1904) in "Scrapbook of Newspaper Clippings Concerning the Musical Career of Arthur Farwell, 1903–1911," Farwell Collection, Sibley Music Library, Eastman School of Music, Rochester, N.Y.

Ellingson, Ter. *The Myth of the Noble Savage.* Berkeley: University of California Press, 2001.

Elson, Louis C. *The History of American Music.* 2nd ed. New York: Burt Franklin, 1925.

——. The National Music of America and Its Sources. Boston: L. C. Page, 1911.

Etude's special issue on Indianist music. *Etude* 38 (October 1920).

Fahrner, Robert. *The Theater Career of Charles Dibdin.* London: Peter Lang, 1989.

Farrell, Gerry. *Indian Music and the West.* Oxford University Press, 1997.

Farwell, Arthur. "Aspects of Indian Music." *Southern Workman* 31, no. 4 (Apr. 1902): 211–17.

——. "A Brief View of American Indian Music." *The Messenger* [Music Teachers' National Association] 4, no. 6 (Aug. 1903): 276–79.

——. "Discovery of Indian Music." *Musical America* 9 (20 Mar. 1909). Reprinted in *"Wanderjahre of a Revolutionist" and Other Essays on American Music,* edited by Thomas Stoner,76–80.

——. "Indian and Negro: How Various Composers Have Made Use of the Music of Both Races." *Musical America* 16, no. 4 (1 June 1912): 24.

——. "Indian Music, a Wealth of Legendary Lore." *Presto,* no. 863 (22 Jan. 1903): 32–33.

——. "Indian Music of a Genuine Sort (On Henry Gilbert)." *Musical America* 14 (25 Nov. 1911): 21.

——. "Introduction to *American Indian Melodies.*" Newton Center, Mass.: Wa-Wan Press, 1901.

——. "A Letter to American Composers." [1903]. Reprinted in *The Wa-Wan Press,* edited by Vera Brodsky Lawrence, vol. 1. New York: Arno Press, 1970.

——. "Negro and Indian: Why Our American Composers Have Turned Their Attention Chiefly to the Red Man." *Musical America* 15 (25 May 1912): 24.

——. "The New Gospel of Music." *Musical America* 19 (4 Apr. 1914). Reprinted in *"Wanderjahre of a Revolutionist" and Other Essays on American Music,* edited by Thomas Stoner, 222–26.

——. "Pioneering for American Music." *Modern Music* 12 (Mar.–Apr. 1935): 116–22.

——. "A Publishing Project in New York." *Musical America* 9 (27 Mar. 1909). Reprinted in *"Wanderjahre of a Revolutionist" and Other Essays on American Music,* edited by Thomas Stoner, 81–86.

——. "Scrapbook of Newspaper Clippings Concerning the Musical Career of Arthur Farwell, 1903–1911." Farwell Collection, Sibley Music Library, Eastman School of Music, Rochester, N.Y.

——. "Second Trip West." *Musical America* 9 (8 May 1909): 23, 31. Reprinted in *"Wanderjahre of a Revolutionist" and Other Essays on American Music,* edited by Thomas Stoner, 118–26.

——. "Toward American Music." *Out West* 20, no. 5 (May 1904): 454–58. Reprinted in *"Wanderjahre of a Revolutionist" and Other Essays on American Music,* edited by Thomas Stoner, 185–90.

——. "Victor Herbert's *Natoma.*" *American Review of Reviews* (Apr. 1911): 441.

——. *"Wanderjahre of a Revolutionist" and other Essays on American Music.* Edited by Thomas Stoner. Rochester, N.Y.: University of Rochester Press, 1995.

——. *The Wa-Wan Press.* 1901–1910. Reprint, edited by Vera Brodsky Lawrence. 5 vols. New York: Arno Press, 1970.

Farwell, Arthur, and W. Dermot Darby, eds. *Music in America.* Vol. 4, *The Art of Music.* New York: National Society for Music, 1915.

Farwell, Arthur, and Louis Laloy. "La musique américaine." *Mercure Musicale* 3, no. 10 (15 Oct. 1907): 1039–45.

Farwell, Brice, ed. *A Guide to the Music of Arthur Farwell and to the Microfilm Collection of His Work.* Briarcliff Manor, N.Y.: privately printed, 1972.

Fassett, Agatha. *The Naked Face of Genius: Béla Bartók's American Years.* Boston: Houghton Mifflin, 1958.

Fawcett, Walden. "How Our Government Is Perpetuating the Indian's Music." *Musical America* 14, no. 8 (1 July 1909): 3–4.

——. "Music of the Red Indian." *Music News* 41 (12 Aug. 1911): 137–38.

Feest, Christian F. "The Indian in Non-English Literature." In *History of Indian-White Relations,* edited by Wilcomb E. Washburn, 582–86. Vol. 4, *Handbook of North American Indians,* edited by William C. Sturtevant. Washington, D.C.: Smithsonian Institution, 1988.

——, ed. *Indians and Europe: An Interdisciplinary Collection of Essays*. Rev. ed. Lincoln: University of Nebraska Press, 1999.

Fenby, Eric. *Delius*. London: Faber and Faber, 1971.

Fenner, Theodore. *Opera in London: Views of the Press: 1785–1830*. Carbondale: Southern Illinois University Press, 1994.

Fewkes, J. W. "On the Use of the Phonograph among the Zuni Indians." *American Naturalist* (July 1890): 687–91.

"Fifth Summer Season at Hollywood Bowl." *Musical Courier* 93, no. 1 (1 July 1926): 1.

Fillmore, John C. "Professor Stumpf on Mr. [Benjamin Ives] Gilman's Transcriptions of the Zuni Songs." *Music* 5 (1893–94): 649–52.

——. "Report on the Structural Peculiarities of the Music." In Alice C. Fletcher and Francis LaFlesche, *A Study of Omaha Indian Music*, 59–77.

——. "A Study of Indian Music." *Century Magazine* 47, no. 4 (Feb. 1894): 616–23.

——. "A Woman's Song of the Kwakiutl Indians." *Journal of the American Folklore Society* 6 (1893): 285–90.

"Film: Smoke Signals, Beyond Silence, and Pi." *In These Times* 22, no. 17 (26 July 1998): 24.

Filson, John. *Filson's Kentucke: A Facsimile Reproduction of the Original Wilmington Edition of 1784, with Paged Critique, Sketch of Filson's Life, and Bibliography, by Willard Rouse Jillson*. Louisville, Ky.: J. P. Morton, 1929.

Finck, Henry T. "An American Composer: Edward A. MacDowell." *Century* 53 (1897): 449–54.

——. *My Adventures in the Golden Age of Music*. New York: Funk and Wagnalls, 1926.

——. "What Is American Music?" *Etude* 7 (1906): 12–13.

Finson, Jon W. "The Romantic Savage: American Indians in the Parlor." Chap. 7 in *The Voices That Are Gone: Themes in Nineteenth-Century American Popular Song*. New York: Oxford University Press, 1994.

"First Production of 3–act American Grand Opera [*The Sacrifice*] by a Bostonian [Converse]." *New York Times* (4 Mar. 1911): 11:1.

Fiske, Roger. *English Theatre Music in the Eighteenth Century*. 2nd ed. New York: Oxford University Press, 1986.

——. *Scotland in Music: A European Enthusiasm*. Cambridge: Cambridge University Press, 1983.

Fletcher, Alice C. *Indian Games and Dances, with Native Songs*. Boston: C. C. Brichard, 1916.

——. "Indian Music: An Address Delivered in Washington, D.C., April 1894." *Music* 6 (1894): 188–99.

——. "Indian Songs." *Century Illustrated Monthly Magazine* 47 (Jan. 1894): 421–31.

——. "Indian Songs and Music." *Journal of American Folklore* 11, no. 41 (Apr.–June 1898): 85–104.

——. *Indian Story and Song from North America*. [1900]. Reprint, New York: AMS Press, 1970.

——. "Music as Found in Certain North American Indian Tribes." *Music* 4 (1893): 457–67. Reprinted in *Music Review* 2 (Aug. 1893): 534–38.

——. "The Sun Dance of the Ogalala Sioux." Proceedings of the American Association for the Advancement of Science 31 (1882): 580–84.

——. "The 'Wa-wan' or Pipe Dance of the Omahas." *Peabody Museum of American Archaeology and Ethnology Reports* 3 (1880–86): 308–33. [Includes music.]

Fletcher, Alice C., and Francis LaFlesche. The Omaha Tribe. 2 vols. 27th Annual Report of the Bureau of American Ethnology to the Secretary of the Smithsonian Institution, 1905–1906. [1911]. Reprint, Lincoln: University of Nebraska Press, 1992.

——. *A Study of Omaha Indian Music.* [1893]. Reprint, with an introduction by Helen Myers, Lincoln: University of Nebraska Press, 1994.

Fletcher, Alice C., and James R. Murie. "The Hako: A Pawnee Ceremony." In *Bureau of American Ethnology 22nd Annual Report, 1900–1901,* 5–372. Washington, D.C.: Government Printing Office, 1904.

Flynn, Joyce. "Academics on the Trail of the Stage 'Indian': A Review Essay." *Studies in American Indian Literature* 2, no. 1 (Winter 1987): 1–16.

Foreman, Carolyn Thomas. *Indians Abroad, 1493–1938.* Norman: University of Oklahoma Press, 1943.

"40,000 Witness 'Shanewis.'" *Pacific Coast Musician* (5 July 1926): 1, 12.

Franko, Mark. *Dance as Text: Ideologies of the Baroque Body.* Cambridge: Cambridge University Press, 1993.

Friar, Ralph E., and Natasha A. *The Only Good Indian . . . : The Hollywood Gospel.* New York: Drama Book Specialists, 1972.

Friberg, Eino, trans. *The Kalevala: Epic of the Finnish People.* Helsinki: Otava Publishing, 1988.

"From Broadway to the Pueblos: Thurlow Lieurance and Rudolf Friml." *Etude* 41 (1923): 231.

"Full Blooded Chippewa Indian C. Kawbawgam, Former Medical Doctor, Being Hailed in Berlin as Another Caruso." *New York Times* (24 Nov. 1912): pt. 3, 5:3.

Garland, Hamlin. *Roadside Meetings.* New York: Macmillan, 1930.

Garrett, Porter. *The Bohemian Jinks: A Treatise.* San Francisco: Bohemian Club, 1908.

Gathorne-Hardy, Geoffrey Malcolm, trans. *The Norse Discoverers of America, the Winland Sagas.* Oxford: Clarendon Press, 1921.

Gidley, Mick. "'The Vanishing Race' in Sight and Sound: Edward S. Curtis's Musicale of North American Indian Life." *Prospects: An Annual of American Cultural Studies* 12 (1987): 59–87.

Gilbert, Henry F. "Indian Music." *New Music Review* 11 (1911): 56–59.

——. "Indian Sketches." *Boston Symphony Programme Notes* (4 and 5 Mar. 1921): 1074.

——. "Native American Indian Music." *Harvard Musical Review* 1, no. 6 (1913): 5–7.

——. "Personal Recollections of Edward MacDowell." *New Music Review* 11 (1912): 494–98.

Gilman, Lawrence. *Edward MacDowell: A Study.* New York: John Lane, 1915.

Giordano, Fedora. "The Anxiety of Discovery: The Italian Interest in Native American Studies." Italian Association for North American Studies. Online at http://www.aisna.org/rsajournal5/giordano.html.

Girdlestone, Cuthbert. *Jean-Philippe Rameau: His Life and Work.* London: Cassell, 1957.

Glassberg, David. *American Historical Pageantry: The Uses of Tradition in the Early Twentieth Century.* Chapel Hill: University of North Carolina Press, 1990.

Gorbman, Claudia. "Scoring the Indian: Music in the Liberal Western." In *Western Music and Its Others,* edited by Georgina Born and David Hesmondhalgh, 234–53.

——. *Unheard Melodies: Narrative Film Music.* Bloomington: Indiana University Press, 1987.

Gottschalk, Louis Moreau. *Notes of a Pianist.* Edited by Clara Gottschalk. Translated by Robert E. Peterson. Philadelphia: Lippincott, 1881.

Grabócz, Márta. "The Role of Semiotical Terminology in Musical Analysis." In *Musical Semiotics in Growth,* edited by Eero Tarasti, 195–218. Bloomington: Indiana University Press, 1996.

Graves, Gary John. *The Bohemian Grove Theatrics: A History and Analysis from the Club's Beginnings in 1872 Up to the Encampment of 1992.* Ph.D. diss., University of California, Berkeley, 1994.

Gray, Edward F. *Leif Eriksson: Discoverer of America, A.D. 1003.* London: Oxford University Press, 1930.

Gray, Judith A. "A Guide to Early Field Recordings (1900–1949) at the Lowie Museum of Anthropology by Richard Keeling." *American Indian Culture and Research Journal* 16, no. 3 (1992): 209.

——. "When Cultures Meet." *Folklife Center News* 14, no. 4 (Fall 1992): 3–9. [Published by the American Folklife Center, Library of Congress.]

Greeley, Horace. "The Plains: As I Crossed Them Ten Years Ago." *Harper's Magazine* (1869). Excerpted in *Harper's: An American Perspective, 1850–1984,* edited by Ann Marie Cunningham. New York: Harper's, 1985.

Green, Rayna D. "The Indian in Popular American Culture." In *History of Indian-White Relations,* edited by Wilcomb E. Washburn, 587–606. Vol. 4, *Handbook of North American Indians,* edited by William C. Sturtevant. Washington, D.C.: Smithsonian Institution, 1988.

Greenblatt, Stephen. *Marvelous Possessions: The Wonder of the New World.* Chicago: University of Chicago Press, 1991.

Grimsted, David. *Melodrama Unveiled: American Theater and Culture, 1800–1850.* Chicago: University of Chicago Press, 1968.

Guion, David M. "From Yankee Doodle Thro' to Handel's Largo: Music at the World's Columbian Exposition." *College Music Symposium* 24, no. 1 (Spring 1984): 81–96.

Hagan, Dorothy Veinus. *Félicien David, 1810–1876: A Composer and a Cause.* Syracuse, N.Y.: Syracuse University Press, 1985.

Haine, W. Scott, "The Development of Leisure and the Transformation of Working-Class Adolescence, Paris 1830–1940." *Journal of Family History* 17, no. 4 (1992): 451–76.

Hale, Henry. "Hiawatha Played by Real Indians." *The Critic* 47, no. 1 (1905): 41–50.

Hale, Philip. "MacDowell's Suite and 'Indian Tunes.'" *Musical Courier* 32, no. 6 (5 Feb. 1896). Rev. and adapted from an earlier review, "Symphony Concert: MacDowell's *Indian Suite.*" *Boston Journal* 2 (Feb. 1896).

Hall, Roger A. *Performing the American Frontier, 1870–1906.* Cambridge: Cambridge University Press, 2001.

Hallowell, A. Irving. "The Impact of the American Indian on American Culture." *American Anthropologist* [1957]. Reprinted in *Folklore in Action: Essays for Discussion in Honor of MacEdward Leach* (vol. 14, *Bibliographical and Special Series*), edited by Horace P. Beck. Philadelphia: American Folklore Society, 1962.

Halpin, Marjorie. Introduction to *Letters and Notes on the Manners, Customs, and Condition of the North American Indians. Written During Eight Years Travel among the Wildest Tribes. . . . by George Catlin.* New York: Dover, 1973.

Hamell, George R. "Mohawks Abroad: The 1764 Amsterdam Etching of Sychnecta." In *Indians and Europe,* edited by Christian F. Feest, 175–97.

Hamm, Charles. *Music in the New World.* New York: Norton, 1983.

——. Yesterdays: Popular Song in America. New York: Norton, 1983.

Hankins, Roger. "Sounds Familiar: Those Indian Songs." *The Ragtimer* (May–June 1970): 5.

Hanley, Jason. "Natural Born Killers: Music and Image in Postmodern Film." In *Postmodern Music/Postmodern Thought,* edited by Judy Lockhead and Joseph Auner, 335–60. New York: Garland, 2002.

Hargrove, John. "The War Dance No War Whoop: Being a Reply to a Letter from George Dashiell." Baltimore: privately printed pamphlet, 1804.

Harker, David. *Fakesong: The Manufacture of British "Folksong," 1700 to the Present Day.* Milton Keynes, U.K.: Open University Press, 1985.

Haun, Eugene. *But Hark! More Harmony: The Libretti of Restoration Opera in English.* Ypsilanti: Eastern Michigan University Press, 1971.

Hawley, Oscar Hatch. "Indian Music." *Musical Courier* 60, no. 13 (1910): 42.

Haywood, Charles. *The American Indians North of Mexico, Including Eskimos.* Vol. 2, *A Bibliography of North American Folklore and Folksong.* 2nd ed. rev. New York: Dover, 1951. [Contains copious bibliographical citations for anthropological studies of Indian music to 1950.]

Heizer, R. F., and M. A. Whipple, eds. *The California Indians : A Source Book.* Berkeley: University of California Press, 1970.

Helm, Ernest Eugene. *Music at the Court of Frederick the Great.* Norman: University of Oklahoma Press, 1960.

Hemming, John. *Red Gold: The Conquest of the Brazilian Indians.* London: Macmillan, 1978.

Hepokoski, James. "Culture Clash." *Musical Times* (Dec. 1991): 686–88.

"Herbert, Composer of *Natoma.*" *Music News* 3 (3 Mar. 1911): 13.

"Herbert Discusses His *Natoma.*" *Musical America* 13 (4 Feb. 1911): 28.

Heth, Charlotte, ed. *Native American Dance: Ceremonies and Social Traditions.* Washington, D.C.: National Museum of the American Indian, Smithsonian Institution, 1992.

Highfill, Philip H., Kalman A. Burnim, and Edward A. Langhans. Biographical Dictionary of Actors, Actresses, Musicians, D*ancers, Managers, and Other Stage Personnel* in London, 1660–1800. Carbondale: Southern Illinois University Press, 1973.

Hilen, Andrew, ed. *The Letters of Henry Wadsworth Longfellow.* 6 vols. Cambridge, Mass: Belknap Press of Harvard University Press, 1966–82.

Hilger, Michael. *The American Indian in Film.* Metuchen, N.J.: Scarecrow Press, 1986.

——. From Savage to Nobleman: Images of Native Americans in Film. Lanham, Md.: Scarecrow Press, 1995.

Hilton, James L., and William von Hippel. "Introduction on the Question of 'Why?': The Context-Dependent Function of Stereotypic Thinking." *Annual Review of Psychology* 47 (1996): 237–71.

Hitchcock, H. Wiley. "An Early American Melodrama: *The Indian Princess* of J. N. Barker and John Bray." *Notes* [Music Library Association] 12 (1954–55): 375–88.

Hofstadter, Richard. *The Progressive Historians: Turner, Beard, Parrington.* New York: Alfred A. Knopf, 1968.

Hogan, Agnes. Notice of Victor Herbert's *Natoma. Philadelphia Record* (19 Feb. 1911): sec. 4, p. 5.

Hoig, Stanley W. *The Cherokees and Their Chiefs in the Wake of Empire.* Fayetteville: University of Arkansas Press, 1998.

Honour, Hugh. *The New Golden Land.* New York: Pantheon Books, 1975.

Horn, David. "Bibliography of Music of the American Indians." In *The Literature of American Music in Books and Folk Music Collections: A Fully Annotated Bibliography,* 141–52. Metuchen, N.J.: Scarecrow Press, 1977.

Hovgaard, William. *Voyages of the Norsemen to America.* New York: American Scandinavian Foundation, 1914.

Hovland, Michael A., comp. *Musical Settings of American Poetry: A Bibliography.* Westport, Conn.: Greenwood Press, 1986.

Howard, James H. "The Native American Image in Western Europe." *American Indian Quarterly* 4, no. 1 (1978): 33–56.

Howard, John Tasker. *Our American Music.* Rev. ed. New York: Thomas Y. Crowell, 1939.

Hudson, Richard. *Passacaglio and Ciaccona: From Guitar Music to Italian Keyboard Variations in the Seventeenth Century.* Ann Arbor, Mich.: UMI Research Press, 1981.

Hughes, Rupert. *Contemporary American Composers, Being a Study of the Music of This Country, Its Present Conditions and Its Future, with Critical Estimates and Biographies of the Principal Living Composers.* Boston: Page, 1900.

Hunter, Anne Home. *Poems.* London: Printed for T. Payne, 1802.

Hunter, Mary. "The *Alla Turca* Style in the Late Eighteenth Century: Race and Gender in the Symphony and the Seraglio." In *The Exotic in Western Music,* edited by Jonathan Bellman, 44–47.

Hutchinson, John W. *Story of the Hutchinsons (Tribe of Jesse).* Compiled and edited by Charles E. Mann with an introduction by Frederick Douglass. Boston: Lee and Shepard, 1896.

"Indian Flute, The." *The Musical Visitor* [Cincinnati] 25, no. 9 (Sept. 1896): 258.

Indian Melodies; Eight Songs, Words and Music, by the Women's Board of Home Missions, Presbyterian Church. New York: Women's Board of Home Missions, Presbyterian Church, n.d.

Indian Music. Bulletin no. 3, School of American Research, Archaeological Institute of America. Santa Fe, N.M.: School of American Research, 1926.

Irving, Washington. "Traits of Indian Character." In *The Sketch-book of Geoffrey Crayon, Gent.* [pseud., 1819]. Reprint, New York: Macmillan, 1915.

Isherwood, Robert M. *Music in the Service of the King.* Ithaca, N.Y.:Cornell University Press, 1973.

Jablonski, Edward. *The Encyclopedia of American Music.* Garden City, N.Y.: Doubleday, 1981.

Jackson, Helen Hunt. *A Century of Dishonor.* New York: Harper and Bros., 1881.
——. *Ramona.* Boston: Little, Brown, 1930.
Jacobi, Frederick. "Modern Music in Gallup, New Mexico." *Modern Music* 2, no. 2 (Apr. 1925): 28–31.
"Jacobi's Indian Dances." *Musical Courier* 97 (20 Dec. 1928): 50.
James, Edwin. *Accounts of S. H. Long's Expedition from Pittsburgh to the Rocky Mountains, 1819–32.* Reprinted in Reuben G. Thwaites, Early Western Travels, 1748–1846, vols. 14–17. Cleveland: Arthur H. Clark, 1906.
Janta, Aleksander. "The First American National Opera: The Story of Edward Sobolewski." In *A History of Nineteenth-Century American-Polish Music,* 11–22. New York: Kosciuszko Foundation, 1982.
Johnson, H. Earle. *Operas on American Subjects.* New York: Coleman-Ross, 1964.
Jones, Eugene H. *Native Americans as Shown on the Stage, 1753–1916.* Metuchen, N.J.: Scarecrow Press, 1988.
Jones, Henry Broadus. The Death Song of the "Noble Savage": A Study in the Idealization of the American Indian. Ph.D. diss., University of Chicago, 1924.
Jorgensen, Joseph G. *The Sun Dance Religion: Power for the Powerless.* Chicago: University of Chicago Press, 1972.
Kasson, Joy. *Buffalo Bill's Wild West: Celebrity, Memory, and Popular History.* New York: Hill and Wang, 2000.
Keillor, Elaine, ed. *The Canadian Musical Heritage,* vol. 1. Ottawa: Canadian Musical Heritage Society, 1983.
——. "Indigenous Music as a Compositional Source: Parallels and Contrasts in Canadian and American Music." in *Taking a Stand: Essays in Honour of John Beckwith,* edited by Timothy J. McGee, 185–218. Toronto: University of Toronto Press, 1995.
Keiser, Albert. *The Indian in American Literature.* New York: Oxford University Press, 1933.
Kelly, Michael. *Reminiscences of Michael Kelly of the King's Theatre and Theatre Royal Drury Lane.* [2nd ed., 1826]. Reprint, with a new introduction by A. Hyatt King. New York: Da Capo Press, 1968.
Kennedy, William Sloane. *Henry W. Longfellow: Biography, Anecdote, Letters, Criticism.* Cambridge, Mass.: Moses King, 1882.
Kilpatrick, Jacquelyn. *The Celluloid Indian: Native Americans in Film.* Lincoln: University of Nebraska Press, 1999.
Kilroe, Edwin P. Saint Tammany *and the Origin of the Society of Tammany, or Columbian Order in the City of New York.* Ph.D. diss., Columbia University, 1913.
Kinscella, Hazel Gertrude. "American Index to *The Musical Quarterly* [1915–57]." *Journal of Research in Music Education* 6, no. 2 (Fall 1958): 1–151.
——. "Lieurance Sings of Green Timber Country in New Cycle." *Musical America* 36 (6 May 1922): 5, 40.
——. "Preserving the Music of a Vanishing Race." *Musical America* 24, no. 8 (24 June 1916): 3–4, 8.
——. "Thurlow Lieurance's Researches in Indian Song Disclose Rich Material for Our Composers." *Musical America* 29, no. 26 (26 Apr. 1919): 3–4.
Kirk, Elise K. *Music at the White House: A History of the American Spirit.* Urbana: University of Illinois Press, 1986.

K. K. "Music of Indians Offers Rich Field to Our Composers, Says Harold Loring." *Musical America* 37, no. 3 (Dec. 1922): 64–68.

Koegel, John. " 'The Indian Chief' and 'Morality': Eighteenth-Century British Popular Song Transformed into Nineteenth-Century American Shape-Note Hymn." In *Music in Performance and Society: Essays in Honor of Roland Jackson,* edited by Malcolm Cole and John Koegel, 437–508. Warren, Mich.: Harmonie Park Press, 1997.

Krehbiel, Henry. "Folk-Music in Chicago, I: Songs of the Omaha Indians." *New York Tribune* (6 Aug. 1893): II:14.

——. "Folk-Music in Chicago, II: Cannibal Songs of the Indians" *New York Tribune* (6 Aug. 1893): II:14.

——. "Folk-Music Studies: Songs of the American Indians (in 3 parts)." *New York Tribune* (24 Sept. 1899, 1 Oct. 1899, and 8 Oct. 1899): all three beginning on p. 15.

——. "Indian Dances—Indian Music." *Musical Courier* 25 (8 Oct. 1892): 9.

——. "Indian Melodies." *New York Daily Tribune* (1902), undated clipping in Krehbiel scrapbook, New York Public Library.

——. "Music at Worcester [on MacDowell's 'Indian' Suite]." *New York Daily Tribune* (23 Sept. 1897).

——. "Music of the Omahas." *New York Tribune* (10 Sept. 1893): II:14.

——. [On MacDowell]. *New York Daily Tribune* (11 Oct. 1896): II:3.

——. Review of the New York Musical Season, 1885–1890. 4 vols. New York: Novello, 1886–1890.

Krohn, Ernst. *A Century of Missouri Music.* [1924]. Reprint, New York: Da Capo Press, 1971.

Krummel, D. W., Jean Geil, Doris J. Dyen, and Deane L. Root. *Resources of American Music History: A Directory of Source Materials from Colonial Times to World War II.* Urbana: University of Illinois Press, 1981.

Lacroix, Paul, ed. *Ballets et mascarades de cour de Henri III à Louis XIV (1581–1692).* Recueillis et publiés, d'après les éditions originales. Geneva: J. Gay et fils, 1868–70.

LaFarge, Oliver. *A Pictorial History of the American Indian.* New York: Crown Publishers, 1956.

Lafitau, Joseph-François. *Mœurs des sauvages américains, comparées aux mœurs des premiers temps.* [1724]. Translated by William N. Fenton and Elizabeth L. Moore. Toronto: Champlain Society, 1974.

LaFlesche, Francis. "The Osage Tribe: Rite of the Chiefs; Sayings of the Ancient Men." In *36th Annual Report of the Bureau of American Ethnology, 1914–15,* 35–604. Washington, D.C.: U.S. Government Printing Office, 1921.

Lancefield, Robert. *Hearing Orientality in (White) America, 1900–1930.* Ph.D. diss., Wesleyan University, in progress.

Land, Edith, and George West, *Musical Accompaniment of Moving Pictures.* [1920]. Reprint, New York: Arno Press, 1970.

Läng-Hemd, Hans. "The Indian Influence in European Music." *Bulletin de la Societé Suisse des Americanistes* 38 (1974): 49–54. [In German.]

Lanier, Sidney. *Letters of Sidney Lanier: Selections from His Correspondence, 1866–1881.* New York: Charles Scribner's Sons, 1899.

Laubin, Reginald and Gladys. *Indian Dances of North America: Their Importance to Indian Life.* Norman: University of Oklahoma Press, 1977.

Lawrence, Vera Brodsky. *Strong on Music: The New York Music Scene in the Days of George Templeton Strong*. 3 vols. Chicago: University of Chicago Press, 1987–95.

Lears, T. Jackson. *No Place of Grace: Antimodernism and the Transformation of American Culture, 1880–1920*. New York: Pantheon Books, 1981.

Lee, Dorothy Sara, ed. *Early Anthologies*. Vol. 8, *The Federal Cylinder Project: A Guide to Field Cylinder Collections in Federal Agencies,* edited by Erika Brady et al. Washington: American Folklife Center, Library of Congress, 1984.

Leichtentritt, Hugo. *Serge Koussevitzky, the Boston Symphony Orchestra, and the New American Music*. Cambridge, Mass.: Harvard University Press, 1946.

Lepore, Jill. *The Name of War: King Philip's War and the Origins of American Identity.* New York: Alfred A. Knopf, 1998.

Leppert, Richard. *Arcadia at Versailles: Noble Amateur Musicians and Their Musettes and Hurdy-gurdies at the French Court (c. 1660–1789), A Visual Study.* Amsterdam: Swets and Zeitlinger, 1978.

Lester S. Levy Collection of American Sheet Music. Special collections, Milton S. Eisenhower Library of the Johns Hopkins University, Baltimore. Online at http://levysheetmusic.mse.jhu.edu.

Leuthold, Steven M. *Indigenous Aesthetics: Native Art, Media, and Identity.* Austin: University of Texas Press, 1998.

———. "Native American Responses to the Western." *American Indian Culture and Research Journal* 19, no. 1 (1995): 153–89.

Levine, Henry. "Indian Opera *Osseo* Is a Feature of Boston's Week." *Musical America* 36 (20 May 1922): 37.

Levine, Lawrence W. *Highbrow/Lowbrow: The Emergence of Cultural Hierarchy in America*. Cambridge, Mass.: Harvard University Press, 1988.

Levine, Victoria Lindsay. *Writing American Indian Music: Historic Transcriptions, Notations, and Arrangements*. Vol. 11, *Music in the United States of America*. Middleton, Wis.: Published for the American Musicological Society by A-R Editions, 2002.

Levy, Alan H. *Edward MacDowell: An American Master.* Lanham, Md.: Scarecrow Press, 1998.

Levy, Beth E. *Frontier Figures: American Music and the Mythology of the American West, 1895–1945*. Ph.D. diss., University of California, Berkeley, 2002.

———. " 'In the Glory of the Sunset': Arthur Farwell, Charles Wakefield Cadman, and Indianism in American Music." *Repercussions* 5, nos. 1 and 2 (Spring–Fall 1996): 128–83.

Lewis, Meriwether. *History of the Expedition under the Command of Captains Lewis and Clark, 1804–6*. Philadelphia: Bradford and Inskeep, 1814.

Libby, Dennis Albert. *Gaspare Spontini and His French and German Operas*. Ph.D. diss., Princeton University, 1969.

Lichtenwanger, William. *The Music of Henry Cowell: A Descriptive Catalog*. Brooklyn, N.Y.: Institute for Studies in American Music, City University of New York, 1986.

Liebersohn, Harry. *Aristocratic Encounters: European Travelers and North American Indians*. New York: Cambridge University Press, 1998.

Lieurance, Thurlow. "Beauties in the Music of the American Indian." *Etude* 36, no. 1 (Jan. 1918): 13.

———. "The Musical Soul of the American Indian." *Etude* 38, no. 10 (Oct. 1920): 655–56. Reprinted in Thurlow Lieurance, Charles Wakefield Cadman, and Arthur Nevin, *Indian Music. The Etude* Musical Booklet Library. Philadelphia: Theodore Presser, 1928.

———. "Stories of Famous Concert Songs: *By the Waters of the Minnetonka.*" *Etude* 50, no. 6 (June 1932): 396, 449.

"Lieurance Recognized Authority on Aboriginal Indian Melodies." *Musical America* 34, no. 12 (3 Sept. 1921): 1, 8.

"Lieurance with his American Indian Proteges." *Music News* 14 (28 Apr. 1922): cover.

L. M. "The Melodrama of *Hiawatha.*" *Musical Leader and Concert-Goer* [Chicago] 6, no. 14 (1903): 9.

Locke, Ralph. "Exoticism." In *The New Grove Dictionary of Music and Musicians,* edited by Stanley Sadie. New York: Grove's Dictionaries, 2000.

Longfellow, Henry Wadsworth. *The Poetical Works of Henry Wadsworth Longfellow,* vol. 1. Boston: Houghton, Mifflin, 1879.

———. *The Song of Hiawatha, with Illustrations from Designs by Frederic Remington.* Boston: Houghton, Mifflin, 1891.

Longfellow, Samuel, ed. *Life of Henry Wadsworth Longfellow, with Extracts from his Journals and Correspondence.* Boston: Houghton Mifflin, 1851.

Longyear, Katherine Marie. *Henry Franklin Gilbert: His Life and Works.* Ph.D. diss., Eastman School of Music, University of Rochester, 1968.

Lott, Eric. *Love and Theft: Blackface Minstrelsy and the American Working Class.* New York: Oxford University Press, 1993.

Lovejoy, Arthur O., and George Boas. *Primitivism and Related Ideas in Antiquity.* Baltimore: Johns Hopkins University Press, 1935.

Lowe, Donald. *Sir Carl Busch: His Life and Work as a Teacher, Conductor, and Composer.* D.M.A. thesis, University of Missouri–Kansas City, 1972.

Lowe, Rachel. *Frederick Delius, 1862–1934: A Catalogue of the Music Archives of the Delius Trust.* London: Delius Trust, 1974.

Lowens, Margery Morgan. *The New York Years of Edward MacDowell.* Ph.D. diss., University of Michigan, 1971.

Lubbers, Klaus. *Born for the Shade: Stereotypes of the Native American in United States Literature and the Visual Arts, 1776–1894.* Amsterdam: Rodopi Bv Editions, 1994.

Lucas, Phil, and Robert Hagopian. *Images of Indians.* Five-part documentary. KCTS–9 Seattle and United Indians of All Tribes Foundation. American Public Broadcasting Consortium, 1979.

Lurie, Nancy O. "Relations between Indians and Anthropologists." In *History of Indian-White Relations,* edited by Wilcomb E. Washburn, 548–56. Vol. 4, *Handbook of North American Indians,* edited by William C. Sturtevant. Washington, D.C.: Smithsonian Institution, 1988.

Lutz, Harmut. "Indians/Native Americans." In *The BFI Companion to the Western,* edited by Edward Buscombe, 155–59. New York: Da Capo Press, 1991.

Lyman, Christopher M. *The Vanishing Race and Other Illusions: Photographs of Indians by Edward S. Curtis.* Washington, D.C.: Smithsonian Institution Press, 1982.

MacDowell, Edward. *Critical and Historical Essays,* edited by W. J. Baltzell. [1912]. Reprint, New York: Da Capo Press, 1969.

——. "Folk Song and Its Relation to Nationalism in Music." In *Critical and Historical Essays,* edited by W. J. Baltzell, 151–53. [1912]. Reprint, New York: Da Capo Press, 1969.

MacDowell, Marian. *Random Notes on Edward MacDowell and His Music.* Boston: Arthur P. Schmidt, 1910.

"MacDowell's Indian Suite." *Presto* (23 Jan. 1902): 8.

Maehder, Jürgen. "The Representation of the 'Discovery' on the Opera Stage." In *Musical Repercussions of 1492: Encounters in Text and Performance,* edited by Carol E. Robertson, 257–87. Washington, D.C.: Smithsonian Institution Press, 1992.

Manchel, Frank. "Cultural Confusion: *Broken Arrow* (1950)." In *Hollywood's Indian: The Portrayal of the Native American on Film,* edited by Peter C. Rollins and John E. O'Connor, 91–106.

Mark, Joan. *A Stranger in Her Native Land: Alice Fletcher and the American Indians.* Lincoln: University of Nebraska Press, 1988.

Marks, Martin Miller. *Music and the Silent Film: Contexts and Case Studies, 1895–1924.* New York: Oxford University Press, 1997.

Marrocco, W. Thomas, and Harold Gleason, eds. *Music in America: An Anthology from the Landing of the Pilgrims to the Close of the Civil War, 1620–1865.* New York: Norton, 1964.

Marsden, Michael T., and Jack G. Nachbar. "The Indian in the Movies." In *History of Indian-White Relations*, edited by Wilcomb E. Washburn, 607–16. Vol. 4, *Handbook of North American Indians,* edited by William C. Sturtevant. Washington, D.C.: Smithsonian Institution, 1988.

Martens, Frederick H. "[Aztecs]." *Musical Quarterly* 14, no. 3 (July 1928): 413–37.

——. *A Thousand and One Nights of Opera.* New York: D. Appleton, 1926.

Masayesva Jr., Victor [writer and director]. *Imagining Indians.* Video recording. Watertown, Mass.: Documentary Educational Resources, 1992.

Mason, Daniel Gregory. "Folksong and American Music (A Plea for the Unpopular Point of View)." *Musical Quarterly* 3 (Oct. 1917): 323–32.

Mason, Peter. *Deconstructing America: Representations of the Other.* London: Routledge, 1990.

Masson, Paul-Marie. *L'opéra de Rameau.* Paris: H. Laurens, 1930.

Masterson, Michael Lee. *Sounds of the Frontier: Music in Buffalo Bill's Wild West.* Ph.D. dissertation, University of New Mexico, 1990.

Mathes, Valerie Shere. *Helen Hunt Jackson and Her Indian Reform Legacy.* Austin: University of Texas Press, 1990.

Mathews, John Joseph. *The Osages: Children of the Middle Waters.* Norman: University of Oklahoma Press, 1961.

——. *Wah-Kon-Tah: The Osage and the White Man's Road.* Norman: University of Oklahoma Press, 1932.

Matz, Duane Allen. *Images of Indians in American Popular Culture since 1865.* D.A. diss., Illinois State University, 1988.

Maust, Wilbur R. "The American Indian in the Orchestral Music of Anthony Philip Heinrich." In *Music East and West: Essays in Honor of Walter Kaufmann,* edited by Thomas Noblitt, 309–25. New York: Pendragon Press, 1981.

May, Karl. *Winnetou I (Der rote Gentleman).* Freiburg, Germany: Fehsenfeld, 1893. Reprinted in Karl May, *Gesammelte Werke,* vol. 7 (1992).

McAllester, David P. "North America/Native America." Chap. 2 in *Worlds of Music: An Introduction to the Music of the World's Peoples.* 2nd ed. New York: Schirmer Books, 1992.

McClatchie, J. D., ed. *Henry Wadsworth Longfellow: Poems and Other Writings.* New York: Library of America, 2001.

McClintock, Walter. "Arthur Nevin and His Indian Opera." *The Metronome* 21, no. 3 (Mar. 1905): 9.

———. "An Illustrated Lecture by Mr. Arthur Nevin on the Music of the Blackfeet Indians and the New Indian Opera *Poia.*" Privately printed [1906?]. Copy at the Wisconsin Historical Society, Madison.

McCreless, Patrick. "Music and Rhetoric." Chap. 27 in *The Cambridge History of Western Music Theory,* edited by Thomas Christensen. Cambridge: Cambridge University Press, 2002.

McGowan, Margaret M. *L'art du ballet de cour en France, 1581–1643.* Paris: Éditions du Centre National de la Recherche Scientifique, 1963.

McKenney, Thomas L., and James Hall. *History of the Indian Tribes of North America.* Philadelphia: E. C. Biddle, 1837–44.

McNickle, D'Arcy. *They Came Here First: The Epic of the American Indian.* 2nd ed. rev. New York: Octagon Books, 1975.

McNutt, James C. "John Comfort Fillmore: A Student of Indian Music Reconsidered." *American Music* 2, no. 1 (Spring 1983): 61–70.

———. "Reply to Pantaleoni." *American Music* 3 (Summer 1984): 229.

Mellers, Wilfrid. *Music in a New Found Land: Themes and Developments in the History of American Music.* [1965]. 2nd ed. rev. London: Faber and Faber, 1987.

"The Melodrama of *Hiawatha.*" *Musical Leader and Concert-Goer* [Chicago] 6, no. 14 (1903): 9.

Meyer, Carter Jones, and Diana Royer. *Selling the Indian: Commercializing and Appropriating American Indian Cultures.* Tucson: University of Arizona Press, 2001.

Mihelich, John. "Smoke or Signals? American Popular Culture and the Challenge to Hegemonic Images of American Indians in Native American Film." *Wicazo Sa Review* 16, no. 2 (2001): 129–37.

Mihesuah, Devon A. *American Indians: Stereotypes and Realities.* Regina, Sask.: Clarity International, 1996.

Miller, Horace Alden. *Modal Trends in Modern Music.* Altadena, Calif.: Cornell Music Publishing, 1941.

———. New Harmonic Devices: A Treatise on Modern Harmonic Problems. Philadelphia: Oliver Ditson, 1930.

Miller, Malloy. "Using American Indian Music in Orchestral Compositions." *Ethnomusicology* 3, no. 2 (May 1959): 102.

Millington, C. Norris. "Only Indians Can Write Real Indian Music." *Musical America* 53, no. 3 (10 Feb. 1933): 12, 14.

Mitchell, David T., and Melissa Hearn. "Colonial Savages and Heroic Tricksters: Native Americans in the American Tradition." *Journal of Popular Culture* 32, no. 4 (Spring 1999): 101–19.

Moffitt, John F., and Santiago Sebastián. *O Brave New People: The European Invention of the American Indian.* Albuquerque: University of New Mexico Press, 1996.

Moine, Marie-Christine. *Les fêtes à la cour du Roi Soleil, 1653–1715.* Paris: F. Lanore, 1984.

Montaigne, Michel de. "On the Cannibals." In *The Complete Essays,* translated and edited by M. A. Screech, 228–41. London: Penguin Books, 1993.

Moogk, Peter N. *La Nouvelle France: The Making of French Canada—A Cultural History.* East Lansing: Michigan State University Press, 2000.

Mooney, James. "Cherokee Ball Play." *American Anthropologist* 3 (1890): 118.

——. "The Ghost Dance Religion and Sioux Outbreak of 1890." In *14th Annual Report of the Bureau of American Ethnology,* part 2. Washington, D.C.: Government Publishing Office, 1893.

——. "Ghost Dance Song: Arapaho." *Southern Workman* 36 (1907): 111.

Moses, Montrose J. The Fabulous Forrest: The Record of an American Actor. Boston: Little, Brown, 1929.

Moyne, Ernest J. "Hiawatha" and "Kalevala": A Study of the Relationship between Longfellow's "Indian Edda" and the Finnish Epic. Helsinki: Academia Scientiarum Fennica, 1965.

——. "Parodies of Longfellow's *Song of Hiawatha.*" *Delaware Notes,* 13th ser. (1957): 93–108.

Mulvey, Christopher. "Among the Sag-a-noshes: Ojibwa and Iowa Indians with George Catlin in Europe, 1843–1848." In *Indians and Europe,* edited by Christian F. Feest, 253–75.

"Music among the Aztecs." *Musical America* 11 (12 Feb. 1910): 18.

Music for the Nation. American sheet music collection at the Library of Congress. 1820–1860 and 1870–1885 currently available. Online at http://memory.loc.gov/ammem/smhtml/smhome.html.

"Music of the Indians [at the Chicago Columbian Exposition]." *Music* 1 (Dec. 1891): 189–91.

"Music of the Remote Past in Hopi . . ." *Musical America* 44 (14 Aug. 1926): 18.

"Music of the Zuni Indians of New Mexico." *Musical Courier* 37 (4 July 1898): [27].

Music of Victor Herbert. The Smithsonian American Musical Theater Series. RCA 3–LP record set. R 017, DPM 30366 (1986).

"National Congress of Musicians: Omaha (I)." *Musical Courier* 36, no. 20 (18 May 1898): 27–28.

"National Congress of Musicians: Omaha (II)." *Musical Courier* 37, no. 3 (20 July 1898): 11–12.

Natoma articles in *New York Times:* 22 Jan. 1911, pt. 5, p. 13; 26 Feb. 1911, pt. 2, p. 1:5; 26 Feb. 1911, pt. 5, p. 10; 26 Feb. 1911, pt. 7, p. 7:1; 28 Feb. 1911, p. 11:2; 1 Mar. 1911, pt. 8, pp. 1–5; 5 Mar. 1911, pt. 1, p. 6; 5 Mar. 1911, pt. 5, p. 16.

Nettl, Bruno. "The American Indians." In *Folk and Traditions of the Western Continents,* 147–68. Englewood Cliffs, N.J.: Prentice-Hall, 1965.

Nettl, Paul. "The Moresca." *Archiv für Musikwissenschaft* 14, no. 3 (1957): 165–74.

Nevin, Arthur. "Explains Berlin's Attack upon *Poia.*" *Musical America* 12, no. 2 (1910): 25.

——. "Impressions of Indian Music as Heard in the Woods, Prairies, Mountains and Wigwams." *Etude* 38, no. 10 (Oct. 1920): 663–64.

——. "Two Summers with the Blackfeet Indians of Montana." *Musical Quarterly* 2 (1916): 257–70.

Newton, Nell Jessup. "Memory and Misrepresentation: Representing Crazy Horse in Tribal Court." In *Borrowed Power: Essays on Cultural Appropriation,* edited by Bruce Ziff and Pratima V. Rao, 195–224.

Niedermeyer, Louis. *Traité théorique et pratique de l'accompagnement du plain-chant.* Paris: Heugel, 1876.

Nixon, Charles E. "*Natoma* Has Chicago Premiere." *Musical America* 14 (23 Dec. 1911): 34.

"On Indian Music and Henry Gilbert." *Musical America* 15, no. 13 (1912): 2.

"On the Field and Work of a Journal of American Folklore." *Journal of American Folklore* 1, no. 1 (Apr.–June 1888): 3–7.

Odell, George C. D. *Annals of the New York Stage.* 15 vols. New York: Columbia University Press, 1927–1949.

Oja, Carol, ed. *American Music Recordings: A Discography of 20th-Century U.S. Composers.* Brooklyn, N.Y.: Institute for Studies in American Music, 1982.

Osman, Deborah Margaret. *The American "Indianist" Composers: A Critical Review of their Sources, Their Aims, and Their Compositional Procedures.* Doctoral thesis, University of South Carolina, 1992.

O'Toole, Fintan. *A Traitor's Kiss: The Life of Richard Brinsley Sheridan, 1751–1816.* New York: Farrar, Straus, and Giroux, 1997.

Painter, George D. *The Longed-for Tempests, 1768–93.* Vol. 1, *Chateaubriand: A Biography.* London: Chatto and Windus, 1977.

Palmer, A[llen] Dean. "Tsianina Blackstone: A Chapter in the History of the American Indian in Opera." *Liberal Arts Review* 7 (Spring 1979): 40–64.

Pantaleoni, Hewitt. "A Reconsideration of Fillmore Reconsidered." *American Music* 3, no. 2 (Summer 1984): 217–28.

Parakilas, James. "How Spain Got a Soul." In *The Exotic in Western Music,* edited by Jonathan Bellman, 137–93.

——. "The Soldier and the Exotic: Operatic Variations on a Theme of Racial Encounter, Part II." *Opera Quarterly* 10, no. 3 (1994): 55–59.

Parton, James. *Life of Voltaire.* 2 vols. Cambridge, Mass.: Riverside Press, 1881.

Pearce, Roy Harvey. *The Savages of America: A Study of the Indian and the Idea of Civilization.* Baltimore: Johns Hopkins University Press, 1953. Rev. as *Savagism and Civilization: A Study of the Indian and the American Mind.* Baltimore: Johns Hopkins University Press, 1965.

Perdue, Theda, and Michael D. Green. *The Cherokee Removal: A Brief History with Documents.* Boston: Bedford Books of St. Martin's Press, 1995.

Perison, Harry D. *Charles Wakefield Cadman: His Life and Works.* Ph.D. diss., Eastman School of Music, University of Rochester, 1978.

——. "The *Indian* Operas of Charles Wakefield Cadman." *College Music Symposium* 22, no. 2 (1982): 48.

Peyser, Herbert F. "Native Composers Achieve Success at Metropolitan." *Musical America* (30 Mar. 1918): 2. [On *Shanewis.*]

Pinnock, Andrew. "Play into Opera: Purcell's *The Indian Queen.*" *Early Music* 18, no. 1 (1990): 3–21.

Pisani, Michael. *Exotic Sounds in the Native Land: Portrayals of North American Indians in Western Music.* Ph.D. diss., Eastman School of Music, University of Rochester, 1996.

——"I'm an Indian Too: Creating Indian Identities in 19th- and 20th-Century Music." In *The Exotic in Western Music,* edited by Jonathan Bellman, 218–57.

——"The Indian Music Debate and 'American' Music in the Progressive Era." *College Music Symposium* 37 (1997): 73–96.

Porter, Susan L. *With an Air Debonair: Musical Theatre in America, 1785–1815.* Washington, D.C.: Smithsonian Institution Press, 1991.

"Portrait of Thurlow Lieurance." *Music News* 7 (23 Apr. 1911): 23.

Powers, William K. "The Indian Hobbyist Movement in North America." In *History of Indian-White Relations,* edited by Wilcomb E. Washburn, 557–561. Vol. 4, *Handbook of North American Indians*, edited by William C. Sturtevant. Washington, D.C.: Smithsonian Institution, 1988.

——. *War Dance: Plains Indian Musical Performance.* Tucson: University of Arizona Press, 1990.

Prats, Armando José. *Invisible Natives: Myth and Identity in the American Western.* Ithaca, N.Y.: Cornell University Press, 2002.

Pratt, Stephanie. "Reynolds' 'King of the Cherokees' and Other Mistaken Identities in the Portraiture of Native American Delegations, 1710–1762." *Oxford Art Journal* 21, no. 2 (1998): 133–50.

Prevots, Naima. *American Pageantry: A Movement for Art and Democracy.* Ann Arbor, Mich.: UMI Research Press, 1990.

Price, Curtis. *Henry Purcell and the London Stage.* Cambridge: Cambridge University Press, 1984.

——. "The Indian Queen." In *The New Grove Dictionary of Opera,* vol. 2, edited by Stanley Sadie. New York: Grove's Dictionaries of Music, 1992.

"Primitive Beat of Indian Music in Jacobi's Quartet." *Musical America* 43 (2 Jan. 1926): 35.

Prucha, Prancis Paul. *The Great Father: The United States Government and the American Indians.* Abr. ed. Lincoln: University of Nebraska Press, 1986.

Purdy, John. "Tricksters of the Trade: 'Remagining' the Filmic Image of Native Americans." In *Native American Representations: First Encounters, Distorted Images, and Literary Appropriations,* edited by Gretchen Bataille, 100–119.

Ramsey, Jarold. "Francis LaFlesche." In *Native American Writers of the United States: Dictionary of Literary Biography,* vol. 175, edited by Kenneth Roemer, 148–53. Detroit: Gale Research, 1997.

Ranger, Paul. "Terror and Pity Reign in Every Breast": Gothic Drama in the London Patent Theatres, 1750–1820. London: Society for Theatre Research, 1991.

Rapée, Erno. *Encyclopedia of Music for Pictures.* New York: Belwin, 1925.

——. Motion Picture Moods for Pianists and Organists. New York: Schirmer, 1924.

Ratner, Leonard. *Classic Music.* New York: Schirmer Books, 1980.

Read, Angelo. "The North American Indian and Music." *Musical America* 6, no. 9 (13 July 1907): 9.

Redfeather, Tsianina. "On Wings of Song." *Music of the West* (Feb. 1948): 7–9.

Reeves, Arthur Middleton. *The Finding of Wineland the Good.* London: Oxford University Press, 1890.

Reidel, Johannes. "Henry Russell's American Experience." In *Festival Essays for Pauline Alderman,* edited by Burton L. Karson, 209–25. Provo, Utah: Brigham Young University Press, 1976.

"Review of Several Books on Indian Ceremonial Dances." *Nature* 58 (1898): 125–27.

Reviews of Coleridge-Taylor's *Hiawatha*: *London Musical Times* (1 Nov. 1899): 364; *Musical Record* (May 1900): 208; *Musical Times* (Apr. 1900): 246.

Rhodes, Willard. "On the Warpath, 1942." *Modern Music* 20, no. 3 (Mar.–Apr. 1943): 160.

Rice, Eric. "Representations of Janissary Music (*Mehter*) as Musical Exoticism in Western Compositions, 1670–1824." *Journal of Musicological Research* 19, no. 1 (1999): 41–88.

Richards, Jeffrey, ed. *Imperialism and Juvenile Literature.* Manchester, U.K.: Manchester University Press, 1989.

Riley, Glenda. *The Life and Legacy of Annie Oakley.* Norman: University of Oklahoma Press, 1994.

Ritson, Joseph. *Scotish Songs.* 2 vols. [1794]. Reprint of 1869 2nd ed., New York: AMS Press, 1975.

Roberts, Helen H. Form in Primitive Music: An Analytical and Comparative Study of the Melodic Form of Some Ancient Southern California Indian Songs. New York: Norton, 1933.

Robertson, Wesley L. "Art and Life in Indian Music." *Etude* 59, no. 3 (Mar. 1941): 161–62.

Rollins, Peter C. "The Hollywood Indian: Still on a Scholarly Frontier?" *Film & History* 23, no. 1 (1993): 1–6.

Rollins, Peter C., and John E. O'Connor, eds. *Hollywood's Indian: The Portrayal of the Native American in Film.* Lexington: University Press of Kentucky, 1998.

Root, Deane L. *American Popular Stage Music, 1860–1880.* Ann Arbor, Mich.: UMI Research Press, 1981.

Rosaldo, Renato. *Culture and Truth: The Remaking of Social Analysis.* Boston: Beacon Press, 1989.

Rosar, William. "Movie Indian Music and Film Music Convention: Identifying Themes, Signs, and Physiognomic Synesthesia." Draft of an unpublished paper, Claremont Graduate School, Claremont, Calif., ca. 1994.

Ross, Bruce Clunies. "Percy Grainger's 'Nordic Revolt against Civilization.'" *Musicology Australia* 9 (1986): 53–65.

Rourke, Constance. *The Roots of American Culture and Other Essays.* Edited by Van Wyck Brooks. [1942]. Reprint, Port Washington, N.Y.: Kennikat Press, 1985.

Rouse, Irving. *The Tainos: Rise and Decline of the People Who Greeted Columbus.* New Haven, Conn.: Yale University Press, 1992. [Contains glossary.]

Rousseau, Jean-Jacques. *Discours sur l'origine et les fondemens de l'inégalité parmi les hommes*. Amsterdam: Marc Michel Rey, 1755.

Rowell, George. *Victorian Theatre, 1792–1914: A Survey.* 2nd ed. Cambridge: Cambridge University Press, 1978.

Runge, Edith Amelie. *Primitivism and Related Ideas in* Sturm und Drang *Literature.* Baltimore: Johns Hopkins University Press, 1946.

Russell, Henry. *Cheer! Boys, Cheer! Memories of Men and Music.* London: John MacQueen, 1895.

Rydell, Robert W. *All the World's a Fair: Visions of Empire at American International Expositions, 1876–1916.* Chicago: University of Chicago Press, 1987.

Sachs, Curt. *World History of the Dance.* Translated by Bessie Schönberg. New York: Norton, 1937.

Sadler, Graham. "Les Indes Galantes." In *The New Grove Dictionary of Opera,* vol. 2, edited by Stanley Sadie. New York: Grove's Dictionaries of Music, 1992.

Said, Edward. *Orientalism.* [1978]. New York: Vintage Books, 1979.

Salisbury, Neal. "The Indians' Old World: Native Americans and the Coming of Europeans." In *American Encounters: Natives and Newcomers from European Contact to Indian Removal, 1500–1850,* edited by Peter Mancall and James H. Merrell, 438–49. New York: Routledge, 2000.

——. "Native People and European Settlers in Eastern North America, 1600–1783." Chap. 7 in *North America, Part 1,* edited by Bruce G. Trigger and Wilcomb E. Washburn. Vol. 1, *The Cambridge History of the Native Peoples of the Americas.* Cambridge: Cambridge University Press, 1996.

Samuels, Charles E. *Thomas Bailey Aldrich.* New York: Twayne Publishers, 1965.

Savage, Roger. "Rameau's American Dancers." *Early Music* 11, no. 4 (Oct. 1983): 441–52.

Sayre, Gordon M. *Les Sauvages Américains: Representations of Native Americans in French and English Colonial Literature.* Chapel Hill: University of North Carolina Press, 1997.

Schafer, William J., and Johannes Riedel. *The Art of Ragtime: Form and Meaning of an Original Black American Art.* Baton Rouge: Louisiana State University Press, 1973.

Scheckel, Susan. *The Insistence of the Indian: Race and Nationalism in Nineteenth-Century American Culture.* Princeton, N.J.: Princeton University Press, 1998.

Schele, Linda, and David Freidel. *A Forest of Kings: The Untold Story of the Ancient Maya.* New York: William Morrow, 1990.

Schleifer, Martha Furman, and Sam Dennison, eds. *Three Centuries of American Music: A Collection of American Sacred and Secular Music.* Vols. 2 and 3. [Boston]: G. K. Hall, 1989–92.

Schoolcraft, Henry Rowe. *Algic Researches: Comprising Inquiries Respecting the Mental Characteristics of the North American Indians.* First series: Indian Tales and Legends. 2 vols. [1839]. Reprint, Mineola, N.Y.: Dover, 1999.

——. *Historical and Statistical Information Respecting the History, Condition, and Prospects of the Indian Tribes of the United States, Part 5.* Philadelphia: Lippincott, Grambo, 1855.

Schramm, Wilbur Lang. "*Hiawatha* and Its Predecessors." *Philological Quarterly* 11, no. 4 (Oct. 1932): 321–43.

See, Adeline. "Gathering the Music of [the Indian] for Posterity." *Musical America* 44, no. 1 (24 Apr. 1926): 5.

Seidl, Anton, ed. *Music in the Modern World.* New York: D. Appleton, 1895.

Self, Geoffrey. *The Hiawatha Man: The Life and Work of Samuel Coleridge-Taylor.* Aldershot, Hants, U.K.: Scolar Press, 1995.

Sheppard, W. Anthony. "An Exotic Enemy: Anti-Japanese Musical Propaganda in World War II Hollywood." *Journal of the American Musicological Society* 54, no. 2 (Summer 2001): 302–57.

Sherk, Warren. "The Western Film Scores of Hans Salter." *Cue Sheet* 11, no. 2 (Apr. 1995): 12–18.

Sidney Lanier. *Letters, 1869–1873.* Edited by Charles R. Anderson and Aubrey H. Starke. Baltimore: Johns Hopkins University Press, 1945.

Singer, Beverly R. *Wiping the War Paint off the Lens: Native American Film and Video.* Minneapolis: University of Minnesota Press, 2001.

Skilton, Charles Sanford. "American Indian Music." In *International Cyclopedia of Music and Musicians,* edited by Oscar Thompson. 8th ed. New York: Dodd, Mead, 1939.

——. "Indian Music at Home." *Musician* 23 (July 1918): 459.

——. "Realism in Indian Music." In *Studies in Musical Education, History, and Aesthetics,* 106–14. Papers and Proceedings of the Music Teachers' National Association 40, Thirteenth Series, 1919. Excerpted in *Musician* 24 (Feb. 1919): 17.

——. "Shawnee Indian Hunting Dance." *Violinist* 33 (Dec. 1923): 226–27.

Slotkin, Richard. *The Fatal Environment: The Myth of the Frontier in the Age of Industrialization, 1800–1890.* New York: Atheneum, 1985.

——. *Gunfighter Nation: The Myth of the Frontier in Twentieth-Century America.* New York: Atheneum, 1992.

——. *Regeneration through Violence: The Mythology of the American Frontier, 1600–1860.* Middletown, Conn.: Wesleyan University Press, 1973.

Smaczny, Jan. "E-flat Major String Quintet." In *Dvořák in America,* edited by John C. Tibbetts, 238–42.

Smith, Catherine Parsons, and Cynthia S. Richardson. *Mary Carr Moore, American Composer.* Ann Arbor: University of Michigan Press, 1987.

Smith, James A. "American Indian Music and Its Use by American Composers." In "Charles Sanford Skilton (1868–1941): Kansas Composer," 49–67. Master's thesis, University of Kansas, 1979.

Smith, Jonathan Z. "Close Encounters of Diverse Kinds." Chap. 1 in *Religion and Cultural Studies,* edited by Susan L. Mizruchi. Princeton, N.J.: Princeton University Press, 2001.

Smith, Sherry L. "Among the Blackfeet: Walter McClintock and Mary Roberts Rinehart." In *Reimagining Indians: Native American through Anglo Eyes, 1880–1940,* 62–76. New York: Oxford University Press, 2000.

Sonneck, O[scar] G. "An American School of Composition: Do We Want and Need It?" In *Papers and Proceedings of the Music Teachers' National Association* (1928). Reprinted in *Oscar Sonneck and American Music,* edited by William Lichtenwanger, 158–66. Urbana: University of Illinois Press, 1983.

——. *Catalogue of the First Editions of Edward MacDowell.* Washington, D.C.: Government Printing Office, 1917.

——. "A Survey of Music in America." [1913]. In *Suum cuique: Essays in Music.* Reprint, Freeport, N.Y.: Books for Libraries Press, 1969.

Sorce, Richard. *An Investigation of Compositional Techniques in the Orchestral Works of Edward MacDowell.* Ph.D. diss., New York University, 1999.

Sousa, John Philip. *National, Patriotic, and Typical Airs of All Lands.* Philadelphia: Coleman, 1890.

"Spanish American Incidents . . . *Natoma* and *The Sacrifice.*" *Musical America* 12 (22 Oct. 1910): 28.

Spears, Jack. "The Indian on the Screen." Chap. 12 in *Hollywood: The Golden Era.* South Brunswick, N.J.: A. S. Barnes, 1971.

Les spectacles à travers les âges. Vol. 1: *Musique, Danse.* Paris: Aux Éditions du Cygne, 1932.

Spector, Irwin. "Dvořák's American Period." *Illinois Quarterly* 33, no. 3 (Feb. 1971): 8.

Spiess, Lincoln Burne. "Church Music in Seventeenth-Century New Mexico." *New Mexico Historical Review* 40, no. 1 (Jan. 1965): 5–21.

Spitzer, Michael. *Metaphor and Musical Thought.* Chicago: University of Chicago Press, 2004.

Steblin, Rita. *History of Key Characteristics in the Eighteenth and Early Nineteenth Centuries.* Rochester, N.Y.: University of Rochester Press, 1996.

Stedman, Raymond William. *Shadows of the Indian: Stereotypes in American Culture.* Norman: University of Oklahoma Press, 1982.

Stensland, Anna Lee. *Literature by and about the American Indian: An Annotated Bibliography with Contributions by Anne M. Fadun.* 2nd ed. Urbana, Ill.: National Council of Teachers of English, 1979.

Stevens, Walter B. *St. Louis: The Fourth City, 1763–1909.* St. Louis: S. J. Clarke, 1909.

Stevenson, Robert M. "American Tribal Music at Contact." *Inter-American Music Review* 14, no. 1 (Spring/Summer 1994): 1–56.

———. "English Sources for Indian Music until 1882." *Ethnomusicology* 17, no. 3 (Sept. 1973): 399–442.

———. *Music in Aztec and Inca Territory.* Berkeley: University of California Press, 1968.

———. *Music in Mexico: A Historical Survey.* New York: Thomas Y. Crowell, 1952.

———. "Written Sources for Indian Music until 1882." *Ethnomusicology* 17, no. 1 (Jan. 1973): 1–40.

Stewart, Hilary, annotator. *The Adventures and Sufferings of John R. Jewitt, Captive of Maquinna.* Seattle: University of Washington Press, 1987.

St. John de Crèvecoeur, J. Hector. *Letters from an American Farmer.* [1782]. London: Penguin Books, 1981.

Stopp [Bolton], Jacklin Talmage. *Religious Influences on American Secular Cantatas, 1850–1930.* Ph.D. diss., University of Michigan, 1964.

Stopp, Jacklin B. "The Secular Cantata in the United States: 1850–1919." *Journal of Research in Music Education* 17 (1969): 388–98.

Stowe, David W. "Dances with Ghosts." Chap. 5 in *How Sweet the Sound: Music in the Spiritual Lives of Americans.* Cambridge, Mass.: Harvard University Press, 2004.

Strickland, Rennard. *Tonto's Revenge: Reflections on American Indian Culture and Policy.* Albuquerque: University of New Mexico Press, 1997.

Strohm, Reinhard. *Dramma per musica: Italian Opera Seria of the Eighteenth Century.* New Haven, Conn.: Yale University Press, 1997.

Stuart, James. *Three Years in North America.* 2 vols. New York: Harper, 1833.

Stumpf, Carl. "Lieder der Bellakula-Indianer" (Songs of the Bella Coolas). *Vierteljahrsschrift für Musikwissenschaft* 2 (1886): 405–26.

"'Suite Primeval' by Charles Sanford Skilton in New York, July 29, 1927." *Musical Courier* 95 (11 Aug. 1927): 5.

Switzer, Richard. *Chateaubriand.* New York: Twayne Publishers, 1971.

Tagg, Philip, and Robert Clarida. *Ten Little Title Tunes: Towards a Musicology of the Mass Media.* New York: Mass Media Music Scholars' Press, 2003.

Tarasti, Eero. *Myth and Music: A Semiotic Approach to the Aesthetics of Myth in Music, Especially That of Wagner, Sibelius, and Stravinsky.* Vol. 51, Approaches to Semiotics. The Hague: Mouton Publishers, 1979.

Taruskin, Richard. "Classical View: 'Nationalism': Colonialism in Disguise?" *New York Times* (22 Aug. 1993): 69.

——. *Defining Russia Musically.* Princeton, N.J.: Princeton University Press, 1997.

——. "Nationalism." In *The New Grove Dictionary of Music and Musicians,* edited by Stanley Sadie. New York: Grove's Dictionaries, 2000.

Tawa, Nicholas. "The Pursuit of National Music." In *Mainstream Music of Early Twentieth-Century America,* 103–40. Westport, Conn.: Greenwood Press, 1992.

——. *Sweet Songs for Gentle Americans: The Parlor Song in America, 1790–1860.* Bowling Green, Ohio: Bowling Green University Popular Press, 1980.

Taylor, Colin F. "The Indian Hobbyist Movement in Europe." In *History of Indian-White Relations,* edited by Wilcomb E. Washburn, 562–69. Vol. 4, *Handbook of North American Indians,* edited by William C. Sturtevant. Washington, D.C.: Smithsonian Institution, 1988.

Tedlock, Barbara. "Songs of the Zuni Kachina Society: Composition, Rehearsal, and Performance." In *Southwestern Indian Ritual Drama,* 7–35. Albuquerque: University of New Mexico Press, 1980.

Temperley, Nicholas, ed. *The Romantic Age: 1800–1914.* Vol. 5, The Athlone Series of Music in Britain. London: Athlone Press, 1981.

Thayer, Stuart. *Annals of the American Circus, 1793–1829.* Manchester, Mich.: Rymack Press, 1976.

Threlfall, Robert. *A Catalogue of the Compositions of Frederick Delius: Sources and References.* London: Delius Trust, 1977.

Thurber, Jeannette. "Dvořák as I Knew Him." *Etude* 37, no. 12 (Nov. 1919): 693–94. Reprinted in *Dvořák in America,* edited by John C. Tibbetts, 382.

Tibbetts, John C., ed. *Dvorák in America: 1892–1895.* Portland, Ore.: Amadeus Press, 1993.

Tiomkin, Dimitri. "Composing for Films." *Films in Review* 2, no. 9 (1951): 17–22.

Todorov, Tzvetan. *The Conquest of America: The Question of the Other.* [1984]. Translated by Richard Howard. Norman: University of Oklahoma Press, 1999.

Tomatz, David. *Rubin Goldmark, Post-Romantic: Trial Balances in American Music.* Ph.D. diss., Catholic University of America, 1966.

Tomlinson, Gary. "Ideologies of Aztec Song." *Journal of the American Musicological Society* 48, no. 3 (Fall, 1995): 343–79.

Tompkins, Eugene. *History of the Boston Theatre, 1854–1901.* Boston: Houghton Mifflin, 1908.

Torgovnick, Marianna. *Gone Primitive: Savage Intellects, Modern Lives.* Chicago: University of Chicago Press, 1990.

Tortolano, William. *Samuel Coleridge-Taylor: Anglo-Black Composer, 1875–1912.* Metuchen, N.J.: Scarecrow Press, 1977.

Trachtenberg, Alan. *The Incorporation of America: Culture and Society in the Gilded Age.* New York: Hill and Wang, 1982.

Trennert, Robert A. "A Resurrection of Native Arts and Crafts: The St. Louis World's Fair, 1904." *Missouri Historical Review* 87, no. 3 (Apr. 1993): 274–92.

Troyer, Carlos. *Indian Music Lecture: The Zuñi Indians and Their Music.* Philadelphia: Theodore Presser, 1913.

True, Lyle C. *How and What to Play for Moving Pictures.* San Francisco: Music Supply, 1914.

Tsou, Judy. "Gendering Race: Stereotypes of Chinese Americans in Popular Sheet Music." *Repercussions: Critical and Alternative Viewpoints on Music and Scholarship* 6, no. 2 (Fall 1997): 25–62.

Turino, Thomas. "Signs of Imagination, Identity, and Experience: A Peircian Semiotic Theory for Music." *Ethnomusicology* 43, no. 2 (Spring/Summer 1999): 221–55.

Turner, Frederick Jackson. "The Significance of the Frontier in American History." In *Annual Report of the American History Association, 1893.* [1894]. Reprinted in *Yearbook of the National Society for the Study of Education* 5. Chicago: National Society for the Study of Education, 1899.

Underwood, Anne. "Thurlow Lieurance . . . Interpreter of Song." *Southwestern Musician* 18, no. 23 (July 1952): 9, 15.

Unsigned review of the Desbarats *Hiawatha. Boston Transcript.* [1902]. Reprinted in *Musical Courier* 45 (1902): 33.

Upton, George P. "Musical Societies of the United States and Their Representation at the World's Fair." *Scribner's Magazine* 14 (July 1893): 68–83.

Upton, William Treat. *Anthony Philip Heinrich: A Nineteenth-Century Composer in America.* [1939]. Reprint, New York: AMS Press, 1967.

Urrows, David Francis. "Apollo in Athens: Otto Dresel and Boston, 1850–90." *American Music* 12, no. 4 (Winter 1994): 345–88.

"The Use of Indian Themes in Composition." *Pan Pipes of Sigma Alpha Iota* 46, no. 2 (Jan. 1954): 65.

Tran, Van Khe. "Is the Pentatonic Universal? A Few Reflections on Pentatonicism." *World of Music* 19, nos. 1–2 (1977): 76–84.

Variety Film Reviews. Vol. 5: *1934–1937.* New York: Garland, 1983.

Vickers, Scott. *Native American Identities: From Stereotype to Archetype in Art and Literature.* Albuquerque: University of New Mexico, 1998.

Vincent, John. *The Diatonic Modes in Modern Music.* Berkeley: University of California Press, 1951.

Viola, Herman J. *After Columbus: The Smithsonian Chronicle of the North American Indians.* Washington, D.C.: Smithsonian Books, 1990.

Voyage en musique: Cent ans d'exotisme: Décors et costumes dans le spectacle lyrique en France. Boulogne-Billancourt, France: Centre Culturel de Boulogne-Billancourt, 1990.

Walker, Cheryl. *Indian Nation: Native American Literature and Nineteenth-Century Nationalisms.* Durham, N.C.: Duke University Press, 1997.

Wallaschek, Richard. *Primitive Music: An Inquiry into the Origins and Development of Music; Songs, Instruments, Dances, and Pantomimes of Savage Races, with Musical Examples.* [1893]. Reprint, New York: Da Capo Press, 1970.

Wallschläger, Hans. *Karl May in Selbstzeugnissen und Bilddokumenten.* Hamburg: Rowolt, 1965.

Warner, Thomas E. *Periodical Literature on American Music, 1620–1920.* Bibliographies in American Music, edited by J. Bunker Clark. Harmonie Park Press, 1988.

Washburn, Wilcomb E. *The American Indian and the United States: A Documentary History.* 4 vols. New York: Random House, 1973.

Watahwaso, Princess. "New Indian Songs." *Musical Courier* 80, no. 13 (25 Mar. 1920): 46.

Waters, Edward N. *Victor Herbert: A Life in Music.* New York: Macmillan, 1955.

———. "The Wa-Wan Press, an Adventure in Musical Idealism." In *A Birthday Offering for Carl Engel,* edited by Gustave Reese, 214–33. New York: G. Schirmer, 1943.

Watkins, Glenn. *Pyramids at the Louvre: Music, Culture, and Collage from Stravinsky to the Postmodernists.* Cambridge, Mass.: Belknap Press of Harvard University Press, 1994.

Weber, David J. *The Mexican Frontier, 1821–1846: The American Southwest under Mexico.* Albuquerque: University of New Mexico Press, 1982.

Wertheimer, Eric. *Imagined Empires: Incas, Aztecs, and the New World of American Literature, 1771–1876.* Cambridge: Cambridge University Press, 1999.

West, Dennis and Joan. "Sending Cinematic Smoke Signals: An Interview with Sherman Alexie." *Cineaste* 23, no. 4 (Winter 1998): 28–31.

Whaples, Miriam K[arpilow]. "Early Exoticism Revisited." In *The Exotic in Western Music,* edited by Jonathan Bellman, 3–25.

———. *Exoticism in Dramatic Music: 1600–1800.* Ph.D. diss., Indiana University, 1958.

White, Richard. "It's Your Misfortune and None of My Own": *A History of the American West.* Norman: University of Oklahoma Press, 1991.

Wied, Maximilian, Prince of. *Travels in the Interior of North America, 1832–34.* [1843]. Reprinted in Reuben G. Thwaites, *Early Western Travels, 1748–1846,* vol. 23. Cleveland: Arthur H. Clark, 1907.

Wiget, Andrew O. "Ghost Dance Songs." In *The Heath Anthology of American Literature,* vol. 2, 742–43. Lexington, Mass.: D. C. Heath, 1990.

Williams, Daniel E. "Until They Are Contaminated by Their More Refined Neighbors: The Images of the Native Americans in Carver's *Travels through the Interior* and Its Influence on the Euro-American Imagination." In *Indians and Europe,* edited by Christian F. Feest, 195–214.

Williams, Mentor L., ed. *Schoolcraft's Indian Legends.* East Lansing: Michigan State University Press, 1991.

Wilmeth, Don B. "Noble or Ruthless Savage? The American Indian Onstage in the Drama." *Journal of American Drama and Theatre* 1, no. 2 (Spring 1989): 34–78. [Includes an extensive "Tentative Checklist of Indian Plays (1606–1987)."]

Wintroub, Michael. "Civilizing the Savage and Making a King: The Royal Entry Festival of Henri II (Rouen, 1550)." *Sixteenth Century Journal* 29 (1998): 465–95.

Wiora, Walter. "Of Art Music and Cultural Classes." In *Music and Civilization: Essays in Honor of Paul Henry Lang,* edited by Edmond Strainchamps and Maria Rika Maniates, 472–77. New York: Norton, 1984.

Wright, Farnsworth. "Chicago Composer Finds Omaha Legend a Source of Inspiration (on H. P. Eames)." *Musical America* 24, no. 5 (3 June 1916): 40.

Wu, Arlouine G. *Constance Eberhart: A Musical Career in the Age of Cadman.* Edited by Leland Fox. National Opera Association Monograph Series, vol. 4. Oxford, Miss.: National Opera Association, 1983.

Wyndham, Henry Saxe. *The Annals of Covent Garden Theatre, from 1732 to 1897.* 2 vols. London: Chatto and Windus, 1906.

Yoder, Robert M. "Tin-Pan Alley's Wonderful Monopoly." *Saturday Evening Post,* 25 Nov. 1950, 39.

Youens, Susan. *Schubert's Poets and the Making of Lieder.* New York: Cambridge University Press, 1996.

Zak, Vladimir. "Asaf'ev's Theory of Intonation and the Analysis of Popular Song." *Popular Music* 2 (1982): 91–111.

Zamecnik, J. S. *Sam Fox Moving Picture Music,* vols. 1 and 2. Cleveland: Sam Fox, 1913.

Ziff, Bruce, and Pratima V. Rao, eds. *Borrowed Power: Essays on Cultural Appropriation.* New Brunswick, N.J.: Rutgers University Press, 1997.

Zuck, Barbara A. "The Impact of European Nationalism: Dvořák, MacDowell, Farwell, Cadman, and the Issue of 'American' Music." In *A History of Musical Americanism,* 56–73. Ann Arbor, Mich.: UMI Research Press, 1980.

Index

This is principally a topical index, with only some of the more prominent individuals and titles referenced. For specific Indian groups see the entry "Indian peoples." An asterisk indicates the presence of a musical example, figure, or table.

	DATE DUE